THE BOOK

VW Golf & Vento
Service and Repair Manual

Mark Coombs and Spencer Drayton

Models covered

(3097-288)

VW Golf & Vento front-wheel-drive models with four-cylinder petrol and diesel engines, including special/limited editions; Hatchback, Saloon and Estate
1391 cc, 1598 cc, 1781 cc & 1984 cc (inc. DOHC) petrol engines
1896 cc diesel and Turbo diesel engines

Covers major mechanical features of Cabriolet
Also covers Saloon models badged "VW Jetta" in certain markets
Does not cover 2792 cc VR6 engine or four-wheel-drive models

© Haynes Publishing 1996

A book in the **Haynes Service and Repair Manual Series**

ABCDE
FGHIJ
KLMNO
PQRST

ISBN 1 85960 097 2

British Library Cataloguing in Publication Data
A catalogue record for this book is available from the British Library.

Printed by **J H Haynes & Co. Ltd, Sparkford, Nr Yeovil, Somerset BA22 7JJ**

Haynes Publishing
Sparkford, Nr Yeovil, Somerset BA22 7JJ, England

Haynes North America, Inc
861 Lawrence Drive, Newbury Park, California 91320, USA

Editions Haynes S.A.
147/149, rue Saint Honoré, 75001 PARIS, France

Contents

LIVING WITH YOUR VW GOLF/VENTO

MAINTENANCE

Routine Maintenance and Servicing

Contents

The new VW Golf range was introduced in the Spring of 1992. Originally, the Golf was available with a choice of 1.4 litre (1391 cc), 1.6 litre (1598 cc), 1.8 litre (1781 cc) and 2.0 litre (1984 cc) petrol engines, as well as a 1.9 litre (1896 cc) diesel engine; both normally-aspirated and turbo versions of the diesel engine being fitted. At first, models were only available in a three and five-door Hatchback form.

All engines are derived from the well-proven engines which have appeared in many VW/Audi vehicles. The engine is of four-cylinder overhead camshaft design, mounted transversely, with the transmission mounted on the left-hand side. All models have a four or five-speed manual transmission.

In Autumn 1992 the four-door Saloon, known as the Vento, was introduced to the range. At the same time a four-speed automatic transmission was offered as an alternative to the manual transmission.

In late 1993 the 2.0 litre (1984 cc) 16-valve engine was introduced.

The engine uses the same bottom end as the 8-valve engine, but with a double overhead camshaft, 16-valve top end to increase power.

In early 1994, a Cabriolet and an Estate model were introduced to complete the range of body styles available.

All models have fully-independent front suspension. The rear suspension is semi-independent, with suspension struts and trailing arms.

A wide range of standard and optional equipment is available within the Golf/Vento range to suit most tastes, including central locking, electric windows, an electric sunroof, an anti-lock braking system, and an air bag. An anti-lock braking system and air conditioning system are available as options on certain models.

Provided that regular servicing is carried out in accordance with the manufacturer's recommendations, the VW Golf/Vento should prove reliable and economical. The engine compartment is well-designed, and most of the items needing frequent attention are easily accessible.

VW Golf 1.8 CL Hatchback

VW Vento 1.8 CL Saloon

The VW Golf/Vento Team

Haynes manuals are produced by dedicated and enthusiastic people working in close co-operation. The team responsible for the creation of this book included:

Authors	Mark Coombs Spencer Drayton
Sub-editors	Sophie Yar Carole Turk
Editor & Page Make-up	Bob Jex
Workshop manager	Paul Buckland
Photo Scans	John Martin Paul Tanswell
Cover illustration & Line Art	Roger Healing
Wiring diagrams	Matthew Marke

We hope the book will help you to get the maximum enjoyment from your car. By carrying out routine maintenance as described you will ensure your car's reliability and preserve its resale value.

Your VW Golf/Vento manual

The aim of this manual is to help you get the best value from your vehicle. It can do so in several ways. It can help you decide what work must be done (even should you choose to get it done by a garage). It will also provide information on routine maintenance and servicing, and give a logical course of action and diagnosis when random faults occur. However, it is hoped that you will use the manual by tackling the work yourself. On simpler jobs it may even be quicker than booking the car into a garage and going there twice, to leave and collect it. Perhaps most important, a lot of money can be saved by avoiding the costs a garage must charge to cover its labour and overheads.

The manual has drawings and descriptions to show the function of the various components so that their layout can be understood. Tasks are described and photographed in a clear step-by-step sequence.

Acknowledgements

Thanks are due to Champion Spark Plug, who supplied the illustrations showing spark plug conditions. Special thanks to Loders of Yeovil who provided several of the project vehicles used in the origination of this manual. Thanks are also due to Sykes-Pickavant Limited, who provided some of the workshop tools, and to all those people at Sparkford and Newbury Park who helped in the production of this manual.

This manual is not a direct reproduction of the vehicle manufacturers' data, and its publication should not be taken as implying any technical approval by the vehicle manufacturers or importers.

We take great pride in the accuracy of information given in this manual, but vehicle manufacturers make alterations and design changes during the production run of a particular vehicle of which they do not inform us. No liability can be accepted by the authors or publishers for loss, damage or injury caused by any errors in, or omissions from, the information given.

Working on your car can be dangerous. This page shows just some of the potential risks and hazards, with the aim of creating a safety-conscious attitude.

General hazards

Scalding

• Don't remove the radiator or expansion tank cap while the engine is hot.
• Engine oil, automatic transmission fluid or power steering fluid may also be dangerously hot if the engine has recently been running.

Burning

• Beware of burns from the exhaust system and from any part of the engine. Brake discs and drums can also be extremely hot immediately after use.

Crushing

• When working under or near a raised vehicle, always supplement the jack with axle stands, or use drive-on ramps. *Never venture under a car which is only supported by a jack.*

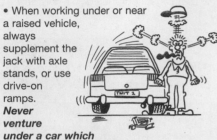

• Take care if loosening or tightening high-torque nuts when the vehicle is on stands. Initial loosening and final tightening should be done with the wheels on the ground.

Fire

• Fuel is highly flammable; fuel vapour is explosive.
• Don't let fuel spill onto a hot engine.
• Do not smoke or allow naked lights (including pilot lights) anywhere near a vehicle being worked on. Also beware of creating sparks (electrically or by use of tools).
• Fuel vapour is heavier than air, so don't work on the fuel system with the vehicle over an inspection pit.
• Another cause of fire is an electrical overload or short-circuit. Take care when repairing or modifying the vehicle wiring.
• Keep a fire extinguisher handy, of a type suitable for use on fuel and electrical fires.

Electric shock

• Ignition HT voltage can be dangerous, especially to people with heart problems or a pacemaker. Don't work on or near the ignition system with the engine running or the ignition switched on.

• Mains voltage is also dangerous. Make sure that any mains-operated equipment is correctly earthed. Mains power points should be protected by a residual current device (RCD) circuit breaker.

Fume or gas intoxication

• Exhaust fumes are poisonous; they often contain carbon monoxide, which is rapidly fatal if inhaled. Never run the engine in a confined space such as a garage with the doors shut.
• Fuel vapour is also poisonous, as are the vapours from some cleaning solvents and paint thinners.

Poisonous or irritant substances

• Avoid skin contact with battery acid and with any fuel, fluid or lubricant, especially antifreeze, brake hydraulic fluid and Diesel fuel. Don't syphon them by mouth. If such a substance is swallowed or gets into the eyes, seek medical advice.
• Prolonged contact with used engine oil can cause skin cancer. Wear gloves or use a barrier cream if necessary. Change out of oil-soaked clothes and do not keep oily rags in your pocket.
• Air conditioning refrigerant forms a poisonous gas if exposed to a naked flame (including a cigarette). It can also cause skin burns on contact.

Asbestos

• Asbestos dust can cause cancer if inhaled or swallowed. Asbestos may be found in gaskets and in brake and clutch linings. When dealing with such components it is safest to assume that they contain asbestos.

Special hazards

Hydrofluoric acid

• This extremely corrosive acid is formed when certain types of synthetic rubber, found in some O-rings, oil seals, fuel hoses etc, are exposed to temperatures above 400ºC. The rubber changes into a charred or sticky substance containing the acid. *Once formed, the acid remains dangerous for years. If it gets onto the skin, it may be necessary to amputate the limb concerned.*
• When dealing with a vehicle which has suffered a fire, or with components salvaged from such a vehicle, wear protective gloves and discard them after use.

The battery

• Batteries contain sulphuric acid, which attacks clothing, eyes and skin. Take care when topping-up or carrying the battery.
• The hydrogen gas given off by the battery is highly explosive. Never cause a spark or allow a naked light nearby. Be careful when connecting and disconnecting battery chargers or jump leads.

Air bags

• Air bags can cause injury if they go off accidentally. Take care when removing the steering wheel and/or facia. Special storage instructions may apply.

Diesel injection equipment

• Diesel injection pumps supply fuel at very high pressure. Take care when working on the fuel injectors and fuel pipes.

⚠ *Warning: Never expose the hands, face or any other part of the body to injector spray; the fuel can penetrate the skin with potentially fatal results.*

Remember...

DO

• Do use eye protection when using power tools, and when working under the vehicle.

• Do wear gloves or use barrier cream to protect your hands when necessary.

• Do get someone to check periodically that all is well when working alone on the vehicle.

• Do keep loose clothing and long hair well out of the way of moving mechanical parts.

• Do remove rings, wristwatch etc, before working on the vehicle – especially the electrical system.

• Do ensure that any lifting or jacking equipment has a safe working load rating adequate for the job.

DON'T

• Don't attempt to lift a heavy component which may be beyond your capability – get assistance.

• Don't rush to finish a job, or take unverified short cuts.

• Don't use ill-fitting tools which may slip and cause injury.

• Don't leave tools or parts lying around where someone can trip over them. Mop up oil and fuel spills at once.

• Don't allow children or pets to play in or near a vehicle being worked on.

The following pages are intended to help in dealing with common roadside emergencies and breakdowns. You will find more detailed fault finding information at the back of the manual, and repair information in the main chapters.

If your car won't start and the starter motor doesn't turn

- ☐ If it's a model with automatic transmission, make sure the selector is in 'P' or 'N'.
- ☐ Open the bonnet and make sure that the battery terminals are clean and tight.
- ☐ Switch on the headlights and try to start the engine. If the headlights go very dim when you're trying to start, the battery is probably flat. Get out of trouble by jump starting (see next page) using a friend's car.

If your car won't start even though the starter motor turns as normal

- ☐ Is there fuel in the tank?
- ☐ Is there moisture on electrical components under the bonnet? Switch off the ignition, then wipe off any obvious dampness with a dry cloth. Spray a water-repellent aerosol product (WD-40 or equivalent) on ignition and fuel system electrical connectors like those shown in the photos. Pay special attention to the ignition coil wiring connector and HT leads. (Note that Diesel engines don't normally suffer from damp.)

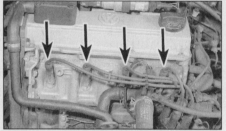

A Check that the spark plug HT leads are securely connected by pushing them onto the plugs.

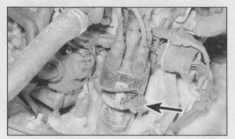

B Check that the HT leads are securely connected to the distributor (where fitted) and the wiring connector (arrowed) is securely connected.

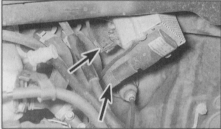

C Check that the HT lead and wiring connector (arrows) are securely connected to the ignition HT coil.

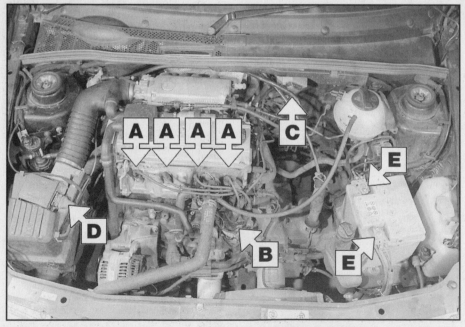

Check that electrical connections are secure (with the ignition switched off) and spray them with a water dispersant spray like WD40 if you suspect a problem due to damp

D Check the airflow meter wiring connector (where applicable) with the ignition switched off.

E Check the security and condition of the battery terminals.

Jump starting

HAYNES HiNT

Jump starting will get you out of trouble, but you must correct whatever made the battery go flat in the first place. There are three possibilities:

1 *The battery has been drained by repeated attempts to start, or by leaving the lights on.*

2 *The charging system is not working properly (alternator drivebelt slack or broken, alternator wiring fault or alternator itself faulty).*

3 *The battery itself is at fault (electrolyte low, or battery worn out).*

When jump-starting a car using a booster battery, observe the following precautions:

✔ Before connecting the booster battery, make sure that the ignition is switched off.

✔ Ensure that all electrical equipment (lights, heater, wipers, etc) is switched off.

✔ Make sure that the booster battery is the same voltage as the discharged one in the vehicle.

✔ If the battery is being jump-started from the battery in another vehicle, the two vehcles MUST NOT TOUCH each other.

✔ Make sure that the transmission is in neutral (or PARK, in the case of automatic transmission).

1 Connect one end of the red jump lead to the positive (+) terminal of the flat battery

2 Connect the other end of the red lead to the positive (+) terminal of the booster battery.

3 Connect one end of the black jump lead to the negative (-) terminal of the booster battery

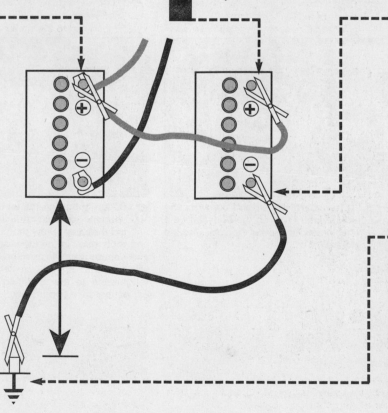

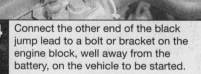

4 Connect the other end of the black jump lead to a bolt or bracket on the engine block, well away from the battery, on the vehicle to be started.

5 Make sure that the jump leads will not come into contact with the fan, drive-belts or other moving parts of the engine.

6 Start the engine using the booster battery, then with the engine running at idle speed, disconnect the jump leads in the reverse order of connection.

Wheel changing

Some of the details shown here will vary according to model. For instance, the location of the spare wheel and jack is not the same on all cars. However, the basic principles apply to all vehicles.

Warning: Do not change a wheel in a situation where you risk being hit by other traffic. On busy roads, try to stop in a lay-by or a gateway. Be wary of passing traffic while changing the wheel – it is easy to become distracted by the job in hand.

Preparation

☐ When a puncture occurs, stop as soon as it is safe to do so.
☐ Park on firm level ground, if possible, and well out of the way of other traffic.
☐ Use hazard warning lights if necessary.

☐ If you have one, use a warning triangle to alert other drivers of your presence.
☐ Apply the handbrake and engage first or reverse gear.
☐ Chock the wheel diagonally opposite the

one being removed – a couple of large stones will do for this.
☐ If the ground is soft, use a flat piece of wood to spread the load under the foot of the jack.

Changing the wheel

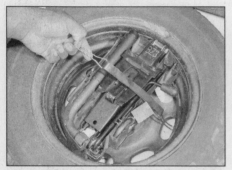

1 The spare wheel and tools are stored in the luggage compartment (Hatchback model shown). Release the retaining strap, and lift out the jack and wheel changing tools out from the centre of the wheel.

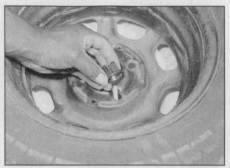

2 Unscrew the retaining nut and lift the wheel out of the vehicle.

3 Remove the wheel trim/hub cap, then slacken each wheel bolt by a half turn.

4 Locate the jack below the reinforced point on the sill (don't jack the vehicle at any other point of the sill) and on firm ground then turn the jack handle clockwise until the wheel is raised clear of the ground. Unscrew the wheel bolts and remove the wheel.

5 Fit the spare wheel, and screw in the bolts. Lightly tighten the bolts with the wheelbrace then lower the vehicle to the ground.

6 Securely tighten the wheel bolts in the sequence shown then refit the wheel trim/hub cap. Stow the punctured wheel and tools back in the luggage compartment and secure them in position. Note that the wheel bolts should be slackened and retightened to the specified torque at the earliest possible opportunity.

Finally...

☐ Remove the wheel chocks.

☐ Stow the jack and tools in the correct locations in the car.

☐ Check the tyre pressure on the wheel just fitted. If it is low, or if you don't have a pressure gauge with you, drive slowly to the nearest garage and inflate the tyre to the right pressure.

Identifying leaks

Puddles on the garage floor or drive, or obvious wetness under the bonnet or underneath the car, suggest a leak that needs investigating. It can sometimes be difficult to decide where the leak is coming from, especially if the engine bay is very dirty already. Leaking oil or fluid can also be blown rearwards by the passage of air under the car, giving a false impression of where the problem lies.

⚠️ **Warning: Most automotive oils and fluids are poisonous. Wash them off skin, and change out of contaminated clothing, without delay.**

HAYNES HiNT *The smell of a fluid leaking from the car may provide a clue to what's leaking. Some fluids are distinctively coloured. It may help to clean the car and to park it over some clean paper as an aid to locating the source of the leak. Remember that some leaks may only occur while the engine is running.*

Sump oil

Engine oil may leak from the drain plug...

Oil from filter

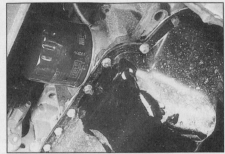

...or from the base of the oil filter.

Gearbox oil

Gearbox oil can leak from the seals at the inboard ends of the driveshafts.

Antifreeze

Leaking antifreeze often leaves a crystalline deposit like this.

Brake fluid

A leak occurring at a wheel is almost certainly brake fluid.

Power steering fluid

Power steering fluid may leak from the pipe connectors on the steering rack.

Towing

When all else fails, you may find yourself having to get a tow home – or of course you may be helping somebody else. Long-distance recovery should only be done by a garage or breakdown service. For shorter distances, DIY towing using another car is easy enough, but observe the following points:
☐ Use a proper tow-rope – they are not expensive. The vehicle being towed must display an 'ON TOW' sign in its rear window.
☐ Always turn the ignition key to the 'on' position when the vehicle is being towed, so that the steering lock is released, and that the direction indicator and brake lights will work.
☐ Only attach the tow-rope to the towing eyes provided **(see illustration)**.
☐ Before being towed, release the handbrake and select neutral on the transmission.

☐ Note that greater-than-usual pedal pressure will be required to operate the brakes, since the vacuum servo unit is only operational with the engine running.
☐ On models with power steering, greater-than-usual steering effort will also be required.
☐ The driver of the car being towed must keep the tow-rope taut at all times to avoid snatching.
☐ Make sure that both drivers know the route before setting off.
☐ Only drive at moderate speeds and keep the distance towed to a minimum. Drive smoothly and allow plenty of time for slowing down at junctions.
☐ On models with automatic transmission, special precautions apply. If in doubt, do not tow, or transmission damage may result.

☐ The front towing eye is supplied as part of the toolkit stored in the luggage compartment. To fit the eye, prise out the reflector next to the direction indicator light in the front bumper. Securely screw the eye into position anti-clockwise - it has a left-handed thread, and tighten using the wheelbrace handle.

Introduction

There are some very simple checks which need only take a few minutes to carry out, but which could save you a lot of inconvenience and expense.

These "Weekly checks" require no great skill or special tools, and the small amount of time they take to perform could prove to be very well spent, for example;

☐ Keeping an eye on tyre condition and pressures, will not only help to stop them wearing out prematurely, but could also save your life.

☐ Many breakdowns are caused by electrical problems. Battery-related faults are particularly common, and a quick check on a regular basis will often prevent the majority of these.

☐ If your car develops a brake fluid leak, the first time you might know about it is when your brakes don't work properly. Checking the level regularly will give advance warning of this kind of problem.

☐ If the oil or coolant levels run low, the cost of repairing any engine damage will be far greater than fixing the leak, for example.

Underbonnet check points

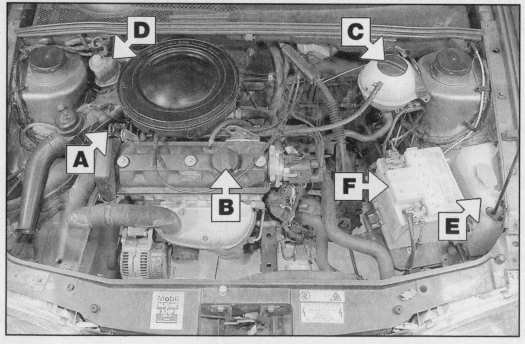

◀ **1.4 litre petrol**

A *Engine oil level dipstick*
B *Engine oil filler cap*
C *Coolant expansion tank*
D *Brake fluid reservoir*
E *Screen washer fluid reservoir*
F *Battery*

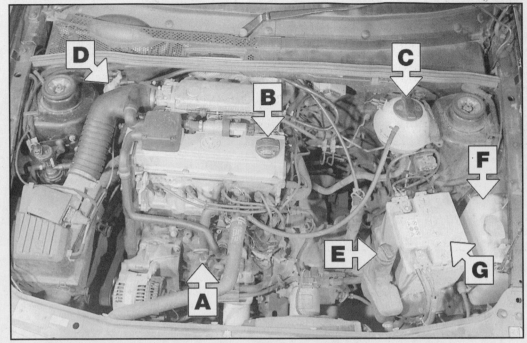

◄ **2.0 litre
8-valve petrol**

A *Engine oil level dipstick*
B *Engine oil filler cap*
C *Coolant expansion tank*
D *Brake fluid reservoir*
E *Power steering fluid reservoir*
F *Screen washer fluid reservoir*
G *Battery*

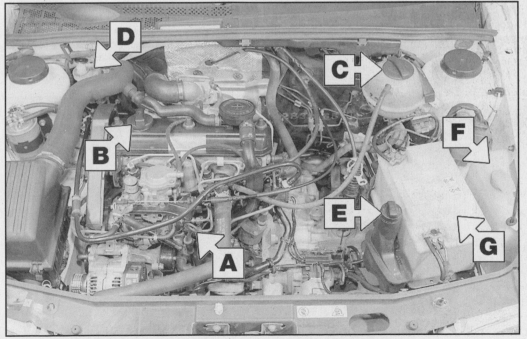

◄ **Turbo diesel**

A *Engine oil level dipstick*
B *Engine oil filler cap*
C *Coolant expansion tank*
D *Brake fluid reservoir*
E *Power steering fluid reservoir*
F *Screen washer fluid reservoir*
G *Battery*

Engine oil level

Before you start

✔ Make sure that your car is on level ground.
✔ Check the oil level before the car is driven, or at least 5 minutes after the engine has been switched off.

 HAYNES HINT *If the oil is checked immediately after driving the vehicle, some of the oil will remain in the upper engine components, resulting in an inaccurate reading on the dipstick!*

The correct oil

Modern engines place great demands on their oil. It is very important that the correct oil for your car is used (See "Lubricants, fluids and tyre pressures" on page 0•17).

Car Care

● If you have to add oil frequently, you should check whether you have any oil leaks. Place some clean paper under the car overnight, and check for stains in the morning. If there are no leaks, the engine may be burning oil *(see "Fault Finding")*.

● Always maintain the level between the upper and lower dipstick marks (see photo 3). If the level is too low severe engine damage may occur. Oil seal failure may result if the engine is overfilled by adding too much oil.

1 The dipstick top is often brightly coloured for easy identification (see *"Underbonnet check points"* on pages 0•10 and 0•11 for exact location). Withdraw the dipstick.

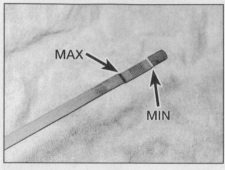

MAX
MIN

3 Note the oil level on the end of the dipstick, which should be between the upper ("MAX") mark and lower ("MIN") mark. Approximately 1.0 litre of oil will raise the level from the lower mark to the upper mark.

2 Using a clean rag or paper towel remove all oil from the dipstick. Insert the clean dipstick into the tube as far as it will go, then withdraw it again.

4 Oil is added through the filler cap. Unscrew the cap and top-up the level; a funnel may help to reduce spillage. Add the oil slowly, checking the level on the dipstick often. Don't overfill (see *"Car Care"* left).

Coolant level

 Warning: DO NOT attempt to remove the expansion tank pressure cap when the engine is hot, as there is a very great risk of scalding. Do not leave open containers of coolant about, as it is poisonous.

Car Care

● With a sealed-type cooling system, adding coolant should not be necessary on a regular basis. If frequent topping-up is required, it is likely there is a leak. Check the radiator, all hoses and joint faces for signs of staining or wetness, and rectify as necessary.

● It is important that antifreeze is used in the cooling system all year round, not just during the winter months. Don't top-up with water alone, as the antifreeze will become too diluted.

1 The coolant level varies with the temperature of the engine. When the engine is cold, the coolant level should be between the "MAX" and "MIN" marks. When the engine is hot, the level may rise slightly above the "MAX" mark.

2 If topping up is necessary, **wait until the engine is cold**. Slowly unscrew the expansion tank cap, to release any pressure present in the cooling system, and remove it.

3 Add a mixture of water and antifreeze to the expansion tank until the coolant level is halfway between the level marks. Refit the cap and tighten it securely.

Brake (and clutch*) fluid level

*On models with a hydraulically-operated clutch, this information is also applicable to the clutch fluid level

Warning:
● **Brake fluid can harm your eyes and damage painted surfaces, so use extreme caution when handling and pouring it.**
● **Do not use fluid that has been standing open for some time, as it absorbs moisture from the air, which can cause a dangerous loss of braking effectiveness.**

 HAYNES HINT
• *Make sure that your car is on level ground.*
• *The fluid level in the reservoir will drop slightly as the brake pads wear down, but the fluid level must never be allowed to drop below the "MIN" mark.*

Safety First!

● If the reservoir requires repeated topping-up this is an indication of a fluid leak somewhere in the system, which should be investigated immediately.

● If a leak is suspected, the car should not be driven until the braking system has been checked. Never take any risks where brakes are concerned.

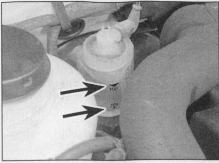

1 The "MAX" and "MIN" marks are indicated on the front of the reservoir. The fluid level must be kept between the marks at all times.

2 If topping-up is necessary, first wipe clean the area around the filler cap to prevent dirt entering the hydraulic system.

3 Unscrew the reservoir cap and carefully lift it out of position, taking care not to damage the level switch float. Inspect the reservoir, if the fluid is dirty the hydraulic system should be drained and refilled (see Chapter 1).

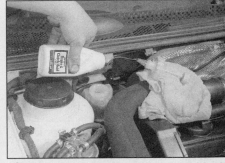

4 Carefully add fluid, taking care not to spill it onto the surrounding components. Use only the specified fluid; mixing different types can cause damage to the system. After topping-up to the correct level, securely refit the cap and wipe off any spilt fluid.

Power steering fluid level

Before you start:

✔ Park the vehicle on level ground.
✔ Set the steering wheel straight-ahead.
✔ The engine should be turned off.

 HAYNES HINT
For the check to be accurate, the steering must not be turned once the engine has been stopped.

Safety First!

● The need for frequent topping-up indicates a leak, which should be investigated immediately.

1 The reservoir is located in the front left-hand corner of the engine compartment, next to the battery. Wipe clean the area around the reservoir filler neck and unscrew the filler cap/dipstick from the reservoir.

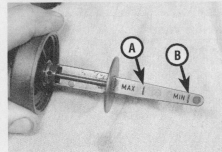

2 Dip the fluid with the reservoir cap/dipstick (do not screw the cap into position). When the engine is cold, the fluid level should be up to the "MIN" mark (B); when hot, it should be on the "MAX" mark (A).

3 When topping-up, use the specified type of fluid and do not overfill the reservoir. When the level is correct, securely refit the cap.

Tyre condition and pressure

It is very important that tyres are in good condition, and at the correct pressure - having a tyre failure at any speed is highly dangerous. Tyre wear is influenced by driving style - harsh braking and acceleration, or fast cornering, will all produce more rapid tyre wear. As a general rule, the front tyres wear out faster than the rears. Interchanging the tyres from front to rear ("rotating" the tyres) may result in more even wear. However, if this is completely effective, you may have the expense of replacing all four tyres at once! Remove any nails or stones embedded in the tread before they penetrate the tyre to cause deflation. If removal of a nail does reveal that the tyre has been punctured, refit the nail so that its point of penetration is marked. Then immediately change the wheel, and have the tyre repaired by a tyre dealer.

Regularly check the tyres for damage in the form of cuts or bulges, especially in the sidewalls. Periodically remove the wheels, and clean any dirt or mud from the inside and outside surfaces. Examine the wheel rims for signs of rusting, corrosion or other damage. Light alloy wheels are easily damaged by "kerbing" whilst parking; steel wheels may also become dented or buckled. A new wheel is very often the only way to overcome severe damage.

New tyres should be balanced when they are fitted, but it may become necessary to re-balance them as they wear, or if the balance weights fitted to the wheel rim should fall off. Unbalanced tyres will wear more quickly, as will the steering and suspension components. Wheel imbalance is normally signified by vibration, particularly at a certain speed (typically around 50 mph). If this vibration is felt only through the steering, then it is likely that just the front wheels need balancing. If, however, the vibration is felt through the whole car, the rear wheels could be out of balance. Wheel balancing should be carried out by a tyre dealer or garage.

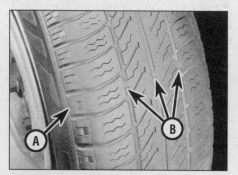

1 Tread Depth - visual check
The original tyres have tread wear safety bands (B), which will appear when the tread depth reaches approximately 1.6 mm. The band positions are indicated by a triangular mark on the tyre sidewall (A).

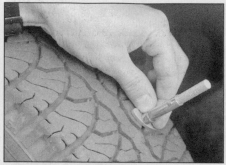

2 Tread Depth - manual check
Alternatively, tread wear can be monitored with a simple, inexpensive device known as a tread depth indicator gauge.

3 Tyre Pressure Check
Check the tyre pressures regularly with the tyres cold. Do not adjust the tyre pressures immediately after the vehicle has been used, or an inaccurate setting will result.

Tyre tread wear patterns

Shoulder Wear

Underinflation (wear on both sides)
Under-inflation will cause overheating of the tyre, because the tyre will flex too much, and the tread will not sit correctly on the road surface. This will cause a loss of grip and excessive wear, not to mention the danger of sudden tyre failure due to heat build-up.
Check and adjust pressures
Incorrect wheel camber (wear on one side)
Repair or renew suspension parts
Hard cornering
Reduce speed!

Centre Wear

Overinflation
Over-inflation will cause rapid wear of the centre part of the tyre tread, coupled with reduced grip, harsher ride, and the danger of shock damage occurring in the tyre casing.
Check and adjust pressures

If you sometimes have to inflate your car's tyres to the higher pressures specified for maximum load or sustained high speed, don't forget to reduce the pressures to normal afterwards.

Uneven Wear

Front tyres may wear unevenly as a result of wheel misalignment. Most tyre dealers and garages can check and adjust the wheel alignment (or "tracking") for a modest charge.
Incorrect camber or castor
Repair or renew suspension parts
Malfunctioning suspension
Repair or renew suspension parts
Unbalanced wheel
Balance tyres
Incorrect toe setting
Adjust front wheel alignment
Note: *The feathered edge of the tread which typifies toe wear is best checked by feel.*

Screen washer fluid level*

*On models with a headlight washer system, the screen wash is also used to clean the headlights

Screenwash additives not only keep the winscreen clean during foul weather, they also prevent the washer system freezing in cold weather - which is when you are likely to need it most. Don't top up using plain water as the screenwash will become too diluted, and will freeze during cold weather. On no account use coolant antifreeze in the washer system - this could discolour or damage paintwork.

1 The screen washer fluid reservoir (arrowed) is located in the front left-hand corner of the engine compartment, next to the battery.

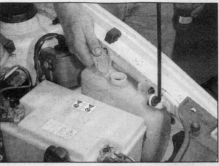

2 The screen washer level can be seen through the reservoir body. If topping-up is necessary, open the cap.

3 When topping-up the reservoir, add a screenwash additive in the quantities recommended on the bottle.

Wiper blades

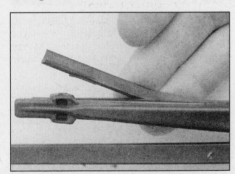

1 Check the condition of the wiper blades; if they are cracked or show any signs of deterioration, or if the glass swept area is smeared, renew them. Wiper blades should be renewed annually.

2 To remove a windscreen wiper blade, pull the arm fully away from the screen until it locks. Swivel the blade through 90°, press the locking tab with your fingers and slide the blade out of the arm's hooked end.

3 Don't forget to check the tailgate wiper blade as well. To remove the blade, depress the retaining tab and slide the blade out of the hooked end of the arm.

Battery

Caution: Before carrying out any work on the vehicle battery, read the precautions given in "Safety first" at the start of this manual.

✔ Make sure that the battery tray is in good condition, and that the clamp is tight. Corrosion on the tray, retaining clamp and the battery itself can be removed with a solution of water and baking soda. Thoroughly rinse all cleaned areas with water. Any metal parts damaged by corrosion should be covered with a zinc-based primer, then painted.

✔ Periodically (approximately every three months), check the charge condition of the battery as described in Chapter 5A.

✔ If the battery is flat, and you need to jump start your vehicle, see *Roadside Repairs*.

1 The battery is located on the left-hand side of the engine compartment. The exterior of the battery should be inspected periodically for damage such as a cracked case or cover.

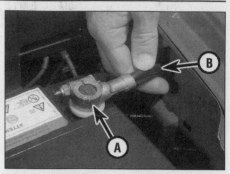

2 Check the tightness of battery clamps (A) to ensure good electrical connections. You should not be able to move them. Also check each cable (B) for cracks and frayed conductors.

HAYNES HINT

Battery corrosion can be kept to a minimum by applying a layer of petroleum jelly to the clamps and terminals after they are reconnected.

3 If corrosion (white, fluffy deposits) is evident, remove the cables from the battery terminals, clean them with a small wire brush, then refit them. Automotive stores sell a useful tool for cleaning the battery post...

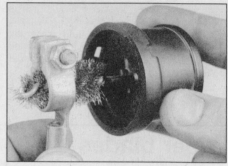

4 ...as well as the battery cable clamps

Bulbs and fuses

✔ Check all external lights and the horn. Refer to the appropriate Sections of Chapter 12 for details if any of the circuits are found to be inoperative.

✔ Visually check all accessible wiring connectors, harnesses and retaining clips for security, and for signs of chafing or damage.

HAYNES HINT

If you need to check your brake lights and indicators unaided, back up to a wall or garage door and operate the lights. The reflected light should show if they are working properly.

1 If a single indicator light, stop-light or headlight has failed, it is likely that a bulb has blown and will need to be replaced. Refer to Chapter 12 for details. If both stop-lights have failed, it is possible that the switch has failed (see Chapter 9).

2 If more than one indicator light or tail light has failed it is likely that either a fuse has blown or that there is a fault in the circuit (see Chapter 12). The fuses are located behind a panel on the bottom of the driver's side lower facia panel.

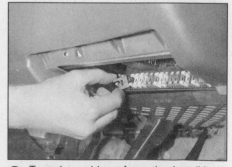

3 To replace a blown fuse, simply pull it out and fit a new fuse of the correct rating (see Chapter 12). If the fuse blows again, it is important that you find out why - a complete checking procedure is given in Chapter 12.

Lubricants and fluids

Engine . . . . Multigrade engine oil, viscosity SAE 10W/40 to 20W/50, to API SG/CD

Cooling system . . . . Ethylene glycol based antifreeze

Manual transmission . . . . VW specification G50 gear oil, viscosity SAE 75W/90

Automatic transmission . . . . Dexron II type ATF

Braking system . . . . Hydraulic fluid to SAE J1703F or DOT 4

Power steering . . . . Dexron II type ATF

Tyre pressures

	Front	Rear
Hatchback petrol models		
Up to half load:		
1.4 litre models	1.8 bar (26 psi)	1.8 bar (26 psi)
1.6 and 1.8 litre models	2.1 bar (30 psi)	1.9 bar (27 psi)
2.0 litre 8-valve models:		
185/60 R 14 and 195/50 R 15 tyres	2.3 bar (33 psi)	2.1 bar (30 psi)
205/50 R 15 tyres	2.0 bar (29 psi)	1.8 bar (26 psi)
2.0 litre 16 valve models:		
195/50 R 15 tyres	2.6 bar (38 psi)	2.4 bar (35 psi)
205/50 R 15 tyres	2.2 bar (32 psi)	2.0 bar (29 psi)
Up to full load:		
1.4 litre models	2.0 bar (29 psi)	2.2 bar (32 psi)
1.6 and 1.8 litre models	2.4 bar (35 psi)	2.6 bar (38 psi)
2.0 litre 8-valve models:		
185/60 R 14 and 195/50 R 15 tyres	2.5 bar (36 psi)	2.7 bar (39 psi)
205/50 R 15 tyres	2.2 bar (32 psi)	2.4 bar (35 psi)
2.0 litre 16 valve models:		
195/50 R 15 tyres	2.8 bar (41 psi)	3.0 bar (44 psi)
205/50 R 15 tyres	2.4 bar (35 psi)	2.6 bar (38 psi)
Hatchback diesel models		
Up to half load:		
Non-turbo models	1.8 bar (26 psi)	1.8 bar (26 psi)
Turbo models	2.1 bar (30 psi)	1.9 bar (27 psi)
Up to full load:		
Non-turbo models	2.0 bar (29 psi)	2.2 bar (32 psi)
Turbo models	2.4 bar (35 psi)	2.6 bar (38 psi)
Saloon petrol models		
Up to half load:		
1.6 and 1.8 litre (55 kW) models	2.0 bar (29 psi)	1.8 bar (26 psi)
1.8 litre (66 KW) models	2.2 bar (32 psi)	2.0 bar (29 psi)
2.0 litre models:		
185/60 R 14 and 195/50 R 15 tyres	2.2 bar (32 psi)	2.0 bar (29 psi)
205/50 R 15 tyres	1.9 bar (27 psi)	1.9 bar (27 psi)
Up to full load:		
1.6 and 1.8 litre (55 KW) models	2.2 bar (32 psi)	2.6 bar (38 psi)
1.8 litre (66 KW) models	2.4 bar (35 psi)	2.8 bar (41 psi)
2.0 litre models:		
185/60 R 14 and 195/50 R 15 tyres	2.4 bar (35 psi)	2.8 bar (41 psi)
205/50 R 15 tyres	2.1 bar (30 psi)	2.5 bar (36 psi)

Tyre pressures (continued)

Saloon diesel models	Front	Rear
Up to half load:		
Non-turbo models	2.0 bar (29 psi)	1.8 bar (26 psi)
Turbo models:		
55 KW models	2.2 bar (32 psi)	2.0 bar (29 psi)
66 KW models	2.3 bar (33 psi)	2.1 bar (30 psi)
Up to full load:		
Non-turbo models	2.2 bar (32 psi)	2.6 bar (38 psi)
Turbo models:		
55 KW models	2.4 bar (35 psi)	2.8 bar (41 psi)
66 KW models	2.6 bar (38 psi)	3.0 bar (44 psi)
Estate petrol models		
Up to half load:		
1.4 litre models	1.8 bar (26 psi)	1.8 bar (26 psi)
1.6 and 1.8 litre models:		
185/60 R 14 and 195/50 R 15 tyres	2.1 bar (30 psi)	2.1 bar (30 psi)
195/60 R 14 tyres	1.8 bar (26 psi)	1.8 bar (26 psi)
Up to full load:		
1.4 litre models	2.0 bar (29 psi)	2.6 bar (38 psi)
1.6 and 1.8 litre models:		
185/60 R 14 and 195/50 R 15 tyres	2.4 bar (35 psi)	3.0 bar (44 psi)
195/60 R 14 tyres	2.1 bar (30 psi)	2.7 bar (39 psi)
Estate diesel models		
Up to half load:		
Non-turbo models and turbo (55 KW) models:		
185/60 R 14 and 195/50 R 15 tyres	2.2 bar (32 psi)	2.2 bar (32 psi)
195/60 R 14 tyres	1.9 bar (27 psi)	1.9 bar (27 psi)
Turbo (66 KW) models:		
195/60 R 14 tyres	1.9 bar (27 psi)	1.9 bar (27 psi)
195/50 R 15 tyres	2.0 bar (29 psi)	2.0 bar (29 psi)
Up to full load:		
Non-turbo models and turbo (55 KW) models:		
185/60 R 14 and 195/50 R 15 tyres	2.4 bar (35 psi)	3.0 bar (44 psi)
195/60 R 14 tyres	2.1 bar (30 psi)	2.7 bar (39 psi)
Turbo (66 KW) models:		
195/60 R 14 tyres	2.2 bar (32 psi)	2.8 bar (41 psi)
195/50 R 15 tyres	2.6 bar (38 psi)	3.2 bar (47 psi)

Note: *Pressures apply to original-equipment tyres, and may vary if any other make of tyre is fitted; check with the tyre manufacturer or supplier for the correct pressures if necessary. Note that the correct pressures for each individual vehicle are given on a sticker which is either inside the glovebox lid or inside the fuel filler flap. The information on this sticker may vary slightly with that quoted above - if so, consult your VAG dealer for the latest recommendations.*

The spare wheel should be run at the maximum full-load pressure for the vehicle.

Chapter 1 Part A:
Routine maintenance and servicing - petrol models

Contents

Degrees of difficulty

Easy, suitable for novice with little experience	**Fairly easy,** suitable for beginner with some experience	**Fairly difficult,** suitable for competent DIY mechanic	**Difficult,** suitable for experienced DIY mechanic	**Very difficult,** suitable for expert DIY or professional

Lubricants and fluids

Refer to end of *"Weekly checks"*

Capacities

Engine oil

Excluding filter
Engine codes ABD, ABU, AEA .... 3.0 litres
All other engine codes .... 3.5 litres
Including filter:
Engine codes ABD, ABU, AEA .... 3.5 litres
All other engine codes .... 4.0 litres

Cooling system

All models (approximate) .... 6.3 litres

Transmission

Manual transmission
4-speed 1.4 litre models .... 2.2 litres
5-speed 1.4 and 1.6 litre models .... 3.1 litres
5-speed (all other models) .... 2.0 litres
Automatic transmission .... 5.6 litres (fluid change 3.0 litres)

Power-assisted steering

All models (approximate) .... 1.5 litres

Fuel tank

All models (approximate) .... 62 litres

Washer reservoirs

Models with headlight washers .... 7.0 litres
Models without headlight washers .... 4.0 litres

Engine

Oil filter:
Engine code ABD (to May 1992) .... Champion C160
Engine code ABD (from June 1992) .... Champion C161
Engine codes AAM, ABS, 2E and ABF .... Champion C160

Cooling system

Antifreeze mixture:
28% antifreeze .... Protection down to -15°C (5°F)
50% antifreeze .... Protection down to -30°C (-22°F)
Note: *Refer to antifreeze manufacturer for latest recommendations.*

Fuel system

Air filter element:
Engine code ABD (to May 1992) .... Champion W102
Engine code ABD (from June 1992), and all other engine codes .... Champion U583
Fuel filter .... Champion L206

Ignition system

Ignition timing .... Refer to Chapter 5B
Spark plugs:
Engine codes ABD and ABS .... Champion N7BYC
Engine codes ABU and AAM .... Champion N9BYC4
Engine code 2E .... Champion N7BMC
Engine code ABF .... Champion C6BYC
Spark plug electrode gap:
All engine codes except ABU and AAM .... 0.8 mm (0.032 in)
Engine codes ABU and AAM .... 1.0 mm (0.039 in)

Brakes

Brake pad minimum thickness .... 7.0 mm
Brake shoe friction material minimum thickness .... 2.5 mm

Torque wrench settings

	Nm	lbf ft
Roadwheel bolts	110	81
Spark plugs:		
Engine codes 2E, AEK, ADY, ABF	30	22
Engine codes AAM, ABS, ADZ, ABD, ABU, AEA	25	18
Sump drain plug	30	22

The maintenance intervals in this manual are provided with the assumption that you, not the dealer, will be carrying out the work. These are the minimum intervals recommended by us for vehicles driven daily. If you wish to keep your vehicle in peak condition at all times, you may wish to perform some of these procedures more often. We encourage frequent maintenance, since it enhances the efficiency, performance and resale value of your vehicle.

When the vehicle is new, it should be serviced by a dealer service department, in order to preserve the factory warranty.

All VW Golf/Vento models are equipped with a service interval display indicator in the instrument panel. Every time the engine is started the panel will illuminate for a few seconds, displaying either of the following. This provides a handy reminder of when the next service is required:

Display shows "IN 00" - no service required
Display shows "OEL" - 10 000 mile (15 000 km) service required
Display shows "IN 01" - 12 monthly service required
Display shows "IN 02" - 20 000 mile (30 000 km) service required

Every 250 miles (400 km) or weekly

☐ Refer to *"Weekly Checks"*

Every 10 000 miles (15 000 km) - "OEL" on interval display

☐ Renew the engine oil and filter (Section 3)
☐ Check the front brake pad thickness (Section 4)
☐ Reset the service interval display (Section 5)

Every 12 months - "IN 01" on interval display

Note: *If the vehicle is covering less 10 000 miles (15 000 km) a year, also carry out the tasks listed above*

☐ Check the automatic transmission fluid level (Section 6)
☐ Check all underbonnet components and hoses for fluid leaks (Section 7)
☐ Check the rear brake pad thickness - rear disc brake models (Section 8)
☐ Check the rear brake shoe lining thickness - rear drum brake models (Section 9)
☐ Check the operation of the handbrake (Section 10)
☐ Check the steering and suspension components for condition and security (Section 11)
☐ Check the condition of the driveshaft gaiters (Section 12)
☐ Check the condition of the exhaust system and its mountings (Section 13)
☐ Check the headlight beam adjustment (Section 14)
☐ Check the operation of the windscreen/tailgate/headlight washer system(s) (as applicable) (Section 15)
☐ Check the condition of the airbag unit(s) (Section 16)
☐ Lubricate all hinges and locks (Section 17)
☐ Carry out a road test (Section 18)
☐ Reset service interval display (Section 5)

Every 20 000 miles (30 000 km) - "IN 02" on interval display

Note: *If the vehicle is covering more than 20 000 miles (30 000 km) a year, also carry out all the operations described above*

☐ Renew the spark plugs (Section 19)
☐ Renew the air filter element (Section 20)
☐ Renew the automatic transmission fluid (Section 21)
☐ Renew the pollen filter element (Section 22)
☐ Check the ignition system (Section 23)
☐ Check the manual transmission oil level (Section 24)
☐ Check the condition of the auxiliary drivebelt(s), and renew if necessary (Section 25)
☐ Reset service interval display (Section 5)

Every 60 000 miles (90 000 km)

☐ Renew the timing belt (Section 26)
☐ Renew the fuel filter (Section 27)

Every 2 years (regardless of mileage)

☐ Renew the coolant (Section 28)
☐ Renew the brake fluid (Section 29)
☐ Check the engine management system (Section 30)

1A

Underbonnet view of a 1.4 litre model

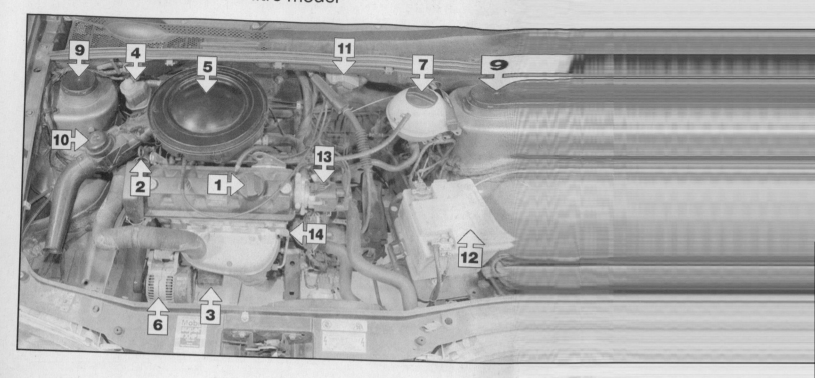

Underbonnet view of a 2.0 litre 8-valve model

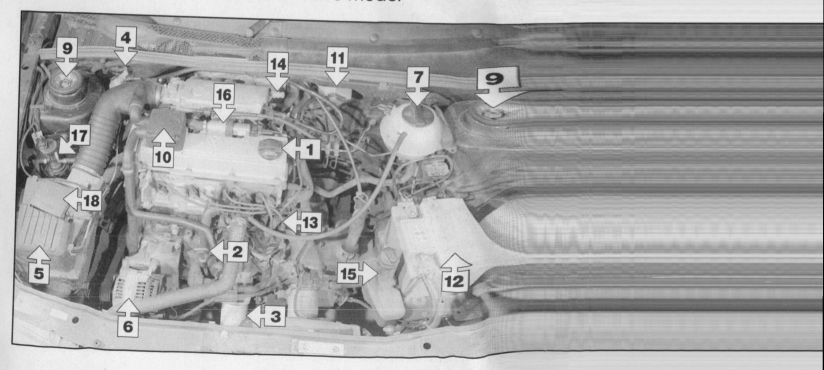

The maintenance intervals in this manual are provided with the assumption that you, not the dealer, will be carrying out the work. These are the minimum intervals recommended by us for vehicles driven daily. If you wish to keep your vehicle in peak condition at all times, you may wish to perform some of these procedures more often. We encourage frequent maintenance, since it enhances the efficiency, performance and resale value of your vehicle.

When the vehicle is new, it should be serviced by a dealer service department, in order to preserve the factory warranty.

All VW Golf/Vento models are equipped with a service interval display indicator in the instrument panel. Every time the engine is started the panel will illuminate for a few seconds, displaying either of the following. This provides a handy reminder of when the next service is required:

Display shows "IN 00" - no service required

Display shows "OEL" - 10 000 mile (15 000 km) service required

Display shows "IN 01" - 12 monthly service required

Display shows "IN 02" - 20 000 mile (30 000 km) service required

Every 250 miles (400 km) or weekly
☐ Refer to *"Weekly Checks"*

Every 10 000 miles (15 000 km) - "OEL" on interval display
☐ Renew the engine oil and filter (Section 3)
☐ Check the front brake pad thickness (Section 4)
☐ Reset the service interval display (Section 5)

Every 12 months - "IN 01" on interval display
Note: *If the vehicle is covering less 10 000 miles (15 000 km) a year, also carry out the tasks listed above*
☐ Check the automatic transmission fluid level (Section 6)
☐ Check all underbonnet components and hoses for fluid leaks (Section 7)
☐ Check the rear brake pad thickness - rear disc brake models (Section 8)
☐ Check the rear brake shoe lining thickness - rear drum brake models (Section 9)
☐ Check the operation of the handbrake (Section 10)
☐ Check the steering and suspension components for condition and security (Section 11)
☐ Check the condition of the driveshaft gaiters (Section 12)
☐ Check the condition of the exhaust system and its mountings (Section 13)
☐ Check the headlight beam adjustment (Section 14)
☐ Check the operation of the windscreen/tailgate/headlight washer system(s) (as applicable) (Section 15)
☐ Check the condition of the airbag unit(s) (Section 16)
☐ Lubricate all hinges and locks (Section 17)
☐ Carry out a road test (Section 18)
☐ Reset service interval display (Section 5)

Every 20 000 miles (30 000 km) - "IN 02" on interval display
Note: *If the vehicle is covering more than 20 000 miles (30 000 km) a year, also carry out all the operations described above*
☐ Renew the spark plugs (Section 19)
☐ Renew the air filter element (Section 20)
☐ Renew the automatic transmission fluid (Section 21)
☐ Renew the pollen filter element (Section 22)
☐ Check the ignition system (Section 23)
☐ Check the manual transmission oil level (Section 24)
☐ Check the condition of the auxiliary drivebelt(s), and renew if necessary (Section 25)
☐ Reset service interval display (Section 5)

Every 60 000 miles (90 000 km)
☐ Renew the timing belt (Section 26)
☐ Renew the fuel filter (Section 27)

Every 2 years (regardless of mileage)
☐ Renew the coolant (Section 28)
☐ Renew the brake fluid (Section 29)
☐ Check the engine management system (Section 30)

1A

Underbonnet view of a 1.4 litre model

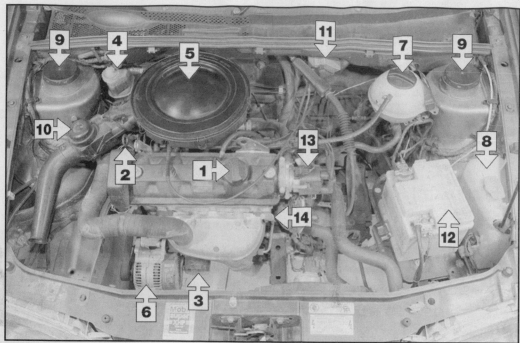

1 Engine oil filler cap
2 Engine oil dipstick
3 Oil filter
4 Master cylinder brake fluid reservoir
5 Air cleaner housing
6 Alternator
7 Coolant expansion tank
8 Windscreen/tailgate washer fluid reservoir
9 Suspension strut upper mounting
10 Air cleaner air temperature control valve
11 Ignition HT coil
12 Battery
13 Distributor
14 Exhaust gas take-off pipe

Underbonnet view of a 2.0 litre 8-valve model

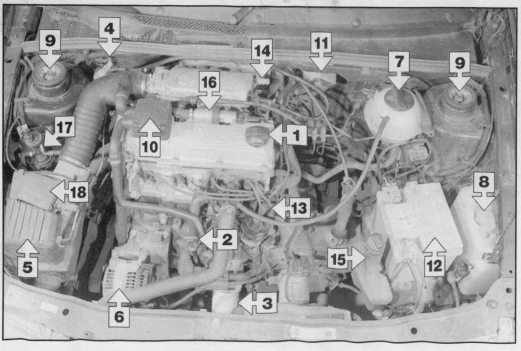

1 Engine oil filler cap
2 Engine oil dipstick
3 Oil filter
4 Master cylinder brake fluid reservoir
5 Air cleaner housing
6 Alternator
7 Coolant expansion tank
8 Windscreen/tailgate washer fluid reservoir
9 Suspension strut upper mounting
10 Crankcase pressure regulating valve
11 Ignition HT coil
12 Battery
13 Distributor
14 Exhaust gas take-off pipe
15 Power steering fluid reservoir
16 Idle speed control valve
17 Evaporative emission system purge valve
18 Airflow meter

Front underbody view (1.4 litre model shown - other models similar)

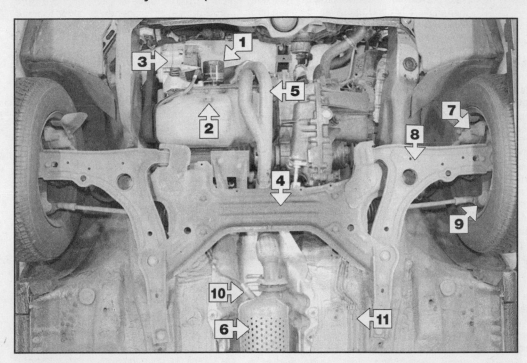

1 Engine oil filter
2 Sump drain plug
3 Alternator
4 Front suspension subframe
5 Exhaust front pipe
6 Catalytic converter
7 Front brake caliper
8 Front suspension lower arm
9 Track rod balljoint
10 Lambda sensor
11 Brake pipes

Rear underbody view (1.4 litre model shown - other models similar)

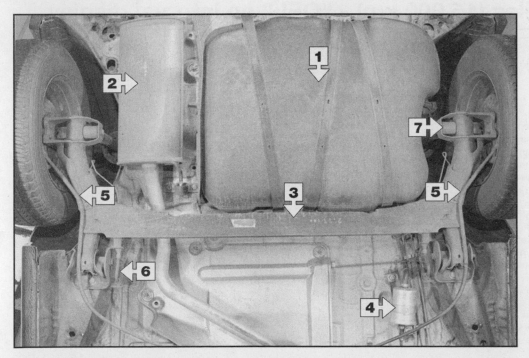

1 Fuel tank
2 Exhaust tailpipe
3 Rear axle assembly
4 Fuel filter
5 Handbrake cable
6 Brake hose
7 Suspension strut lower
  mounting

1 Introduction

General information

This Chapter is designed to help the home mechanic maintain his/her vehicle for safety, economy, long life and peak performance.

The Chapter contains a master maintenance schedule, followed by Sections dealing specifically with each task in the schedule. Visual checks, adjustments, component renewal and other helpful items are included. Refer to the accompanying illustrations of the engine compartment and the underside of the vehicle for the locations of the various components.

Servicing your vehicle in accordance with the mileage/time maintenance schedule and the following Sections will provide a planned maintenance programme, which should result in a long and reliable service life. This is a comprehensive plan, so maintaining some items but not others at the specified service intervals, will not produce the same results.

As you service your vehicle, you will discover that many of the procedures can - and should - be grouped together, because of the particular procedure being performed, or because of the proximity of two otherwise unrelated components to one another. For example, if the vehicle is raised for any reason, the exhaust can be inspected at the same time as the suspension and steering components.

The first step in this maintenance programme is to prepare yourself before the actual work begins. Read through all the Sections relevant to the work to be carried out, then make a list and gather all the parts and tools required. If a problem is encountered, seek advice from a parts specialist, or a dealer service department.

2 Intensive maintenance

1 If, from the time the vehicle is new, the routine maintenance schedule is followed closely, and frequent checks are made of fluid levels and high-wear items, as suggested throughout this manual, the engine will be kept in relatively good running condition, and the need for additional work will be minimised.
2 It is possible that there will be times when the engine is running poorly due to the lack of regular maintenance. This is even more likely if a used vehicle, which has not received regular and frequent maintenance checks, is purchased. In such cases, additional work may need to be carried out, outside of the regular maintenance intervals.
3 If engine wear is suspected, a compression test (refer to the relevant Part of Chapter 2) will provide valuable information regarding the overall performance of the main internal components. Such a test can be used as a basis to decide on the extent of the work to be carried out. If, for example, a compression test indicates serious internal engine wear, conventional maintenance as described in this Chapter will not greatly improve the performance of the engine, and may prove a waste of time and money, unless extensive overhaul work is carried out first.

4 The following series of operations are those most often required to improve the performance of a generally poor-running engine:

Primary operations

a) Clean, inspect and test the battery (See "Weekly Checks").
b) Check all the engine-related fluids (See "Weekly Checks").
c) Check the condition and tension of the auxiliary drivebelt (Section 25).
d) Renew the spark plugs (Section 19).
e) Inspect the distributor cap and rotor arm (Section 23).
f) Check the condition of the air filter, and renew if necessary (Section 20).
g) Check the fuel filter (Section 27).
h) Check the condition of all hoses, and check for fluid leaks (Section 7).
i) Check the exhaust gas emissions (Section 30).

5 If the above operations do not prove fully effective, carry out the following secondary operations:

Secondary operations

All items listed under "Primary operations", plus the following:
a) Check the charging system (see relevant Part of Chapter 5).
b) Check the ignition system (see relevant Part of Chapter 5).
c) Check the fuel system (see relevant Part of Chapter 4).
d) Renew the distributor cap and rotor arm (Section 23).
e) Renew the ignition HT leads (Section 23)

Every 10 000 miles (15 000 km) - "OEL" on interval display

3 Engine oil and filter renewal

1 Frequent oil and filter changes are the most important maintenance procedures which can be undertaken by the DIY owner. As engine oil ages, it becomes diluted and contaminated, which leads to premature engine wear.
2 Before starting this procedure, gather all the necessary tools and materials. Also make sure that you have plenty of clean rags and newspapers handy, to mop up any spills. Ideally, the engine oil should be warm, as it will drain better, and more built-up sludge will be removed with it. Take care, however, not to touch the exhaust or any other hot parts of the engine when working under the vehicle. To avoid any possibility of scalding, and to protect yourself from possible skin irritants and other harmful contaminants in used engine oils, it is advisable to wear gloves when carrying out this work. Access to the underside of the vehicle will be greatly improved if it can be raised on a lift, driven onto ramps, or jacked up and supported on axle stands (see "Jacking and Vehicle Support"). Whichever method is chosen, make sure that the vehicle remains level, or if it is at an angle, that the drain plug is at the lowest point.
3 Using a socket and wrench or a ring spanner, slacken the drain plug about half a turn (see illustration). Position the draining container under the drain plug, then remove the plug completely (see Haynes Hint). Recover the sealing ring from the drain plug.

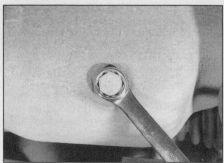

3.3 Slackening the sump drain plug

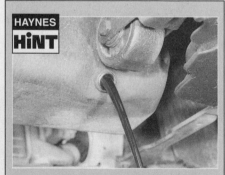

Keep the drain plug pressed into the sump while unscrewing it by hand last couple of turns. As the plug releases, move it away sharply so the stream of oil issuing from the sump runs into the container, not up your sleeve!

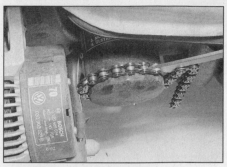

3.7 Using a chain wrench to slacken the oil filter

4 Allow some time for the old oil to drain, noting that it may be necessary to reposition the container as the oil flow slows to a trickle.
5 After all the oil has drained, wipe off the drain plug with a clean rag, and fit a new sealing washer. Clean the area around the drain plug opening, and refit the plug. Tighten the plug securely.
6 If the filter is also to be renewed, move the container into position under the oil filter, which is located on the front side of the cylinder block, below the inlet manifold.
7 Using an oil filter removal tool if necessary, slacken the filter initially, then unscrew it by hand the rest of the way **(see illustration)**. Empty the oil in the filter into the container.
8 Use a clean rag to remove all oil, dirt and sludge from the filter sealing area on the engine. Check the old filter to make sure that the rubber sealing ring has not stuck to the engine. If it has, carefully remove it.
9 Apply a light coating of clean engine oil to the sealing ring on the new filter, then screw it into position on the engine. Tighten the filter firmly by hand only - **do not** use any tools.
10 Remove the old oil and all tools from under the car then lower the car to the ground (if applicable).

OIL CARE
OIL BANK LINE
0800 66 33 66

Note: It is antisocial and illegal to dump oil down the drain. To find the location of your local oil recycling bank, call this number free.

11 Remove the dipstick, then unscrew the oil filler cap from the cylinder head cover or oil filler/breather neck (as applicable). Fill the engine, using the correct grade and type of oil (see *"Lubricants fluids and capacities"*). An oil can spout or funnel may help to reduce spillage. Pour in half the specified quantity of oil first then wait a few minutes for the oil to fall to the sump. Continue adding oil a small quantity at a time until the level is up to the lower mark on the dipstick. Adding around 1.0 litre will bring the level up to the upper mark on the dipstick. Refit the filler cap.
12 Start the engine and run it for a few minutes; check for leaks around the oil filter seal and the sump drain plug. Note that there may be a few seconds delay before the oil pressure warning light goes out when the engine is started, as the oil circulates through the engine oil galleries and the new oil filter (where fitted) before the pressure builds up.
13 Switch off the engine, and wait a few minutes for the oil to settle in the sump once more. With the new oil circulated and the filter completely full, recheck the level on the dipstick, and add more oil as necessary.
14 Dispose of the used engine oil safely, with reference to *"General repair procedures"* in the *Reference* section of this manual.

4 Front brake pad check

1 Firmly apply the handbrake, then jack up the front of the car and support it securely on axle stands. Remove the front roadwheels.
2 For a comprehensive check, the brake pads should be removed and cleaned. The operation of the caliper can then also be checked, and the condition of the brake disc itself can be fully examined on both sides. Refer to Chapter 9 **(see Haynes Hint)**.
3 If any pad's friction material is worn to the specified thickness or less, *all four pads must be renewed as a set.*

5 Resetting the service interval display

1 After all necessary maintenance work has been completed, the relevant service interval

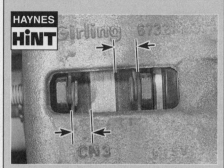

For a quick check, the thickness of the friction material on each brake pad can be measured through the aperture in the caliper body

display code must be reset. If more than one service schedule is carried out, note that the relevant display intervals must be reset individually.
2 The display is reset using the reset button on the left-hand side of the instrument panel (below the speedometer) and the clock setting button on the right-hand side of the panel (below the clock/tachometer); on models with a digital clock the lower (minute) button is used. Resetting is carried out as follows.
3 Turn the ignition switch and check that the speedometer mileage indicator is set to the mileage setting and not the trip meter setting. When this is so, press and hold in the button on the left of the instrument panel. Keeping the button depressed, switch off the ignition and release the button. The word "OEL" should be shown on the display, by depressing the left-hand button again the display will change to "IN 01" followed by "IN 02". Set the display to the relevant service which has just been performed, then depress the clock adjustment button briefly until "———-" is displayed; this indicates that the service interval display has been reset. Repeat the reset procedure for all the relevant service display intervals.
4 Once the resetting procedure is complete, switch on the ignition and check that "IN 00" is shown in the display.

1A

Every 12 months - "IN 01" on interval display

6 Automatic transmission fluid level check

1 Take the vehicle on a short journey, to warm the transmission up to normal operating temperature, then park the vehicle on level ground. The fluid level is checked using the dipstick located at the front of the engine

compartment, on the front of the transmission unit.
2 With the engine idling and the selector lever in the "P" (Park) position, withdraw the dipstick from the tube, and wipe all the fluid from its end with a clean rag or paper towel. Insert the clean dipstick back into the tube as far as it will go, then withdraw it once more. Note the fluid level on the end of the dipstick;

it should be between the MAX and MIN marks. **Note:** *If the engine has not been warmed up, the fluid level should be at the 20°C mark.*
3 If topping-up is necessary, add the required quantity of the specified fluid to the transmission through the dipstick tube. Use a funnel with a fine mesh gauze, to avoid spillage, and to ensure that no foreign matter

A leak in the cooling system will usually show up as white - or rust - coloured deposits on the area adjoining the leak

enters the transmission. **Note:** *Never overfill the transmission so that the fluid level is above the upper mark.*

4 After topping-up, take the vehicle on a short run to distribute the fresh fluid, then recheck the level again, topping-up if necessary.

5 Always maintain the level between the two dipstick marks. If the level is allowed to fall below the lower mark, fluid starvation may result, which could lead to severe transmission damage. If the level is too high, the excess fluid may be ejected. In either case, an incorrect level will adversely affect the operation of the transmission.

6 Frequent need for topping-up indicates that there is a leak, which should be found and corrected before it becomes serious.

7 Hose and fluid leak check

1 Visually inspect the engine joint faces, gaskets and seals for any signs of water or oil leaks. Pay particular attention to the areas around the camshaft cover, cylinder head, oil filter and sump joint faces. Bear in mind that, over a period of time, some very slight seepage from these areas is to be expected - what you are really looking for is any indication of a serious leak **(see Haynes Hint)**. Should a leak be found, renew the offending gasket or oil seal by referring to the appropriate Chapters in this manual.

2 Also check the security and condition of all the engine-related pipes and hoses. Ensure that all cable-ties or securing clips are in place and in good condition. Clips which are broken or missing can lead to chafing of the hoses, pipes or wiring, which could cause more serious problems in the future.

3 Carefully check the radiator hoses and heater hoses along their entire length. Renew any hose which is cracked, swollen or deteriorated. Cracks will show up better if the hose is squeezed. Pay close attention to the hose clips that secure the hoses to the cooling system components. Hose clips can pinch and puncture hoses, resulting in cooling system leaks.

4 Inspect all the cooling system components (hoses, joint faces etc.) for leaks. A leak in the cooling system will usually show up as white- or rust-coloured deposits on the area adjoining the leak. Where any problems of this nature are found on system components, renew the component or gasket with reference to Chapter 3.

5 Where applicable, inspect the automatic transmission fluid cooler hoses for leaks or deterioration.

6 With the vehicle raised, inspect the petrol tank and filler neck for punctures, cracks and other damage. The connection between the filler neck and tank is especially critical. Sometimes a rubber filler neck or connecting hose will leak due to loose retaining clamps or deteriorated rubber.

7 Carefully check all rubber hoses and metal fuel lines leading away from the petrol tank. Check for loose connections, deteriorated hoses, crimped lines, and other damage. Pay particular attention to the vent pipes and hoses, which often loop up around the filler neck and can become blocked or crimped. Follow the lines to the front of the vehicle, carefully inspecting them all the way. Renew damaged sections as necessary.

8 From within the engine compartment, check the security of all fuel hose attachments and pipe unions, and inspect the fuel hoses and vacuum hoses for kinks, chafing and deterioration.

9 Where applicable, check the condition of the power steering fluid hoses and pipes.

8 Rear brake pad check - models with rear disc brakes

1 Chock the front wheels, then jack up the rear of the vehicle and support it on axle stands. Remove the rear roadwheels.

2 For a quick check, the thickness of friction material remaining on each brake pad can be measured through the top of the caliper body. If any pad's friction material is worn to the specified thickness or less, all four pads must be renewed as a set.

3 For a comprehensive check, the brake pads should be removed and cleaned. This will permit the operation of the caliper to be checked, and the condition of the brake disc itself to be fully examined on both sides. Refer to Chapter 9 for further information.

9 Rear brake shoe check - models with rear drum brakes

1 Chock the front wheels, then jack up the rear of the vehicle, and support it securely on axle stands.

2 For a quick check, the thickness of friction material remaining on one of the brake shoes can be observed through the hole in the brake backplate which is exposed by prising out the sealing grommet **(see illustration)**. If a rod of

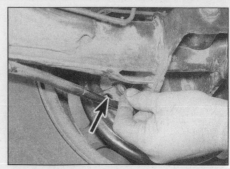

9.2 Remove the rubber plug and check the brake friction material thickness through the backplate aperture (arrowed)

the same diameter as the specified minimum friction material thickness is placed against the shoe friction material, the amount of wear can be assessed. A torch or inspection light will probably be required. If the friction material on any shoe is worn down to the specified minimum thickness or less, all four shoes must be renewed as a set.

3 For a comprehensive check, the brake drum should be removed and cleaned. This will allow the wheel cylinders to be checked, and the condition of the brake drum itself to be fully examined (see Chapter 9).

10 Handbrake check and adjustment

Refer to Chapter 9

11 Steering and suspension check

Front suspension and steering check

1 Raise the front of the vehicle, and securely support it on axle stands.

2 Visually inspect the balljoint dust covers and the steering rack-and-pinion gaiters for splits, chafing or deterioration. Any wear of these components will cause loss of lubricant, together with dirt and water entry, resulting in rapid deterioration of the balljoints or steering gear.

3 On vehicles with power steering, check the fluid hoses for chafing or deterioration, and the pipe and hose unions for fluid leaks. Also check for signs of fluid leakage under pressure from the steering gear rubber gaiters, which would indicate failed fluid seals within the steering gear.

4 Grasp the roadwheel at the 12 o'clock and 6 o'clock positions, and try to rock it **(see illustration)**. Very slight free play may be felt, but if the movement is appreciable, further investigation is necessary to determine the source. Continue rocking the wheel while an assistant depresses the footbrake. If the movement is now eliminated or significantly reduced, it is likely that the hub bearings are

11.4 Check for wear in the hub bearings by grasping the wheel and trying to rock it

12.1 Check the condition of the driveshaft gaiters (arrowed)

at fault. If the free play is still evident with the footbrake depressed, then there is wear in the suspension joints or mountings.

5 Now grasp the wheel at the 9 o'clock and 3 o'clock positions, and try to rock it as before. Any movement felt now may again be caused by wear in the hub bearings or the steering track-rod balljoints. If the inner or outer balljoint is worn, the visual movement will be obvious.

6 Using a large screwdriver or flat bar, check for wear in the suspension mounting bushes by levering between the relevant suspension component and its attachment point. Some movement is to be expected as the mountings are made of rubber, but excessive wear should be obvious. Also check the condition of any visible rubber bushes, looking for splits, cracks or contamination of the rubber.

7 With the car standing on its wheels, have an assistant turn the steering wheel back and forth about an eighth of a turn each way. There should be very little, if any, lost movement between the steering wheel and roadwheels. If this is not the case, closely observe the joints and mountings previously described, but in addition, check the steering column universal joints for wear, and the rack-and-pinion steering gear itself.

Suspension strut/ shock absorber check

8 Check for any signs of fluid leakage around the suspension strut/shock absorber body, or from the rubber gaiter around the piston rod. Should any fluid be noticed, the suspension strut/shock absorber is defective internally, and should be renewed. **Note:** *Suspension struts/shock absorbers should always be renewed in pairs on the same axle.*

9 The efficiency of the suspension strut/shock absorber may be checked by bouncing the vehicle at each corner. Generally speaking, the body will return to its normal position and stop after being depressed. If it rises and returns on a rebound, the suspension strut/shock absorber is probably suspect. Examine also the suspension strut/shock absorber upper and lower mountings for any signs of wear.

12 Driveshaft gaiter check

1 With the vehicle raised and securely supported on stands, turn the steering onto full lock, then slowly rotate the roadwheel. Inspect the condition of the outer constant velocity (CV) joint rubber gaiters, squeezing the gaiters to open out the folds. Check for signs of cracking, splits or deterioration of the rubber, which may allow the grease to escape, and lead to water and grit entry into the joint. Also check the security and condition of the retaining clips. Repeat these checks on the inner CV joints **(see illustration)**. If any damage or deterioration is found, the gaiters should be renewed (see Chapter 8).

2 At the same time, check the general condition of the CV joints themselves by first holding the driveshaft and attempting to rotate the wheel. Repeat this check by holding the inner joint and attempting to rotate the driveshaft. Any appreciable movement indicates wear in the joints, wear in the driveshaft splines, or a loose driveshaft retaining nut.

13 Exhaust system check

1 With the engine cold (at least an hour after the vehicle has been driven), check the complete exhaust system from the engine to the end of the tailpipe. The exhaust system is most easily checked with the vehicle raised on a hoist, or suitably supported on axle stands, so that the exhaust components are readily visible and accessible.

2 Check the exhaust pipes and connections for evidence of leaks, severe corrosion and damage. Make sure that all brackets and mountings are in good condition, and that all relevant nuts and bolts are tight. Leakage at any of the joints or in other parts of the system will usually show up as a black sooty stain in the vicinity of the leak.

3 Rattles and other noises can often be traced to the exhaust system, especially the brackets and mountings. Try to move the

pipes and silencers. If the components are able to come into contact with the body or suspension parts, secure the system with new mountings. Otherwise separate the joints (if possible) and twist the pipes as necessary to provide additional clearance.

14 Headlight beam alignment check

Accurate adjustment of the headlight beam is only possible using optical beam-setting equipment, and this work should therefore be carried out by a VW dealer or service station with the necessary facilities.

Basic adjustments can be carried out in an emergency, and further details are given in Chapter 12.

15 Windscreen/tailgate/ headlight washer system(s) check

Check that each of the washer jet nozzles are clear and that each nozzle provides a strong jet of washer fluid. The tailgate and headlight jets should be aimed to spray at a point slightly above the centre of the screen/headlight. On the windscreen washer nozzles where there are two jets, aim one of the jets slightly above then centre of the screen and aim the other just below to ensure complete coverage of the screen. If necessary, adjust the jets using a pin.

16 Airbag unit check

Where fitted, inspect the airbag(s) exterior condition checking for signs of damage or deterioration. If an airbag shows signs of damage, it must be renewed (see Chapter 12).

17 Hinge and lock lubrication

Lubricate the hinges of the bonnet, doors and tailgate with a light general-purpose oil. Similarly, lubricate all latches, locks and lock strikers. At the same time, check the security and operation of all the locks, adjusting them if necessary (see Chapter 11).

Lightly lubricate the bonnet release mechanism and cable with a suitable grease.

18 Road test

Instruments and electrical equipment

1 Check the operation of all instruments and electrical equipment.

2 Make sure that all instruments read correctly,

1A

and switch on all electrical equipment in turn, to check that it functions properly.

Steering and suspension

3 Check for any abnormalities in the steering, suspension, handling or road "feel".
4 Drive the vehicle, and check that there are no unusual vibrations or noises.
5 Check that the steering feels positive, with no excessive "sloppiness", or roughness, and check for any suspension noises when cornering and driving over bumps.

Drivetrain

6 Check the performance of the engine, clutch (where applicable), gearbox/transmission and driveshafts.
7 Listen for any unusual noises from the engine, clutch and gearbox/transmission.
8 Make sure the engine runs smoothly at idle, and there is no hesitation on accelerating.
9 Check that, where applicable, the clutch action is smooth and progressive, that the drive is taken up smoothly, and that the pedal

travel is not excessive. Also listen for any noises when the clutch pedal is depressed.
10 On manual gearbox models, check that all gears can be engaged smoothly without noise, and that the gear lever action is not abnormally vague or "notchy".
11 On automatic transmission models, make sure that all gearchanges occur smoothly, without snatching, and without an increase in engine speed between changes. Check that all the gear positions can be selected with the vehicle at rest. If any problems are found, they should be referred to a VW dealer.
12 Listen for a metallic clicking sound from the front of the vehicle, as the vehicle is driven slowly in a circle with the steering on full-lock. Carry out this check in both directions. If a clicking noise is heard, this indicates wear in a driveshaft joint, in which case renew the joint if necessary.

Check the operation and performance of the braking system

13 Make sure that the vehicle does not pull to

one side when braking, and that the wheels do not lock prematurely when braking hard.
14 Check that there is no vibration through the steering when braking.
15 Check that the handbrake operates correctly without excessive movement of the lever, and that it holds the vehicle stationary on a slope.
16 Test the operation of the brake servo unit as follows. With the engine off, depress the footbrake four or five times to exhaust the vacuum. Hold the brake pedal depressed, then start the engine. As the engine starts, there should be a noticeable "give" in the brake pedal as vacuum builds up. Allow the engine to run for at least two minutes, and then switch it off. If the brake pedal is depressed now, it should be possible to detect a hiss from the servo as the pedal is depressed. After about four or five applications, no further hissing should be heard, and the pedal should feel considerably harder.

Every 20 000 miles (30 000 km) - "IN 02" on interval display

19 Spark plug renewal

1 The correct functioning of the spark plugs is vital for the correct running and efficiency of the engine. It is essential that the plugs fitted are appropriate for the engine (a suitable type is specified at the beginning of this Chapter). If this type is used and the engine is in good condition, the spark plugs should not need attention between scheduled replacement intervals. Spark plug cleaning is rarely necessary, and should not be attempted unless specialised equipment is available, as damage can easily be caused to the firing ends.
2 If the marks on the original-equipment spark plug (HT) leads cannot be seen, mark the leads "1" to "4", to correspond to the cylinder the lead serves (No 1 cylinder is at the

timing belt end of the engine). Pull the leads from the plugs by gripping the end fitting, not the lead, otherwise the lead connection may be fractured **(see illustration)**.
3 It is advisable to remove the dirt from the spark plug recesses using a clean brush, vacuum cleaner or compressed air before removing the plugs, to prevent dirt dropping into the cylinders **(see illustration)**. **Note:** *On engine codes ABU, ABD and AEA it will be necessary to remove the air cleaner/throttle body air box to gain access to the spark plugs.*
4 Unscrew the plugs using a spark plug spanner, suitable box spanner or a deep socket and extension bar. Keep the socket aligned with the spark plug - if it is forcibly moved to one side, the ceramic insulator may be broken off **(see illustration)**. As each plug is removed, examine it as follows.
5 Examination of the spark plugs will give a good indication of the condition of the engine. If the insulator nose of the spark plug is clean

and white, with no deposits, this is indicative of a weak mixture or too hot a plug (a hot plug transfers heat away from the electrode slowly, a cold plug transfers heat away quickly).
6 If the tip and insulator nose are covered with hard black-looking deposits, then this is indicative that the mixture is too rich. Should the plug be black and oily, then it is likely that the engine is fairly worn, as well as the mixture being too rich.
7 If the insulator nose is covered with light tan to greyish-brown deposits, then the mixture is correct and it is likely that the engine is in good condition.
8 The spark plug electrode gap is of considerable importance as, if it is too large or too small, the size of the spark and its efficiency will be seriously impaired. The gap should be set to the value given in the Specifications at the beginning of this Chapter.
9 To set the gap, measure it with a feeler blade and then bend open, or closed, the

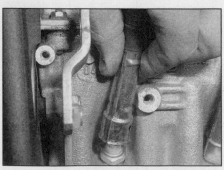

19.2 Pull the HT leads from the plugs by gripping the end fitting, not the lead, or the lead connection may be fractured

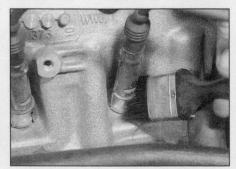

19.3 Using a clean brush to remove the dirt from the spark plug recesses

19.4 Removing a spark plug (engine code 2E shown)

19.9 Adjusting a spark plug electrode gap

19.12 Tightening a spark plug (engine code ABD shown, air cleaner removed for access)

outer plug electrode until the correct gap is achieved. The centre electrode should never be bent, as this may crack the insulator and cause plug failure, if nothing worse. If using feeler blades, the gap is correct when the appropriate-size blade is a firm sliding fit **(see illustration)**.

10 Special spark plug electrode gap adjusting tools are available from most motor accessory shops, or from some spark plug manufacturers.

11 Before fitting the spark plugs, check that the threaded connector sleeves are tight, and that the plug exterior surfaces and threads are clean. It's often difficult to screw in new spark plugs without cross-threading them - this can be avoided using a piece of rubber hose **(see Haynes Hint)**.

12 Remove the rubber hose (if used), and tighten the plug to the specified torque using the spark plug socket and a torque wrench **(see illustration)**. Refit the remaining spark plugs in the same manner.

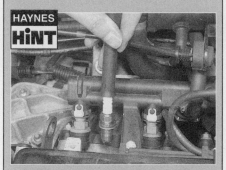

HAYNES HINT

It is very often difficult to insert spark plugs into their holes without cross-threading them. To avoid this possibility, fit a short length of 5/16 inch internal diameter rubber hose over the end of the spark plug. The flexible hose acts as a universal joint to help align the plug with the plug hole. Should the plug begin to cross-thread, the hose will slip on the spark plug, preventing thread damage to the aluminium cylinder head

13 Connect the HT leads in their correct order, and refit any components removed for access.

20 Air filter renewal

1 Prise open the spring clips and lift off the air cleaner top cover. *Caution: On certain models, the airflow meter is integral with the air cleaner top cover. Handle the airflow meter very carefully, as it easily damaged.*

2 Lift out the filter element **(see illustration)**.

3 Remove any debris that may have collected inside the air cleaner.

4 Fit a new air filter element in position, ensuring that the edges are securely seated **(see illustration)**.

20.2 Lifting out the air cleaner element (engine code ABD shown)

20.4 Fit a new air filter element in position, ensuring that the edges are securely seated (engine code 2E shown)

5 Refit the air cleaner top cover and snap the retaining clips into position. On models with a throttle body mounted air cleaner, the alignment arrows on the top cover must line up **(see illustration)**.

21 Automatic transmission fluid renewal

As the automatic transmission is not fitted with a drain plug; the transmission fluid must be pumped out using a special adapter. For this reason, it is recommended that automatic transmission fluid renewal is carried out by a VAG dealer.

22 Pollen filter renewal

1 The pollen filter (where fitted) is located beneath the windscreen wiper motor cover panels; it is located on the right-hand side on left-hand drive models, and the left-hand side on right-hand drive models.

2 Unclip the rubber seal from relevant end of the top of the engine compartment bulkhead.

3 Unscrew the fastener screws and pull out the fasteners securing the relevant half of the windscreen wiper motor cover panel. Release the half of the cover panel from the windscreen and remove it from the vehicle.

4 Pivot the pollen filter cover upwards and away then release the retaining clips and withdraw the from its housing.

5 Wipe clean the filter housing then fit the new filter. Clip the filter securely in position and refit the cover.

6 Refit the trim cover, securing it in position with the fasteners, and seat the rubber seal on the bulkhead.

23 Ignition system check

⚠️ *Warning: Voltages produced by an electronic ignition system are considerably higher than those produced by conventional ignition systems. Extreme care must be*

20.5 Air cleaner top cover alignment arrows (early-engine code ABD)

1A

taken when working on the system with the ignition switched on. Persons with surgically-implanted cardiac pacemaker devices should keep well clear of the ignition circuits, components and test equipment.

1 The ignition system components should be checked for damage or deterioration as follows.

General component check

2 The spark plug (HT) leads should be checked whenever new spark plugs are fitted.
3 Pull the leads from the plugs by gripping the end fitting, not the lead, otherwise the lead connection may be fractured.

HAYNES HiNT *Ensure that the leads are numbered before removing them, to avoid confusion when refitting*

4 Check inside the end fitting for signs of corrosion, which will look like a white crusty powder. Push the end fitting back onto the spark plug, ensuring that it is a tight fit on the plug. If not, remove the lead again and use pliers to carefully crimp the metal connector inside the end fitting until it fits securely on the end of the spark plug.
5 Using a clean rag, wipe the entire length of the lead to remove any built-up dirt and grease. Once the lead is clean, check for burns, cracks and other damage. Do not bend the lead too much, nor pull the lead lengthwise - the conductor inside might break.
6 Disconnect the other end of the lead from the distributor cap. Again, pull only on the end fitting. Check for corrosion and a tight fit in the same manner as the spark plug end. If an ohmmeter is available, check the resistance of the lead by connecting the meter between the spark plug end of the lead and the segment inside the distributor cap. Refit the lead securely on completion.
7 Check the remaining leads one at a time, in the same way.
8 If new spark plug (HT) leads are required, buy a set for your specific car and engine.
9 Unscrew its retaining screws and remove the distributor cap. Wipe it clean, and carefully inspect it inside and out for signs of cracks, black carbon tracks (tracking) and worn, burned or loose contacts; check that the cap's carbon brush is unworn, free to move against spring pressure, and making good contact with the rotor arm. Also inspect the cap seal for signs of wear or damage, and renew if necessary **(see Haynes Hint).** Remove the rotor arm from the distributor

HAYNES HiNT *When fitting a new cap, remove the leads from the old cap one at a time, and fit them to the new cap in the same location*

shaft and inspect the rotor arm. It is common practice to renew the cap and rotor arm whenever new spark plug (HT) leads are fitted.
10 Do not simultaneously remove all the leads from the old cap, or firing order confusion may occur. When refitting, ensure that the arm is securely pressed onto the shaft, and tighten the cap retaining screws securely.
11 Even with the ignition system in first-class condition, some engines may still occasionally experience poor starting attributable to damp ignition components. To disperse moisture, a water-dispersant aerosol should be liberally applied.

Ignition timing - check and adjustment

12 Check the ignition timing as described in Chapter 5A or B as applicable.

24 Manual transmission oil level check

1 Park the car on a level surface. The oil level must be checked before the car is driven, or at least 5 minutes after the engine has been switched off. If the oil is checked immediately after driving the car, some of the oil will remain distributed around the transmission components, resulting in an inaccurate level reading.
2 Remove the retaining clips and screws, then lower the undertray away from the engine bay.

3 Wipe clean the area around the filler/level plug, which is situated in the following locations:
a) *4-speed 1.4 litre engines (084 transmission)- the filler/level plug is situated on the differential casin.* **(see illustration).**
b) *5-speed 1.4 and 1.6 litre engines (085 transmission) - the filler/level plug is situated on the left hand end of the transmission casing* **(see illustration).**
c) *5-speed 1.8 and 2.0 litre SOHC engines (020 transmission)- the filler/level plug is situated on the differential casing* **(see illustration).**
d) *5-speed 2.0 litre DOHC engines (02A transmission) - the filler/level plug is situated on the front of the differential casing* **(see illustration).**

4 The oil level should reach the lower edge of the filler/level hole. A certain amount of oil will have gathered behind the filler/level plug, and will trickle out when it is removed; this does **not** necessarily indicate that the level is correct. To ensure that a true level is established, wait until the initial trickle has stopped, then add oil as necessary until a trickle of new oil can be seen emerging. The level will be correct when the flow ceases; use only good-quality oil of the specified type.
5 Filling the transmission with oil is an extremely awkward operation; above all, allow plenty of time for the oil level to settle properly before checking it. If a large amount is added to the transmission, and a large amount flows out on checking the level, refit the filler/level

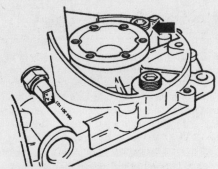
24.3a Manual transmission filler level plug, 4-speed 1.4 litre engines

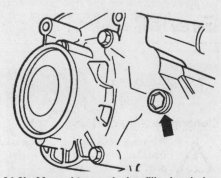
24.3b Manual transmission filler level plug, 5-speed 1.4 and 1.6 litre engines

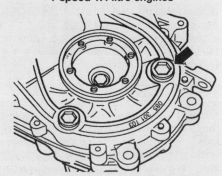
24.3c Manual transmission filler level plug, 5-speed 1.8 and 2.0 litre SOHC engines

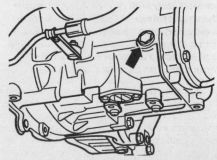
24.3d Manual transmission filler level plug, 5-speed 2.0 litre DOHC engines

plug and take the vehicle on a short journey so that the new oil is distributed fully around the transmission components, then recheck the level when it has settled again.

6 If the transmission has been overfilled so that oil flows out when the filler/level plug is removed, check that the car is completely level (front-to-rear and side-to-side), and allow the surplus to drain off into a suitable container.

7 When the level is correct, fit a new sealing washer to the filler/level plug. Refit the plug, tightening it securely. Wash off any spilt oil then refit the engine bay undertray securing it in position with the retaining clips and screws.

25 Auxiliary drivebelt check and renewal
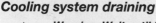

Checking

1 Disconnect the battery negative cable and position it away from the terminal.

2 Park the vehicle on a level surface, apply the handbrake and chock the rear wheels.

3 Raise the front of the vehicle, rest it securely on axle stands and remove the roadwheels.

4 Turn the steering to full right hand lock, then remove the screws and clips and lower the undertray away from the engine bay.

5 Using a socket and wrench on the crankshaft sprocket bolt, rotate the crankshaft so that the full length of the auxiliary drivebelts can be examined. Look for cracks, splitting and fraying on the surface of the belt; check also for signs of glazing (shiny patches) and separation of the belt plies. If damage or wear is visible, the belt should be renewed.

Renewal

6 For details of auxiliary drivebelt renewal, refer to the relevant part of Chapter 2B.

Every 60 000 miles (90 000 km)

26 Timing belt renewal

Refer to the relevant Part of Chapter 2

27 Fuel filter renewal

 Warning: Refer to the notes in "Safety first!", and follow them implicitly. Petrol is a highly-dangerous and volatile liquid, and the precautions necessary when handling it cannot be overstressed.

1 The fuel filter is situated underneath the rear of the vehicle, on the right-hand side in front of the fuel tank. To gain access to the filter, chock the front wheels, then jack up the rear of the vehicle and support it on axle stands.

2 Refer to Section 9 of Chapter 4A or B as applicable, and depressurise the fuel system.

3 Slacken the hose clips and disconnect the fuel lines from either side of the filter unit. If the clips are of the crimp type, snip them off with cutters and replace them with equivalent size worm drive clips upon reconnection.

4 Release the filter retaining clip, remove the cover bracket and lower the filter unit away from its mounting bracket.

5 Fit the new filter into position, ensuring that the arrow on the filter body is pointing towards the front of the vehicle, in the direction of the fuel flow.

6 Connect the fuel hoses to the filter, securing them in position with their retaining clips.

7 Fit the cover bracket then tighten the filter strap securing screws securely.

8 Start the engine, check the filter hose connections for leaks, then lower the vehicle to the ground.

 Warning: Dispose safely of the old filter; it will be highly flammable, and may explode if thrown on a fire.

1A

Every 2 years (regardless of mileage)

28 Coolant renewal

Cooling system draining

 Warning: Wait until the engine is cold before starting this procedure. Do not allow antifreeze to come in contact with your skin, or with the painted surfaces of the vehicle. Rinse off spills immediately with plenty of water. Never leave antifreeze lying around in an open container, or in a puddle in the driveway or on the garage floor. Children and pets are attracted by its sweet smell, but antifreeze can be fatal if ingested.

1 With the engine completely cold, cover the expansion tank cap with a wad of rag, and slowly turn the cap anti-clockwise to relieve the pressure in the cooling system (a hissing sound will normally be heard). Wait until any pressure remaining in the system is released, then continue to turn the cap until it can be removed.

2 Position a suitable container beneath the radiator bottom hose connection, then release the retaining clip and ease the hose from the radiator stub. If the hose joint has not been disturbed for some time, it will be necessary to gently manipulate the hose to break the joint. Do not use excessive force, or the radiator stub could be damaged. Allow the coolant to drain into the container.

3 If the coolant has been drained for a reason other than renewal, then provided it is clean and less than two years old, it can be re-used, though this is not recommended.

4 Once all the coolant has drained, reconnect the hose to the radiator and secure it in position with the retaining clip.

Cooling system flushing

5 If coolant renewal has been neglected, or if the antifreeze mixture has become diluted, then in time, the cooling system may gradually lose efficiency, as the coolant passages become restricted due to rust, scale deposits, and other sediment. The cooling system efficiency can be restored by flushing the system clean.

6 The radiator should be flushed independently of the engine, to avoid unnecessary contamination.

Radiator flushing

7 To flush the radiator disconnect the top and bottom hoses and any other relevant hoses from the radiator, with reference to Chapter 3.

8 Insert a garden hose into the radiator top inlet. Direct a flow of clean water through the radiator, and continue flushing until clean water emerges from the radiator bottom outlet.

9 If after a reasonable period, the water still does not run clear, the radiator can be flushed with a good proprietary cooling system cleaning agent. It is important that their manufacturer's instructions are followed carefully. If the contamination is particularly bad, insert the hose in the radiator bottom outlet, and reverse-flush the radiator.

Engine flushing

10 To flush the engine, remove the thermostat as described in Chapter 3, then temporarily refit the thermostat cover.

11 With the top and bottom hoses disconnected from the radiator, insert a garden hose into the radiator top hose. Direct a clean flow of water through the engine, and continue flushing until clean water emerges from the radiator bottom hose.

12 On completion of flushing, refit the thermostat and reconnect the hoses with reference to Chapter 3.

Cooling system filling

13 Before attempting to fill the cooling system, make sure that all hoses and clips are in good condition, and that the clips are tight. Note that an antifreeze mixture must be used all year round, to prevent corrosion of the engine components (see following sub-Section).

14 Remove the expansion tank filler cap, and fill the system by slowly pouring the coolant into the expansion tank to prevent airlocks from forming.

15 If the coolant is being renewed, begin by pouring in a couple of litres of water, followed by the correct quantity of antifreeze, then top-up with more water.

16 Once the level in the expansion tank starts to rise, squeeze the radiator top and bottom hoses to help expel any trapped air in the system. Once all the air is expelled, top-up the coolant level to the "MAX" mark and refit the expansion tank cap.

17 Start the engine and run it until it reaches normal operating temperature, then stop the engine and allow it to cool.

18 Check for leaks, particularly around disturbed components. Check the coolant level in the expansion tank, and top-up if necessary. Note that the system must be cold before an accurate level is indicated in the expansion tank. If the expansion tank cap is removed while the engine is still warm, cover the cap with a thick cloth, and unscrew the cap slowly to gradually relieve the system pressure (a hissing sound will normally be heard). Wait until any pressure remaining in the system is released, then continue to turn the cap until it can be removed.

Antifreeze mixture

19 The antifreeze should always be renewed at the specified intervals. This is necessary not only to maintain the antifreeze properties, but also to prevent corrosion which would otherwise occur as the corrosion inhibitors become progressively less effective.

20 Always use an ethylene-glycol based antifreeze which is suitable for use in mixed-metal cooling systems. The quantity of antifreeze and levels of protection are indicated in the Specifications.

21 Before adding antifreeze, the cooling system should be completely drained, preferably flushed, and all hoses checked for condition and security.

22 After filling with antifreeze, a label should be attached to the expansion tank, stating the type and concentration of antifreeze used, and the date installed. Any subsequent topping-up should be made with the same type and concentration of antifreeze.

23 Do not use engine antifreeze in the windscreen/tailgate washer system, as it will cause damage to the vehicle paintwork. A screenwash additive should be added to the washer system in the quantities stated on the bottle (see "Weekly Checks").

29 Brake fluid renewal

⚠️ *Warning: Brake hydraulic fluid can harm your eyes and damage painted surfaces, so use extreme caution when handling and pouring it. Do not use fluid that has been standing open for some time, as it absorbs moisture from the air. Excess moisture can cause a dangerous loss of braking effectiveness.*

1 The procedure is similar to that for the bleeding of the hydraulic system as described in Chapter 9, except that the brake fluid reservoir should be emptied by siphoning, using a clean poultry baster or similar before starting, and allowance should be made for the old fluid to be expelled when bleeding a section of the circuit.

2 Working as described in Chapter 9, open the first bleed screw in the sequence, and pump the brake pedal gently until nearly all the old fluid has been emptied from the master cylinder reservoir.

 Old hydraulic fluid is often much darker in colour than the new, making it easy to distinguish the two.

3 Top-up to the "MAX" level with new fluid, and continue pumping until only the new fluid remains in the reservoir, and new fluid can be seen emerging from the bleed screw. Tighten the screw, and top the reservoir level up to the "MAX" level line.

4 Work through all the remaining bleed screws in the sequence until new fluid can be seen at all of them. Be careful to keep the master cylinder reservoir topped-up to above the "MIN" level at all times, or air may enter the system and greatly increase the length of the task.

5 When the operation is complete, check that all bleed screws are securely tightened, and that their dust caps are refitted. Wash off all traces of spilt fluid, and recheck the master cylinder reservoir fluid level.

6 Check the operation of the brakes before taking the car on the road.

30 Engine management system check

1 This check is part of the manufacturer's maintenance schedule, and involves testing the engine management system using special dedicated test equipment. Such testing will allow the test equipment to read any fault codes stored in the electronic control unit memory.

2 Unless a fault is suspected, this test is not essential, although it should be noted that it is recommended by the manufacturers.

3 If access to suitable test equipment is not possible, make a thorough check of all ignition, fuel and emission control system components, hoses, and wiring, for security and obvious signs of damage. Further details of the fuel system, emission control system and ignition system can be found in Chapter 4A and 4B, and in Chapter 5B.

Chapter 1 Part B:
Routine maintenance and servicing - diesel models

Contents

Degrees of difficulty

Easy, suitable for novice with little experience		**Fairly easy,** suitable for beginner with some experience		**Fairly difficult,** suitable for competent DIY mechanic		**Difficult,** suitable for experienced DIY mechanic		**Very difficult,** suitable for expert DIY or professional	

Lubricants and fluids

Refer to the end of *"Weekly checks"*

Capacities

Engine oil
Excluding filter .... 3.8 litres
Including filter .... 4.3 litres

Cooling system
All models (approximate) .... 6.3 litres

Transmission
Manual transmission:
  02A .... 2.0 litres
  020 .... 2.0 litres
Automatic transmission .... 5.6 litres (fluid change 3.0 litres)

Power-assisted steering
All models (approximate) .... 1.5 litres

Fuel tank
All models (approximate) .... 62 litres

Washer reservoirs
Models with headlight washers .... 7.0 litres
Models without headlight washers .... 4.0 litres

Engine
Oil filter .... Champion C150

Cooling system
Antifreeze mixture:
  28% antifreeze .... Protection down to -15°C (5°F)
  50% antifreeze .... Protection down to -30°C (-22°F)
Note: *Refer to antifreeze manufacturer for latest recommendations.*

Fuel system
Air filter element .... Champion U583
Fuel filter .... Champion L114

Brakes
Brake pad minimum thickness .... 7.0 mm
Brake shoe friction material minimum thickness .... 2.5 mm

Torque wrench settings

	Nm	lbf ft
Sump drain plug	30	22
Roadwheel bolts	110	81

The maintenance intervals in this manual are provided with the assumption that you, not the dealer, will be carrying out the work. These are the minimum intervals recommended by us for vehicles driven daily. If you wish to keep your vehicle in peak condition at all times, you may wish to perform some of these procedures more often. We encourage frequent maintenance, since it enhances the efficiency, performance and resale value of your vehicle.

When the vehicle is new, it should be serviced by a dealer service department, in order to preserve the factory warranty.

All VW Golf/Vento models are equipped with a service interval display indicator in the instrument panel. Every time the engine is started the panel will illuminate for a few seconds, displaying either of the following. This provides a handy reminder of when the next service is required:

Display shows "IN 00" - no service required

Display shows "OEL" - 10 000 mile (15 000 km) service required

Display shows "IN 01" - 12 monthly service required

Display shows "IN 02" - 20 000 mile (30 000 km) service required

Every 250 miles (400 km) or weekly

☐ Refer to *"Weekly checks"*

Every 5000 miles (7500 km) - normally-aspirated models ("OEL" on interval display)

☐ Renew the engine oil and filter (Section 3)
☐ Drain the water from the fuel filter (Section 4)
☐ Check the front brake pad thickness (Section 5)
☐ Reset the service interval display (Section 6)

Every 10 000 miles (15 000 km) - turbo models ("OEL" on interval display)

☐ Renew the engine oil and filter (Section 3)
☐ Drain the water from the fuel filter (Section 4)
☐ Check the front brake pad thickness (Section 5)
☐ Reset the service interval display (Section 6)

Every 12 months - "IN 01" on interval display

Note: *If the vehicle is a normally-aspirated model travelling less 5000 miles (7500 km) or a turbo model travelling less than 10 000 miles (15 000 km) a year, also carry out the tasks listed above*

☐ Check the automatic transmission fluid level (Section 7)
☐ Check and, if necessary, adjust the engine idle speed (Section 8)
☐ Check all underbonnet components and hoses for fluid leaks (Section 9)
☐ Check the rear brake pad thickness - rear disc brake models (Section 10)
☐ Check the rear brake shoe lining thickness - rear drum brake models (Section 11)
☐ Check the operation of the handbrake (Section 12)
☐ Check the steering and suspension components for condition and security (Section 13)
☐ Check the condition of the driveshaft gaiters (Section 14)

Every 12 months - "IN 01" on interval display (continued)

☐ Check the condition of the exhaust system and its mountings (Section 15)
☐ Check the headlight beam adjustment (Section 16)
☐ Check the operation of the windscreen/tailgate/headlight washer system(s) (as applicable) (Section 17)
☐ Check the condition of the airbag unit(s) (Section 18)
☐ Lubricate all hinges and locks (Section 19)
☐ Carry out a road test (Section 20)
☐ Reset service interval display (Section 6)

Every 20 000 miles (30 000 km) - "IN 02" on interval display

Note: *If the vehicle is travelling more than 20 000 miles (30 000 km) a year, also carry out all the operations described above*

☐ Renew the fuel filter (Section 21)
☐ Renew the air filter element (Section 22)
☐ Renew the automatic transmission fluid (Section 23)
☐ Renew the pollen filter element (Section 24)
☐ Check the condition of the timing belt and adjust if necessary (Section 25)
☐ Check the manual transmission oil level (Section 26)
☐ Check the condition of the auxiliary drivebelt(s), and renew if necessary (Section 27)
☐ Reset service interval display (Section 6)

Every 60 000 miles (90 000 km)

☐ Renew the timing belt (Section 28)

Every 2 years (regardless of mileage)

☐ Renew the coolant (Section 29)
☐ Renew the brake fluid (Section 30)
☐ Check the exhaust emissions (Section 31)

1B

Underbonnet view of an early Turbo model

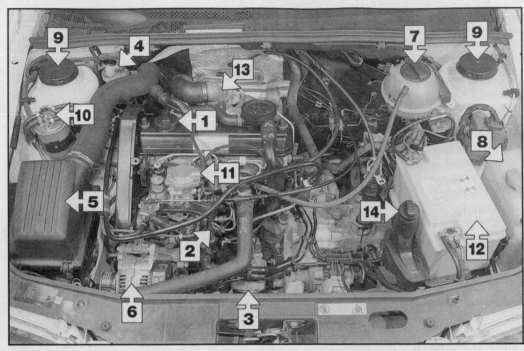

1 Engine oil filler cap
2 Engine oil dipstick
3 Oil filter housing
4 Master cylinder brake fluid reservoir
5 Air cleaner housing
6 Alternator
7 Coolant expansion tank
8 Windscreen/tailgate washer fluid reservoir
9 Suspension strut upper mounting
10 Fuel filter
11 Injection pump
12 Battery
13 Turbocharger
14 Power steering fluid reservoir

Front underbody view (early Turbo model shown - other models similar)

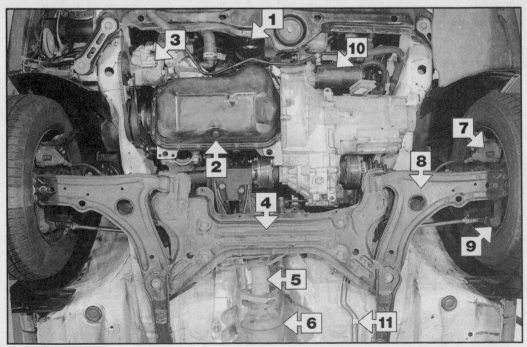

1 Engine oil filter
2 Sump drain plug
3 Power steering pump
4 Front suspension subframe
5 Exhaust front pipe
6 Catalytic converter
7 Front brake caliper
8 Front suspension lower arm
9 Track rod balljoint
10 Starter motor
11 Brake pipes

Rear underbody view (early Turbo model shown - other models similar)

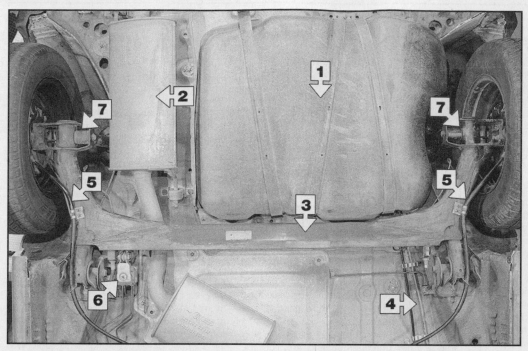

1 Fuel tank
2 Exhaust tailpipe
3 Rear axle assembly
4 Fuel pipes
5 Handbrake cable
6 Rear brake pressure regulating valve
7 Suspension strut lower mounting

1 Introduction

General information

This Chapter is designed to help the home mechanic maintain his/her vehicle for safety, economy, long life and peak performance.

The Chapter contains a master maintenance schedule, followed by Sections dealing specifically with each task in the schedule. Visual checks, adjustments, component renewal and other helpful items are included. Refer to the accompanying illustrations of the engine compartment and the underside of the vehicle for the locations of the various components.

Servicing your vehicle in accordance with the mileage/time maintenance schedule and the following Sections will provide a planned maintenance programme, which should result in a long and reliable service life. This is a comprehensive plan, so maintaining some items but not others at the specified service intervals, will not produce the same results.

As you service your vehicle, you will discover that many of the procedures can - and should - be grouped together, because of the particular procedure being performed, or because of the proximity of two otherwise-unrelated components to one another. For example, if the vehicle is raised for any reason, the exhaust can be inspected at the same time as the suspension and steering components.

The first step in this maintenance programme is to prepare yourself before the actual work begins. Read through all the Sections relevant to the work to be carried out, then make a list and gather all the parts and tools required. If a problem is encountered, seek advice from a parts specialist, or a dealer service department.

2 Intensive maintenance

1 If, from the time the vehicle is new, the routine maintenance schedule is followed closely, and frequent checks are made of fluid levels and high-wear items, as suggested throughout this manual, the engine will be kept in relatively good running condition, and the need for additional work will be minimised.
2 It is possible that there will be times when the engine is running poorly due to the lack of regular maintenance. This is even more likely if a used vehicle, which has not received regular and frequent maintenance checks, is purchased. In such cases, additional work may need to be carried out, outside of the regular maintenance intervals.
3 If engine wear is suspected, a compression test (refer to the relevant Part of Chapter 2) will provide valuable information regarding the overall performance of the main internal components. Such a test can be used as a basis to decide on the extent of the work to be carried out. If, for example, a compression test indicates serious internal engine wear, conventional maintenance as described in this Chapter will not greatly improve the performance of the engine, and may prove a waste of time and money, unless extensive overhaul work is carried out first.

4 The following series of operations are those most often required to improve the performance of a generally poor-running engine:

Primary operations

a) Clean, inspect and test the battery (See "Weekly checks").
b) Check all the engine-related fluids (See "Weekly checks").
c) Drain the water from the fuel filter (Section 4).
d) Check the condition and tension of the auxiliary drivebelt (Section 27).
e) Check the condition of the air filter, and renew if necessary (Section 22).
f) Check the condition of all hoses, and check for fluid leaks (Section 9).
g) Check the engine idle speed setting (Section 8).
h) Check the exhaust gas emissions (Section 31).

5 If the above operations do not prove fully effective, carry out the following secondary operations:

Secondary operations

All items listed under "Primary operations", plus the following:

a) Check the charging system (see relevant Part of Chapter 5).
b) Check the ignition system (see relevant Part of Chapter 5).
c) Renew the fuel filter (Section 21) and check the fuel system (see relevant Part of Chapter 4).

Every 5000/10 000 miles - "OEL" on interval display

3 Engine oil and filter renewal

1 Frequent oil and filter changes are the most important preventative maintenance procedures which can be undertaken by the DIY owner. As engine oil ages, it becomes diluted and contaminated, which leads to premature engine wear.

2 Before starting this procedure, gather all the necessary tools and materials. Also make sure that you have plenty of clean rags and newspapers handy, to mop up any spills. Ideally, the engine oil should be warm, as it will drain better, and more built-up sludge will be removed with it. Take care, however, not to touch the exhaust or any other hot parts of the engine when working under the vehicle. To avoid any possibility of scalding, and to protect yourself from possible skin irritants and other harmful contaminants in used engine oils, it is advisable to wear gloves when carrying out this work. Access to the underside of the vehicle will be greatly improved if it can be raised on a lift, driven onto ramps, or jacked up and supported on axle stands (see *"Jacking and Vehicle Support"*). Whichever method is chosen, make sure that the vehicle remains level, or if it is at an angle, that the drain plug is at the lowest point.

3 Slacken the sump drain plug about half a turn **(see illustration)**. Position the draining container under the drain plug, then remove the plug completely **(see Haynes Hint)**. Recover the sealing ring from the drain plug.

4 Allow some time for the old oil to drain, noting that it may be necessary to reposition the container as the oil flow slows to a trickle.

5 After all the oil has drained, wipe off the drain plug with a clean rag, and fit a new sealing washer. Clean the area around the drain plug opening, and refit the plug. Tighten the plug securely.

6 If the filter is also to be renewed, move the container into position under the oil filter, which is located on the front side of the cylinder block, next to the front engine mounting.

HAYNES HINT

Keep the drain plug pressed into the sump while unscrewing it by hand last couple of turns. As the plug releases, move it away sharply so the stream of oil issuing from the sump runs into the container, not up your sleeve!

7 Using an oil filter removal tool if necessary, slacken the filter initially, then unscrew it by hand the rest of the way. Empty the oil in the old filter into the container.

8 Use a clean rag to remove all oil, dirt and sludge from the filter sealing area on the engine. Check the old filter to make sure that the rubber sealing ring has not stuck to the engine. If it has, carefully remove it.

9 Apply a light coating of clean engine oil to the sealing ring on the new filter, then screw it into position on the engine **(see illustration)**. Tighten the filter firmly by hand only - **do not** use any tools.

10 Remove the old oil and all tools from under the car then lower the car to the ground (if applicable).

11 Remove the dipstick, then unscrew the oil filler cap from the cylinder head cover or oil filler/breather neck (as applicable). Fill the engine, using the correct grade and type of oil (see *"Lubricants, fluids and tyre pressures"*). An oil can spout or funnel may help to reduce spillage. Pour in half the specified quantity of oil first, then wait a few minutes for the oil to fall to the sump (see *"Weekly Checks"*). Continue adding oil a small quantity at a time until the level is up to the lower mark on the

OIL CARE
FOLLOW THE CODE

OIL BANK LINE
0800 66 33 66

Note: It is antisocial and illegal to dump oil down the drain. To find the location of your local oil recycling bank, call this number free.

dipstick. Adding about 1.0 litre will bring the level up to the upper mark on the dipstick. Refit the filler cap.

12 Start the engine and run it for a few minutes; check for leaks around the oil filter seal and the sump drain plug. Note that there may be a few seconds delay before the oil pressure warning light goes out when the engine is started, as the oil circulates through the engine oil galleries and the new oil filter (where fitted) before the pressure builds up.

13 Switch off the engine, and wait a few minutes for the oil to settle in the sump once more. With the new oil circulated and the filter completely full, recheck the level on the dipstick, and add more oil as necessary.

14 Dispose of the used engine oil safely, with reference to *"General repair procedures"* in the *Reference* section of this manual.

4 Fuel filter water draining

1 From time to time, the water collected from the fuel by the filter unit must be drained out.

2 The fuel filter is mounted on the inner wing, above the right hand wheel arch. At the top of the filter unit, release the clip and lift out the control valve, leaving the fuel hoses attached.

3 Slacken the screw and raise the filter in its retaining bracket

4 Position a container below the filter unit and pad the surrounding area with rags to absorb any fuel that may be spilt.

5 Unscrew the drain valve at the base of the filter unit, until fuel starts to run out into the container **(see illustration)**. Keep the valve open until about 100 cc of fuel has been collected.

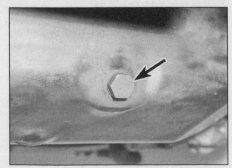

3.3 Drain plug (arrowed), situated to the rear of the sump

3.9 Fitting a new oil filter

4.5 Unscrew the drain valve (arrowed) at the base of the filter unit

6 Refit the control valve to the top of the filter and insert the retaining clip. Close the drain valve and wipe off any surplus fuel from the nozzle.

7 Remove the collecting container and rags, then push the filter unit back into the retaining bracket and tighten the bracket securing screw.

8 Run the engine at idle and check around the fuel filter for fuel leaks.

9 Raise the engine speed to about 2000 rpm several times, then allow the engine to idle again. Observe the fuel flow through the transparent hose leading to the fuel injection pump and check that it is free of air bubbles.

5 Front brake pad check

1 Firmly apply the handbrake, then jack up the front of the car and support it securely on axle stands. Remove the front roadwheels.

2 For a comprehensive check, the brake pads should be removed and cleaned. The operation of the caliper can then also be checked, and the condition of the brake disc itself can be fully examined on both sides. Refer to Chapter 9 for further information **(see Haynes Hint)**.

For a quick check, the thickness of the friction material on each brake pad can be measured through the aperture in the caliper body

3 If any pad's friction material is worn to the specified thickness or less, *all four pads must be renewed as a set.*

6 Resetting the service interval display

1 After all necessary maintenance work has been completed, the relevant service interval display code must be reset. If more than one service schedule is carried out, note that the relevant display intervals must be reset individually.

2 The display is reset using the reset button on the left-hand side of the instrument panel (below the speedometer) and the clock setting button on the right-hand side of the panel (below the clock/tachometer); on models with a digital clock the lower (minute) button is used. Resetting is carried out as follows.

3 Turn the ignition switch and check that the speedometer mileage indicator is set to the mileage setting and not the trip meter setting. When this is so, press and hold in the button on the left of the instrument panel. Keeping the button depressed, switch off the ignition and release the button. The word "OEL" should be shown on the display, by depressing the left-hand button again the display will change to "IN 01" followed by "IN 02". Set the display to the relevant service which has just been performed, then depress the clock adjustment button briefly until "——-" is displayed; this indicates that the service interval display has been reset. Repeat the reset procedure for all the relevant service display intervals.

4 On completion, switch on the ignition and check that "IN 00" is shown in the display.

Every 12 months - "IN 01" on interval display

7 Automatic transmission fluid level check

1 Take the vehicle on a short journey, to warm the transmission up to normal operating temperature, then park the vehicle on level ground. The fluid level is checked using the dipstick located at the front of the engine compartment, on the front of the transmission unit.

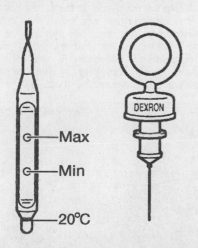

7.2 Note the fluid level on the end of the dipstick; it should be between the MAX and MIN marks

2 With the engine idling and the selector lever in the "P" (Park) position, withdraw the dipstick from the tube, and wipe all the fluid from its end with a clean rag or paper towel. Insert the clean dipstick back into the tube as far as it will go, then withdraw it once more. Note the fluid level on the end of the dipstick; it should be between the MAX and MIN marks. **Note:** *If the engine has not been warmed up, the fluid level should be at the 20°C mark* **(see illustration).**

3 If topping-up is necessary, add the required quantity of the specified fluid to the transmission through the dipstick tube. Use a funnel with a fine mesh gauze, to avoid spillage, and to ensure that no foreign matter enters the transmission. **Note:** *Never overfill the transmission so that the fluid level is above the upper mark.*

4 After topping-up, take the vehicle on a short run to distribute the fresh fluid, then recheck the level again, topping-up if necessary.

5 Always maintain the level between the two dipstick marks. If the level is allowed to fall below the lower mark, fluid starvation may result, which could lead to severe transmission damage. If the level is too high, the excess fluid may be ejected. In either case, an incorrect level will adversely affect the operation of the transmission.

6 Frequent need for topping-up indicates that there is a leak, which should be found and corrected before it becomes serious.

8 Idle speed check and adjustment

Engine codes AAZ and 1Y

1 Start the engine and run it until it reaches its normal operating temperature. With the handbrake applied and the transmission in neutral, allow the engine to idle. Check that the cold start knob is pushed in to the fully 'off' position.

2 Using a diesel tachometer, check the idle speed against Chapter 4C Specifications.

3 If necessary, adjust the engine idle speed by rotating the adjustment knob at the fuel injection pump **(see illustration).**

8.3 Adjust the engine idle speed by rotating the adjustment knob at the fuel injection pump (arrowed)

1B

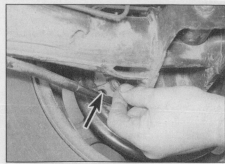

A leak in the cooling system will usually show up as white - or rust-coloured deposits on the area adjoining the leak

Engine code 1Z

4 The engine idle speed must be checked and adjusted by a VAG dealer using dedicated electronic test equipment.

9 Hose and fluid leak check

1 Visually inspect the engine joint faces, gaskets and seals for any signs of water or oil leaks. Pay particular attention to the areas around the camshaft cover, cylinder head, oil filter and sump joint faces. Bear in mind that, over a period of time, some very slight seepage from these areas is to be expected - what you are really looking for is any indication of a serious leak **(see Haynes Hint)**. Should a leak be found, renew the offending gasket or oil seal by referring to the appropriate Chapters in this manual.
2 Also check the security and condition of all the engine-related pipes and hoses. Ensure that all cable-ties or securing clips are in place and in good condition. Clips which are broken or missing can lead to chafing of the hoses, pipes or wiring, which could cause more serious problems in the future.
3 Carefully check the radiator hoses and heater hoses along their entire length. Renew any hose which is cracked, swollen or deteriorated. Cracks will show up better if the hose is squeezed. Pay close attention to the hose clips that secure the hoses to the cooling system components. Hose clips can pinch and puncture hoses, resulting in cooling system leaks.
4 Inspect all the cooling system components (hoses, joint faces etc.) for leaks. A leak in the cooling system will usually show up as white or rust coloured deposits on the area adjoining the leak. Where any problems of this nature are found on system components, renew the component or gasket with reference to Chapter 3.
5 Where applicable, inspect the automatic transmission fluid cooler hoses for leaks or deterioration.
6 With the vehicle raised, inspect the petrol tank and filler neck for punctures, cracks and

other damage. The connection between the filler neck and tank is especially critical. Sometimes a rubber filler neck or connecting hose will leak due to loose retaining clamps or deteriorated rubber.
7 Carefully check all rubber hoses and metal fuel lines leading away from the petrol tank. Check for loose connections, deteriorated hoses, crimped lines, and other damage. Pay particular attention to the vent pipes and hoses, which often loop up around the filler neck and can become blocked or crimped. Follow the lines to the front of the vehicle, carefully inspecting them all the way. Renew damaged sections as necessary.
8 From within the engine compartment, check the security of all fuel hose attachments and pipe unions, and inspect the fuel hoses and vacuum hoses for kinks, chafing and deterioration.
9 Where applicable, check the condition of the power steering fluid hoses and pipes.

10 Rear brake pad check - models with rear disc brakes

1 Chock the front wheels, then jack up the rear of the vehicle and support it on axle stands. Remove the rear roadwheels.
2 For a quick check, the thickness of friction material remaining on each brake pad can be measured through the top of the caliper body. If any pad's friction material is worn to the specified thickness or less, all four pads must be renewed as a set.
3 For a comprehensive check, the brake pads should be removed and cleaned. This will permit the operation of the caliper to be checked, and the condition of the brake disc itself to be fully examined on both sides. Refer to Chapter 9 for further information.

11 Rear brake shoe check - models with rear drum brakes

1 Chock the front wheels, then jack up the rear of the vehicle, and support it securely on axle stands.
2 For a quick check, the thickness of friction material remaining on one of the brake shoes can be observed through the hole in the brake backplate which is exposed by prising out the sealing grommet **(see illustration)**. If a rod of the same diameter as the specified minimum friction material thickness is placed against the shoe friction material, the amount of wear can be assessed. A torch or inspection light will probably be required. If the friction material on any shoe is worn down to the specified minimum thickness or less, all four shoes must be renewed as a set.
3 For a comprehensive check, the brake drum should be removed and cleaned. This will allow the wheel cylinders to be checked, and the condition of the brake drum itself to be fully examined (see Chapter 9).

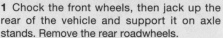

11.2 Remove the rubber plug and check the brake friction material thickness through the back plate aperture (arrowed)

12 Handbrake check and adjustment

Refer to Chapter 9.

13 Steering and suspension check

Front suspension and steering check

1 Raise the front of the vehicle, and securely support it on axle stands.
2 Visually inspect the balljoint dust covers and the steering rack-and-pinion gaiters for splits, chafing or deterioration. Any wear of these components will cause loss of lubricant, together with dirt and water entry, resulting in rapid deterioration of the balljoints or steering gear.
3 On vehicles with power steering, check the fluid hoses for chafing or deterioration, and the pipe and hose unions for fluid leaks. Also check for signs of fluid leakage under pressure from the steering gear rubber gaiters, which would indicate failed fluid seals within the steering gear.
4 Grasp the roadwheel at the 12 o'clock and 6 o'clock positions, and try to rock it **(see illustration)**. Very slight free play may be felt, but if the movement is appreciable, further investigation is necessary to determine the source. Continue rocking the wheel while an assistant depresses the footbrake. If the

13.4 Check for wear in the hub bearings by grasping the wheel and trying to rock it

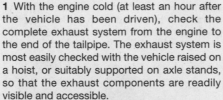

14.1 Check the condition of the driveshaft gaiters (arrowed)

movement is now eliminated or significantly reduced, it is likely that the hub bearings are at fault. If the free play is still evident with the footbrake depressed, then there is wear in the suspension joints or mountings.

5 Now grasp the wheel at the 9 o'clock and 3 o'clock positions, and try to rock it as before. Any movement felt now may again be caused by wear in the hub bearings or the steering track-rod balljoints. If the inner or outer balljoint is worn, the visual movement will be obvious.

6 Using a large screwdriver or flat bar, check for wear in the suspension mounting bushes by levering between the relevant suspension component and its attachment point. Some movement is to be expected as the mountings are made of rubber, but excessive wear should be obvious. Also check the condition of any visible rubber bushes, looking for splits, cracks or contamination of the rubber.

7 With the car standing on its wheels, have an assistant turn the steering wheel back and forth about an eighth of a turn each way. There should be very little, if any, lost movement between the steering wheel and roadwheels. If this is not the case, closely observe the joints and mountings previously described, but in addition, check the steering column universal joints for wear, and the rack-and-pinion steering gear itself.

Suspension strut/ shock absorber check

8 Check for any signs of fluid leakage around the suspension strut/shock absorber body, or from the rubber gaiter around the piston rod. Should any fluid be noticed, the suspension strut/shock absorber is defective internally, and should be renewed. **Note:** *Suspension struts/shock absorbers should always be renewed in pairs on the same axle.*

9 The efficiency of the suspension strut/shock absorber may be checked by bouncing the vehicle at each corner. Generally speaking, the body will return to its normal position and stop after being depressed. If it rises and returns on a rebound, the suspension strut/shock absorber is probably suspect. Examine also the suspension strut/shock absorber upper and lower mountings for any signs of wear.

14 Driveshaft gaiter check

1 With the vehicle raised and securely supported on stands, turn the steering onto full lock, then slowly rotate the roadwheel. Inspect the condition of the outer constant velocity (CV) joint rubber gaiters, squeezing the gaiters to open out the folds. Check for signs of cracking, splits or deterioration of the rubber, which may allow the grease to escape, and lead to water and grit entry into the joint. Also check the security and condition of the retaining clips. Repeat these checks on the inner CV joints **(see illustration)**. If any damage or deterioration is found, the gaiters should be renewed (see Chapter 8).

2 At the same time, check the general condition of the CV joints themselves by first holding the driveshaft and attempting to rotate the wheel. Repeat this check by holding the inner joint and attempting to rotate the driveshaft. Any appreciable movement indicates wear in the joints, wear in the driveshaft splines, or a loose driveshaft retaining nut.

15 Exhaust system check

1 With the engine cold (at least an hour after the vehicle has been driven), check the complete exhaust system from the engine to the end of the tailpipe. The exhaust system is most easily checked with the vehicle raised on a hoist, or suitably supported on axle stands, so that the exhaust components are readily visible and accessible.

2 Check the exhaust pipes and connections for evidence of leaks, severe corrosion and damage. Make sure that all brackets and mountings are in good condition, and that all relevant nuts and bolts are tight. Leakage at any of the joints or in other parts of the system will usually show up as a black sooty stain in the vicinity of the leak.

3 Rattles and other noises can often be traced to the exhaust system, especially the brackets and mountings. Try to move the pipes and silencers. If the components are able to come into contact with the body or suspension parts, secure the system with new mountings. Otherwise separate the joints (if possible) and twist the pipes as necessary to provide additional clearance.

16 Headlight beam alignment check

Accurate adjustment of the headlight beam is only possible using optical beam-setting equipment, and this work should therefore be carried out by a VW dealer or service station with the necessary facilities.

Basic adjustments can be carried out in an emergency, and further details are given in Chapter 12.

17 Windscreen/tailgate/ headlight washer system(s) check

Check that each of the washer jet nozzles are clear and that each nozzle provides a strong jet of washer fluid. The tailgate and headlight jets should be aimed to spray at a point slightly above the centre of the screen/headlight. On the windscreen washer nozzles where there are two jets, aim one of the jets slightly above then centre of the screen and aim the other just below to ensure complete coverage of the screen. If necessary, adjust the jets using a pin.

18 Airbag unit check

Where fitted, inspect the airbag(s) exterior condition checking for signs of damage or deterioration. If an airbag shows signs of damage, it must be renewed (see Chapter 12).

19 Hinge and lock lubrication

Lubricate the hinges of the bonnet, doors and tailgate with a light general-purpose oil. Similarly, lubricate all latches, locks and lock strikers. At the same time, check the security and operation of all the locks, adjusting them if necessary (see Chapter 11).

Lightly lubricate the bonnet release mechanism and cable with a suitable grease.

20 Road test

Instruments and electrical equipment

1 Check the operation of all instruments and electrical equipment.

2 Make sure all instruments read correctly, and switch on all electrical equipment in turn, to check that it functions properly.

Steering and suspension

3 Check for any abnormalities in the steering, suspension, handling or road "feel".

4 Drive the vehicle, and check that there are no unusual vibrations or noises.

5 Check that the steering feels positive, with no excessive "sloppiness", or roughness, and check for any suspension noises when cornering and driving over bumps.

Drivetrain

6 Check the performance of the engine, clutch (where applicable), gearbox/transmission and driveshafts.

1B

7 Listen for any unusual noises from the engine, clutch and gearbox/transmission.

8 Make sure that the engine runs smoothly when idling, and that there is no hesitation when accelerating.

9 Check that, where applicable, the clutch action is smooth and progressive, that the drive is taken up smoothly, and that the pedal travel is not excessive. Also listen for any noises when the clutch pedal is depressed.

10 On manual gearbox models, check that all gears can be engaged smoothly without noise, and that the gear lever action is not abnormally vague or "notchy".

11 On automatic transmission models, make sure that all gearchanges occur smoothly, without snatching, and without an increase in engine speed between changes. Check that all the gear positions can be selected with the vehicle at rest. If any problems are found, they should be referred to a VW dealer.

12 Listen for a metallic clicking sound from the front of the vehicle, as the vehicle is driven slowly in a circle with the steering on full-lock. Carry out this check in both directions. If a clicking noise is heard, this indicates wear in a driveshaft joint, in which case renew the joint if necessary.

Check the operation and performance of the braking system

13 Make sure that the vehicle does not pull to one side when braking, and that the wheels do not lock prematurely when braking hard.

14 Check that there is no vibration through the steering when braking.

15 Check that the handbrake operates correctly without excessive movement of the lever, and that it holds the vehicle stationary on a slope.

16 Test the operation of the brake servo unit as follows. With the engine off, depress the footbrake four or five times to exhaust the vacuum. Hold the brake pedal depressed, then start the engine. As the engine starts, there should be a noticeable "give" in the brake pedal as vacuum builds up. Allow the engine to run for at least two minutes, and then switch it off. If the brake pedal is depressed now, it should be possible to detect a hiss from the servo as the pedal is depressed. After about four or five applications, no further hissing should be heard, and the pedal should feel much harder.

Every 20 000 miles (30 000 km) - "IN 02" on interval display

21 Fuel filter renewal

1 The fuel filter is mounted on the inner wing, above the right hand wheel arch. Position a container underneath the filter unit and pad the surrounding area with rags to absorb any fuel that may be spilt.

2 At the top of the filter unit, release the clip and lift out the control valve, leaving the fuel hoses attached to it (see illustrations).

3 Slacken the hose clips and pull the fuel supply and delivery hoses from the ports on the of the filter unit. If crimp-type clips are fitted, cut them off using snips, and use equivalent size worm-drive clips on refitting. Note the fitted position of each hose, to aid correct refitting later. *Caution: Be prepared for an amount of fuel loss.*

4 Slacken the securing screw and raise the filter out its retaining bracket (see illustrations).

5 Fit a new fuel filter into the retaining bracket and tighten the securing screw.

6 Refit the control valve to the top of the filter and insert the retaining clip.

7 Reconnect the fuel supply and delivery hoses, using the notes made during removal - note the fuel flow arrow markings next to each port. Where crimp-type hoses were originally fitted, use equivalent size worm-drive clips on refitting (see illustration). Remove the collecting container and rags,

8 Start and run the engine at idle, then check around the fuel filter for fuel leaks. **Note:** *It may take a few seconds of cranking before the engine starts.*

9 Raise the engine speed to about 2000 rpm several times, then allow the engine to idle again. Observe the fuel flow through the transparent hose leading to the fuel injection pump and check that it is free of air bubbles.

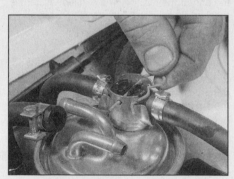
21.2a release the clip . . .

21.2b . . .and lift out the control valve, leaving the fuel hoses attached to it

22 Air filter renewal

1 The air filter is housed in the air cleaner, which is situated on the right hand side of the inner wing.

2 Prise open the spring clips and lift off the air cleaner top cover (see illustration). *Caution: On engine code 1Z, the airflow meter is integral with the air cleaner top cover, handle this component very carefully, as it easily damaged.*

21.4a Slacken the securing screw . . .

21.4b . . .and raise the filter out its retaining bracket

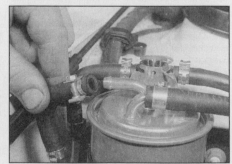
21.7 Reconnect the fuel supply and delivery hoses

22.2 Prise open the spring clips, and lift off the air cleaner top cover

3 Lift out the air filter element.
4 Remove any debris that may have collected inside the air cleaner.
5 Fit a new air filter element in position, ensuring that the edges are securely seated **(see illustration)**.
6 Refit the air cleaner top cover and snap the retaining clips into position.

23 Automatic transmission fluid renewal

As the automatic transmission is not fitted with a drain plug; the transmission fluid must be pumped out using a special adapter. For this reason, it is recommended that automatic transmission fluid renewal is carried out by a VAG dealer.

24 Pollen filter renewal

1 The pollen filter (where fitted) is located beneath the windscreen wiper motor cover panels; it is located on the right-hand side on left-hand drive models, and the left-hand side on right-hand drive models.
2 Unclip the rubber seal from relevant end of the top of the engine compartment bulkhead.
3 Unscrew the retaining fastener screws and pull out the fasteners securing the relevant half of the windscreen wiper motor cover panel in position. Release the half of the cover panel from the windscreen and remove it from the vehicle.
4 Pivot the pollen filter cover upwards and away then release the retaining clips and withdraw the from its housing.
5 Wipe clean the filter housing then fit the new filter. Clip the filter securely in position and refit the cover.
6 Refit the trim cover, securing it in position with the fasteners, and seat the rubber seal on the bulkhead.

25 Timing belt check and adjustment

1 Referring to Chapter 2B remove the timing belt cover and inspect the timing belt for signs of damage or deterioration. Check the timing

22.5 Fit a new air filter element in position, ensuring the edges are securely seated

belt carefully for any signs of uneven wear, splitting, or oil contamination. Pay particular attention to the roots of the teeth. Renew the belt if there is the slightest doubt about its condition. The cost of a new belt is nothing when compared to the cost of repairs, should the belt break in service.
2 If signs of oil contamination are found, trace the source of the leak, and rectify it. Wash the engine timing belt area and all related components, to remove all traces of oil.
3 Check and if necessary adjust the belt tension, as described in Chapter 2B. On completion, refit the belt cover.

26 Manual transmission oil level check

1 Park the car on a level surface. The oil level must be checked before the car is driven, or at least 5 minutes after the engine has been switched off. If the oil is checked just after driving the car, some of the oil will remain distributed around the transmission, resulting in an inaccurate level reading.
2 Remove the retaining clips and screws, then lower the undertray away from the engine bay.
3 Wipe clean the area around the filler/level plug, which is situated on the differential casing on engine codes AAZ and 1Y or on the front of the left hand end of the transmission on engine code 1Z. Unscrew the plug and clean it; discard the sealing washer **(see illustrations)**.

26.3a Manual transmission oil filler/level plug location (engine codes AAZ and 1Y)

4 The oil level should reach the lower edge of the filler/level hole. A certain amount of oil will have gathered behind the filler/level plug, and will trickle out when it is removed; this does **not** necessarily indicate that the level is correct. To ensure that a true level is established, wait until the initial trickle has stopped, then add oil as necessary until a trickle of new oil can be seen emerging. The level will be correct when the flow ceases. When topping-up, use only good-quality oil of the specified type (refer to "*Lubricants, fluids and tyre pressures*" at the end of "*Weekly Checks*").
5 Filling the transmission with oil is an extremely awkward operation; above all, allow plenty of time for the oil level to settle properly before checking it. If a large amount is added to the transmission, and a large amount flows out on checking the level, refit the filler/level plug and take the vehicle on a short journey so that the new oil is distributed fully around the transmission components, then recheck the level when it has settled again.
6 If the transmission has been overfilled so that oil flows out when the filler/level plug is removed, check that the car is completely level (front-to-rear and side-to-side), and allow the surplus to drain off into a suitable container.
7 When the level is correct, fit a new sealing washer to the filler/level plug. Refit the plug, tightening it securely. Wash off any spilt oil then refit the engine bay undertray securing it in position with the retaining clips and screws.

1B

27 Auxiliary drivebelt check and renewal

Checking

1 Disconnect the battery negative cable and position it away from the terminal.
2 Park the vehicle on a level surface, apply the handbrake and chock the rear wheels.
3 Raise the front of the vehicle, rest it securely on axle stands and remove the roadwheels.
4 Turn the steering to full right hand lock, then remove the screws and clips and lower the undertray away from the engine bay.

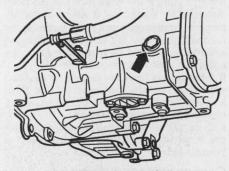

26.3b Manual transmission oil filler/level plug location (engine code 1Z)

5 Using a socket and wrench on the crankshaft sprocket bolt, rotate the crankshaft so that the full length of the auxiliary drivebelts can be examined. Look for cracks, splitting and fraying on the surface of the belt; check also for signs of glazing (shiny patches) and separation of the belt plies. If damage or wear is visible, the belt should be renewed.

Renewal

6 For details of auxiliary drivebelt renewal, refer to the relevant Section of Chapter 2B.

Every 60 000 miles (90 000 km)

28 Timing belt renewal

Refer to Chapter 2B.

Every 2 years (regardless of mileage)

29 Coolant renewal

Cooling system draining

Warning: Wait until the engine is cold before starting this procedure. Do not allow antifreeze to come in contact with your skin, or with the painted surfaces of the vehicle. Rinse off spills immediately with plenty of water. Never leave antifreeze lying around in an open container, or in a puddle in the driveway or on the garage floor. Children and pets are attracted by its sweet smell, but antifreeze can be fatal if ingested.

1 With the engine completely cold, cover the expansion tank cap with a wad of rag, and slowly turn the cap anti-clockwise to relieve the pressure in the cooling system (a hissing sound will normally be heard). Wait until any pressure remaining in the system is released, then continue to turn the cap until it can be removed.
2 Position a suitable container beneath the radiator bottom hose connection, then release the retaining clip and ease the hose from the radiator stub. If the hose joint has not been disturbed for some time, it will be necessary to gently manipulate the hose to break the joint. Do not use excessive force, or the radiator stub could be damaged. Allow the coolant to drain into the container.
3 If the coolant has been drained for a reason other than renewal, then provided it is clean and less than two years old, it can be re-used, though this is not recommended.
4 Once all the coolant has drained, reconnect the hose to the radiator and secure it in position with the retaining clip.

Cooling system flushing

5 If coolant renewal has been neglected, or if the antifreeze mixture has become diluted, then in time, the cooling system may gradually lose efficiency, as the coolant passages become restricted due to rust, scale deposits, and other sediment. The cooling system efficiency can be restored by flushing the system clean.
6 The radiator should be flushed independently of the engine, to avoid unnecessary contamination.

Radiator flushing

7 To flush the radiator disconnect the top and bottom hoses and any other relevant hoses from the radiator, with reference to Chapter 3.
8 Insert a garden hose into the radiator top inlet. Direct a flow of clean water through the radiator, and keep flushing until clean water emerges from the radiator bottom outlet.
9 If after a reasonable period, the water still does not run clear, the radiator can be flushed with a good proprietary cooling system cleaning agent. It is important that their manufacturer's instructions are followed carefully. If the contamination is particularly bad, insert the hose in the radiator bottom outlet, and reverse-flush the radiator.

Engine flushing

10 To flush the engine, remove the thermostat as described in Chapter 3, then temporarily refit the thermostat cover.
11 With the top and bottom hoses disconnected from the radiator, insert a garden hose into the radiator top hose. Direct a clean flow of water through the engine, and continue flushing until clean water emerges from the radiator bottom hose.
12 On completion, refit the thermostat and reconnect the hoses (refer to Chapter 3).

Cooling system filling

13 Before attempting to fill the cooling system, make sure that all hoses and clips are in good condition, and that the clips are tight. Note that an antifreeze mixture must be used all year round, to prevent corrosion of the engine components (see following sub-Section).

14 Remove the expansion tank filler cap, and fill the system by slowly pouring the coolant into the expansion tank to prevent airlocks from forming.
15 If the coolant is being renewed, begin by pouring in a couple of litres of water, followed by the correct quantity of antifreeze, then top-up with more water.
16 Once the level in the expansion tank starts to rise, squeeze the radiator top and bottom hoses to help expel any trapped air in the system. Once all the air is expelled, top-up the coolant level to the "MAX" mark and refit the expansion tank cap.
17 Start the engine and run it until it reaches normal operating temperature, then stop the engine and allow it to cool.
18 Check for leaks, particularly around disturbed components. Check the coolant level in the expansion tank, and top-up if necessary. Note that the system must be cold before an accurate level is indicated in the expansion tank. If the expansion tank cap is removed while the engine is still warm, cover the cap with a thick cloth, and unscrew the cap slowly to gradually relieve the system pressure (a hissing sound will normally be heard). Wait until any pressure remaining in the system is released, then continue to turn the cap until it can be removed.

Antifreeze mixture

19 The antifreeze should always be renewed at the specified intervals. This is necessary not only to maintain the antifreeze properties, but also to prevent corrosion which would otherwise occur as the corrosion inhibitors become progressively less effective.
20 Always use an ethylene-glycol based antifreeze which is suitable for use in mixed-metal cooling systems. The quantity of antifreeze and levels of protection are indicated in the Specifications.
21 Before adding antifreeze, the cooling system should be completely drained, preferably flushed, and all hoses checked for condition and security.

22 After filling with antifreeze, a label should be attached to the expansion tank, stating the type and concentration of antifreeze used, and the date installed. Any subsequent topping-up should be made with the same type and concentration of antifreeze.

23 Do not use engine antifreeze in the windscreen/tailgate washer system, as it will cause damage to the vehicle paintwork. A screenwash additive should be added to the washer system in the quantities stated on the bottle (see "*Weekly Checks*").

30 Brake fluid renewal

⚠ *Warning: Brake fluid can harm your eyes and damage painted surfaces, so use extreme caution when handling and pouring it. Do not use fluid that has been standing open for some time, as it absorbs moisture from the air. Excess moisture content can cause a dangerous loss of braking effectiveness.*

1 The procedure is similar to that for the bleeding of the hydraulic system as described in Chapter 9, except that the brake fluid reservoir should be emptied by siphoning, using a clean poultry baster or similar before starting, and allowance should be made for the old fluid to be expelled when bleeding a section of the circuit.

2 Working as described in Chapter 9, open the first bleed screw in the sequence, and pump the brake pedal gently until nearly all the old fluid has been emptied from the master cylinder reservoir.

HAYNES HiNT | *Old hydraulic fluid is often much darker in colour than the new, making it easy to distinguish the two.*

3 Top-up to the "MAX" level with new fluid, and continue pumping until only the new fluid remains in the reservoir, and new fluid can be seen emerging from the bleed screw. Tighten the screw, and top the reservoir level up to the "MAX" level line.

4 Work through all the remaining bleed screws in the sequence until new fluid can be seen at all of them. Be careful to keep the master cylinder reservoir topped-up to above the "MIN" level at all times, or air may enter the system and greatly increase the length of the task.

5 When the operation is complete, check that all bleed screws are securely tightened, and that their dust caps are refitted. Wash off all traces of spilt fluid, and recheck the master cylinder reservoir fluid level.

6 Check the operation of the brakes before taking the car on the road.

31 Exhaust gas emissions check

1 This task should be entrusted to a VW dealer or another suitable specialist equipped with the necessary gas analyser needed to check diesel exhaust gas emissions.

1B

Chapter 2 Part A:
Petrol engine in-car repair procedures

Contents

Degrees of difficulty

Easy, suitable for novice with little experience	Fairly easy, suitable for beginner with some experience	Fairly difficult, suitable for competent DIY mechanic	Difficult, suitable for experienced DIY mechanic	Very difficult, suitable for expert DIY or professional

2A

Specifications

General

Engine code*

1391cc, Bosch Mono-Motronic injection, 44kW	ABD
1598cc:	
Bosch Mono-Motronic injection, 55kW, 08/92 to 09/94	ABU
Bosch Mono-Motronic injection, 55kW, 10/94 on	AEA
Bosch Motronic injection, cross-flow cylinder head, 74kW	AEK
1781cc:	
Bosch Mono-Motronic injection, 55kW	AAM
Bosch Mono-Motronic injection, 66kW, to 10/94	ABS
Bosch Mono-Motronic injection, 66kW, 10/94 on	ADZ
1984 cc:	
Digifant multi-point injection, 85kW, to 10/94	2E
Simos multi-point injection, 85kW, 10/94 on	ADY
Digifant multi-point injection, DOHC, 110kW	ABF

* Note: *See 'Buying Spare Parts and Vehicle Identification' for the location of code marking on the engine.*

Bore:

ABD	75.0 mm
ABU, AEA	76.5 mm
AEK, AAM, ABS, ADZ	81.0 mm
2E, ADY, ABF	82.5 mm

Stroke:

ABD:	
to 07/92	79.14 mm
07/92 on	78.70 mm
ABU, AEA	86.9 mm
AEK	77.4 mm
AAM, ABS, ADZ	86.4 mm
2E, ADY, ABF	92.8 mm

Compression ratio:
AAM	9.0:1
ABU	9.3:1
ABD	9.5:1
AEA, ABS, 2E, ADZ, ADY	10.0:1
AEK	10.3:1
ABF	10.5:1

Compression pressures (wear limit):
ABU, AEA, ABD, AAM	7.0 bar
ADY, ADZ, ABS, 2E, ABF, AEK	7.5 bar
Firing order	1 - 3 - 4 - 2
No 1 cylinder location	Timing belt end

Timing belt tension:
Engine code ABF (measured using Volkswagen tool VW 210)	Scale reading of 13 to 14 units

Lubrication system

Oil pump type:
ABU, ABD, AEA	Sump-mounted, chain-driven from crankshaft
AAM, ABS, 2E, ADZ, ADY, ABF, AEK	Sump-mounted, driven indirectly from intermediate shaft
Normal operating oil pressure	2.0 bar minimum (at 2000 rpm, oil temperature 80°C)
Oil pump backlash	0.2 mm (wear limit)
Oil pump axial clearance	0.15 mm (wear limit)
Oil pump drive chain tension (where applicable)	3 to 4 mm (approx) deflection at mid-point between sprockets

Torque wrench settings

	Nm	lbf ft
Alternator mounting bolts	25	18
Auxiliary belt pulley bolts	20	15
Camshaft cover retaining screws/nuts	10	7
Camshaft sprocket bolt:		
Engine code ABF	65	48
All other engine codes	80	59
Coolant pump bolts (engine codes ABD, ABU, AEA), M6 bolts	10	7
Coolant pump bolts (engine codes ABD, ABU, AEA), M8 bolts	20	15
Crankshaft oil seal housing bolts	10	7
Crankshaft sprocket bolt:		
Engine codes ABU, ABD, AEA:		
Stage 1	90	66
Stage 2 (angle tighten)	Angle-tighten a further 120°	
All other engine codes		
Stage 1	90	66
Stage 2 (angle tighten)	Angle-tighten a further 90°	
Cylinder head bolts:		
Stage 1	40	30
Stage 2	60	44
Stage 3	Angle-tighten a further 90°	
Stage 4	Angle-tighten a further 90°	
Engine mountings:		
Front block bolt	50	37
Front bracket bolts	50	37
Left rear mounting bracket bolts	25	18
Rear block-to-body bolts	25	18
Right rear mounting bracket bolts	25	18
Through-bolts	50	37
Exhaust manifold nuts, M8 nuts	25	18
Exhaust manifold nuts, M10 nuts	40	30
Flywheel mounting bolts:		
Stage 1	60	44
Stage 2	Angle-tighten a further 90°	
Oil pickup-to-oil pump bolts	10	7
Oil pump cover bolts	10	7
Oil pump drive chain guide rail-to-crankcase bolts	10	7
Oil pump-to-crankcase bolts	20	15
Power steering pump mounting bolts	25	18
Sump retaining bolts	20	15
Timing belt tensioner centre nut/bolt	45	33
Torque converter driveplate bolts:		
Stage 1	60	44
Stage 2	Angle-tighten a further 90°	

1 General information

Using this Chapter

Chapter 2 is divided into three Parts; A, B and C. Repair operations that can be carried out with the engine in the vehicle are described in Parts A (petrol engines) and B (diesel engines). Part C covers the removal of the engine/transmission as a unit, and describes the engine dismantling and overhaul procedures.

In Parts A and B, the assumption is made that the engine is installed in the vehicle, with all ancillaries connected. If the engine has been removed for overhaul, the preliminary dismantling information which precedes each operation may be ignored.

Access to the engine bay can be improved by removing the bonnet and the front lock carrier assembly; for details, see Chapter 11 and Chapter 2C respectively.

Engine description

Throughout this Chapter, engines are identified and referred to by the manufacturer's code letters, rather than capacity. A listing of all engines covered, together with their code letters, is given in the Specifications.

The engines are water-cooled, single or double overhead camshaft, in-line four-cylinder units, with cast-iron cylinder blocks and aluminium-alloy cylinder heads. All are mounted transversely at the front of the vehicle, with the transmission bolted to the left-hand side of the engine.

The cylinder head carries the camshaft(s), which are driven by a toothed timing belt. It also houses the inlet and exhaust valves, which are closed by single or double coil springs, and which run in guides pressed into the cylinder head. The camshaft actuates the valves directly via hydraulic tappets, mounted in the cylinder head. The cylinder head contains integral oilways which supply and lubricate the tappets.

The crankshaft is supported by five main bearings, and endfloat is controlled by a thrust bearing fitted between cylinder Nos 2 and 3.

Engine coolant is circulated by a pump, driven either by the camshaft timing belt or the auxiliary drivebelt. For details of the cooling system, refer to Chapter 3.

Larger engines are fitted with a timing belt-driven intermediate shaft, which provides drive for the distributor and the oil pump.

Lubricant is circulated under pressure by a pump, driven either by the crankshaft or by the intermediate shaft, depending on engine type. Oil is drawn from the sump through a strainer, and then forced through an externally-mounted, replaceable screw-on filter. From there, it is distributed to the cylinder head, where it lubricates the camshaft journals and hydraulic tappets, and also to the crankcase, where it lubricates the main bearings, connecting rod big- and small-ends, gudgeon pins and cylinder bores. Larger engines are fitted with oil jets, mounted at the base of each cylinder - these spray oil onto the underside of the pistons, to improve cooling. An oil cooler, supplied with engine coolant, reduces the temperature of the oil before it re-enters the engine.

Repairs possible with the engine installed in the vehicle :

The following operations can be performed without removing the engine:-

a) Auxiliary drivebelts - removal and refitting.
b) Camshaft(s) - removal and refitting. *
c) Camshaft oil seal - renewal.
d) Camshaft sprocket - removal and refitting.
e) Coolant pump - removal and refitting (refer to Chapter 3).
f) Crankshaft oil seals - renewal.
g) Crankshaft sprocket - removal and refitting.
h) Cylinder head - removal and refitting. *
i) Engine mountings - inspection and renewal.
j) Intermediate shaft oil seal - renewal.
k) Oil pump and pickup assembly - removal and refitting.
l) Sump - removal and refitting.
m) Timing belt, sprockets and cover - removal, inspection and refitting.

*Cylinder head dismantling procedures are detailed in Chapter 2C, with details of camshaft and hydraulic tappet removal.
Note: It is possible to remove the pistons and connecting rods (after removing the cylinder head and sump) without removing the engine . However, this is not recommended. Work of this nature is more easily and thoroughly completed with the engine on the bench, as described in Chapter 2C.

2 Engine assembly and valve timing marks - general information and usage

General information

Note: This sub-section has been written with the assumption that the distributor, HT leads and timing belt are correctly fitted.

1 The crankshaft, camshaft (and on certain engines, the intermediate shaft) sprockets are driven by the timing belt, and rotate in phase with each other. When the timing belt is removed during servicing or repair, it is possible for the shafts to rotate independently of each other, and the correct phasing is then lost.

2 The design of the engines covered in this Chapter is such that potentially damaging piston-to-valve contact may occur if the camshaft is rotated when any of the pistons are stationary at, or near, the top of its stroke.

3 For this reason, it is important that the correct phasing between the camshaft, crankshaft and intermediate shaft is preserved whilst the timing belt is off the engine. This is achieved by setting the engine in a reference condition (known as Top Dead Centre or TDC) before the timing belt is removed, and then preventing the shafts from rotating until the belt is refitted. Similarly, if the engine has been dismantled for overhaul, the engine can be set to TDC during reassembly to ensure that the correct shaft phasing is restored.

Note: On engine codes ABU and ABD, the coolant pump is also driven by the timing belt, but the pump alignment with respect to the crankshaft and camshaft is not critical. On engine code ABF, the intermediate shaft drives only the oil pump, so its alignment with the crankshaft and camshaft is not critical.

4 TDC is the highest position a piston reaches within its respective cylinder - in a four-stroke engine, each piston reaches TDC twice per cycle; once on the compression stroke, and once on the exhaust stroke. In general, TDC normally refers to No 1 cylinder on the compression stroke. (Note that the cylinders are numbered one to four, starting from the timing belt end of the engine).

5 The crankshaft sprocket is equipped with a marking which, when aligned with a reference marking on the timing belt cover or intermediate shaft sprocket (depending on engine type), indicates that No 1 cylinder (and hence also No 4 cylinder) is at TDC **(see illustrations)**. Note that on some engines, the pulley for the ribbed auxiliary drivebelt must

2A

2.5a Crankshaft/intermediate shaft sprocket timing marks: engine codes AAM, ABS, ADZ, ADY, 2E

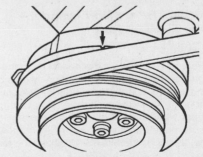

2.5b Crankshaft ribbed drivebelt pulley timing marks: engine code AEK, ABF

2.5c Crankshaft sprocket timing marks: engine codes ABU, ABD

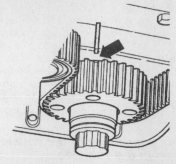

2.5d Crankshaft sprocket timing marks - bevelled tooth (arrowed): engine code AEA

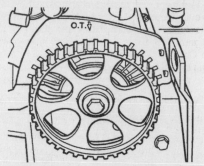

2.6a Camshaft timing marks: engine codes AEK, ABF, AAM, ABS, ADZ, ADY, 2E

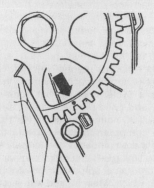

2.6b Camshaft timing marks: engine code AEA

2.6c Camshaft timing marks: engine codes ABU, ABD

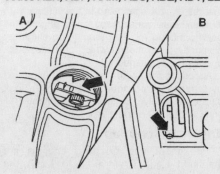

2.7 Flywheel/driveplate timing marks: engine codes AEK, ABF

A Flywheel   B Driveplate

be temporarily fitted to obtain the crankshaft marks.

6 The camshaft sprocket is also equipped with a timing mark - when this is similarly aligned, the engine is correctly synchronised, and the timing belt can then be refitted and tensioned **(see illustrations)**.

7 In addition, on certain engines the flywheel/driveplate has markings which can be observed by removing a protective cap from the transmission bellhousing. When this mark is aligned with a corresponding reference mark on the bellhousing casting, it indicates that No 1 cylinder is at TDC **(see illustration)**. Note, however, that these markings cannot be used if the transmission has been removed from the engine for repair or overhaul.

8 The following sub-Sections describe setting the engine to TDC on No 1 cylinder.

Setting TDC on No 1 cylinder - timing belt fitted

All engines

9 Before starting work, disconnect the battery negative cable. Disable the ignition system by removing the distributor centre HT lead and grounding it on the cylinder block, using a jumper wire. Prevent any vehicle movement by putting the transmission in neutral, applying the handbrake and chocking the rear wheels.

10 On the distributor cap, note the position of the No 1 cylinder HT terminal with respect

to the distributor body. On some models, the manufacturer provides a marking in the form of a small cut-out . If the terminal is not marked, follow the HT lead from the No 1 cylinder spark plug back to the distributor cap - No 1 cylinder is at the timing end of the engine - and using chalk or a pen (*not* a pencil), place a mark on the distributor body directly under the terminal.

11 Remove the distributor cap, as described in Chapter 5B.

12 Disconnect the HT leads from the spark plugs, noting their order of connection.

13 To bring any piston up to TDC, it will be necessary to rotate the crankshaft manually. This can be done by using a wrench and socket on the bolt that retains the crankshaft pulley (refer to Section 5 for more detail).

14 Rotate the crankshaft in its normal direction of rotation until the distributor rotor arm electrode begins to approach the mark that was made on the distributor body.

HAYNES HiNT *Remove all four spark plugs; this will make the engine easier to turn; refer to Chapter 1A for details.*

15 With reference to Section 4, remove the upper timing belt outer covers to expose the camshaft timing belt sprocket beneath.

16 Identify the timing marks on both the camshaft sprocket and the inner section of the timing belt cover (or cylinder head cover, as applicable) - refer to the accompanying

illustrations. Continue turning the crankshaft clockwise until these marks are exactly aligned with each other.

17 At this point, identify the timing marks on the crankshaft sprocket (or pulley, as applicable) and the timing belt cover (or intermediate shaft, as applicable) and check that they are correctly aligned; refer to the illustrations in *General Information*. **Note**: *On some engines, the outer part of the lower timing belt cover must be removed to expose the crankshaft sprocket timing marks.*

Engine codes ABF, AEK only

18 Locate the timing inspection hole on the transmission bellhousing, and remove the protective cap. This exposes the edge of the flywheel, on which there is a set of timing marks.

19 With the camshaft timing marks aligned, the timing mark on the flywheel should be aligned exactly with the pointer marked on the bellhousing - refer to the illustrations in *General Information*. **Note**: *Observe from directly above the inspection hole to ensure correct alignment.*

20 On engine code AEK, note that the intermediate shaft sprocket has no timing markings - alignment is achieved by checking that the centre of the rotor arm electrode is lined up with the No 1 terminal marking on the distributor body.

All engines

21 Check that the centre of the distributor rotor arm electrode is now aligned with the No

1 terminal mark on the distributor body. If it proves impossible to align the rotor arm with the No 1 terminal whilst maintaining the alignment of the camshaft timing marks, refer to Chapter 5B and check that the distributor has been fitted correctly.

22 When all the above steps have been completed successfully, the engine will be set to TDC on No 1 cylinder.

Caution: If the timing belt is to be removed, ensure that the crankshaft, camshaft and intermediate shaft alignment is preserved by preventing the sprockets from rotating with respect to each other.

Setting TDC on No 1 cylinder - timing belt removed

23 This procedure has been written with the assumption that the timing belt has been removed and that the alignment between the camshaft, crankshaft and where applicable, intermediate shaft has been lost, for example following engine removal and overhaul.

24 On all the engines covered in this manual, it is possible for damage to be caused by the piston crowns striking the valve heads, if the camshaft is rotated with the timing belt removed and the crankshaft set to TDC. For this reason, the TDC setting procedure must be carried out in a particular order, as described in the following paragraphs.

25 Before the cylinder head is refitted, use a wrench and socket on the crankshaft pulley centre bolt to turn the crankshaft in its normal direction of rotation, until all four pistons are positioned **halfway down** their bores, with No 1 piston on its upstroke - i.e. around 90° before TDC.

26 With the cylinder head and camshaft sprocket fitted, identify the timing marks on both the camshaft sprocket and the inner section of the timing belt cover or cylinder head cover, as applicable; refer to the illustrations in *General Information*.

27 Turn the camshaft sprocket in its normal direction of rotation until the timing marks on the sprocket and timing belt inner cover (or cylinder head cover, on engine code ABF); are exactly aligned.

28 On engine code AEK *only*, check that the centre of the rotor arm electrode is lined up with the No 1 cylinder terminal marking on the distributor; if this is not the case, rotate the intermediate shaft sprocket to bring them into alignment.

29 Identify the timing marks on the crankshaft sprocket (or pulley, as applicable) and the timing belt cover (or intermediate shaft, as applicable); refer to the illustrations in *General Information*. Using a socket and wrench on the crankshaft sprocket retaining bolt, turn the crankshaft through 90° (quarter of a turn) in its normal direction of rotation, to bring the timing marks into alignment.

30 On engine codes ABF and AEK only, if the transmission is fitted to the engine, the crankshaft alignment can be verified by

observing the timing marks on the flywheel and transmission bellhousing. Remove the protective cap from the timing inspection hole on the bellhousing, and check that the marks are aligned as described in paragraph 7. **Note:** *Observe from directly above the inspection hole, to ensure correct alignment.*

31 Check that the centre of the distributor rotor arm electrode is now aligned with No 1 cylinder terminal marking on the distributor body. If it proves impossible to align the rotor arm with the No 1 terminal whilst maintaining the alignment of the camshaft timing marks, refer to Chapter 5B and check that the distributor has been fitted correctly.

32 When all the above steps have been completed successfully, the engine will be set at TDC on No 1 cylinder. The timing belt can now be fitted as described in Section 4.

Caution: Until the timing belt is fitted, ensure that the crankshaft, camshaft and intermediate shaft alignment is preserved by preventing the sprockets from rotating with respect to each other.

3 Cylinder compression test

1 When engine performance is down, or if misfiring occurs which cannot be attributed to the ignition or fuel systems, a compression test can provide diagnostic clues as to the engine's condition. If the test is performed regularly, it can give warning of trouble before any other symptoms become apparent.

2 The engine must be fully warmed-up to normal operating temperature, the battery must be fully charged, and all the spark plugs must be removed (refer to Chapter 1). The aid of an assistant will also be required.

3 Disable the ignition system by disconnecting the ignition HT coil lead from the distributor cap and earthing it on the cylinder block. Use a jumper lead or similar wire to make a good connection.

4 Fit a compression tester to the No 1 cylinder spark plug hole - the type of tester which screws into the plug thread is preferable.

5 Have an assistant hold the throttle wide open, then crank the engine on the starter motor; after one or two revolutions, the compression pressure should build up to a maximum figure, and then stabilise. Record the highest reading obtained.

6 Repeat the test on the remaining cylinders, recording the pressure in each. Keep the throttle wide open.

7 All cylinders should produce very similar pressures; a difference of more than 2 bars between any two cylinders indicates a fault. Note that the compression should build up quickly in a healthy engine; low compression on the first stroke, followed by gradually-increasing pressure on successive strokes, indicates worn piston rings. A low compression reading on the first stroke, which

does not build up during successive strokes, indicates leaking valves or a blown head gasket (a cracked head could also be the cause). Deposits on the undersides of the valve heads can also cause low compression.

8 Refer to the Specifications section of this Chapter, and compare the recorded compression figures with those stated by the manufacturer.

9 If the pressure in any cylinder is low, carry out the following test to isolate the cause. Introduce a teaspoonful of clean oil into that cylinder through its spark plug hole, and repeat the test.

10 If the addition of oil temporarily improves the compression pressure, this indicates that bore or piston wear is responsible for the pressure loss. No improvement suggests that leaking or burnt valves, or a blown head gasket, may be to blame.

11 A low reading from two adjacent cylinders is almost certainly due to the head gasket having blown between them; the presence of coolant in the engine oil will confirm this.

12 If one cylinder is about 20 percent lower than the others and the engine has a slightly rough idle, a worn camshaft lobe could be the cause.

13 If the compression reading is unusually high, the combustion chambers are probably coated with carbon deposits. If this is the case, the cylinder head should be removed and decarbonised.

14 On completion of the test, refit the spark plugs and restore the ignition system.

4 Camshaft timing belt and outer covers - removal and refitting

General information

1 The primary function of the toothed timing belt is to drive the camshaft(s), but it is also used to drive the coolant pump or intermediate shaft, depending on the engine specification. Should the belt slip or break in service, the valve timing will be disturbed and piston-to-valve contact may occur, resulting in serious engine damage.

2 For this reason, it is important that the timing belt is tensioned correctly, and inspected regularly for signs of wear or deterioration.

3 Note that the removal of the *inner* section of the timing belt cover is described as part of the cylinder head removal procedure; see Section 11 later in this Chapter.

Removal

4 Before starting work, immobilise the engine and vehicle as follows:

a) *Disable the ignition system by removing the distributor centre HT lead and grounding it on the cylinder block, using a jumper wire.*

b) *Disable the fuel system by removing the fuel pump relay from its socket.*

2A

4.6 Removing the timing belt outer cover (engine code ABD shown)

4.12 Relieve the tension on the timing belt by slackening the tensioner mounting nut (arrowed): engine code 2E shown

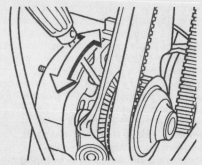

4.13 Release the tension on the timing belt by rotating the pump towards the engine - use a screwdriver as a lever

c) *Unplug the electrical wiring from the starter solenoid at the connector; refer to Chapter 5A for guidance.*

d) *Prevent any vehicle movement by applying the handbrake and chocking the rear wheels.*

5 Access to the timing belt covers can be improved by removing the air cleaner housing-to-throttle body ducting, and on all engine codes except ABU, AEA and AEA, by removing the crankcase breather hose.

6 Release the uppermost part of the timing belt cover by prising open the metal spring clips and where applicable, removing the retaining screws. Lift the cover away from the engine **(see illustration)**.

7 With reference to Section 6, remove the auxiliary drive V-belt (where fitted), then remove the ribbed auxiliary drivebelt.

8 Refer to Section 2 and using the engine alignment markings, set the engine to TDC on No 1 cylinder. Note that on some engines, it will be necessary to remove the pulley for the ribbed auxiliary drivebelt (together with the V-belt pulley, where fitted) and timing belt lower cover first, to gain access to the engine alignment markings on the crankshaft sprocket - this operation is described in the next paragraph.

9 Slacken and withdraw the retaining screws, then remove the pulley for the ribbed auxiliary drivebelt (together with the V-belt pulley, where fitted) from the crankshaft sprocket. On completion, check that the engine is still set to TDC.

HAYNES HiNT *To prevent the auxiliary drivebelt pulley from rotating whilst the mounting bolts are being slackened, select top gear (manual transmission) or 'PARK' (automatic transmission) and get an assistant to apply the footbrake firmly. Failing this, grip the sprocket by wrapping a length of old rubber hose or inner tube around it.*

10 All engine codes *except* ABU, ABD, AEA, refer to Chapter 3 and remove the coolant pump pulley to allow removal of the timing belt lower cover.

11 Remove the retaining screws and clips, and lift off the timing belt lower cover.

12 All engines *except* ABD, ABU, refer to Section 5 and relieve the tension on the timing belt by slackening the tensioner mounting nut slightly, allowing it to pivot away from the belt **(see illustration)**.

13 On engine codes ABD and ABU only, slacken the coolant pump mounting bolts, then release the tension on the timing belt by rotating the pump towards the engine - use a stout screwdriver, inserted between the lugs on the pump casting, as a lever **(see illustration)**.

14 Examine the timing belt for manufacturer's markings that indicate the direction of rotation. If none are present, make your own using typist's correction fluid.

Caution: If the belt appears to be in good condition and can be re-used, it is essential that it is refitted the same way around, otherwise accelerated wear will result, leading to premature failure.

15 Slide the belt off the sprockets, taking care to avoid twisting or kinking it excessively. Ensure that the sprockets remain aligned with their respective timing markings once the timing belt has been removed.

Caution: It is potentially damaging to allow the camshaft to turn with the timing belt removed and the engine set at TDC, as piston-to-valve contact may occur.

16 Examine the belt for evidence of contamination by coolant or lubricant. If this is the case, identify the source of the contamination before progressing any further. Check the belt for signs of wear or damage, particularly around the leading edges of the belt teeth. Renew the belt if its condition is in doubt; the cost of belt renewal is negligible compared with potential cost of the engine repairs, should the belt fail in service. Similarly, if the belt is known to have covered more than 36 000 miles, it is prudent to renew it regardless of condition, as a precautionary measure.

17 If the timing belt is not going to be refitted for some time, it is a wise precaution to hang a warning label on the steering wheel, to remind yourself (and others) not to attempt starting the engine.

Refitting

18 Ensure that the crankshaft, camshaft and where applicable, intermediate shaft timing marks, are still correctly aligned in the TDC on No 1 cylinder position, as described in Section 2.

Engine codes ABD and ABU

19 Loop the timing belt under the crankshaft sprocket loosely, observing the direction of rotation markings.

20 Refit the lower section of the timing belt cover.

21 Fit the pulley for the ribbed auxiliary drivebelt to the crankshaft sprocket, noting that the offset of the mounting holes allows only one fitting position, then insert and tighten the bolts to the specified torque.

22 Ensure that the timing marks on the crankshaft pulley and camshaft sprocket are correctly aligned with their corresponding reference marks on the timing belt inner cover; refer to Section 2 for details.

23 Engage the timing belt teeth with the crankshaft sprocket, then manoeuvre it into position over the coolant pump and camshaft sprockets - avoid bending the belt back on itself or twisting it excessively as you do this. Ensure that the 'front run' of the belt is taut - ie all the slack should be in the section of the belt that passes over the coolant pump pulley.

24 Insert a stout screwdriver between the lugs on the coolant pump casting, then using the screwdriver as a lever, turn the coolant pump so that the slack in the belt is taken up **(refer to illustration 4.13)**.

25 Test the belt tension by grasping it between the fingers at a point mid-way between the coolant pump and camshaft sprockets and twisting it; the belt tension is correct when it can just be twisted through 90° (quarter of a turn) and no further.

26 When the correct belt tension has been achieved, tighten the coolant pump mounting bolts to the specified torque.

27 Using a spanner or wrench and socket on the crankshaft pulley centre bolt, rotate the crankshaft through two complete revolutions, and reset the engine to TDC on No 1 cylinder, with reference to Section 2. Re-check the belt tension, and adjust it if necessary.

4.31a Turn the tensioner with an Allen key until the slack in the belt is taken up

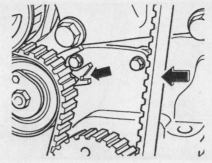

4.31b Sliding pointer should line up with the groove in the tensioner baseplate

Engine code AEA

28 Ensure that the timing marks on the crankshaft and camshaft sprockets are correctly aligned with their corresponding TDC reference marks on the timing belt inner cover; refer to Section 2 for details.

29 Engage the timing belt teeth with the crankshaft sprocket, then manoeuvre it into position over the coolant pump and camshaft sprockets. Observe the direction of rotation markings on the belt.

30 Pass the flat side of the belt over the tensioner roller - avoid bending the belt back on itself or twisting it excessively as you do this. Ensure the 'front run' of the belt is taut - ie all the slack should be in the section of the belt that passes over the tensioner roller.

31 Tension the belt as follows: tighten the tensioner securing bolt lightly, then insert an Allen key into the adjustment hole, and turn the eccentrically-mounted tensioner clockwise until the slack in the belt is taken up. Continue turning the tensioner until the sliding pointer lines up with the groove in the tensioner baseplate **(see illustrations)**. On completion, tighten the tensioner securing bolt to the specified torque.

32 Using a spanner or wrench and socket on the crankshaft pulley centre bolt, rotate the crankshaft through two complete revolutions, and reset the engine to TDC on No 1 cylinder, with reference to Section 2. Re-check the alignment of the tensioner, and adjust it if necessary.

33 Refer to Section 5 and test the operation of the tensioner.

34 Refit the lower and upper sections of the timing belt outer cover, tightening the retaining screws securely.

35 Refit the pulley for the ribbed auxiliary drivebelt to the crankshaft sprocket, noting that the offset of the mounting holes allows only one fitting position, then insert and tighten the retaining bolts to the specified torque.

Engine codes ABF and AEK

36 Ensure that the timing marks on the flywheel and camshaft sprocket are correctly aligned with their corresponding TDC reference marks on the transmission bellhousing and timing belt inner

cover/cylinder head cover respectively; refer to Section 2 for details.

37 Loop the timing belt under the crankshaft sprocket loosely, observing the direction of rotation markings.

38 Refit the lower section of the timing belt cover.

39 Fit the pulley for the ribbed auxiliary drivebelt to the crankshaft sprocket, noting that the offset of the mounting holes allows only one fitting position, then insert and tighten the retaining bolts to the specified torque.

40 On engine code AEK only, ensure that the intermediate shaft has not moved since the removal of the timing belt. Check that the marking for the No 1 cylinder terminal on the distributor body is still aligned with the centre of the rotor arm electrode (see Section 2).

41 Fully engage the timing belt teeth with the crankshaft sprocket, then manoeuvre the belt into position over the intermediate shaft and camshaft sprocket(s). Observe the direction of rotation markings on the belt.

42 Pass the flat side of the belt over the tensioner roller - avoid bending the belt back on itself or twisting it excessively as you do this. Ensure that the 'front run' of the belt is taut - i.e. all the slack should be in the section of the belt that passes over the tensioner roller.

43 Tension the belt by turning the eccentrically-mounted tensioner clockwise; two holes are provided in the side of the tensioner hub for this purpose - a pair of right-angled circlip pliers is an ideal substitute for the correct VAG tool **(see illustration)**.

44 On engine code ABF only, at this point, the belt tension must be accurately checked, and if necessary adjusted to specification - as this involves the use of dedicated belt tension measuring device (Volkswagen tool No VW 210), it is advisable to have this operation carried out by a VAG dealer.

45 On engine code AEK only, test the timing belt tension by grasping it between the fingers at a point mid-way between the intermediate shaft and camshaft sprockets and twisting it; the belt tension is correct when it can just be twisted through 90° (quarter of a turn) and no further.

46 When the correct belt tension has been

achieved, tighten the tensioner locknut to the specified torque.

47 Using a spanner or wrench and socket on the crankshaft pulley centre bolt, rotate the crankshaft through two complete revolutions and reset the engine to TDC on No 1 cylinder, with reference to Section 2. Re-check the timing belt tension and adjust it, if necessary.

48 Refit the upper section of the timing belt outer cover, and tighten the retaining screws securely.

Engine codes AAM, ABS, 2E, ADZ and ADY

49 Ensure that the timing mark on the camshaft sprocket is correctly aligned with the corresponding TDC reference mark on the timing belt inner cover; refer to Section 2 for details.

50 Loop the timing belt under the crankshaft sprocket loosely, observing the direction of rotation markings.

51 Temporarily refit the pulley for the ribbed auxiliary drivebelt to the crankshaft sprocket, using two of the retaining screws - note that the offset mounting holes allow only one fitting position.

52 Verify that the timing marks on the crankshaft pulley and the intermediate shaft sprocket are still correctly aligned; refer to Section 2 for details.

53 Engage the timing belt teeth with the crankshaft sprocket, then manoeuvre it into position over the intermediate shaft and camshaft sprockets. Observe the direction of rotation markings on the belt.

54 Pass the flat side of the belt over the tensioner roller - avoid bending the belt back on itself or twisting it excessively as you do this. Ensure that the 'front run' of the belt is taut - ie all the slack should be in the section of the belt that passes over the tensioner roller.

55 Tension the belt by turning the eccentrically-mounted tensioner clockwise; two holes are provided in the side of the tensioner hub for this purpose - a pair of sturdy right-angled circlip pliers is a suitable substitute for the correct VAG tool **(refer to illustration 4.43)**.

56 Test the timing belt tension by grasping it between the fingers at a point mid-way between the intermediate shaft and camshaft

4.43 Tension the belt by turning the tensioner clockwise using circlip pliers

2A

sprockets and twisting it; the belt tension is correct when it can just be twisted through 90° (quarter of a turn) and no further.

57 When the correct belt tension has been achieved, tighten the tensioner locknut to the specified torque.

58 Using a spanner or wrench and socket on the crankshaft pulley centre bolt, rotate the crankshaft through two complete revolutions. Reset the engine to TDC on No 1 cylinder with reference to Section 2, and check that the crankshaft pulley and intermediate shaft and camshaft sprocket timing marks are re-aligned. Re-check the timing belt tension and adjust it, if necessary.

59 Remove the pulley for the ribbed auxiliary drivebelt from the crankshaft sprocket, to allow the lower section of the outer timing belt cover to be refitted, then refit the pulley, noting that the offset of the mounting holes allows only one fitting position. Finally, insert and tighten the retaining bolts to the specified torque.

All engine codes

60 Refer to Chapter 3 and refit the coolant pump pulley, where applicable.

61 Working from Section 6, refit and tension the auxiliary drivebelt(s).

62 Restore ignition system by reconnecting the HT lead to the distributor cap, then restore the fuelling system by refitting the fuel pump relay.

63 On completion, refer to Chapter 5B and check the ignition timing; adjust it if necessary.

---

5 Timing belt sprockets and tensioner - removal, inspection and refitting

1 Before starting work, immobilise the engine and vehicle as follows:
  a) *Disable the ignition system by removing the distributor centre HT lead and grounding it on the cylinder block, using a jumper wire.*
  b) *Disable the fuelling system by removing the fuel pump relay from its socket.*
  c) *Unplug the electrical wiring from the starter solenoid at the connector; refer to Chapter 5A for guidance.*
  d) *Prevent any vehicle movement by applying the handbrake and chocking the rear wheels.*

2 To gain access to the components detailed in this Section, carry out the following:
  a) *Refer to Section 6 and remove the auxiliary drivebelt(s)*
  b) *All engine codes except ABU, ABD and AEA, refer to Chapter 3 and remove the coolant pump pulley.*

Timing belt tensioner

Removal - engine codes ABD and ABU

3 These engines are not fitted with separate timing belt tensioning devices - the timing belt

5.6 Slide the tensioner off its mounting stud

tension is set by altering the position of the coolant pump; refer to Section 4 for details.

Removal - all other engines

4 With reference to the relevant paragraphs of Sections 2 and 4, set the engine to TDC on No 1 cylinder, then remove the timing belt upper and lower covers.

5 Slacken the retaining nut at the hub of the tensioner pulley, and allow the assembly to rotate anti-clockwise, relieving the tension on the timing belt. Remove the nut and recover the washer.

6 Slide the tensioner off its mounting stud **(see illustration)**.

Inspection

7 Wipe the tensioner clean, but do not use solvents that may contaminate the bearings. Spin the tensioner pulley on its hub by hand. Stiff movement or excessive freeplay is an indication of severe wear; the tensioner is not a serviceable component, and should be renewed.

Refitting

8 Slide the tensioner pulley over the mounting stud, then refit the washer and retaining nut - do not fully tighten the nut at this stage.

9 With reference to Section 4, tension the timing belt and refit the timing belt covers.

10 On engine code AEA only, the operation of the semi-automatic belt tensioner can be tested as follows. Apply finger pressure to the timing belt at a point mid-way between the camshaft and crankshaft sprockets. The sliding pointer that protrudes from behind the tensioner roller should slide away from the alignment groove in the tensioner baseplate as pressure is applied, and then move back as the pressure is removed (refer to the illustrations in Section 4).

11 Restore the ignition and fuelling systems by reconnecting the distributor HT lead and refitting the fuel pump relay.

12 With reference to Chapter 5B, check that the ignition timing is still within specifications; adjust it if necessary.

Camshaft timing belt sprocket

Removal

13 With reference to Section 4, remove the timing belt covers and set the engine to TDC

To make a camshaft sprocket holding tool, obtain two lengths of steel strip about 6mm thick by 30 mm wide or similar, one 600 mm long, the other 200 mm long (all dimensions approximate). Bolt the two strips together to form a forked end, leaving the bolt slack so that the shorter strip can pivot freely. At the end of each 'prong' of the fork, secure a bolt with a nut and a locknut, to act as the fulcrums; these will engage with the cut-outs in the sprocket, and should protrude by about 30mm

on No 1 cylinder. Slacken the tensioner hut (or coolant pump mounting bolts on engine codes ABD and ABU) and rotate it anti-clockwise to relieve the tension on the timing belt. Carefully slide the timing belt off the camshaft sprocket.

14 The camshaft sprocket must be held stationary whilst its retaining bolt is slackened; if access to the correct VAG special tool is not possible, a simple home-made tool using basic materials may be fabricated **(see Tool Tip)**.

15 Using the home-made tool, brace the camshaft sprocket. Slacken and remove the retaining bolt; recover the washer (if fitted).

16 Slide the camshaft sprocket from the end of the camshaft. Where applicable, recover the Woodruff key from the keyway.

17 With the sprocket removed, examine the camshaft oil seal for signs of leaking. If necessary, refer to Section 8 and renew it.

18 Wipe the sprocket and camshaft mating surfaces clean.

Refitting

19 Where applicable, fit the Woodruff key into the keyway, with the plain surface facing upwards. Offer up the sprocket to the camshaft, engaging the slot in the sprocket with the Woodruff key. On engines where a key is not used, ensure that the lug in the sprocket hub engages with recess in the end of the camshaft.

20 Working from Section 4, check that the engine is still set to TDC on No 1 cylinder, then refit and tension the timing belt. Refit the timing belt covers.

21 Refit the crankshaft (and where applicable, coolant pump) auxiliary belt

5.25 Removing the crankshaft sprocket

pulley(s), then insert the retaining bolts and tighten them to the specified torque.

22 With reference to Section 6, refit and tension the auxiliary drivebelt(s).

Crankshaft timing belt sprocket

Removal

23 With reference to Sections 2, 4 and 5, remove the timing belt covers and set the engine to TDC on No 1 cylinder. Slacken the tensioner centre hut (or coolant pump mounting bolts on engine codes ABD and ABU) and rotate it anti-clockwise to relieve the tension on the timing belt. Carefully slide the timing belt off the crankshaft sprocket.

24 The crankshaft sprocket must be held stationary whilst its retaining bolt is slackened. If access to the correct VAG flywheel locking tool is not available, lock the crankshaft in position by removing the starter motor, as described in Chapter 5A, to expose the flywheel ring gear. Then get an assistant insert a stout lever between the gear teeth and the transmission bellhousing whilst the sprocket retaining bolt is slackened.

25 Withdraw the bolt, recover the washer and lift off the sprocket (see illustration).

26 With the sprocket removed, examine the crankshaft oil seal for signs of leaking. If necessary, refer to Section 10 and renew it.

27 Wipe the sprocket and crankshaft mating surfaces clean.

Refitting

28 Offer up the sprocket, engaging the lug on the inside of the sprocket with the recess in the end of the crankshaft. Insert the bolt and tighten it to the specified torque.

29 Working from Section 4, check that the engine is still set to TDC on No 1 cylinder, then refit and tension the timing belt. Refit the timing belt covers.

30 Refit the crankshaft (and where applicable, coolant pump) auxiliary belt pulley(s), then insert the retaining bolts and tighten them to the specified torque.

31 With reference to Section 6, refit and tension the auxiliary drivebelt(s).

Coolant pump timing belt sprocket - engine codes ABD, ABU and AEA only

32 The coolant pump sprocket is an integral part of the coolant pump assembly, and cannot be renewed as a separate item.

Intermediate shaft sprocket

Removal

33 With reference to Section 4, remove the timing belt covers, and set the engine to TDC on No 1 cylinder. Slacken the tensioner centre nut, and rotate it anti-clockwise to relieve the tension on the timing belt. Carefully slide the timing belt off the camshaft sprocket.

34 The intermediate shaft sprocket must be held stationary whilst its retaining bolt is slackened; if access to the correct VAG special tool is not possible, a simple home-made tool using basic materials made be fabricated as described in the camshaft sprocket removal sub-Section.

35 Using the home-made tool, brace the intermediate shaft sprocket and slacken and remove the retaining bolt; recover the washer where fitted.

36 Slide the sprocket from the end of the intermediate shaft. Where applicable, recover the Woodruff key from the keyway.

37 With the sprocket removed, examine the intermediate shaft oil seal for signs of leaking. If necessary, refer to Section 8 and renew it.

38 Wipe the sprocket and shaft mating surfaces clean.

Refitting

39 Where applicable, fit the Woodruff key into the keyway, with the plain surface facing upwards. Offer up the sprocket to the intermediate shaft, engaging the slot in the sprocket with the Woodruff key.

40 With reference to Section 2, check that the engine is still set to TDC on No 1 cylinder. Where applicable, align the intermediate shaft sprocket with the crankshaft pulley timing marks.

41 Tighten the sprocket retaining bolt to the specified torque; hold the sprocket using the method employed during removal.

42 With reference to Section 4, refit and tension the timing belt, then refit the timing belt covers.

43 Refit the crankshaft auxiliary belt pulley(s), then insert the retaining bolts and tighten them to the specified torque.

44 With reference to Section 6, refit and tension the auxiliary drivebelt(s).

6 Auxiliary drivebelts - removal and refitting

General information

1 Depending on the vehicle specification and engine type, one or two auxiliary drivebelts may be fitted. Both are driven from pulleys mounted on the crankshaft, and provide drive for the alternator, coolant pump, power steering pump and on vehicles with air conditioning, the refrigerant compressor.

2 The run of the belts and the components they drive are also dependent on vehicle specification and engine type, and because of this, the coolant pump and power steering pump may be fitted with pulleys to suit either a ribbed belt or a V-belt.

3 The ribbed auxiliary belt may be fitted with an automatic tensioning device, depending on its run (and hence the number of components it is driving). Otherwise, the belt is tensioned by the alternator mountings, which have an in-built tensioning spring. The V-belt is tensioned by pivoting the power steering pump on its mounting.

4 On refitting, the auxiliary belt must be tensioned correctly, to ensure correct operation under all conditions and prolonged service life.

Auxiliary V-belt

Removal

5 Park the vehicle on a level surface, and apply the handbrake. Jack up the front of the vehicle and rest it securely on axle stands - refer to "Jacking and Vehicle Support". Disable the starting system by unplugging the starter solenoid at the connector; see Chapter 5A.

6 Turn the steering to full right lock, then refer to Chapter 11 and remove the plastic air ducting from underneath the right-hand front wing.

7 With reference to Chapter 10, slacken the power steering pump mounting bolts and allow the pump body to pivot around its uppermost mounting towards the engine.

8 Guide the V-belt off the power steering pump pulley and where applicable, the coolant pump pulley.

9 Examine the belt for signs or wear or damage, and renew it if necessary.

Refitting and tensioning

10 Refit the belt by reversing the removal procedure, ensuring that it seats evenly in the pulleys.

11 Set the belt tension by grasping the underside of the power steering pump and drawing it towards the front of the vehicle. The tension is correct when the midpoint of the belt's longest run can be deflected by no more than 5 mm. Tighten the power steering pump mounting bolts to the specified torque.

12 Rotate the crankshaft in its normal direction of rotation through two turns, then re-check and if necessary adjust the tension.

Auxiliary ribbed belt

Removal

13 Park the vehicle on a level surface, and apply the handbrake. Jack up the front of the vehicle and rest it on axle stands - refer to "Jacking and Vehicle Support". Disable the starting system by unplugging the starter solenoid at the connector - see Chapter 5A.

14 Turn the steering to full right lock, then refer to Chapter 11 and remove the plastic air ducting from underneath the right-hand front wing.

2A

15 Where applicable, remove the auxiliary V-belt as described in the previous sub-Section.
16 Examine the ribbed belt for manufacturer's markings, indicating the direction of rotation. If none are present, make some using typist's correction fluid or a dab of paint - do not cut or score the belt in any way.

Vehicles with a roller-arm automatic tensioning device

17 Rotate the tensioner roller arm clockwise against its spring tension, so that the roller is forced away from the belt - use an adjustable spanner as a lever.

Vehicles with rotary automatic tensioning device

18 Fit a ring spanner to the tensioner centre nut, and rotate the assembly anti-clockwise, against its spring tension.

Vehicles without an automatic tensioning device

19 Slacken the alternator upper and lower mounting bolts by between one and two turns.
20 Push the alternator down to its stop against the spring tension, so that it rotates around its uppermost mounting.

All vehicles

21 Pull the belt off the alternator pulley, then release it from the remaining pulleys.

Refitting and tensioning

Caution: Observe the manufacturer's direction of rotation markings on the belt, when refitting.

22 Pass the ribbed belt underneath the crankshaft pulley, ensuring that the ribs seat in the channels on the surface of the pulley.

Vehicles with roller-arm automatic tensioning device

23 Rotate the tensioner roller arm clockwise against its spring tension - use an adjustable spanner as a lever.
24 Pass the belt around the coolant pump pulley or air conditioning refrigerant pump pulley (as applicable), then fit it over the alternator pulley.
25 Release the tensioner pulley arm, and allow the roller to bear against the flat surface of the belt.

Vehicles with rotary automatic tensioning device

26 Fit a ring spanner to the tensioner centre nut, and rotate the assembly anti-clockwise, against its spring tension.
27 Pass the flat side of the belt underneath the tensioner roller, then fit it over the power steering pump and alternator pulleys.
28 Release the spanner and allow the tensioner roller to bear against the flat side of the belt.

Vehicles without an automatic tensioning device

29 Repeatedly push the alternator down to its stop against the spring tension, so that it rotates around its uppermost mounting, and check that it moves back freely when released. If necessary, slacken the alternator mounting bolts by a further half a turn.

30 Keep the alternator pushed down against its stop, pass the belt over the alternator pulley, then release the alternator and allow it to tension the belt.
31 Restore the starting system, then start the engine and allow it to idle for about 10 seconds.
32 Switch the engine off, then tighten first the lower, then the upper alternator mounting bolts to the specified torque.

All vehicles

33 Refer to Chapter 11 and refit the plastic air ducts to the underside of the wing.
34 Where applicable, refer to the previous sub-Section and refit the auxiliary V-belt.
35 Lower the vehicle to the ground, then (if not already done) restore the starting system with reference to Chapter 5A.

7 Camshaft cover - removal and refitting

Removal

1 Immobilise the engine by:
a) *Unplugging the fuel pump relay from its socket.*
b) *Disconnecting the HT king lead from the distributor and earthing it on the engine block using a jumper wire.*
c) *Unplugging the electrical wiring from the starter solenoid at the connector; refer to Chapter 5A for guidance.*

Engine codes ABU, ABD, AEA

2 Remove disconnect the crankcase breather hose from the cover; cut off retaining clip, if it is of the crimp type - fit a worm-drive clip in its place on refitting.
3 To gain greater working space, refer to Chapter 4A and disconnect the throttle cable from the throttle housing.
4 Slacken and withdraw the three camshaft cover retaining bolts - recover the washers and seals.

Engine code AEK

5 With reference to Chapter 4B, remove the upper section of the inlet manifold and throttle body from the engine.
6 Prise the crankcase breather pressure-regulating valve from the port on the cylinder head cover.
7 Working around the edge of the camshaft cover, progressively slacken and remove the retaining nuts.

Engine codes ADY, 2E

8 Disconnect the crankcase breather hoses from the pressure regulator valve, mounted on top of the camshaft cover. If crimp-type hose clips are used, cut them off and replace them with standard worm-drive clips on refitting. Slacken and withdraw the retaining screws and remove the regulator valve.
9 On engine code 2E, access may be improved by removing the idling stabilisation valve; refer to Chapter 4B.

10 Working around the edge of the camshaft cover, progressively slacken and remove the retaining nuts.

Engine codes ADZ, ABS, AAM

11 Remove crankcase breather hose from the cover; cut off the crimp-type clip - use an equivalent sized worm-drive clip on refitting.
12 To gain greater working space, refer to Chapter 4A and disconnect throttle cable from throttle housing.
13 Working around the edge of the camshaft cover, progressively slacken and remove the retaining nuts.
14 Lift the cover away from the cylinder head; if it sticks, do not attempt to lever it off with an implement - instead free it by working around the cover and tapping it lightly with a soft-faced mallet.
15 Lift the baffle plate off the camshaft bearing caps.
16 Recover the three pieces of the gasket and discard them; a new set must be used on refitting. Clean the mating surfaces of the cylinder head and camshaft cover thoroughly, removing all traces of oil and old gasket. Take care, however, not to damage the surfaces.

Engine code ABF

17 Refer to Chapter 5B and disconnect the HT leads from the spark plugs.
18 Refer to Chapter 4B and remove the upper section of the inlet manifold and throttle body.
19 With reference to Chapter 1A, remove the spark plugs from the cylinder head.
20 Working around the edge of the camshaft cover, progressively slacken and remove the outer retaining screws. Where applicable, remove the reinforcement plates from the edge of the cover. Slacken and withdraw the two inner retaining screws from between the spark plug apertures - recover the washers.

All engine codes

21 Lift the cover away from the cylinder head; if it sticks, do not attempt to lever it off with an implement - instead free it by working around the cover and tapping it lightly with a soft-faced mallet.
22 Where applicable, lift the oil baffle plate off the camshaft bearing cap studs, noting its orientation.
23 Recover the camshaft cover gasket; note that the gasket may be made up of several pieces, depending on engine specification. Inspect each piece carefully - renew the entire gasket if damage or deterioration is evident.
Note: *On engine codes ADZ, ABS, AAM, the gasket must be discarded and renewed, regardless of condition.*
24 Clean the mating surfaces of the cylinder head and camshaft cover thoroughly, removing all traces of oil and old gasket - take care to avoid damaging the surfaces as you do this.

Refitting

25 Refit the camshaft cover by following the

removal procedure in reverse, noting the following points:

a) Ensure that all sections of the gasket are correctly seated on the cylinder head, and take care to avoid displacing it as the camshaft cover is lowered into position.

b) Tighten the camshaft cover retaining screws/nuts to the specified torque.

c) When refitting hoses that were originally secured with crimp-type clips, use standard worm-drive clips in their place on refitting.

26 On completion, restore the fuel and ignition systems by refitting the fuel pump relay and reconnecting the distributor HT lead.

8 Camshaft oil seal - renewal

1 Immobilise the engine by:

a) Unplugging the fuel pump relay.

b) Disconnecting the HT king lead from the distributor and earthing it on the engine block using a jumper wire.

c) Unplugging the electrical wiring from the starter solenoid at the connector; refer to Chapter 5A for guidance.

2 Refer to Section 6 and remove the auxiliary drivebelt(s).

3 With reference to Sections 2, 4 and 5 of this Chapter, remove the auxiliary belt pulleys and timing belt cover, then set the engine to TDC on No 1 cylinder and remove the timing belt, timing belt tensioner (where applicable) and camshaft sprocket.

4 After removing the retaining screws, lift the inner timing belt cover away from the engine block - this will expose the oil seal . **Note:** On engine codes ABU, ABD and AEA, the coolant pump retaining bolts pass through the timing belt inner cover; with reference to Chapter 3, drain the coolant from the engine and remove the coolant pump.

5 Drill two small holes into the existing oil seal, diagonally opposite each other. Thread two self-tapping screws into the holes, and using two pairs of pliers, pull on the heads of the screws to extract oil seal. Take great care to avoid drilling through into the seal housing or camshaft sealing surface.

6 Clean out the seal housing and sealing surface of the camshaft by wiping it with a lint-free cloth - avoid using solvents that may enter the cylinder head and affect component lubrication. Remove any swarf or burrs that may cause the seal to leak.

7 Lubricate the lip of the new oil seal with clean engine oil, and push it over the camshaft until it is positioned above its housing.

8 Using a hammer and a socket of suitable diameter, drive the seal squarely into its housing **(see illustration). Note:** Select a socket that bears only on the hard outer surface of the seal, not the inner lip which can easily be damaged.

9 With reference to Sections 2, 4 and 5 of this

8.8 Drive the camshaft oil seal squarely into its housing

Chapter, refit the inner timing belt cover and the timing sprockets, then refit and tension the timing belt. On completion, refit the timing belt outer cover.

10 With reference to Section 6, refit and tension the auxiliary drivebelt(s).

9 Intermediate shaft oil seal - renewal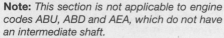

Note: This section is not applicable to engine codes ABU, ABD and AEA, which do not have an intermediate shaft.

1 Immobilise the engine by:

a) Unplugging the fuel pump relay from its socket.

b) Disconnecting the HT king lead from the distributor and earthing it on the engine block using a jumper wire.

c) Unplugging the electrical wiring from the starter solenoid at the connector; refer to Chapter 5A for guidance.

2 Refer to Chapter 1 and remove the auxiliary drivebelt(s).

3 With reference to Sections 4 and 5 of this Chapter, remove the auxiliary belt pulleys, timing belt outer cover, timing belt, tensioner (where applicable) and intermediate shaft sprocket.

4 After removing the retaining screws, lift the inner timing belt cover away from the engine block - this will expose the intermediate shaft sealing flange.

5 With reference to Section 7 of Chapter 2C, remove the intermediate shaft flange, and renew the shaft and flange oil seals.

10.9 Lubricate the new crankshaft oil seal, and position it over the housing

6 Referring to Sections 4 and 5 of this Chapter, carry out the following:

a) Refit the inner timing belt cover.

b) Refit the intermediate shaft timing belt sprocket.

c) Refit and tension the timing belt.

d) Refit the timing belt outer cover.

7 With reference to Section 6 of this Chapter, refit and tension the auxiliary drivebelt(s).

10 Crankshaft oil seals - renewal

Crankshaft front oil seal

1 Immobilise the engine by:

a) Unplugging the fuel pump relay.

b) Disconnecting the HT king lead from the distributor and earthing it on the engine block using a jumper wire.

c) Unplugging the electrical wiring from the starter solenoid at the connector; refer to Chapter 5A for guidance.

2 Drain the engine oil - see Chapter 1A.

3 With reference to "Jacking and Vehicle Support", raise the front of the vehicle and rest it securely on axle stands.

4 Working from Chapter 11, remove the screws and detach the plastic air ducting from underneath the right-hand front wing.

5 Remove the auxiliary drivebelt(s) - see Section 6.

6 With reference to Sections 4 and 5 of this Chapter, remove the auxiliary belt pulleys, timing belt outer covers, timing belt and crankshaft sprocket.

7 Remove the oil seal, using the same method as that described for the camshaft oil seal removal, in Section 8.

8 Clean out the seal housing and sealing surface of the crankshaft by wiping it with a lint-free cloth - avoid using solvents that may enter the crankcase and affect component lubrication. Remove any swarf or burrs that could cause the seal to leak.

9 Lubricate the lip of the new oil seal with clean engine oil, and position it over the housing **(see illustration)**.

10 Using a hammer and a socket of suitable diameter, drive the seal squarely into its housing **(see illustration). Note:** Select a socket that bears only on the hard outer

10.10 Using a hammer and a socket, drive the seal squarely into its housing

surface of the seal, not the inner lip which can easily be damaged.

11 With reference to Sections 2, 4 and 5 of this Chapter, refit the crankshaft timing belt sprocket, then refit and tension the timing belt. On completion, refit the timing belt outer cover, and auxiliary drivebelt pulley(s).

12 The remainder of the refitting procedure is a reversal of removal, as follows:
 a) *With reference to Section 6, refit and tension the auxiliary drivebelt(s).*
 b) *Refit the plastic air ducting to the underside of the wing, working from Chapter 11.*
 c) *Refer to Chapter 1A and refill the engine with the correct grade and quantity of oil.*
 d) *Restore the ignition, fuelling and starting systems.*

Crankshaft front oil seal housing - gasket renewal

13 Proceed as described in paragraphs 1 to 6 above, then refer to Section 15 and remove the sump.

14 Progressively slacken and then remove the oil seal housing retaining bolts.

15 Lift the housing away from the cylinder block, together with the crankshaft oil seal, using a twisting motion to ease the seal along the shaft.

16 Recover the old gasket from the seal housing on the cylinder block. If it has disintegrated, scrape the remains off with a trimming knife blade. Take care to avoid damaging the mating surfaces.

17 Prise the old oil seal from the housing using a stout screwdriver.

18 Wipe the oil seal housing clean, and check it visually for signs of distortion or cracking. Lay the housing on a work surface, with the mating surface face down. Press in a new oil seal, using a block of wood as a press to ensure that the seal enters the housing squarely.

19 Smear the crankcase mating surface with multi-purpose grease, and lay the new gasket in position.

20 Pad the end of the crankshaft with a layer of PVC tape; this will protect the oil seal as it is being fitted.

21 Lubricate the inner lip of the crankshaft oil seal with clean engine oil, then offer up the seal and its housing to the end of the crankshaft. Ease the seal along the shaft using a twisting motion, until the housing is flush with the crankcase.

22 Insert the retaining bolts and tighten them progressively to the specified torque **(see illustration)**. *Caution: The housing is fabricated from a light alloy, and may be distorted if the bolts are not tightened progressively.*

23 Refer to Section 15 and refit the sump.

24 With reference to Sections 2, 4 and 5 of this Chapter, refit the crankshaft timing belt sprocket, then refit and tension the timing belt. On completion, refit the timing belt outer cover, and auxiliary drivebelt pulley(s).

10.22 Tighten the front oil seal housing bolts to the specified torque

25 The remainder of the refitting procedure is a reversal of removal, as follows:
 a) *With reference to Section 6, refit and tension the auxiliary drivebelt(s).*
 b) *Refit the plastic air ducting to the underside of the wing, working from Chapter 11.*
 c) *Refer to Chapter 1A and refill the engine with the correct grade and quantity of oil.*
 d) *Restore the ignition, fuelling and starting systems.*

Crankshaft rear oil seal (flywheel end)

26 Proceed as described in paragraphs 1 to 3 above, then refer to Section 15 and remove the sump.

27 Working from Chapter 11, remove the screws and detach the plastic air ducting from underneath the left-hand front wing.

28 Refer to Chapter 7A or B as applicable, and remove the transmission from the engine.

29 On vehicles with manual transmission, refer to Section 13 of this Chapter and remove the flywheel, then refer to Chapter 6 and remove the clutch friction plate and pressure plate.

30 On vehicles with automatic transmission, refer to Section 13 of this Chapter and remove the driveplate from the crankshaft.

31 Where applicable, remove the retaining bolts and lift the intermediate plate away from the cylinder block.

32 Progressively slacken and then remove the oil seal housing retaining bolts.

33 Lift the housing away from the cylinder block, together with the crankshaft oil seal, using a twisting motion to ease the seal along the shaft.

34 Recover the old gasket from the seal housing on the cylinder block. If it has disintegrated, scrape the remains off with a trimming knife blade. Take care to avoid damaging the mating surfaces.

35 Prise the old oil seal from the housing using a stout screwdriver.

36 Wipe the oil seal housing clean, and check it visually for signs of distortion or cracking. Lay the housing on a work surface, with the mating surface face down. Press in a new oil seal, using a block of wood as a press to ensure that the seal enters the housing squarely.

10.40 Tighten the rear oil seal housing bolts to the specified torque

37 Smear the crankcase mating surface with multi-purpose grease, and lay the new gasket in position.

38 A protective plastic cap is supplied with genuine VAG crankshaft oil seals; when fitted over the end of the crankshaft, the cap prevents damage to the inner lip of the oil seal as it is being fitted. Use PVC tape to pad the end of the crankshaft if a cap is not available.

39 Lubricate the inner lip of the crankshaft oil seal with clean engine oil, then offer up the seal and its housing to the end of the crankshaft. Ease the seal along the shaft using a twisting motion, until the housing is flush with the crankcase.

40 Insert the retaining bolts and tighten them progressively to the specified torque **(see illustration)**. *Caution: The housing is fabricated from a light alloy, and may be distorted if the bolts are not tightened progressively.*

41 Refer to Section 15 and refit the sump.

42 Fit the intermediate plate to the cylinder block, then insert and tighten the bolts.

43 On vehicles with automatic transmission, work from Section 13 of this Chapter and refit the driveplate to the crankshaft.

44 On vehicles with manual transmission, refer to Section 13 of this Chapter and refit the flywheel, then refer to Chapter 6 and refit the clutch friction plate and pressure plate.

45 Referring to Chapter 7A or B as applicable, refit the transmission to the engine.

46 The remainder of the refitting procedure is a reversal of removal, as follows:
 a) *Refit the plastic air ducting to the underside of the wing, working from Chapter 11.*
 b) *Refer to Chapter 1A and refill the engine with the correct grade and quantity of oil.*
 c) *Restore the ignition, fuelling and starting systems.*

11 Cylinder head and manifolds - removal, separation and refitting

Removal

1 Select a solid, level surface to park the vehicle upon. Give yourself enough space to move around it easily.

2 Refer to Chapter 11 and remove the bonnet from its hinges.

3 Disconnect the battery negative cable, and position It away from the terminal. **Note:** *If the vehicle has a security-coded radio, check that you have a copy of the code number before disconnecting the battery cable. Refer to your VAG dealer if in doubt.*

4 Referring to Chapter 1A, carry out the following :
   a) *Drain the engine oil.*
   b) *Drain the cooling system.*

5 Refer to Section 6 and remove the auxiliary drivebelt(s).

6 With reference to Section 2, set the engine to TDC on No 1 cylinder.

7 Refer to Chapter 3 and perform the following:
   a) *Slacken the clips and disconnect the radiator top and bottom hoses from the ports on the cylinder head and coolant pump/thermostat housing (as applicable).*
   b) *Slacken the clips and disconnect the expansion tank and cabin heater inlet and outlet coolant hoses from the ports on the cylinder head.*

8 The "lock carrier" is a panel assembly comprising the front bumper moulding, radiator and grille, cooling fan(s) headlight units, front valence and bonnet lock mechanism. Although its removal is not essential, its does give greatly-improved access to the engine. Its removal is described at the beginning of the engine removal procedure - refer to Chapter 2C for details.

9 With reference to Chapter 4D, unplug the lambda sensor cabling from the main harness at the multiway connector (where applicable).

10 With reference to Chapter 5B and Chapter 1A, carry out the following:
   a) *Remove the HT leads from the spark plugs and the distributor.*
   b) *On engine codes ABF, ABU, ABD and AEA, remove the distributor.*

11 On multi-point fuel-injected models, refer to Chapter 4B and remove the throttle body, the upper section of the inlet manifold (engine codes AEK and ABF only), the fuel rail and the fuel injectors.

12 On single-point fuel-injected models, refer to Chapter 4A, remove the throttle body air box, and then remove the throttle body.

13 With reference to Sections 2, 4 and 6, carry out the following:
   a) *Remove the camshaft cover.*
   b) *Remove the timing belt outer covers, and disengage the timing belt from the camshaft sprocket.*

14 On engine codes ABD, AEA and ABU, refer to Section 5 and remove the camshaft sprocket.

15 Slacken and withdraw the retaining screws, and lift off the inner timing belt cover(s). Note that on engine codes ABU, AEA and ABD, the coolant pump securing bolts double up as fixings for inner timing belt cover - refer to Chapter 3 and remove the coolant pump from the engine block.

16 With reference to Chapter 4A or B as

applicable, unplug wiring harness from the coolant temperature sensor at the connector.

17 Refer to Chapter 4D and separate the exhaust downpipe from the exhaust manifold flange.

18 Where applicable, detach the warm-air inlet hose from the exhaust manifold heat shield.

19 Slacken and remove the bolt securing the engine oil dipstick tube to the cylinder head.

20 Remove the retaining screw and detach the engine harness connector bracket from the cylinder head.

21 Following the reverse of the tightening sequence shown in illustration 11.37, progressively slacken the cylinder head bolts, by half a turn at a time, until all bolts can be unscrewed by hand.

22 Check that nothing remains connected to the cylinder head, then lift the head away from the cylinder block; seek assistance if possible, as it is a heavy assembly, especially if it is being removed complete with the manifolds.

23 Remove the gasket from the top of the block, noting the locating dowels. If the dowels are a loose fit, remove them and store them with the head for safe-keeping. Do not discard the gasket - on some models it will be needed for identification purposes.

24 If the cylinder head is to be dismantled for overhaul refer to Chapter 2C.

Manifold separation

25 Inlet manifold removal and refitting is described in Chapter 4A or B as applicable.

26 Progressively slacken and remove the exhaust manifold retaining nuts. Lift the manifold away from the cylinder head and recover the gaskets. Where applicable, slacken the union and detach the CO sampling pipe from the manifold.

27 Ensure that the mating surfaces are completely clean, then refit the exhaust manifold, using new gaskets. Tighten the retaining nuts to the specified torque.

Preparation for refitting

28 The mating faces of the cylinder head and cylinder block/crankcase must be perfectly clean before refitting the head. Use a hard plastic or wood scraper to remove all traces of gasket and carbon; also clean the piston crowns. Take particular care during the cleaning operations, as aluminium alloy is easily damaged. Also, make sure that the carbon is not allowed to enter the oil and water passages - this is particularly important for the lubrication system, as carbon could block the oil supply to the engine's components. Using adhesive tape and paper, seal the water, oil and bolt holes in the cylinder block/crankcase.

29 Check the mating surfaces of the cylinder block/crankcase and the cylinder head for nicks, deep scratches and other damage. If slight, they may be removed carefully with a file, but if excessive, machining may be the only alternative to renewal.

30 If warpage of the cylinder head gasket surface is suspected, use a straight-edge to check it for distortion. Refer to Part C of this Chapter if necessary.

31 Check the condition of the cylinder head bolts, and particularly their threads, whenever they are removed. Wash the bolts in suitable solvent, and wipe them dry. Check each for any sign of visible wear or damage, renewing any bolt if necessary. Measure the length of each bolt, to check for stretching (although this is not a conclusive test, if all bolts have stretched by the same amount). VW do not actually specify that the bolts must be renewed, however, it is strongly recommended that the bolts should be renewed as a complete set whenever they are disturbed.

32 On all the engines covered in this Chapter, it is possible for the piston crowns to strike and damage the valve heads, if the camshaft is rotated with the timing belt removed and the crankshaft set to TDC. For this reason, the crankshaft must be set to a position other than TDC on No 1 cylinder, before the cylinder head is refitted: use a wrench and socket on the crankshaft pulley centre bolt to turn the crankshaft in its normal direction of rotation, until all four pistons are positioned halfway down their bores, with No 1 piston on its upstroke - ie 90° before TDC.

Refitting

33 Lay a new head gasket on the cylinder block, engaging it with the locating dowels. Ensure that the manufacturer's "TOP" and part number markings are face up **(see illustrations)**.

2A

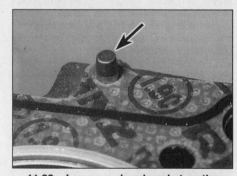

11.33a Lay a new head gasket on the block, enaging it with the locating dowels

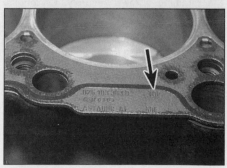

11.33b Ensure that the manufacturer's "TOP" mark and part number are face up

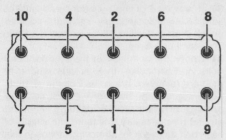

11.37 Cylinder head bolt tightening sequence

34 With the help of an assistant, place the cylinder head and manifolds centrally on the cylinder block, ensuring that the locating dowels engage with the recesses in the cylinder head. Check that the head gasket is correctly seated before allowing the weight the full weight of the cylinder head to rest upon it.

35 Apply a smear of grease to the threads, and to the underside of the heads, of the cylinder head bolts; use a good-quality high-melting point grease.

36 Carefully enter each bolt into its relevant hole (*do not drop them in*) and screw in, by hand only, until finger-tight.

37 Working progressively and in the sequence shown, tighten the cylinder head bolts to their Stage 1 torque setting, using a torque wrench and suitable socket **(see illustration)**. Repeat the exercise in the same sequence for the Stage 2 torque setting.

38 Once all the bolts have been tightened to their Stage 2 settings, working again in the given sequence, angle-tighten the bolts through the specified Stage 3 angle, using a socket and extension bar. It is recommended that an angle-measuring gauge is used during this stage of the tightening, to ensure accuracy. If a gauge is not available, use white paint to make alignment marks between the bolt head and cylinder head prior to tightening; the marks can then be used to check that the bolt has been rotated through the correct angle during tightening. Repeat the exercise for the Stage 4 setting.

39 Where applicable on engine codes ABU, AEA and ABD, refit the coolant pump with reference to Chapter 3.

40 Refit the timing belt inner cover, tightening the retaining screws securely. On engine codes ABU, ABD and AEA, refer to Section 5 and refit the camshaft sprocket.

41 Refer to Section 2 and follow the procedure for setting the engine to TDC on No 1 cylinder with the timing belt removed. On completion, refer to Section 4 and refit the camshaft timing belt.

42 The remainder of the refitting sequence is a reversal of the removal procedure, as follows:

a) *Bolt the engine dipstick tube to the cylinder head, where applicable.*

b) *Refer to Chapter 4D and reconnect the exhaust downpipe to the exhaust manifold.*

c) *On multipoint fuel-injected systems, refer to Chapter 4B and refit the fuel injectors, fuel rail, upper section of the inlet manifold (where applicable) and the throttle body.*

d) *On single-point fuel-injected models, refer to Chapter 4A and refit the throttle body and air box.*

e) *Refer to Chapter 5B and refit the distributor (where applicable) and the ignition HT leads.*

f) *Refer to Sections 6 and refit the camshaft cover.*

g) *With reference to the information in Chapter 2C, refit the lock carrier assembly, if it was removed for greater access.*

h) *Reconnect the radiator, expansion tank and heater coolant hoses, referring to Chapter 3 for guidance. Reconnect the coolant temperature sensor wiring.*

i) *Refer to Section 6 and refit the auxiliary drivebelt(s).*

j) *Restore the battery connection.*

k) *Refer to Chapter 11 and refit the bonnet.*

43 On completion, refer to Chapter 1A and carry out the following:

a) *Refill the engine cooling system with the correct quantity of new coolant.*

b) *Refill the engine lubrication system with the correct grade and quantity of oil.*

12 Hydraulic tappets - operation check

⚠️ **Warning: After fitting hydraulic tappets, wait a minimum of 30 minutes (or preferably, leave overnight) before starting the engine, to allow the tappets time to settle, otherwise the pistons may strike the valve heads.**

1 The hydraulic tappets are self-adjusting, and require no attention whilst in service.

2 If the hydraulic tappets become excessively noisy, their operation can be checked as described below.

3 Run the engine until it reaches its normal operating temperature. Switch off the engine, then refer to Section 6 and remove the camshaft cover.

4 Rotate the camshaft by turning the crankshaft with a socket and wrench, until the first cam lobe over No 1 cylinder is pointing upwards.

5 Using a feeler blade, measure the clearance between the base of the cam lobe and the top of the tappet. If the clearance is greater than 0.1mm, then the tappet is defective and must be renewed.

6 If the clearance is less than 0.1 mm, press down on the top of the tappet, until it is felt to contact the top of the valve stem **(see illustration)**. Use a wooden or plastic implement that will not damage the surface of the tappet.

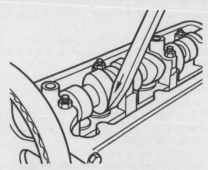

12.6 Press down on the tappet, until it contacts the top of the valve stem

7 If the tappet travels more than 0.1 mm before making contact, then it is defective and must be renewed.

8 Hydraulic tappet removal and refitting is described as part of the cylinder head overhaul sequence - see Chapter 2C for details.

13 Flywheel/driveplate - removal, inspection and refitting

General information

Manual transmission models

1 The mounting arrangement of the flywheel and clutch components depends on the type of transmission fitted.

2 On vehicles fitted with the 020 (5-speed) transmission, the clutch pressure plate is bolted directly to the end of the crankshaft. The flywheel is then bolted to the pressure plate. Removal of these components is therefore described in Chapter 6.

3 On vehicles fitted with the 020A, 085 (5-speed) and 084 (4-speed) transmission, the layout is more conventional; the flywheel is mounted on the crankshaft, with the pressure plate bolted to it. Removal of the flywheel is as described below.

Automatic transmission models

4 The torque converter driveplate is bolted directly to the end of the crankshaft; removal is as described below. Removal of the automatic transmission and torque converter is described in Chapter 7B.

Driveplate

Removal

5 Remove the transmission as described in Chapter 7B.

6 Lock the driveplate in position by bolting a piece of scrap metal between the driveplate and one of the transmission bellhousing mounting holes. Mark the position of the driveplate with respect to the crankshaft using a dab of paint.

7 Slacken and withdraw the driveplate mounting bolts, then lift off the driveplate. Recover the packing plate and the shim (where applicable) **(see illustration)**.

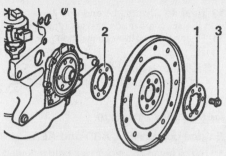

13.7 Driveplate components
1 Packing plate 2 Shim 3 Mounting bolt

Refitting

8 Refitting is a reversal of removal, using the alignment marks made during removal. Fit new mounting bolts and tighten them to the specified torque. Remove the locking tool, and refit the transmission as described in Chapter 7B.

Flywheel

Removal

9 Remove the transmission and clutch as described in Chapter 7A and Chapter 6.
10 Lock the flywheel in position using a home-made locking tool, fabricated from a piece of scrap metal. Bolt it to one of the transmission bellhousing mounting holes **(see illustration)**. Mark the position of the flywheel with respect to the crankshaft using a dab of paint.
11 Slacken and withdraw the flywheel mounting bolts, then lift off the flywheel. *Caution: Get an assistant to help, as the flywheel is extremely heavy.*

Inspection

12 If the flywheel's clutch mating surface is deeply scored, cracked or otherwise damaged, the flywheel must be renewed. However, it may be possible to have it surface-ground; seek the advice of a VAG dealer or engine reconditioning specialist.
13 If the ring gear is badly worn or has missing teeth, the flywheel must be renewed.

Refitting

14 Clean the mating surfaces of the flywheel and crankshaft. Remove any remaining

13.10 Flywheel locked in position with a home-made tool

locking compound from the threads of the crankshaft holes, using the correct-size tap, if available.

 HAYNES HiNT *If a suitable tap is not available, cut two slots down the threads of one of the old flywheel bolts with a hacksaw, and use the bolt to remove the locking compound from the threads.*

15 If the new flywheel retaining bolts are not supplied with their threads already pre-coated, apply a suitable thread-locking compound to the threads of each bolt **(see illustration)**.
16 Offer up the flywheel to the crankshaft, using the alignment marks made during removal, and fit the new retaining bolts.
17 Lock the flywheel using the method employed on dismantling, and tighten the retaining bolts to the specified torque **(see illustration)**.
18 Refit the clutch as described in Chapter 6. Remove the locking tool, and refit the transmission as described in Chapter 7B.

14 Engine mountings - inspection and renewal

Inspection

1 If improved access is required, raise the front of the car and support it securely on axle stands.

2 Check the mounting rubbers to see if they are cracked, hardened or separated from the metal at any point; renew the mounting if any such damage or deterioration is evident.
3 Check that all the mounting's fasteners are securely tightened; use a torque wrench to check if possible.
4 Using a large screwdriver or a crowbar, check for wear in the mounting by carefully levering against it to check for free play. Where this is not possible, enlist the aid of an assistant to move the engine/transmission back and forth, or from side to side, while you watch the mounting. While some free play is to be expected even from new components, excessive wear should be obvious. If excessive free play is found, check first that the fasteners are correctly secured, then renew any worn components as described below.

Renewal

Front engine mounting

5 Disconnect the battery negative cable, and position it away from the terminal.
6 Position a trolley jack underneath the engine and position it such that the jack head is directly underneath the engine/bellhousing mating surface.
7 Raise the jack until it just takes the weight of the engine off the front engine mounting.
8 Slacken and withdraw the engine mounting through-bolt.
9 On all engine codes except ABU, ABD and AEA, refer to Chapter 5B and remove the starter motor.
10 Slacken and withdraw the engine mounting-to-transmission bellhousing bolts and remove the bracket.
11 Working under the engine mounting front crossmember, remove the engine mounting block retaining screw.
12 Lift the engine mounting block out of the crossmember cup.
13 Refitting is a reversal of removal, noting the following points:
a) Ensure that the orientation lug that protrudes from the top of surface of the engine mounting block engages with the recess in the mounting bracket **(see illustration)**.
b) Tighten all bolts to the specified torque.

2A

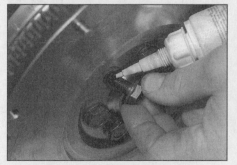

13.15 If necessary, apply locking compound to the new flywheel bolts

13.17 Tighten the flywheel bolts to the specified torque

14.13 Lug (arrowed) on top of the mounting block engages in the recess in the bracket

14.25 Removing the rear left-hand engine mounting block

Rear right-hand engine mounting

14 Disconnect the battery negative cable.

15 Mount an engine lifting beam across the engine bay, and attach the jib to the engine lifting eyes on the cylinder head. Alternatively, an engine hoist can be used. Raise the hoist/lifting beam jib to take the weight of the engine off the engine mounting.

16 Slacken and withdraw the engine mounting through-bolt.

17 Unbolt the engine mounting bracket from the cylinder block.

18 Unbolt the engine mounting block from the body, and remove it from the engine bay.

19 Refitting is a reversal of removal, noting the following points:

a) *Ensure that the orientation lug that protrudes from the top of surface of the engine mounting block engages with the recess in the mounting bracket.*

b) *Tighten all bolts to the specified torque.*

Rear left-hand mounting

20 Disconnect the battery negative cable, and position it away from the terminal.

21 Position a trolley jack below the engine, with the jack head directly underneath the engine/bellhousing mating surface.

22 Raise the jack until it just takes the weight of the engine off the rear right-hand engine mounting.

23 Slacken and withdraw the engine mounting through-bolt.

24 Unbolt the engine mounting bracket from the end of the transmission casing.

25 Unbolt the engine mounting block from the body, and remove it from the engine bay **(see illustration)**.

26 Refitting is a reversal of removal, noting the following points:

a) *Ensure that the orientation lug that protrudes from the top of surface of the engine mounting block engages with the recess in the mounting bracket.*

b) *Tighten all bolts to the specified torque.*

15 Sump - removal and refitting

Removal

1 Disconnect the battery negative cable, and

15.6 Removing the sump bolts (engine removed and inverted for clarity)

position it away from the terminal. Refer to Chapter 1A and drain the engine oil. Where applicable, remove the screws and lower the engine undertray away from the vehicle.

2 Park the vehicle on a level surface, apply the handbrake and chock the rear wheels.

3 Raise the front of the vehicle, rest it securely on axle stands or wheel ramps; refer to *"Jacking and Vehicle Support"*.

4 On engine codes ABU, AEA and ABD, remove the exhaust system downpipe, as described in Chapter 4D.

5 To improve access to the sump, refer to Chapter 8 and disconnect the right-hand driveshaft from the transmission output flange.

6 Working around the outside of the sump, progressively slacken and withdraw the sump retaining bolts **(see illustration)**. Where applicable, unbolt and remove the flywheel cover plate from the transmission to gain access to the left-hand sump fixings.

7 Break the joint by striking the sump with the palm of your hand, then lower the sump and withdraw it from underneath the vehicle. Recover and discard the sump gasket. Where a baffle plate is fitted, note that it can only be removed once the oil pump has been unbolted (see Section 16).

8 While the sump is removed, take the opportunity to check the oil pump pick-up/strainer for signs of clogging or disintegration. If necessary, remove the pump as described in Section 16, and clean or renew the strainer.

Refitting

9 Clean all traces of sealant from the mating surfaces of the cylinder block/crankcase and sump, then use a clean rag to wipe out the sump.

10 Ensure that the sump and cylinder block/crankcase mating surfaces are clean and dry, then apply a coating of suitable sealant to the sump and crankcase mating surfaces.

11 Lay a new sump gasket in position on the sump mating surface, then offer up the sump and refit the retaining bolts. Tighten the nuts and bolts evenly and progressively to the specified torque.

12 Where applicable, refit the driveshaft, exhaust downpipe and engine bay undertray.

13 Refer to Chapter 1A and refill the engine with the specified grade and quantity of oil.

14 Restore the battery connection.

16 Oil pump and pickup - removal, inspection and refitting

General information

Engine codes ABU, ABD and AEA

1 The oil pump and pickup are both mounted at the timing belt end of the crankcase. Drive is taken from the crankshaft via a chain and sprocket.

Engine codes AEK, AAM, ABS, ADZ, ADY, 2E and ABF

2 The oil pump and pickup are both mounted in the sump. Drive is taken from the intermediate shaft, which rotates at half crankshaft speed.

Removal

Engine codes ABU, ABD and AEA

3 Refer to Section 15 and remove the sump from the crankcase.

4 With reference to Section 10, remove the front (timing belt end) crankshaft oil seal and housing.

5 Slacken and remove the bolts securing the oil pump to the end of the crankcase. Where applicable, remove the bolts and lift off the guide rail **(see illustration)**.

6 Remove the screws securing the oil pump pickup to the crankcase bracket.

7 Disengage the pump sprocket from the drive chain, and remove the oil pump and pickup from the engine.

Engine codes AEK, AAM, ABS, ADZ, ADY, 2E and ABF

8 Refer to Section 15 and remove the sump from the crankcase.

9 Slacken and remove the bolts securing the oil pump to the base of the crankcase **(see illustration)**.

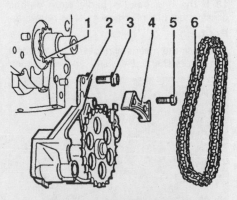

16.5 Oil pump components - engine codes ABU, ABD, AEA

1 Crank sprocket   4 Guide rail
2 Pump body   5 Guide rail bolts
3 Mounting bolts   6 Drive chain

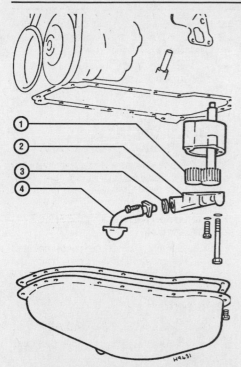

16.9 Oil pump components - engine codes AEK, ABF, AAM, ABS, ADZ, ADY, 2E

1 Oil pump gears   3 O-ring seal
2 Oil pump cover   4 Pickup tube

10 Lower the oil pump and pickup away from the crankcase. Where applicable, recover the baffle plate.

Inspection

11 Remove the screws from the mating flange, and lift off the pickup tube. Recover the O-ring seal. Slacken and withdraw the screws, then remove the oil pump cover.
12 Clean the pump thoroughly, and inspect the gear teeth for signs of damage or wear.
13 Where applicable, check the condition of the oil pump drive chain; if the links appear

16.14 Checking the oil pump backlash (engine code 2E shown)

excessively worn or are particularly loose, renew the chain.
14 Check the pump backlash by inserting a feeler blade between the meshed gear teeth; rotate the gears against each other slightly, to give the maximum clearance **(see illustration)**. Compare the measurement with the limit quoted in Specifications.
15 Check the pump axial clearance as follows. Lay an engineer's straight edge across the oil pump casing, then using a feeler blade, measure the clearance between the straight edge and the pump gears **(see illustration)**. Compare the measurement with the limit quoted in Specifications.
16 If either measurement is outside of the specified limit, this indicates that the pump is worn and must be renewed.

Refitting

Engine codes ABU, ABD and AEA

17 Refit the oil pump cover, then fit the screws and tighten them to the specified torque.
18 Reassemble the oil pickup to the oil pump, using a new O-ring seal. Tighten the retaining screws to the specified torque.
19 Offer up the oil pump to the end of the crankcase. Fit the drive chain over the oil pump sprocket, then engage it with the crankshaft sprocket.

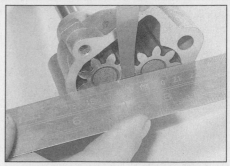

16.15 Checking the oil pump axial clearance (engine code 2E shown)

20 Fit the pump mounting bolts and hand-tighten them. Where applicable, fit the chain guide rail and tighten the retaining bolts to the specified torque.
21 Tension the drive chain by applying finger pressure to it at a point midway between the two sprockets. Adjust the position of the pump on its mountings until the tension is within the range given in the Specifications. On completion, tighten the mounting bolts to the specified torque.
22 Fit and tighten the fixings for the pickup tube to crankcase bracket.
23 With reference to Section 10, refit the crankshaft oil seal housing, using a new gasket and oil seal.
24 Refer to Section 15 and refit the sump.

Engine codes AEK, AAM, ABS, ADZ, ADY, 2E and ABF

25 Refit the oil pump cover, then fit and tighten the screws to the specified torque.
26 Reassemble the oil pickup to the oil pump, using a new O-ring seal. Tighten the retaining screws to the specified torque.
27 Where applicable, fit the crankcase baffle plate in place.
28 Offer up the oil pump to the crankcase, then fit the mounting bolts and tighten them to the specified torque.
29 Refer to Section 15 and refit the sump.

2A

Notes

Chapter 2 Part B:
Diesel engine in-car repair procedures

Contents

Degrees of difficulty

Easy, suitable for novice with little experience		Fairly easy, suitable for beginner with some experience		Fairly difficult, suitable for competent DIY mechanic		Difficult, suitable for experienced DIY mechanic		Very difficult, suitable for expert DIY or professional	

Specifications

General

Engine code: *

1896cc, mechanical fuel injection, normally-aspirated, 47kW	1Y
1896cc, mechanical fuel injection, turbocharged, 55 kW	AAZ
1896cc, electronic direct fuel injection, turbocharged, 66kW	1Y

* Note: See "Buying Spare Parts and Vehicle Identification" for the location of the code marking on the engine.

Bore	79.5 mm
Stroke	95.5 mm
Compression ratio:	
1Y	22.5:1
AAZ	22.5:1
1Z	19.5:1
Compression pressures (wear limit):	
1Z	19 Bar
AAZ, 1Y	26 Bar
Firing order	1 - 3 - 4 - 2
Cylinder No 1 location	Timing belt end
Timing belt tension:	
Engine code 1Z (measured using Volkswagen tool VW 210)	Scale reading of 13 - 14 units

Lubrication system

Oil pump type	Sump-mounted, driven indirectly from intermediate shaft
Normal operating oil pressure	2.0 bar minimum (at 2000 rpm, oil temperature 80°C)
Oil pump backlash	0.2 mm (wear limit)
Oil pump axial clearance	0.15 mm (wear limit)

Torque wrench settings

	Nm	lbf ft
Alternator mounting bolts	25	18
Camshaft cover screws	10	7
Camshaft bearing cap nuts/bolts:		
Engine codes ABU, ABD, AEA:		
Stage 1	6	4
Stage 2	Angle-tighten a further 90°	
Engine code ABF	15	11
All other engine codes	20	15
Camshaft sprocket bolt	45	33
Crankshaft auxiliary belt pulley screws	25	18
Crankshaft front oil seal housing bolts	25	18
Crankshaft rear oil seal housing bolts	10	7
Crankshaft sprocket bolt:		
Stage 1	90	66
Stage 2	Angle-tighten a further 90°	
Cylinder head bolts:		
Stage 1	40	30
Stage 2	60	44
Stage 3	Angle-tighten a further 90°	
Stage 4	Angle-tighten a further 90°	
Engine mountings:		
Through-bolts	50	37
Front mounting block bolt	50	37
Front mounting bracket bolts	55	41
Left rear mounting bracket bolts	25	18
Rear mounting block-to-body bolts	25	18
Right rear mounting bracket bolts	25	18
Exhaust manifold nuts	25	18
Idler roller to timing belt cover (engine code 1Z only)	25	18
Inlet manifold bolts	25	18
Intermediate shaft sprocket bolt	45	33
Oil pump cover screws	10	7
Oil pump mounting bolts	25	18
Oil pump pickup tube screws	10	7
Power steering pump mounting bolts	25	18
Sump retaining bolts	20	15
Timing belt tensioner locknut	20	15

1 General information

Using this Chapter

Chapter 2 is divided into three parts; A, B and C. Repair operations that can be carried out with the engine in the vehicle are described in Parts A (petrol engines) and B (diesel engines). Part C covers the removal of the engine/transmission as a unit and describes the engine dismantling and overhaul procedures.

In Parts A and B, the assumption is made that the engine is installed in the vehicle, with all ancillaries connected. If the engine has been removed for overhaul, the preliminary dismantling information which precedes each operation may be ignored.

Access to the engine bay can be improved by removing the bonnet and the front lock carrier assembly; these procedures are described in Chapter 11 and Chapter 2C respectively.

Engine description

Throughout this Chapter, engines are identified and referred to by manufacturer's code letters, rather than capacity. A listing of all engines covered, together with their code letters, is given in the Specifications at the start of this Chapter.

The engines are water-cooled, single overhead camshaft, in-line four cylinder units with cast-iron cylinder blocks and aluminium-alloy cylinder heads. All are mounted transversely at the front of the vehicle, with the transmission bolted to the left-hand side of the engine.

The cylinder head carries the camshaft(s), which are driven by a toothed timing belt. It also houses the inlet and exhaust valves, which are closed by single or double coil springs, and which run in guides pressed into the cylinder head. The camshaft actuates the valves directly via hydraulic tappets, mounted in the cylinder head. The cylinder head contains integral oilways which supply and lubricate the tappets.

On engine codes AAZ, 1Y (indirect injection engines), the cylinder head incorporates renewable swirl chambers. On engine code 1Z (direct injection engine), the piston crowns are shaped to form combustion chambers.

The crankshaft is supported by five main bearings, and endfloat is controlled by a thrust bearing fitted between cylinders No 2 and 3.

All diesel engines are fitted with a timing belt-driven intermediate shaft, which provides drive for the brake servo vacuum pump and the oil pump.

Engine coolant is circulated by a pump, driven by the auxiliary drivebelt. For details of the cooling system, refer to Chapter 3.

Lubricant is circulated under pressure by a pump, driven either by the crankshaft or by the intermediate shaft, depending on engine type. Oil is drawn from the sump through a strainer, and then forced through an externally-mounted, replaceable screw-on filter. From there, it is distributed to the cylinder head, where it lubricates the camshaft journals and hydraulic tappets, and also to the crankcase, where it lubricates the main bearings, connecting rod big- and small-ends, gudgeon pins and cylinder bores. Oil jets are fitted to the base of each cylinder - these spray oil onto the underside of the pistons, to improve cooling. An oil cooler, supplied with engine coolant, reduces the temperature of the oil before it re-enters the engine.

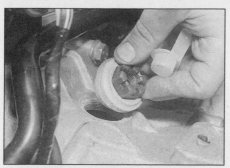

2.2a Remove the inspection bung from the transmission bellhousing

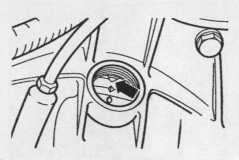

2.2b Timing mark on the edge of the flywheel (arrowed) lined up with pointer on bellhousing casting

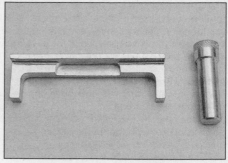

2.3 Engine locking tools

Repairs possible with the engine installed in the vehicle

The following operations can be performed without removing the engine:

a) *Auxiliary drivebelts - removal and refitting.*
b) *Camshaft(s) - removal and refitting. **
c) *Camshaft oil seal - renewal.*
d) *Camshaft sprocket - removal and refitting.*
e) *Coolant pump - removal and refitting (refer to Chapter 3)*
f) *Crankshaft oil seals - renewal.*
g) *Crankshaft sprocket - removal and refitting.*
h) *Cylinder head - removal and refitting. **
i) *Engine mountings - inspection and renewal.*
j) *Intermediate shaft oil seal - renewal.*
k) *Oil pump and pickup assembly - removal and refitting.*
l) *Sump - removal and refitting.*
m) *Timing belt, sprockets and cover - removal, inspection and refitting.*

*Cylinder head dismantling procedures are in Chapter 2C, and also contain details of camshaft and hydraulic tappet removal.

Note: *It is possible to remove the pistons and connecting rods (after removing the cylinder head and sump) without removing the engine from the vehicle. However, this procedure is not recommended. Work of this nature is more easily and thoroughly completed with the engine on the bench - refer to Chapter 2C.*

1 Remove camshaft cover, auxiliary drivebelts and timing belt outer covers as described in Sections 7, 6 and 4 respectively.
2 Remove the inspection bung from the transmission bellhousing. Rotate the crankshaft clockwise with a wrench and socket, or a spanner, until the timing mark machined onto the edge of the flywheel lines up with pointer on the bellhousing casting **(see illustrations)**.
3 To lock the engine in the TDC position, the camshaft (not the sprocket) and fuel injection pump sprocket must be secured in a reference position, using special locking tools. Improvised tools may be fabricated, but due to the exact measurements and machining involved, it is strongly recommended that a kit of locking tools is either borrowed or hired from a VAG dealer, or purchased from a reputable tool manufacturer - for example, Sykes Pickavant produce a kit of camshaft and fuel injection pump sprocket locking tools specifically for the range of engines covered in this Chapter **(see illustration)**.
4 Engage the edge of the locking bar with the slot in the end of the camshaft **(see illustration)**.
5 With the locking bar still inserted, turn the camshaft slightly (by turning the crankshaft clockwise, as before), so that the locking bar rocks to one side, allowing one end of the bar

to contact the cylinder head surface. At the other side of the locking bar, measure the gap between the end of the bar and the cylinder head using a feeler blade.
6 Turn the camshaft back slightly, then pull out the feeler blade. The idea now is to level the locking bar by inserting two feeler blades, each with a thickness equal to *half* the originally measured gap, on either side of the camshaft between each end of the locking bar and the cylinder head. This centres the camshaft, and sets the valve timing in reference condition **(see illustration)**.
7 Insert the locking pin through the fuel injection pump sprocket alignment hole, and thread it into the support bracket behind the sprocket. This locks the fuel injection pump in a reference condition **(see illustration)**.
8 The engine is now set to TDC on No 1 cylinder.

Compression test

Note: *A compression tester specifically designed for Diesel engines must be used for this test.*

1 When engine performance is down, or if misfiring occurs, a compression test can provide diagnostic clues as to the engine's condition. If the test is performed regularly, it can give warning of trouble before any other symptoms become apparent.

2.4 Engage the locking bar with the slot in the camshaft

2.6 Camshaft centred and locked using locking bar and feeler gauges

2.7 Injection pump sprocket locked using locking pin (arrowed): engine code AAZ

2B

2 A compression tester specifically intended for Diesel engines must be used, because of the higher pressures involved. The tester is connected to an adapter which screws into the glow plug or injector hole. It is unlikely to be worthwhile buying such a tester for occasional use, but it may be possible to borrow or hire one - if not, have the test performed by a garage.

3 Unless specific instructions to the contrary are supplied with the tester, observe the following points:

a) *The battery must be in a good state of charge, the air filter must be clean, and the engine should be at normal operating temperature.*

b) *All the injectors or glow plugs should be removed before starting the test. If removing the injectors, also remove the flame shield washers, otherwise they may be blown out.*

c) *The stop solenoid must be disconnected, to prevent the engine from running or fuel from being discharged.*

4 There is no need to hold the accelerator pedal down during the test, because the Diesel engine air inlet is not throttled.

5 VAG specify wear limits for compression pressures - refer to the Specifications. Seek the advice of a VAG dealer or other Diesel specialist if in doubt as to whether a particular pressure reading is acceptable.

6 The cause of poor compression is less easy to establish on a Diesel engine than on a petrol one. The effect of introducing oil into the cylinders ("wet" testing) is not conclusive, because there is a risk that the oil will sit in the swirl chamber or in the recess on the piston crown, instead of passing to the rings. However, the following can be used as a rough guide to diagnosis.

7 All cylinders should produce very similar pressures; a difference of more than 5 bars between any two cylinders indicates the existence of a fault. Note that the compression should build up quickly in a healthy engine; low compression on the first stroke, followed by gradually-increasing pressure on successive strokes, indicates worn piston rings. A low compression reading on the first stroke, which does not build up during successive strokes, indicates leaking valves or a blown head gasket (a cracked head could also be the cause).

8 A low reading from two adjacent cylinders is almost certainly due to the head gasket having blown between them; the presence of coolant in the engine oil will confirm this.

9 If the compression reading is unusually high, the cylinder head surfaces, valves and pistons are probably coated with carbon deposits. If this is the case, the cylinder head should be removed and decarbonised (refer to Part C of this Chapter).

Leakdown test

10 A leakdown test measures the rate at which compressed air fed into the cylinder is

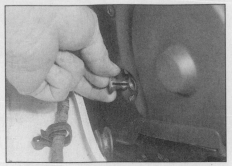

4.6 Removing the press-stud fixings from the timing belt upper cover

lost. It is an alternative to a compression test, and in many ways it is better, since the escaping air provides easy identification of where pressure loss is occurring (piston rings, valves or head gasket).

11 The equipment needed for leakdown testing is unlikely to be available to the home mechanic. If poor compression is suspected, have the test performed by a suitably-equipped garage.

4 Camshaft timing belt and outer covers - removal and refitting

General information

1 The primary function of the toothed timing belt is to drive the camshaft(s), but it is also used to drive the coolant pump or intermediate shaft, depending on the engine specification. Should the belt slip or break in service, the valve timing will be disturbed and piston-to-valve contact may occur, resulting in serious engine damage.

2 For this reason, it is important that the timing belt is tensioned correctly, and inspected regularly for signs of wear or deterioration.

3 Note that the removal of the *inner* section of the timing belt cover is described as part of the cylinder head removal procedure; see Section 11 later in this Chapter.

Removal

4 Before starting work, immobilise the engine by disconnecting the fuel cut-off solenoid cable (see Chapter 4C). Prevent any vehicle movement by applying the handbrake and chocking the rear wheels.

5 Access to the timing belt covers can be improved by removing the air cleaner housing - refer to Chapter 4C.

6 Release the uppermost part of the timing belt outer cover by prising open the metal spring clips and where applicable, removing the press-stud fixings **(see illustration)**. Lift the cover away from the engine

7 With reference to Section 6, remove the auxiliary drivebelt(s). Slacken and withdraw the screws, and lift off the coolant pump pulley

8 Refer to Section 2, and using the engine

4.9 Removing the crankshaft auxiliary belt pulleys

alignment markings, set the engine to TDC on No 1 cylinder.

9 Slacken and withdraw the retaining screws, then remove the pulley for the ribbed auxiliary belt (together with the V-belt pulley, where fitted) from the crankshaft sprocket **(see illustration)**. On completion, check that the engine is still set to TDC.

> **HAYNES HiNT** *To prevent the auxiliary belt pulley from rotating whilst the mounting bolts are being slackened, select top gear (manual transmission) or 'PARK' (automatic transmission) and get an assistant to apply the footbrake firmly. Failing this, grip the sprocket by wrapping a length of old rubber hose or inner tube around it.*

10 Remove the retaining screws and clips, and lift off the timing belt lower cover.

11 On engines with a two-part fuel injection pump sprocket, ensure that the sprocket locking pin is firmly in position (see Section 2), then loosen the outer sprocket securing bolts by half a turn. *Caution: Do not loosen the sprocket centre bolt, as this will alter the fuel injection pump's basic timing setting.*

12 With reference to Section 5, relieve the tension on the timing belt by slackening the tensioner mounting nut slightly, allowing it to pivot away from the belt.

13 On engine code 1Z, slacken and withdraw the bolt and remove the idler roller from the timing belt inner cover.

14 Examine the timing belt for manufacturer's markings that indicate the direction of rotation. If none are present, make your own using typist's correction fluid or a dab of paint - do not cut or score the belt in any way. *Caution: If the belt appears to be in good condition and can be re-used, it is essential that it is refitted the same way around, otherwise accelerated wear will result, leading to premature failure.*

15 Slide the belt off the sprockets, taking care to avoid twisting or kinking it excessively.

16 Examine the belt for evidence of contamination by coolant or lubricant. If this is the case, find the source of the contamination before progressing any further. Check the belt

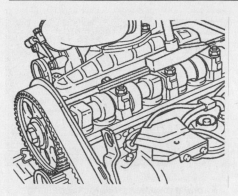

4.19 Releasing the camshaft sprocket from the taper using a pin punch

for signs of wear or damage, particularly around the leading edges of the belt teeth. Renew the belt if its condition is in doubt; the cost of belt renewal is negligible compared with potential cost of the engine repairs, should the belt fail in service. Similarly, if the belt is known to have covered more than 36 000 miles, it is prudent to renew it regardless of condition, as a precautionary measure.

17 If the timing belt is not going to be refitted for some time, it is a wise precaution to hang a warning label on the steering wheel, to remind yourself (and others) not to start the engine.

Refitting

18 Ensure that the crankshaft is still set to TDC on No 1 cylinder, as described in Section 2.

19 Refer to Section 5 and slacken the camshaft sprocket bolt by half a turn. Release the sprocket from the camshaft taper mounting by carefully tapping it with a pin punch, inserted through the hole provided in the timing belt inner cover **(see illustration)**.

20 Loop the timing belt loosely under the crankshaft sprocket. *Caution: Observe the direction of rotation markings on the belt.*

21 Engage the timing belt teeth with the crankshaft sprocket, then manoeuvre it into position over the camshaft and injection pump sprockets. Ensure the belt teeth seat correctly on the sprockets. **Note:** *Slight adjustments to the position of the camshaft sprocket (and*

where applicable, injection pump sprocket) may be necessary to achieve this.

22 Pass the flat side of the belt over the intermediate shaft pulley and tensioner roller - avoid bending the belt back on itself or twisting it excessively as you do this.

23 On engine code 1Z only, refit the idler roller to the timing belt inner cover, and tighten the retaining bolt to the specified torque.

24 On engines with a single-part fuel injection pump sprocket, remove the locking pin from the fuel injection pump sprocket (see Section 2).

25 Ensure that the 'front run' of the belt is taut - ie all the slack should be in the section of the belt that passes over the tensioner roller.

26 Tension the belt by turning the eccentrically-mounted tensioner clockwise; two holes are provided in the side of the tensioner hub for this purpose - a pair of sturdy right-angled circlip pliers is a suitable substitute for the correct VAG tool. **(see illustrations)**.

27 On engines with a semi-automatic belt tensioner, turn the tensioner clockwise until the alignment markings on the pulley and hub are lined up **(see illustration)**.

28 Test the timing belt tension by grasping it between the fingers at a point mid-way between the intermediate shaft and camshaft sprockets, and twisting it. The belt tension is correct when the belt can just be twisted through 90° (quarter of a turn) and no further.

29 When the correct belt tension has been achieved, tighten the tensioner locknut to the specified torque.

30 On engines without a semi-automatic tensioner, the belt tension must be accurately checked, and if necessary adjusted - this involves the use of dedicated belt tension measuring device (Volkswagen tool VW 210), and it is advisable to have this operation carried out by a VAG dealer.

31 At this point, check the crankshaft is still set to TDC on No 1 cylinder (see Section 2).

32 Refer to Section 5 and tighten the camshaft sprocket bolt to the specified torque.

33 On engines with a two-part fuel injection

pump sprocket, tighten the outer sprocket bolts, then remove the sprocket locking pin.

34 With reference to Section 2, remove the camshaft locking bar.

35 Using a spanner or wrench and socket on the crankshaft pulley centre bolt, rotate the crankshaft through two complete revolutions. Reset the engine to TDC on No 1 cylinder, with reference to Section 2 and check that the fuel injection pump sprocket locking pin can be inserted. Re-check the timing belt tension and adjust it, if necessary.

36 Refit the upper and lower sections of the timing belt outer cover, tightening the retaining screws securely.

37 Where applicable, refit the coolant pump pulley and tighten the retaining screws to the specified torque.

38 Refit the crankshaft auxiliary belt pulley and tighten the retaining screws to the specified torque, using the method employed during removal. Note that the offset of the pulley mounting holes allows only one fitting position.

39 Working from Section 6, refit and tension the auxiliary drivebelt(s).

40 Restore the fuelling system by reconnecting the fuel cut-off solenoid wiring (see Chapter 4C).

41 On completion, refer to Chapter 4C and check the fuel injection pump timing.

5 Timing belt tensioner and sprockets - removal and refitting

1 Before starting work, disable the fuelling system by disconnecting the wiring from the fuel cut-off solenoid (see Chapter 4C). Prevent any vehicle movement by applying the handbrake and chocking the rear wheels.

2 To gain access to the components detailed in this Section, refer to Section 6 and remove the auxiliary drivebelt(s).

Timing belt tensioner

Removal

3 With reference to the relevant paragraphs of Sections 2 and 4, set the engine to TDC on No 1 cylinder, then remove the upper and lower sections of the timing belt outer cover.

2B

4.26a Tensioning the timing belt using a pair of circlip pliers in the belt tensioner

4.26b Timing belt correctly fitted

4.27 Alignment marks on pulley and hub - engines with semi-automatic tensioner

5.4 Remove the tensioner nut and recover the washer

5.5 Slide the tensioner off its mounting stud

TOOL TIP

To make a camshaft sprocket holding tool, obtain two lengths of steel strip about 6mm thick by 30 mm wide or similar, one 600 mm long, the other 200 mm long (all dimensions approximate). Bolt the two strips together to form a forked end, leaving the bolt slack so that the shorter strip can pivot freely. At the end of each 'prong' of the fork, secure a bolt with a nut and a locknut, to act as the fulcrums; these will engage with the cut-outs in the sprocket, and should protrude by about 30mm

4 Slacken the retaining nut at the hub of the tensioner pulley and allow the assembly to rotate anti-clockwise, relieving the tension on the timing belt. Remove the nut and recover the washer **(see illustration)**.

5 Slide the tensioner off its mounting stud **(see illustration)**.

Inspection

6 Wipe the tensioner clean, but do not use solvents that may contaminate the bearings. Spin the tensioner pulley on its hub by hand. Stiff movement or excessive freeplay is an indication of severe wear; the tensioner is not a serviceable component, and should be renewed.

Refitting

7 Slide the tensioner pulley over the mounting stud. On engines with a semi-automatic tensioner, engage the forked end of the backplate with the timing belt pillar.

8 Refit the tensioner washer and retaining nut - do not fully tighten the nut at this stage.

9 With reference to Section 4, refit and tension the timing belt.

10 On engines with a semi-automatic tensioner, the operation of the tensioner can be tested as follows: apply finger pressure to the timing belt at a point mid-way between the camshaft and crankshaft sprockets. The tensioner pulley alignment marks should move apart as pressure is applied, and then move back and line up again as the pressure is removed **(refer to illustration 4.27)**.

11 Restore the fuelling system by reconnecting the fuel cut-off solenoid wiring.

12 Refer to Section 4 and refit the timing belt covers.

Camshaft timing belt sprocket

Removal

13 Refer to Section 2 and 4, set the engine to TDC on No 1 cylinder, then remove the timing belt outer covers. With reference to the previous sub-Section, slacken the tensioner centre hut and allow it to rotate anti-clockwise, to relieve the tension on the timing belt. Carefully slide the timing belt off the camshaft sprocket.

14 The camshaft sprocket must be held stationary whilst its retaining bolt is slackened; if access to the correct VAG

special tool is not possible, a simple home-made tool using basic materials may be fabricated **(see Tool Tip)**.

15 Using the home-made tool, brace the camshaft sprocket and slacken and remove the retaining bolt; recover the washer where fitted.

16 Slide the camshaft sprocket from the end of the camshaft **(see illustration)**. Where applicable, recover the Woodruff key from the keyway.

17 With the sprocket removed, examine the camshaft oil seal for signs of leaking. If necessary, refer to Section 8 and renew it.

18 Wipe the sprocket and camshaft mating surfaces clean.

Refitting

19 Where applicable, fit the Woodruff key into the keyway with the plain surface facing upwards. Fit the sprocket to the camshaft, engaging the slot in the sprocket with the Woodruff key. Where a key is not used, ensure the lug in the sprocket hub engages with recess in the end of the camshaft.

20 Working from Sections 2 and 4, check that the engine is still set to TDC on No 1 cylinder, then refit and tension the timing belt. Refit the timing belt covers.

21 Refit the crankshaft auxiliary belt pulley(s), then insert the retaining screws and tighten them to the specified torque.

22 With reference to Section 6, refit and tension the auxiliary drivebelt(s).

Crankshaft timing belt sprocket

Removal

23 Refer to Section 2 and 4, set the engine to

5.16 Removing the camshaft sprocket

TDC on No 1 cylinder, then remove the timing belt outer covers. With reference to the previous sub-Section, slacken the tensioner centre hut and allow it to rotate anti-clockwise, to relieve the tension on the timing belt. Carefully slide the timing belt off the camshaft sprocket.

24 The crankshaft sprocket must be held stationary whilst its retaining bolt is slackened. If access to the correct VAG flywheel locking tool is not available, lock the crankshaft in position by removing the starter motor, as described in Chapter 5A, to expose the flywheel ring gear. Get an assistant insert a stout lever between the ring gear teeth and the transmission bellhousing whilst the sprocket retaining bolt is slackened.

25 Withdraw the bolt, recover the washer and lift off the sprocket.

26 With the sprocket removed, examine the crankshaft oil seal for signs of leaking. If necessary, refer to Section 10 and renew it.

27 Wipe the sprocket and crankshaft mating surfaces clean.

Refitting

28 Offer up the sprocket to the crankshaft, engaging the lug on the inside of the sprocket with the recess in the end of the crankshaft. Insert the retaining bolt and tighten it to the specified torque **(see illustrations)**.

29 Working from Sections 2 and 4, check that the engine is still set to TDC on No 1 cylinder, then refit and tension the timing belt. Refit the timing belt covers.

30 Refit the crankshaft auxiliary belt pulley(s).

31 With reference to Section 6, refit and tension the auxiliary drivebelt(s).

5.28a Insert the camshaft sprocket bolt . . .

5.28b . . . tighten it to the Stage 1 torque . . .

5.28c . . . then through the Stage 2 angle

5.34 Brace the intermediate shaft sprocket, then remove the retaining bolt

Intermediate shaft sprocket

Removal

32 With reference to Sections 2 and 4, remove the timing belt covers and set the engine to TDC on No 1 cylinder. Slacken the tensioner centre nut and rotate it anti-clockwise to relieve the tension on the timing belt. Carefully slide the timing belt off the camshaft sprocket.

33 The intermediate shaft sprocket must be held stationary whilst its retaining bolt is slackened; if access to the correct VAG special tool is not possible, a simple home-made tool using basic materials may be fabricated as described in the camshaft sprocket removal sub-Section.

34 Using a socket and extension bar, brace the intermediate shaft sprocket. Slacken and remove the retaining bolt; recover the washer, where fitted **(see illustration)**.

35 Slide the sprocket from the end of the intermediate shaft. Where applicable, recover the Woodruff key from the keyway.

36 With the sprocket removed, examine the intermediate shaft oil seal for signs of leaking. If necessary, refer to Section 8 and renew it.

37 Wipe the sprocket and shaft mating surfaces clean.

Refitting

38 Where applicable, fit the Woodruff key into the keyway with the plain surface facing upwards. Offer up the sprocket to the intermediate shaft, engaging the slot in the sprocket with the Woodruff key.

39 Tighten the sprocket retaining bolt to the specified torque; hold the sprocket using the method employed during removal.

40 With reference to Section 2, check that the engine is still set to TDC on No 1 cylinder. Working from Section 4, refit and tension the timing belt, then refit the timing belt covers.

41 Refit the crankshaft auxiliary belt pulley(s), then insert the retaining screws and tighten them to the specified torque.

42 With reference to Section 6, refit and tension the auxiliary drivebelt(s).

---

6 Auxiliary drivebelts - removal and refitting

General information

1 Depending on the vehicle specification and engine type, one or two auxiliary drivebelts may be fitted. Both are driven from pulleys mounted on the crankshaft, and provide drive for the alternator, coolant pump, power steering pump and on vehicles with air conditioning, the refrigerant compressor.

2 The run of the belts and the components they drive are also dependent on vehicle specification and engine type. Because of this, the coolant pump and power steering pump may have pulleys to suit either a ribbed belt or a V-belt.

3 The ribbed auxiliary belt may have an automatic tensioning device, depending on its run (and hence the number of components it is driving). Otherwise, the belt is tensioned by the alternator mountings, which have an in-built tensioning spring. The V-belt is tensioned by pivoting the power steering pump on its mounting.

4 On refitting, the auxiliary belt must be tensioned correctly to ensure correct operation and prolonged service life.

Auxiliary V-belt

Removal

5 Park the vehicle on a level surface and apply the handbrake. Jack up the front of the vehicle and rest it on axle stands - refer to "Jacking and Vehicle Support". Disable the starting system by unplugging the starter solenoid at the connector; see Chapter 5A.

6 Turn the steering to full right lock, then refer to Chapter 11 and remove the plastic air ducting from below the right-hand front wing.

7 With reference to Chapter 10, slacken the power steering pump mounting bolts and allow the pump body to pivot around its uppermost mounting towards the engine.

8 Guide the V-belt off the power steering pump pulley and where applicable, the coolant pump pulley **(see illustration)**.

9 Examine the belt for signs or wear or damage, and renew it if necessary.

Refitting and tensioning

10 Refit the belt by reversing the removal procedure, ensuring that it seats evenly in the pulleys.

11 Set the belt tension by grasping the underside of the power steering pump and drawing it towards the front of the vehicle. The tension is correct when the midpoint of the belt's longest run can be deflected by no more than 5 mm. Tighten the power steering pump bolt to the correct torque **(see illustration)**

12 Rotate the crankshaft in its normal direction of rotation through two turns, then re-check and if necessary adjust the tension.

2B

6.8 Removing the auxiliary V-belt

6.11 Tightening the steering pump bolt

6.17 Rotate the tensioner roller arm clockwise - use an adjustable spanner - and remove the belt

Auxiliary ribbed belt

Removal

13 Park the vehicle on a level surface and apply the handbrake. Jack up the front of the vehicle and rest it securely on axle stands - refer to "*Jacking and Vehicle Support*". Disable the starting system by unplugging the starter solenoid at the connector; refer to Chapter 5A.

14 Turn the steering to full right lock, then refer to Chapter 11 and remove the plastic air ducting from underneath the right-hand front wing.

15 Where applicable, remove the auxiliary V-belt as described in the previous sub-Section.

16 Examine the ribbed belt for manufacturer's markings, indicating the direction of rotation. If none are present, make some using typist's correction fluid or a dab of paint - do not cut or score the belt in any way.

Vehicles with a roller-arm automatic tensioning device

17 Rotate the tensioner roller arm clockwise against its spring tension so that the roller is forced away from the belt - use an adjustable spanner as a lever **(see illustration)**.

Vehicles with rotary automatic tensioning device

18 Fit a ring spanner to the tensioner centre nut and rotate the assembly anti-clockwise, against its spring tension.

Vehicles without an automatic tensioning device

19 Slacken the alternator upper and lower mounting bolts by between one and two turns.

20 Push the alternator down to its stop against the spring tension, so that it rotates around its uppermost mounting.

All vehicles

21 Pull the belt off the alternator pulley, then release it from the remaining pulleys.

Refitting and tensioning

Caution: Observe the manufacturer's direction of rotation markings on the belt, when refitting.

22 Pass the ribbed belt underneath the crankshaft pulley, ensuring that the ribs seat securely in the channels on the surface of the pulley.

Vehicles with roller-arm automatic tensioning device

23 Rotate the tensioner roller arm clockwise against its spring tension - use an adjustable spanner as a lever **(refer to illustration 6.17)**.

24 Pass the belt around the coolant pump pulley or air conditioning refrigerant pump pulley (as applicable), then fit it over the alternator pulley.

25 Release the tensioner pulley arm and allow the roller to bear against the flat surface of the belt.

Vehicles with rotary automatic tensioning device

26 Fit a ring spanner to the tensioner centre nut and rotate the assembly anti-clockwise, against its spring tension.

27 Pass the flat side of the belt underneath the tensioner roller, then fit it over the power steering pump and alternator pulleys.

28 Release the spanner, and let the tensioner roller bear against the flat side of the belt.

Vehicles without an automatic tensioning device

29 Repeatedly push the alternator down to its stop against the spring tension, so that it rotates around its uppermost mounting and check that it moves back freely when released. If necessary, slacken the alternator mounting bolts by a further half a turn.

30 Keep the alternator pushed down against its stop, pass the belt over the alternator pulley, then release the alternator and allow it to tension the belt.

31 Restore the starting system, then start the engine and allow it to idle for approximately ten seconds.

7.2 Crankcase breather regulator valve

7.4 Lift the camshaft cover away from the cylinder head

32 Switch the engine off, then tighten first the lower, then the alternator upper mounting bolts to the specified torque.

All vehicles

33 Refer to Chapter 11 and refit the plastic air ducts to the underside of the wing.

34 Where applicable, refer to the previous sub-Section and refit the auxiliary V-belt.

35 Lower the vehicle to the ground, then (if not already carried out) restore the starting system with reference to Chapter 5A.

7 Camshaft cover - removal and refitting

Removal

1 Immobilise the engine by unplugging the electrical wiring from the fuel cut-off solenoid at the connector; refer to Chapter 4C for guidance.

2 Disconnect the crankcase breather hose and regulator valve from the camshaft cover **(see illustration)**.

3 Slacken and withdraw the three camshaft cover retaining nuts - recover the washers and seals **(see illustration)**.

4 Lift the cover away from the cylinder head **(see illustration)**; if it sticks, do not attempt to lever it off - instead free it by working around the cover and tapping it lightly with a soft-faced mallet.

5 Recover the camshaft cover gasket **(see illustration)**. Inspect the gasket carefully, and renew it if damage or deterioration is evident.

6 Clean the mating surfaces of the cylinder

7.3 Camshaft cover retaining nut

7.5 Recover the camshaft cover gasket

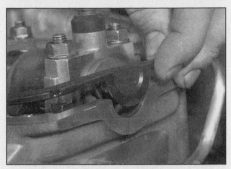

7.7 Ensure that the camshaft cover gasket is correctly seated on the cylinder head

head and camshaft cover thoroughly, removing all traces of oil and old gasket - take care to avoid damaging the surfaces as you do this.

Refitting

7 Refit the camshaft cover by following the removal procedure in reverse, noting the following points:
a) *Ensure that the gasket is correctly seated on the cylinder head, and take care to avoid displacing it as the camshaft cover is lowered into position (see illustration).*
b) *Tighten the camshaft cover retaining screws/nuts to the specified torque.*
c) *When refitting hoses that were originally secured with crimp-type clips, use standard worm-drive clips in their place on refitting.*

8 On completion, restore the fuelling system by reconnecting the fuel cut-off solenoid lead.

8 Camshaft oil seal - renewal

1 Immobilise the engine by unplugging the electrical wiring from the fuel cut-off solenoid at the connector; refer to Chapter 4C for guidance.
2 Refer to Section 6 and remove the auxiliary drivebelt(s).
3 With reference to Sections 2, 4 and 5 of this Chapter, remove the auxiliary belt pulleys and timing belt cover; set the engine to TDC on No 1 cylinder and remove the timing belt, timing belt tensioner (where applicable) and camshaft sprocket.
4 After removing the retaining screws, lift the timing belt inner cover away from the engine block.
5 Working from the relevant Section of Chapter 2C, carry out the following:
a) *Unbolt the camshaft No 1 bearing cap, and slide off the camshaft oil seal.*
b) *Lubricate the surface of a new camshaft oil seal with clean engine oil, and fit it over the end of the camshaft.*
c) *Apply a suitable sealant to the mating surface of the bearing cap, then refit it and tighten its mounting nuts progressively to the specified torque (see illustration).*

6 Refer to Section 7 and refit the camshaft cover.
7 With reference to Sections 2, 4 and 5 of this Chapter, refit the timing belt inner cover and timing sprockets, then refit and tension the timing belt. On completion, refit the timing belt outer cover.
8 With reference to Section 6, refit and tension the auxiliary drivebelt(s).

9 Intermediate shaft oil seal - renewal

1 Immobilise the engine by unplugging the electrical wiring from the fuel cut-off solenoid at the connector; refer to Chapter 4C for guidance.
2 Refer to Section 6 and remove the auxiliary drivebelt(s).
3 With reference to Sections 4 and 5 of this Chapter, remove the auxiliary belt pulleys, timing belt outer cover, timing belt, tensioner (where applicable) and intermediate shaft sprocket.
4 After removing the retaining screws, lift the inner timing belt cover away from the engine block - this will expose the intermediate shaft sealing flange.
5 With reference to Section 7 of Chapter 2C, remove the intermediate shaft flange and renew the shaft and flange oil seals.
6 Refer to Sections 4 and 5 of this Chapter, carry out the following:
a) *Refit the timing belt inner cover.*
b) *Refit the intermediate shaft timing belt sprocket.*
c) *Refit and tension the timing belt.*
d) *Refit the timing belt outer cover.*

7 With reference to Section 6 of this Chapter, refit and tension the auxiliary drivebelt(s).

10 Crankshaft oil seals - renewal

Crankshaft front oil seal

1 Immobilise the engine by unplugging the electrical wiring from the fuel cut-off solenoid at the connector; refer to Chapter 4C for guidance.
2 Refer to Chapter 1B and drain the engine oil.

8.5 Refitting the camshaft bearing cap

10.7 Removing the crankshaft front oil seal using self-tapping screws

3 With reference to "*Jacking and Vehicle Support*", raise the front of the vehicle and rest it securely on axle stands.
4 Working from Chapter 11, remove the screws and detach the plastic air ducting from underneath the right-hand front wing.
5 Refer to Section 6 and remove the auxiliary drivebelt(s).
6 With reference to Sections 4 and 5 of this Chapter, remove the auxiliary belt pulleys, timing belt outer covers, timing belt and crankshaft sprocket.
7 Drill two small holes into the existing oil seal, diagonally opposite each other. Thread two self-tapping screws into the holes and using two pairs of pliers, pull on the heads of the screws to extract the oil seal (**see illustration**). Take great care to avoid drilling through into the seal housing or crankshaft sealing surface.
8 Clean out the seal housing and sealing surface of the crankshaft by wiping it with a lint-free cloth - avoid using solvents that may enter the crankcase and affect component lubrication. Remove any swarf or burrs that could cause the seal to leak.
9 Smear the lip of the new oil seal with clean engine oil, and position it over the housing.
10 Using a hammer and a socket of suitable diameter, drive the seal squarely into its housing. **Note:** *Select a socket that bears only on the hard outer surface of the seal, not the inner lip, which can easily be damaged.*
11 With reference to Sections 2, 4 and 5 of this Chapter, refit the crankshaft timing belt sprocket, then refit and tension the timing belt. On completion, refit the timing belt outer cover, and auxiliary drivebelt pulley(s).
12 The remainder of the refitting procedure is a reversal of removal, as follows:
a) *With reference to Section 6, refit and tension the auxiliary drivebelt(s).*
b) *Refit the plastic air ducting to the underside of the wing - see Chapter 11.*
c) *Refer to Chapter 1B and refill the engine with the correct grade and quantity of oil.*
d) *Restore the fuelling system.*

Crankshaft front oil seal housing - gasket renewal

13 Proceed as described in paragraphs 1 to 6 above, then refer to Section 15 and remove the sump.

2B

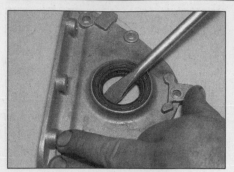

10.17 Prise the old oil seal from the housing

10.19 Locate the new crankshaft front oil seal housing gasket in position

10.21 Offer up the seal and its housing to the end of the crankshaft

14 Progressively slacken and then remove the oil seal housing retaining bolts.

15 Lift the housing away from the cylinder block, together with the crankshaft oil seal, using a twisting motion to ease the seal along the shaft.

16 Recover the old gasket from the seal housing on the cylinder block. If it has disintegrated, scrape the remains off with a trimming knife blade. Take care to avoid damaging the mating surfaces.

17 Prise the old oil seal from the housing using a stout screwdriver (see illustration).

18 Wipe the oil seal housing clean, and check it visually for signs of distortion or cracking. Lay the housing on a work surface, with the mating surface face down. Press in a new oil seal, using a block of wood as a press to ensure that the seal enters the housing squarely.

19 Smear the crankcase mating surface with multi-purpose grease, and lay the new gasket in position (see illustration).

20 Pad the end of the crankshaft with a layer of PVC tape; this will protect the oil seal as it is being fitted.

21 Lubricate the inner lip of the crankshaft oil seal with clean engine oil, then offer up the seal and its housing to the end of the crankshaft. Ease the seal along the shaft using a twisting motion, until the housing is flush with the crankcase (see illustration).

22 Insert the bolts and tighten them to the specified torque. *Caution: The housing is light alloy, and may be distorted if the bolts are not tightened progressively.*

23 Refer to Section 15 and refit the sump.

24 With reference to Sections 2, 4 and 5 of this Chapter, refit the crankshaft timing belt sprocket, then refit and tension the timing belt. On completion, refit the timing belt outer cover, and auxiliary drivebelt pulley(s).

25 The remainder of the refitting procedure is a reversal of removal, as follows:

a) *With reference to Section 6, refit and tension the auxiliary drivebelt(s).*

b) *Refit the plastic air ducting to the underside of the wing, working from Chapter 11.*

c) *Refer to Chapter 1B and refill the engine with the correct grade and quantity of oil.*

d) *Restore the fuelling system.*

Crankshaft rear oil seal (flywheel end)

26 Proceed as described in paragraphs 1 to 3 above, then refer to Section 15 remove the sump.

27 Working from Chapter 11, remove the screws and detach the plastic air ducting from underneath the left-hand front wing.

28 Refer to Chapter 7A or B as applicable, and remove the transmission from the engine.

29 On vehicles with manual transmission, refer to Section 13 of this Chapter and remove the flywheel; refer to Chapter 6 and remove the clutch friction plate and pressure plate.

30 On vehicles with automatic transmission, refer to Section 13 of this Chapter and remove the driveplate from the crankshaft.

31 Where applicable, remove the retaining bolts and lift the intermediate plate away from the cylinder block.

32 Progressively slacken and then remove the oil seal housing retaining bolts.

33 Lift the housing away from the cylinder block, together with the crankshaft oil seal, using a twisting motion to ease the seal along the shaft.

34 Recover the old gasket from the seal housing cylinder block. If it has disintegrated, scrape the remains off with a trimming knife blade. Take care to avoid damaging the mating surfaces.

35 Prise the old oil seal from the housing using a stout screwdriver (see illustration).

36 Wipe the oil seal housing clean, and check it visually for signs of distortion or cracking. Lay the housing on a work surface, with the mating surface face down. Press in a new oil seal, using a block of wood as a press to ensure that the seal enters the housing squarely (see illustration).

37 Smear the crankcase mating surface with multi-purpose grease, and lay the new gasket in position (see illustration).

38 A protective plastic cap is supplied with genuine VAG crankshaft oil seals; when fitted over the end of the crankshaft, the cap prevents damage to the inner lip of the oil seal as it is being fitted (see illustration). Use PVC tape to pad the end of the crankshaft if a cap is not available.

39 Lubricate the inner lip of the crankshaft oil seal with clean engine oil, then offer up the seal and its housing to the end of crankshaft. Ease the seal along the shaft using a twisting motion, until the housing is flush with the crankcase (see illustration).

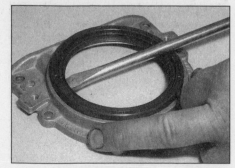

10.35 Prise the crankshaft rear oil seal from the housing

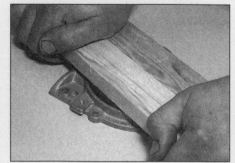

10.36 Press in a new oil seal, using a block of wood

10.37 Locate the new crankshaft rear oil seal housing gasket in position

10.38 A protective plastic cap is supplied with genuine VAG crankshaft oil seals

10.39 Fitting the crankshaft rear oil seal and housing

10.40 Tightening the crankshaft rear oil seal housing retaining bolts

40 Insert the retaining bolts and tighten them progressively to the specified torque **(see illustration)**. *Caution: The housing is light alloy, and may be distorted if the bolts are not tightened progressively.*

41 Refer to Section 15 and refit the sump.

42 Fit the intermediate plate to the cylinder block, then insert and tighten the retaining bolts.

43 On vehicles with automatic transmission, work from Section 13 of this Chapter and refit the driveplate to the crankshaft.

44 On vehicles with manual transmission, refer to Chapter 6 and refit the flywheel, pressure plate and clutch friction plate.

45 With reference to Chapter 7A or B as applicable, refit the transmission to the engine.

46 The remainder of the refitting procedure is a reversal of removal, as follows:

a) Refit the plastic air ducting to the underside of the wing, working from Chapter 11.

b) Refer to Chapter 1B and refill the engine with the correct grade and quantity of oil.

c) Restore the fuelling systems.

11 Cylinder head, inlet and exhaust manifolds - removal, separation and refitting

Removal

1 Select a level surface to park the vehicle upon. Give yourself enough space to move around it easily.

2 Refer to Chapter 11 and remove the bonnet from its hinges.

3 Disconnect the battery negative cable, and position It away from the terminal. **Note:** *If the vehicle has a security-coded radio, check that you have a copy of the code number before disconnecting the battery cable.*

4 With reference to Chapter 1B, carry out the following:

a) Drain the engine oil.

b) Drain the cooling system.

5 Refer to Section 6 and remove the auxiliary drivebelt(s).

6 With reference to Section 2, set the engine to TDC on No 1 cylinder.

7 Refer to Chapter 3 and perform the following:

a) Slacken the clips and disconnect the radiator hoses from the ports on the cylinder head.

b) Slacken the clips and disconnect the expansion tank hose, and the heater inlet and outlet coolant hoses, from the ports on the cylinder head **(see illustration)**.

8 The "lock carrier" is a panel assembly comprising the front bumper moulding, radiator and grille, cooling fan(s) headlight units, front valence and bonnet lock mechanism. Although its removal is not essential, its does give greatly-improved access to the engine; refer to the beginning of the engine removal procedure, in Chapter 2C.

9 Refer to Chapter 4C and carry out the following:

a) Disconnect and remove the injector fuel supply hoses from the injectors and the injection pump head.

b) Disconnect the injector bleed hose from the injection pump fuel return port.

c) Unplug all fuel system electrical cabling at the relevant connectors, labelling each cable to aid refitting later.

10 With reference to Sections 2, 4 and 7, carry out the following:

a) Remove the camshaft cover.

b) Remove the timing belt outer covers, and disengage the timing belt from the camshaft sprocket.

c) Remove the timing belt tensioner, camshaft sprocket and fuel injection pump sprocket.

11 Slacken and withdraw the retaining screws and lift off the timing belt inner covers **(see illustrations)**.

12 With reference to Chapter 3 and 4C (as applicable), disconnect the wiring plug from the coolant temperature sensor **(see illustration)**.

2B

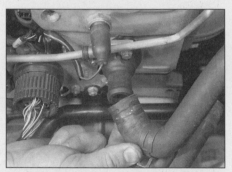

11.7 Disconnect the heater coolant hoses from the ports on the cylinder head

11.11a Slacken and withdraw the retaining screws . . .

11.11b . . . and lift off the timing belt inner covers

11.12 Disconnect the wiring plug from the coolant temperature sensor

11.13 Unbolt the electrical supply cable from No 4 cylinder glow plug

11.14 Removing the engine harness connector bracket from the cylinder head

11.16 Lifting the cylinder head away from the engine

13 Refer to Chapter 4D and carry out the following:
a) *Remove the bolts and separate the exhaust downpipe from the exhaust manifold flange.*
b) *Where applicable, remove the turbocharger from the exhaust manifold.*
c) *Where applicable, remove the EGR valve and its connecting pipework from the inlet and exhaust manifolds.*
d) *Unbolt the supply cable from the glow plug in cylinder No 4 (see illustration).*

14 Remove the retaining screw and detach the engine harness connector bracket from the cylinder head (see illustration).

15 Working in the reverse of the sequence shown in illustration 11.37a, progressively slacken the cylinder head bolts, by half a turn at a time, until all bolts can be unscrewed by hand. Discard the bolts - new ones must be fitted on reassembly.

16 Check that nothing remains connected to the cylinder head, then lift the head away from the cylinder block; seek assistance if possible, as it is a heavy assembly, especially if it is being removed complete with the manifolds (see illustration).

17 Remove the gasket from the top of the block, noting the locating dowels. If the dowels are a loose fit, remove them and store them with the head for safe-keeping. Do not discard the gasket - it will be needed for identification purposes.

18 If the cylinder head is to be dismantled for overhaul refer to Chapter 2C.

Manifold separation

19 With the cylinder head on a work surface, slacken and withdraw the inlet manifold securing bolts. Lift the manifold away, and recover the gasket.

20 Unbolt the heat shield (see illustration),

then progressively slacken and remove the exhaust manifold retaining nuts. Lift the manifold away from the cylinder head, and recover the gaskets.

21 Ensure that the inlet and exhaust manifold mating surfaces are completely clean. Refit the exhaust manifold, using new gaskets. Ensure that the gaskets are fitted the correct way around, otherwise they will obstruct the inlet manifold gasket. Tighten the exhaust manifold retaining nuts to the specified torque (see illustrations).

22 Refit the heat shield to the studs on the exhaust manifold, then fit and tighten the retaining nuts.

23 Fit a new inlet manifold gasket to the cylinder head, then lift the inlet manifold into position. Insert the retaining bolts and tighten them to the specified toque (see illustrations).

11.20 Unbolt and remove the exhaust manifold heat shield

11.21a Fit the exhaust manifold gaskets . . .

11.21b . . . then refit the exhaust manifold. Tighten the nuts to the specified torque

11.23a Fit a new inlet manifold gasket to the cylinder head . . .

11.23b . . . then lift the inlet manifold into position

11.23c Insert the retaining bolts and tighten them to the specified toque

Preparation for refitting

24 The mating faces of the cylinder head and cylinder block/crankcase must be perfectly clean before refitting the head. Use a hard plastic or wood scraper to remove all traces of gasket and carbon; also clean the piston crowns. Take particular care during the cleaning operations, as aluminium alloy is easily damaged. Also, make sure that the carbon is not allowed to enter the oil and water passages - this is particularly important for the lubrication system, as carbon could block the oil supply to the engine's components. Using adhesive tape and paper, seal the water, oil and bolt holes in the cylinder block/crankcase.

25 Check the mating surfaces of the cylinder block/crankcase and the cylinder head for nicks, deep scratches and other damage. If slight, they may be removed carefully with abrasive paper, but note that head machining will not be possible - refer to Chapter 2C.

26 If warpage of the cylinder head gasket surface is suspected, use a straight-edge to check it for distortion. Refer to Part C of this Chapter if necessary.

27 Clean out the cylinder head bolt drillings using a suitable tap. If a tap is not available, make a home-made substitute (see Tool Tip).

28 On all the engines covered in this Chapter, it is possible for the piston crowns to strike and damage the valve heads, if the camshaft is rotated with the timing belt removed and the crankshaft set to TDC. For this reason, the crankshaft must be set to a position other than TDC on No 1 cylinder, before the cylinder head is refitted. Use a wrench and socket on the crankshaft pulley centre bolt to turn the crankshaft in its normal direction of rotation, until all four pistons are positioned halfway down their bores, with No 1 piston on its upstroke - approximately 90° before TDC.

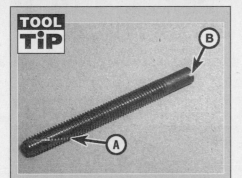

TOOL TiP

If a tap is not available, make a home-made substitute by cutting a slot (A) down the threads of one of the old cylinder head bolts. After use, the bolt head can be cut off, and the shank can then be used as an alignment dowel to assist cylinder head refitting. Cut a screwdriver slot (B) in the top of the bolt, to allow it to be unscrewed

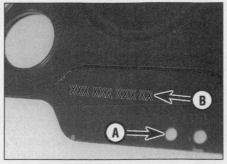

11.29 Cylinder head gasket punched holes (A) and part number (B)

11.36 Oil the cylinder head bolt threads, then place each bolt into its relevant hole

Refitting

29 Examine the old cylinder head gasket for manufacturer's identification markings. These will either be in the form of punched holes or a part number, on the edge of the gasket (see illustration). Unless new pistons have been fitted, the new cylinder head gasket must be the same type as the old one.

30 If new piston assemblies have been fitted as part of an engine overhaul, before purchasing the new cylinder head gasket, refer to Section 13 of Chapter 2C and measure the piston projection. Purchase a new gasket according to the results of the measurement (see Chapter 2C Specifications).

31 Lay the new head gasket on the cylinder block, engaging it with the locating dowels. Ensure that the manufacturer's "TOP" and part number markings are face up.

32 Cut the heads from two of the old cylinder head bolts. Cut a slot, big enough for a screwdriver blade, in the end of each bolt. These can be used as alignment dowels to assist in cylinder head refitting (see illustration).

33 With the help of an assistant, place the cylinder head and manifolds centrally on the cylinder block, ensuring that the locating dowels engage with the recesses in the cylinder head. Check that the head gasket is correctly seated before allowing the full weight of the cylinder head to rest upon it.

34 Unscrew the home-made alignment dowels, using a flat bladed screwdriver.

35 Apply a smear of grease to the threads, and to the underside of the heads, of the new cylinder head bolts.

11.32 Two of the old head bolts (arrowed) used as cylinder head alignment dowels

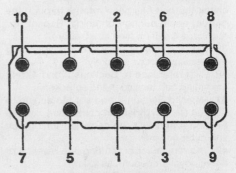

11.37a Cylinder head bolt tightening sequence

11.37b Tightening the cylinder head bolts using a torque wrench and socket

36 Oil the bolt threads, then carefully enter each bolt into its relevant hole (*do not drop them in*) and screw in, by hand only, until finger-tight (see illustration).

37 Working progressively and in the sequence shown, tighten the cylinder head bolts to their Stage 1 torque setting, using a torque wrench and suitable socket (see illustrations). Repeat the exercise in the same sequence for the Stage 2 torque setting.

38 Once all the bolts have been tightened to their Stage 2 settings, working again in the given sequence, angle-tighten the bolts through the specified Stage 3 angle, using a socket and extension bar. It is recommended that an angle-measuring gauge is used during this stage of the tightening, to ensure accuracy. If a gauge is not available, use white paint to make alignment marks between the bolt head and cylinder head prior to tightening; the marks can then be used to

2B

11.38 Angle-tightening a cylinder head bolt

check the bolt has been rotated through the correct angle during tightening. Repeat for the Stage 4 setting **(see illustration)**.

39 Refit the timing belt inner cover, tightening the retaining screws securely.

40 With reference to Sections 2 and 4, refit the timing belt tensioner and sprockets.

41 Refer to Section 2 and set the engine to TDC on No 1 cylinder. On completion, refer to Section 4 and refit the camshaft timing belt and outer covers.

42 The remainder of refitting is a reversal of the removal procedure, as follows:

a) *Refer to Chapter 4D and refit the turbocharger (where applicable), the exhaust downpipe, the EGR valve (where applicable) and the glow plug cabling.*

b) *Refer to Chapter 4C and refit the injector fuel supply hoses to the injectors and the injection pump head. Reconnect all fuel system electrical cabling. Refit the injector bleed hose to the injection pump fuel return port.*

c) *Refit the engine harness connector bracket to the cylinder head.*

d) *Refit the camshaft cover (see Section 7).*

e) *With reference to the information in Chapter 2C, refit the lock carrier assembly, if it was removed for greater access.*

f) *Reconnect the radiator, expansion tank and heater coolant hoses, referring to Chapter 3 for guidance. Reconnect the coolant temperature sensor wiring.*

g) *Refer to Section 6 and refit the auxiliary drivebelt(s).*

h) *Restore the battery connection.*

i) *Refer to Chapter 11 and refit the bonnet.*

43 On completion, refer to Chapter 1B and carry out the following:

a) *Refill the engine cooling system with the correct quantity of new coolant.*

b) *Refill the engine lubrication system with the correct grade and quantity of oil.*

Note: *No further tightening of the cylinder head bolts is required.*

12 Hydraulic tappets - operation check

1 The hydraulic tappets are self-adjusting, and require no attention whilst in service.

2 If the hydraulic tappets become excessively noisy, their operation can be checked as described below.

3 Run the engine until it reaches its normal operating temperature. Switch off the engine, then refer to Section 7 and remove the camshaft cover.

4 Rotate the camshaft by turning the crankshaft with a socket and wrench, until the first cam lobe over No 1 cylinder is pointing upwards.

5 Using a feeler blade, measure the clearance between the base of the cam lobe and the top of the tappet. If the clearance is greater than 0.1mm, then the tappet is defective and must be renewed.

6 If the clearance is less than 0.1 mm, press down on the top of the tappet, until it is felt to contact the top of the valve stem. Use a wooden or plastic implement that will not damage the surface of the tappet.

7 If the tappet travels more than 1.0 mm before making contact, then it is defective and must be renewed.

8 Hydraulic tappet removal and refitting is described as part of the cylinder head overhaul sequence - see Chapter 2C for details.

⚠️ **Warning:** *After fitting hydraulic tappets, wait a minimum of 30 minutes (or leave overnight) before starting the engine, to allow the tappets time to settle, otherwise the pistons may strike the valve heads.*

13 Flywheel/driveplate - removal, inspection and refitting

General information

1 The mounting arrangement of the flywheel and clutch components depends on the type of transmission fitted.

2 On vehicles fitted with the 020 (5-speed) transmission, the clutch pressure plate is bolted directly to the end of the crankshaft. The flywheel is then bolted to the pressure plate. Removal of these components is therefore described in Chapter 6.

3 On vehicles fitted with the 020A, 085 (5-speed) and 084 (4-speed) transmission, the

14.10a Remove the engine mounting-to-transmission bellhousing bolts . . .

layout is more conventional; the flywheel is mounted on the crankshaft, with the pressure plate bolted to it. Removal of the flywheel is as described in Section 13 of Chapter 2A.

14 Engine mountings - inspection and renewal

Inspection

1 If improved access is required, raise the front of the car and support it securely on axle stands.

2 Check the mounting rubbers to see if they are cracked, hardened or separated from the metal at any point; renew the mounting if any such damage or deterioration is evident.

3 Check that all the mounting's fasteners are securely tightened; use a torque wrench to check if possible.

4 Using a large screwdriver or a crowbar, check for wear in the mounting by carefully levering against it to check for free play. Where this is not possible, enlist the aid of an assistant to move the engine/transmission back and forth, or from side to side, while you watch the mounting. While some free play is to be expected even from new components, excessive free play should be obvious. If excessive free play is found, check first that the fasteners are correctly secured, then renew any worn components as described below.

Renewal

Front engine mounting

5 Disconnect the battery negative cable, and position it away from the terminal.

6 Position a trolley jack underneath the engine, and position it such that the jack head is directly underneath the engine/bellhousing mating surface.

7 Raise the jack until it just takes the weight of the engine off the front engine mounting.

8 Slacken and withdraw the engine mounting through-bolt.

9 Refer to Chapter 5B and remove the starter motor.

10 Slacken and withdraw the engine mounting-to-transmission bellhousing bolts, and remove the bracket **(see illustrations)**.

14.10b . . . and remove the bracket

14.11 Remove the engine mounting block retaining screw

14.12 Lift the engine mounting block out of the crossmember cup

14.13 Lug (arrowed) on top of the mounting engages with the recess in the bracket

11 Working under the engine mounting front crossmember, remove the engine mounting block retaining screw **(see illustration)**.

12 Lift the engine mounting block out of the crossmember cup **(see illustration)**.

13 Refitting is a reversal of removal, noting the following points:

a) *Ensure that the orientation lug that protrudes from the top of surface of the engine mounting block engages with the recess in the mounting bracket* **(see illustration)**.

b) *Tighten all bolts to the specified torque.*

Rear right-hand engine mounting

14 Disconnect the battery negative cable, and position it away from the terminal.

15 Mount an engine lifting beam across the engine bay, and attach the jib to the engine lifting eyes on the cylinder head. Alternatively, an engine hoist can be used. Raise the hoist/lifting beam jib to take the weight of the engine off the engine mounting.

16 Slacken and withdraw the engine mounting through-bolt.

17 Unbolt the engine mounting bracket from the cylinder block.

18 Unbolt the engine mounting block from the body, and remove it from the engine bay.

19 Refitting is a reversal of removal, noting the following points:

a) *Ensure that the orientation lug that protrudes from the top of surface of the engine mounting block engages with the recess in the mounting bracket.*

b) *Tighten all bolts to the specified torque.*

Rear left-hand mounting

20 Disconnect the battery negative cable, and position it away from the terminal.

21 Position a trolley jack underneath the engine, and position it such that the jack head is directly underneath the engine/bellhousing mating surface.

22 Raise the jack until it just takes the weight of the engine off the rear right-hand engine mounting.

23 Slacken and withdraw the engine mounting through-bolt.

24 Unbolt the engine mounting bracket from the end of the transmission casing.

25 Unbolt the engine mounting block from the body, and remove it from the engine bay **(see illustration)**.

26 Refitting is a reversal of removal, noting the following points:

a) *Ensure that the orientation lug that protrudes from the top of surface of the engine mounting block engages with the recess in the mounting bracket.*

b) *Tighten all bolts to the specified torque.*

15 Sump - removal, inspection and refitting

Removal

1 Disconnect the battery negative cable, and position it away from the terminal. Refer to Chapter 1B and drain the engine oil. Where applicable, remove the screws and lower the engine undertray away from the vehicle.

2 Park the vehicle on a level surface, apply the handbrake and chock the rear wheels.

3 Raise the front of the vehicle, rest it securely on axle stands or wheel ramps; refer to *"Jacking and Vehicle Support"*.

4 To improve access to the sump, refer to Chapter 8 and disconnect the right-hand driveshaft from the transmission output flange.

5 Working around the outside of the sump, progressively slacken and withdraw the sump retaining bolts. Where applicable, unbolt and remove the flywheel cover plate from the

14.25 Removing the rear left-hand engine mounting

transmission to gain access to the left-hand sump fixings.

6 Break the joint by striking the sump with the palm of your hand, then lower the sump and withdraw it from underneath the vehicle. Recover and discard the sump gasket. Where a baffle plate is fitted, note that it can only be removed once the oil pump has been unbolted (see Section 16).

7 While the sump is removed, take the opportunity to check the oil pump pick-up/strainer for signs of clogging or disintegration. If necessary, remove the pump as described in Section 16, and clean or renew the strainer.

Refitting

8 Clean all traces of sealant from the mating surfaces of the cylinder block/crankcase and sump, then use a piece of clean rag to wipe out the sump.

9 Ensure that the sump and cylinder block/crankcase mating surfaces are clean and dry, then apply a coating of suitable sealant to the sump and crankcase mating surfaces.

10 Lay a new sump gasket in position on the sump mating surface, then offer up the sump and refit the retaining bolts. Tighten the nuts and bolts evenly and progressively to the specified torque.

11 Where applicable, refit the driveshaft, exhaust downpipe and engine undertray.

12 Refer to Chapter 1B and refill the engine with the specified grade and quantity of oil.

13 Restore the battery connection.

16 Oil pump and pickup - removal and refitting

General information

1 The oil pump and pickup are both mounted in the sump. Drive is taken from the intermediate shaft, which rotates at half crankshaft speed.

2 The oil pump arrangement is identical to that described for engine codes ADZ, ADY, 2E, ABF, AEK, AAM and ABS: refer to Chapter 2A for further details.

2B

Notes

Chapter 2 Part C:
Engine removal and overhaul procedures

Contents

Degrees of difficulty

Easy, suitable for novice with little experience	**Fairly easy,** suitable for beginner with some experience	**Fairly difficult,** suitable for competent DIY mechanic	**Difficult,** suitable for experienced DIY mechanic	**Very difficult,** suitable for expert DIY or professional

2C

Specifications

Engine codes
See Chapter 2A or B.

Cylinder head
Cylinder head gasket surface, maximum distortion:
  Engine codes ABF, ABD, AEA, ABU . . . . .0.05 mm
  Engine codes AAZ, 1Z, 1Y, AAM, ABS,
    2E, ADZ, ADY, AEK . . . . .0.1 mm
Minimum cylinder head height:
  Engine codes ABU, ABD, AEA . . . . .135.6 mm
  Engine codes AAM, ABS, ADZ, ADY, 2E, AEK . . . . .132.6 mm
  Engine code ABF . . . . .118.1 mm
  Engine codes AAZ, 1Y, 1Z . . . . .Head reworking not possible
Maximum swirl chamber projection
(engine codes 1Z, 1Y, AAZ) . . . . .0.07 mm

Cylinder head gasket
Identification markings (punched holes),
engine codes AAZ, 1Z and 1Y only*:
  Engine code 1Z:
    Piston projection:
      0.91 to 1.00 mm . . . . .1 hole
      1.01 to 1.10 mm . . . . .2 holes
      1.11 to 1.20 mm . . . . .3 holes
  Engine codes 1Y, AAZ:
    Piston projection:
      0.66 to 0.86 mm . . . . .1 hole
      0.87 to 0.90 mm . . . . .2 holes
      0.91 to 1.02 mm . . . . .3 holes

***Note:** See text in Chapter 2B and in
Sections 4 and 13 of this Chapter for details.*

Valves
Valve stem diameter:
  Inlet:
    Engine codes AAM, ADZ, ADY:
      Up to November 1994 . . . . .7.97 mm
      From December 1994 . . . . .6.92 ± 0.02 mm
    Engine codes 2E, ABS,1Y, 1Z, AAZ . . . . .7.97 mm
    Engine code AEK:
      Up to November 1994 . . . . .7.94 mm
      From December 1994 . . . . .6.92 ± 0.02 mm
    Engine code ABF . . . . .6.97 mm
    Engine code ABD:
      Up to July 1992 . . . . .7.965 mm
      From August 1992 . . . . .6.97 mm
    Engine codes ABU, AEA . . . . .6.963 mm
  Exhaust:
    Engine codes AAM, ADZ, ADY:
      Up to November 1994 . . . . .7.95 mm
      From December 1994 . . . . .6.92 ± 0.02 mm
    Engine codes 2E, ABS, 1Y, 1Z, AAZ . . . . .7.95 mm
    Engine code AEK:
      Up to November 1994 . . . . .7.95 mm
      From December 1994 . . . . .6.92 ± 0.02 mm
    Engine code ABF . . . . .6.94 mm
    Engine code ABD:
      Up to July 1992 . . . . .7.945 mm
      From August 1992 . . . . .6.95 mm
    Engine code ABU, AEA . . . . .6.943 mm

Valves (continued)

Maximum valve head deflection
(end of valve stem flush with top of guide):
  Inlet:
    Engine codes AAZ, 1Y, 1Z ....1.3 mm
    All other engine codes 1.0mm
  Exhaust:
    All engine codes ....1.3 mm
Valve spring free length:
  Standard ....N/A
  Service limit ....N/A
Valve spring squareness limit ....N/A

Camshaft

Maximum shaft runout ....N/A
Cam height:
  Inlet ....N/A
  Exhaust ....N/A
Endfloat, all engine codes ....0.15 mm
Maximum runout, all engine codes ....0.01 mm
Maximum running clearance:
  Engine code AAZ, 1Z, 1Y ....0.11 mm
  All other engine codes ....0.1 mm
Camshaft identification codes:
  Engine code ABF:
    Inlet 051 101, 051 101A
    Exhaust 051 102
  Engine code AEK ....D 048
  Engine code ABD:
    Up to September 1994 ....030 AH
    From October 1994 ....032 Q
  Engine code ABU 032
  Engine code AEA ....032 N, 032 P
  Engine code 1Z ....W 028F
  Engine codes AAZ, 1Y ....W 028D
  Engine code AAM ....M 026
  Engine codes ABS, ADZ ....Q 026
  Engine code 2E ....A 026
  Engine code ADY ....D 048

Intermediate shaft

Maximum endfloat:
  Engine codes ABF, ADZ, ADY, AAM, ABS, 2E, AEK ......0.25 mm

Cylinder block

Bore diameter:
  Engine code ABF, ADY, 2E:
    Standard ....82.51 mm
    1st oversize ....82.76 mm
    2nd oversize ....83.01 mm
    Maximum bore wear ....0.08 mm
  Engine codes ADZ, AAM, ABS:
    Standard ....81.01 mm
    1st oversize ....81.26 mm
    2nd oversize ....81.51 mm
    Maximum bore wear ....0.08 mm
  Engine codes AAZ, 1Y, 1Z:
    Standard ....79.51 mm
    1st oversize ....79.76 mm
    2nd oversize ....80.01 mm
    Maximum bore wear ....0.10 mm
  Engine code AEK:
    Standard ....81.01 mm
    1st oversize ....81.51 mm
    Maximum bore wear ....0.08 mm

Engine codes ABU, AEA:
  Standard ....76.51 mm
  1st oversize ....76.76 mm
  2nd oversize ....77.01 mm
  3rd oversize ....77.26 mm
  Maximum bore wear ....0.08 mm
Engine code ABD:
  Standard ....75.01 mm
  1st oversize ....75.26 mm
  2nd oversize ....75.51 mm
  3rd oversize ....75.76 mm
  Maximum bore wear ....0.08 mm

Pistons and piston rings

Piston diameter:
  Engine code ABF, ADY, 2E:
    Standard ....82.485 mm
    1st oversize ....82.735 mm
    2nd oversize ....82.985 mm
    Maximum deviation ....0.04 mm
  Engine codes ADZ, AAM, ABS:
    Standard ....80.985 mm
    1st oversize ....81.235 mm
    2nd oversize ....81.585 mm
    Maximum deviation ....0.04 mm
  Engine codes AAZ, 1Y:
    Standard ....79.48 mm
    1st oversize ....79.73 mm
    2nd oversize79.98 mm
    Maximum deviation ....0.04 mm
  Engine code 1Z:
    Standard79.47 mm
    1st oversize ....79.92 mm
    2nd oversize ....79.97 mm
    Maximum deviation ....0.04 mm
  Engine code AEK:
    Standard ....80.965 mm
    1st oversize ....81.485 mm
    Maximum deviation ....0.04 mm
  Engine codes ABU, AEA:
    Standard ....76.470 mm
    1st oversize ....76.720 mm
    2nd oversize ....76.970 mm
    3rd oversize ....77.220 mm
    Maximum deviation ....0.04 mm
  Engine code ABD:
    Standard ....74.985 mm
    1st oversize ....75.235 mm
    2nd oversize ....75.485 mm
    3rd oversize ....75.735 mm
    Maximum deviation ....0.04 mm
Gudgeon pin external diameter:
  Engine codes AAZ, 1Z ....26.0 mm
  Engine codes 1Y ....24.0 mm
  All other engine codes ....N/A
Piston ring-to-groove wall clearance:
  Engine code ABF:
    Top compression ring:
      Standard ....0.02 to 0.07 mm
      Service limit ....0.15 mm
    2nd compression ring:
      Standard ....0.02 to 0.07 mm
      Service limit ....0.15 mm
    Oil scraper ring:
      Standard ....0.02 to 0.06 mm
      Service limit ....0.15 mm

Pistons and piston rings (continued)

Engine codes ADZ, ADY, AAM, ABS, 2E:
    Top compression ring:
        Standard . . . . .0.02 to 0.05 mm
        Service limit . . . . .0.15 mm
    2nd compression ring:
        Standard . . . . .0.02 to 0.05 mm
        Service limit . . . . .0.15 mm
    Oil scraper ring:
        Standard . . . . .0.02 to 0.05 mm
        Service limit . . . . .0.15 mm
Engine code 1Z:
    Top compression ring:
        Standard . . . . .0.06 to 0.09 mm
        Service limit . . . . .0.25 mm
    2nd compression ring:
        Standard . . . . .0.05 to 0.08 mm
        Service limit . . . . .0.25 mm
    Oil scraper ring:
        Standard . . . . .0.03 to 0.06 mm
        Service limit . . . . .0.15 mm
Engine codes AAZ, 1Y:
    Top compression ring:
        Standard . . . . .0.09 to 0.12 mm
        Service limit . . . . .0.25 mm
    2nd compression ring:
        Standard . . . . .0.05 to 0.08 mm
        Service limit . . . . .0.25 mm
    Oil scraper ring:
        Standard . . . . .0.03 to 0.06 mm
        Service limit . . . . .0.15 mm
Engine code AEK:
    Top compression ring:
        Standard . . . . .0.02 to 0.05 mm
        Service limit . . . . .0.15 mm
    2nd compression ring:
        Standard . . . . .0.02 to 0.05 mm
        Service limit . . . . .0.15 mm
    Oil scraper ring:
        Standard . . . . .0.02 to 0.05 mm
        Service limit . . . . .0.15 mm
Engine codes ABU, ABD, AEA:
    Top compression ring:
        Standard . . . . .0.04 to 0.08 mm
        Service limit . . . . .0.15 mm
    2nd compression ring:
        Standard . . . . .0.04 to 0.08 mm
        Service limit . . . . .0.15 mm
    Oil scraper ring*:
        Standard . . . . .0.04 to 0.08 mm
        Service limit . . . . .0.15 mm
*Note: 3-part oil scraper ring: clearances not measurable.
Piston ring end gap:
    Engine codes ABF, ADZ, ADY, AAM, ABS, 2E, 1Z, AEK:
        Top compression ring:
             Standard . . . . .0.20 to 0.40 mm
             Service limit . . . . .1.0 mm
        2nd compression ring:
             Standard . . . . .0.20 to 0.40 mm
             Service limit . . . . .1.0 mm
        Oil scraper ring:
             Standard . . . . .0.25 to 0.50 mm
             Service limit . . . . .1.0 mm

Engine codes AAZ, 1Y:
    Top compression ring:
        Standard . . . . .0.20 to 0.40 mm
        Service limit . . . . .1.2 mm
    2nd compression ring:
        Standard . . . . .0.20 mm to 0.40 mm
        Service limit . . . . .0.6 mm
    Oil scraper ring:
        Standard . . . . .0.25 to 0.50 mm
        Service limit . . . . .1.2 mm
Engine codes ABU, AEA:
    Top compression ring:
        Standard . . . . .0.20 to 0.50 mm
        Service limit . . . . .1.0 mm
    2nd compression ring:
        Standard . . . . .0.40 to 0.70 mm
        Service limit . . . . .1.0 mm
    Oil scraper ring, single part:
        Standard . . . . .0.25 to 0.50 mm
        Service limit . . . . .1.0 mm
    Oil scraper ring, 3-part:
        Standard . . . . .0.40 to 1.40 mm
        Service limit . . . . .N/A
Engine code ABD:
    Top compression ring:
        Standard . . . . .0.20 to 0.50 mm
        Service limit . . . . .1.0 mm
    2nd compression ring:
        Standard . . . . .0.40 to 0.60 mm
        Service limit . . . . .1.0 mm
    Oil scraper ring, single part:
        Standard . . . . .0.25 to 0.50 mm
        Service limit . . . . .1.0 mm
    Oil scraper ring, 3-part:
        Standard . . . . .0.40 to 1.40 mm
        Service limit . . . . .N/A

Connecting rods

Length:
    Engine codes 1Z, AAZ . . . . .144 mm
    Engine code 1Y . . . . .150 mm
    All other engine codes . . . . .N/A
Big-end thrust clearance:
    Engine code ABF, ADZ, ADY, 2E, AAM, ABS, AEK:
        Standard . . . . .0.05 to 0.31 mm
        Service limit . . . . .0.37 mm
    Engine code AAZ, 1Y, 1Z:
        Standard . . . . .N/A
        Service limit . . . . .0.37 mm
    Engine codes ABU, ABD, AEA:
        Standard . . . . .N/A
        Service limit . . . . .N/A
Minimum big-end bearing shell pretension:
    Engine code ABD . . . . .0.5 mm
    Engine code ABU, AEA . . . . .1.5 mm
    All other engine codes . . . . .N/A

Crankshaft

Maximum shaft runout . . . . .N/A
Maximum endfloat:
    Engine codes ABF, ADZ, ADY, 2E, ABS, AAM, AEK:
        Standard . . . . .0.07 to 0.17 mm
        Service limit . . . . .0.25 mm
    Engine codes AAZ, 1Y, 1Z:
        Standard . . . . .0.07 to 0.17 mm
        Service limit . . . . .0.37 mm

Crankshaft (continued)

Maximum endfloat:
Engine codes ABD, AEA, ABU:
Standard ....0.07 to 0.18 mm
Service limit ....0.20 mm
Main bearing journal diameters:
All engine codes:
Standard ....54.00 mm
1st undersize ....53.75 mm
2nd undersize ....53.50 mm
3rd undersize ....53.25 mm
Tolerance:
Engine codes ABD, AEA, ABU ....-0.022 to -0.037 mm
All other engine codes ....-0.022 to -0.042 mm
Main bearing running clearances:
Engine codes ABF, AAM, ABS, ADZ, ADY, 2E, AEK:
Standard ....0.02 to 0.06 mm
Service limit ....0.17 mm
Engine codes AAZ, 1Y, 1Z, ABU, ABD, AEA:
Standard ....0.03 to 0.08 mm
Service limit ....0.17 mm
Crankpin journal diameters:
Engine code ABD:
Standard ....42.00 mm
1st undersize ....41.75 mm
2nd undersize ....41.50 mm
3rd undersize ....41.25 mm
Tolerance ....-0.020 to -0.035 mm
All other engine codes:
Standard ....47.80 mm
1st undersize ....47.55 mm
2nd undersize ....47.30 mm
3rd undersize ....47.05 mm

Tolerance:
Engine codes ABU, AEA ....-0.022 to -0.037 mm
All other engine codes ....-0.022 to -0.042 mm
Big-end running clearance:
Engine codes ABF, AAM, ABS, ADZ, ADY, 2E, AEK:
Standard ....0.01 to 0.06 mm
Service limit ....0.12 mm
Engine codes AAZ, 1Y, 1Z:
Standard ....N/A
Service limit ....0.08 mm
Engine code ABD:
Standard ....0.010 to 0.051 mm
Service limit ....0.095 mm
Engine code ABU, AEA:
Standard ....0.006 to 0.047 mm
Service limit ....0.091 mm

Oil pump

Gear backlash, all engine codes:
Standard ....0.05 mm
Service limit ....0.20 mm
Gear axial clearance, all engine codes:
Service limit 0.15mm
Drive chain tension (deflection),
engine codes ABU, ABD and AEA only:
Engine codes ABD to 12/93 and ABU to 01/93 ......2.0 to 3.0 mm
Engine codes ABD from 01/94 on,
ABU from 02/94 on and AEA:
Test limit ....4.0 to 5.0 mm
Adjustment setting ....3.5 to 4.5 mm

Torque wrench settings

	Nm	lbf ft
Big-end bearing caps bolts/nuts:		
Stage 1	30	22
Stage 2	Angle-tighten a further 90°	
Camshaft bearing cap nuts/bolts:		
Engine codes ABU, ABD, AEA:		
Stage 1	6	4
Stage 2	Angle-tighten a further 90°	
Engine code ABF	15	11
All other engine codes	20	15
Crankshaft main bearing cap bolts:		
Engine codes 1Y, AAZ, 1Z, ADZ, ADY, AEK:		
Stage 1	65	48
Stage 2	Angle-tighten a further 90°	
Engine codes AAM, ABS, 2E, ABF	65	48
Engine codes ABD, ABU, AEA:		
Bolts with full-length threads:		
Stage 1	65	48
Stage 2	Angle-tighten a further 90°	
Bolts with part-length threads	65	48
Engine crossmember-to-body bolts	50	37
Intermediate shaft flange bolts	25	18
Intermediate shaft sprocket bolt:		
Engine codes 1Y, AAZ, 1Z	45	33
Engine code ABF	65	48
All other engine codes	80	59
Lock carrier-to-chassis bolts	23	17
Lock carrier-to-wing screws	5	4
Piston oil jet/pressure relief valve	27	19
Transmission bellhousing to engine:		
M10 bolts (engine code ABD, ABU, AEA only)	45	33
M10 bolts (all other engine codes)	60	44
M12 bolts	80	59

1 Engine and transmission removal - preparation and precautions

If you have decided that the engine must be removed for overhaul or major repair work, several preliminary steps should be taken.

Locating a suitable place to work is extremely important. Adequate work space, along with storage space for the vehicle, will be needed. If a workshop or garage is not available, at the very least a solid, level, clean work surface is required.

If possible, clear some shelving close to the work area and use it to store the engine components and ancillaries as they are removed and dismantled. In this manner, the components stand a better chance of staying clean and undamaged during the overhaul. Laying out components in groups together with their fixings bolts, screws etc will save time and avoid confusion when the engine is refitted.

Clean the engine compartment and engine/transmission before beginning the removal procedure; this will help visibility and help to keep tools clean.

The help of an assistant should be available; there are certain instances when one person cannot safely perform all of the operations required to remove the engine from the vehicle. Safety is of primary importance, considering the potential hazards involved in this kind of operation. A second person should always be in attendance to offer help in an emergency. If this is the first time you have removed an engine, advice and aid from someone more experienced would also be beneficial.

Plan the operation ahead of time. Before starting work, obtain (or arrange for the hire of) all of the tools and equipment you will need. Access to the following items will allow the task of removing and refitting the engine/transmission to be completed safely and with relative ease: a heavy-duty trolley jack - rated in excess of the combined weight of the engine and transmission, complete sets of spanners and sockets as described in the front of this manual, wooden blocks, and plenty of rags and cleaning solvent for mopping up spilled oil, coolant and fuel. A selection of different sized plastic storage bins will also prove useful for keeping dismantled components grouped together. If any of the equipment must be hired, make sure that you arrange for it in advance, and perform all of the operations possible without it beforehand; this may save you time and money.

Plan on the vehicle being out of use for quite a while, especially if you intend to carry out an engine overhaul. Read through the whole of this Section and work out a strategy based on your own experience and the tools, time and workspace available to you. Some of the overhaul processes may have to carried out by a VAG dealer or an engineering works - these establishments often have busy schedules, so it would be prudent to consult them before removing or dismantling the engine, to get an idea of the amount of time required to carry out the work.

When removing the engine from the vehicle, be methodical about the disconnection of external components. Labelling cables and hoses as they are removed will greatly assist the refitting process.

Always be extremely careful when lifting the engine/transmission assembly from the engine bay. Serious injury can result from careless actions. If help is required, it is better to wait until it is available rather than risk personal injury and/or damage to components by continuing alone. By planning ahead and taking your time, a job of this nature, although major, can be accomplished successfully and without incident.

On all models described in this manual, the engine and transmission are removed as a complete assembly through the front of the vehicle. This involves the removal of the lock carrier, which is the panel assembly that forms the front of the engine bay. Although the lock carrier is a large assembly, its removal is not difficult, and the benefits in terms of ease of access are well worth the effort involved. It should be noted, however, that engine codes ABU, ABD and AEA can removed through the top of the engine bay, without removing the lock carrier, if required.

Note that the engine and transmission should ideally be removed with the vehicle standing on all four roadwheels, but access to the driveshafts and exhaust system downpipe will be improved if the vehicle can be temporarily raised onto axle stands.

2 Engine and transmission - removal, separation and refitting

Removal

All models

1 Select a solid, level surface to park the vehicle upon. Give yourself enough space to move around it easily.

2 Refer to Chapter 11 and remove the bonnet from its hinges.

3 Disconnect the battery negative cable, and position It away from the terminal. **Note:** *If the vehicle has a security-coded radio, check that you have a copy of the code number before disconnecting the battery cable; refer to Chapter 12 for details.*

4 With reference to Chapter 1A or B as applicable, carry out the following :

a) *If the engine is to be dismantled, drain the engine oil.*

b) *Drain the cooling system.*

c) *Where applicable, remove the auxiliary drive V-belt.*

d) *Remove the ribbed auxiliary drivebelt.*

5 Refer to Chapter 3 and perform the following:

a) *Slacken the clips and disconnect the radiator top and bottom hoses from the ports on the cylinder head, and from the thermostat housing/coolant pump (as applicable).*

b) *Disconnect the coolant hoses from the expansion tank and heater inlet and outlet ports at the bulkhead.*

6 On vehicles with air conditioning, refer to Chapter 3 and carry out the following additional operations:

a) *Unbolt the air conditioning fluid reservoir from its mountings, and allow it to rest on the engine front crossmember.*

b) *Remove the retaining bolts from the clips that secure the refrigerant condenser supply and return pipes to the engine crossmember.*

c) *Unbolt the air conditioning compressor from the engine, and allow it to rest on the engine front crossmember.*

7 Make reference to Chapter 11 and carry out the following:

a) *Remove the undertray from the underside of the engine.*

b) *Remove the screws and clips that secure the plastic inner wheel arch liners to the front valance.*

8 The "lock carrier" is a panel assembly comprising the front bumper moulding, radiator and grille, cooling fan(s) headlight units, front valance and bonnet lock mechanism. Its removal gives greatly-improved access to the engine and transmission, and allows them to be lifted out of the vehicle via the front of the engine bay. To remove the lock carrier, carry out the following:

a) *Unplug the wiring harness at the multiway connector. The connector is a bayonet fit; twist the housing to unlock the two halves, then pull them apart. Recover the internal seal if it has become loose and cover the connector housings with a plastic bag to prevent the ingress of dirt.. Release the harness from all the metal retaining clips.*

b) *Refer to Chapter 11 and detach the bonnet lock release cable form the lock mechanism.*

c) *Remove the lock carrier fixings at the following locations: two flange screws on the uppermost edge above the headlight units, four bolts (two on each side) behind fog lamp units/reflector panels, threaded into the ends of the chassis rails.*

d) *Lift the lock carrier assembly away from the front of the vehicle and rest it on a dust sheet; tilt the assembly forward as you remove it, to avoid spilling any coolant that may remain in the radiator.* **Note:** *On vehicles with air conditioning, the compressor remains connected to the refrigerant condenser by the supply and return hoses and is removed together with the lock carrier assembly.* **Caution: Take care to avoid kinking the air conditioning refrigerant hoses.**

2C

Petrol models

9 With reference to Chapter 4D, unplug the lambda sensor cabling from the main harness at the multiway connector.

10 Disconnect the ignition HT king lead from the centre terminal of the distributor cap, and tie it back away from the engine.

11 Refer to Chapter 9 and disconnect the brake servo vacuum hose from the port on the inlet manifold.

12 On vehicles with an Exhaust Gas Recirculation (EGR) system, refer to Chapter 4D and disconnect the vacuum hoses from the connection points on the EGR valve, brake servo vacuum hose, air inlet hose and where applicable, fuel injection pump. Make a careful note of the order of connection to ensure correct refitting.

13 On vehicles with an activated charcoal canister emission control system, refer to Chapter 4D and disconnect the vacuum hose from the port on the throttle body. Make a careful note of the point of connection to ensure correct refitting.

Single-point injection models

14 With reference to Chapter 4A, carry out the following operations:
  a) Depressurise the fuel system
  b) Remove the exhaust manifold-to-air cleaner and throttle body airbox-to-air cleaner ducting from the engine bay.
  c) Remove the airbox from the top of the throttle body; make a note of the vacuum hose connections to ensure correct refitting later.
  d) Disconnect the accelerator cable from the throttle spindle lever.
  e) Disconnect the fuel supply and return hoses from the throttle body - observe the precautions at the start of Chapter 4A.

Multipoint injection models

15 With reference to Chapter 4B, carry out the following operations:
  a) Depressurise the fuel system.
  b) Slacken the clips and remove the exhaust manifold-to-air cleaner and throttle body-to-airflow meter ducting from the engine bay.
  c) Disconnect the accelerator cable from the throttle spindle lever.
  d) Disconnect the fuel supply and return hoses from the throttle body - observe the precautions at the start of Chapter 4B.

16 On vehicles with automatic transmission, extra clearance is required when removing the engine and transmission as one assembly. Removing the ribbed auxiliary belt pulleys from the crankshaft and where applicable, coolant pump achieves this - see Chapter 2A.

Diesel models

 Warning: When dismantling any part of the air inlet system on a turbocharged vehicle, ensure that no foreign material can get into the turbo air inlet port; cover the opening with a sheet of plastic, secured with an elastic band. The turbocharger compressor blades could be severely damaged if debris is allowed to enter.

17 Refer to Chapter 9 and disconnect the brake servo vacuum hose from the vacuum pump on the cylinder block.

18 On vehicles with an Exhaust Gas Recirculation (EGR) system, refer to Chapter 4D and disconnect the vacuum hoses from the connection points on the EGR valve, brake servo vacuum hose, air inlet hose and where applicable, fuel injection pump. Make a careful note of the order of connection to ensure correct refitting.

19 Refer to Chapter 4C and carry out the following operations:
  a) Slacken and withdraw the banjo bolts, then disconnect the fuel supply and return hoses from the fuel injection pump.
  b) Release the clip, then disconnect the injector bleed hose from the port on the fuel return union.

Engine codes AAZ, 1Y
  c) Slacken the clips and remove the inlet air hose from the air cleaner, crankcase ventilation hose and inlet manifold (engine code 1Y) or turbocharger inlet (engine code AAZ) as applicable.
  d) Disconnect the accelerator cable from the fuel injection pump.
  e) Where applicable, disconnect the cold start accelerator cable from the fuel injection pump.

Engine code 1Z
  f) Slacken the clips and remove the inlet air hose from the air mass meter, turbocharger inlet and crankcase ventilation hose.
  g) Slacken the clips and remove the supply and return inlet air hoses that run from the turbocharger to the intercooler and back. It will be necessary to unplug the cabling from the inlet air temperature sensor at the connector.
  h) Disconnect the vacuum control hose from the port on the boost pressure control diaphragm, at the side of the turbocharger; refer to Chapter 4D for greater details.

All models

20 Isolate the main engine harness from the vehicle at the connector, which is mounted on a bracket at transmission end of the cylinder block. The connector is a bayonet fit; twist the housing to unlock the two halves, then pull them apart. Recover the internal seal if it has become loose. Cover the connector housings with a plastic bag to prevent the ingress of dirt **(see illustration)**.

21 Refer to Chapter 5A and disconnect the wiring from the alternator, starter motor and solenoid.

22 With reference to Chapter 5B and Chapter 4A, B or C as applicable, identify those sections of the ignition and fuelling system electrical harness that remain

2.20 Main engine harness connector

connected to sensors and actuators on the engine, that are not part of the main engine harness. These sections will not be isolated at the engine harness connector, and must be disconnected individually. Label each connector carefully to ensure correct refitting.

23 On vehicles with power steering, refer to Chapter 10 and carry out the following:
  a) Slacken the retaining screws and release the clips that secure the power steering supply and return pipes to the engine front crossmember.
  b) Remove the power steering fluid reservoir retaining screws and lower it away from the battery tray, allowing it to rest on the engine crossmember.
  c) Unbolt the power steering pump, together with its mounting brackets from the engine and hang it from the engine crossmember using wire or a large cable-tie. **Note:** The power steering hoses can remain connected to the pump and reservoir, so there is no need to drain the hydraulic fluid from the system.

24 On manual transmission models, refer to Chapter 7A and carry out the following:
  a) At the top of the transmission casing, disconnect the wiring from the speedometer drive transducer and reversing light switch.
  b) Disconnect the gear selection mechanism from the transmission.
  c) Vehicles with a cable operated clutch: Refer to Chapter 6 and disconnect the clutch cable from the release mechanism at the front of the transmission casing.
  d) Vehicles with a hydraulically operated clutch: With reference to Chapter 6, remove the clutch slave cylinder from the transmission casing.

25 On automatic transmission models, refer to Chapter 7B and carry out the following:
  a) Release the selector cable from the selector lever at the top of the transmission casing.
  b) Clamp the coolant hoses leading to the transmission fluid cooler, then release the clips and disconnect the hoses from the cooler ports.
  c) Unplug the wiring harness from the transmission at the connectors; label each connector to aid refitting later.

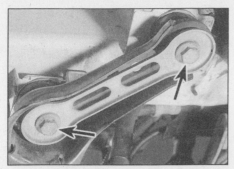

2.32 Front crossmember mounting bolts (left-hand side shown)

2.33 Car supported on stands, with engine and transmission removed

26 Refer to Chapter 8 and separate the driveshafts from the transmission differential output shafts.

27 With reference to Chapter 4D, unbolt the exhaust down pipe from the exhaust manifold (or turbocharger on engine codes AAZ and 1Z). Recover and discard the gasket.

28 Unbolt the engine and transmission earthing straps from the bodywork.

29 With reference to Chapter 2A, slacken and withdraw the through-bolts from all three engine mountings.

30 Attach the jib of an engine lifting beam or hoist to the lifting eyelets at the front of the cylinder head. Raise the jib slightly and tilt the engine towards the rear of the engine bay, so that the front engine mounting is raised above the front crossmember.

31 Unscrew the retaining bolts and withdraw the starter motor; refer to Chapter 5A for greater detail. Remove the front engine mounting bracket.

32 Working under the front of the vehicle, slacken and withdraw the retaining bolts, then lower the front crossmember to the ground, together with the power steering pump. Remove the retaining bolt from underneath, and extract the engine mounting rubber block **(see illustration)**.

33 Carry out a final check to ensure that nothing else remains connected to the engine, then slowly wheel the hoist back from the vehicle, and manoeuvre the engine and transmission out through the front of the engine bay. Rotate the assembly slightly as it is withdrawn, so that the timing belt end of the engine emerges first. Guide the pulleys past the inner wing to avoid damaging the paintwork **(see illustration)**.

Separation

34 Rest the engine and transmission assembly on a firm, flat surface, and use wooden blocks as wedges to keep the unit steady.

Manual transmission

35 The transmission is secured to the engine by a combination of machine screws and studs, threaded into the cylinder block and bellhousing - the total number of fixings depends on the type of transmission and vehicle specification. Note that two of these

fixings also serve as mountings for the starter motor and the front engine mounting.

36 Starting at the bottom, remove all the screws and nuts then carefully draw the transmission away from the engine, resting it securely on wooden blocks. Collect the locating dowels if they are loose enough to be extracted. *Caution: Take care to prevent the transmission from tilting, until the input shaft is fully disengaged from the clutch friction plate.*

37 Refer to Chapter 6, and remove the clutch release mechanism, pressure plate and friction plate.

Automatic transmission

38 Unbolt the skid plate from the underside of the transmission oil pan.

39 Unbolt the protection plate from the bottom of the transmission bellhousing, this will expose the rear face of the driveplate.

40 Mark the position of the torque converter with respect to the driveplate, using chalk or a marker pen. Remove the three nuts that secure the driveplate to the torque converter; turn the engine over using a socket and wrench on the crankshaft sprocket to rotate the driveplate and expose each nut in turn.

41 The transmission is secured to the engine by a combination of machine screws and studs with nuts, threaded into the cylinder block and bellhousing - the total number of fixings depends on the type of transmission and vehicle specification. Note that two of these fixings also serve as mountings for the starter motor.

42 Starting at the bottom, remove all the screws and nuts then carefully draw the transmission away from the engine, resting it securely on wooden blocks. Collect the locating dowels if they are loose enough to be extracted. *Caution: Take care to prevent the torque converter from sliding off the transmission input shaft - hold it in place as the transmission is withdrawn.*

43 Place a length of batten across the open face of the bellhousing, fastening it with cable-ties, to keep the torque converter in place in its housing.

Refitting

44 If the engine and transmission have not been separated, go to paragraph 50.

Manual transmission

45 Smear a little high-melting-point grease on the splines of the transmission input shaft. Do not use an excessive amount as there is the risk of contaminating the clutch friction plate. Carefully offer up the transmission to the cylinder block, guiding the dowels into the mounting holes in cylinder block.

46 Refit the bellhousing bolts and nuts, hand tightening them to secure the transmission in position. **Note:** *Do not tighten them to force the engine and transmission together.* Ensure that the bellhousing and cylinder block mating faces will butt together evenly without obstruction, before tightening the bolts and nuts to their specified torque.

Automatic transmission

47 Remove the torque converter restraint from the face of the bellhousing. Check that the drive lugs on the torque converter hub are correctly engaged with the recesses in the inner wheel of the automatic transmission fluid pump.

48 Carefully offer up the transmission to the cylinder block, guiding the dowels into the mounting holes in cylinder block. Observe the markings made during the removal, to ensure correct alignment between the torque converter and the driveplate.

49 Refit the bellhousing bolts and nuts, hand-tightening them to secure the transmission in position. **Note:** *Do not tighten them to force the engine and transmission together.* Ensure that the bellhousing and cylinder block mating faces will butt together evenly without obstruction, before tightening the bolts and nuts to their specified torque.

All models

50 With reference to Chapter 5A, refit the starter motor, together with the front engine mounting bracket and tighten the retaining bolts to the specified torque.

51 Attach the jib of an engine hoist to the lifting eyelets on the cylinder head, and raise the engine and transmission from the ground.

52 Wheel the hoist up to the front of the vehicle and with the help of an assistant, guide the engine and transmission in through the front of the engine bay. Rotate the assembly slightly so that the transmission casing enters first, then guide the auxiliary belt pulleys past the bodywork.

53 Align the rear engine mounting brackets with the mounting points on the body. Note that alignment lugs protrude from the metal discs that are bonded to the top of each of each engine mounting; these must engage with the recesses on the underside of the engine mounting brackets (Chapter 2A or 2B).

54 Lift the front engine mounting crossmember into position. Apply a little clean engine oil to the threads of the retaining bolts, then insert and tighten them to the correct torque. *Caution: Ensure that no weight bears on the crossmember until the bolts are tightened.*

2C

55 Fit the front engine mounting rubber block into the cup in the crossmember, then insert the retaining bolt through the underside of the crossmember and tighten it to the specified torque.

56 Lower the engine and transmission into position, ensuring that the locating lugs on the front engine mounting engage with the recess in the mounting bracket. Insert the front and rear engine mounting through-bolts, tightening them by hand initially.

57 Detach the engine hoist jib from the lifting eyelets.

58 Settle the engine and transmission assembly on its mountings by rocking it backwards and forwards, then tighten the mounting through-bolts to the specified torque.

59 Refer to Chapter 8 and reconnect the driveshafts to the transmission.

60 The remainder of the refitting sequence is the direct reverse of the removal procedure, noting the following points:

a) *Ensure that all sections of the wiring harness follow their original routing; use new cable-ties to secure the harness in position, keeping it away from sources of heat and abrasion.*

b) *On vehicles with manual transmission, refer to Chapter 7A and reconnect the gear shift mechanism to the transmission, then check the overall operation of the gear shift mechanism. If necessary, adjust the gear shift rod/cables.* **Note:** *On engine codes ABU, ABD and AEA with manual transmission, refer to the notes in Chapter 7A on renewal of the locking screw on the selector rod shift finger.*

c) *On vehicles with a hydraulically-operated clutch, refer to Chapter 6 and refit the slave cylinder, then bleed the clutch hydraulic system.*

d) *On vehicles with a cable-operated clutch, refer to Chapter 6 and reconnect the cable to the transmission, then check the operation of the automatic adjustment mechanism.*

e) *On vehicles with automatic transmission, refer to Chapter 7B and reconnect the selector cable to the transmission, then check (and if necessary adjust) the overall operation of the gear selection mechanism.*

f) *Refer to Chapter 11 and refit the lock carrier assembly to the front of the vehicle; ensure that all wiring harness connections are remade correctly and tighten the retaining fixings to the specified torque.*

g) *Ensure that all hoses are correctly routed and are secured with the correct hose clips, where applicable. If the hose clips originally fitted were of the crimp variety, they cannot be used again; proprietary worm drive clips must be fitted in their place, unless otherwise specified.*

h) *Refill the cooling system as described in Chapter 1A or B.*

i) *Refill the engine with appropriate grades and quantities of oil (Chapter 1A or B).*

Diesel models

j) *Engine codes 1Y and AAZ: with reference to Chapter 4D, after reconnecting the cold start accelerator cable to fuel injection pump, check and if necessary adjust the operation of the cold start acceleration system.*

Petrol models

k) *With reference to Chapter 4A or B as applicable, reconnect the throttle cable and adjust it as necessary.*

l) *With reference to Chapter 5B, check and adjust the engine idle speed and where applicable, the ignition timing.*

All models

61 When the engine is started for the first time, check for air, coolant, lubricant and fuel leaks from manifolds, hoses etc. If the engine has been overhauled, read the notes in Section 14 before attempting to start it.

3 Engine overhaul - preliminary information

It is much easier to dismantle and work on the engine if it is mounted on a portable engine stand. These stands can often be hired from a tool hire shop. Before the engine is mounted on a stand, the flywheel should be removed, so that the stand bolts can be tightened into the end of the cylinder block/ crankcase.

If a stand is not available, it is possible to dismantle the engine with it blocked up on a sturdy workbench, or on the floor. Be very careful not to tip or drop the engine when working without a stand.

If you intend to obtain a reconditioned engine, all ancillaries must be removed first, to be transferred to the replacement engine (just as they will if you are doing a complete engine overhaul yourself). These components include the following:

Petrol engines

a) *Power steering pump (Chapter 10) - where applicable.*

b) *Air conditioning compressor (Chapter 3) - where applicable.*

c) *Alternator (including mounting brackets)and starter motor (Chapter 5A).*

d) *The ignition system and HT components including all sensors, distributor, HT leads and spark plugs (Chapters 1 and 5).*

e) *The fuel injection system components (Chapter 4A and B)*

f) *All electrical switches, actuators and sensors, and the engine wiring harness (Chapter 4A and B, Chapter 5B).*

g) *Inlet and exhaust manifolds (Chapter 2C).*

h) *Engine oil dipstick and tube (Chapter 2C)*

i) *Engine mountings (Chapter 2A and B).*

j) *Flywheel/driveplate (Chapter 2C).*

k) *Clutch components (Chapter 6) - manual transmission.*

Diesel engines

a) *Power steering pump (Chapter 10) - where applicable.*

b) *Air conditioning compressor (Chapter 3) - where applicable.*

c) *Alternator (including mounting brackets)and starter motor (Chapter 5A).*

d) *The glow plug/pre-heating system components (Chapter 4D).*

e) *All fuel system components, including the fuel injection pump, all sensors and actuators (Chapter 4C)*

f) *The vacuum pump (Chapter 2B).*

g) *All electrical switches, actuators and sensors, and the engine wiring harness (Chapter 4A and B, Chapter 5B).*

h) *Inlet and exhaust manifolds and where applicable, the turbocharger (Chapter 2C).*

i) *The engine oil level dipstick and its tube (Chapter 2C)*

j) *Engine mountings (Chapter 2A and B).*

k) *Flywheel/driveplate (Chapter 2C).*

l) *Clutch components (Chapter 6) - manual transmission.*

Note: *When removing the external components from the engine, pay close attention to details that may be helpful or important during refitting. Note the fitted position of gaskets, seals, spacers, pins, washers, bolts, and other small components.*

If you are obtaining a "short" engine (the engine cylinder block/ crankcase, crankshaft, pistons and connecting rods, all fully assembled), then the cylinder head, sump and baffle plate, oil pump, timing belt (together with its tensioner and covers), auxiliary belt (together with its tensioner), coolant pump, thermostat housing, coolant outlet elbows, oil filter housing and where applicable oil cooler will also have to be removed.

If you are planning a full overhaul, the engine can be dismantled in the order given below:

a) *Inlet and exhaust manifolds.*

b) *Timing belt, sprockets and tensioner.*

c) *Cylinder head.*

d) *Flywheel/driveplate.*

e) *Sump.*

f) *Oil pump.*

g) *Piston/connecting rod assemblies.*

h) *Crankshaft.*

4 Cylinder head - dismantling, cleaning, inspection and assembly

Note: *New and reconditioned cylinder heads are available from VW, and from engine specialists. Specialist tools are required for the dismantling and inspection procedures, and new components may not be readily available. It may, therefore, be more practical for the home mechanic to buy a reconditioned head, rather than to dismantle, inspect and recondition the original head.*

When dealing with the DOHC engine (engine code ABF), the operations described

4.6 Keep groups of components together in labelled bags or boxes

in this Section are equally applicable to both the inlet and exhaust camshafts, unless specifically stated otherwise.

Dismantling

1 Remove the cylinder head from the engine block, and separate the inlet and exhaust manifolds from it (Part A or B of this Chapter).

2 On diesel models, remove the injectors and glow plugs (see Chapter 4C and Chapter 5C).

3 Refer to Chapter 3 and remove the coolant outlet elbow together with its gasket/O-ring.

4 Where applicable, unscrew the coolant sensor and oil pressure switch from the cylinder head.

5 Remove the timing belt sprocket from the camshaft (Part A or B of this Chapter).

6 It is important that groups of components are kept together when they are removed and, if still serviceable, refitted in the same groups. If they are refitted randomly, accelerated wear leading to early failure will occur. Stowing groups of components in plastic bags or storage bins will help to keep everything in the right order - label them according to their fitted location, eg 'No 1 exhaust', 'No 2 inlet', etc **(see illustration)**. (Note that No 1 cylinder is nearest the timing belt end of the engine.)

7 Check that the manufacturer's identification markings are visible on camshaft bearing caps; if none can be found, make your own using a scriber or centre-punch.

8 The camshaft bearing cap nuts must be removed progressively and in sequence to avoid stressing the camshaft, as follows.

Engine codes AAZ, 1Y, 1Z (diesels), ABU, AEA, ABD and AEK

9 Slacken the nuts from bearing caps Nos 5, 1 and 3 first, then at bearing caps 2 and 4. Slacken the nuts alternately and diagonally half a turn at a time until they can be removed by hand. **Note:** *Camshaft bearing caps are numbered 1 to 5 from the timing belt end.*

Engine codes ADZ, ADY, AAM, ABS and 2E

10 Slacken and remove the retaining nuts from bearing caps Nos 1 and 3 first, then at bearing caps 2 and 5. Slacken the nuts alternately and diagonally half a turn at a time until they can be removed by hand. **Note:** *Camshaft bearing caps are numbered 1 to 5 from the timing belt end - there is no bearing cap fitted at cylinder No 4 (see illustration).*

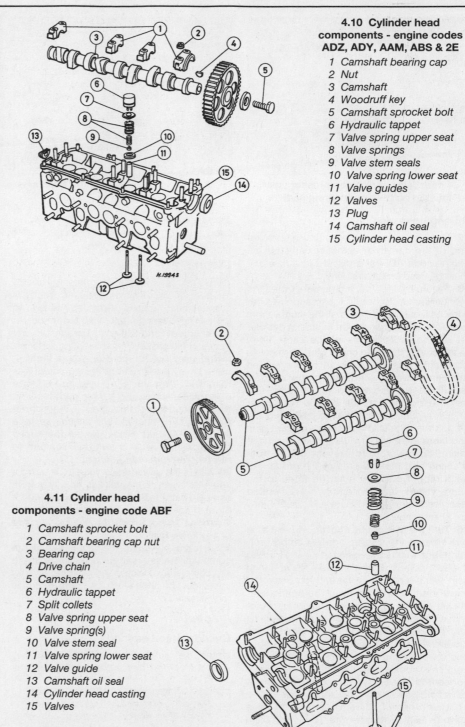

4.10 Cylinder head components - engine codes ADZ, ADY, AAM, ABS & 2E

1 Camshaft bearing cap
2 Nut
3 Camshaft
4 Woodruff key
5 Camshaft sprocket bolt
6 Hydraulic tappet
7 Valve spring upper seat
8 Valve springs
9 Valve stem seals
10 Valve spring lower seat
11 Valve guides
12 Valves
13 Plug
14 Camshaft oil seal
15 Cylinder head casting

4.11 Cylinder head components - engine code ABF

1 Camshaft sprocket bolt
2 Camshaft bearing cap nut
3 Bearing cap
4 Drive chain
5 Camshaft
6 Hydraulic tappet
7 Split collets
8 Valve spring upper seat
9 Valve spring(s)
10 Valve stem seal
11 Valve spring lower seat
12 Valve guide
13 Camshaft oil seal
14 Cylinder head casting
15 Valves

Engine code ABF

11 At the inlet camshaft, slacken and remove the retaining nuts from bearing caps 5 and 7 plus the additional cap adjacent to the drive chain sprocket, then at bearing caps 6 and 8. Slacken the nuts alternately and diagonally half a turn at a time until they can be removed by hand. At the exhaust camshaft, slacken and remove the retaining nuts from bearing caps 1 and 3 plus the additional caps adjacent to the drive chain and timing belt sprockets, then at bearing caps 2 and 4. Slacken the nuts alternately and diagonally half a turn at a time until they can be removed by hand. **Note:** *The exhaust camshaft bearing caps are numbered 1 to 4 from timing belt end - inlet camshaft bearing caps are numbered 5 to 8 from the same end (see illustration).*

2C

4.15a Valve spring compressor jaws located on the upper spring seat . . .

4.15b . . . and on the valve head

4.18 Swirl chamber removal (diesel models)

All engine codes

12 Slide the oil seal from the timing sprocket end of the camshaft (exhaust camshaft on engine code ABF) and discard it; a new one must be used on reassembly.

13 Carefully lift the camshaft from the cylinder head; do not tilt it and support both ends as it is removed so that the journals and lobes are not damaged. On engine code ABF, lift out both camshafts at the same time, together with the drive chain. Mark the chain's direction of rotation, to ensure that it is refitted the same way around, when the head is rebuilt later - use a dab of paint for this purpose, do not mark the chain with a scriber or centre-punch as this will risk damaging it.

14 Lift the hydraulic tappets from their bores and store them with the valve contact surface facing downwards, to prevent the oil from draining out. Make a note of the position of each tappet, as they must be fitted to the same valves on reassembly - accelerated wear leading to early failure will result if they are interchanged.

15 Turn the cylinder head over, and rest it on one side. Using a valve spring compressor, compress each valve spring in turn, extracting the split collets when the upper valve spring seat has been pushed far enough down the valve stem to free them. If the spring seat sticks, tap the upper jaw of the compressor with a hammer to free it **(see illustrations)**.

16 Release the valve spring compressor and remove the upper spring seat, valve spring(s) and lower spring seat. **Note:** *Depending on age and specification, engines may have concentric double valve springs, or single valve springs with no lower spring seat.*

17 Use a pair of pliers to extract the valve stem oil seal. Withdraw the valve itself from the head gasket side of the cylinder head. If the valve sticks in the guide, carefully deburr the end face with fine abrasive paper. Repeat this process for the remaining valves.

18 On diesel models, if the swirl chambers are badly coked or burned and are in need of renewal, insert a pin punch through each injector hole, and carefully drive out the swirl chambers using a mallet **(see illustration)**. **Note:** *On diesel models up to October 1993 with a fibre head gasket, a metal head gasket must be used on reassembly - under these*

circumstances, new swirl chambers **must** be fitted to match the new type of gasket - refer to Chapter 2B for greater detail.

Cleaning

19 Using a suitable degreasing agent, remove all traces of oil deposits from the cylinder head, paying particular attention to the journal bearings, hydraulic tappet bores, valve guides and oilways. Scrape off any traces of old gasket from the mating surfaces, taking care not to score or gouge them. If using emery paper, do not use a grade of less than 100. Turn the head over and using a blunt blade, scrape any carbon deposits from the combustion chambers and ports. **Caution: Do not erode the sealing surface of the valve seat. Finally, wash the entire head casting with a suitable solvent to remove the remaining debris.**

20 Clean the valve heads and stems using a fine wire brush. If the valve is heavily coked, scrape off the majority of the deposits with a blunt blade first, then use the wire brush. **Caution: Do not erode the sealing surface of the valve face.**

21 Thoroughly clean the remainder of the components using solvent and allow them to dry completely. Discard the oil seals, as new items must be fitted when the cylinder head is reassembled.

Inspection

Cylinder head casting

Note: *On diesel engines (engine codes 1Z, 1Y, AAZ) the cylinder heads and valves cannot be*

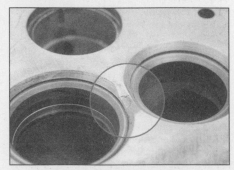

4.22 Look for cracking between the valve seats

reworked (although valves may be lapped in); new or exchange units must be obtained.

22 Examine the head casting closely to identify any damage sustained or cracks that may have developed **(see illustration)**. Pay particular attention to the areas around the mounting holes, valve seats and spark plug holes. If cracking is discovered between the valve seats, Volkswagen state that the cylinder head may be re-used, provided the cracks are no larger than 0.5 mm wide. More serious damage will mean the renewal of the cylinder head casting.

23 Moderately pitted and scorched valve seats can be repaired by lapping the valves in during reassembly, as described later in this Chapter. Badly worn or damaged valve seats may be restored by recutting; this is a highly specialised operation involving precision machining and accurate angle measurement and as such should be entrusted to a professional cylinder head re-builder.

24 Measure any distortion of the gasketed surfaces using a straight edge and a set of feeler blades. Take one measurement longitudinally on both the inlet and exhaust manifold mating surfaces. Take several measurements across the head gasket surface, to assess the level of distortion in all planes **(see illustration)**. Compare the measurements with the figures in the Specifications. On petrol engines, if the head is distorted out of specification, it may be possible to repair it by smoothing down any high-spots on the surface with fine abrasive paper.

25 Minimum cylinder head heights (measured

4.24 Measuring the distortion of the cylinder head gasketed surface

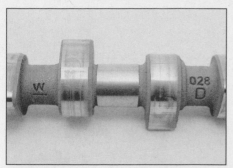

4.26 Camshaft identification markings

4.30 Checking camshaft endfloat using a DTI gauge

between the cylinder head gasket surface and the cylinder head cover gasket surface), where quoted by the manufacturer, are listed in Specifications. If the cylinder head is to be professionally machined, bear in mind the following:

a) *The minimum cylinder head height dimension (where specified) must be adhered to.*

b) *The valve seats will need to be recut to suit the new height of the cylinder head, otherwise valve to piston crown contact may occur.*

c) *Before the valve seats can be recut, check that there is enough material left on the cylinder head to allow repair; if too much material is removed, the valve stem may protrude too far above the top of the valve guide and this would prevent the hydraulic tappets from operating correctly. Refer to a professional head rebuilder or machine shop for advice.* **Note:** *Depending on engine type, it may be possible to obtain new valves with shorter valve stems - refer to your VAG dealer for advice.*

Camshaft

26 The camshaft is identified by means of markings stamped onto the side of the shaft, between the inlet and exhaust lobes - refer to Specifications for details **(see illustration)**.

27 Visually inspect the camshaft for evidence of wear on the surfaces of the lobes and journals. Normally their surfaces should be smooth and have a dull shine; look for scoring, erosion or pitting and areas that appear highly polished - these are signs that wear has begun to occur. Accelerated wear will occur once the hardened exterior of the camshaft has been damaged, so always renew worn items. **Note:** *If these symptoms are visible on the tips of the camshaft lobes, check the corresponding tappet, as it will probably be worn as well.*

28 Where applicable, examine the distributor drive gear for signs of wear or damage. Slack in the drive caused by worn gear teeth will affect ignition timing.

29 If the machined surfaces of the camshaft appear discoloured or "blued", it is likely that it has been overheated at some point, probably due to inadequate lubrication. This

may have distorted the shaft, so check the runout as follows: place the camshaft between two V-blocks and using a DTI gauge, measure the runout at the centre journal. A maximum runout figure is not quoted by the manufacturer, but use 0.1 mm as a rough guide. If it exceeds this figure, camshaft renewal should be considered.

30 To measure the camshaft endfloat, temporarily refit the camshaft to the cylinder head, then fit the first and last bearing caps and tighten the retaining nuts to the specified first stage torque setting (on engine codes ABD, ABU and AEA, only fit the third bearing cap) - refer to "Reassembly" for details. Anchor a DTI gauge to the timing pulley end of the cylinder head and align the gauge probe with the camshaft axis. Push the camshaft to one end of the cylinder head as far as it will travel, then rest the DTI gauge probe on the end of the camshaft, and zero the gauge display. Push the camshaft as far as it will go to the other end of the cylinder head, and record the gauge reading. Verify the reading by pushing the camshaft back to its original position and checking that the gauge indicates zero again **(see illustration)**. **Note:** *The hydraulic tappets must not be fitted to the cylinder whilst this measurement is being taken.*

31 Check that the camshaft endfloat measurement is within the limit listed in the Specifications. Wear outside of this limit is unlikely to be confined to any one component, so renewal of the camshaft, cylinder head and bearing caps must be considered; seek the advice of a cylinder head rebuilding specialist.

32 The difference between the outside diameters of the camshaft bearing surfaces and the internal diameters formed by the bearing caps and the cylinder head must now be measured, this dimension is known as the camshaft "running clearance".

33 The dimensions of the camshaft bearing journals are not quoted by the manufacturer, so running clearance measurement by means of a micrometer and a bore gauge or internal vernier calipers cannot be recommended in this case.

34 Another (more accurate) method of measuring the running clearance involves the use of Plastigage. This is a soft, plastic

material supplied in thin "sticks" of about the same diameter as a sewing needle. Lengths of Plastigage are cut to length as required, laid on the camshaft bearing journals and crushed as the bearing caps are temporarily fitted and tightened. The Plastigage spreads widthways as it is crushed; the running clearance can then be determined by measuring the increase in width using the card gauge supplied with the Plastigage kit.

35 The following paragraphs describe this measurement procedure step by step, but note that a similar method is used to measure the crankshaft running clearances; refer to the illustrations in Section 11 for further guidance.

36 Ensure that the cylinder head, bearing cap and camshaft bearing surfaces are completely clean and dry. Lay the camshaft in position in the cylinder head.

37 Lay a length of Plastigage on top of each of the camshaft bearing journals.

38 Lubricate each bearing cap with a little silicone release agent, then place them in position over the camshaft and tighten the retaining nuts down to the specified torque - refer to *Reassembly* later in this Section for guidance. **Note:** *Where the torque setting is expressed in several stages, tighten the cap fixings to the first stage only. Do not rotate the camshaft whilst the bearing caps are in place, as the measurements will be affected.*

39 Carefully remove the bearing caps again, lifting them vertically away from the camshaft to avoid disturbing the Plastigage. The Plastigage should remain on the camshaft bearing surface, squashed into a uniform sausage shape. If it disintegrates as the bearing caps are removed, re-clean the components and repeat the exercise, using a little more release agent on the bearing cap.

40 Hold the scale card supplied with the kit against each bearing journal, and match the width of the crushed Plastigage with the graduated markings on the card, use this to determine the running clearances.

41 Compare the camshaft running clearance measurements with those listed in the Specifications; if any are outside the specified tolerance, the camshaft and cylinder head should be renewed. Note that undersize camshafts with bearing shells may be obtained from VAG dealers, but only as part of an exchange cylinder head package.

42 On engine code ABF, running clearance measurements must be carried out on both camshafts.

43 On completion, remove the bearing caps and camshaft, and clean of all remaining traces of Plastigage and silicone release agent.

Valves and associated components

Note: *On all engines, the valve heads cannot be re-cut (although they may be lapped in); new or exchange units must be obtained.*

44 Examine each valve closely for signs of wear. Inspect the valve stems for wear ridges, scoring or variations in diameter; measure

2C

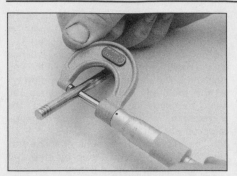

4.44 Measure the diameter of a valve stem with a micrometer

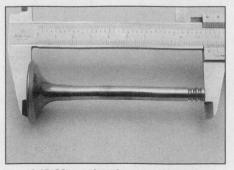

4.45 Measuring the overall length of a valve

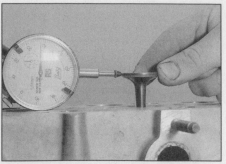

4.49 Measure the maximum deflection of the valve in its guide, using a DTI gauge

their diameters at several points along their lengths with a micrometer **(see illustration)**.
45 Check the overall length of each valve, and compare the measurements with the figure in the Specifications **(see illustration)**.
46 The valve heads should not be cracked, badly pitted or charred. Note that light pitting of the valve head can be rectified by grinding-in the valves during reassembly, as described later in this Section. Measure the valve head diameter using a micrometer; the valve cannot be re-used if this dimension is too small.
47 Check that the valve stem end face is free from excessive pitting or indentation; this would be caused by defective hydraulic tappets.
48 Place the valves in a V-block and using a DTI gauge, measure the runout at the valve head. A maximum figure is not quoted by the manufacturer, but the valve should be renewed if the runout appears excessive.
49 Insert each valve into its respective guide in the cylinder head and set up a DTI gauge against the edge of the valve head. With the valve end face flush with the top of the valve guide, measure the maximum side to side deflection of the valve in its guide **(see illustration)**. If the measurement is out of tolerance, the valve and valve guide should be renewed as a pair. **Note:** *Valve guides are an interference fit in the cylinder head and their removal requires access to a hydraulic press. For this reason, it would be wise to entrust the job to an engineering workshop or head rebuilding specialist.*
50 Using vernier callipers, measure the free length of each of the valve springs. As a

manufacturer's figure is not quoted, the only way to check the length of the springs is by comparison with a new component. Note that valve springs are usually renewed during a major engine overhaul **(see illustration)**.
51 Stand each spring on its end on a flat surface, against an engineers square **(see illustration)**. Check the squareness of the spring visually; if it appears distorted, renew the spring.
52 Measuring valve spring pre-load involves compressing the valve by applying a specified weight and measuring the reduction in length. This may be a difficult operation to conduct in the home workshop, so it would be wise to approach your local garage or engineering workshop for assistance. Weakened valve springs will at best, increase engine running noise and at worst, cause poor compression, so defective items should be renewed.

Reassembly

Caution: Unless all new components are to be used, maintain groups when refitting valve train components - do not mix components between cylinders and ensure that components are refitted in their original positions.

53 To achieve a gas-tight seal between the valves and their seats, it will be necessary to grind, or 'lap', the valves in. To complete this process you will need a quantity of fine/coarse grinding paste and a grinding tool - this can either be of the dowel and rubber sucker type, or the automatic type which are driven by a rotary power tool.
54 Smear a small quantity of *fine* grinding

paste on the sealing face of the valve head. Turn the cylinder head over so that the combustion chambers are facing upwards and insert the valve into the correct guide. Attach the grinding tool to the valve head and using a backward/forward rotary action, grind the valve head into its seat. Periodically lift the valve and rotate it to redistribute the grinding paste **(see illustration)**.
55 Continue this process until the contact between valve and seat produces an unbroken, matt grey ring of uniform width, on both faces. Repeat the operation for the remaining valves.
56 If the valves and seats are so badly pitted that coarse grinding paste must be used, check first that there is enough material left on both components to make this operation worthwhile - if too little material is left remaining, the valve stems may protrude too far above their guides, impeding the correct operation of the hydraulic tappets. Refer to a machine shop or cylinder head rebuilding specialist for advice.
57 Assuming the repair is feasible, work as described in the previous paragraph but use the coarse grinding paste initially, to achieve a dull finish on the valve face and seat. Then, wash off coarse paste with solvent and repeat the process using fine grinding paste to obtain the correct finish.
58 When all the valves have been ground in, remove all traces of grinding paste from the cylinder head and valves with solvent, and allow them to dry completely.
59 Where necessary on diesel engines, fit new swirl chambers by driving them squarely

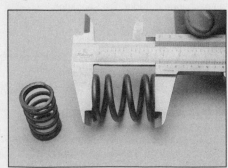

4.50 Measure the free length of each of the valve springs

4.51 Checking the squareness of a valve spring

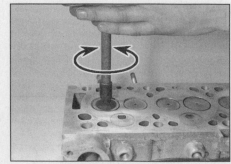

4.54 Grinding-in a valve

4.59a Fitting a swirl chamber
(diesel engines)

4.59b Swirl chamber locating recess

4.60 Measuring swirl chamber projection
using a DTI gauge

into their housings with a mallet - use a block of wood to protect the face of the swirl chamber. Note the locating recess on the side of the chamber and the corresponding groove in the housing **(see illustrations)**.

60 On completion, the projection of the swirl chamber from the face of the cylinder head must be measured using a DTI gauge and compared with the limit quoted in the Specifications **(see illustration)**. If this limit is exceeded, there is a risk that the chamber may be struck by the piston, and in this case the advice of a professional cylinder head rebuilder or machine shop should be sought.

61 Turn the head over and place it on a stand, or wooden blocks. Where applicable, fit the first lower spring seat into place, with the convex side facing the cylinder head **(see illustration)**.

62 Working on one valve at a time, lubricate the valve stem with clean engine oil, and

insert it into the guide. Fit one of the protective plastic sleeves supplied with the new valve stem oil seals over the valve end face - this will protect the oil seal whilst it is being fitted **(see illustrations)**.

63 Dip a new valve stem seal in clean engine oil, and carefully push it over the valve and onto the top of the valve guide - take care not to damage the stem seal as it passes over the valve end face. Use a suitable long reach socket to press it firmly into position **(see illustrations)**.

64 Locate the valve spring(s) over the valve stem **(see illustration)**. Where a lower spring seat is fitted, ensure that the springs locate squarely on the stepped surface of the seat. **Note:** *Depending on age and specification, engines may have either concentric double valve springs, **or** single valve springs with no lower spring seat.*

65 Fit the upper seat over the top of the

springs, then using a valve spring compressor, compress the springs until the upper seat is pushed beyond the collet grooves in the valve stem. Refit the split collet, using a dab of grease to hold the two halves in the grooves **(see illustrations)**. Gradually release the spring compressor, checking that the collet remains correctly seated as the spring extends. When correctly seated, the upper seat should force the two halves of the collet together, and hold them securely in the grooves in the end of the valve.

66 Repeat this process for the remaining sets of valve components. To settle the components after installation, strike the end of each valve stem with a mallet, using a block of wood to protect the stem from damage. Check before progressing any further that the split collets remain firmly held in the end of the valve stem by the upper spring seat.

67 Smear some clean engine oil onto the

2C

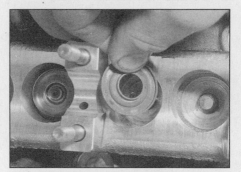

4.61 Fit the lower spring set in place, with the convex face facing the cylinder head

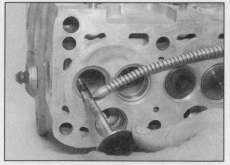

4.62a Lubricate the valve stem with clean engine oil and insert it into the guide

4.62b Fit one of the protective plastic sleeves over the valve end face

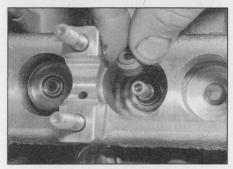

4.63a Fit a new valve stem seal over the valve

4.63b Use a long-reach socket to press on the oil seal

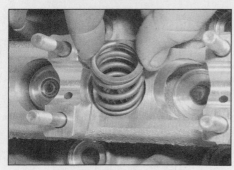

4.64 Fitting a valve spring

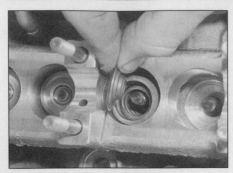

4.65a Fit the upper seat over the top of the valve spring

4.65b Use grease to hold the two halves of the split collet in the groove

4.67 Fit the tappets into their bores in the cylinder head

sides of the hydraulic tappets, and fit them into position in their bores in the cylinder head. Push them down until they contact the valves, then lubricate the camshaft lobe contact surfaces **(see illustration)**.

68 Lubricate the camshaft and cylinder head bearing journals with clean engine oil, then carefully lower the camshaft into position on the cylinder head. Support the ends of the shaft as it is inserted, to avoid damaging the lobes and journals **(see illustrations)**.

69 On engine ABF, locate the drive chain on the inlet and exhaust camshafts (observing the direction of rotation markings made earlier) such that the timing marks line up as shown. Lower the camshafts and chain onto the cylinder head, ensuring that the marks remain aligned **(see illustration)**.

70 On all engine codes except ABD, AEA, ABU and ABF, turn the camshaft so that the lobes for No 1 cylinder are pointing upwards.

71 On diesel engines (engine codes 1Z, 1Y and AAZ), with reference to Chapter 2B, lubricate the lip of a new camshaft oil seal with clean engine oil and locate it over the end of the camshaft. Slide the seal along the camshaft until it locates in the lower half of its housing in the cylinder head **(see illustration)**.

72 Oil the upper surfaces of the camshaft bearing journals, then fit the bearing caps in place. Ensure that they fitted the right way around and in the correct locations, then fit and tighten the retaining nuts, as follows:

Note: *New bearing cap retaining nuts must be used on reassembly for all engine codes.*

Engine code ABF

73 The bearing caps have recesses machined into one corner; these recesses must face the inlet side of the cylinder head **(see illustration)**.

74 Fit caps Nos 6 and 8 over the inlet

camshaft, and tighten the retaining nuts alternately and diagonally to the specified torque.

75 Fit the remaining inlet camshaft caps and tighten the nuts to the specified torque.

76 Fit caps Nos 2 and 4 to the exhaust camshaft and tighten the retaining nuts to the specified torque.

77 Smear the mating surfaces of the remaining caps with sealant, locate them over the exhaust camshaft, then fit and tighten the nuts to the specified torque **(refer to illustration 4.87)**.

Engine codes ABU, AEA and ABD

78 The bearing caps have their respective cylinder numbers stamped onto them, and have an elongated lug on one side. When correctly fitted, the numbers should be readable from the exhaust side of the cylinder head, and the lugs should face the inlet side of the cylinder head **(see illustration)**.

4.68a Lubricate the camshaft bearings with clean engine oil . . .

4.68b . . . then lower the camshaft into position on the cylinder head

4.69 On engine code ABF, ensure that the timing marks remain aligned

4.71 Fitting the camshaft oil seal (engine codes 1Z, 1Y, and AAZ)

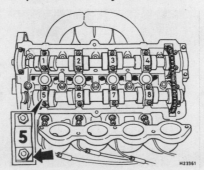

4.73 On engine code ABF, the bearing caps have recesses (arrowed)

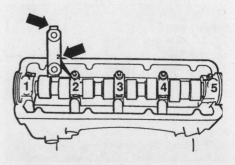

4.78 On engine codes ABU, ABD & AEA, the bearing caps are fitted as shown

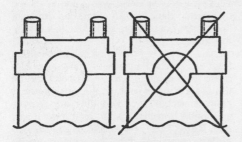

4.85 On engine codes AAM, ABS, 2E, ADZ, ADY, AAZ, 1Y, 1Z and AEK, the camshaft bearing cap holes are drilled off-centre

4.88 Fitting a new camshaft oil seal

4.87 Smear the mating surfaces of caps Nos 1 and 5 with sealant

4.89 Fit the coolant elbow, using a new O-ring or gasket

79 Fit caps Nos 2 and 4 over the camshaft and tighten the retaining nuts alternately and diagonally to the specified Stage 1 torque.

80 Smear the mating surfaces of caps Nos 1 and 5 with sealant then fit them, together with cap No 3, over the camshaft and tighten the nuts to the specified first stage torque (**refer to illustration 4.87**).

81 Tighten all bearing caps to the Stage 2 torque, then fit the bolts to bearing cap No 5 and tighten them to the specified torque.

Engine codes AAM, ABS, 2E, ADZ and ADY

82 The bearing cap mounting holes are drilled off-centre; ensure they are fitted the correct way round (**refer to illustration 4.85**).

83 Fit caps Nos 2 and 5 over the camshaft and tighten the retaining nuts alternately and diagonally to the specified torque.

84 Smear the mating surfaces of caps Nos 1 and 5 with sealant, locate them over the camshaft then fit and tighten the nuts to the specified torque (**refer to illustration 4.87**).

Engine codes AAZ, 1Y, 1Z (diesels) and AEK

85 The bearing cap mounting holes are drilled off-centre; ensure that they are fitted the correct way around (**see illustration**).

86 Fit caps Nos 2 and 4 over the camshaft, and tighten the retaining nuts alternately and diagonally to the specified torque.

87 Smear the mating surfaces of caps Nos 1 and 5 with sealant then fit them, together with cap No 3, over the camshaft and tighten the nuts to the specified first stage torque (**see illustration**).

All engine codes except AAZ, 1Y and 1Z (diesels)

88 With reference to Chapter 2A or B as applicable, lubricate the lip of a new camshaft oil seal with clean engine oil, and locate it over the end of the camshaft. Using a mallet and a long-reach socket of an appropriate diameter, drive the seal squarely into its housing until it bears against the inner stop - do not attempt to force it in any further (**see illustration**).

All engine codes

89 Refit the coolant outlet elbow, using a new gasket/O-ring as necessary (**see illustration**).

90 Refit the coolant sensor and oil pressure switch.

91 With reference to Chapter 2A or B as applicable, carry out the following:

a) *Refit the timing belt sprocket to the camshaft.*

b) *Refit the inlet and exhaust manifolds, complete with new gaskets.*

5.5a Remove the piston cooling jet retaining screw (arrowed) . . .

92 On diesel engines, refit the fuel injectors and glow plugs, with reference to Chapter 4C and 4D).

93 Refer to Chapter 2A or B as applicable refit the cylinder head to the cylinder block.

5 Pistons and connecting rods - removal and inspection

Removal

1 Refer to Part A or B of this Chapter (as applicable) and remove the cylinder head, flywheel, sump and baffle plate, oil pump and pickup.

2 Inspect the tops of the cylinder bores; any wear ridges found at the point where the pistons reach top dead centre must be removed; otherwise the pistons may be damaged when they are pushed out of their bores. This can be accomplished with a scraper or ridge reamer.

3 Scribe the number of each piston on its crown, to allow identification later; note that No 1 is at the timing belt end of the engine.

4 Using a set of feeler blades, measure the big-end to crankpin web thrust clearance at each connecting rod, and record the measurements for later reference.

5 Where applicable, remove the retaining screw and withdraw the piston cooling jets from their mounting holes. On engine codes 2E and ABF, the jet mounting incorporates a pressure relief valve, take care to avoid damaging it during removal (**see illustrations**).

6 Rotate the crankshaft until pistons No 1 and 4 are at bottom dead centre. Unless they are already identified, mark the big-end bearing caps and connecting rods with their respective piston numbers, using a centre-punch or a scribe (**see illustration**). Note the orientation of the bearing caps in relation to the connecting rod; it may be difficult to see the manufacturer's markings at this stage, so scribe alignment arrows on them both to ensure correct reassembly. Unbolt the bearing cap bolts/nuts, half a turn at a time, until they can be removed by hand. Recover the bottom shell bearing, and tape it to the cap for safe keeping. Note that if the shell bearings are to be re-used, they must be refitted to the same connecting rod.

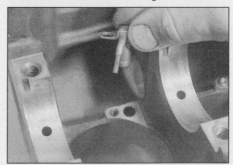

5.5b . . . and withdraw the jet from its mounting hole

2C

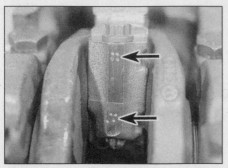

5.6 Mark the big-end caps and connecting rods with their piston numbers (arrowed)

5.7 Pad the bolt threads with tape

7 On certain engines, the bearing cap bolts will remain in the connecting rod; in this case the threads of the bolts should be padded with insulating tape, to prevent them from scratching the crankpins when the pistons are removed from their bores **(see illustration)**.

8 Drive the pistons out of the top of their bores by pushing on the underside of the piston crown with a piece of dowel or a hammer handle. As the piston and connecting rod emerge, recover the top shell bearing and tape it to the connecting rod for safekeeping.

9 Turn the crankshaft through half a turn and working as described above, remove No 2 and 3 pistons and connecting rods. Remember to maintain the components in their cylinder groups, whilst they are in a dismantled state.

10 Insert a small flat-bladed screwdriver into the removal slot and prise the gudgeon pin circlips from each piston. Push out the

gudgeon pin, and separate the piston and connecting rod **(see illustrations)**. Discard the circlips as new items must be fitted on reassembly. If the pin proves difficult to remove, heat the piston to 60°C with hot water - the resulting expansion will then allow the two components to be separated.

Inspection

11 Before an inspection of the pistons can be carried out, the existing piston rings must be removed, using a removal/installation tool, or an old feeler blade if such a tool is not available. Always remove the upper piston rings first, expanding them to clear the piston crown. The rings are very brittle and will snap if they are stretched too much - sharp edges are produced when this happens, so protect your eyes and hands. Discard the rings on removal, as new items must be fitted when the engine is reassembled **(see illustration)**.

12 Use a section of old piston ring to scrape the carbon deposits out of the ring grooves, taking care not to score or gouge the edges of the groove.

13 Carefully scrape away all traces of carbon from the top of the piston. A hand-held wire brush (or a piece of fine emery cloth) can be used, once the majority of the deposits have been scraped away. Be careful not to remove any metal from the piston, as it is relatively soft. **Note:** *Take care to preserve the piston number markings that were made during removal.*

14 Once the deposits have been removed, clean the pistons and connecting rods with paraffin or a suitable solvent, and dry thoroughly. Make sure that the oil return holes in the ring grooves are clear.

15 Examine the piston for signs of terminal wear or damage. Some normal wear will be apparent, in the form of a vertical 'grain' on the piston thrust surfaces and a slight looseness of the top compression ring in its groove. Abnormal wear should be carefully examined, to assess whether the component is still serviceable and what the cause of the wear might be.

16 Scuffing or scoring of the piston skirt may indicate that the engine has been overheating, through inadequate cooling, lubrication or abnormal combustion temperatures. Scorch marks on the skirt indicate that blow - by has occurred, perhaps caused by worn bores or piston rings. Burnt areas on the piston crown are usually an indication of pre-ignition, pinking or detonation. In extreme cases, the piston crown may be melted by operating under these conditions. Corrosion pit marks in the piston crown indicate that coolant has seeped into the combustion chamber and/or the crankcase. The faults causing these symptoms must be corrected before the engine is brought back into service, or the same damage will recur.

17 Check the pistons, connecting rods, gudgeon pins and bearing caps for cracks. Lay the connecting rods on a flat surface, and look along the length to see if it appears bent or twisted. If you have doubts about their condition, get them measured at an engineering workshop. Inspect the small-end bush bearing for signs of wear or cracking.

18 Using a micrometer, measure the diameter of all four pistons at a point 10 mm from the bottom of the skirt, at right angles to the gudgeon pin axis **(see illustration)**. Compare the measurements with those listed in the Specifications. If the piston diameter is out of the tolerance band listed for its particular size, then it must be renewed. Note: If the cylinder block was re - bored during a previous overhaul, oversize pistons may have been fitted. Record the measurements and use them to check the piston clearances when the cylinder bores are measured, later in this Chapter.

19 Hold a new piston ring in the appropriate groove and measure the ring-to-groove

5.10a Insert a small screwdriver into the slot and prise off the gudgeon pin circlips

5.10b Push out the gudgeon pin and separate the piston and connecting rod

5.11 Piston rings can be removed using an old feeler blade

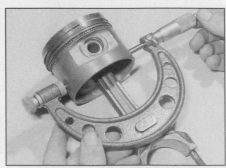

5.18 Using a micrometer, measure the diameter of all four pistons

5.19 Measuring the piston ring-to-groove clearance using a feeler blade

clearance using a feeler blade **(see illustration)**. Note that the rings are of different widths, so use the correct ring for the groove. Compare the measurements with those listed; if the clearances are outside of the tolerance band, then the piston must be renewed. Confirm this by checking the width of the piston ring with a micrometer.

20 Using internal/external vernier callipers, measure the connecting rod small-end internal diameter and the gudgeon pin external diameter. Subtract the gudgeon pin diameter from the small-end diameter to obtain the clearance. If this measurement is outside its specification, then the piston and connecting rod bush will have to be resized and a new gudgeon pin installed. An engineering workshop will have the equipment needed to undertake a job of this nature.

21 The orientation of the piston with respect to the connecting rod must be correct when the two are reassembled. The piston crown is marked with an arrow (which may be obscured by carbon deposits); this must point towards the timing belt end of the engine when the piston is installed. The connecting rod and its bearing cap both have recesses machined into them, close to their mating surfaces - these recesses must both face the same way as the arrow on the piston crown (ie towards the timing belt end of the engine) when correctly installed **(see illustration)**. Reassemble the two components to satisfy this requirement. **Note:** *On certain engines, the connecting rod big-ends are provided with offset dowels which locate in holes in the bearing caps.*

22 Lubricate the gudgeon pin and small-end bush with clean engine oil. Slide the pin into the piston, engaging the connecting rod small-end. Fit two new circlips to the piston at either end of the gudgeon pin, such that their open ends are facing 180° away from the removal slot in the piston. Repeat this operation for the remaining pistons.

6 Crankshaft - removal and inspection

Removal

1 Note: *If no work is to be done on the pistons and connecting rods, then removal of*

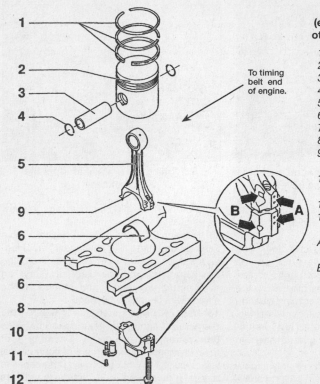

5.21 Piston assembly (engine code AAZ shown - other engine codes similar)

1 Piston rings
2 Piston
3 Gudgeon pin
4 Circlip
5 Connecting rod
6 Big-end bearing shell
7 Top of cylinder block
8 Big-end bearing cap
9 Locating dowel (where applicable)
10 Oil jet for piston cooling (where applicable)
11 Oil jet retaining screw
12 Big-end bearing cap bolts
A Connecting rod/bearing cap identification marks
B Connecting rod/bearing cap orientation marks

To timing belt end of engine.

2C

the cylinder head and pistons will not be necessary. Instead, the pistons need only be pushed far enough up the bores so that they are positioned clear of the crankpins. The use of an engine stand is strongly recommended.

2 With reference to Chapter 2A or B as applicable, carry out the following:

a) *Remove the crankshaft timing belt sprocket.*
b) *Remove the clutch components and flywheel.*
c) *Remove the sump, baffle plate, oil pump and pickup.*
d) *Remove the front and rear crankshaft oil seals and their housings.*

3 Remove the pistons and connecting rods, as described in Section 5 (refer to the Note above).

4 Carry out a check of the crankshaft endfloat, as follows. **Note:** *This can only be accomplished when the crankshaft is still*

installed in the cylinder block/crankcase, but is free to move. Set up a DTI gauge so that the probe is in line with the crankshaft axis and is in contact with a fixed point on end of the crankshaft. Push the crankshaft along its axis to the end of its travel, and then zero the gauge. Push the crankshaft fully the other way, and record the endfloat indicated on the dial **(see illustration)**. Compare the result with the figure given in the Specifications and establish whether new thrustwashers are required.

5 If a dial gauge is not available, feeler blades can be used. First push the crankshaft fully towards the flywheel end of the engine, then use a feeler blade to measure the gap between cylinder No 2 crankpin web and the main bearing thrustwasher **(see illustration)**. Compare the results with the Specifications.

6 Observe the manufacturer's identification marks on the main bearing caps. The number

6.4 Measuring crankshaft endfloat using a DTI gauge

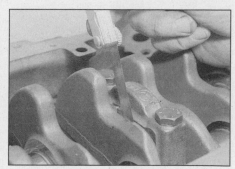

6.5 Measuring crankshaft endfloat using feeler blades

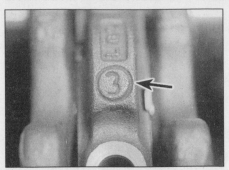

6.6 Manufacturer's identification markings on the main bearing caps (arrowed)

6.8 Lifting the crankshaft from the crankcase

6.13 Use a micrometer to measure the diameter of each main bearing journal

relates to the position in the crankcase, as counted from the timing belt end of the engine **(see illustration)**.

7 Loosen the main bearing cap bolts one quarter of a turn at a time, until they can be removed by hand. Using a soft-faced mallet, strike the caps lightly to free them from the crankcase. Recover the lower main bearing shells, taping them to the cap for safekeeping. Mark them with indelible ink to aid identification, but do not score or scratch them in any way.

8 Carefully lift the crankshaft out, taking care not to dislodge the upper main bearing shells **(see illustration)**. It would be wise to get an assistant's help, as the crankshaft is heavy. Set it down on a clean, level surface and chock it with blocks to prevent it from rolling.

9 Extract the upper main bearing shells from the crankcase, and tape them to their respective bearing caps. Remove the two thrustwasher bearings from either side of No 3 crank web.

10 With the shell bearings removed, observe the recesses machined into the bearing caps and crankcase - these provide location for the lugs which protrude from the shell bearings and so prevent them from being fitted incorrectly.

Inspection

11 Wash the crankshaft in a suitable solvent and allow it to dry. Flush the oil holes thoroughly, to ensure that are not blocked - use a pipe cleaner or a needle brush if necessary. Remove any sharp edges from the

edge of the hole which may damage the new bearings when they are installed.

12 Inspect the main bearing and crankpin journals carefully; if uneven wear, cracking, scoring or pitting are evident then the crankshaft should be reground by an engineering workshop, and refitted to the engine with undersize bearings.

13 Use a micrometer to measure the diameter of each main bearing journal **(see illustration)**. Taking a number of measurements on the surface of each journal will reveal if it is worn unevenly. Differences in diameter measured at 90° intervals indicate that the journal is out of round. Differences in diameter measured along the length of the journal, indicate that the journal is tapered. Again, if wear is detected, the crankshaft must be reground by an engineering workshop, and undersize bearings will be needed (refer to "*Reassembly*")

14 Check the oil seal journals at either end of the crankshaft. If they appear excessively scored or damaged, they may cause the new seals to leak when the engine is reassembled. It may be possible to repair the journal; seek the advice of an engineering workshop or your VAG dealer.

15 Measure the crankshaft runout by setting up a DTI gauge on the centre main bearing and rotating the shaft in V-blocks. The maximum deflection of the gauge will indicate the runout. Take precautions to protect the bearing journals and oil seal mating surfaces from damage during this procedure. A maximum runout figure is not quoted by the

manufacturer, but use the figure of 0.05 mm as a rough guide. If the runout exceeds this figure, crankshaft renewal should be considered - consult your VAG dealer or an engine rebuilding specialist for advice.

16 Refer to Section 8 for details of main and big-end bearing inspection.

7 Intermediate shaft - removal and refitting

Note: *This Section does not apply to engine codes ABU, ABD, AEA.*

Removal

1 Refer to Chapter 1A or B and carry out the following:
  a) *Remove the timing belt.*
  b) *Remove the intermediate shaft sprocket.*

2 Before the shaft is removed, the endfloat must be checked. Anchor a DTI gauge to the cylinder block with its probe in line with the intermediate shaft centre axis. Push the shaft into the cylinder block to the end of its travel, zero the DTI gauge and then draw the shaft out to the opposite end of its travel. Record the maximum deflection and compare the figure with that listed in Specifications - renew the shaft if the endfloat exceeds this limit **(see illustration)**.

3 Slacken the retaining bolts and withdraw the intermediate shaft flange. Recover the O-ring seal, then press out the oil seal **(see illustrations)**.

4 Withdraw the intermediate shaft from the cylinder block and inspect the drive gear at

7.2 Check the intermediate shaft endfloat using a DTI gauge

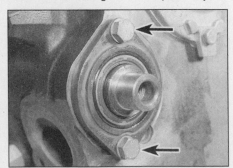

7.3a Slacken the retaining bolts (arrowed) . . .

7.3b . . . and withdraw the intermediate shaft flange

7.3c Press out the oil seal . . .

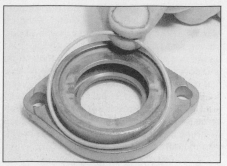

7.3d . . . then recover the O-ring seal

the end of the shaft; if the teeth show signs of excessive wear, or are damaged in any way, the shaft should be renewed.

5 If the oil seal has been leaking, check the shaft mating surface for signs of scoring or damage.

Refitting

6 Liberally oil the intermediate shaft bearing surfaces and drive gear, then carefully guide the shaft into the cylinder block and engage the journal at the leading end with its support bearing.

7 Press a new shaft oil seal into its housing in the intermediate shaft flange and fit a new O-ring seal to the inner sealing surface of the flange.

8 Lubricate the inner lip of the seal with clean engine oil, and slide the flange and seal over the end of the intermediate shaft. Ensure that the O-ring is correctly seated, then fit the flange retaining bolts and tighten them to the specified torque. Check that the intermediate shaft can rotate freely.

9 With reference to Chapter 2A or B, carry out the following:

a) *Refit the timing belt sprocket to the intermediate shaft and tighten the centre bolt to the specified torque.*

b) *Refit the timing belt. Where applicable on petrol models, follow the intermediate sprocket alignment instructions carefully to ensure that the distributor drive gear alignment is preserved.*

8 Cylinder block/crankcase casting - cleaning and inspection

Cleaning

1 Remove all external components and electrical switches/sensors from the block. For complete cleaning, the core plugs should ideally be removed. Drill a small hole in the plugs, then insert a self-tapping screw into the hole. Extract the plugs by pulling on the screw with a pair of grips, or by using a slide hammer.

2 Scrape all traces of gasket and sealant from the cylinder block/crankcase, taking care not to damage the sealing surfaces.

3 Remove all oil gallery plugs (where fitted).

The plugs are usually very tight - they may have to be drilled out, and the holes re-tapped. Use new plugs when the engine is reassembled.

4 If the casting is extremely dirty, it should be steam-cleaned. After this, clean all oil holes and galleries one more time. Flush all internal passages with warm water until the water runs clear. Dry thoroughly, and apply a light film of oil to all mating surfaces and cylinder bores, to prevent rusting. If you have access to compressed air, use it to speed up the drying process, and to blow out all the oil holes and galleries.

> ⚠ **Warning: Wear eye protection when using compressed air!**

5 If the castings are not very dirty, you can do an adequate cleaning job with hot, soapy water and a stiff brush. Take plenty of time, and do a thorough job. Regardless of the cleaning method used, be sure to clean all oil holes and galleries very thoroughly, and to dry all components well. Protect the cylinder bores as described above, to prevent rusting.

6 All threaded holes must be clean, to ensure accurate torque readings during reassembly. To clean the threads, run the correct-size tap into each of the holes to remove rust, corrosion, thread sealant or sludge, and to restore damaged threads **(see illustration)**. If possible, use compressed air to clear the holes of debris produced by this operation. **Note:** *Take extra care to exclude all cleaning liquid from blind tapped holes, as the casting may be cracked by hydraulic action if a bolt is threaded into a hole containing liquid.*

8.6 To clean the cylinder block threads, run a correct-size tap into the holes

7 Apply suitable sealant to the new oil gallery plugs, and insert them into the holes in the block. Tighten them securely.

8 If the engine is not going to be reassembled immediately, cover it with a large plastic bag to keep it clean; protect all mating surfaces and the cylinder bores as described above, to prevent rusting.

Inspection

9 Visually check the casting for cracks and corrosion. Look for stripped threads in the threaded holes. If there has been any history of internal water leakage, it may be worthwhile having an engine overhaul specialist check the cylinder block/crankcase with professional equipment. If defects are found, have them renewed or if possible, repaired.

10 Check the cylinder bores for scuffing or scoring. Any evidence of this kind of damage should be cross-checked with an inspection of the pistons: see Section 5 of this Chapter. If the damage is in its early stages, it may be possible to repair the block by reboring it. Seek the advice of an engineering workshop before you progress.

11 To allow an accurate assessment of the wear in the cylinder bores to be made, their diameter must be measured at a number of points, as follows. Insert a bore gauge into bore No 1 and take three measurements in line with the crankshaft axis; one at the top of the bore, roughly 10 mm below the bottom of the wear ridge, one halfway down the bore and one at a point roughly 10 mm the bottom of the bore. **Note:** *Stand the cylinder block squarely on a workbench during this procedure, inaccurate results may be obtained if the measurements are taken when the engine mounted on a stand.*

12 Rotate the bore gauge through 90°, so that it is at right angles to the crankshaft axis and repeat the measurements detailed in paragraph 11 **(see illustration)**. Record all six measurements, and compare them with the

2C

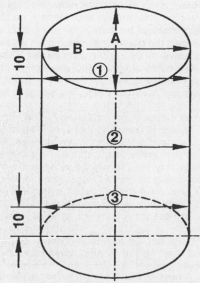

8.12 Bore measurement points

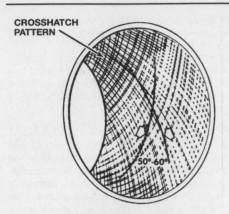

8.17 Cylinder bore honing pattern

data listed in the Specifications. If the difference in diameter between any two cylinders exceeds the wear limit, or if any one cylinder exceeds its maximum bore diameter, then *all four* cylinders will have to be rebored and oversize pistons will have to be fitted. Note that the imbalances produced by not reboring all the cylinders together would render the engine unusable.

13 Use the piston diameter measurements recorded earlier (see Section 5) to calculate the piston-to-bore clearances. Figures are not available from the manufacturer, so seek the advice of your VAG dealer or engine reconditioning specialist.

14 Place the cylinder block on a level work surface, crankcase downwards. Use a straight edge and a set of feeler blades to measure the distortion of the cylinder head mating surface in both planes. A maximum figure is not quoted by the manufacturer, but use the figure of 0.05 mm as a rough guide. If the measurement exceeds this figure, repair may be possible by machining - consult your dealer for advice.

15 Before the engine can be reassembled, the cylinder bores must be honed. This process involves using an abrasive tool to produce a fine, cross-hatch pattern on the inner surface of the bore. This has the effect of seating the piston rings, resulting in a good seal between the piston and cylinder. There are two types of honing tool available to the home mechanic, both are driven by a rotary power tool, such as a drill. The 'bottle brush' hone is a stiff, cylindrical brush with abrasive stones bonded to its bristles. The more conventional surfacing hone has abrasive stones mounted on spring-loaded legs. For the inexperienced home mechanic, satisfactory results will be achieved more easily using the Bottle Brush hone. **Note:** *If you are unwilling to tackle cylinder bore honing, an engineering workshop will be able to carry out the job for you at a reasonable cost.*

16 Carry out the honing as follows; you will need one of the honing tools described above, a power drill/air wrench, a supply of clean rags, some honing oil and a pair of safety glasses.

17 Fit the honing tool in the drill chuck. Lubricate the cylinder bores with honing oil and insert the honing tool into the first bore, compressing the stones to allow it to fit. Turn on the drill and as the tool rotates, move it up and down in the bore at a rate that produces a fine cross-hatch pattern on the surface. The lines of the pattern should ideally cross at about 50 to 60° **(see illustration)**, although some piston ring manufacturer's may quote a different angle; check the literature supplied with the new rings.

⚠️ *Warning: Wear safety glasses to protect your eyes from debris flying off the honing tool.*

18 Use plenty of oil during the honing process. Do not remove any more material than is necessary to produce the required finish. When removing the hone tool from the bore, do not pull it out whilst it is still rotating; maintain the up/down movement until the chuck has stopped, then withdraw the tool whilst rotating the chuck by hand, in the normal direction of rotation.

19 Wipe out the oil and swarf with a rag and proceed to the next bore. When all four bores have been honed, thoroughly clean the whole cylinder block in hot soapy water to remove all traces of honing oil and debris. The block is clean when a clean rag, moistened with new engine oil does not pick up any grey residue when wiped along the bore.

20 Apply a light coating of engine oil to the mating surfaces and cylinder bores to prevent rust forming. Store the block in a plastic bag until reassembly.

9 Main and big-end bearings - inspection and selection

Inspection

1 Even though the main and big-end bearings should be renewed during the engine overhaul, the old bearings should be retained for close examination, as they may reveal valuable information about the condition of the engine **(see illustration)**.

2 Bearing failure can occur due to lack of lubrication, the presence of dirt or other foreign particles, overloading the engine, or corrosion. Regardless of the cause of bearing failure, the cause must be corrected before the engine is reassembled, to prevent it from happening again.

3 When examining the bearing shells, remove them from the cylinder block/crankcase, the main bearing caps, the connecting rods and the connecting rod big-end bearing caps. Lay them out on a clean surface in the same general position as their location in the engine. This will enable you to match any bearing problems with the corresponding crankshaft journal. *Do not* touch any shell's internal bearing surface with your fingers while checking it, or the delicate surface may be scratched.

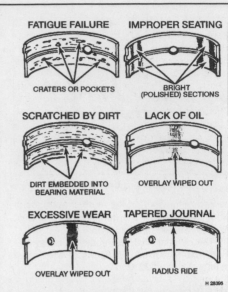

9.1 Typical bearing failures

4 Dirt and other foreign matter gets into the engine in a variety of ways. It may be left in the engine during assembly, or it may pass through filters or the crankcase ventilation system. It may get into the oil, and from there into the bearings. Metal chips from machining operations and normal engine wear are often present. Abrasives are sometimes left in engine components after reconditioning, especially when parts are not thoroughly cleaned using the proper cleaning methods. Whatever the source, these foreign objects often end up embedded in the soft bearing material, and are easily recognised. Large particles will not embed in the bearing, but will score or gouge the bearing and journal. The best prevention for this cause of bearing failure is to clean all parts thoroughly, and keep everything spotlessly-clean during engine assembly. Frequent and regular engine oil and filter changes are also recommended.

5 Lack of lubrication (or lubrication breakdown) has a number of interrelated causes. Excessive heat (which thins the oil), overloading (which squeezes the oil from the bearing face) and oil leakage (from excessive bearing clearances, worn oil pump or high engine speeds) all contribute to lubrication breakdown. Blocked oil passages, which usually are the result of misaligned oil holes in a bearing shell, will also oil-starve a bearing, and destroy it. When lack of lubrication is the cause of bearing failure, the bearing material is wiped or extruded from the steel backing of the bearing. Temperatures may increase to the point where the steel backing turns blue from overheating.

6 Driving habits can have a definite effect on bearing life. Full-throttle, low-speed operation (labouring the engine) puts very high loads on bearings, tending to squeeze out the oil film. These loads cause the bearings to flex, which produces fine cracks in the bearing face (fatigue failure). Eventually, the bearing material will loosen in pieces, and tear away from the steel backing.

7 Short-distance driving leads to corrosion of bearings, because insufficient engine heat is produced to drive off the condensed water and corrosive gases. These products collect in the engine oil, forming acid and sludge. As the oil is carried to the engine bearings, the acid attacks and corrodes the bearing material.

8 Incorrect bearing installation during engine assembly will lead to bearing failure as well. Tight-fitting bearings leave insufficient bearing running clearance, and will result in oil starvation. Dirt or foreign particles trapped behind a bearing shell result in high spots on the bearing, which lead to failure.

9 *Do not* touch any shell's internal bearing surface with your fingers during reassembly; there is a risk of scratching the delicate surface, or of depositing particles of dirt on it.

10 As mentioned at the beginning of this Section, the bearing shells should be renewed as a matter of course during engine overhaul; to do otherwise is false economy.

Selection - main and big-end bearings

11 Main and big-end bearings for the engines described in this Chapter are available in standard sizes and a range of undersizes to suit reground crankshafts - refer to Specifications for details.

12 The running clearances will need to be checked when the crankshaft is refitted with its new bearings (see Section 11).

10 Engine overhaul - reassembly sequence

1 Before reassembly begins, ensure that all new parts have been obtained, and that all necessary tools are available. Read through the entire procedure to familiarise yourself with the work involved, and to ensure that all items necessary for reassembly of the engine are at hand. In addition to all normal tools and materials, thread-locking compound will be needed. A suitable tube of liquid sealant will also be required for the joint faces that are without gaskets. It is recommended that the manufacturer's own products are used, which are specially formulated for this purpose; the relevant product names are quoted in the text of each Section where they are required.

2 In order to save time and avoid problems, engine reassembly should ideally be carried out in the following order:
  a) Crankshaft.
  b) Piston/connecting rod assemblies.
  c) Oil pump (see Chapter 2A or B)
  d) Sump (see Chapter 2A or B)
  e) Flywheel (see Chapter 2A or B)
  f) Cylinder head and gasket (Chapter 2A or B)
  g) Timing belt tensioner, sprockets and timing belt (see Chapter 2A or B)
  h) Engine external components and ancillaries.
  i) Auxiliary drivebelts, pulleys and tensioners.

3 At this stage, all engine components should be absolutely clean and dry, with all faults repaired. The components should be laid out (or in individual containers) on a completely clean work surface.

11 Crankshaft - refitting and running clearance check

1 Crankshaft refitting is the first stage of engine reassembly following overhaul. At this point, it is assumed that the crankshaft, cylinder block/crankcase and bearings have been cleaned, inspected and reconditioned or renewed.

2 Place the cylinder block on a clean, level worksurface, with the crankcase facing upwards. Unbolt the bearing caps and carefully release them from the crankcase; lay them out in order to ensure correct reassembly. If they are still in place, remove the bearing shells from the caps and the crankcase and wipe out the inner surfaces with a clean rag - they must be kept spotlessly clean.

3 Clean the rear surface of the new bearing shells with a rag and lay them on the bearing saddles. Ensure that the orientation lugs on the shells engage with the recesses in the saddles, and that the oil holes are correctly aligned **(see illustration)**. Do not hammer or otherwise force the bearing shells into place. It is critically important that the surfaces of the bearings are kept free from damage and contamination.

4 Give the newly-fitted bearing shells and the crankshaft journals a final clean with a rag. Check that the oil holes in the crankshaft are free from dirt, as any left here will become embedded in the new bearings when the engine is first started.

5 Carefully lay the crankshaft in the crankcase, taking care not to dislodge the bearing shells.

Running clearance check

6 When the crankshaft and bearings are refitted, a clearance must exist between them to allow lubricant to circulate. This clearance is impossible to check using feeler blades, so Plastigage is used. This is a thin strip of soft plastic that is crushed between the bearing

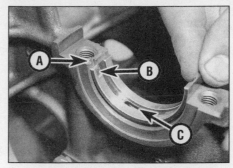

11.3 Bearing shells correctly refitted
  A Recess in bearing saddle
  B Lug on bearing shell
  C Oil hole

shells and journals when the bearing caps are tightened up. The change in its width then indicates the size of the clearance gap.

7 Cut off five pieces of Plastigage, just shorter than the length of the crankshaft journal. Lay a piece on each journal, in line with its axis **(see illustration)**.

8 Wipe off the rear surfaces of the new lower half main bearing shells and fit them to the main bearing caps, ensuring the locating lugs engage correctly **(see illustration)**.

9 Wipe the front surfaces of the bearing shells and give them a light coating of silicone release agent - this will prevent the Plastigage from sticking to the shell. Fit the caps in their correct locations on the bearing saddles, using the manufacturer's markings as a guide. Ensure that they are correctly orientated - the caps should be fitted such that the recesses for the bearing shell locating lugs are on the same side as those in the bearing saddle.

10 Working from the centre bearing cap, tighten the bolts one half turn at a time until they are all correctly torqued *to their first stage only*. Do not let the crankshaft turn at all whilst the Plastigage is in place. Progressively unbolt the bearing caps and remove them, taking care not to dislodge the Plastigage.

11 The width of the crushed Plastigage can now be measured, using the scale provided **(see illustration)**. Use the correct scale, as both imperial and metric are printed. This measurement indicates the running clearance - compare it with that listed in Specifications. If the clearance is outside the tolerance, it

11.7 Lay a piece of Plastigage on each journal, in line with the crankshaft axis

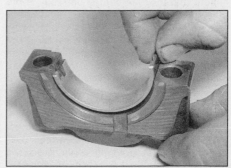

11.8 Fit the new lower half main bearing shells to the main bearing caps

2C

11.11 **Measure the width of the crushed Plastigage using the scale provided**

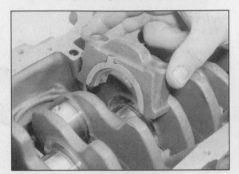

11.17 **Fitting a main bearing cap in place**

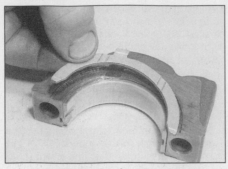

11.16 **Fitting the thrustwashers to No 3 bearing cap**

11.18 **Tighten the bearing cap bolts to the specified torque**

may be due to dirt or debris trapped under the bearing surface; try cleaning them again and repeat the clearance check. If the results are still unacceptable, re-check the journal diameters and the bearing sizes. If the Plastigage is thicker at one end, the journals may be tapered, and will require regrinding.

12 When you are satisfied that the clearances are correct, carefully remove the remains of the Plastigage from the journals and bearings faces. Use a soft, plastic or wooden scraper as anything metallic is likely to damage the surfaces.

Crankshaft - final refitting

13 Lift the crankshaft out of the crankcase. Wipe off the surfaces of the bearings in the crankcase and the bearing caps. Fit the thrust bearings either side of the No 3 bearing saddle, between cylinders No 2 and 3. Use a small quantity of grease to hold them in place; ensure that they are seated correctly in the machined recesses, with the oil grooves facing outwards

14 Liberally coat the bearing shells in the crankcase with clean engine oil of the appropriate grade.

15 Lower the crankshaft into position so that No 2 and 3 cylinder crankpins are at TDC; No 1 and 4 cylinder crankpins will then be at BDC, ready for fitting No 1 piston.

16 Lubricate the lower bearing shells in the main bearing caps with clean engine oil, then fit the thrustwashers to either side of bearing cap No 3, noting that the lugs protruding from the washers engage the recesses in the side of the bearing cap **(see illustration)**. Make

sure that the locating lugs on the shells are still engaged with the corresponding recesses in the caps.

17 Fit the main bearing caps in the correct order and orientation - No 1 bearing cap must be at the timing belt end of the engine and the bearing shell locating recesses in the bearing saddles and caps must be adjacent to each other **(see illustration)**. Insert the bearing cap bolts and hand tighten them only.

18 Working from the centre bearing cap outwards, tighten the retaining bolts to their specified torques. Where the torque is expressed in several stages, tighten all the bolts to the first stage, then repeat the exercise in the same sequence for the subsequent stage(s) **(see illustrations)**.

19 Refit the crankshaft rear oil seal housing, together with a new oil seal; refer to Part A or B (as applicable) of this Chapter for details.

20 Check that the crankshaft rotates freely by turning it by manually. If resistance is felt, re-check the running clearances, as described above.

21 Carry out a check of the crankshaft endfloat as described at the beginning of Section 6. If the thrust surfaces of the crankshaft have been checked and new thrust bearings have been fitted, then the endfloat should be within specification.

12 Pistons and piston rings - assembly

1 At this point it is assumed that the pistons have been correctly assembled to their

respective connecting rods and that the piston ring-to-groove clearances have been checked. If not, refer to the end of Section 5.

2 Before the rings can be fitted to the pistons, the end gaps must be checked with the rings fitted into the cylinder bores.

3 Lay out the piston assemblies and the new ring sets on a clean work surface so that the components are kept together in their groups during and after end gap checking. Place the crankcase on the work surface on its side, allowing access to the top and bottom of the bores.

4 Take the No 1 piston top ring and insert it into the top of the bore. Using the No 1 piston as a ram, push the ring close to the bottom of the bore, at the lowest point of the piston travel. Ensure that it is perfectly square in the bore by pushing firmly against the piston crown.

5 Use a set of feeler blades to measure the gap between the ends of the piston ring; the correct blade will just pass through the gap with a minimal amount of resistance **(see illustration)**. Compare this measurement with that listed in Specifications. Check that you have the correct ring before deciding that a gap is incorrect. Repeat the operation for all twelve rings.

6 If new rings are being fitted, it is unlikely that the end gaps will be too small. If a measurement is found to be undersize, it must be corrected or there is the risk that the ends of the ring may contact each other during operation, possibly resulting in engine damage. This is achieved by gradually filing down the ends of the ring, using a file clamped in a vice. Fit the ring over the file such that both its ends contact opposite faces of the file. Move the ring along the file, removing small amounts of material at a time. Take great care as the rings are brittle and form sharp edges if they fracture. Remember to keep the rings and piston assemblies in the correct order.

7 When all the piston ring end gaps have been verified, they can be fitted to the pistons. Work from the lowest ring groove (oil control ring) upwards. Note that the oil control ring comprises two side rails separated by a expander ring. Note also that the two compression rings are different in cross-section, and so must be fitted in the correct

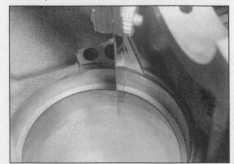

12.5 **Checking a piston ring end gap using a feeler blade**

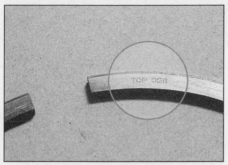

12.7 Piston ring "TOP" marking

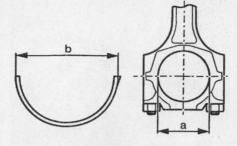

13.11 Dimensions for calculation of big-end bearing shell pre-tension (engine codes ABU, ABD and AEA)

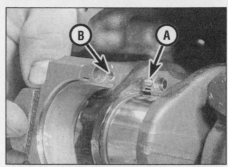

13.19 Fitting a big-end bearing cap
A Dowel   B Locating hole

groove and the right way up, using a piston ring fitting tool. Both of the compression rings have marks stamped on one side to indicate the top facing surface. Ensure that these marks face up when the rings are fitted **(see illustration)**.

8 Distribute the end gaps around the piston, spaced at 120° intervals to the each other. **Note:** *If the piston ring manufacturer supplies specific fitting instructions with the rings, follow these exclusively.*

13 Piston and connecting rod assemblies - refitting and big-end bearing clearance check

Big-end running clearance check

Note: *At this point, it is assumed that the crankshaft has been fitted to the engine, as described in Section 11.*

1 As with the main bearings (Section 10), a running clearance must exist between the big-end crankpin and its bearing shells to allow oil to circulate. There are two methods of checking the size of the running clearance, as described in the following paragraphs.

2 Place the cylinder block on a clean, level worksurface, with the crankcase facing upwards. Position the crankshaft such that crankpins No 1 and 4 are at BDC.

3 The first method is the least accurate and involves bolting bearing caps to the big-ends, away from the crankshaft, with the bearing shells in place. **Note:** *Correct orientation of the bearing caps is critical; refer to the notes in Section 5. The internal diameter formed by the assembled big-end is then measured using internal vernier callipers. The diameter of the respective crankpin is then subtracted from this measurement and the result is the running clearance.*

4 The second method of carrying out this check involves the use of Plastigage, in the same manner as the main bearing running clearance check (see Section 11) and is much more accurate than the previous method. Clean all four crankpins with a clean rag. With crankpins No 1 and 4 at BDC initially, place a strand of Plastigage on each crankpin journal.

5 Fit the upper big-end bearing shells to the connecting rods, ensuring that the locating lugs and recesses engage correctly. Temporarily refit the piston/connecting rod assemblies to the crankshaft; refit the big-end bearing caps, using the manufacturer's markings to ensure that they are fitted the correct way around - refer to *"Final refitting"* for details.

6 Tighten the bearing cap nuts/bolts as described below. Take care not to disturb the Plastigage or rotate the connecting rod during the tightening process.

7 Dismantle the assemblies without rotating the connecting rods. Use the scale printed on the Plastigage envelope to determine the big-end bearing running clearance and compare it with the figures listed in Specifications.

8 If the clearance is significantly different from that expected, the bearing shells may be the wrong size (or excessively worn, if the original shells are being re-used). Make sure that no dirt or oil was trapped between the bearing shells and the caps or connecting rods when the clearance was measured. Re-check the diameters of the crankpins. Note that if the Plastigage was wider at one end than at the other, the crankpins may be tapered. When the problem is identified, fit new bearing shells or have the crankpins reground to a listed undersize, as appropriate.

9 Upon completion, carefully scrape away all traces of the Plastigage material from the crankshaft and bearing shells. Use a plastic or wooden scraper, which will be soft enough to prevent scoring of the bearing surfaces.

Engine codes ABU, ABD and AEA only

10 Determine the pre-tension of the big-end shell bearings, as follows. Temporarily fit the big-end bearing caps to the connecting rods (without the bearing shells), then using internal vernier calipers or a bore gauge, measure the big-end internal diameter (dimension "a").

11 Now measure the *external* diameter of the bearing shell using a micrometer or vernier calipers (dimension "b"). The pre-tension is given by dimension "a" subtracted from dimension "b" **(see illustration)**. Compare the figure with that listed in the Specifications - if it is less than the minimum limit, then the bearing shell must be renewed.

Piston and connecting rod assemblies - final refitting

12 Note that the following procedure assumes that the crankshaft main bearing caps are in place (see Section 10).

13 Ensure that the bearing shells are correctly fitted, as described at the beginning of this Section. If new shells are being fitted, ensure that all traces of the protective grease are cleaned off using paraffin. Wipe dry the shells and connecting rods with a lint-free cloth.

14 Lubricate the cylinder bores, the pistons, and piston rings with clean engine oil. Lay out each piston/connecting rod assembly in order on a worksurface. On engines where the big-end bolts are captive in the connecting rods, fit short sections of rubber hose or tape over the bolt threads, to protect the cylinder bores during reassembly.

15 Start with piston/connecting rod assembly No 1. Make sure that the piston rings are still spaced as described in Section 12, then clamp them in position with a piston ring compressor.

16 Insert the piston/connecting rod assembly into the top of cylinder No 1. Lower the big-end in first, guiding it to protect the big-end bolts and the cylinder bores.

17 Ensure that the orientation of the piston in its cylinder is correct - the piston crown, connecting rods and big-end bearing caps have markings, which must point towards the timing belt end of the engine when the piston is installed in the bore - refer to Section 5 for details.

18 Using a block of wood or hammer handle against the piston crown, tap the assembly into the cylinder until the piston crown is flush with the top of the cylinder.

19 Ensure that the bearing shell is still correctly installed. Liberally lubricate the crankpin and both bearing shells with clean engine oil. Taking care not to mark the cylinder bores, tap the piston/connecting rod assembly down the bore and onto the crankpin. Refit the big-end bearing cap, tightening its retaining nuts/bolts finger-tight at first **(see illustration)**. Note that the orientation of the bearing cap with respect to the connecting rod must be correct when the

2C

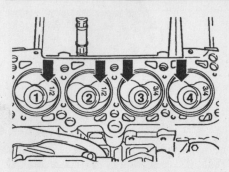

13.20 Piston orientation and fitting order (engine code 1Z)

13.21a Tightening the big-end bearing cap bolts to the Stage 1 . . .

13.21b . . . and Stage 2 torque settings

two components are reassembled. The connecting rod and its corresponding bearing cap both have recesses machined into them, close to their mating surfaces - these recesses must both face in the same direction as the arrow on the piston crown (ie towards the timing belt end of the engine) when correctly installed - refer to the illustrations in Section 5 for details. **Note:** *On certain engines, the connecting rod big-ends are provided with offset dowels which locate in holes in the bearing caps.*

20 On engine code 1Z, the piston crowns are specially shaped to improve the engine's combustion characteristics. Because of this, pistons 1 and 2 are different to pistons 3 and 4. When correctly fitted, the larger inlet valve chambers on pistons 1 and 2 must face the flywheel end of the engine, and the larger inlet valve chambers on pistons 3 and 4 must face the timing belt end of the engine. New pistons have number markings on their crowns to indicate their type - "1/2" denotes piston 1 or 2, "3/4" indicates piston 3 or 4 **(see illustration)**.

21 Working progressively around each bearing cap, tighten the retaining nuts half a turn at a time to the specified torque **(see illustrations)**.

22 Refit the remaining three piston/connecting rod assemblies in the same way.

23 Rotate the crankshaft by hand. Check that it turns freely; some stiffness is to be expected if new parts have been fitted, but there should be no binding or tight spots.

Engine codes 1Z, 1Y and AAZ (diesels) only

24 If new pistons are to be fitted, or if a new short engine is to be installed, the projection of the piston crowns above the cylinder head at TDC must be measured, to determine the type of head gasket that should be fitted.

25 Turn the cylinder block over (so that the crankcase is facing downwards) and rest it on a stand or wooden blocks. Anchor a DTI gauge to the cylinder block, and zero it on the head gasket mating surface. Rest the gauge probe on No 1 piston crown and turn the crankshaft slowly by hand so that the piston reaches and then passes through TDC. Measure and record the maximum deflection at TDC.

26 Repeat the measurement at piston No 4, then turn the crankshaft through 180° and take measurements at pistons Nos 2 and 3.

27 If the measurements differ from piston to piston, take the highest figure and use this to determine the head gasket type that must be used - refer to the Specifications for details.

28 Note that if the original pistons have been refitted, then a new head gasket of the same type as the original item must be fitted; refer to Chapter 2B for details of how to identify different head gasket types.

14 Engine - initial start-up after overhaul and reassembly

1 Refit the remainder of the engine components in the order listed in Section 10 of this Chapter, referring to Part A or B where necessary. Refit the engine (and transmission) to the vehicle as described in Section 2 of this Chapter. Double-check the engine oil and coolant levels and make a final check that everything has been reconnected. Make sure that there are no tools or rags left in the engine compartment.

Petrol models

2 Remove the spark plugs, referring to Chapter 1A for details.

3 The engine must be immobilised such that it can be turned over using the starter motor, without starting - disable the fuel pump by unplugging the fuel pump power relay from the relay board; refer to the relevant Part of Chapter 4 for details. *Caution: If the vehicle has a catalytic converter, it is potentially damaging to immobilise the engine by disabling the ignition system without first disabling the fuel system, as unburnt fuel could be supplied to the catalyst.*

4 Turn the engine using the starter motor until the oil pressure warning lamp goes out. If the lamp fails to extinguish after several seconds of cranking, check the engine oil level and oil filter security. Assuming these are correct, check the security of the oil pressure switch cabling - do not progress any further until you are satisfied that oil is being pumped around the engine at sufficient pressure.

5 Refit the spark plugs, and reconnect the fuel pump relay.

Diesel models

6 Disconnect the electrical cable from the fuel cut-off valve at the fuel injection pump - refer to Chapter 4C for details.

7 Turn the engine using the starter motor until the oil pressure warning lamp goes out.

8 If the lamp fails to extinguish after several seconds of cranking, check the engine oil level and oil filter security. Assuming these are correct, check the security of the oil pressure switch cabling - do not progress any further until you are satisfied that oil is being pumped around the engine at sufficient pressure.

9 Reconnect the fuel cut-off valve cable.

All models

10 Start the engine, but be aware that as fuel system components have been disturbed, the cranking time may be a little longer than usual.

11 While the engine is idling, check for fuel, water and oil leaks. Don't be alarmed if there are some odd smells and the occasional plume of smoke as components heat up and burn off oil deposits.

12 Assuming all is well, keep the engine idling until hot water is felt circulating through the top hose.

13 On petrol models, check the ignition timing, idle speed and idle mixture settings (see Chapter 1A), then switch the engine off.

14 On diesel models, check the fuel injection pump timing and engine idle speed, as described in Chapter 4C and Chapter 1B.

15 After a few minutes, recheck the oil and coolant levels, and top-up as necessary.

16 On all the engines described in this Chapter, there is no need to re-tighten the cylinder head bolts once the engine has been run following reassembly.

17 If new pistons, rings or crankshaft bearings have been fitted, the engine must be treated as new, and run-in for the first 600 miles (1000 km). *Do not* operate the engine at full-throttle, or allow it to labour at low engine speeds in any gear. It is recommended that the engine oil and filter are changed at the end of this period.

Chapter 3
Cooling, heating and ventilation systems

Contents

Degrees of difficulty

Easy, suitable for novice with little experience	**Fairly easy,** suitable for beginner with some experience	**Fairly difficult,** suitable for competent DIY mechanic	**Difficult,** suitable for experienced DIY mechanic	**Very difficult,** suitable for expert DIY or professional

Specifications

General

Expansion tank cap opening pressure ....   1.3 to 1.5 bars

Thermostat

Opening temperatures:
  1.4 and 1.6 litre models:
    Starts to open .... 84°C
    Fully open .... 98°C
  All other models:
    Starts to open .... 85°C
    Fully open .... 105°C

Electric cooling fan(s)

Cooling fan(s) cut in:
  Stage 1 speed:
    Switches on... 92 to 97°C
    Switches off .... 84 to 91°C
  Stage 2 speed:
    Switches on... 99 to 105°C
    Switches off .... 91 to 98°C
  Stage 3 speed (where fitted - see Section 5)):
    Switches on... 110 to 115°C
    Switches off .... 105 to 110°C

Torque wrench settings

	Nm	lbf ft
Alternator mounting bracket nuts	30	22
Coolant pump - 1.6 litre (AEK engine), 1.8, 1.9 and 2.0 litre models:		
Retaining bolts	10	7
Pulley bolts	25	18
Coolant pump/thermostat housing retaining bolts/studs:		
Stage 1	20	15
Stage 2	Angle-tighten a further 90°	
Cooling fan retaining nuts	10	7
Cooling fan thermostatic switch	35	26
Radiator mounting bolts	10	7
Temperature gauge sender unit (16 valve models)	10	7
Thermostat cover bolts.............................	10	7

1 General information and precautions

General information

The cooling system is of pressurised type, comprising of a pump, an aluminium crossflow radiator, an electric cooling fan, and a thermostat. The system functions as follows. Cold coolant from the radiator passes through the hose to the coolant pump where it is pumped around the cylinder block and head passages. After cooling the cylinder bores, combustion surfaces and valve seats, the coolant reaches the underside of the thermostat, which is initially closed. The coolant passes through the heater and is returned through the cylinder block to the coolant pump.

When the engine is cold the coolant circulates only through the cylinder block, cylinder head, expansion tank and heater. When the coolant reaches a predetermined temperature, the thermostat opens and the coolant passes through to the radiator. As the coolant circulates through the radiator it is cooled by the inrush of air when the car is in forward motion. Airflow is supplemented by the action of the electric cooling fan(s) when necessary. Upon reaching the radiator, the coolant is now cooled and the cycle is repeated.

The electric cooling fan(s) mounted on the rear of the radiator are controlled by a thermostatic switch. At a preset coolant temperature, the switch actuates the fan(s).

Refer to Section 11 for information on the air conditioning system.

Precautions

 Warning: Do not attempt to remove the expansion tank filler cap or disturb any part of the cooling system while the engine is hot, as there is a high risk of scalding. If the expansion tank filler cap must be removed before the engine and radiator have fully cooled (even though this is not recommended) the pressure in the cooling system must first be relieved.

Cover the cap with a thick layer of cloth, to avoid scalding, and slowly unscrew the filler cap until a hissing sound can be heard. When the hissing has stopped, indicating that the pressure has reduced, slowly unscrew the filler cap until it can be removed; if more hissing sounds are heard, wait until they have stopped before unscrewing the cap completely. At all times keep well away from the filler cap opening.

Do not allow antifreeze to come into contact with skin or painted surfaces of the vehicle. Rinse off spills immediately with plenty of water. Never leave antifreeze lying around in an open container or in a puddle in the driveway or on the garage floor. Children and pets are attracted by its sweet smell. Antifreeze can be fatal if ingested.

If the engine is hot, the electric cooling fan may start rotating even if the engine is not running, so be careful to keep hands, hair and loose clothing well clear when working in the engine compartment.

Refer to Section 11 for precautions to be observed when working on models with air conditioning.

2 Cooling system hoses - disconnection and renewal

Note: *Refer to the warnings given in Section 1 of this Chapter before proceeding.*

1 If the checks described in Chapter 1 reveal a faulty hose, it must be renewed as follows.

2 First drain the cooling system (see Chapter 1). If the coolant is not due for renewal, it may be re-used if it is collected in a clean container.

3 To disconnect a hose, release its retaining clips, then move them along the hose, clear of the relevant inlet/outlet union **(see illustration)**. Carefully work the hose free. While the hoses can be removed with relative ease when new or hot, **do not** attempt to disconnect any part of the system while it is still hot.

4 Note that the radiator inlet and outlet unions are fragile; do not use excessive force when attempting to remove the hoses. If a

hose proves to be difficult to remove, try to release it by rotating the hose ends before attempting to free it.

HAYNES HiNT *If all else fails, cut the hose with a sharp knife, then slit it so that it can be peeled off in two pieces. Although this may prove expensive if the hose is otherwise undamaged, it is preferable to buying a new radiator.*

5 When fitting a hose, first slide the clips onto the hose, then work the hose into position. If clamp type clips were originally fitted, it is a good idea to replace them with screw type clips when refitting the hose. If the hose is stiff, use a little soapy water as a lubricant, or soften the hose by soaking it in hot water.

6 Work the hose into position, checking that it is correctly routed, then slide each clip along the hose until it passes over the flared end of the relevant inlet/outlet union, before securing it in position with the retaining clip.

7 Refill the cooling system (see Chapter 1).

8 Check thoroughly for leaks as soon as possible after disturbing any part of the cooling system.

3 Radiator - removal, inspection and refitting

HAYNES HiNT *If leakage is the reason for wanting to remove the radiator, bear in mind that minor leaks can often be cured using a radiator sealant with the radiator in situ.*

Removal

1 Disconnect the battery negative lead.

2 Drain the cooling system (see Chapter 1).

3 Remove the front bumper as described in Chapter 11.

4 Remove both headlights as described in Chapter 12.

5 Release the retaining clips and disconnect the coolant hoses from the radiator **(see illustrations)**.

2.3 Disconnect the thermostat housing hose (1.9 litre Diesel shown)

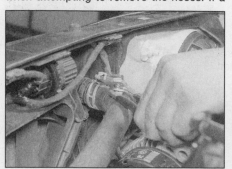

3.5a Release the retaining clips and disconnect the top . . .

3.5b . . . and bottom hoses from the radiator

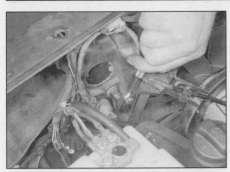

3.8a Removing a radiator retaining bolt

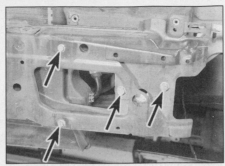

3.8b It may be necessary to undo the bolts (left-hand bolts arrowed) . . .

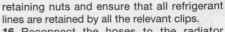

3.8c . . . and remove the crossmember to remove the radiator

3.8d Removing the radiator

6 Disconnect the wiring connector from the cooling fan switch on the left-hand end of the radiator.

7 On models equipped with air conditioning, in order to gain the clearance required to remove the radiator carry out the following. Unscrew the retaining nuts and release the air conditioning system fluid reservoir/drier assembly from its mounting bracket. Release the refrigerant lines from all the relevant retaining clips then undo the retaining bolts and move the condenser forwards as far as possible, taking great care not to place any excess strain on the refrigerant lines. **Do not** disconnect the refrigerant lines from the condenser (refer to the warnings given in Section 11).

8 On all models, slacken and remove the four retaining bolts from the rear of the radiator then manoeuvre the radiator out from the front of the vehicle. On some models, it will be necessary to unbolt the crossmember from the front of the vehicle to gain the necessary clearance required to withdraw the radiator **(see illustrations)**.

Inspection

9 If the radiator has been removed due to suspected blockage, reverse flush it as described in Chapter 1. Clean dirt and debris from the radiator fins, using an air line (in which case, wear eye protection) or a soft brush. Be careful, as the fins are sharp and easily damaged.

10 If necessary, a radiator specialist can perform a "flow test" on the radiator, to establish whether an internal blockage exists.

11 A leaking radiator must be referred to a specialist for permanent repair. Do not attempt to weld or solder a leaking radiator, as damage may result.

12 In an emergency, minor leaks from the radiator can be cured using a suitable radiator sealant in accordance with the manufacturers instructions with the radiator *in situ*.

13 If the radiator is to be sent for repair or renewed, remove the cooling fan switch.

Refitting

14 Manoeuvre the radiator into position and refit its retaining bolts, tightening them to the specified torque setting. Where necessary, refit the crossmember and securely tighten all its mounting bolts.

15 On models with air conditioning, seat the condenser in position and securely tighten its retaining bolts. Refit the reservoir/drier

retaining nuts and ensure that all refrigerant lines are retained by all the relevant clips.

16 Reconnect the hoses to the radiator unions and securely tighten their clips.

17 Reconnect the wiring connector to the cooling fan switch.

18 Refit the headlights and front bumper as described in Chapters 11 and 12.

19 On completion, reconnect the battery and refill the cooling system (see Chapter 1).

4 Thermostat -
removal, testing and refitting

Removal

1 Disconnect the battery negative lead.
2 Drain the cooling system (see Chapter 1).

**1.4 litre and all 1.6 litre
(except AEK engine) models**

3 On these models the thermostat housing is on the left-hand end of the cylinder head.

4 Release the retaining clip and disconnect the coolant hose from the thermostat housing.

5 Slacken and remove the two bolts and remove the thermostat housing cover.

6 Recover the sealing ring and withdraw the thermostat. Discard the sealing ring; a new one should be used on refitting.

**1.6 litre (AEK engine) models
and all 1.8, 1.9 and 2.0 litre models**

7 On these models the thermostat is in the base of the coolant pump housing which is on the front, right-hand end of the engine.

8 On models with power steering, remove the pump drivebelt (see Chapter 1). Slacken and remove the bolts securing the power steering pump mounting bracket to the engine and position the pump assembly clear of the engine. It is not necessary to disconnect the hydraulic hose/pipe from the pump.

9 Release the retaining clip and disconnect the coolant hose from the thermostat cover.

10 Slacken and remove the two retaining bolts and remove the thermostat cover from the coolant pump housing **(see illustration)**.

11 Recover the sealing ring and withdraw the thermostat. Discard the sealing ring; a new one should be used on refitting **(see illustration)**.

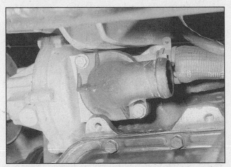

4.10 Undo the retaining bolts and remove the thermostat cover

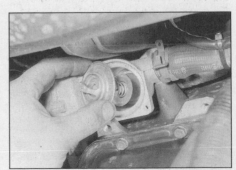

4.11 Recover the sealing ring, then withdraw the thermostat from its housing, noting its orientation

Testing

12 A rough test of the thermostat may be made by suspending it with a piece of string in a container full of water. Heat the water to bring it to the boil - the thermostat must open by the time the water boils. If not, renew it.

13 If a thermometer is available, the precise opening temperature of the thermostat may be determined, and compared with the figures given in the Specifications. The opening temperature is also marked on the thermostat.

14 A thermostat which fails to close as the water cools must also be renewed.

Refitting

1.4 litre and all 1.6 litre (except AEK engine) models

15 Refitting is a reversal of removal, bearing in mind the following points:

a) Ensure that the thermostat is correctly located in the housing then fit the new sealing ring.

b) Tighten the thermostat cover bolts to the specified torque setting.

c) On completion refill the cooling system as described in Chapter 1.

1.6 litre (AEK engine) models and all 1.8, 1.9 and 2.0 litre models

16 Refitting is the reverse of the removal sequence noting the following points:

a) Ensure that the thermostat is correctly located in the housing and fit the new sealing ring.

b) Tighten the cover bolts to the specified torque setting.

c) On models with power steering, tighten the mounting bracket bolts to the specified torque (see Chapter 10) and refit the drivebelt as described in Chapter 1.

d) On completion refill the cooling system as described in Chapter 1.

5 Electric cooling fan - testing, removal and refitting

Testing

1 The cooling fan is supplied with current through the ignition switch, cooling fan control unit (mounted on the left-hand front suspension turret), the relay(s) and fuses/fusible link (see Chapter 12). The circuit is completed by the cooling fan thermostatic switch, which is mounted in the left-hand end of the radiator. The cooling fan has two speed settings; the thermostatic switch actually contains two switches, one for the stage 1 fan speed setting and another for the stage 2 fan speed setting. **Note:** *On some models equipped with air conditioning, there is also a second switch (fitted into one of the coolant outlet housings/hoses on the cylinder head). This switch controls the cooling fan stage 3 speed setting.* Testing of the cooling fan circuit is as follows noting that the following check should be carried out on both the stage 1

speed circuit and speed 2 circuit (see wiring diagrams at the end of Chapter 12). **Note:** *On models with a twin cooling fan arrangement, if only one fan is working, the drivebelt linking the fans has broken.*

2 If a fan does not appear to work, first check the fuses/fusible links. If they are good, run the engine until normal operating temperature is reached, then allow it to idle. If the fan does not cut in within a few minutes, switch off the ignition and disconnect the wiring plug from the cooling fan switch. Bridge the relevant two contacts in the wiring plug using a length of spare wire, and switch on the ignition. If the fan now operates, the switch is probably faulty and should be renewed.

3 If the switch appears to work, the motor can be checked by disconnecting the motor wiring connector and connecting a 12 volt supply directly to the motor terminals. If the motor is faulty, it must be renewed, as no spares are available.

4 If the fan still fails to operate, check that the cooling fan circuit wiring (Chapter 12). Check each wire for continuity and ensure all connections are clean and free of corrosion.

5 If no fault can be found with the fuses/fusible links, wiring, fan switch, or fan motor then it is likely that the cooling fan control unit is faulty. Testing of the unit should be entrusted to a VW dealer; if the unit is faulty it must be renewed.

Removal

6 Remove the radiator (refer to Section 3). Disconnect the wiring connector from the rear of the cooling fan motor **(see illustration)**.

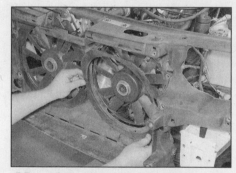

5.7 . . . then remove the fan retaining ring

5.8b On models with twin cooling fans, release the drivebelt from the fan pulley . . .

7 Press out the pins from the centre of the fan retaining ring fasteners and unclip the ring from the shroud **(see illustration)**.

8 Slacken and remove the motor retaining nuts and remove the cooling fan assembly from the front of the vehicle **(see illustrations)**. On models with twin cooling fans, as the motor is removed free it from the drivebelt linking the fans and remove the belt; if necessary undo the retaining nuts and remove the second fan. No spare parts are available for the motor, and if the unit is faulty, it must be renewed.

Refitting

9 Refitting is a reversal of removal, tightening the cooling fan retaining nuts to the specified torque. On models with twin fans, prior to refitting inspect the fan drivebelt for signs of damage or deterioration and renew if necessary.

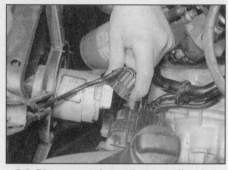

5.6 Disconnect the radiator cooling fan wiring connector . . .

5.8a Slacken and remove the fan retaining nuts from the rear of the shroud

5.8c . . . and remove the fan from the vehicle

10 Refit the radiator (see Section 3) then start the engine and run it until it reaches normal operating temperature. Continue to run the engine and check that the cooling fan cuts in and functions correctly.

6 Cooling system electrical switches - testing, removal and refitting

Electric cooling fan thermostatic switch

Testing

1 Testing of the switch is described in Section 5, as part of the electric cooling fan test procedure.

Removal

2 The switch is located in the left-hand side of the radiator. The engine and radiator should be cold before removing the switch.
3 Disconnect the battery negative lead.
4 Either drain the cooling system to below the level of the switch (as described in Chapter 1), or have ready a suitable plug which can be used to plug the switch aperture in the radiator whilst the switch is removed. If a plug is used, take great care not to damage the radiator, and do not use anything which will allow foreign matter to enter the radiator.
5 Disconnect the wiring plug from the switch.
6 Carefully unscrew the switch from the radiator.

Refitting

7 Refitting is a reversal of removal, applying a smear of suitable sealant to the threads of the switch and tightening it to the specified torque setting. On completion, refill the cooling system as described in Chapter 1 or top-up as described in "Weekly checks".
8 Start the engine and run it until it reaches normal operating temperature, then continue to run the engine and check that the cooling fan cuts in and functions correctly.

Coolant temperature gauge sensor

Note: On all models except the 2.0 litre 16-valve, the sender unit is an integral part of the fuel system/preheating system (as applicable) temperature sender unit.

Testing

9 The coolant temperature gauge, mounted in the instrument panel, is fed with a stabilised voltage supply from the instrument panel feed (through the ignition switch and a fuse), and its earth is controlled by the sensor.
10 The sensor unit is screwed into the left-hand end of the cylinder head on 2.0 litre 16-valve models and is clipped into the coolant outlet elbow on the front of the cylinder head on all other models. The sensor contains a thermistor, which consists of an electronic component whose electrical resistance decreases at a predetermined rate as its temperature rises. When the coolant is cold, the sensor resistance is high, current flow through the gauge is reduced, and the gauge needle points towards the "cold" end of the scale. If the sensor is faulty, it must be renewed.
11 If the gauge develops a fault, first check the other instruments; if they do not work at all, check the instrument panel electrical feed. If the readings are erratic, there may be a fault in the instrument panel assembly. If the fault lies in the temperature gauge alone, check it as follows.
12 If the gauge needle remains at the "cold" end of the scale, disconnect the wiring connector from the sensor unit, and earth the temperature gauge wire (see "Wiring diagrams" for details) to the cylinder head. If the needle then deflects when the ignition is switched on, the sensor unit is proved faulty, and should be renewed. If the needle still does not move, remove the instrument panel (Chapter 12) and check the continuity of the wiring between the sensor unit and the gauge, and the feed to the gauge unit. If continuity is shown, and the fault still exists, then the gauge is faulty and should be renewed.
13 If the gauge needle remains at the "hot" end of the scale, disconnect the sensor wire. If the needle then returns to the "cold" end of the scale when the ignition is switched on, the sensor unit is proved faulty and should be renewed. If the needle still does not move, check the remainder of the circuit as described previously.

Removal

14 Either partially drain the cooling system to just below the level of the sensor (as described in Chapter 1), or have ready a suitable plug which can be used to plug the sensor aperture whilst it is removed. If a plug is used, take great care not to damage the sensor unit aperture, and do not use anything which will allow foreign matter to enter the cooling system.
15 Disconnect the battery negative lead.
16 Disconnect the wiring from the sensor.
17 On 2.0 litre 16-valve models, unscrew the sensor unit from the end of the cylinder head and recover its sealing washer.
18 On all other models, depress the sensor unit and slide out its retaining clip. Withdraw the sensor from the coolant elbow and recover its sealing ring.

Refitting

19 On 2.0 litre 16-valve models, fit a new sealing washer to the sensor unit and fit it to the head, tightening it to the specified torque setting.
20 On all other models, fit a new sealing ring to the sensor unit. Push the sensor fully into the coolant elbow and secure it in position with the retaining clip.
21 Reconnect the wiring connector then refill the cooling system as described in Chapter 1 or top-up as described in "Weekly checks".

Fuel injection/preheating system coolant temperature sensor

22 On all models except the 2.0 litre 16-valve, the sensor is combined with the coolant temperature gauge sensor (see above). Testing of the sensor should be entrusted to a VW dealer.
23 On 2.0 litre 16-valve models, a separate sensor is fitted; the sensor being screwed into the left-hand end of the cylinder head. Testing of the sensor should be entrusted to a VW dealer and removal and refitting is as described above for the coolant temperature gauge sensor.

7 Coolant pump - removal and refitting

Removal

1.4 litre and all 1.6 litre (except AEK engine) models

1 Drain the cooling system as described in Chapter 1.
2 Remove the timing belt inner cover as described in the relevant Part of Chapter 2.
3 Withdraw the coolant pump from the cylinder block. Discard the sealing ring, a new one should be used on refitting. Note it is not possible to overhaul the pump. If it is faulty, the unit must be renewed.

1.6 litre (AEK engine) models and all 1.8, 1.9 and 2.0 litre models

Note: New coolant pump/thermostat housing assembly retaining studs/bolts will be required on refitting.
4 Drain the cooling system as described in Chapter 1.
5 Remove the alternator as described in 5.
6 On models equipped with power steering, remove the power steering pump as described in Chapter 10.
7 On models equipped with air conditioning, unbolt the compressor from its mounting bracket and position it clear of the engine. **Note:** Do not disconnect the refrigerant lines from the compressor (see Warnings in Section 11).
8 Slacken and remove the retaining bolts and remove the pulley from the coolant pump **(see illustrations)**.
9 Slacken and remove the nuts securing the alternator mounting bracket assembly to the side of the cylinder block and remove the bracket.
10 Release the retaining clips and disconnect the coolant hoses from the back of the coolant pump housing and the thermostat housing.
11 Unscrew the retaining studs/bolts (as applicable) securing the coolant pump/thermostat housing to the block and remove the housing assembly from the engine. **Note:** On some engines it will be necessary to unscrew the bolt(s) that secure the timing belt cover to the housing assembly

3

7.8a On 1.6 (AEK engine), 1.8, 1.9 and 2.0 litre models, undo the retaining bolts . . .

(see Chapter 2). Recover the sealing ring which is fitted between the housing and block and discard it; a new one should be used on refitting **(see illustrations)**.

12 With the assembly on a bench, unscrew the retaining bolts and remove the pump from the housing. Discard the gasket, a new one must be used on refitting **(see illustration)**. Note it is not possible to overhaul the pump. If it is faulty, the unit must be renewed.

Refitting

1.4 litre and all 1.6 litre (except AEK engine) models

13 Fit the new sealing ring to the rear of the pump and locate the pump in the cylinder block.

14 Refit the timing belt inner cover as described in the relevant Part of Chapter 2.

15 On completion refill the cooling system as described in Chapter 1.

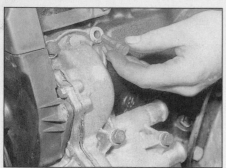

7.11a Slacken and remove the retaining bolts/studs . . .

the block . . .
7.11c . . . and recover its sealing ring

7.8b . . . and remove the pulley from the coolant pump

1.6 litre (AEK engine) models and all 1.8, 1.9 and 2.0 litre models

16 Ensure that the pump and housing mating surfaces are clean and dry and position a new gasket on the housing.

17 Fit the coolant pump to the housing and evenly tighten its retaining bolts to the specified torque setting.

18 Fit the new sealing ring to the housing assembly recess and refit the housing to the cylinder block. Fit the retaining studs/bolts (as applicable) and tighten them to the specified stage 1 torque setting and then through the specified stage 2 angle.

19 Connect the coolant hoses to the housing and securely tighten their retaining clips.

20 Refit the alternator mounting bracket to the engine and tighten its retaining nuts to the specified torque setting.

21 Refit the pulley to the coolant pump and tighten its retaining bolts to the specified

7.11b . . . then remove the coolant pump/thermostat housing assembly from

7.12 Undo the retaining bolts and remove the pump and gasket from housing

torque setting (this can be done once the drivebelt is refitted and tensioned).

22 Where necessary, refit the power steering pump as described in Chapter 10 and the air conditioning compressor.

23 Refit the alternator as described in Chapter 5.

24 On completion refill the cooling system as described in Chapter 1.

8 Heating and ventilation system - general information

1 The heating/ventilation system consists of a four-speed blower motor (housed in the passenger compartment), face-level vents in the centre and at each end of the facia, and air ducts to the front and rear footwells.

2 The control unit is located in the facia, and the controls operate flap valves to deflect and mix the air flowing through the various parts of the heating/ventilation system. The flap valves are contained in the air distribution housing, which acts as a central distribution unit, passing air to the various ducts and vents.

3 Cold air enters the system through the grille at the rear of the engine compartment. On some models (depending on specification) a pollen filter is fitted to the ventilation inlet to filter out dust, soot, pollen and spores from the air entering the vehicle.

4 The airflow, which can be boosted by the blower, then flows through the various ducts, according to the settings of the controls. Stale air is expelled through ducts behind the rear bumper. If warm air is required, the cold air is passed through the heater matrix, which is heated by the engine coolant.

5 If necessary, the outside air supply can be closed off, allowing the air inside the vehicle to be recirculated. This can be useful to prevent unpleasant odours entering from outside the vehicle, but should only be used briefly, as the recirculated air inside the vehicle will soon deteriorate.

6 Certain models may be fitted with heated front seats. The heat is produced by electrically-heated mats in the seat and backrest cushions (see Chapter 12). The temperature is regulated automatically by a thermostat, and cannot be adjusted.

9 Heater/ventilation components - removal and refitting

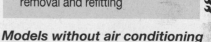

Models without air conditioning

Heater/ventilation control unit

1 Disconnect the battery negative lead.

2 Remove the cigarette lighter/facia switch panel as described in Section 11 of Chapter 12.

3 Withdraw the control unit from the facia and disconnect its wiring connectors.

4 Unclip the control cables and release each cable from the control unit, noting each

9.4a Release the outer cable retaining clip . . .

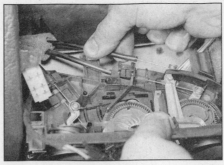

9.4b . . . and detach the control cable from the heater control unit

cable's correct fitted location and routing; to avoid confusion on refitting, label each cable as it is disconnected. The outer cables are released by simply lifting the retaining clips **(see illustrations)**.

5 Refitting is reversal of removal. Ensure that the control cables are correctly routed and reconnected to the control panel, as noted before removal. Clip the outer cables in position and check the operation of each knob/lever before refitting the centre facia panel.

Heater/ventilation control cables

6 Remove the heater/ventilation control unit from the facia as described above in paragraphs 1 to 4, detaching the relevant cable from the control unit.
7 Slacken and remove the passenger side facia shelf retaining screws. Move the shelf downwards, to release its upper retaining clips and remove it from the facia.
8 Release the retaining clips and remove the insulating sheet from underneath the air distribution/blower motor housing.
9 Follow the run of the cable behind the facia, taking note of its routing, and disconnect the cable from the lever on the air distribution/blower motor housing. Note that the method of fastening is the same as that used at the control unit.
10 Fit the new cable, ensuring that it is correctly routed and free from kinks and obstructions.
11 Connect the cable to the control unit and air distribution/blower motor housing making sure the outer cable is clipped securely in position.

12 Check the operation of the control knob then refit the control unit as described previously in this Section. Finally refit the insulating sheeting and facia shelf.

Heater matrix

13 Unscrew the expansion tank cap (referring to the Warning note in Section 1) to release any pressure present in the cooling system then securely refit the cap.
14 Clamp both heater hoses as close to the bulkhead as possible to minimise coolant loss. Alternatively, drain the cooling system as described in Chapter 1.
15 Release the retaining clips and disconnect both hoses from the heater matrix unions which are located in the centre of the engine compartment bulkhead **(see illustrations)**.
16 Remove the facia panel as described in Chapter 12.
17 Slacken the retaining nuts and free the earth terminal block and earth strap from both

the left- and right-hand ends of the facia mounting frame **(see illustration)**.
18 Release the plastic retaining clips securing the fusebox/relay plate assembly to the base of the facia mounting frame. Unhook the fusebox/relay plate assembly pivots and position it clear of the facia frame.
19 Unscrew the centre screw from the passenger side sill trim panel retaining clip then remove the retaining clip. Press down on the top of the front trim panel, to release its lower edge from the sill, then pull the panel upwards and remove it from the vehicle.
20 Undo the passenger side footwell panel retaining screw and remove the panel from the vehicle.
21 Using a pencil or felt tip pen, mark the outline of the outer facia mounting frame retaining bolts relative to the door pillars, to use as a guide on refitting.
22 Release the wiring harness from any retaining clips securing it to the facia frame.
23 Slacken and remove the nuts and bolts securing the centre mounting brackets to the frame and the two bolts securing the frame to the pedal bracket assembly **(see illustrations)**.
24 With the aid of an assistant, undo the four bolts securing the frame to the door pillars then ease the frame rearwards and remove it from the vehicle **(see illustrations)**.
25 Slacken the retaining screws and remove the rear footwell duct joining pieces from the base of the air distribution housing **(see illustrations)**.
26 Remove the retaining screw and fastener and remove the front footwell duct assembly

3

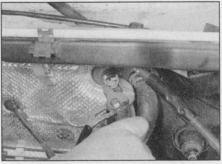

9.15a Release the retaining clips . . .

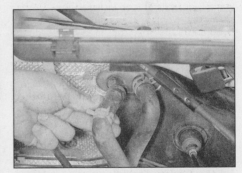

9.15b . . . and detach the coolant hoses from the heater matrix unions

9.17 Unscrew the nut and detach the earth block and strap (arrowed) from the facia

9.23a Slacken the bolts securing the facia frame to its lower centre bracket . . .

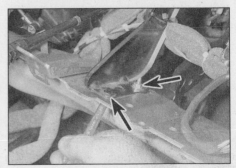

9.23b . . . and the nuts (locations arrowed) securing it to the upper centre bracket

9.24a Undo the bolts (arrowed) securing the mounting frame to the door pillars . . .

9.24b . . . and remove the frame from the vehicle

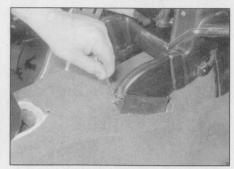

9.25a Undo the retaining screw . . .

9.25b . . . and remove the rear footwell duct pieces from the distribution housing

9.26a Slacken and remove the retaining screw and fastener (arrowed) . . .

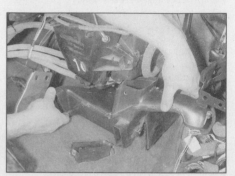

9.26b . . . and remove the front footwell duct assembly

from the base of the air distribution housing **(see illustrations)**.

27 Release the retaining clip and free the wiring connector from the side of the air distribution housing. Disconnect the wiring connector and those connected to the blower motor and resistor **(see illustrations)**.

28 From within the engine compartment, slacken and remove the three nuts securing the air distribution/blower motor housing in position, there are two nuts securing the air distribution housing to the bulkhead and a single nut securing the blower motor housing in position. **Note:** *The nuts are hidden behind the engine compartment bulkhead sound insulation material; if the insulation material is examined closely it will be seen that access holes are already provided.*

29 From inside the vehicle manoeuvre the air distribution/blower motor housing assembly out of position **(see illustration)**. **Note:** *Keep*

the matrix unions uppermost as the matrix is removed to prevent coolant spillage. Mop up any spilt coolant immediately and wipe the affected area with a damp cloth to prevent staining.

30 Recover the seal which is fitted between

the matrix union and bulkhead; the seal should be renewed if it shows signs of damage or deterioration.

31 Release the retaining clips and withdraw the matrix from the air distribution housing **(see illustrations)**.

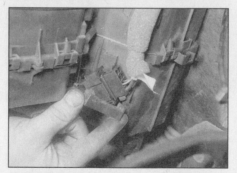

9.27a Release the wiring connector from the side of the air distribution housing . . .

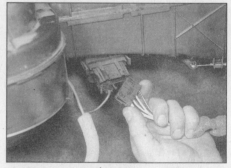

9.27b . . . and disconnect the wiring from the blower motor resistor

9.29 Removing the air distribution/blower motor housing assembly

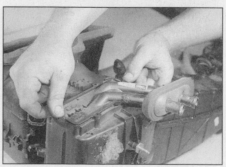

9.31a Release the retaining clips . . .

9.31b . . . and withdraw the heater matrix from the housing

32 Refitting is a reversal of removal, bearing in mind the following points:

a) *Ensure that the matrix is clipped securely into the air distribution housing.*

b) *Prior to refitting, make sure the foam seals on the top of the housings are in good condition and refit the seal to the matrix unions.*

c) *When tightening the air distribution/blower motor housing retaining nuts, have an assistant hold the assembly fully upwards to ensure an airtight seal between the housings and bulkhead.*

d) *Manoeuvre the facia mounting frame into position and refit all its retaining bolts. Align the end retaining bolts with the marks made prior to removal then go around and tighten all the retaining bolts securely.*

e) *On completion, refill the cooling system as described in Chapter 1.*

Heater blower motor

33 Disconnect the battery negative lead.

34 Slacken and remove the passenger side facia shelf retaining screws. Move the shelf downwards, to release its upper retaining clips and remove it from the facia **(see illustration)**.

35 Release the retaining clips and remove the insulating sheet from underneath the air distribution/blower motor housing.

36 Disconnect the motor wiring connectors from the resistor and the earth block on the facia frame.

37 Release the retaining clip then rotate the motor assembly and lower it out from the base of the housing **(see illustration)**.

38 Refitting is a reversal of the removal procedure making sure the motor is correctly clipped into the housing.

Heater blower motor resistor

39 Carry out the operations described in paragraphs 33 to 35.

40 Disconnect the wiring connectors from the resistor then release the retaining clips and withdraw the resistor from the housing **(see illustrations)**.

41 Refitting is the reverse of removal.

Models with air conditioning

Note: *The following information is only applicable to manually controlled air conditioning systems. At the time of writing no information was available on models with the automatic "Climatronic" system.*

Heater control unit

42 Refer to the information given in paragraphs 1 to 5.

Heater matrix

43 On models equipped with air conditioning it is not possible to remove the heater matrix without opening the refrigerant circuit (See Section 11). Therefore this task must be entrusted to a VW dealer.

9.34 Removing the passenger side facia shelf

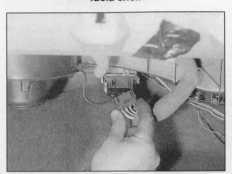

9.40a Disconnect the wiring connectors . . .

Heater blower motor

44 Carry out the operations described in paragraphs 33 to 35.

45 Disconnect the wiring connector from the motor then undo the retaining screws and lower the motor assembly out of position.

46 Refitting is the reverse of removal.

Heater blower motor resistor

47 On models equipped with a passenger side airbag, remove the airbag unit as described in Chapter 12.

48 On models not equipped with a passenger side airbag, remove the glovebox as described in Chapter 11, Section 28.

49 Disconnect the wiring connector then undo the retaining screw and remove the resistor from the housing.

50 Refitting is the reverse of removal.

10 Heater/ventilation vents and housings - removal and refitting

Vents

1 All vents can be carefully levered out of position with a small flat-bladed screwdriver, taking great care not to mark the vent housing **(see illustration)**.

2 On refitting, carefully manoeuvre the vent back into position ensuring it is correctly engaged with the locating pegs.

Driver's side facia vent housing

3 Remove the lighting switch as described in Chapter 12.

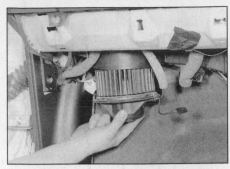

9.37 Removing the heater blower motor

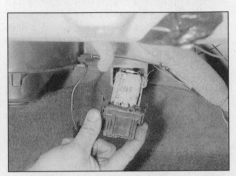

9.40b . . . then release the clips and withdraw the blower motor resistor

4 Remove the vent as described in paragraph 1.

5 Undo the retaining screws and remove the vent housing from the facia.

6 Refitting is the reverse of removal.

Passenger's side facia vent housing

7 Remove the vent as described in paragraph 1.

8 Undo the retaining screws and withdraw the vent housing from the facia.

9 Refitting is the reverse of removal.

Central facia vent housing

10 Remove the radio/cassette unit as described in Chapter 12.

11 Slacken and remove the vent housing retaining screws and withdraw the housing from the facia.

12 Refitting is the reverse of removal.

10.1 Removing a facia vent

3

11 Air conditioning system - general information and precautions

General information

An air conditioning system is available on certain models. It enables the temperature of incoming air to be lowered, and dehumidifies the air, which makes for rapid demisting and increased comfort.

The cooling side of the system works in the same way as a domestic refrigerator. Refrigerant gas is drawn into a belt-driven compressor and passes into a condenser mounted in front of the radiator, where it loses heat and becomes liquid. The liquid passes through an expansion valve to an evaporator, where it changes from liquid under high pressure to gas under low pressure. This change is accompanied by a drop in temperature, which cools the evaporator. The refrigerant returns to the compressor and the cycle begins again.

Air blown through the evaporator passes to the air distribution unit, where it is mixed with hot air blown through the heater matrix to achieve the desired temperature in the passenger compartment.

The heating side of the system works in the same way as on models without air conditioning (see Section 8).

The operation of the system is controlled electronically by coolant temperature switches (see Section 5), and pressure switches which are screwed into the compressor high-pressure line. Any problems with the system should be referred to a VW dealer.

Precautions

 Warning: The refrigeration circuit contains a liquid refrigerant (Freon) and it is therefore dangerous to disconnect any part of the system without specialised knowledge and equipment. The refrigerant is potentially dangerous and should only be handled by qualified persons. If it is splashed onto the skin it can cause frostbite. It is not itself poisonous, but in the presence of a naked flame (including a cigarette) it forms a poisonous gas. Uncontrolled discharging of the refrigerant is dangerous and potentially damaging to the environment. Do not operate the air conditioning system if it is known to be short of refrigerant, as this may damage the compressor.

When an air conditioning system is fitted, it is necessary to observe special precautions whenever dealing with any part of the system, its associated components and any items which require disconnection of the system. If for any reason the system must be disconnected, entrust this task to your VW dealer or a refrigeration engineer.

12 Air conditioning system components - removal and refitting

 Warning: Do not attempt to open the refrigerant circuit. Refer to the precautions given in Section 11.

1 The only operation which can be carried out easily without discharging the refrigerant is the renewal of the compressor drivebelt, which is covered in Chapter 1. All other operations must be referred to a VW dealer or an air conditioning specialist.
2 If necessary the compressor can be unbolted and moved aside, without disconnecting its flexible hoses, after removing the drivebelt.

Chapter 4 Part A:
Fuel system - single-point petrol injection

Contents

Degrees of difficulty

Easy, suitable for novice with little experience	Fairly easy, suitable for beginner with some experience	Fairly difficult, suitable for competent DIY mechanic	Difficult, suitable for experienced DIY mechanic	Very difficult, suitable for expert DIY or professional

Specifications

System type
All engine codes . . . . Bosch Mono-Motronic

Fuel system data
Fuel pump type . . . . Electric, immersed in fuel tank
Fuel pump delivery rate . . . . 1000 cm^3 / min (battery voltage of 12.5 V)
Regulated fuel pressure . . . . 0.8 to 1.2 bar
Engine idle speed . . . . 700-1000 rpm (non-adjustable, electronically controlled)
Maximum engine speed . . . . 6300 rpm (governed electronically)
Injector electrical resistance . . . . 1.2 to 1.6 ohms at 15°C

Recommended fuel
Minimum octane rating:
  Engine code ABU . . . . 91 RON
  Engine code ABD . . . . 91 RON
  Engine code AEA:
    With catalyst . . . . 95 RON
    Without catalyst . . . . Leaded
  Engine code AAM . . . . 91 RON
  Engine code ABS . . . . 95 RON
  Engine code ADZ . . . . 95 RON

Torque wrench settings	Nm	lbf ft
CO sampling pipe bracket to inlet manifold	20	15
Fuel pipe to throttle body banjo bolts (engine code ABD)	25	18
Fuel tank strap bolts	25	18
Injector cap/inlet air temperature sensor housing screw	5	4
Inlet manifold heater retaining screws	10	7
Inlet manifold retaining bolts	25	18
Lambda sensor (engine codes AAM, ABS, ADZ)	50	37
Lambda sensor (engine codes ABU, AEA, ABD)	55	41
Throttle body air box retaining screw	10	7
Throttle body retaining screws (engine codes AAM, ABS, ADZ)	10	7
Throttle body retaining screws (engine codes ABU, AEA, ABD)	15	11
Throttle valve positioning module screws	6	4
Warm-air collection plate to inlet manifold	25	18

1 General information and precautions

General information

The Bosch Mono-Motronic system is a self-contained engine management system, which controls both the fuel injection and ignition. This Chapter deals with the fuel injection system components only - refer to Chapter 5B for details of the ignition system components.

The fuel injection system comprises a fuel tank, an electric fuel pump, a fuel filter, fuel supply and return lines, a throttle body with an integral electronic fuel injector, and an Electronic Control Unit (ECU) together with its associated sensors, actuators and wiring.

The fuel pump delivers a constant supply of fuel through a cartridge filter to the throttle body, at a slightly higher pressure than required - the fuel pressure regulator (integral with the throttle body) maintains a constant fuel pressure at the fuel injector and returns excess fuel to the tank via the return line. This constant flow system also helps to reduce fuel temperature and prevents vaporisation.

The fuel injector is opened and closed by an Electronic Control Unit (ECU), which calculates the injection timing and duration according to engine speed, throttle position and rate of opening, inlet air temperature, coolant temperature, road speed and exhaust gas oxygen content information, received from sensors mounted on the engine.

Inlet air is drawn into the engine through the air cleaner, which contains a renewable paper filter element. The inlet air temperature is regulated by a vacuum operated valve mounted in the air cleaner, which blends air at ambient temperature with hot air, drawn from over the exhaust manifold.

Idle speed control is achieved partly by an electronic throttle positioning module, mounted on the side of the throttle body and partly by the ignition system, which gives fine control of the idle speed by altering the ignition timing. As a result, manual adjustment of the engine idle speed is not necessary.

To improve cold starting and idling (and fuel economy), an electric heating element is mounted on the underside of the inlet manifold; this prevents fuel vapour condensation when the engine is cold. Power is supplied to the heater by a relay, which is in turn controlled by the ECU.

The exhaust gas oxygen content is constantly monitored by the ECU via the Lambda sensor, which is mounted in the exhaust pipe. The ECU then uses this information to modify the injection timing and duration to maintain the optimum air/fuel ratio - a result of this is that manual adjustment of the idle exhaust CO content is not necessary. In addition, certain models are fitted with an exhaust catalyst - see Chapter 4D for details.

In addition, the ECU controls the operation of the activated charcoal filter evaporative loss system - refer to Chapter 4D for further details.

It should be noted that fault diagnosis of the Bosch Mono-Motronic system is only possible with dedicated electronic test equipment. Problems with the systems operation should therefore be referred to a VAG dealer for assessment. Once the fault has been identified, the removal/refitting sequences detailed in the following Sections will then allow the appropriate component(s) to be renewed as required.

Note: *Throughout this Chapter, vehicles are frequently referred to by their engine code, rather than by engine capacity - refer to Chapter 2A for engine code listings.*

Precautions

 Warning: Petrol is extremely flammable - great care must be taken when working on any part of the fuel system.

Do not smoke, or allow any naked flames or uncovered light bulbs near the work area. Note that gas powered domestic appliances with pilot flames, such as heaters boilers and tumble-dryers, also present a fire hazard - bear this in mind if you are working in an area where such appliances are present. Always keep a suitable fire extinguisher close to the work area and familiarise yourself with its operation before starting work. Wear eye protection when working on fuel systems and wash off any fuel spilt on bare skin immediately with soap and water. Note that fuel vapour is just as dangerous as liquid fuel; a vessel that has been emptied of liquid fuel will still contain vapour and can be potentially explosive.

Many of the operations described in this Chapter involve the disconnection of fuel lines, which may cause an amount of fuel spillage. Before commencing work, refer to the above Warning and the information in "Safety first!" at the beginning of this manual.

Residual fuel pressure always remain in the fuel system, long after the engine has been switched off. This pressure must be relieved in a controlled manner before work can commence on any component in the fuel system - refer to Section 9 for details.

When working with fuel system components, pay particular attention to cleanliness - dirt entering the fuel system may cause blockages which will lead to poor running.

In the interests of personal safety and equipment protection, many of the procedures in this Chapter suggest that the negative cable be removed from the battery terminal. This firstly eliminates the possibility of accidental short circuits being caused as the vehicle is being worked upon, and secondly prevents damage to electronic components (eg sensors, actuators, ECU's) which are particularly sensitive to the power surges caused by disconnection or reconnection of the wiring harness whilst they are still "live".

It should be noted, however, that many of the engine management systems described in this Chapter (and Chapter 5B) have a "learning" capability, that allows the system to adapt to the engine's running characteristics as it wears with use. This "learnt" information is lost when the battery is disconnected and the system will then take a short period of time to "re-learn" the engine's characteristics - this may be manifested (temporarily) as rough idling, reduced throttle response and possibly a slight increase in fuel consumption, until the system re-adapts. The re-adaptation time will depend on how often the vehicle is used and the driving conditions encountered.

2 Air cleaner and inlet system - removal and refitting

Removal

1 Slacken the worm drive clips and disconnect the air ducting from the air cleaner assembly.

2 Lift off the plastic cap, remove the retaining screw **(see illustration)** and lift off the throttle body air box, recovering the seal.

3 Disconnect the vacuum hoses from the inlet air temperature regulator vacuum switch, noting their order of fitment.

4 Unhook the rubber loops from the lugs on the chassis member.

5 Pull the air cleaner towards the engine and withdraw the air inlet hose from the port on the inner wing.

6 Lift the air cleaner out of the engine bay.

7 Prise open the retaining clips and lift the top cover from the air cleaner. Remove the air cleaner filter element (see Chapter 1A for more details).

8 On models with a round-type air cleaner, prise open the retaining clips and lift the cover

2.2 Remove the throttle body air box retaining screws (arrowed)

2.8 On the round-type air cleaner, prise open the air cleaner cover retaining clips

from the top of the air cleaner **(see illustration)**. Recover the filter element, then remove the retaining nuts and lift the air cleaner from the top of the throttle body.

Refitting

9 Refit the air cleaner by following the removal procedure in reverse.

3 Inlet air temperature regulator - removal and refitting

Removal

1 Disconnect the vacuum hoses from the temperature regulator, noting their locations.
2 Remove the throttle body air box/air cleaner, as described in Section 2.
3 Prise off the metal retaining plate **(see illustration)** and remove the temperature regulator from the throttle body air box/air cleaner. Recover the gasket.

Refitting

4 Refit the regulator by following the removal procedure in reverse.

4 Accelerator cable - removal, refitting and adjustment

Removal

1 Remove the throttle body air box/air cleaner as described in Section 2.

4.2 Throttle body accelerator cable mounting arrangement

A Throttle valve spindle plate
B Adjustment clip

3.3 Temperature regulator metal plate (arrowed)- wing-mounted air cleaner

2 At the throttle body, disconnect the accelerator cable inner from the throttle valve spindle plate **(see illustration)**.
3 Remove the adjustment clip and extract the cable outer from the mounting bracket `(refer to illustration 4.2).
4 Refer to Chapter 11 and remove the facia trim panels from underneath the steering column.
5 Working under the facia, depress the accelerator pedal slightly, then unclip the accelerator cable end from the pedal extension lever.
6 At the point where the cable passes through the bulkhead, unscrew the cap from the two-piece grommet so that the cable can move freely.
7 Release the cable from its clips and guide it out through the bulkhead grommet.

Refitting

8 Refit the accelerator cable by following the removal procedure in reverse.

Adjustment

Vehicles with manual transmission

9 At the throttle body, fix the position of the cable outer in its mounting bracket by inserting the metal clip in one of the locating slots, such that when the accelerator is depressed fully, the throttle valve is held wide open to its end stop.

Vehicles with automatic transmission

10 On vehicles with automatic transmission, place a block of wood 15 mm thick between the underside of the accelerator pedal and the stop on the floorpan, then hold the accelerator pedal down onto the block of wood.
11 At the throttle body, fix the position of the cable outer in its mounting bracket by inserting the metal clip in one of the locating slots, such that when the accelerator is depressed fully (onto the block of wood), the throttle valve is held wide open to its end stop.
12 Remove the block of wood and release the accelerator pedal. Refer to Chapter 7B and using a continuity tester, check that the kickdown switch contacts close as the accelerator pedal is depressed past the full throttle position, just before it contacts the stop on the floorpan.

5 Bosch Mono Motronic engine management system components - removal and refitting

Note: *Observe the precautions in Section 1 before working on any component in the fuel system.*

Throttle body

Removal

1 Refer to Section 2 and remove the air cleaner/throttle body air box.
2 Refer to Section 9 and depressurise the fuel system, then disconnect the battery negative cable and position it away from the terminal.
3 Disconnect the fuel supply and return hoses from the ports on the side of the throttle body. Note the arrows that denote the direction of fuel flow, and mark the hoses accordingly **(see illustration)**.
4 Unplug the wiring harness from the throttle body at the connectors, labelling them to aid correct refitting later.
5 Refer to Section 4 and disconnect the accelerator cable from the throttle body.
6 Remove the through-bolts and lift the throttle body away from the inlet manifold, recovering the gasket.

Refitting

7 Refitting is a reversal of removal; renew all gaskets where appropriate. On completion, check and if necessary adjust the accelerator cable. If the lower section of the throttle body has been renewed (with integral throttle potentiometer) in vehicles with electronic automatic transmission control, the new potentiometer must be matched to the transmission ECU; refer to a VAG dealer for advice as this operation requires access to dedicated test equipment.

Fuel injector

Removal

8 Refer to Section 2 and remove the air cleaner/throttle body air box.
9 Refer to Section 9 and depressurise the fuel system, then disconnect the battery negative cable and position it away from the terminal.

5.3 Throttle body fuel supply and return ports (engine code ABD shown)

4A

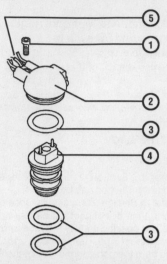

**5.11 Injector components
(engine code ABD shown)**

1 Screw
2 Injector cap/inlet air temperature
sensor housing
3 O-ring seals
4 Injector
5 Wiring harness connection

10 Unplug the wiring harness from the injector at the connector(s), labelling them to aid correct refitting later.
11 Remove the screw and lift off the injector retaining cap/ inlet air temperature sensor housing **(see illustration)**.
12 Lift the injector out of the throttle body, recovering the O-ring seals.
13 Check the injector electrical resistance using a multimeter and compare the result with the Specifications.

Refitting

14 Refit the injector by following the removal procedure in reverse, renewing all O-ring seals. Tighten the retaining screw to the specified torque.

Inlet air temperature sensor

15 The inlet air temperature sensor is an integral part of the injector retaining cap. Removal is as described in the previous sub-Section. Check its electrical resistance using a multimeter with a resistance measurement function **(refer to illustration 5.11)**.

Fuel pressure regulator

Removal

16 If the operation of the fuel pressure regulator is in question, dismantle the unit as described below, then check the cleanliness and integrity of the internal components.
17 Remove the air cleaner/throttle body air box, with reference to Section 2.
18 Refer to Section 9 and depressurise the fuel system, then disconnect the battery negative cable and position it away from the terminal.

19 With reference to the relevant sub-Section, remove the screw and lift off the inlet air temperature/injector cap.
20 Slacken and withdraw the retaining screws and lift off the fuel pressure regulator retaining frame **(see illustration)**.
21 Lift out the upper cover, spring and membrane.
22 Clean all the components thoroughly, then inspect the membrane for cracks or splits - renew it if necessary.

Refitting

23 Reassemble the pressure regulator by following the removal procedure in reverse.

Throttle valve positioning module

Removal

24 Disconnect the battery negative cable and position it away from the terminal. Remove the air cleaner/throttle body air box, with reference to Section 2.
25 Refer to Section 4 and disconnect the accelerator cable from the throttle body.
26 Unplug the connector from the side of the throttle valve positioning module.
27 Remove the retaining screws and lift the module together with the accelerator cable outer mounting bracket away from the throttle body.

Refitting

28 Refitting is a reversal of removal. Note that if a new module has been fitted, the adjustment of the idle switch will need to be checked - refer to a VAG dealer for advice as this operation requires access to dedicated test equipment.

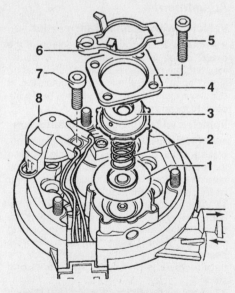

5.20 Fuel pressure regulator components

1 Membrane
2 Spring
3 Upper cover
4 Retaining frame
5 Screws
6 Cable guide
7 Injector retaining
  screw
8 Injector cap

**5.33 Lambda sensor
(engine code ABD shown)**

Throttle valve potentiometer

29 Refer to the relevant sub-Section and remove the throttle body. The throttle valve potentiometer is an integral part of the lower section of the throttle body and cannot be renewed separately.
30 Where a new lower throttle body (with throttle potentiometer) has been fitted in vehicles with electronic automatic transmission control, the potentiometer must be matched to the transmission ECU; refer to a VAG dealer for advice as this operation requires access to dedicated test equipment.

Idle switch

31 Refer to the relevant sub-Section and remove the throttle valve positioning module. The idle switch is an integral part of the module and cannot be renewed separately.
32 Where a new throttle valve positioning module has been fitted, the adjustment of the idle switch will need to be checked - refer to a VAG dealer for advice as this operation requires access to dedicated test equipment.

Lambda sensor

Removal

33 On engine codes ABU, ABD and AEA, the lambda sensor is threaded into the exhaust pipe, at the front of the first silencer/catalyst, as applicable. On engine codes AAM, ABS and ADZ, the lambda sensor is threaded into the exhaust manifold **(see illustration)**. Refer to Chapter 4D for details.
34 Disconnect the battery negative cable and position it away from the terminal, then unplug the wiring harness from the lambda sensor at the connector, located adjacent to the right hand rear engine mounting.
35 Note: *As a flying lead remains connected to the sensor after it has been disconnected, if the correct size spanner is not available, a slotted socket will be required to remove the sensor. Working under the vehicle, slacken and withdraw the sensor, taking care to avoid damaging the sensor probe as it is removed.*

Refitting

36 Apply a little anti-seize grease to the sensor threads only - keep the probe tip clean.
37 Refit the sensor to its housing, tightening it to the correct torque. Restore the harness

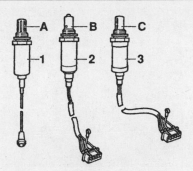

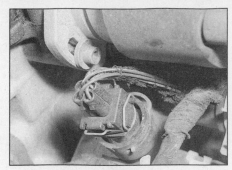

5.37 Lambda sensor versions
1 *Unheated probe - fitted up to September 1994 (manual transmission and catalyst)*
2 *Heated probe - fitted up to September 1994 (without catalyst)*
3 *Heated probe - fitted from October 1994 (automatic transmission and catalyst)*
A *Many slots*
B *Drillings*
C *Few slots*

connection. Note that the type of lambda sensor fitted depends on vehicle specification **(see illustration)**.

Coolant temperature sensor

Removal

38 Disconnect the battery negative cable and position it away from the terminal, then refer to Chapter 3 and drain approximately one quarter of the coolant from the engine.
39 On engine codes ABD, AEA and ABU the temperature sensor is located on the left hand side of the cylinder head, under the heater coolant outlet elbow **(see illustration)**. On engine codes AAM, ABS and ADZ, the sensor is mounted at the top coolant outlet elbow, at the front of the cylinder head.
40 Unscrew/unclip the sensor from its housing and recover the sealing washer(s) and O-ring - be prepared for an amount of coolant loss.

Refitting

41 Refit the sensor by reversing the removal procedure, using new sealing washers and rings where appropriate. Refer to Chapter 1A and top-up the cooling system.

6 Fuel filter - removal and refitting

Note: *Observe the precautions in Section 1 before working on any component in the fuel system.*

Removal

1 The fuel filter is mounted in the fuel supply line, in front of the fuel tank. Access is from the underside of the vehicle.
2 Refer to Section 9 and depressurise the fuel system.
3 Park the car on a level surface, then apply the handbrake and select 1st gear (manual

5.39 Coolant temperature sensor (engine code ABD shown)

transmission) or 'P' (automatic transmission) and chock the front roadwheels. Raise the rear of the vehicle, support it securely on axle stands and remove the roadwheels; refer to *"Jacking and vehicle support"* for guidance.
4 Slacken the hose clips and disconnect the fuel lines from either side of the filter unit **(see illustration)**. If the clips are of the crimp type, snip them off with cutters and replace them with equivalent size worm drive clips upon reconnection.
5 Release the filter retaining clip/remove the cover bracket (where applicable) and lower the filter unit away from its mounting bracket.

Refitting

6 Refitting is a reversal of removal. Note the direction of flow arrow marked on the side of the filter unit casing - this must point towards the engine when fitted **(see illustration)**.

6.4 Fuel filter hose clips (arrowed)

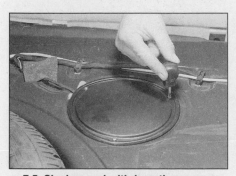

7.5 Slacken and withdraw the access hatch screws from the floorpan

7 Fuel pump and gauge sender unit - removal and refitting

Note: *Observe the precautions in Section 1 before working on any component in the fuel system.*

⚠ **Warning: Avoid direct skin contact with fuel - wear protective clothing and gloves when handling fuel system components. Ensure that the work area is well ventilated to prevent the build-up of fuel vapour.**

General information

1 The fuel pump and gauge sender unit are combined in one assembly, which is mounted on the top of the fuel tank. Access is via a hatch provided in the load space floor. The unit protrudes into the fuel tank and its removal involves exposing the contents of the tank to the atmosphere.

Removal

2 Depressurise the fuel system (Section 9).
3 Ensure that the vehicle is parked on a level surface, then disconnect the battery negative cable and position it away from the terminal.
4 Refer to Chapter 11 and remove the trim from the load space floor.
5 Slacken and withdraw the access hatch screws and lift the hatch away from the floorpan **(see illustration)**.
6 Unplug the wiring harness connector from the pump/sender unit **(see illustration)**.

6.6 Note the direction of flow arrow marked on the side of the filter unit

7.6 Unplug the wiring harness connector from the pump/sender unit

4A

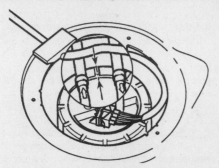

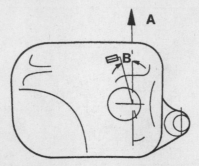

7.13a Arrow markings on the sender unit body and the fuel tank must be aligned

7.13b Pump/sender unit float arm must be installed as shown

A To front of vehicle   B Angle = 5°

7.13c Reconnect the fuel hoses to the correct ports - observe the direction of flow arrow markings

7 Pad the area around the supply and return fuel hoses with rags to absorb any spilt fuel, then slacken the hose clips and remove them from the ports at the sender unit. Observe the supply and return arrows markings on the ports - label the fuel hoses accordingly to ensure correct refitting later.

8 Unscrew the plastic securing ring and lift it out. Use a pair of water pump pliers to grip and rotate the plastic securing ring.

Turn the pump/sender unit to the left to release it from its bayonet fitting and lift it out, holding it above the level of the fuel in the tank until the excess fuel has drained out. Recover the rubber seal.

9 Remove the pump/sender unit from the vehicle and lay it on an absorbent card or rag. Inspect the float at the end of the sender unit swinging arm for punctures and fuel ingress - renew the unit if it appears damaged.

10 The fuel pick-up incorporated in the assembly is spring loaded to ensure that it always draws fuel from the lowest part of the tank. Check that the pick-up is free to move under spring tension with respect to the sender unit body.

11 Inspect the rubber seal from the fuel tank aperture for signs of fatigue - renew it if necessary.

12 Inspect the sender unit wiper and track; clean off any dirt and debris that may have accumulated and look for breaks in the track.

Refitting

13 Refit the sender unit by following the removal procedure in reverse, noting the following points:
- a) The arrow markings on the sender unit body and the fuel tank must be aligned.
- b) Smear the tank aperture rubber seal with clean fuel before fitting it in position.
- c) When correctly installed, the pump/sender unit float arm must point towards the front left hand side of the vehicle, by an angle that depends on vehicle model.
- d) Reconnect the fuel hoses to the correct ports - observe the direction of flow arrow markings **(see illustrations)**.

8 Fuel tank - removal and refitting

Note: *Observe the precautions in Section 1 before working on any component in the fuel system.*

Removal

1 Before the tank can be removed, it must be drained of as much fuel as possible. As no drain plug is provided, it is preferable to carry out this operation with the tank almost empty.

2 Disconnect the battery negative cable and position it away from the terminal. Using a hand pump or syphon, remove any remaining fuel from the bottom of the tank.

3 Refer to Section 7 and carry out the following:
- a) Disconnect the wiring harness from the top of the pump sender unit at the multiway connector.
- b) Disconnect the fuel supply and return hoses from the pump/sender unit.

4 Position a trolley jack under the centre of the tank. Insert a block of wood between the jack head and the tank to prevent damage to the tank surface. Raise the jack until it just takes the weight of the tank.

5 Working inside the rear right hand wheel arch, slacken and withdraw the screws that secure the tank filler neck inside of the wheel arch. Open the fuel filler flap and peel the rubber sealing flange away from the bodywork.

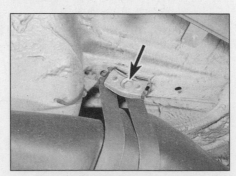

8.6 Remove the retaining screws from the tank securing straps (arrowed)

6 Remove the retaining screws from the tank securing straps **(see illustration)**, keeping one hand on the tank to steady it, as it is released from its mountings.

7 Lower the jack and tank away from the underside of the vehicle; disconnect the charcoal canister vent pipe from the port on the filler neck as it is exposed. Locate the earthing strap and disconnect it from the terminal at the filler neck.

8 If the tank is contaminated with sediment or water, remove the fuel pump/sender unit (see Section 7) and swill the tank out with clean fuel. The tank is injection moulded from a synthetic material and if damaged, it should be renewed. However, in certain cases it may be possible to have small leaks or minor damage repaired. Seek the advice of a suitable specialist before attempting to repair the fuel tank.

Refitting

9 Refitting is the reverse of the removal procedure noting the following points:
- a) When lifting the tank back into position make sure the mounting rubbers are correctly positioned and take care to ensure none of the hoses get trapped between the tank and vehicle body.
- b) Ensure that all pipes and hoses are correctly routed and securely held in position with their retaining clips.
- c) Reconnect the earth strap to its terminal on the filler neck.
- d) Tighten the tank retaining strap bolts to the specified torque.
- e) On completion, refill the tank with fuel and exhaustively check for signs of leakage prior to taking the vehicle out on the road.

9 Fuel injection system - depressurisation

Note: *Observe the precautions in Section 1 before working on any component in the fuel system.*

⚠️ **Warning: The following procedure will merely relieve the pressure in the fuel system - remember that fuel will still be** *present in the system components and take precautions accordingly before disconnecting any of them.*

1 The fuel system referred to in this Section is defined as the tank-mounted fuel pump, the fuel filter, the fuel injector, the throttle body-mounted fuel pressure regulator and the metal pipes and flexible hoses of the fuel lines between these components. All these contain fuel which will be under pressure while the engine is running and/or while the ignition is switched on. The pressure will remain for some time after the ignition has been switched off and must be relieved before any of these components are disturbed for servicing work. Ideally, the engine should be allowed to cool completely before work commences.

2 Refer to Chapter 12 and locate the fuel pump relay. Remove the relay from its housing, then crank the engine for a few seconds. The engine may fire and run for a while, but continue cranking until it stops. The fuel injector should have opened enough times during cranking to considerably reduce the line fuel pressure.

3 Disconnect the battery negative terminal.

4 Place a suitable container beneath the relevant connection/union to be disconnected, and have a large rag ready to soak up any escaping fuel not being caught by the container.

5 Slowly loosen the connection or union nut (as applicable) to avoid a sudden release of pressure and position the rag around the connection to catch any fuel spray which may be expelled. Once the pressure has been released, disconnect the fuel line and insert plugs to minimise fuel loss and prevent the entry of dirt into the fuel system.

10 Inlet manifold - removal and refitting

Note: *Observe the precautions in Section 1 before working on any component in the fuel system.*

Removal

1 Disconnect the battery negative cable and position it away from the terminal, then refer to Chapter 3 and drain the coolant from the engine.

2 With reference to Section 5, remove the throttle body from the inlet manifold. Recover and discard the gasket and where applicable, remove the intermediate flange.

3 Slacken the clips and remove the coolant hoses from the inlet manifold.

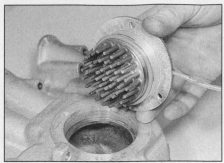

10.8 Remove the retaining screws and lift out the manifold heater unit

4 Refer to Chapter 9 and disconnect the brake servo vacuum hose from the port on the inlet manifold.

5 On engine codes ABU, AEA and ABD, carry out the following:
a) *Remove the screws and lift off the warm air collection plate.*
b) *Remove the screws and disconnect the exhaust CO sampling pipe from the inlet manifold.*

6 Disconnect the harness wiring from the inlet manifold heater at the connector.

7 Progressively slacken and remove the inlet manifold nuts and screws, then loosen the manifold from the cylinder head.

8 Make a final check to ensure that nothing remains connected to the manifold, then manoeuvre it out of the engine bay and recover the gasket. If required, remove the retaining screws and lift out the manifold heater unit **(see illustration)**.

Refitting

9 Refitting is the reverse of the removal procedure, noting the following points:
a) *Ensure that the manifold and cylinder head mating surfaces are clean and dry. Install the manifold with a new gasket and tighten its retaining nuts to the specified torque setting.*
b) *Ensure that all relevant hoses are reconnected to their original positions and are securely held (where necessary) by their retaining clips.*
c) *Refit the throttle body as described in Section 5.*
d) *On completion, refill the cooling system as described in Chapter 1.*

11 Fuel injection system - testing and adjustment

1 If a fault appears in the fuel injection system first ensure that all the system wiring connectors are securely connected and free

of corrosion. Then ensure that the fault is not due to poor maintenance; ie, check that the air cleaner filter element is clean, the spark plugs are in good condition and correctly gapped, the cylinder compression pressures are correct, the ignition timing is correct and the engine breather hoses are clear and undamaged, referring to Chapter 1A, Chapter 2A and Chapter 5B for further information.

2 If these checks fail to reveal the cause of the problem the vehicle should be taken to a suitably equipped VAG dealer for testing. A diagnostic connector is incorporated in the engine management system wiring harness, into which a dedicated electronic test equipment can be plugged. The test equipment is capable of "interrogating" the engine management system ECU electronically and accessing its internal fault log. In this manner, faults can be pinpointed quickly and simply, even if their occurrence is intermittent. Testing all the system components individually in an attempt to locate the fault by elimination is a time consuming operation that is unlikely to be fruitful (particularly if the fault occurs dynamically) and carries high risk of damage to the ECU's internal components.

3 Experienced home mechanics equipped with an accurate tachometer and a carefully-calibrated exhaust gas analyser may be able to check the exhaust gas CO content and the engine idle speed; if these are found to be out of specification, then the vehicle must be taken to a suitably-equipped VAG dealer for assessment. Neither the air/fuel mixture (exhaust gas CO content) nor the engine idle speed are manually adjustable; incorrect test results indicate a fault within the fuel injection system.

12 Unleaded petrol - general information and usage

Note: *The information given in this Chapter is correct at the time of writing and applies only to petrols currently available in the UK. Check with a VAG dealer as more up-to-date information may be available. If travelling abroad consult one of the motoring organisations (or a similar authority) for advice on the petrols available and their suitability for your vehicle.*

1 The fuel recommended by VAG is given in the Specifications of this Chapter.

2 RON and MON are different testing standards; RON stands for Research Octane Number (also written as RM), while MON stands for Motor Octane Number (also written as MM).

4A

Notes

Chapter 4 Part B:
Fuel system - multipoint petrol injection

Contents

Degrees of difficulty

Easy, suitable for novice with little experience	Fairly easy, suitable for beginner with some experience	Fairly difficult, suitable for competent DIY mechanic	Difficult, suitable for experienced DIY mechanic	Very difficult, suitable for expert DIY or professional

Specifications

System type
Engine code ADY	Simos
Engine code 2E	Digifant
Engine code ABF	Digifant 3.0, 3.2
Engine code AEK	Bosch Motronic

Fuel system data
Fuel pump type	Electric, immersed in fuel tank
Fuel pump delivery rate	1100 cm^3 / min (battery voltage of 12.6 V)
Regulated fuel pressure	2.5 bar
Engine idle speed (non-adjustable, electronically controlled):	
Engine code ADY	750 to 850 rpm
Engine code 2E	770 to 870 rpm
Engine code ABF	770 to 890 rpm
Engine code AEK	800 to 880 rpm
Idle CO content (non-adjustable, electronically controlled):	
Engine code ADY	N/A
Engine code 2E	0.2 to 1.2 %
Engine code ABF	0.3 to 1.2 %
Engine code AEK	N/A
Injector electrical resistance:	
Engine codes ADY, 2E, ABF	15 to 20 ohms
Engine code AEK	14 to 21.5 ohms

Recommended fuel
Minimum octane rating (all models)	95 RON

Torque wrench settings
	Nm	lbf ft
Fuel rail upper to lower section screw (engine codes ABF and 2E)	10	7
Inlet manifold temperature sensor (engine code AEK)	10	7
Inlet manifold to cylinder head	25	18
Lambda sensor	50	37
Throttle body through-bolts (M6 bolts)	10	7
Throttle body through-bolts (M8 bolts)	20	15
Upper inlet manifold to lower inlet manifold bolts (ABF and AEK)	20	15

4B

1 General information and precautions

General information

The Bosch Motronic, Digifant and Simos systems are self-contained engine management systems, which control both the fuel injection and ignition. This Chapter deals with the fuel system components only - see Chapter 5B for details of the ignition system.

The fuel injection system comprises a fuel tank, an electric fuel pump, a fuel filter, fuel supply and return lines, a throttle body, a fuel rail, a fuel pressure regulator, four electronic fuel injectors, and an Electronic Control Unit (ECU) together with its associated sensors, actuators and wiring. The component layout varies from system to system - refer to the relevant Section for details.

The fuel pump delivers a constant supply of fuel through a cartridge filter to the fuel rail, at a slightly higher pressure than required - the fuel pressure regulator maintains a constant fuel pressure to the fuel injectors and returns excess fuel to the tank via the return line. This constant flow system also helps to reduce fuel temperature and prevents vaporisation.

The fuel injectors are opened and closed by an Electronic Control Unit (ECU), which calculates the injection timing and duration according to engine speed, crankshaft position, throttle position and rate of opening, inlet manifold depression (or inlet air volume flow rate, depending on system type), inlet air temperature, coolant temperature, road speed and exhaust gas oxygen content information, received from sensors mounted on and around the engine. Refer to the relevant Section for specific details of the components utilised in each system.

Inlet air is drawn into the engine through the air cleaner, which contains a renewable paper filter element. The inlet air temperature is regulated by a vacuum operated valve mounted in the air cleaner, which blends air at ambient temperature with hot air, drawn from over the exhaust manifold.

Idle speed control is achieved partly by an electronic throttle valve positioning module, on the side of the throttle body and partly by the ignition system, which gives fine control of the idle speed by altering the ignition timing. As a result, manual adjustment of the engine idle speed is not necessary or possible.

The exhaust gas oxygen content is constantly monitored by the ECU via the Lambda sensor, which is mounted in the exhaust pipe. The ECU then uses this information to modify the injection timing and duration to maintain the optimum air/fuel ratio - a result of this is that manual adjustment of the idle exhaust CO content is not necessary or possible. In addition, certain models are fitted with an exhaust catalyst - see Chapter 4D.

Where fitted, the ECU controls the operation of the activated charcoal filter

evaporative loss system - refer to Chapter 4D for further details.

It should be noted that fault diagnosis of all the engine management systems described in this Chapter is only possible with dedicated electronic test equipment. Problems with the systems operation should therefore be referred to a VAG dealer for assessment. Once the fault has been identified, the removal/refitting sequences detailed in the following Sections will then allow the appropriate component(s) to be renewed as required.

Note: *Throughout this Chapter, vehicles are frequently referred to by their engine code, rather than by engine capacity - refer to Chapter 2A for engine code listings.*

Precautions

Warning: Petrol is extremely flammable - great care must be taken when working on any part of the fuel system.

Do not smoke, or allow any naked flames or uncovered light bulbs near the work area. Note that gas powered domestic appliances with pilot flames, such as heaters, boilers and tumble-dryers, also present a fire hazard - bear this in mind if you are working in an area where such appliances are present. Always keep a suitable fire extinguisher to hand and familiarise yourself with its operation before starting work. Wear eye protection when working on fuel systems and wash off any fuel spilt on bare skin immediately with soap and water. Note that fuel vapour is just as dangerous as liquid fuel; a vessel that has been emptied of liquid fuel will still contain vapour and can be potentially explosive.

Many of the operations described in this Chapter involve the disconnection of fuel lines, which may cause some fuel spillage. Before commencing work, refer to the above Warning and the information in "Safety first!" at the start of this manual.

Residual fuel pressure always remain in the fuel system, long after the engine has been switched off. This pressure must be relieved in a controlled manner before work can commence on any component in the fuel system - refer to Section 10 for details.

When working with fuel system components, pay particular attention to cleanliness - dirt entering the fuel system may cause blockages which will lead to poor running.

In the interests of personal safety and equipment protection, many of the procedures in this Chapter suggest that the negative cable be removed from the battery terminal. This firstly eliminates the possibility of accidental short-circuits being caused as the vehicle is being worked upon, and secondly prevents damage to electronic components (eg sensors, actuators, ECU's) which are very

sensitive to the power surges caused by disconnection or reconnection of the wiring harness whilst they are still "live".

It should be noted, however, that many of the engine management systems described in this Chapter (and Chapter 5B) have a "learning" capability, that allows the system to adapt to the engine's running characteristics as it wears with normal use. This "learnt" information is lost when the battery is disconnected and on reconnection, the system will then take a short period of time to "re-learn" the engine's characteristics - this may be manifested (temporarily) as rough idling, reduced throttle response and possibly a slight increase in fuel consumption, until the system re-adapts. The re-adaptation time will depend on how often the vehicle is used and the driving conditions encountered.

2 Air cleaner and inlet system - removal and refitting

Removal

1 Slacken the worm-drive clips and disconnect the air ducting from the air cleaner assembly.

2 Where applicable, slacken the clip and disconnect the warm air duct from the base of the air cleaner.

3 On all engine codes except ABF, refer to Section 5, 6 or 7 and remove the airflow meter from the air cleaner. *Caution: The airflow meter is a delicate component - handle it carefully.*

4 Disconnect the vacuum hoses from the inlet air temperature regulator vacuum switch, noting their order of fitment.

5 Unhook the rubber loops from the lugs on the chassis member.

6 Pull the air cleaner towards the engine and withdraw the air inlet hose from the port on the inner wing.

7 Lift the air cleaner out of the engine bay and recover the rubber mountings.

8 Prise open the retaining clips and lift the top cover from the air cleaner. Remove the air cleaner filter element (see Chapter 1A for more details).

Refitting

9 Refit the air cleaner by following the removal procedure in reverse.

3 Inlet air temperature regulation system - general information and component renewal

General information

1 The inlet air regulation system consists of a temperature controlled vacuum switch, mounted in the air cleaner housing, a vacuum operated flap valve and several lengths of interconnecting vacuum hose. The switch senses the temperature of the inlet air and opens when a preset lower limit is reached. It then directs the manifold vacuum to the flap valve which opens, allowing warm air drawn from around the exhaust manifold to blend with the inlet air.

Component renewal

Temperature switch

2 With reference to Section 2, release the clips and remove the top cover from the air cleaner.

3 Disconnect the vacuum hoses from the temperature switch, noting their order of connection to ensure correct refitting.

4 Prise the metal retaining clip off the temperature switch ports, then press the switch body through into the top of the air cleaner. Recover the gasket.

5 Refitting is a reversal of removal.

Flap valve

6 The flap valve is integrated with the lower section of the air cleaner and cannot be renewed separately.

4 Accelerator cable - removal, refitting and adjustment

Note: *Observe the precautions in Section 1 before working on any component in the fuel system.*

Removal

1 Remove the throttle body air box/air cleaner as described in Section 2.

2 At the throttle body, prise off the clip and disconnect the accelerator cable inner from the throttle valve spindle **(see illustrations)**.

3 Remove the metal clip and extract the cable outer from the mounting bracket **(see illustrations)**.

4 Refer to Chapter 11 and remove the facia trim panels from underneath the steering column.

5 Depress the accelerator pedal slightly, then unclip the accelerator cable end from the pedal extension lever.

6 At the point where the cable passes through the bulkhead, unscrew the cap from the two-piece grommet so that the cable can move freely.

7 Release the cable from its securing clips and guide it out through the bulkhead grommet.

Refitting

8 Refit the accelerator cable by following the removal procedure in reverse.

Adjustment

Vehicles with manual transmission

9 At the throttle body, fix the position of the cable outer in its mounting bracket by inserting the metal clip in one of the locating slots, such that when the accelerator is depressed fully, the throttle valve is held wide open to its end stop.

Vehicles with automatic transmission

10 On vehicles with automatic transmission, place a block of wood 15 mm thick between the underside of the accelerator pedal and the stop on the floorpan, then hold the accelerator pedal down onto the block of wood.

11 At the throttle body, fix the position of the cable outer in its bracket by inserting the metal clip in one of the locating slots, such that when the accelerator is depressed fully (onto the block of wood), the throttle valve is held wide open to its end stop.

12 Remove the block of wood and release the accelerator pedal. Refer to Chapter 7B and using a continuity tester, check that the kickdown switch contacts close as the accelerator pedal is depressed past the full throttle position, just before it contacts the stop on the floorpan.

5 Bosch Motronic engine management system components - removal and refitting

Note: *Observe the precautions in Section 1 before working on any component in the fuel system.*

Airflow meter

Removal

1 Disconnect the battery negative cable and position it away from the terminal.

2 With reference to Section 2 , slacken the clips and disconnect the air ducting from the airflow meter, at the rear of the air cleaner housing.

3 Unplug the harness connector from the airflow meter.

4 Remove the retaining screws and extract the meter from the air cleaner housing. Recover the O-ring seal. *Caution: Handle the airflow meter carefully - its internal components are easily damaged.*

Refitting

5 Refitting is a reversal of removal. Renew the O-ring seal if it appears damaged.

Throttle valve potentiometer

Removal

6 Disconnect the battery negative cable and position it away from the terminal.

7 Unplug the harness connector from the potentiometer.

8 Remove the retaining screws and lift the potentiometer away from the throttle body. Recover the O-ring seal.

Refitting

9 Refitting is a reversal of removal, noting the following:

　a) Renew the O-ring seal if it is damaged.

　b) Ensure that the potentiometer drive engages correctly with the throttle spindle extension.

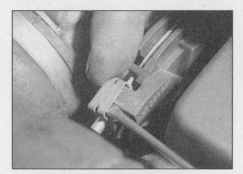

4.2a At the throttle body, prise off the clip . . .

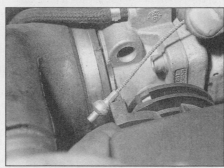

4.2b . . . and disconnect the accelerator cable inner from the throttle valve

4.3a Remove the metal clip . . .

4.3b . . . and extract the cable outer from the bracket (engine code 2E shown)

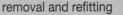

c) *On vehicles with automatic transmission, the potentiometer must be matched to the automatic transmission Electronic Control Unit (ECU) - this operation requires access to dedicated electronic test equipment, refer to a VAG dealer for advice.*

Inlet manifold temperature sensor

Removal

10 The sensor is threaded into the right hand side of the upper section of the inlet manifold.
11 Disconnect the battery negative cable and position it away from the terminal. Unplug the harness connector from the sensor.
12 Unscrew the sensor from the manifold using a suitable spanner.

Refitting

13 Refitting is a reversal of removal, observe the correct tightening torque.

Idling stabilisation valve

Removal

14 The valve is mounted on a bracket on the rear of the upper section of the inlet manifold.
15 Disconnect the battery negative cable and position it away from the terminal. Unplug the harness connector from the sensor.
16 Slacken the clips and disconnect the inlet air duct hose and the inlet silencer unit hose from the ports on the idle stabilisation valve.
17 Slacken the mounting bracket retaining clip and remove the valve from the manifold.

Refitting

18 Refitting is a reversal of removal.

Road speed sensor

19 The road speed sensor is mounted on the transmission - refer to Chapter 7A or B as applicable.

Coolant temperature sensor

Removal

20 The coolant temperature sensor is mounted in the coolant outlet elbow on the front of the cylinder head (see Chapter 3).
21 Disconnect the battery negative cable and position it away from the terminal, then unplug the harness connector from the sensor.
22 Refer to Chapter 3 and drain approximately one quarter of the coolant from the engine.
23 Extract the retaining clip and lift the sensor from the coolant elbow - be prepared for an amount of coolant loss. Recover the O-ring.

Refitting

24 Refit the sensor by reversing the removal procedure, using a new O-ring. Refer to Chapter 1A and top-up the cooling system.

Engine speed sensor

Removal

25 The engine speed sensor is mounted on the front cylinder block, adjacent to the mating surface of the block and transmission bellhousing. If necessary, drain the engine oil and remove the oil filter and cooler to improve access - see Chapter 2A for details.
26 Disconnect the battery negative cable and position it away from the terminal, then unplug the harness connector from the sensor.
27 Remove the retaining screw and withdraw the sensor from the cylinder block.

Refitting

28 Refit the sensor by reversing the removal procedure.

Throttle body

29 Refer to Section 4 and detach the accelerator cable from the throttle valve lever.
30 Slacken the clips and detach the inlet air ducting from the throttle body.
31 Disconnect the battery negative cable and position it away from the terminal, then unplug the harness connector from the throttle potentiometer.
32 Disconnect the vacuum hose from the port on the throttle body, then release the wiring harness from the guide clip.
33 Slacken and withdraw the through-bolts, then lift the throttle body away from the inlet manifold. Recover and discard the gasket.
34 If required, refer to the relevant sub-Section and remove the throttle potentiometer.

Refitting

35 Refitting is a reversal of removal, noting the following:

a) *Use a new throttle body-to-inlet manifold gasket.*
b) *Observe the correct tightening torque when refitting the throttle body through-bolts.*
c) *Ensure that all vacuum hoses and electrical connectors are refitted securely.*
d) *With reference to Section 4, check and if necessary adjust the accelerator cable.*

Fuel injectors and fuel rail

Note: *Observe the precautions in Section 1 before working on any component in the fuel system.*

Removal

36 Disconnect the battery negative cable and position it away from the terminal.
37 Refer to the relevant sub-Section in this Chapter and remove the throttle body, then refer to Section 12 and remove the upper section of the inlet manifold.
38 Unplug the injector harness connectors, labelling them to aid correct refitting later.
39 Refer to Section 10 and depressurise the fuel system.
40 Disconnect the vacuum hose from the port on the top of the fuel pressure regulator.
41 Slacken the clips and disconnect the fuel supply and return hoses from the end of the fuel rail. *Carefully* note the fitted positions of the hoses - the supply hose is marked with a white arrow and the return hose is marked with a blue arrow.
42 Slacken and withdraw the fuel rail retaining screws, then carefully lift the rail away from the inlet manifold, together with the injectors. Recover the injector lower O-ring seals as they emerge from the manifold **(see illustration)**.
43 The injectors can be removed individually from the fuel rail by extracting the relevant metal clip and easing the injector out of the rail. Recover the injector upper O-ring seals.
44 If required, remove the fuel pressure regulator, referring to the relevant sub-Section for guidance.
45 Check the electrical resistance of the injector using a multimeter and compare it with the Specifications. **Note:** *If a faulty injector is suspected, before condemning the injector, it is worth trying the effect of one of the proprietary injector-cleaning treatments.*

Refitting

46 Refit the injectors and fuel rail by following

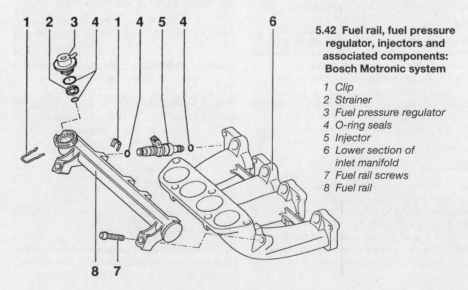

5.42 Fuel rail, fuel pressure regulator, injectors and associated components: Bosch Motronic system

1 *Clip*
2 *Strainer*
3 *Fuel pressure regulator*
4 *O-ring seals*
5 *Injector*
6 *Lower section of inlet manifold*
7 *Fuel rail screws*
8 *Fuel rail*

the removal procedure in reverse, noting the following points:

a) Renew the injector O-ring seals if they appear worn or damaged.

b) Ensure that the injector retaining clips are securely seated.

c) Check that the fuel supply and return hoses are reconnected correctly - refer to the colour coding described in "Removal".

d) Use a new gasket when refitting the upper section of the inlet manifold.

e) Check that all vacuum and electrical connections are remade correctly and securely.

f) On completion, check exhaustively for fuel leaks before bringing the vehicle back into service.

Fuel pressure regulator

Note: *Observe the precautions in Section 1 before working on any component in the fuel system.*

Removal

47 Disconnect the battery negative cable and position it away from the terminal.

48 Remove the screws and lift the deflector plate away from the regulator housing.

49 Refer to Section 10 and depressurise the fuel system.

50 Disconnect the vacuum hose from the port on the top of the fuel pressure regulator.

51 Slacken the clip and disconnect the fuel supply hose from the end of the fuel rail **(refer to illustration 5.42)**. This will allow the majority of fuel in the regulator to drain out. Be prepared for an amount of fuel loss - position a small container and some old rags underneath the fuel regulator housing. **Note:** *The supply hose is marked with a white arrow.*

52 Extract the retaining clip from the side of the regulator housing and lift out the regulator body, recovering the O-ring seals and the strainer plate.

53 Examine the strainer plate for contamination and clean it in fuel if necessary.

Refitting

54 Refit the fuel pressure regulator by following the removal procedure in reverse, noting the following points:

a) Renew the O-ring seals if they appear worn or damaged.

b) Ensure that the regulator retaining clip is securely seated.

c) Refit the regulator vacuum hose securely.

Lambda sensor

Removal

55 The lambda sensor is threaded into the exhaust pipe, at the front of the catalytic converter. Refer to Chapter 4D for details

56 Disconnect the battery negative cable and position it away from the terminal, then unplug the wiring harness from the lambda sensor at the connector, located adjacent to the right hand rear engine mounting.

57 Working under the vehicle, slacken and withdraw the sensor, taking care to avoid damaging the sensor probe as it is removed. **Note:** *As a flying lead remains connected to the sensor after is has been disconnected, if the correct size spanner is not available, a slotted socket will be required to remove the sensor.*

Refitting

58 Apply a little anti-seize grease to the sensor threads - avoid contaminating the probe tip.

59 Refit the sensor to its housing, tightening it to the correct torque. Restore the harness connection.

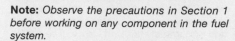

6 Simos engine management system components - removal and refitting

Note: *Observe the precautions in Section 1 before working on any component in the fuel system.*

Airflow meter

Removal

1 Disconnect the battery negative cable and position it away from the terminal.

2 With reference to Section 2 , slacken the clips and disconnect the air ducting from the airflow meter, at the rear of the air cleaner housing.

3 Unplug the harness connector from the airflow meter.

4 Remove the retaining screws and extract the meter from the air cleaner housing. Recover the O-ring seal. *Caution: Handle the airflow meter carefully - its internal components are easily damaged.*

Refitting

5 Refitting is a reversal of removal. Renew the O-ring seal if it appears damaged.

Throttle valve potentiometer

6 The throttle valve potentiometer is an integral part of the throttle body - refer to the information in the relevant sub-Section.

Inlet manifold temperature sensor

Removal

7 The sensor is mounted on the side of the air cleaner housing.

8 Disconnect the battery negative cable and position it away from the terminal. Unplug the harness connector from the sensor.

9 Extract the retaining clip and withdraw the sensor from its housing.

Refitting

10 Refitting is a reversal of removal.

Road speed sensor

11 The road speed sensor is mounted on the transmission - refer to Chapter 7A or B as applicable.

Coolant temperature sensor

Removal

12 The coolant temperature sensor is mounted in the coolant outlet elbow on the front of the cylinder head (see Chapter 3).

13 Disconnect the battery negative cable and position it away from the terminal, then unplug the harness connector from the sensor.

14 Refer to Chapter 3, and drain approximately one quarter of the coolant from the engine.

15 Extract the retaining clip and lift the sensor from the coolant elbow - be prepared for an amount of coolant loss. Recover the O-ring.

Refitting

16 Refit the sensor by reversing the removal procedure, using a new O-ring. Refer to Chapter 1A and top-up the cooling system.

Engine speed sensor

Removal

17 The engine speed sensor is mounted on the front cylinder block, adjacent to the mating surface of the block and transmission bellhousing. If necessary, drain the engine oil and remove the oil filter (and where applicable oil cooler) to improve access - see Chapter 2A for details.

18 Disconnect the battery negative cable and position it away from the terminal, then unplug the harness connector from the sensor.

19 Remove the retaining screw and withdraw the sensor from the cylinder block.

Refitting

20 Refit the sensor by reversing the removal procedure.

Throttle body

21 Refer to Section 4 and detach the accelerator cable from the throttle valve lever.

22 Slacken the clips and detach the inlet air ducting from the throttle body.

23 Disconnect the battery negative cable and position it away from the terminal, then unplug the harness connector from the throttle positioning valve module, mounted at the rear of the throttle body.

24 Disconnect the vacuum hose from the port on the throttle body, then release the wiring harness from the guide clip.

25 Refer to Chapter 3, and drain approximately one quarter of the coolant from the engine. Slacken the clips and disconnect the coolant hoses from the ports at the base of the throttle body, making a careful note of their fitted positions.

26 Disconnect the charcoal filter emission control system vacuum hose from the port at the top of the throttle body.

27 Slacken and withdraw the through-bolts, then lift the throttle body away from the inlet manifold. Recover and discard the gasket.

4B

Refitting

28 Refitting is a reversal of removal, noting the following:
a) Use a new throttle body-to-inlet manifold gasket.
b) Observe the correct tightening torque when refitting the throttle body through-bolts.
c) Ensure that the coolant hoses are correctly refitted - the hose from the cylinder head connects to the port furthest from the inlet manifold.
d) Ensure that all the vacuum hoses and electrical connectors are refitted securely.
e) Refer to Chapter 1A and top-up the cooling system.
f) Check and if necessary adjust the accelerator cable.

Fuel injectors and fuel rail

Note: *Observe the precautions in Section 1 before working on any component in the fuel system.*

Removal

29 Disconnect the battery negative cable and position it away from the terminal.
30 Unplug the injector harness connectors, labelling them to aid correct refitting later.
31 Depressurise the fuel system (Section 10).
32 Disconnect the vacuum hose from the port on the top of the fuel pressure regulator.
33 Slacken the clips and disconnect the fuel supply and return hoses from the end of the fuel rail. *Carefully* note the fitted positions of the hoses and label them to aid refitting later.
34 Slacken and withdraw the fuel rail screws, then carefully lift the rail away from the inlet manifold, together with the injectors. Recover the injector inserts and lower O-ring seals as they emerge from the manifold.
35 The injectors can be removed individually from the fuel rail by extracting the relevant metal clip and easing the injector out of the rail. Recover the injector upper O-ring seals.
36 If required, remove the fuel pressure regulator, referring to the relevant sub-Section for guidance.
37 Check the electrical resistance of the injector using a multimeter and compare it with the Specifications. **Note:** *If a faulty injector is suspected, before condemning the injector, it is worth trying the effect of one of the proprietary injector-cleaning treatments.*

Refitting

38 Refit the injectors and fuel rail by following the removal procedure in reverse, noting the following points:
a) Renew the injector O-ring seals if they appear worn or damaged.
b) Ensure that the injector retaining clips are securely seated.
c) Check that the fuel supply and return hoses are reconnected correctly, according to the notes made during "Removal" - the fuel return port faces downwards.

d) Check that all vacuum and electrical connections are remade correctly and securely.
e) On completion, check exhaustively for fuel leaks before bringing the vehicle back into service.

Fuel pressure regulator

Note: *Observe the precautions in Section 1 before working on any component in the fuel system.*

Removal

39 Disconnect the battery negative cable and position it away from the terminal.
40 Refer to Section 10 and depressurise the fuel system.
41 Disconnect the vacuum hose from the port on the top of the fuel pressure regulator.
42 Slacken the clip and disconnect the fuel return hose from the end of the fuel rail. This will allow the majority of fuel in the fuel rail to drain out. Be prepared for an amount of fuel loss - position a small container and some old rags underneath the port. **Note:** *The return port faces downwards.*
43 Extract the retaining clip from the side of the regulator housing and lift out the regulator body, recovering the O-ring seals and the strainer plate.
44 Examine the strainer plate for contamination and clean it if necessary, using neat fuel.

Refitting

45 Refit the fuel pressure regulator by following the removal procedure in reverse, noting the following points:
a) Renew the O-ring seals if they appear worn or damaged.
b) Ensure that the regulator retaining clip is securely seated.
c) Refit the regulator vacuum hose securely.

Lambda sensor

Removal

46 The lambda sensor is threaded into the exhaust pipe, at the front of the catalytic converter. Refer to Chapter 4D for details.
47 Disconnect the battery negative cable and position it away from the terminal, then unplug the wiring harness from the lambda sensor at the connector, located adjacent to the right hand rear engine mounting.
48 Working under the car, slacken and withdraw the sensor, taking care to avoid damaging the sensor probe as it is removed. **Note:** *As a flying lead remains connected to the sensor after is has been disconnected, if the correct spanner is not available, a slotted socket will be required to remove the sensor.*

Refitting

49 Apply a little anti-seize grease to the sensor threads - avoid contaminating the probe tip.
50 Refit the sensor to its housing, tightening it to the correct torque. Restore the harness connection.

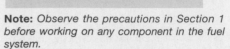

7 Digifant engine management system components - removal and refitting

Note: *Observe the precautions in Section 1 before working on any component in the fuel system.*

Airflow meter (engine code 2E only)

Note: *An airflow meter is not used on engine code ABF. Engine load is sensed using a manifold pressure sensor, which is an integral part of the Electronic Control Unit and hence cannot be renewed separately.*

Removal

1 Disconnect the battery negative cable and position it away from the terminal.
2 With reference to Section 2, slacken the clips and disconnect the air ducting from the airflow meter, at the rear of the air cleaner housing.
3 Unplug the harness connector from the airflow meter **(see illustration)**.
4 Remove the retaining screws and extract the meter from the air cleaner housing. Recover the seal. *Caution: Handle the airflow meter carefully - its internal components are easily damaged.*

Refitting

5 Refitting is a reversal of removal. Renew the O-ring seal if it appears damaged. **Note:** *On completion, the airflow meter must be "matched" electronically to the Digifant Electronic Control Unit (ECU) - this operation requires access to dedicated electronic test equipment, refer to a VAG dealer for advice.*

Throttle valve potentiometer

Removal

6 Disconnect the battery negative cable and position it away from the terminal.
7 Unplug the harness connector from the potentiometer **(see illustration)**.
8 Remove the retaining screws and lift the potentiometer away from the throttle body. Where applicable, recover the O-ring seal.

7.3 Unplug the harness connector from the airflow meter (engine code 2E only)

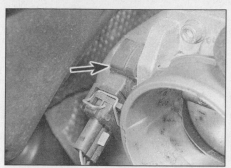

7.7 Unplug the harness connector (arrowed) from the throttle potentiometer - inlet air duct removed for clarity

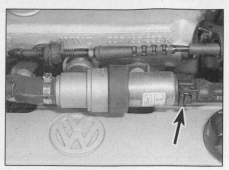

7.16 Idling stabilisation valve harness connector (arrowed)

7.22 Unplug the harness connector (arrowed) from the coolant temperature sensor (engine code 2E shown)

Refitting

9 Refitting is a reversal of removal, noting the following:

a) Where applicable, renew the O-ring seal if it appears damaged.

b) Ensure that the potentiometer drive engages correctly with the throttle spindle extension.

c) On completion, the potentiometer must be "matched" electronically to the Digifant Electronic Control Unit (ECU) - this operation requires access to dedicated electronic test equipment, refer to a VAG dealer for advice.

d) On vehicles with automatic transmission, the potentiometer must be matched to the automatic transmission Electronic Control Unit (ECU) - this operation requires access to dedicated electronic test equipment, refer to a VAG dealer for advice.

Inlet air temperature sensor

Removal

10 On engine code 2E, the sensor is an integral part of the airflow meter and cannot be renewed separately.

11 On engine code ABF, the sensor is located in the inlet air duct, downstream of the air cleaner.

12 Disconnect the battery negative cable and position it away from the terminal. Unplug the harness connector from the sensor.

13 Extract the retaining clip and withdraw the sensor from its housing. Recover the O-ring.

Refitting

14 Refitting is a reversal of removal. Renew the O-ring if it appears damaged.

Idling stabilisation valve

Removal

15 The valve is mounted on a bracket on the inlet manifold, above the camshaft cover. On engine code ABF, remove the retaining screws and lift off the protective cover plate.

16 Disconnect the battery negative cable and position it away from the terminal. Unplug the harness connector from the valve **(see illustration)**.

17 Slacken the clip and disconnect the inlet air duct hose from the port on the idle stabilisation valve.

18 Slacken the mounting bracket retaining clip and carefully extract the valve from the inlet manifold.

Refitting

19 Refitting is a reversal of removal.

Road speed sensor

20 The road speed sensor is mounted on the transmission - refer to Chapter 7A or B as applicable.

Coolant temperature sensor

Removal - engine code 2E

21 The coolant temperature sensor is mounted in the coolant outlet elbow on the front of the cylinder head (see Chapter 3).

22 Disconnect the battery negative cable, then unplug the harness connector from the sensor **(see illustration)**.

23 Refer to Chapter 3 and drain approximately one quarter of the coolant from the engine.

24 Extract the retaining clip and lift the sensor from the coolant elbow - be prepared for an amount of coolant loss. Recover the O-ring.

Removal - engine code ABF

25 The coolant temperature sensor is mounted on the side of the cylinder head, below and to the left of the ignition distributor.

26 Disconnect the battery negative cable and position it away from the terminal, then unplug the harness connector from the sensor.

27 Refer to Chapter 3 and drain approximately one quarter of the coolant from the engine.

28 Unscrew the sensor and recover the sealing washer.

Refitting

29 Refit the sensor by reversing the removal procedure, using a new O-ring/sealing washer as applicable. Refer to Chapter 1A and top-up the cooling system.

Engine speed sensor

Removal

30 The engine speed sensor is mounted on the front cylinder block, adjacent to the mating surface of the block and transmission bellhousing.

31 Disconnect the battery negative cable and position it away from the terminal, then unplug the harness connector from the sensor.

32 Remove the sensor retaining screw, and carefully withdraw the sensor from the cylinder block.

Refitting

33 Refit the sensor by reversing the removal procedure.

Cold start valve (engine code 2E up to July 1993)

Removal

34 Refer to Section 10 and depressurise the fuel system.

35 Disconnect the battery negative cable and position it away from the terminal.

36 Unplug the harness connection from the cold start valve.

37 Slacken the clip and pull the fuel hose off the port at the rear of the cold start valve.

38 Remove the retaining screw and withdraw the cold start valve from the inlet manifold. Recover and discard the gasket.

Refitting

39 Refit the cold start valve by reversing the removal procedure, using a new gasket.

Throttle body

40 Refer to Section 4 and detach the accelerator cable from the throttle valve lever.

41 Slacken the clips and detach the inlet air ducting from the throttle body.

42 Disconnect the battery negative cable and position it away from the terminal, then unplug the harness connector from the throttle potentiometer.

43 Disconnect the vacuum hoses from the ports on the throttle body, noting their order of fitment. Release the wiring harness from the guide clip.

44 Slacken and withdraw the upper and

4B

7.44 Throttle body upper through-bolts (arrowed)

lower through-bolts **(see illustration)**, then lift the throttle body away from the inlet manifold. Recover and discard the gasket.

45 If required, refer to the relevant sub-Section and remove the throttle potentiometer.

Refitting

46 Refitting is a reversal of removal, noting the following:

a) *Use a new throttle body-to-inlet manifold gasket.*

b) *Observe the correct tightening torque when refitting the throttle body through-bolts.*

c) *Ensure that all vacuum hoses and electrical connectors are refitted securely.*

d) *With reference to Section 4, check and if necessary adjust the accelerator cable.*

Fuel injectors and fuel rail

Note: *Observe the precautions in Section 1 before working on any component in the fuel system.*

Removal

47 Disconnect the battery negative cable and position it away from the terminal.

48 Refer to the relevant sub-Section in this Chapter and remove the throttle body.

49 On engine code ABF, refer to Section 12 and remove the upper section of the inlet manifold.

50 Unplug the injector harness at the multiway connector.

51 Refer to Section 10 and depressurise the fuel system.

52 Disconnect the vacuum hose from the port on the top of the fuel pressure regulator.

53 Slacken the clips and disconnect the fuel supply and return hoses from the end of the fuel rail. *Carefully* note the fitted positions of the hoses - the supply hose is colour-coded black/white and the return hose is colour-coded blue.

54 Slacken and withdraw the fuel rail retaining screws, then carefully lift the fuel rail away from the inlet manifold, together with the injectors. Recover the injector lower O-ring seals as they emerge from the manifold.

55 Remove the retaining screws and lift the upper section of the fuel rail away from the lower section; recover and discard the gasket.

56 The injectors can now be carefully pressed from the fuel rail individually. Recover the injector upper O-ring seals.

57 If required, remove the fuel pressure regulator, referring to the relevant sub-Section for guidance.

58 Check the electrical resistance of the injector using a multimeter set to the resistance measurement function connected across the injector terminals and compare it with the Specifications. **Note:** *If a faulty injector is suspected, before condemning the injector, it is worth trying the effect of one of the proprietary injector-cleaning treatments.*

59 Refit the injectors to the fuel rail, noting that the recesses in the side of each injector body must align with the lugs in the lower section of the fuel rail. Moisten the lower O-ring seals with clean engine oil before refitting.

60 Refit the upper section of the fuel rail, together with a new gasket and tighten the retaining screw to the specified torque.

Refitting

61 Refit the injectors and fuel rail by following the removal procedure in reverse, noting the following points:

a) *Renew the injector O-ring seals if they appear worn or damaged.*

b) *Ensure that the injector retaining clips are securely seated.*

c) *Check that the fuel supply and return hoses are reconnected correctly - refer to the colour coding described in "Removal".*

d) *On engine code ABF, use a new gasket when refitting the upper section of the inlet manifold to the lower section.*

e) *Check that all vacuum and electrical connections are remade correctly and securely.*

f) *On completion, check exhaustively for fuel leaks before bringing the vehicle back into service.*

Fuel pressure regulator

Note: *Observe the precautions in Section 1 before working on any component in the fuel system.*

Removal

62 Disconnect the battery negative cable and position it away from the terminal.

63 Refer to Section 10 and depressurise the fuel system.

64 Disconnect the vacuum hose from the port on the top of the fuel pressure regulator.

65 Slacken the clip and disconnect the fuel supply hose from the end of the fuel rail. This will allow the majority of fuel in the regulator to drain out. Be prepared for an amount of fuel loss - position a small container and some old rags underneath the fuel regulator housing.

66 Extract the retaining clip from the side of the regulator housing and lift out the regulator body, recovering the O-ring seal.

Refitting

67 Refit the fuel pressure regulator by following the removal procedure in reverse, noting the following points:

a) *Renew the O-ring seals if they appear worn or damaged.*

b) *Ensure that the regulator retaining clip is securely seated.*

c) *Refit the regulator vacuum hose securely.*

Lambda sensor

Removal

68 The lambda sensor is threaded into the exhaust pipe, at the front of the catalytic converter. Refer to Chapter 4D for details.

69 Disconnect the battery negative cable and position it away from the terminal, then unplug the wiring harness from the lambda sensor at the connector, located adjacent to the right-hand rear engine mounting.

70 Working under the vehicle, slacken and withdraw the sensor, taking care to avoid damaging the sensor probe as it is removed. **Note:** *As a flying lead remains connected to the sensor after is has been disconnected, if the correct size spanner is not available, a slotted socket will be required to remove the sensor.*

Refitting

71 Apply a little anti-seize grease to the sensor threads - avoid contaminating the probe tip.

72 Refit the sensor to its housing, tightening it to the correct torque. Restore the harness connection.

8 Fuel filter - renewal

Note: *Observe the precautions in Section 1 before working on any component in the fuel system.*

Refer to the information in Chapter 4A, Section 6.

9 Fuel pump and gauge sender unit - removal and refitting

Note: *Observe the precautions in Section 1 before working on any component in the fuel system.*

Refer to the information in Chapter 4A, Section 7.

10 Fuel injection system - depressurisation

Note: *Observe the precautions in Section 1 before working on any component in the fuel system.*

Refer to the information in Chapter 4A, Section 9.

11 Fuel tank -
removal and refitting

Note: *Observe the precautions in Section 1 before working on any component in the fuel system.*

Refer to the information in Chapter 4A, Section 8.

12 Inlet manifold -
removal and refitting

Note: *Observe the precautions in Section 1 before working on any component in the fuel system.*

Engine code AEK

Removal

1 Refer to Section 10 and depressurise the fuel system, then disconnect the battery negative cable and position it away from the terminal.

2 Refer to Section 2 and disconnect the air inlet ducting from the throttle body.

3 Refer to Section 5 and remove the throttle body from the upper section of the inlet manifold.

4 Remove the retaining screws and lift the deflector plate away from the fuel pressure regulator.

5 Unplug the wiring harness from the inlet manifold temperature sensor (see Section 5).

6 Disconnect the brake servo vacuum hose from the port on the side of the inlet manifold.

7 Slacken and withdraw the through-bolts, then separate the upper and lower sections of the inlet manifold. **Note:** *Remove the retaining screw from the support bracket between the upper section of the inlet manifold and the cylinder head. Check that nothing remains connected to the upper section, then lift it out of the engine bay. Recover the gasket.*

8 Refer to Section 5 and remove the fuel rail and fuel injectors. **Note:** *The fuel rail may be moved to one side, leaving the fuel lines connected to it, but take care to avoid straining them.*

9 Progressively slacken and remove the inlet manifold-to-cylinder head bolts. Lift the manifold away from the head and recover the gasket.

Refitting

10 Refit the inlet manifold by following the removal procedure in reverse, noting the following points:
   a) *Use new manifold gaskets.*
   b) *Tighten the manifold-to-cylinder head and upper-to-lower manifold bolts to the specified torque.*
   c) *Check that all vacuum and electrical connections are remade correctly and securely.*
   d) *On completion, check exhaustively for fuel leaks before bringing the vehicle back into service.*

Engine codes 2E, ADY

Removal

11 Refer to Section 10 and depressurise the fuel system, then disconnect the battery negative cable and position it away from the terminal.

12 Refer to Section 2 and disconnect the air inlet ducting from the throttle body.

13 Refer to Section 5 and remove the throttle body from the inlet manifold.

14 Unplug the wiring harness from the temperature switch at the side of the inlet manifold.

15 Disconnect the brake servo vacuum hose from the port on the side of the inlet manifold.

16 Refer to Section 6 and remove the fuel rail and fuel injectors, together with the fuel pressure regulator. **Note:** *The fuel rail may be moved to one side, leaving the fuel lines connected to it, but take care to avoid straining them.*

17 Progressively slacken and remove the inlet manifold-to-cylinder head bolts. Lift the manifold away from the head and recover the gasket.

Refitting

18 Refit the inlet manifold by following the removal procedure in reverse, noting the following points:
   a) *Use a new manifold-to-cylinder head gasket.*
   b) *Tighten the manifold-to-cylinder head bolts to the specified torque.*
   c) *Check that all vacuum and electrical connections are remade correctly and securely.*
   d) *On completion, check exhaustively for fuel leaks before bringing the vehicle back into service.*

Engine code ABF

Removal

19 Refer to Section 10 and depressurise the fuel system, then disconnect the battery negative cable and position it away from the terminal.

20 Refer to Section 2 and disconnect the air inlet ducting from the throttle body.

21 With reference to Section 5, remove the throttle body and the idling stabilisation valve from the upper section of the inlet manifold.

22 Disconnect the brake servo vacuum hose from the port on the side of the inlet manifold.

23 Slacken and withdraw the through-bolts, then separate the upper and lower sections of the inlet manifold. Check that nothing remains connected to the upper section, then lift it out of the engine bay. Recover the gasket.

24 Refer to Section 5 and remove the fuel rail and fuel injectors.

25 Progressively slacken and remove the inlet manifold-to-cylinder head bolts. Lift the manifold away from the head and recover the gasket.

Refitting

26 Refit the inlet manifold by following the removal procedure in reverse, noting the following points:
   a) *Use new manifold gaskets.*
   b) *Tighten the manifold-to-cylinder head and upper-to-lower manifold bolts to the specified torque.*
   c) *Check that all vacuum and electrical connections are remade correctly and securely.*
   d) *On completion, check exhaustively for fuel leaks before bringing the vehicle back into service.*

13 Fuel injection system -
testing and adjustment

1 If a fault appears in the fuel injection system first ensure that all the system wiring connectors are securely connected and free of corrosion. Then ensure that the fault is not due to poor maintenance; ie, check that the air cleaner filter element is clean, the spark plugs are in good condition and correctly gapped, the cylinder compression pressures are correct, the ignition timing is correct and the engine breather hoses are clear and undamaged, referring to Chapter 1A, Chapter 2A and Chapter 5B.

2 If these checks fail to reveal the cause of the problem the vehicle should be taken to a suitably equipped VAG dealer for testing. A diagnostic connector is incorporated in the engine management system wiring harness, into which a dedicated electronic test equipment can be plugged. The test equipment is capable of "interrogating" the engine management system ECU electronically and accessing its internal fault log. In this manner, faults can be pinpointed quickly and simply, even if their occurrence is intermittent. Testing all the system components individually in an attempt to locate the fault by elimination is a time consuming operation that is unlikely to be fruitful (particularly if the fault occurs dynamically) and carries high risk of damage to the ECU's internal components.

3 Experienced home mechanics equipped with an accurate tachometer and a carefully-calibrated exhaust gas analyser may be able to check the exhaust gas CO content and the engine idle speed; if these are found to be out of specification, then the vehicle must be taken to a suitably-equipped VAG dealer for assessment. Neither the air/fuel mixture (exhaust gas CO content) nor the engine idle speed are manually adjustable; incorrect test results indicate a fault within the fuel injection system.

4B

14 Unleaded petrol - general information and usage

Note: *The information given in this Chapter is correct at the time of writing and applies only* to petrols currently available in the UK. Check with a VAG dealer as more up to date information may be available. If travelling abroad, consult one of the motoring organisations (or a similar authority) for advice on the petrols available and their suitability for your vehicle.

1 The fuel recommended by VAG is given in the Specifications of this Chapter.
2 RON and MON are different testing standards; RON stands for Research Octane Number (also written as RM), while MON stands for Motor Octane Number (also written as MM).

Chapter 4 Part C :
Fuel system - diesel

Contents

Degrees of difficulty

| Easy, suitable for novice with little experience | Fairly easy, suitable for beginner with some experience | Fairly difficult, suitable for competent DIY mechanic 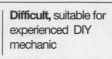 | Difficult, suitable for experienced DIY mechanic | Very difficult, suitable for expert DIY or professional |

Specifications

General

Firing order	1-3-4-2
Maximum engine speed (engine codes AAZ and 1Y)	5200 ± 100 rpm
Engine idle speed (engine codes AAZ and 1Y)	900 ± 30 rpm
Engine fast idle speed (engine codes AAZ and 1Y)	1050 ± 50 rpm

Fuel injection pump

Injection pump timing, DTI reading (engine codes AAZ and 1Y):
Test	0.83 to 0.97 mm
Setting	0.90 ± 0.02 mm

Torque wrench settings

	Nm	lbf ft
Fuel tank retaining strap bolts	25	18
Injection pump fuel supply and return banjo bolts	25	18
Injection pump fuel union lock nuts	20	15
Injection pump head fuel unions	25	18
Injection pump timing plug	15	11
Injection pump to front support bracket bolts	25	18
Injection pump to rear support bracket bolts	25	18
Injection pump top cover screws (engine code 1Z)	10	7
Injector fuel pipe unions	25	18
Injectors	70	52

1 General information and precautions

General information

Engine codes AAZ and 1Y

The fuel system comprises a fuel tank, a fuel injection pump, an engine-bay mounted fuel filter with an integral water separator, fuel supply and return lines and four fuel injectors.

The injection pump is driven at half crankshaft speed by the camshaft timing belt. Fuel is drawn from the fuel tank, through the filter by the injection pump, which then distributes the fuel under very high pressure to the injectors via separate delivery pipes.

The injectors are spring loaded mechanical valves, which open when the pressure of the fuel supplied to them exceeds a specific limit. Fuel is then sprayed from the injector nozzle into the cylinder via a swirl chamber (indirect injection). Engine code AAZ is fitted with two-stage injectors which open in steps as the supplied fuel pressure rises; this improves the engines combustion characteristics.

The basic injection timing is set by the position of the injection pump on its mounting bracket. When the engine is running, the injection timing is advanced and retarded mechanically by the injection pump itself and is influenced primarily by the accelerator position and engine speed.

The engine is stopped by means of a solenoid operated fuel cut-off valve which interrupts the flow of fuel to the injection pump when de-activated.

On cars registered before October 1994, when starting from cold, the engine idle speed could be raised manually by means of a cold start accelerator cable, controlled via a knob on the facia. From this date onwards, the cold start accelerator cable was replaced by an automatic idle boost actuator, mounted on the side of the injection pump.

It should be noted that from 10/94, the fuel injection pump is equipped with an electronic self-diagnosis and fault logging system. Servicing of this system is only possible with dedicated electronic test equipment. Problems with the systems operation should therefore be referred to a VAG dealer for assessment. Once the fault has been identified, the removal/refitting sequences detailed in the following Sections will then allow the appropriate component(s) to be renewed as required.

Engine code 1Z

The direct-injection fuelling system is controlled electronically by a Diesel engine management system, comprising an Electronic Control Unit (ECU) and its associated sensors, actuators and wiring.

Basic injection timing is set mechanically by the position of the pump on its mounting bracket. Dynamic timing and injection duration are controlled by the ECU and are dependant on engine speed, throttle position and rate of opening, inlet air flow , inlet air temperature, coolant temperature, fuel temperature, ambient pressure (altitude) and manifold depression information, received from sensors mounted on and around the engine. Closed loop control of the injection timing is achieved by means of an injector needle lift sensor.

Two-stage injectors are used, which improve the engine's combustion characteristics, leading to quieter running and better exhaust emissions. Note that injector No 3 is fitted with the needle lift sensor.

In addition, the ECU manages the operation of the Exhaust Gas Recirculation (EGR) emission control system (Chapter 4D), the turbocharger boost pressure control system (Section 13) and the glow plug control system (Chapter 4D).

It should be noted that fault diagnosis of the diesel engine management system fitted to engine code 1Z is only possible with dedicated electronic test equipment. Problems with the system's operation should therefore be referred to a VAG dealer for assessment. Once the fault has been identified, the removal/refitting sequences detailed in the following Sections will then allow the appropriate component(s) to be renewed as required.

Note: *Throughout this Chapter, vehicles are frequently referred to by their engine code, rather than by engine capacity - refer to Chapter 2B for engine code listings.*

Precautions

Many of the operations described in this Chapter involve the disconnection of fuel lines, which may cause an amount of fuel spillage. Before commencing work, refer to the warnings below and the information in *"Safety first!"* at the beginning of this manual.

⚠️ *Warning: When working on any part of the fuel system, avoid direct contact skin contact with diesel fuel - wear protective clothing and gloves when handling fuel system components. Ensure that the work area is well ventilated to prevent the build up of diesel fuel vapour.*

Fuel injectors operate at extremely high pressures and the jet of fuel produced at the nozzle is capable of piercing skin, with potentially fatal results. When working with pressurised injectors, take great to avoid exposing any part of the body to the fuel spray. It is recommended that any pressure testing of the fuel system components should be carried out by a diesel fuel systems specialist.

Under no circumstances should diesel fuel be allowed to come into contact with coolant hoses - wipe off accidental spillage immediately. Hoses that have been contaminated with fuel for an extended period should be renewed. Diesel fuel systems are particularly sensitive to contamination from dirt, air and water. Pay particular attention to cleanliness when working on any part of the fuel system, to prevent the ingress of dirt. Thoroughly clean the area around fuel unions before disconnecting them. Store dismantled components in sealed containers to prevent contamination and the formation of condensation. Only use lint-free cloths and clean fuel for component cleansing. Avoid using compressed air when cleaning components in situ .

2 Air cleaner assembly - removal and refitting

Removal

1 Slacken the worm drive clips and disconnect the air ducting from the air cleaner assembly (engine codes AAZ and 1Y) or airflow meter (engine code 1Z) **(see illustration)**.

2 Unhook the rubber loops from the lugs on the chassis member **(see illustration)**.

3 Pull the air cleaner towards the engine and withdraw the air inlet hose from the port on the inner wing.

4 Lift the air cleaner out of the engine bay. On engine code 1Z, separate the airflow meter from the air cleaner by removing the retaining screws. Handle the airflow meter carefully, as it is a delicate component.

5 Prise open the retaining clips and lift the top cover from the air cleaner. Remove the air cleaner filter element (see Chapter 1B for more details).

Refitting

6 Refit the air cleaner by following the removal procedure in reverse. Engage the mounting lug with the recess in the inner wing **(see illustration)**.

3 Accelerator cable - removal, refitting and adjustment

1 This Section only applies to engine codes 1Y and AAZ; engine code 1Z is fitted with an electronic accelerator position sensor (see Section 13).

Removal

2 Refer to Chapter 11 and remove the facia trim panels from underneath the steering column.

3 Depress the accelerator pedal slightly, then unclip the accelerator cable end from the pedal extension lever **(see illustration)**.

4 At the point where the cable passes through the bulkhead, unscrew the cap from the two-piece grommet so that the cable can move freely.

5 Working in the engine bay, remove the clip

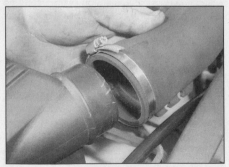

2.1 Disconnect the air ducting from the air cleaner assembly

2.2 Unhook the rubber loops from the lugs on the chassis member

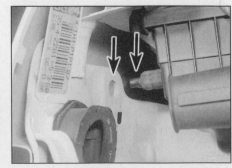

2.6 Engage the mounting lug with the recess (arrowed) in the inner wing

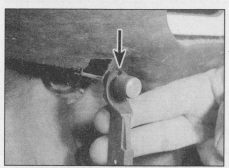

3.3 Unclip the accelerator cable end (arrowed) from the pedal extension lever

3.5 Detach the accelerator cable inner from the fuel injection pump lever

3.6 Extract the accelerator cable outer from the mounting bracket

and detach the end of the accelerator cable inner from the fuel injection pump lever **(see illustration)**.

6 Slide back the rubber grommet and extract the accelerator cable outer from the mounting bracket **(see illustration)**.

7 Release the cable from its securing clips and guide it out through the bulkhead grommet.

Refitting

8 Refit the accelerator cable by following the removal procedure in reverse.

Adjustment

9 At the fuel injection pump, fix the position of the cable outer in its mounting bracket by inserting the metal clip in one of the locating slots, such that when the accelerator is depressed fully, the throttle lever is held wide open to its end stop.

4 Cold Start Accelerator (CSA) cable - removal, refitting and adjustment

Removal

1 Working in the engine bay at the fuel injection pump, slacken the locking screw and disconnect the CSA cable inner from the injection pump lever.

2 Prise off the retaining clip and withdraw the cable outer from the mounting bracket on the side of the injection pump. Recover the washer.

3 Release the cable from the clips that secure it in position in the engine bay.

4 Remove the trim panels from underneath the steering column (see Chapter 11), to gain access to the inside of the facia.

5 Pull the cold start knob out to expose its rear surface, then prise off the clip and remove the knob from the cable inner.

6 Slacken and remove the retaining nut to release the cable outer from the facia.

7 Pull the cable through into the cabin, guiding it through the bulkhead grommet.

Refitting

8 Refit the CSA cable by reversing the removal procedure.

Adjustment

9 Push the cold start knob into the "fully off" position.

10 Thread the CSA cable inner through the drilling in the lever on the injection pump. Hold the injection pump cold start lever in the closed position, then pull the cable inner taught to take up the slack and tighten the locking screw.

11 Operate the cold start knob from the cabin and check that it is possible to move the injection pump lever through its full range of travel.

12 Push the cold start knob in to its "fully off" position, then start the engine and check the idle speed, as described in Chapter 1B.

13 Pull the cold start knob fully out and check that the idle speed rises to approximately 1050 rpm. Adjust the cable if necessary.

5 Fuel tank sender unit - removal and refitting

1 The fuel tank sender unit is on the top of the fuel tank and is accessible via a hatch in the load space floor. The unit provides a variable voltage signal that drives the facia mounted fuel gauge and also serves as a connection point for the fuel supply and return hoses.

2 The unit protrudes into the fuel tank and its removal involves exposing the contents of the tank to the atmosphere.

⚠️ *Warning: Avoid direct contact skin contact with diesel fuel - wear protective clothing and gloves when handling fuel system components. Ensure that the work area is well ventilated to prevent the build-up of diesel fuel vapour.*

Removal

3 Ensure that the vehicle is parked on a level surface, then disconnect the battery negative cable and position it away from the terminal.

4 Remove the trim from the load space floor.

5 Slacken and withdraw the access hatch screws and lift the hatch away from the floorpan **(see illustration)**.

6 Unplug the wiring harness connector from the sender unit **(see illustration)**.

7 Pad the area around the supply and return fuel hoses with rags to absorb any spilt fuel, then slacken the hose clips and remove them from the ports at the sender unit **(see illustration)**. Observe the supply and return

5.5 Slacken the access hatch screws, and lift the hatch away from the floorpan

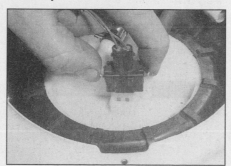

5.6 Unplug the wiring harness connector from the sender unit

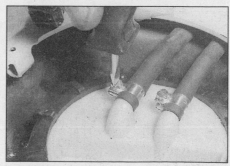

5.7 Slacken the hose clips and remove the fuel pipes from the ports at the sender unit

4C

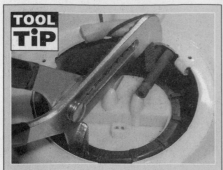

TOOL TiP

Use a pair of water pump pliers to grip and rotate the fuel tank sender unit plastic securing ring

arrows markings on the ports - label the fuel hoses accordingly to ensure correct refitting.

8 Unscrew the plastic securing ring and lift it out **(see Tool Tip)**. Where applicable, turn the sender unit to left to release it from its bayonet fitting and lift it out, holding it above the level of the fuel in the tank until the excess fuel has drained out. Recover the rubber seal **(see illustrations)**.

9 Remove the sender unit from the vehicle and lay it on an absorbent card or rag. Inspect the float at the end of the swinging arm for punctures and fuel ingress - renew the sender unit if it appears damaged.

10 The fuel pick-up incorporated in the sender unit is spring loaded to ensure that it always draws fuel from the lowest part of the tank. Check that the pick-up is free to move under spring tension with respect to the sender unit body.

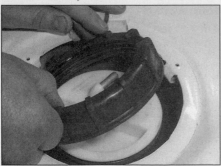

5.8a Unscrew the plastic securing ring and lift it out

5.8c . . . and recover the rubber seal

11 Recover the rubber seal from the fuel tank aperture and inspect for signs of fatigue - renew it if necessary **(see illustration 5.8c)**.

12 Inspect the sender unit wiper and track; clean off any dirt and debris that may have accumulated and look for breaks in the track **(see illustration)**. An electrical specification for the sender unit is not quoted by VW, but the integrity of the wiper and track may be verified by connecting a multimeter, set to the resistance function, across the sender unit connector terminals. The resistance should vary as the float arm is moved up and down, and an open circuit reading indicates that the sender is faulty and should be renewed.

Refitting

13 Refitting is a reversal of removal, noting the following points:

a) *The arrow markings on the sender unit body and the fuel tank must be aligned (see illustration).*

b) *Smear the tank aperture rubber seal with clean fuel before fitting it in position.*

6 Fuel tank - removal and refitting

Note: *Observe the precautions in Section 1 before working on any component in the fuel system.*

Removal

1 Before the tank can be removed, it must be drained of as much fuel as possible. As no drain plug is provided, it is preferable to carry out this operation with the tank almost empty.

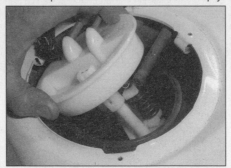

5.8b Lift out the sender unit . . .

5.12 Look for breaks in the sender unit wiper track

2 Disconnect the battery negative cable and position it away from the terminal. Using a hand pump or syphon, remove any remaining fuel from the bottom of the tank.

3 Refer to Section 5 and carry out the following:

a) *Disconnect the wiring harness from the top of the sender unit at the multiway connector.*

b) *Disconnect the fuel supply and return hoses from the sender unit.*

4 Position a trolley jack under the centre of the tank. Insert a block of wood between the jack head and the tank to prevent damage to the tank surface. Raise the jack until it just takes the weight of the tank (see "*Jacking and vehicle support*").

5 Working inside the rear right hand wheelarch, slacken and withdraw the screws that secure the tank filler neck inside of the wheelarch. Open the fuel filler flap and peel the rubber sealing flange away from the bodywork.

6 Remove the retaining screws from the tank securing straps, keeping one hand on the tank to steady it, as it is released from its mountings.

7 Lower the jack and tank away from the underside of the vehicle; disconnect the breather hose(s) from the port on the filler neck as they are exposed. Locate the earthing strap and disconnect it from the terminal at the filler neck.

8 If the tank is contaminated with sediment or water, remove the sender unit (see Section 5) and swill the tank out with clean fuel. The tank is injection moulded from a synthetic material and if damaged, it should be renewed. However, in certain cases it may be possible to have small leaks or minor damage repaired. Seek the advice of a suitable specialist before attempting to repair the fuel tank.

Refitting

9 Refitting is the reverse of the removal procedure, noting the following points:

a) *When lifting the tank back into position make sure the mounting rubbers are correctly positioned and take great care to ensure that none of the hoses become trapped between the tank and vehicle body.*

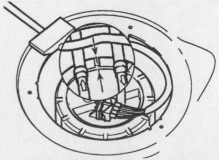

5.13 The arrow marks on the sender unit body and the fuel tank must be aligned

7.4 Attach a two-legged puller to the injection pump sprocket

7.5a Lift off the pump sprocket . . .

7.5b . . . and recover the Woodruff key

7.6a Slacken the rigid fuel pipe unions at the rear of the injection pump

7.6b Lift the fuel pipe assembly away from the engine

b) Ensure that all pipes and hoses are correctly routed and securely held in position with their retaining clips.
c) Reconnect the earth strap to its terminal on the filler neck.
d) Tighten the tank retaining strap bolts to the specified torque.
e) On completion, refill the tank with fuel and exhaustively check for signs of leakage prior to taking the vehicle out on the road.

7 Fuel injection pump - removal and refitting

Note: *On engine code 1Z, the injection pump commencement of injection setting must be checked and if necessary adjusted after refitting. The commencement of injection is controlled by the fuel injection ECU and is influenced by several other engine parameters, including coolant temperature, and engine speed and position. Although the adjustment is a mechanical operation, checking can only be carried out by a VAG dealer, as dedicated electronic test equipment is needed to interface with the fuel injection ECU.*

Removal

1 Disconnect the battery negative cable and position it away from the terminal.
2 With reference to Chapter 2B, carry out the following:
a) Remove the air cleaner (and airflow meter on engine code 1Z) and the associated ducting.

b) Remove the cylinder head cover and timing belt outer cover.
c) Set the engine to TDC on cylinder No 1.
d) Remove the timing belt from the camshaft and fuel injection pump sprockets.

3 Loosen the nut or bolts (as applicable) that secure the timing belt sprocket to the injection pump shaft. The sprocket must be braced whilst its fixings are loosened - a home made tool can easily be fabricated for this purpose; refer to Section 5 of Chapter 2B for further details. *Caution: On engine codes AAZ and 1Y from October 1994 on, the sprocket is a two-piece assembly, secured with three bolts - on no account should the shaft centre nut be slackened, as this will alter the basic injection timing .*

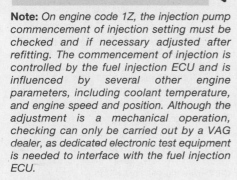

Hint 1: Cut the fingertips from an old pair of rubber gloves and secure them over the fuel ports with elastic bands

4 Attach a two-legged puller to the injection pump sprocket, then gradually tighten the puller until the sprocket is under firm tension (see illustration). *Caution: To prevent damage to the injection pump shaft, insert a piece of scrap metal between the end of the shaft and the puller centre bolt.*
5 Tap sharply on the puller centre bolt with a hammer - this will free the sprocket from the tapered shaft. Detach the puller, then fully slacken and remove the sprocket fixings, lift off the sprocket and recover the Woodruff key (see illustrations).
6 Using a pair of spanners, slacken the rigid fuel pipe unions at the rear of the injection pump and at each end of the injectors, then lift the fuel pipe assembly away from the engine (see illustrations). *Caution: Be prepared for some fuel leakage during this operation, position a small container under the union to be slackened and pad the area with old rags, to catch any spilt diesel. Take great care to avoid stressing the rigid fuel pipes as they are removed.*
7 Cover the open pipes and ports to prevent the ingress of dirt and excess fuel leakage (see Haynes Hint 1).
8 Slacken the fuel supply and return banjo bolts at the injection pump ports, again taking precautions to minimise fuel spillage. Cover the open pipes and ports to prevent the ingress of dirt and excess fuel leakage (see Haynes Hint 2).

4C

Hint 2: Fit a short length of hose over the banjo bolt (arrowed) so that the drillings are covered, then thread the bolt back into its injection pump port

7.9 Disconnect the injector bleed hose from the fuel return union port (arrowed)

7.17 Withdraw the injection pump rear mounting bolt

7.28 Tightening the fuel injection pump sprocket, using a home-made locking tool

9 Disconnect the injector bleed hose from the port on the fuel return union **(see illustration)**.
10 Refer to Section 12 and disconnect the cabling from the stop control valve.
11 All engine codes *except* 1Z: With reference to Sections 3 and 4, disconnect the cold start accelerator cable and accelerator cable from the injection pump.
12 Engine code 1Z only: Unplug the electrical wiring from the fuel cut-off valve/commencement of injection valve and the quantity adjuster module at the connectors, labelling the cables to aid refitting later.
13 All engine codes except post-October 1994 AAZ and 1Y: If the existing injection pump is to be refitted later, use a scriber or a pen to mark the relationship between the injection pump body and the front mounting bracket. This will allow an approximate injection timing setting to be achieved when the pump is refitted.

Engine codes AAZ and 1Y from October 1994 onwards

14 Unplug the electrical wiring from the following components, labelling the connectors to aid refitting later:
a) *Commencement of injection valve.*
b) *Injection period sensor.*
c) *Engine code AAZ: The boost pressure enrichment cut-off valve.*
d) *Engine code 1Y: Full throttle stop valve.*
e) *Vehicles without air conditioning: Idle speed boost actuator.*

15 On later models, where the injection pump wiring is not provided with individual connectors, free the engine harness multiway connector from its bracket, and unbolt the earth connection. **Note:** *New injection pumps are not supplied with harness multiway connector housings; if the pump is to be renewed, then the relevant spade terminal pins must be pushed out of the existing connector housing, to allow those from the new pump to be inserted; refer to the Wiring Diagrams for details of connector pin-outs.*
16 On vehicles with air conditioning, disconnect the vacuum hose from the idle speed boost actuator.

All models

17 Slacken and withdraw the bolt that

secures the injection pump to the rear mounting bracket **(see illustration)**. *Caution: Do not slacken the pump distributor head bolts, as this could cause serious internal damage to the injection pump.*
18 Slacken and withdraw the three nuts/bolts that secure the injection pump to the front mounting bracket. Note that where fixing bolts are used, the two outer bolts are held captive with metal brackets. Support the pump body as the last fixing is removed.
19 Check that nothing remains connected to the injection pump, then lift it away from the engine.

Refitting

20 Offer up the injection pump to the engine, then insert the injection pump-to-rear support bracket bolt and tighten it to the specified torque.
21 Insert the injection pump-to-front support bracket bolts and tighten them to the specified torque. **Note:** *On engine code 1Z and pre-October 1994 engine codes AAZ and 1Y, the mounting holes are elongated to allow adjustment - if a new pump is being fitted, then mount it such that the bolts are initially at the centre of the holes to allow the maximum range of pump timing adjustment. Alternatively, if the existing pump is being refitted, use the markings made during removal for alignment.*
22 On engine code 1Z and post-October 1994 engine codes AAZ and 1Y where a new injection pump is being fitted, prime new injection pumps by fitting a small funnel to the fuel return pipe union and filling the cavity with clean diesel. Pad the area around the union with clean dry rags to absorb any spillage.
23 Reconnect the fuel injector delivery pipes to the injectors and injection pump head, then tighten the unions to the correct torque using a pair of spanners.
24 Reconnect the fuel supply and return pipes to the FIP and tighten the banjo bolts to the specified torque, use new sealing washers. **Note:** *The inside diameter of the banjo bolt for the fuel return pipe is smaller than that of the fuel supply line and is marked "OUT".*
25 Push the injector bleed hose onto the port on the return hose union.

26 Fit the timing belt sprocket to the injection pump shaft, ensuring that the Woodruff key is correctly seated. Fit the washer and retaining nut/bolts (as applicable), hand tightening them only at this stage.
27 Lock the injection pump sprocket in position by inserting a bar or bolt through its alignment hole and into the drilling in the pump front mounting bracket. Ensure that there is minimal play in the sprocket, once it has been locked in position.
28 With reference to Chapter 2B, refit the timing belt, then check and adjust the injection pump to camshaft timing. On completion, tension the timing belt and tighten the fuel injection pump sprocket to the specified torque **(see illustration)**. Refit the timing belt outer cover and cylinder head cover, using a new gasket where necessary.
29 The rest of refitting is a direct reversal of removal, noting the following points:
a) *Reconnect all electrical connections to the pump, using the labels made during removal. When fitting a new injection pump to post-October 1994 engine codes AAZ and 1Y, push the pump wiring terminal pins into their respective locations in the existing engine harness multiway connector; refer to the connector pin-outs in the Wiring Diagrams for greater details.*
b) *All engine codes except 1Z: Reconnect the accelerator and cold start accelerator cables to the pump and adjust them as necessary.*
c) *Refit the air cleaner (and airflow meter on engine code 1Z) and its ducting.*
d) *Reconnect the battery negative cable.*

Engine code 1Z

30 The commencement of injection must now be dynamically checked and if necessary adjusted by a VAG dealer; refer to the note at the beginning of this Section.

Engine code AAZ and 1Y

31 Carry out the following:
a) *Pre-October 1994 engine codes AAZ and 1Y only: Check and if necessary adjust the injection pump static timing as described in Section 10.*
b) *Check and if necessary adjust the engine idling speed as described in Chapter 1B.*

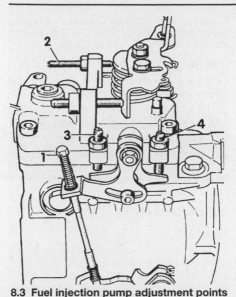

8.3 Fuel injection pump adjustment points (engine codes AAZ and 1Y)

1 Idling speed adjustment screw
2 Maximum engine speed adjustment screw
3 Minimum idling speed stop screw
4 Maximum idling speed stop screw

c) Check and if necessary adjust the maximum no-load engine speed, as described in Section 8.
d) Post October 1994 models only: Check and if necessary adjust the engine idle boost speed, as described in Section 9.

8 Maximum engine speed - checking and adjustment

Note: *This Section does not apply to engine code 1Z.* **Caution: Observe the precautions in Section 1 before working on any component in the fuel system. This operation should not be carried if the condition of the camshaft timing belt is questionable.**

1 Start the engine and with the handbrake applied and the transmission in neutral, have an assistant depress the accelerator fully.
2 Using a diesel tachometer, check that the maximum engine speed is as quoted in the Specifications. **Caution: Do not maintain maximum engine speed for more than two or three seconds.**
3 If necessary, adjust the maximum engine speed by slackening the locknut and rotating the adjusting screw **(see illustration)**.
4 On completion, tighten the locknut.

9 Fast idle speed - checking and adjustment

Note: *This Section does not apply to engine code 1Z.*
Note: *Observe the precautions in Section 1 before working on any component in the fuel system.*

1 With reference to Chapter 1B, check and if necessary adjust the engine idling speed.
2 Pull the facia cold start knob fully out and using a diesel tachometer, check that the idle speed rises to that given in the Specifications.
3 If necessary, adjust the setting by slackening the locknut and rotating the adjusting screw **(refer to illustration 8.3)**.
4 On completion, tighten the locknut.

10 Fuel injection pump timing - testing and adjustment

Note: *On engine code 1Z, the fuel injection pump timing can only be tested and adjusted using dedicated test equipment. Refer to a VAG dealer for advice.*
Note: *Observe the precautions in Section 1 before working on any component in the fuel system.*

Testing

1 Disconnect the battery negative cable and position it away from the terminal.
2 With reference to Chapter 2B, set the engine to TDC on cylinder No 1 then check the valve timing, adjusting it if necessary. On completion, reset the engine to TDC on cylinder No 1.
3 At the rear of the injection pump, unscrew the plug from the pump head and recover the seal **(see illustration)**.
4 Using a suitably threaded adapter, screw a DTI gauge into the pump head **(see illustration)**. Pre-load the gauge by a reading of approximately 2.5 mm.
5 Using a socket and wrench on the crankshaft bolt, slowly rotate the crankshaft anti-clockwise; the DTI gauge will indicate movement - keep turning the crankshaft until the movement just ceases.
6 Zero the DTI gauge, with a pre-load of approximately 1.0 mm.
7 Now turn the crankshaft clockwise to bring the engine back up to TDC on cylinder No 1. Observe the reading indicated by the DTI gauge and compare it with the Specifications.
8 If the reading is within the test tolerance quoted in the Specifications, remove the DTI gauge and refit the pump head plug. Use a new seal and tighten the plug to the specified torque.

9 If the reading is out of tolerance, proceed as described in the next sub-Section.

Adjustment

10 Slacken the pump securing bolts at the front and rear brackets (see Section 7).
11 Rotate the injection pump body until the "Setting" reading (see Specifications) is indicated on the DTI gauge.
12 On completion, tighten the pump securing bolts to the specified torque.
13 Remove the DTI gauge and refit the pump head plug. Use a new seal and tighten the plug to the specified torque.

11 Injectors - general information, removal and refitting

⚠️ **Warning: Exercise extreme caution when working on the fuel injectors. Never expose the hands or any part of the body to injector spray, as the high working pressure can cause the fuel to penetrate the skin, with possibly fatal results. You are strongly advised to have any work which involves testing the injectors under pressure carried out by a dealer or fuel injection specialist. Refer to the precautions given in Section 1 of this Chapter before proceeding.**

General information

1 Injectors do deteriorate with prolonged use and it is reasonable to expect them to need reconditioning or renewal after 60 000 miles (100 000 km) or so. Accurate testing, overhaul and calibration of the injectors must be left to a specialist. A defective injector which is causing knocking or smoking can be located without dismantling as follows.
2 Run the engine at a fast idle. Slacken each injector union in turn, placing rag around the union to catch spilt fuel and being careful not to expose the skin to any spray. When the union on the defective injector is slackened, the knocking or smoking will stop.

Removal

Note: *Take great care not to allow dirt into the injectors or fuel pipes during this procedure.*

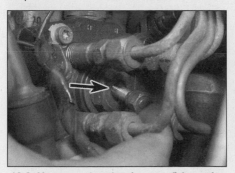

10.3 Unscrew the plug (arrowed) from the pump head and recover the seal

10.4 Screw a DTI gauge into the pump head

4C

11.6 Removing an injector from the cylinder head

11.7 Recover the heat shield washer

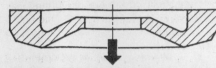

11.8 The heat shield washer must be fitted with its convex side facing downwards (arrow faces the cylinder head)

Do not drop the injectors or allow the needles at their tips to become damaged. The injectors are precision-made to fine limits and must not be handled roughly.

3 Disconnect the battery negative lead and cover the alternator with a clean cloth or plastic bag to prevent the possibility of fuel being spilt onto it.

4 Carefully clean around the injectors and pipe union nuts and disconnect the return pipe from the injector.

5 Wipe clean the pipe unions then slacken the union nut securing the relevant injector pipes to each injector and the relevant union nuts securing the pipes to the rear of the injection pump (pipes are removed as one assembly); as each pump union nut is slackened, retain the adapter with a suitable open-ended spanner to prevent it being unscrewed from the pump. With the union nuts undone remove the injector pipes from the engine. Cover the injector and pipe unions to prevent the entry of dirt into the system.

 HAYNES HiNT *Cut the fingertips from an old rubber glove and secure them over the open unions with elastic bands to prevent dirt ingress (see Section 7).*

6 Unscrew the injector, using a deep socket or box spanner, and remove it from the cylinder head **(see illustration)**.

7 Recover the heat shield washer **(see illustration)**.

Refitting

8 Fit a new heat shield washer to the cylinder head, noting that it must be fitted with its convex side facing downwards (towards the cylinder head) **(see illustration)**.

9 Screw the injector into position and tighten it to the specified torque **(see illustration)**.

11.9 Screw the injector into position and tighten it to the specified torque

10 Refit the injector pipes and tighten the union nuts to the specified torque setting. Position any clips attached to the pipes as noted before removal.

11 Reconnect the return pipe to the injector.

12 Restore the battery connection and check the running of the engine.

12 Fuel cut-off solenoid - removal and refitting

Note: Observe the precautions in Section 1 before working on the fuel system.

Removal

1 The fuel cut-off valve is located at the rear of the injection pump.

2 Disconnect the battery negative cable and position it away from the terminal. Unplug the harness from the connector at the top of the valve **(see illustration)**.

12.2 Fuel cut-off valve connector (arrowed)

3 Slacken and withdraw the valve body from the injection pump. Recover the sealing washer, O-ring seal and the plunger.

Refitting

4 Refitting is a reversal of removal. Use a new sealing washer and O-ring seal.

13 Diesel engine management system (engine code 1Z) - component removal and refitting

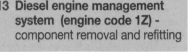

Note: Observe the precautions in Section 1 before working on the fuel system.

Accelerator position sensor

Removal

1 Disconnect the battery negative cable and position it away from the terminal.

2 Refer to Chapter 11 and remove the trim panels from under the steering column area of the facia, to gain access to the pedal cluster.

3 Prise the clip from the end of the accelerator pedal spindle, then withdraw the spindle and recover the bush and spring.

4 Lift the accelerator pedal clear of the pedal bracket, disengaging it from the position sensor cable cam plate.

5 Unplug the position sensor from the wiring harness at the connector.

6 Remove the screw that secures the position sensor bracket to the pedal bracket.

7 Remove the sensor from the pedal bracket, then remove the fixings and release it from the mounting bracket.

8 Slacken and remove the spindle nut, then pull the cable cam plate off the spindle.

Refitting

9 Refitting is a reversal of removal, noting the following points:

a) The cable cam plate must be fitted to the position sensor spindle according to the dimensions shown **(see illustration)**.

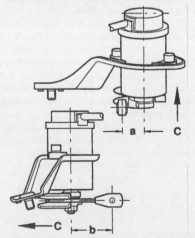

13.9 Mounting arrangement of accelerator position sensor cable cam plate
a 22 ± 0.5 mm   b 41 ± 0.5 mm
C Towards front of vehicle

b) On completion, the adjustment of the position sensor must be verified electronically, using dedicated test equipment - refer to a VAG dealer for advice.

Coolant temperature sensor

Removal

10 Disconnect the battery negative cable and position it away from the terminal, then refer to Chapter 3 and drain approximately one quarter of the coolant from the engine.
11 The sensor is at the top coolant outlet elbow, at the front of the cylinder head. Unplug the wiring from it at the connector.
12 Remove the securing clip and extract the sensor from its housing and recover the O-ring seal - be prepared for coolant loss.

Refitting

13 Refit the coolant temperature sensor by reversing the removal procedure, using a new O-ring seal. Refer to Chapter 1B and top-up the cooling system.

Fuel temperature sensor

Removal

14 Disconnect the battery negative cable and position it away from the terminal.
15 Slacken and withdraw the retaining screws and lift the top cover from the injection pump. Recover the gasket.
16 Remove the screws and lift out the fuel temperature sensor.

Refitting

17 Refitting is a reversal of removal. Tighten the pump top cover screws to the specified torque.

Inlet air temperature sensor

Removal

18 Disconnect the battery negative cable and position it away from the terminal.

19 The sensor is mounted in the air duct between the intercooler and the inlet manifold. Unplug the wiring harness from it at the connector.
20 Remove the securing clip and extract the sensor from its housing and recover the O-ring seal.

Refitting

21 Refit the inlet air temperature sensor by reversing the removal procedure, using a new O-ring seal. Refer to Chapter 1B and top-up the cooling system.

Engine speed signal sensor

Removal

22 The engine speed sensor is mounted on the front cylinder block, adjacent to the mating surface of the block and transmission bellhousing.
23 Disconnect the battery negative cable and position it away from the terminal, then unplug the harness connector from the sensor.
24 Remove the retaining screw and withdraw the sensor from the cylinder block.

Refitting

25 Refit the sensor by reversing the removal procedure.

Airflow meter

Removal

26 Disconnect the battery negative cable and position it away from the terminal.
27 With reference to Section 2 , slacken the clips and disconnect the air ducting from the airflow meter, at the rear of the air cleaner housing.
28 Unplug the harness connector from the airflow meter.
29 Remove the retaining screws and extract the meter from the air cleaner housing. Recover the O-ring seal. **Caution: Handle the airflow meter carefully - its internal components are easily damaged.**

Refitting

30 Refitting is a reversal of removal. Renew the O-ring seal if it appears damaged.

Manifold pressure sensor

31 The manifold pressure sensor is an integral part of the Electronic Control Unit and hence cannot be renewed separately.

Absolute pressure (altitude) sensor

Vehicles up to August 1994

32 The sensor is mounted behind the facia, above the relay board. Refer to Chapter 11 and remove the relevant sections of the facia to gain access.
33 Disconnect the battery negative cable and position it away from the terminal. Unclip the sensor from its bracket and unplug it from the wiring harness at the connector.

Vehicles from August 1994 on

34 The absolute pressure sensor is an integral part of the Electronic Control Unit and hence cannot be renewed separately.

Boost pressure valve

Removal

35 The boost pressure valve is mounted on the inner wing, to the rear of the air cleaner housing.
36 Disconnect the battery negative cable and position it away from the terminal. Unplug the wiring harness from it at the connector.
37 Remove the vacuum hoses from the ports on the boost control valve, noting their order of connection carefully to aid correct refitting.
38 Remove the retaining screw and lift the valve away from the inner wing.

4C

Chapter 4 Part D:
Emission control and exhaust systems

Contents

Degrees of difficulty

Easy, suitable for novice with little experience	**Fairly easy,** suitable for beginner with some experience	**Fairly difficult,** suitable for competent DIY mechanic	**Difficult,** suitable for experienced DIY mechanic	**Very difficult,** suitable for expert DIY or professional

Specifications

Turbocharger

Type	Garrett or KKK
Maximum boost pressure:	
Engine code 1Z	0.50 to 0.65 bar at 3500 to 4000 rpm
Engine code AAZ	0.60 to 0.83 bar at 4000 rpm

Torque wrench settings	Nm	lbf ft
EGR valve-to-exhaust manifold connecting pipe	25	18
EGR valve-to-exhaust manifold connecting pipe clamp		
(engine code 1Y)	10	7
Exhaust downpipe-to-turbocharger nuts	25	18
Exhaust mounting bracket-to-body bolts	40	30
Exhaust system clamp bolts	25	18
Turbocharger-to-exhaust manifold bolts:		
Engine code AAZ	45	33
Engine code 1Z	35	26
Turbocharger oil supply pipe, turbocharger union	25	18
Turbocharger oil return pipe, turbocharger union	40	30
Turbocharger oil return pipe, cylinder block banjo bolt:		
Engine code AAZ	50	37
Engine code 1Z	30	22

1 General information

Emission control systems

All petrol engine models have the ability to use unleaded petrol and are controlled by engine management systems that are "tuned" to give the best compromise between driveability, fuel consumption and exhaust emission production. In addition, a number of systems are fitted that help to minimise other harmful emissions: a crankcase emission-control system that reduces the release of pollutants from the engines lubrication system is fitted to all models, catalytic converters that reduce exhaust gas pollutants are fitted to most models and an evaporative loss emission control system that reduces the release of gaseous hydrocarbons from the fuel tank is fitted to all models.

All diesel engined models also have a crankcase emission control system. In addition, all models are fitted with a catalytic converter and an Exhaust Gas Recirculation (EGR) system to reduce exhaust emissions.

Crankcase emission control

To reduce the emission of unburned hydrocarbons from the crankcase into the atmosphere, the engine is sealed and the blow-by gases and oil vapour are drawn from inside the crankcase, through a wire mesh oil separator, into the inlet tract to be burned by the engine during normal combustion.

Under conditions of high manifold depression (idling, deceleration) the gases will be sucked positively out of the crankcase. Under conditions of low manifold depression (acceleration, full-throttle running) the gases are forced out of the crankcase by the (relatively) higher crankcase pressure; if the engine is worn, the raised crankcase pressure (due to increased blow-by) will cause some of the flow to return under all manifold conditions. On certain engines, a pressure regulating valve (on the camshaft cover) controls the flow of gases from the crankcase.

Exhaust emission control - petrol models

To minimise the amount of pollutants which escape into the atmosphere, most models are fitted with a catalytic converter in the exhaust system. On all models where a catalytic converter is fitted, the fuelling system is of the closed-loop type, in which a lambda sensor in the exhaust system provides the engine management system ECU with constant feedback, enabling the ECU to adjust the air/fuel mixture to optimise combustion.

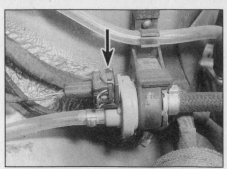

2.3 Unplug the wiring harness from the purge valve at the connector (arrowed)

The lambda sensor has a heating element built-in that is controlled by the ECU through the lambda sensor relay to quickly bring the sensor's tip to its optimum operating temperature. The sensor's tip is sensitive to oxygen and relays a voltage signal to the ECU that varies according on the amount of oxygen in the exhaust gas. If the inlet air/fuel mixture is too rich, the exhaust gases are low in oxygen so the sensor sends a low-voltage signal, the voltage rising as the mixture weakens and the amount of oxygen rises in the exhaust gases. Peak conversion efficiency of all major pollutants occurs if the inlet air/fuel mixture is maintained at the chemically-correct ratio for the complete combustion of petrol of 14.7 parts (by weight) of air to 1 part of fuel (the 'stoichiometric' ratio). The sensor output voltage alters in a large step at this point, the ECU using the signal change as a reference point and correcting the inlet air/fuel mixture accordingly by altering the fuel injector pulse width. Details of the lambda sensor removal and refitting are given in Chapter 4A or B as applicable.

Exhaust emission control - diesel models

An oxidation catalyst is fitted in the line with the exhaust system of all diesel engined models. This has the effect of removing a large proportion of the gaseous hydrocarbons, carbon monoxide and particulates present in the exhaust gas.

An Exhaust Gas Recirculation (EGR) system is fitted to all diesel engined models. This reduces the level of nitrogen oxides produced during combustion by introducing a proportion of the exhaust gas back into the inlet manifold, under certain engine operating conditions, via a plunger valve. The system is controlled electronically by the glow plug control module on engine codes 1Y and AAZ, or by the diesel engine management ECU on engine code 1Z.

Evaporative emission control - petrol models

To minimise the escape of unburned hydrocarbons into the atmosphere, an evaporative loss emission control system is fitted to all petrol models. The fuel tank filler cap is sealed and a charcoal canister is mounted underneath the right-hand wing to collect the petrol vapours released from the fuel contained in the fuel tank. It stores them until they can be drawn from the canister (under the control of the fuel-injection/ignition system ECU) via the purge valve(s) into the inlet tract, where they are then burned by the engine during normal combustion.

To ensure that the engine runs correctly when it is cold and/or idling and to protect the catalytic converter from the effects of an over-rich mixture, the purge control valve(s) are not opened by the ECU until the engine has warmed up, and the engine is under load; the valve solenoid is then modulated on and off to allow the stored vapour to pass into the inlet tract.

Exhaust systems

The exhaust system comprises the exhaust manifold, one or two silencer units (depending on model and specification), a catalytic converter (where fitted), a number of mounting brackets and a series of connecting pipes.

On engine codes AAZ and 1Z, a turbocharger is fitted to the exhaust manifold - refer to Section 6 for further details.

2 Evaporative loss emission control system - general information and component renewal

General information

1 The evaporative loss emission control system consists of the purge valve, the activated charcoal filter canister and a series of connecting vacuum hoses.
2 The purge valve is mounted on a bracket behind the air cleaner housing, and the charcoal canister is mounted on a bracket inside the right-hand front wheel housing.

Component renewal

Purge valve

3 Ensure that the ignition is switched off, then unplug the wiring harness from the purge valve at the connector **(see illustration)**.
4 Slacken the clips and pull the vacuum hoses off the purge valve ports. Make a note of their orientation to aid refitting later.
5 Slide the purge valve out of its retaining ring and remove it from the engine bay.
6 Refitting is a reversal of removal.

Charcoal canister

7 Locate the canister in the wheel housing. Disconnect the vacuum hoses from it, noting which ports they connect to. Depress the locking tab on the side of the securing strap and lift the canister out of the wheel housing.
8 Refitting is a reversal of removal.

3 Crankcase emission system - general information

The crankcase emission control system consists of a series of hoses that connect the crankcase vent to the camshaft cover vent and the air inlet, a pressure regulating valve (where applicable) and an oil separator unit.

The system requires no attention other than to check at regular intervals that the hose(s) are free of blockages and undamaged.

4 Exhaust Gas Recirculation (EGR) system - general information and component removal

General information

1 The EGR system consists of the EGR valve, the EGR solenoid valve (engine codes 1Y and AAZ) or modulator valve (engine code 1Z) and a series of connecting vacuum hoses.
2 The EGR valve is mounted on a flange joint at the inlet manifold and is connected to a second flange joint at the exhaust manifold by a semi-flexible pipe.
3 The EGR solenoid valve/modulator valve is mounted on a bracket on the right-hand front suspension turret, behind the air cleaner.

Component renewal

EGR valve

4 Disconnect the vacuum hose from the port at the top of the EGR valve.
5 Slacken and withdraw the bolts that secure the semi-flexible connecting pipe to the EGR valve flange **(see illustration)**. Recover and

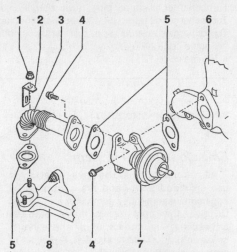

4.5 EGR valve and associated components: engine code 1Z

1 Nut	5 Gaskets
2 Oil supply pipe bracket	6 Inlet manifold
3 Semi-flexible pipe	7 EGR valve
4 Screw	8 Exhaust manifold

discard the gasket from the joint. (On engine code 1Y, slacken the clamp bolt and disconnect the semi-flexible pipe from the EGR valve).

6 Remove the bolts that secure the EGR valve to the inlet manifold flange and lift off the EGR valve. Recover and discard the gasket.

7 Refitting is a reversal of removal, noting the following points:

a) *Use new flange joint gaskets and self-locking nuts.*

b) *When reconnecting the semi-flexible pipe, fit the retaining bolts loosely and ensure that the pipe is unstressed before tightening the bolts to the specified torque.*

EGR solenoid valve/Modulator valve

8 Ensure that the ignition is switched off, then unplug the wiring harness from the valve at the connector.

9 Slacken the clips and pull the vacuum hoses off the valve ports. Make a *careful* note of their orientation to aid refitting later.

10 Remove the retaining screws and lift off the valve.

11 Refitting is a reversal of removal. *Caution: Ensure that the vacuum hoses are refitted correctly; combustion and exhaust smoke production can be drastically affected by an incorrectly operating EGR system.*

5 Exhaust manifold - removal and refitting

The exhaust manifold removal is described as part of the cylinder head dismantling sequence; refer to Chapter 2A or B as applicable.

6 Turbocharger - removal and refitting

General information

1 A turbocharger is fitted on engine codes AAZ and 1Z and is mounted directly on the exhaust manifold. Lubrication is provided by a dedicated oil supply pipe that runs from the the engine oil filter mounting. Oil is returned to the sump via a return pipe that connects to the side of the cylinder block. The turbocharger unit has an integral wastegate valve and vacuum actuator diaphragm, which is used to control the boost pressure applied to the inlet manifold.

2 The turbocharger's internal components rotate at very high speed, and as such are very sensitive to contamination; a great deal of damage can be caused by small particles of dirt, particularly if they strike the delicate turbine blades. *Caution: Thoroughly clean the area around all oil pipe unions before disconnecting them, to prevent the ingress of dirt. Store dismantled components in a*

sealed container to prevent contamination. *Cover the turbocharger air inlet ducts to prevent debris entering, and clean using lint-free cloths only.*

⚠️ *Warning: Do not run the engine with the turbocharger air inlet hose disconnected; the depression at the inlet can build up very suddenly if the engine speed raised and there is the risk of foreign objects being sucked in and ejected at very high speed.*

Engine code AAZ

Removal

3 Disconnect the battery negative cable and position it away from the terminal.

4 Slacken the clips and remove the turbocharger-to-inlet manifold **(see illustrations)** and air cleaner-to-turbocharger ducting.

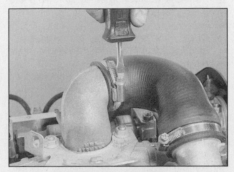

6.4a Slacken the clips . . .

6.4b . . . and remove the turbocharger-to-inlet manifold ducting

6.6a Slackening the oil return pipe union at the turbocharger

6.6b Disconnecting the oil supply pipe at the turbocharger

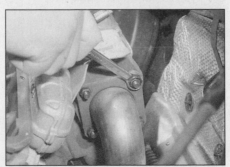

6.7a Remove the nuts and disconnect the downpipe from the turbocharger outlet

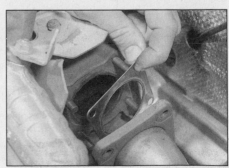

6.7b Recover and discard the gasket

5 Disconnect the vacuum hoses from the wastegate actuator diaphragm housing; note their order of connection and colour coding to aid correct refitting later.

6 Loosen the unions and disconnect the oil supply and return pipes from the turbocharger unit **(see illustrations)**. Recover the sealing washers and discard them - new items must be used on refitting. Free the supply pipe from the clip on the inlet manifold.

7 Remove the nuts and disconnect the exhaust downpipe from the turbocharger outlet. Recover and discard the gasket - a new item must be used on refitting **(see illustrations)**. Slacken the mountings and remove the downpipe from the exhaust manifold support bracket.

8 Slacken and withdraw the turbocharger-to-exhaust manifold bolts. **Note:** *Access to the lowest bolt is restricted; a universal-joint extension bar will ease its removal.* Discard the bolts - new ones must be used on refitting.

4D

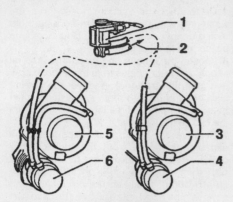

6.10 Wastegate vacuum hose connections: engine code AAZ

1 Two-way valve
2 To vacuum pump
3 Turbocharger (KKK)
4 Wastegate actuator
5 Turbocharger (Garrett)
6 Wastegate actuator

9 Lift the turbocharger unit away from the exhaust manifold.

Refitting

10 Refit the turbocharger by following the removal procedure in reverse, noting the following points:

a) Offer up the turbocharger to the exhaust manifold, then fit and hand tighten the exhaust downpipe nuts.

b) Apply high temperature grease to the threads and heads of the new turbocharger-to-exhaust manifold bolts, then fit and tighten them to the specified torque.

c) Tighten the exhaust downpipe nuts to the specified torque.

d) Prime the oil supply pipe and turbocharger oil inlet port with clean engine oil before reconnecting the union and tightening it to the specified torque.

e) Tighten the oil return union to the specified torque.

f) Reconnect the wastegate actuator vacuum hoses according to the notes made during removal **(see illustration)**.

g) When the engine is started after refitting, allow it idle for approximately one minute to give the oil time to circulate around the turbine shaft bearings.

Engine code 1Z

Removal

11 Disconnect the battery negative cable and position it away from the terminal. Slacken the clips and remove the turbocharger-to-inlet manifold and air cleaner-to-turbocharger ducting.

12 Disconnect the boost control valve vacuum hoses from the wastegate actuator diaphragm housing; note their order of connection and colour coding to aid correct refitting later.

13 Remove the nuts and disconnect the exhaust downpipe from the turbocharger

outlet. Recover and discard the gasket - a new item must be used on refitting.

14 Loosen the unions and disconnect the oil supply and return pipes from the turbocharger unit. Recover the sealing washers and discard them - new items must be used on refitting. Free the supply pipe from the clip on the inlet manifold.

15 Remove the retaining screws and detach the downpipe from the cylinder head support bracket.

16 Slacken and withdraw the two turbocharger-to-inlet manifold bolts from above, then working underneath the exhaust manifold, slacken and remove the retaining nut. Discard the bolts as new items must be used on refitting.

17 Lift the turbocharger unit away from the exhaust manifold.

Refitting

18 Refit the turbocharger by following the removal procedure in reverse, noting the following points:

a) Offer up the turbocharger to the exhaust manifold, then fit and initially hand tighten the exhaust downpipe nuts.

b) Fit the exhaust manifold-to-turbocharger nut and tighten it to the specified torque.

c) Apply high temperature grease to the threads and heads of the new turbocharger-to-exhaust manifold bolts, then fit and tighten them to the specified torque.

d) Tighten the exhaust downpipe nuts to the specified torque.

e) Prime the oil supply pipe and turbocharger oil inlet port with clean engine oil before reconnecting the union and tightening it to the specified torque.

f) Fit a new seal to the oil return union and tighten it to the specified torque.

g) Reconnect the wastegate actuator vacuum hoses according to the notes made during removal **(see illustration)**.

h) When the engine is started after refitting, allow it idle for approximately one minute to give the oil time to circulate around the turbine shaft bearings.

7 Exhaust system - general information and component renewal

General information

1 On engine codes ABU, AEA, ABD, AAM and 1Y the exhaust system is made up of the downpipe, the front silencer (or catalytic converter, depending on specification), the intermediate silencer and the tail section which contains the rear silencer. A flexible coupling is mounted in the downpipe upstream of the catalytic converter/front silencer connection flange.

2 On all other models, the exhaust system is made up of the downpipe, the the front

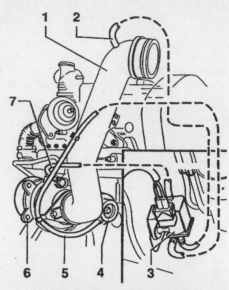

6.18 Wastegate vacuum hose connections: engine code 1Z

1 Inlet hose
2 Hose colour-coded black
3 Boost pressure control solenoid
4 Wastegate actuator
5 Hose colour-coded blue
6 Turbocharger
7 Hose colour-coded red

silencer (or catalytic converter, depending on specification), the intermediate pipe, and the tail section which contains the intermediate and rear silencers. On engine codes AAZ and 1Z, a flexible coupling is fitted in the downpipe, downstream of the exhaust manifold flange. On engine code 2E where a catalytic converter is not fitted, the front silencer is integral with the downpipe.

3 On all models, the system is suspended throughout its entire length by rubber mountings, which are secured to the underside of the vehicle by metal brackets.

Removal

4 Each exhaust section can be removed individually or, alternatively, the complete system can be removed as a unit.

5 To remove the system or part of the system, first jack up the front or rear of the car and support it on axle stands (see "Jacking and Vehicle Support"). Alternatively position the car over an inspection pit or on car ramps.

Downpipe

6 Place blocks of wood under the catalytic converter/front silencer to act as a support. Where applicable, refer to Chapter 4A or B and remove the lambda sensor from the exhaust pipe.

7 Slacken and remove the nuts securing the downpipe to the catalytic converter/front silencer (as applicable). Remove the bolts and recover the sealing olive from the joint.

8 Undo the nuts and separate the downpipe from the exhaust manifold. Recover the gasket then withdraw the downpipe from underneath the vehicle. **Note:** *On engine code ABD from October 1994, the catalytic converter is integral with the downpipe and must be removed complete.*

Catalytic converter

9 Slacken and remove the nuts securing the downpipe to the catalytic converter. Remove the bolts and recover the sealing olive from the joint .

10 Slacken the catalytic converter to intermediate pipe clamping ring bolts.

11 Free the catalytic converter from the intermediate pipe then withdraw it from underneath the vehicle. **Note:** *On engine code ABD from October 1994, the catalytic converter is integral with the downpipe and must be removed complete.*

Intermediate pipe

12 Slacken the clamping ring bolts and disengage the clamp from the intermediate pipe-to-tailpipe joint and the intermediate pipe-to-catalytic converter/front silencer joint.

13 Disengage the intermediate pipe from the tailpipe and the catalytic converter/front silencer and remove it from the vehicle.

Tailpipe

14 Slacken the clamping ring bolts and disengage the tailpipe at the joint.

15 Unhook the tailpipe from its mounting rubbers and remove it from the vehicle. **Note:** *Where applicable, silencers in the tail section can be carefully cut from the exhaust system using a hacksaw and renewed individually; refer to a VAG dealer or an exhaust specialist for further advice.*

Complete system

16 Disconnect the front pipe from the manifold - see paragraphs 6, 7 and 8.

17 With the aid of an assistant, free the system from all its mounting rubbers and manoeuvre it out from underneath the vehicle.

Heatshield(s)

18 The heatshields are secured to the underside of the body by a mixture of nuts, bolts and clips. Each shield can be removed once the relevant exhaust section has been removed. Note that if the shield is being removed to gain access to a component located behind it, in some cases it may prove sufficient to remove the retaining nuts and/or bolts and simply lower the shield, removing the need to disturb the exhaust system.

Refitting

19 Each section is refitted by a reverse of the removal sequence, noting the following points.

a) Ensure that all traces of corrosion have been removed from the flanges and renew all necessary gaskets.

b) Inspect the rubber mountings for signs of damage or deterioration and renew as necessary.

c) Renew the sealing olive in the catalytic converter/front silencer-to-downpipe joint.

d) On joints which are secured by clamping rings, apply a smear of exhaust system jointing paste to the joint mating surfaces to ensure an air-tight seal. Tighten the clamping ring nuts evenly and progressively to the specified torque so that the clearance between the clamp halves is equal on either side.

e) Prior to tightening the exhaust system fasteners, ensure that all rubber mountings are correctly located and that there is adequate clearance between the exhaust system and vehicle underbody.

8 Catalytic converter - general information and precautions

1 The catalytic converter is a reliable and simple device which needs no maintenance in itself, but there are some facts of which an owner should be aware if the converter is to function properly for its full service life.

Petrol models

a) DO NOT use leaded petrol in a car with a catalytic converter - the lead will coat the precious metals reagents, reducing their converting efficiency and will eventually destroy the converter.

b) Always keep the ignition and fuel systems well-maintained in accordance with the manufacturer's schedule.

c) If the engine develops a misfire, do not drive the car at all (or at least as little as possible) until the fault is cured.

d) DO NOT push- or tow-start the car - this will soak the catalytic converter in unburned fuel, causing it to overheat when the engine does start.

e) DO NOT switch off the ignition at high engine speeds.

f) In some cases a sulphurous smell (like that of rotten eggs) may be noticed from the exhaust. This is common to many catalytic converter-equipped cars and once the car has covered a few thousand miles the problem should disappear. Low quality fuel with a high sulphur content will exacerbate this effect.

g) The catalytic converter, used on a well-maintained and well-driven car, should last between 50 000 and 100 000 miles - if the converter is no longer effective it must be renewed.

Petrol and diesel models

h) DO NOT use fuel or engine oil additives - these may contain substances harmful to the catalytic converter.

i) DO NOT continue to use the car if the engine burns oil to the extent of leaving a visible trail of blue smoke.

j) Remember that the catalytic converter operates at very high temperatures. DO NOT, therefore, park the car in dry undergrowth, over long grass or piles of dead leaves after a long run.

k) Remember that the catalytic converter is FRAGILE - do not strike it with tools during servicing work.

4D

Chapter 5 Part A:
Starting and charging systems

Contents

Degrees of difficulty

| Easy, suitable for novice with little experience | Fairly easy, suitable for beginner with some experience | Fairly difficult, suitable for competent DIY mechanic | Difficult, suitable for experienced DIY mechanic | Very difficult, suitable for expert DIY or professional |

Specifications

General
System type .... 12 volt, negative earth

Starter motor
Rating:
  Engine codes ABU, ABD .... 12V, 0.9 kW
  All other engine codes .... 12V, 1.1 kW

Battery
Ratings .... 36 to 110 Ah (depending on model and market)

Alternator
Minimum brush length .... 5 mm (tolerance +1mm, -0 mm)

Torque wrench settings

	Nm	lbf ft
Alternator mounting bolts	25	18
Battery clamping plate screw	20	15
Battery mounting tray screws	15	11
Battery terminal bolts	5	4
Power steering hose guide to starter motor (all engine codes except ABU, ABD)	20	15
Starter motor mounting bolts:		
Engine codes ABU, ABD	20	15
All engine codes except ABU, ABD:		
Lower bolt	45	33
Upper bolt	60	44
Stud	60	44

---

1 General information and precautions

General information

The engine electrical system consists mainly of the charging and starting systems. Because of their engine-related functions, these are covered separately from the body electrical devices such as the lights, instruments, etc (which are covered in Chapter 12). On petrol engine models refer to Part B of this Chapter for information on the ignition system, and on diesel models refer to Part C for the pre-heating system.

The electrical system is of the 12-volt negative earth type.

The battery may of the low maintenance or "maintenance-free" (sealed for life) type and is charged by the alternator, which is belt-driven from the crankshaft pulley.

The starter motor is of the pre-engaged type, with an integral solenoid. On starting, the solenoid moves the drive pinion into engagement with the flywheel ring gear before the starter motor is energised. Once the engine has started, a one-way clutch prevents the motor armature being driven by the engine until the pinion disengages from the flywheel.

Precautions

Further details of the various systems are given in the relevant Sections of this Chapter. While some repair procedures are given, the usual course of action is to renew the component concerned. The owner whose interest extends beyond mere component renewal should obtain a copy of the "Automobile Electrical & Electronic Systems Manual", available from the publishers of this manual.

It is necessary to take extra care when working on the electrical system to avoid damage to semi-conductor devices (diodes and transistors), and to avoid the risk of personal injury. In addition to the precautions given in *"Safety first!"*, observe the following when working on the system:

Always remove rings, watches, etc before working on the electrical system. Even with the battery disconnected, capacitive discharge could occur if a component's live terminal is earthed through a metal object. This could cause a shock or nasty burn.

Do not reverse the battery connections. Components such as the alternator, electronic control units, or any other components having semi-conductor circuitry could be irreparably damaged.

If the engine is being started using jump leads and a slave battery, connect the batteries *positive-to-positive* and *negative-to-negative* (see *"Booster battery (jump) starting"*). This also applies when connecting a battery charger.

Never disconnect the battery terminals, the alternator, any electrical wiring or any test instruments when the engine is running.

Do not allow the engine to turn the alternator when the alternator is not connected.

Never "test" for alternator output by "flashing" the output lead to earth.

Never use an ohmmeter of the type incorporating a hand-cranked generator for circuit or continuity testing.

Always ensure that the battery negative lead is disconnected when working on the electrical system.

Before using electric-arc welding equipment on the car, disconnect the battery, alternator and components such as the fuel injection/ignition electronic control unit to protect them from the risk of damage.

Certain radio/cassette units fitted as standard equipment by VAG are equipped with a built-in security code to deter thieves. If the power source to the unit is cut, the anti-theft system will activate. Even if the power source is immediately reconnected, the radio/cassette unit will not function until the correct security code has been entered. Therefore, if you do not know the correct security code for the radio/cassette unit **do not** disconnect the battery negative terminal of the battery or remove the radio/cassette unit from the vehicle. Refer to your VAG dealer for further information on whether the unit fitted to your car has a security code.

2 Battery - testing and charging

Standard and low maintenance battery - testing

1 If the vehicle covers a small annual mileage it is worthwhile checking the specific gravity of the electrolyte every three months to determine the state of charge of the battery. Use a hydrometer to make the check and compare the results with the following table.

	Ambient temperature above 25°C (77°F)	Ambient temperature below 25°C (77°F)
Fully charged	1.210 to 1.230	1.270 to 1.290
70% charged	1.170 to 1.190	1.230 to 1.250
Discharged	1.050 to 1.070	1.110 to 1.130

Note that the specific gravity readings assume an electrolyte temperature of 15°C (60°F); for every 10°C (48°F) below 15°C (60°F) subtract 0.007. For every 10°C (48°F) above 15°C (60°F) add 0.007.

2 If the battery condition is suspect, first check the specific gravity of electrolyte in each cell. A variation of 0.040 or more between any cells indicates loss of electrolyte or deterioration of the internal plates.

3 If the specific gravity variation is 0.040 or more, the battery should be renewed. If the cell variation is satisfactory but the battery is discharged, it should be charged as described later in this Section.

Maintenance-free battery - testing

4 In cases where a "sealed for life" maintenance-free battery is fitted, topping-up and testing of the electrolyte in each cell is not possible. The condition of the battery can therefore only be tested using a battery condition indicator or a voltmeter.

5 Certain models my be fitted with a maintenance-free battery, with a built-in charge condition indicator. The indicator is located in the top of the battery casing, and indicates the condition of the battery from its colour. If the indicator shows green, then the battery is in a good state of charge. If the indicator turns darker, eventually to black, then the battery requires charging, as described later in this Section. If the indicator shows clear/yellow, then the electrolyte level in the battery is too low to allow further use, and the battery should be renewed. **Do not** attempt to charge, load or jump start a battery when the indicator shows clear/yellow.

6 If testing the battery using a voltmeter, connect the voltmeter across the battery and compare the result with those given in the Specifications under "charge condition". The test is only accurate if the battery has not been subjected to any kind of charge for the previous six hours. If this is not the case, switch on the headlights for 30 seconds, then wait four to five minutes before testing the battery after switching off the headlights. All other electrical circuits must be switched off, so check that the doors and tailgate are fully shut when making the test.

7 If the voltage reading is less than 12.2 volts, then the battery is discharged, whilst a reading of 12.2 to 12.4 volts indicates a partially discharged condition.

8 If the battery is to be charged, remove it from the vehicle and charge it as described later in this Section.

Standard and low maintenance battery - charging

Note: *The following is intended as a guide only. Always refer to the manufacturer's recommendations (often printed on a label attached to the battery) before charging a battery.*

9 Charge the battery at a rate equivalent to 10% of the battery capacity (eg for a 45 Ah battery charge at 4.5 A) and continue to charge the battery at this rate until no further rise in specific gravity is noted over a four hour period.

10 Alternatively, a trickle charger charging at the rate of 1.5 amps can safely be used overnight.

11 Specially rapid "boost" charges which are claimed to restore the power of the battery in 1 to 2 hours are not recommended, as they can cause serious damage to the battery plates through overheating.

12 While charging the battery, note that the temperature of the electrolyte should never exceed 37.8°C (100°F).

Maintenance-free battery - charging

Note: *The following is intended as a guide only. Always refer to the manufacturer's recommendations (often printed on a label attached to the battery) before charging a battery.*

13 This battery type takes considerably longer to fully recharge than the standard type, the time taken being dependent on the extent of discharge, but it can take anything up to three days.

14 A constant voltage type charger is required, to be set, when connected, to 13.9 to 14.9 volts with a charger current below 25 amps. Using this method, the battery should be useable within three hours, giving a voltage reading of 12.5 volts, but this is for a partially discharged battery and, as mentioned, full charging can take far longer.

15 If the battery is to be charged from a fully discharged state (condition reading less than 12.2 volts), have it recharged by your VAG dealer or local automotive electrician, as the charge rate is higher and constant supervision during charging is necessary.

3 Battery - removal and refitting

Removal

1 **Note:** *If the vehicle has a security coded radio, check that you have a copy of the code number before disconnecting the battery cable; refer to Chapter 12 for details.*

2 Slacken the clamp screw and disconnect the battery negative cable from the terminal.

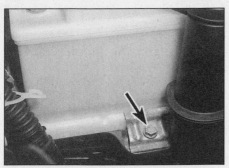

3.4 Battery clamping plate screw (arrowed)

3.7 Battery mounting tray retaining screws (arrowed)

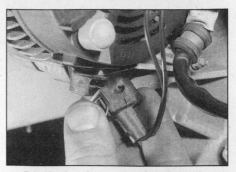

5.3 Unplug the sense cable from the alternator at the connector

3 Unclip the plastic cover and disconnect the battery positive cable in the same manner.

4 At the base of the battery, slacken and withdraw the retaining screw, then lift off the clamping plate **(see illustration)**.

5 Remove the battery from the engine bay.

6 To remove the battery mounting tray, first remove the power steering fluid reservoir mounting screws (where applicable). Lay the reservoir on the inner wing, taking care not to stress the fluid hoses.

7 Slacken and withdraw the four retaining screws **(see illustration)**, then lift off the battery mounting tray, extracting the wiring harness from clips on the underside as they become exposed.

Refitting

8 Refit the battery by following the removal procedure in reverse. Tighten the battery mounting tray and battery clamping plate screws to the correct torque.

4 Alternator/charging system - testing in vehicle

Note: *Refer to "Safety first!" and Section 1 of this Chapter before starting work.*

1 If the ignition warning light fails to illuminate when the ignition is switched on, first check the alternator wiring connections for security. If satisfactory, check that the warning light bulb has not blown, and that the bulbholder is secure in its location in the instrument panel. If the light still fails to illuminate, check the continuity of the warning light feed wire from the alternator to the bulbholder. If all is satisfactory, the alternator is at fault and should be renewed or taken to an auto-electrician for testing and repair.

2 If the ignition warning light illuminates when the engine is running, stop the engine and check that the drivebelt is correctly tensioned (see Chapter 2A or B) and that the alternator connections are secure. If all is so far satisfactory, check the alternator brushes and slip rings as described in Section 8. If the fault persists, the alternator should be renewed, or taken to an auto-electrician for testing and repair.

3 If the alternator output is suspect even though the warning light functions correctly,

the regulated voltage may be checked as follows.

4 Connect a voltmeter across the battery terminals and start the engine.

5 Increase the engine speed until the voltmeter reading remains steady; the reading should be approximately 12 to 13 volts, and no more than 14 volts.

6 Switch on as many electrical accessories (eg, the headlights, heated rear window and heater blower) as possible, and check that the alternator maintains the regulated voltage at around 13 to 14 volts.

7 If the regulated voltage is not as stated, this may be due to worn brushes, weak brush springs, a faulty voltage regulator, a faulty diode, a severed phase winding or worn or damaged slip rings. The brushes and slip rings may be checked (see Section 6), but if the fault persists, the alternator should be renewed or taken to an auto-electrician.

5 Alternator - removal and refitting

Removal

1 Disconnect the battery negative cable and position it away from the terminal.

2 Remove the auxiliary drivebelt from the alternator pulley (see Chapter 2A or 2B).

3 Unplug the sense cable from the alternator at the connector **(see illustration)**.

4 Remove the protective cap, slacken and withdraw the nut and washers, then disconnect the power cable from the alternator at the screw terminal post. Where applicable, unbolt and remove the cable guide **(see illustrations)**.

5 Slacken and remove the lower, then the upper bolts, then lift the alternator away from its bracket **(see illustration)**. Where applicable,

5.4a Remove the protective cap . . .

5.4b . . . remove the nut and washers, then disconnect the power cable

5.4c Where applicable, unbolt and remove the cable guide

5.5 Lifting the alternator away from its mounting bracket (diesel engine shown)

5A

6.3a Remove the retaining screws (arrowed)...

6.3b ...then prise open the clips...

6.3c ...and lift the plastic cover from the rear of the alternator

pivot the tensioner roller out of the way to gain access to the lower mounting bolt.

6 Refer to Section 6 if the removal of the brush holder/voltage regulator module is required.

Refitting

7 Refitting is a reversal of removal. Refer to Chapter 2A or B as applicable for details of refitting and tensioning the auxiliary drivebelt.

8 On completion, tighten the alternator mounting bolts to the specified torque.

6 Alternator - brush holder/ regulator module renewal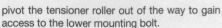

1 Remove the alternator, as described in Section 5.

2 Place the alternator on a clean work surface, with the pulley facing down.

3 Remove the retaining screws, then prise open the clips and lift the plastic cover from the rear of the alternator **(see illustrations)**.

4 Slacken and withdraw the brush holder/voltage regulator module screws, then lift the module away from the alternator **(see illustrations)**.

5 Measure the free length of the brush contacts - take the measurement from the manufacturer's emblem (A) etched on the side of the brush contact, to the shallowest part of the curved end face of the brush (B) **(see illustration)**. Check the measurement with the Specifications; renew the module if the brushes are worn below the minimum limit.

6 Inspect the surfaces of the slip rings, at the end of the alternator shaft **(see illustration)**. If they appear excessively worn, burnt or pitted, then renewal must be considered; refer to an automobile electrical system specialist for further guidance.

7 Reassemble the alternator by following the dismantling procedure in reverse. On completion, refer to Section 5 and refit the alternator.

7 Starting system - testing

Note: *Refer to the precautions given in "Safety first!" and in Section 1 of this Chapter before starting work.*

1 If the starter motor fails to operate when the ignition key is turned to the appropriate position, the following possible causes may be to blame:

a) *The battery is faulty.*

b) *The electrical connections between the switch, solenoid, battery and starter motor are somewhere failing to pass the necessary current from the battery through the starter to earth.*

c) *The solenoid is faulty.*

d) *The starter motor is mechanically or electrically defective.*

2 To check the battery, switch on the headlights. If they dim after a few seconds, this indicates that the battery is discharged - recharge (see Section 3) or renew the battery. If the headlights glow brightly, operate the ignition switch and observe the lights. If they dim, then this indicates that current is reaching the starter motor, therefore the fault must lie in the starter motor. If the lights continue to glow brightly (and no clicking sound can be heard from the starter motor solenoid), this indicates that there is a fault in the circuit or solenoid - see following paragraphs. If the starter motor turns slowly when operated, but the battery is in good condition, then this indicates that either the starter motor is faulty, or there is considerable resistance somewhere in the circuit.

3 If a fault in the circuit is suspected, disconnect the battery leads (including the earth connection to the body), the starter/solenoid wiring and the engine/transmission earth strap. Thoroughly clean the connections, and reconnect the leads and wiring, then use a voltmeter or test lamp to check that full battery voltage is available at the battery positive lead connection to the solenoid, and that the earth

6.4a Remove the brush holder/volatge regulator module screws...

6.4b ...then lift the module away from the alternator

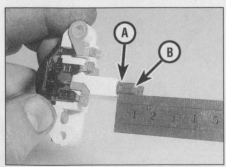

6.5 Measuring the alternator brush length - for A and B, see text

6.6 Inspect the surfaces of the slip rings (arrowed), at the end of the alternator shaft

is sound. Smear petroleum jelly around the battery terminals to prevent corrosion - corroded connections are amongst the most frequent causes of electrical system faults.

4 If the battery and all connections are in good condition, check the circuit by disconnecting the wire from the solenoid blade terminal. Connect a voltmeter or test lamp between the wire end and a good earth (such as the battery negative terminal), and check that the wire is live when the ignition switch is turned to the "start" position. If it is, then the circuit is sound - if not the circuit wiring can be checked as described in Chapter 12.

5 The solenoid contacts can be checked by connecting a voltmeter or test lamp between the battery positive feed connection on the starter side of the solenoid, and earth. When the ignition switch is turned to the "start" position, there should be a reading or lighted bulb, as applicable. If there is no reading or lighted bulb, the solenoid is faulty and should be renewed.

6 If the circuit and solenoid are proved sound, the fault must lie in the starter motor. Begin checking the starter motor by removing it (see Section 8), and checking the brushes. If the fault does not lie in the brushes, the motor windings must be faulty. In this event, it may be possible to have the starter motor overhauled by a specialist, but check on the availability and cost of spares before proceeding, as it may prove more economical to obtain a new or exchange motor.

8 Starter motor - removal and refitting

On engine codes ABU, ABD and AEA, the starter motor is bolted to the transmission bellhousing, at the rear of the engine. On all other engine codes, the starter is situated on the bellhousing at the front of the engine and shares its mounting bolts with the front engine mounting bracket. **Note:** *Removal of the front engine mounting bracket involves supporting the engine with either a lifting beam or an engine hoist whilst the bracket is removed - refer to Chapter 2A or B as applicable for greater detail.*

Removal

Engine codes except ABU, ABD, AEA

1 Disconnect the battery negative cable and position it away from the terminal.

2 Refer to Chapter 2A or B as applicable and remove the front engine mounting bracket from the starter motor.

3 Unhook the wiring connector from the cable guide above the solenoid housing, then remove the cable guide. Unplug the solenoid supply cabling at the connector **(see illustrations).**

4 Where applicable, unbolt the PAS hose guide from the starter motor mountings.

5 At the rear of the solenoid housing, remove the nut and washer from the power cable terminal post and take off the power cables **(see illustration).**

6 Remove the starter upper mounting bolt, then slacken and remove the nut from the mounting stud underneath the starter motor.

7 Guide the starter and solenoid assembly out of the bellhousing aperture **(see illustration).**

Engine codes ABU, ABD, AEA

8 Disconnect the battery negative cable and position it away from the terminal.

9 Unplug the solenoid supply cabling at the connector.

10 At the rear of the solenoid housing, remove the nut and washer from the power cable terminal post and take off the power cable.

11 Remove the starter mounting bolts, then guide the starter and solenoid assembly out of the bellhousing aperture.

Refitting

12 Refit the starter motor by following the removal procedure in reverse. Tighten the mounting bolts to the specified torque. Where applicable, refer to Chapter 2A or B and refit the front engine mounting bracket.

9 Starter motor - testing and overhaul

If the starter motor is thought to be defective, it should be removed from the vehicle and taken to an auto-electrician for assessment. In the majority of cases, new starter motor brushes can be fitted at a reasonable cost. However, check the cost of repairs first as it may prove more economical to purchase a new or exchange motor.

8.3a Remove the cable guide from above the solenoid housing . . .

8.3b . . . then unplug the solenoid supply cabling at the connector

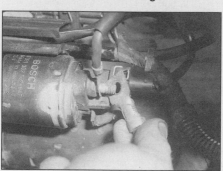

8.5 Remove the nut and washer, and take off the power cables

8.7 Guide the starter and solenoid assembly out of the bellhousing aperture

5A

Chapter 5 Part B:
Ignition system - petrol engines

Contents

Degrees of difficulty

Easy, suitable for novice with little experience	Fairly easy, suitable for beginner with some experience	Fairly difficult, suitable for competent DIY mechanic 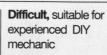	Difficult, suitable for experienced DIY mechanic	Very difficult, suitable for expert DIY or professional

Specifications

General

Type:

Engine code ADY	Simos
Engine code 2E	Digifant
Engine code ABF	Digifant 3.0, 3.2
Engine code AEK	Bosch Motronic
Engine codes ABU, AEA, ABD, AAM, ABS, ADZ	Bosch Mono-Motronic

Ignition coil

Primary winding resistance	0.5 to 1.2Ω

Distributor

Secondary resistance	3 to 4 kΩ
Type	Breakerless
Dwell angle	Controlled by engine management system
Ignition timing	Controlled by engine management system

Spark plugs

See Chapter 1A Specifications

Torque wrench settings

	Nm	lbf ft
Distributor clamp plate bolt	25	18
Distributor clamp bolts (engine codes ABF, ABU, ABD, AEA only)	10	7
Knock sensor mounting bolt	20	15
Spark plugs (engine codes ABF, AEK, ADY)	30	22
Spark plugs (all other engine codes)	25	18

1 General information

The Bosch Motronic, Mono-Motronic, Digifant and Simos systems are self-contained engine management systems, which control both the fuel injection and ignition. This Chapter deals with the ignition system components only - refer to Chapter 4A or B for details of the fuel system components.

The ignition system comprises four spark plugs, five HT leads, the distributor, an electronic ignition coil, and an Electronic Control Unit (ECU) together with its associated sensors, actuators and wiring. The component layout varies from system to system but the basic operation is the same for all models.

The basic operation is as follows: the ECU supplies a voltage to the input stage of the ignition coil which causes the primary windings in the coil to be energised. The supply voltage is periodically interrupted by the ECU and this results in the collapse of primary magnetic field, which then induces a much larger voltage in the secondary coil, called the HT voltage. This voltage is directed, by the distributor via the HT leads, to the spark plug in the cylinder currently on its ignition stroke. The spark plug electrodes form a gap small enough for the HT voltage to arc across, and the resulting spark ignites the fuel/air mixture in the cylinder. The timing of this sequence of events is critical and is regulated solely by the ECU.

The ECU calculates and controls the ignition timing and dwell angle primarily according to engine speed, crankshaft position and inlet manifold depression (or inlet air volume flow rate, depending on system type) information, received from sensors mounted on and around the engine. Other parameters that affect ignition timing are throttle position and rate of opening, inlet air temperature, coolant temperature and on certain systems, engine knock. Again, these are monitored via sensors mounted on the engine.

On systems where knock control is employed, knock sensor(s) are mounted on the cylinder block - these have the ability to detect engine pre-ignition (or 'pinking') before it actually becomes audible. If pre-ignition occurs, the ECU retards the ignition timing of the cylinder that is pre-igniting in steps until the pre-ignition ceases. The ECU then advances the ignition timing of that cylinder in steps until it is restored to normal, or until pre-ignition occurs again.

Idle speed control is achieved partly by an electronic throttle valve positioning module, mounted on the side of the throttle body and partly by the ignition system, which gives fine control of the idle speed by altering the ignition timing. As a result, manual adjustment of the engine idle speed is not necessary or possible.

On certain systems, the ECU has the ability to perform multiple ignition cycles during cold starting. During cranking, each spark plug fires several times per ignition stroke, until the engine starts. This greatly improves the engines cold starting performance.

It should be noted that comprehensive fault diagnosis of all the engine management systems described in this Chapter is only possible with dedicated electronic test equipment. Problems with the systems operation that cannot be pinpointed by following the basic guidelines in Section 2 should therefore be referred to a VAG dealer for assessment. Once the fault has been identified, the removal/refitting sequences detailed in the following Sections will then allow the appropriate component(s) to renewed as required.
Note: *Throughout this Chapter, vehicles are frequently referred to by their engine code, rather than by engine capacity - refer to Chapter 2A for engine code listings.*

2 Ignition system - testing

⚠ *Warning: Extreme care must be taken when working on the system with the ignition switched on; it is possible to get a substantial electric shock from a vehicle's ignition system. Persons with cardiac pacemaker devices should keep well clear of the ignition circuits, components and test equipment. Always switch off the ignition before disconnecting or connecting any component and when using a multi-meter to check resistances.*

General

1 Most ignition system faults are likely to be due to loose or dirty connections or to 'tracking' (unintentional earthing) of HT voltage due to dirt, dampness or damaged insulation, rather than by the failure of any of the system's components. **Always** check all wiring thoroughly before condemning an electrical component and work methodically to eliminate all other possibilities before deciding that a particular component is faulty.
2 The old practice of checking for a spark by holding the live end of an HT lead a short distance away from the engine is not recommended; not only is there a high risk of an electric shock, but the HT coil could be damaged. Similarly, **never** try to 'diagnose' misfires by pulling off one HT lead at a time.

Engine will not start

3 If the engine either will not turn over at all, or only turns very slowly, check the battery and starter motor. Connect a voltmeter across the battery terminals (meter positive probe to battery positive terminal), disconnect the ignition coil HT lead from the distributor cap and earth it, then note the voltage reading obtained while turning over the engine on the starter for (no more than) ten seconds. If the reading obtained is less than approximately 9.5 volts, first check the battery, starter motor and charging systems (see Chapter 5A).
4 If the engine turns over at normal speed but will not start, check the HT circuit by connecting a timing light (following the manufacturer's instructions) and turning the engine over on the starter motor; if the light flashes, voltage is reaching the spark plugs, so these should be checked first. If the light does not flash, check the HT leads themselves followed by the distributor cap, carbon brush and rotor arm using the information given in Chapter 1.
5 If there is a spark, check the fuel system for faults referring to the relevant part of Chapter 4 for further information.
6 If there is still no spark, then the problem must lie within the engine management system. In these cases, the vehicle should be referred to a VAG dealer for assessment.

Engine misfires

7 An irregular misfire suggests either a loose connection or intermittent fault on the primary circuit, or an HT fault on the coil side of the rotor arm.
8 With the ignition switched off, check carefully through the system ensuring that all connections are clean and securely fastened. If the equipment is available, check the LT circuit as described above.
9 Check that the HT coil, the distributor cap and the HT leads are clean and dry. Check the leads themselves and the spark plugs (by substitution, if necessary), then check the distributor cap, carbon brush and rotor arm as described in Chapter 1.
10 Regular misfiring is almost certainly due to a fault in the distributor cap, HT leads or spark plugs. Use a timing light (paragraph 4 above) to check whether HT voltage is present at all leads.
11 If HT voltage is not present on one particular lead, the fault will be in that lead or in the distributor cap. If HT is present on all leads, the fault will be in the spark plugs; check and renew them if there is any doubt about their condition.
12 If no HT voltage is present, check the HT coil; its secondary windings may be breaking down under load.

Other problems

13 Problems with the system's operation that cannot be pinpointed by following the guidelines in the preceding paragraphs should be referred to a VAG dealer for assessment.

3 HT coil - removal and refitting

Removal

1 On all models, the ignition coil is mounted at the rear of the engine bay, on the underside of the vent strip.
2 Disconnect the battery negative cable and position it away from the terminal.
3 Unplug the HT lead from the ignition coil at the connector (**see illustration**).
4 Disconnect the LT cable from the ignition coil at the multiway connector (**see illustration**).
5 Slacken and withdraw the mounting screws and remove the ignition coil.

Refitting

6 Refitting is a reversal of removal.

3.3 Unplug the HT lead from the ignition coil at the connector

3.4 Disconnect the LT cable from the ignition coil at the multiway connector

Chapter 5 Part C:
Pre-heating systems - diesel models

Contents

Degrees of difficulty

Easy, suitable for novice with little experience	Fairly easy, suitable for beginner with some experience	Fairly difficult, suitable for competent DIY mechanic	Difficult, suitable for experienced DIY mechanic	Very difficult, suitable for expert DIY or professional

Specifications

Glow plugs

Electrical resistance
Engine codes AAZ, 1Y	1.5 Ω (approx)
Engine code 1Z	N/A

Current consumption:
Engine codes AAZ, 1Y	8 amps (per glow plug)
Engine code 1Z	N/A

Torque wrench settings	Nm	lbf ft
Glow plug to cylinder head (engine code 1Z)	15	11
Glow plug to cylinder head (engine codes 1Y, AAZ)	25	18

1 General information

To assist cold starting, diesel engined models are fitted with a pre-heating system, which comprises four glow plugs, a glow plug control unit, a facia mounted warning lamp and the associated electrical wiring.

The glow plugs are miniature electric heating elements, encapsulated in a metal case with a probe at one end and electrical connection at the other. Each swirl chamber/inlet tract has a glow plug threaded into it, the glow plug probe is positioned directly in line with incoming spray of fuel. When the glow plug is energised, the fuel passing over it is heated, allowing its optimum combustion temperature to be achieved more readily when it reaches the cylinder.

The duration of the pre-heating period is governed by the glow plug control unit, which monitors the temperature of the engine via the coolant temperature sensor and alters the pre-heating time to suit the conditions.

A facia mounted warning lamp informs the driver that pre-heating is taking place. The lamp extinguishes when sufficient pre-heating has taken place to allow the engine to be started, but power will still be supplied to the glow plugs for a further period until the engine is started. If no attempt is made to start the engine, the power supply to the glow plugs is switched off to prevent battery drain and glow plug burn-out. Note that on certain models, the warning lamp will also illuminate during normal driving if a pre-heating system malfunction occurs.

Generally, pre-heating is triggered by the ignition key being turned to the second position. However, certain models are equipped with a pre-heating system that activates when the drivers door is opened. Refer to the vehicles handbook for further information.

After the engine has been started, the glow plugs continue to operate for a further period of time. This helps to improve fuel combustion whilst the engine is warming up, resulting in quieter, smoother running and reduced exhaust emissions.

2 Glow plug control unit - removal and refitting

1 On engine code 1Z, the pre-heating system is controlled by the diesel engine management system ECU - refer to Chapter 4C.

Removal

2 The glow plug control unit is located behind the facia, above the main relay box - refer to Chapter 11 and remove the relevant sections of trim to gain access.
3 Disconnect the battery negative cable an position it away from the terminal.
4 Unplug the wiring harness from the control unit at the connector.
5 Remove the retaining screws lift the control unit from its mounting bracket.

Refitting

6 Refitting is a reversal of removal.

3 Glow plugs - testing, removal and refitting

Testing

1 If the system malfunctions, testing is ultimately by substitution of known good units, but some preliminary checks may be made as described in the following paragraphs.
2 Connect a voltmeter or 12 volt test lamp to between the glow plug supply cable and a good earth point on the engine. *Caution: Make sure that the live connection is kept well clear of the engine and bodywork.*
3 Have an assistant activate the pre-heating system (either using the ignition key, or opening the drivers door as applicable) and check that a battery voltage is applied to the glow plug electrical connection. (Note that the voltage will drop to zero when the pre-heating period ends).
4 If no supply voltage can be detected at the glow plug, then either the glow plug relay (where applicable) or the supply cabling must be faulty.

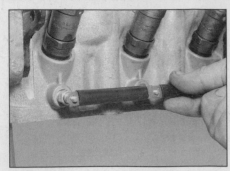

3.10 Remove the nuts and washers from the glow plug terminal. Lift off the bus bar

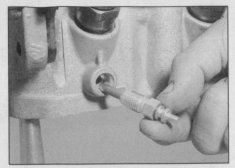

3.11 Slacken and withdraw the glow plug

3.13 Tighten the glow plug to the specified torque

5 To locate a faulty glow plug, first disconnect the battery negative cable and position it away from the terminal.

6 Refer to the next sub-Section and remove the supply cabling from the glow plug terminal. Measure the electrical resistance between the glow plug terminal and the engine earth. A reading of anything more than a few Ohms indicates that the plug is defective.

7 If a suitable ammeter is available, connect it between the glow plug and its supply cable and measure the steady state current consumption (ignore the initial current surge which will be about 50% higher). Compare the result with the Specifications - high current consumption (or no current draw at all) indicates a faulty glow plug.

8 As a final check, remove the glow plugs and inspect them visually, as described in the next sub-Section.

Removal

9 Disconnect the battery negative cable and position it away from the terminal.

10 Remove the nuts and washers from the glow plug terminal. Lift off the bus bar **(see illustration)**.

11 Slacken and withdraw the glow plug **(see illustration)**.

12 Inspect the glow plug probe for signs of damage. A badly burned or charred probe is usually an indication of a faulty fuel injector; refer to Chapter 4C for greater detail.

Refitting

13 Refitting is a reversal of removal; tighten the glow plug to the specified torque **(see illustration)**.

Chapter 6
Clutch

Contents

Degrees of difficulty

Easy, suitable for novice with little experience	Fairly easy, suitable for beginner with some experience	Fairly difficult, suitable for competent DIY mechanic	Difficult, suitable for experienced DIY mechanic	Very difficult, suitable for expert DIY or professional

Specifications

General

Type	Single dry plate, diaphragm spring with spring-loaded hub
Operation:	
084, 085, 020	Cable with automatic adjustment mechanism
02A	Hydraulic with slave and master cylinders
Diameter:	
084 transmission	190 mm
085 transmission	190 mm
020 transmission	210 mm
02A transmission	228 mm

Torque wrench settings

	Nm	lbf ft
Clutch hydraulic pipe unions	20	15
Flywheel-to-pressure plate bolts (020 transmission only)	20	15
Master cylinder-to-bulkhead nuts	25	18
Pressure plate-to-crankshaft bolts (020 transmission only):		
Stage 1	60	44
Stage 2	Angle-tighten a further 90°	
Pressure plate-to-flywheel bolts:		
084. 085 transmission	25	18
02A transmission	20	15
Slave cylinder-to-transmission mounting bolts	25	18

1 General information

Vehicles with manual transmission are fitted with a pedal operated single dry plate clutch system. When the clutch pedal is depressed, effort is transmitted to the clutch release mechanism either mechanically, by means of a cable or hydraulically (transmission 02A only), by means of master and slave cylinders. The release mechanism transfers effort to the pressure plate diaphragm spring, which withdraws from the flywheel and releases the driven plate. The mounting arrangement of the flywheel and clutch components depends on the type of transmission fitted.

On vehicles fitted with the 020 (5-speed) transmission, the clutch system comprises the clutch pedal, a self adjusting clutch cable, the clutch release components, the pressure plate and the driven plate. Note that the clutch pressure plate is bolted directly to the crankshaft flange - the dished flywheel is then mounted on the pressure plate.

On vehicles fitted with the 02A, 085 (5-speed) and 084 (4-speed) transmission, the layout is more conventional; the flywheel is mounted on the crankshaft, with the pressure plate bolted to it. In this case, removal of the flywheel is described in Chapter 2A.

The hydraulic fluid employed in the clutch system is the same as that used in the braking system, hence fluid is supplied to the master cylinder from a tapping on the brake fluid reservoir. The clutch hydraulic system must be sealed before work is carried out on any of its components and then on completion, topped up and bled to remove any air bubbles. Details of these procedures are given in Section 2 of this Chapter.

2 Hydraulic system - draining, refilling and bleeding

⚠ **Warning: Hydraulic fluid is poisonous; thoroughly wash off spills from bare skin without delay. Seek immediate medical advice if any fluid is swallowed or gets into the eyes. Certain types of hydraulic fluid are inflammable and may ignite when brought into contact with hot components; when servicing any hydraulic system, it is safest to assume that the fluid IS inflammable, and to take precautions against the risk of fire as though it were petrol that was being handled. Hydraulic fluid is an effective paint stripper and will also attack many plastics. If spillage occurs onto painted**

bodywork or fittings, it should be washed off immediately, using copious quantities of fresh water. It is also hygroscopic i.e. it can absorb moisture from the air, which then renders it useless. Old fluid may have suffered contamination, and should never be re-used. When topping-up or renewing the fluid, always use the recommended grade, and ensure that it comes from a new sealed container.

Note: *This section applies only to models with transmission type 02A.*

General information

1 Whenever the clutch hydraulic lines are disconnected for service or repair, a certain amount of air will enter the system. The presence of air in any hydraulic system will introduce a degree of elasticity and in the clutch system, this will translate into poor pedal feel and reduced travel, leading to inefficient gear changes and even clutch system failure. For this reason, the hydraulic lines must be sealed using hose clamps before any work is carried out and then on completion, topped up and bled to remove any air bubbles.

2 To seal off the hydraulic supply to the clutch slave cylinder, trace the rigid supply pipe back to the point where it connects to the flexible hydraulic hose. Fit a proprietary brake hose clamp to the flexible section of the hose and tighten it securely **(see illustration)**.

3 Unlike the braking system, the clutch hydraulic system cannot be bled by simply pumping the clutch pedal and catching the ejected fluid in a receptacle connected to the bleed pipe. The system must be pressurised externally; the most effective way of achieving this is to use a pressure brake bleeding kit. These are readily available in motor accessories shops and are extremely effective; the following sub-section describes bleeding the clutch system using such a kit.

Bleeding

4 Locate the slave cylinder bleed nipple, at the end of the slave cylinder housing. Remove the protective cap.

5 Fit a ring spanner over the bleed nipple head, but do not slacken it at this point. Connect a length of clear plastic hose over nipple and insert the other end into a clean container **(see illustration)**. Pour hydraulic fluid into the container, such that the end of the hose is covered.

6 Following the manufacturers instructions, pour hydraulic fluid into the bleeding kit vessel.

7 Unscrew the vehicles fluid reservoir cap, then connect the bleeding kit fluid supply hose to the reservoir.

8 Connect the pressure hose to a supply of compressed air - a spare tyre is convenient source. **Caution: Check that the pressure in the tyre does not exceed the maximum supply pressure quoted by the kit**

2.2 Hydraulic hose clamp in use

manufacturer, let some air escape to reduce the pressure, if necessary. Gently open the air valve and allow the air and fluid pressures to equalise. Check that there are no leaks before proceeding.

9 Using the spanner, slacken the bleed pipe nipple until fluid and air bubbles can be seen to flow through the tube, into the container. Maintain a steady flow until the emerging fluid is free of air bubbles; keep a watchful eye on the level of fluid in the bleeding kit vessel and the vehicles fluid reservoir - if it is allowed to drop too low, air may be forced into the system, defeating the object of the exercise. To refill the vessel, turn off the compressed air supply, remove the lid and pour in an appropriate quantity of clean fluid from a new container - do not re-use the fluid collected in the receiving container. Repeat as necessary until the ejected fluid is bubble-free.

10 On completion, pump the clutch pedal several times to assess its feel and travel. If firm, constant pedal resistance is not felt throughout the pedal stroke, it is probable that air is still present in the system - repeat the bleeding procedure until the pedal feel is restored.

11 Depressurise the bleeding kit and remove it from the vehicle. At this point, the fluid reservoir may be "over-full"; the excess should be removed using a *clean* pipette to reduce the level to the "MAX" mark.

12 Tighten the bleed pipe nipple using the spanner and remove the receiving container. Refit the protective cap.

13 On completion, assess the feel of the clutch pedal; If It exhibits any 'sponginess' or looseness, further bleeding may be required.

14 Finally, road test the vehicle and check the operation of the clutch system whilst changing up and down through the gears, whilst pulling away from a standstill and from a hillstart.

3 Master cylinder - removal and refitting

Note: *This section applies only to transmission 02A.*
Note: *Refer to the warning at the beginning of Section 2 regarding the hazards of working with hydraulic fluid.*

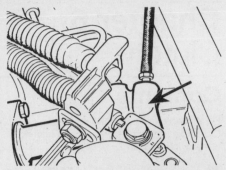

2.5 Hose connected to slave cylinder bleed nipple (arrowed)

Removal

1 Refer to Chapter 11 and remove the facia trim panels from the area underneath the steering column.

2 To separate the master cylinder push rod from the clutch pedal, insert one flat bladed screwdriver in each of the two holes on either side of the clutch pedal. Press in the release tangs and withdraw push rod from the pedal, together with the guide clip.

3 Slacken and remove the master cylinder mounting nuts.

4 Working in the engine bay, clamp off the flexible hydraulic fluid hose leading from the fluid reservoir to the master cylinder using a brake hose clamp, as described in Section 2. Clamp off the supply hose to the slave cylinder in the same manner.

5 Position a small container underneath the master cylinder, then slacken the union and disconnect the hydraulic pipe. **Caution: Be prepared for an amount of hydraulic fluid spillage.**

6 With the mounting nuts removed, the master cylinder can be withdrawn into the engine bay and removed from the vehicle. Recover and discard the gasket; a new item must be used on refitting.

Refitting

7 Refit the master cylinder by following the removal procedure in reverse, noting the following:

a) *Tighten the master cylinder mounting nuts to the specified torque.*
b) *Tighten all hydraulic pipe unions to the specified torque.*
c) *Fit a new master cylinder-to-bulkhead gasket.*
d) *Ensure that the master cylinder push rod and its guide clip locate securely in the clutch pedal recess (see illustration).*

8 On completion, bleed the hydraulic system as described in Section 2.

4 Slave cylinder - removal and refitting

Note: *This section applies only to transmission 02A.*
Note: *Refer to the warning at the beginning of*

3.7 Ensure that the master cylinder push rod and its guide clip locate securely in the clutch pedal recess

A Guide clip
B Master cylinder push rod
C Clutch pedal

Section 2 regarding the hazards of working with hydraulic fluid.

Removal

1 Refer to Chapter 7A and unbolt the gear change/select cable mounting bracket from the top of the transmission casing.
2 Clamp off the slave cylinder hydraulic hose using a brake pipe clamp (see Section 2).
3 Position a small container underneath the end of slave cylinder, then slacken the union and disconnect the hydraulic pipe. *Caution: Be prepared for an amount of hydraulic fluid spillage.*
4 Slacken and withdraw the mounting bolts, then remove the slave cylinder.

Refitting

5 Refit the slave cylinder by following the removal procedure in reverse, noting the following:
a) Tighten the slave cylinder mounting bolts to the specified torque.
b) Tighten all hydraulic pipe unions to the specified torque.

c) Ensure the end of the slave cylinder push rod engages with the clutch release lever as it is fitted into the transmission casing.
d) Refer to Chapter 7B and refit the gear change/select cable mounting bracket to the top of the transmission casing.
6 On completion, bleed the hydraulic system as described in Section 2.

5 Clutch cable - removal and refitting

Note: *This section does not apply to transmission 02A.*

Removal

020 transmission

1 Depress the clutch pedal several times, to settle the automatic adjustment mechanism.
2 Working in the engine bay, slide the locking strap down to the top of the adjustment mechanism protective boot. Grasp the top and bottom of the adjustment mechanism and compress it - at the same time, hook the ends of the locking strap over the lugs protruding from the side of the adjustment mechanism **(see illustration). Note:** *If the locking strap is no longer attached to the clutch cable, a home made strap can be fabricated using nylon cable-ties or a length of electrical cable.*
3 Lift the clutch release lever up and extract the clutch cable inner from it, together with the locking plates and rubber damper.
4 Working inside the vehicle, refer to Chapter 11 and remove the facia trim panels from the area underneath the steering column.
5 Unhook the cable inner from the recess at the top of clutch pedal.
6 Push the clutch cable out through the bulkhead grommet, into the engine bay.
7 Disconnect the clutch cable from its securing clips and lift it out of the engine bay.

085, 084 transmission

8 Depress the clutch pedal several times, to settle the automatic adjustment mechanism.
9 In the engine bay, pull on the clutch release lever so that the clutch cable inner (and adjustment mechanism) is fully extended.
10 Disengage the clutch cable outer from the

clutch release lever, then extract the cable inner termination from the anchor bracket on the transmission casing **(see illustration)**.
11 Working inside the vehicle, refer to Chapter 11 and remove the facia trim panels from the area underneath the steering column.
12 Refer to Chapter 12 and remove the relay plate from the bracket under the facia.
13 Unhook the clutch cable inner from the recess at the top of the clutch pedal.
14 Push the clutch cable out through the bulkhead grommet, into the engine bay.
15 Disconnect the clutch cable from its securing clips and lift it out of the engine bay.

Refitting

020 transmission

16 Feed the clutch cable through the bulkhead grommet, into the cabin area.
17 Apply a smear of multi-purpose grease to the inner clutch cable nipple, then fit the nipple into the recess at the top of the clutch pedal. Refit the facia trim panels.
18 Pre-tension the adjustment mechanism by depressing the clutch pedal whilst an assistant pulls on the clutch cable inner and simultaneously compresses the adjustment mechanism. Use the locking strap to keep the adjustment mechanism compressed, as described in the *Removal* sub-Section.
19 Working in the engine bay, guide the clutch cable inner through the release lever and fit the retaining plates and rubber damper.
20 Fit the base of the adjustment mechanism into the retaining bracket on the transmission casing **(see illustration)**.
21 Unhook the locking strap from the lugs at the side of the adjustment mechanism, then depress the clutch pedal several times, until the cable tension is set.

085, 084 transmission

22 Working from the engine bay, feed the clutch cable through the bulkhead grommet, into the cabin area.
23 Apply a smear of grease to the inner clutch cable nipple, then fit the nipple into the recess at the top of the clutch pedal. Refit the relay plate and facia trim panels.
24 Connect the end of the clutch cable inner to the bracket on the transmission casing.

5.2 Compressing the adjustment mechanism using the locking strap

5.10 Clutch cable mounting arrangement (084, 085 transmission)

A Release lever   *B Anchor bracket*

5.20 Fit the base of the adjustment mechanism into the retaining bracket on the transmission casing

6.5 Home-made flywheel locking tool in use

6.8 Lock the pressure plate in position with a piece of scrap metal

25 Engage the clutch cable outer with the fork at the end of the clutch release lever.
26 Depress the clutch pedal several times until the cable tension is set.

All models

27 On completion, assess the feel of the clutch pedal before bringing the vehicle back into service. If it exhibits any stiffness or shows signs of binding, check the routing of the cable and ensure that there are no sharp bends or kinks along its length.
28 Finally, road test the vehicle and check the operation of the clutch whilst changing up and down through the gears, whilst pulling away from a standstill and from a hillstart.

6 Clutch components - removal and refitting

Warning: Dust created by clutch wear and deposited on the clutch components may contain asbestos, which is a health hazard. DO NOT blow it out with compressed air or inhale any of it. DO NOT use petrol or petroleum-based solvents to clean off the dust. Brake system cleaner or methylated spirit should be used to flush the dust into a suitable receptacle. After the clutch components are wiped clean with clean rags, dispose of the contaminated rags and cleaner in a sealed, marked container.

Note: *Some friction materials may no longer contain asbestos, but it is safest to assume they DO, and to take precautions accordingly*

General information

1 The mounting arrangement of the flywheel and clutch components depends on the type of transmission fitted.
2 On vehicles fitted with the 020 (5-speed) transmission, the clutch pressure plate is bolted directly to the end of the crankshaft. The dished flywheel is then bolted to the pressure plate. Removal of these components is described in the following paragraphs.
3 On vehicles fitted with the 02A, 085 (5-speed) and 084 (4-speed) transmission, the layout is more conventional; the flywheel is mounted on the crankshaft, with the pressure

plate bolted to it. Removal of the flywheel is as described in Chapter 2A or B as appropriate and removal of the clutch components is described in the following paragraphs.

Removal

020 transmission

4 Remove the transmission (see Chapter 7A).
5 Before the flywheel bolts can be removed, the flywheel must be locked in position - a home made flywheel locking tool can be fabricated from scrap metal **(see illustration)**.
6 Slacken the flywheel bolts progressively, then lift the flywheel away from the clutch pressure plate and recover the friction plate.
7 Prise off the spring clip and lift the clutch release plate away.
8 Lock the pressure plate in position by bolting a piece of scrap metal between it and one of the bellhousing mounting bolt holes **(see illustration)**.

9 Progressively slacken the pressure plate bolts until they can be removed by hand. Recover the intermediate plate.
10 Lift the pressure plate away from the crankshaft flange.

02A, 084 and 085 transmissions

11 Refer to Chapter 7A and remove the transmission from the engine.
12 Unclip the release bearing from the release lever and examine it for signs of terminal wear or damage. Spin it by hand and listen to the bearings; if the bearing sticks or is unduly noisy, it should be renewed.
13 Lock the pressure plate in position by bolting a piece of scrap metal between it and one of the bellhousing mounting bolt holes **(see illustration 6.8)**.
14 Progressively slacken the pressure plate bolts until they can be removed by hand. Lift off the pressure plate and recover the friction plate.

Refitting

020 transmission

15 If a new pressure plate is to be fitted, first wipe the protective grease from the friction surface only. Lift the pressure plate up to the crankshaft flange together with the intermediate plate then insert a new set of retaining bolts. Coat the bolt threads with a suitable locking compound, if they are not supplied already coated **(see illustrations)**.
16 Hold the pressure plate still using the method described during removal and tighten the retaining bolts progressively to the specified torque **(see illustration)**.

6.15a Lift the pressure plate up to the crankshaft flange . . .

6.15b . . . together with the intermediate plate . . .

6.15c . . .then insert a new set of retaining bolts

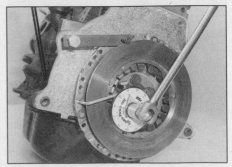

6.16 Tighten the pressure plate retaining bolts progressively to the specified torque

6.17a Fit the release plate . . .

6.17b . . .and secure it in position with the spring clip

17 Fit the release plate and secure it in position with the spring clip **(see illustrations)**. Apply a smear of high temperature grease to the centre of the release plate.

18 Smear a quantity of high temperature grease on the splines at the centre of the friction plate - take care to avoid contaminating the friction surfaces.

19 Hold the friction plate up to the pressure plate, with the spring loaded boss facing outwards, then offer up the flywheel, ensuring that the locating dowels engage with the recess on the edge of the pressure plate **(see illustrations)**. Insert a new set of flywheel retaining bolts - hand tighten them only at this stage.

20 Centre the friction plate using vernier calipers; ensure that there is uniform gap between outer edge of the friction plate and the inner edge of the flywheel, around the whole circumference **(see illustration)**.

21 Tighten the flywheel retaining bolts diagonally and progressively to the specified torque. Re-check the friction plate centralisation.

22 Refer to Chapter 7A and refit the transmission.

02A, 084 and 085 transmissions

23 Smear a quantity of high temperature grease on the splines at the centre of the friction plate - take care to avoid contaminating the friction surfaces.

24 If a new pressure plate is to be fitted, first wipe the protective grease from the friction surface only. Hold the friction plate up to the

6.19a Fit the friction plate, with the spring-loaded boss facing outwards

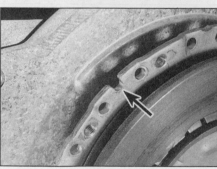

6.19c . . . the recesses on the edge of the pressure plate (arrowed)

pressure plate, with the spring loaded boss facing outwards, then offer up the pressure plate, ensuring that the locating dowels engage with the flywheel. Insert a new set of pressure plate retaining bolts - hand tighten them only at this stage.

25 Centre the friction plate using vernier calipers; ensure that there is uniform gap between outer edge of the friction plate and the inner edge of the pressure plate, around the whole circumference.

26 Tighten the pressure plate bolts diagonally and progressively to the specified torque. Re-check the friction plate centralisation.

27 Refit the release bearing to the release shaft.

28 Refer to Chapter 7A and refit the transmission.

6.19b Ensure that the locating dowels (arrowed) enagage with . . .

6.20 Centre the friction plate using vernier calipers

6

Chapter 7 Part A:
Manual transmission

Contents

Degrees of difficulty

Easy, suitable for novice with little experience	**Fairly easy,** suitable for beginner with some experience	**Fairly difficult,** suitable for competent DIY mechanic 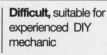	**Difficult,** suitable for experienced DIY mechanic	**Very difficult,** suitable for expert DIY or professional

Specifications

General

Type . . . . Transverse mounted, front wheel drive layout with integral transaxle differential/final drive. 4 or 5 forward speeds, 1 reverse speed

Lubricant capacity:
020 transmission . . . . 2.0 litres
084 transmission . . . . 3.1 litres
085 transmission . . . . 2.2 litres
02A transmission . . . . 2.0 litres

Torque wrench settings

	Nm	lbf ft
Clutch shield plate	15	11
Engine front crossmember-to-body bolts	50	37
Transmission bellhousing-to-engine bolts, M10	60	44
Transmission bellhousing-to-engine bolts, M12	80	59

1 General information

The manual transmission is mounted transversely in the engine bay, bolted directly to the engine. This layout has the advantage of providing the shortest possible drive path to the front wheels, as well as locating the transmission in the airflow through engine bay, optimising cooling. The unit is cased in aluminium alloy.

Drive from the crankshaft is transmitted via the clutch to the gearbox input shaft, which is splined to accept the clutch friction plate.

All forward gears are fitted with syncromeshes. When a gear is selected, the movement of the cabin floor-mounted gear lever is communicated to the gearbox either by a selector rod, or selector and shift cables, depending on the transmission type. This in turn actuates a series of selector forks inside the gearbox which are slotted onto the synchromesh sleeves. The sleeves, which are locked to the gearbox shafts but can slide axially by means of splined hubs, press baulk rings into contact with the respective

gear/pinion. The coned surfaces between the baulk rings and the pinion/gear act as a friction clutch, that progressively matches the speed of the synchromesh sleeve (and hence the gearbox shaft) with that of the gear/pinion. The dog teeth on the outside of the baulk ring prevent the synchromesh sleeve ring from meshing with the gear/pinion until their speeds are exactly matched; this allows gear changes to be carried out smoothly and greatly reduces the noise and mechanical wear caused by rapid gear changes.

Drive is transmitted to the differential crownwheel, which rotates the differential case and planetary gears, thus driving the sun gears and driveshafts. The rotation of the planetary gears on their shaft allows the inner roadwheel to rotate at a slower speed than the outer roadwheel during cornering.

This Chapter covers the 084 4-speed transmission, fitted to 1.4 litre models, the 085 5-speed transmission fitted to 1.4 and 1.6 litre models, the 020 5-speed transmission fitted to 1.8 and 2.0 litre SOHC petrol engines and 1.9 litre normally-aspirated and turbo-diesel engines, and the 02A transmission fitted to the 2.0 litre DOHC petrol engine and the 1.9 litre direct injection turbo-diesel engine.

2 Gearchange linkage - adjustment

084, 085, 020 transmission

1 If the gearchange quality proves unsatisfactory following transmission refitting, proceed as described in the following paragraphs.
2 Refer to Chapter 11 and remove the knob and gaiter from the gear change lever, to expose the adjustment collar.
3 Select first gear, then take up the play in the gear change mechanism by gently pressing the gear change lever to the left.
4 Measure the clearance between the gear change lever stop and the side of the lever housing (see illustration).
5 If the clearance is greater than 1.5 mm, slacken the adjustment collar clamping bolt and rotate the collar until the correct clearance is achieved (refer to illustration 2.4).
6 On completion, tighten the clamping bolt. Refit the gear change lever gaiter and knob.

02A transmission

7 To accurately adjust the operation of the gear selector and shift cables, precisely

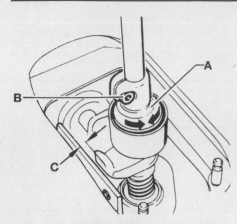

2.4 Gearchange lever adjustment collar (084, 085, 020 transmission)

A Adjustment collar
B Clamp bolt
C Clearance less than 1.5 mm

machined jigs are required to set the gear change lever in a reference position. It is recommended, therefore that this operation be entrusted to a VAG dealer.

3 Manual transmission - removal and refitting

Removal

1 Select a solid, level surface to park the vehicle upon. Give yourself enough space to move around it easily. Apply the handbrake and chock the rear wheels.
2 Raise the front of the vehicle and rest it securely on axle stands (see "Jacking and Vehicle Support").
3 Refer to Chapter 11 and remove the bonnet from its hinges.
4 Disconnect the battery negative cable and position It away from the terminal. **Note:** If the vehicle has a security coded radio, check that you have a copy of the code number before disconnecting the battery cable; refer to Chapter 12 for details.
5 The "lock carrier" is a panel assembly comprising the front bumper moulding, radiator and grille, cooling fan(s) headlight units, front valence and bonnet lock

mechanism. Although its removal is not essential, its does give greatly improved access to the engine. Its removal is relatively simple and is described at the beginning of the engine removal procedure - refer to Chapter 2C for details.
6 Extra working space may be gained on engine codes ABU, AEA and ABD by removing the exhaust downpipe; refer to Chapter 4D for details.
7 On models with transmissions 020, 084 and 085, disconnect the clutch cable from the transmission release lever (see Chapter 6).
8 Unbolt the earth strap from the transmission.
9 Referring to Sections 5 and 6, disconnect the harness cabling from the speedometer transducer and reversing light switch.
10 Position a trolley jack underneath the transmission and raise it to just take the weight of the unit.

Models with transmission 02A

11 Disconnect the shift and selector cables from the transmission levers **(see illustration)**.
12 Unbolt the shift and selector cable support bracket from the top of the transmission casing.
13 Refer to Chapter 6 and remove the slave cylinder from the transmission casing. Insert a 35 mm M8 bolt through the drilling above the slave cylinder aperture, to hold the clutch release lever in position.

Models with transmissions 084, 085 and 020

14 Disconnect the longer of the two gearshift selector rods from the relay lever; prise open

the plastic clip and pull off the balljoint **(see illustration)**.
15 Disconnect the shorter of the two gearshift selector rods with the damper weight from the lever at the transmission and the gear shift shaft; pull out the locking pins to separate the joints **(see illustration)**.

All models

16 On engine codes ABU, ABD and AEA, refer to Chapter 5A and remove the starter motor.
17 Refer to Chapter 2A or B as applicable and carry out the following:
   a) Unbolt and remove the front engine mounting bracket from the transmission bellhousing (support the engine with a lifting beam or hoist).
   b) Unbolt and remove the rear left hand engine mounting bracket from the transmission casing and the bodywork **(see illustration)**.
18 On models with 084, 085 and 020 transmissions, unbolt and remove the relay lever support bracket from the rear of the transmission casing **(see illustration)**
19 Where applicable, unbolt the clutch shield plate from the underside of the transmission bellhousing.
20 Refer to Chapter 8 and unbolt the driveshafts from the transmission output shafts. Suspend the driveshafts as high as possible inside the engine using cable-ties or wire. Turn the steering to full left lock.
21 Starting at the bottom, work around the transmission bellhousing and remove all except the uppermost retaining bolts.
22 Slacken and withdraw the bolts, then

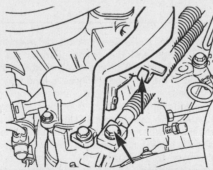

3.11 Disconnect shift and selector cables (arrowed) from 02A transmission levers

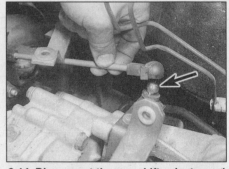

3.14 Disconnect the gearshift selector rod from the relay lever (arrowed)

3.15 Pull out the locking pins to separate the selector shaft joints

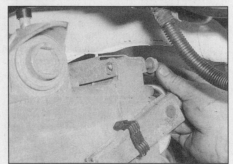

3.17 Unbolting the rear left-hand engine mounting bracket from the transmission

3.18 Unbolt and remove the relay lever support bracket

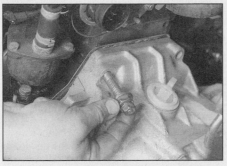

3.24a Remove the last bellhousing bolt . . .

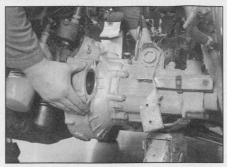

3.24b . . . and pull the transmission away from the engine (transmission 020 shown)

lower the front engine mounting crossmember away from the vehicle.

23 Check that nothing remains connected to the transmission, before attempting to separate it from the engine.

24 Remove the last retaining bolt from the top of the bellhousing and pull the transmission away from the engine **(see illustrations)**.

 Warning: Support the transmission to ensure that it remains steady on the jack head. Keep the transmission level until the input shaft is fully withdrawn from the clutch friction plate.

25 When all the locating dowels are clear of their mounting holes, lower the transmission out of the engine bay using the jack.

Refitting

26 Refitting the transmission is essentially a reversal of the removal procedure, but note the following points:

a) *Apply a smear of high-melting-point grease to the clutch friction plate splines; take care to avoid contaminating the friction surfaces.*

b) *When refitting the engine front crossmember, tighten the bolts to the correct torque before the weight of the engine is allowed to rest upon it.*

c) *Tighten the bellhousing bolts to the specified torque*

d) *Refer to Chapter 2A or B (as applicable) and tighten the engine mounting bolts to the correct torque.*

e) *On models fitted with transmission 02A, refer to Chapter 6 and refit the slave cylinder, then bleed the hydraulic system.*

f) *On models fitted with transmissions 084, 085 and 020, refer to Chapter 6 and refit the clutch cable.*

g) *On completion, refer to Section 2 and check the gearchange linkage adjustment.*

4 Manual transmission overhaul - general information

The overhaul of a manual transmission is a complex (and often expensive) engineering task for the DIY home mechanic to undertake,

which requires access to specialist equipment. It involves dismantling and reassembly of many small components, measuring clearances precisely and if necessary, adjusting them by the selection shims and spacers. Internal transmission components are also often difficult to obtain and in many instances, extremely expensive. Because of this, if the transmission develops a fault or becomes noisy, the best course of action is to have the unit overhauled by a specialist repairer or to obtain an exchange reconditioned unit.

Nevertheless, it is not impossible for the more experienced mechanic to overhaul the transmission if the special tools are available and the job is carried out in a deliberate step-by-step manner, to ensure that nothing is overlooked.

The tools necessary for an overhaul include internal and external circlip pliers, bearing pullers, a slide hammer, a set of pin punches, a dial test indicator and possibly a hydraulic press. In addition, a large, sturdy workbench and a vice will be required.

During dismantling of the transmission, make careful notes of how each component is fitted to make reassembly easier and accurate.

Before dismantling the transmission, it will help if you have some idea of where the problem lies. Certain problems can be closely related to specific areas in the transmission which can make component examination and renewal easier. Refer to the Fault Diagnosis Section in this manual for more information.

5.7 Unplug the wiring harness from the reversing light switch at the connector (084 transmission shown)

5 Reversing light switch - testing, removal and refitting

Testing

1 Ensure that the ignition switch is turned to the 'OFF' position.

2 Unplug the wiring harness from the reversing light switch at the connector. The switch is located on the top of the transmission casing on the 020 and 02A units, and on the underside of the transmission casing on the 084 and 085 units.

3 Connect the probes of a continuity tester, or multimeter set to the resistance measurement function, across the terminals of the reverse light switch.

4 The switch contacts are normally open, so with any gear other than reverse selected, the tester/meter should indicate an open circuit. When reverse gear is then selected, the switch contacts should close, causing the tester/meter to indicate a short circuit.

5 If the switch appears to be constantly open or short circuit, or is intermittent in its operation, it should be renewed.

Removal

6 Ensure that the ignition switch is turned to the 'OFF' position.

7 Unplug the wiring harness from the reversing light switch at the connector **(see illustration)**

8 Slacken the switch body using a ring spanner and withdraw it from the transmission casing. Recover the sealing ring. **(see illustration)**.

Refitting

9 Refit the switch by reversing the removal procedure.

6 Speedometer drive - removal and refitting

General information

1 All transmissions are fitted with an electronic speedometer transducer. This device measures the rotational speed of the

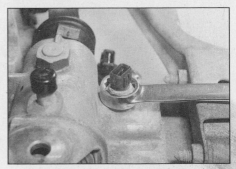

5.8 Slacken the switch body using a ring spanner and withdraw it from the transmission casing

7A

6.4a Remove the transducer retaining screw using an Allen key . . .

6.4b . . . and withdraw the unit from the transmission casing (020 transmission)

transmission final drive and converts the information into an electronic signal, which is then sent to the speedometer module in the instrument panel. On certain models, the signal is also used as an input by the engine management system ECU.

Removal

2 Ensure that the ignition switch is turned to the 'OFF' position.

3 Locate the speed transducer, at the top of the transmission casing. Unplug the wiring harness from the transducer, at the connector.

4 Remove the transducer retaining screw using an Allen key and withdraw the unit from the transmission casing **(see illustrations)**.

5 Recover sealing ring.

Refitting

6 Refit the transducer by following the removal procedure in reverse.

Chapter 7 Part B:
Automatic transmission

Contents

Degrees of difficulty

Easy, suitable for novice with little experience	**Fairly easy,** suitable for beginner with some experience	**Fairly difficult,** suitable for competent DIY mechanic	**Difficult,** suitable for experienced DIY mechanic	**Very difficult,** suitable for expert DIY or professional

Specifications

General

Make and type	Electro-hydraulically controlled planetary gearbox providing four forward speeds and one reverse speed. Drive transmitted through hydrokinetic torque converter
Designation	096
Automatic transmission fluid capacity	5.6 litres total, 3.0 litres approx. for fluid change

Torque wrench settings

	Nm	lbf ft
Torque converter shield plate	15	11
Torque converter-to-driveplate bolts	60	44
Transmission bellhousing-to-engine bolts, M10	60	44
Transmission bellhousing-to-engine bolts, M12	80	59

1 General information

The 096 automatic transmission is a four speed unit, incorporating a hydrokinetic torque converter with and a planetary gearbox.

Gear selection is achieved by means of a cabin floor mounted, seven position selector lever. The transmission operates in different modes, depending on the position of the selector lever.

The overall operation of the transmission is managed by an electronic control unit (ECU) and as a result there are no manual adjustments. Comprehensive fault diagnosis can therefore only be carried out using dedicated electronic test equipment.

Due to the complexity of the transmission and its control system, major repairs and overhaul operations should be left to a VAG dealer, who will be equipped with the necessary equipment for fault diagnosis and repair. The information in this Chapter is therefore limited to a description of the removal and refitting of the transmission as a complete unit. The removal, refitting and adjustment of the selector cable is also described.

2 Automatic transmission - removal and refitting

Removal

1 Select a solid, level surface to park the vehicle upon. Give yourself enough space to move around it easily. Apply the handbrake and chock the rear wheels.

2 Raise the front of the vehicle and rest it securely on axle stands (see "*Jacking and Vehicle Support*").

3 Refer to Chapter 11 and remove the bonnet from its hinges.

4 Disconnect the battery negative cable and position It away from the terminal. **Note:** *If the vehicle has a security coded radio, check that you have a copy of the code number before disconnecting the battery cable; refer to Chapter 12 for details.*

5 The "lock carrier" is a panel assembly comprising the front bumper moulding, radiator and grille, cooling fan(s) headlight units, front valence and bonnet lock mechanism. Although its removal is not essential, its does give greatly improved access to the engine. Its removal is relatively simple and is described at the beginning of the engine removal procedure - refer to Chapter 2C for details.

6 Refer to Section 4 and disconnect the selector cable from the transmission selector shaft.

7 Unbolt the earth strap from the transmission.

8 Clamp off the coolant hoses leading to and from the transmission fluid cooler unit, then slacken the clips and pull off the hoses **(see illustration).** Absorb any coolant that escapes with old rags.

9 Disconnect the wiring harness from the

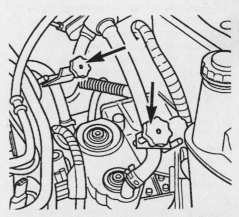

2.8 Clamp off the coolant hoses leading to and from the transmission fluid cooler unit (hose clamps arrowed)

7B

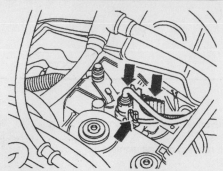

2.9 Disconnect the multiway connectors (arrowed)

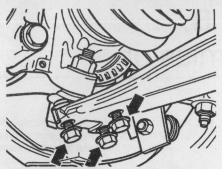

2.16 Suspension lower arm-to-balljoint bolts (arrowed)

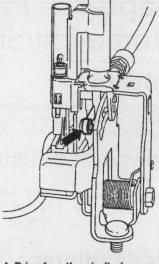

4.4 Prise free the circlip (arrowed) and detach the cable from the shift mechanism

transmission at the multiway connectors, labelling each one to aid refitting later **(see illustration)**.

10 Unbolt the protective plate from the underside of the transmission oil pan.

11 Refer to Chapter 5A and remove the starter motor.

12 Position a trolley jack underneath the transmission and raise it to just take the weight of the unit.

13 Refer to Chapter 2A or B as applicable and carry out the following:

a) *Unbolt and remove the front engine mounting bracket from the transmission bellhousing (support the engine with a lifting beam or hoist).*

b) *Unbolt and remove the rear left hand engine mounting bracket from the transmission casing and the engine mounting block..*

14 Unbolt the torque converter shield plate from the underside of the transmission bellhousing.

15 Refer to Chapter 8 and unbolt the driveshafts from the transmission output shafts.

16 Refer to Chapter 10 and separate the left hand suspension lower arm from the lower balljoint. Pass the left hand driveshaft over the suspension arm and swing it towards the rear of the vehicle, out of the way **(see illustration)**.

17 Suspend the right hand driveshaft as high as possible inside the engine using cable-ties or wire. Turn the steering to full left lock.

18 Working through the starter motor aperture, slacken and withdraw each torque converter-to-driveplate bolt in turn. As each bolt is removed, rotate the crankshaft using a wrench and socket on the crankshaft sprocket to expose the next bolt. Repeat until all the bolts are removed.

19 Slacken and withdraw the bolts, then lower the front engine mounting crossmember away from the vehicle.

20 Starting at the bottom, work around the transmission bellhousing and remove all except the uppermost retaining bolts.

21 Check that nothing remains connected to the transmission, before attempting to separate it from the engine.

22 Remove the last retaining bolt from the top of the bellhousing and pull the transmission away from the engine.

> ⚠ **Warning: Support the transmission to ensure that it remains steady on the jack head. Take care to prevent the torque converter from falling out as the transmission is removed.**

23 When all the locating dowels are clear of their mounting holes, lower the transmission out of the engine bay using the jack. Strap a restraining bar across the front of the bellhousing to keep the torque converter in position.

Refitting

24 Refitting the transmission is essentially a reversal of the removal procedure, but note the following points:

a) *As the torque converter is refitted, ensure that the drive pins at the centre of the torque converter hub engage with the recesses in the automatic transmission fluid pump inner wheel.*

b) *Tighten the bellhousing bolts and torque converter-to-driveplate bolts to the specified torque.*

c) *When refitting the engine front crossmember, tighten the bolts to the correct torque before the weight of the engine is allowed to rest upon it.*

d) *Refer to Chapter 2A or B (as applicable) and tighten the engine mounting bolts to the correct torque.*

e) *On completion, refer to Section 4 and check the gear selector cable adjustment.*

3 Automatic transmission overhaul - general information

In the event of a fault occurring, it will be necessary to establish whether the fault is electrical, mechanical or hydraulic in nature, before repair work can be contemplated. Diagnosis requires detailed knowledge of the transmissions operation and construction, as well as access to specialised test equipment, and so is deemed to be beyond the scope of this manual. It is therefore essential that problems with the automatic transmission are referred to a VAG dealer for assessment.

Note that a faulty transmission should not be removed before the vehicle has been assessed by a dealer, as fault diagnosis is carried out with the transmission in situ.

4 Selector cable - removal, refitting and adjustment

Removal

1 Move the selector lever to the 'P' position

2 At the transmission end of the cable, undo the cable clamp nut and detach the cable from the selector lever cable bracket.

3 Working inside the car, remove the retaining screws securing the selector lever cover to the console, pull the cover up along the lever and move it to one side.

4 Prise free the circlip and detach the cable from the shift mechanism **(see illustration)**.

5 Withdraw the cable from the selector lever housing, then working along its length, release the cable from the securing clips and remove it from the vehicle.

Refitting

6 Refit the selector cable by following the removal procedure in reverse. When fitting the cable to the selector lever, use a new circlip.

7 Before tightening the connection at the transmission selector shaft, adjust the selector cable as described below.

Adjustment

8 Move the selector lever to the 'P' position.

9 At the transmission, slacken the cable locking bolt on the side of the selector shaft lever. Push the selector shaft up against its end stop, corresponding to the 'P' position, then tighten the locking bolt.

10 Verify the operation of the selector lever by shifting through all gear positions and checking that every gear can be selected smoothly and without delay.

Chapter 8
Driveshafts

Contents

Degrees of difficulty

Easy, suitable for novice with little experience	**Fairly easy,** suitable for beginner with some experience	**Fairly difficult,** suitable for competent DIY mechanic	**Difficult,** suitable for experienced DIY mechanic	**Very difficult,** suitable for expert DIY or professional

Specifications

Type	Steel shafts with ball-and-cage type constant velocity joint at each end (later automatic transmission models have a tripod type inner joint)

Torque wrench settings

	Nm	lbf ft
Driveshaft retaining nut:		
2.0 litre (GT specification) models:		
Early models:		
Stage 1	90	66
Stage 2	Angle-tighten through a further 45°	
Later models (with modified hub splines):		
Stage 1	200	150
Fully slacken the nut, then tighten to:		
Stage 2	50	37
Stage 3	Angle-tighten through a further 30°	
All other models	265	197
Inner constant velocity joint retaining bolts	45	33
Lower arm balljoint retaining bolts	35	26
Roadwheel bolts	110	81

1 General information

Drive is transmitted from the differential to the front wheels by means of two solid-steel driveshafts of unequal length. The right-hand driveshaft is longer than the left-hand, due to the position of the transmission.

Both driveshafts are splined at their outer ends to accept the wheel hubs, and are threaded so that each hub can be fastened by a large nut. The inner end of each driveshaft is bolted to the transmission drive flanges.

Constant velocity (CV) joints are fitted to each end of the driveshafts, to ensure the smooth and efficient transmission of drive at all the angles possible as the roadwheels move up and down with the suspension, and as they turn from side to side under steering. On manual transmission and early automatic transmission models, both inner and outer constant velocity joints are of the ball-and-cage type. On later automatic transmission models, the outer joint is of the ball-and-cage type, but the inner joint is of the tripod type.

2 Driveshaft - removal and refitting

Note: *A new driveshaft retaining nut will be required on refitting.*

Removal

Note: *On later automatic transmission models with tripod type inner driveshaft joints (see Section 3, paragraph 1), in order to gain the necessary clearance required to withdraw the left-hand driveshaft, it may be necessary to unbolt the front and rear engine/transmission mountings and lift the engine slightly in order to remove the left-hand driveshaft (refer to Chapter 2 for details).*

1 Remove the wheel trim/hub cap (as applicable) and slacken the driveshaft retaining nut with the vehicle resting on its wheels **(see illustration)**. Also slacken the wheel bolts

2 Chock the rear wheels of the car, firmly apply the handbrake, then jack up the front of the car and support it on axle stands. Remove the front roadwheel.

3 Slacken and remove the bolts securing the inner driveshaft joint to the transmission flange and, where necessary, recover the retaining plates from underneath the bolts. Support the driveshaft by suspending it with

2.1 Remove the trim/hub cap and slacken the driveshaft retaining nut

8

2.3a Slacken the inner driveshaft joint retaining bolts . . .

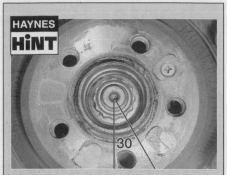

2.3b . . . and remove them along with their retaining plates (arrowed)

HAYNES HiNT

Where a 12-point nut is fitted, the angle between each driveshaft retaining nut flat point is 30°. If an angle-tightening gauge is not available, the angle can be accurately measured by making marks on the hub and the nearest nut flat point and tightening the nut so its mark moves by the correct number of points.

wire or string - do not allow it to hang under its weight, or the joint may be damaged **(see illustrations)**.

4 Using a suitable marker pen, draw around the end of the suspension lower arm, marking the correct fitted position of balljoint. Unscrew the balljoint retaining bolts and remove the retaining plate from the top of the lower arm **Note:** *On some models the balljoint inner retaining bolt hole is slotted; on these models the inner retaining bolt can be slackened, leaving the retaining plate and bolt in position in the arm, and the balljoint disengaged from the bolt.*

5 Unscrew the driveshaft retaining nut and (where necessary) remove its washer.

6 Carefully pull the swivel hub assembly outwards, and withdraw the driveshaft outer constant velocity joint from the hub assembly. The outer joint will be very tight, tap the joint out of the hub using a soft-faced mallet. If this fails to free it from the hub, the joint will have to be pressed out using a suitable tool which is bolted to the hub.

7 Manoeuvre the driveshaft out from underneath the vehicle and (where fitted) recover the gasket from the end of the inner constant velocity joint. Discard the gasket - a new one should be used on refitting.

8 *Do not allow the vehicle to rest on its wheels with one or both driveshaft(s) removed, as damage to the wheel bearing(s) may result.* If moving the vehicle is unavoidable, temporarily insert the outer end of the driveshaft(s) in the hub(s), and tighten the driveshaft retaining nut(s); in this case, the inner end(s) of the driveshaft(s) must be supported, for example by suspending with string from the vehicle underbody. *Do not allow the driveshaft to hang down under its weight, or the joint may be damaged.*

Refitting

9 Ensure that the transmission flange and inner joint mating surfaces are clean and dry. Where necessary, fit a new gasket to the joint by peeling off its backing foil and sticking it in position.

10 Ensure that the outer joint and hub splines are clean and dry. On all models except later 2.0 litre (GT specification) models, remove all traces of locking compound from both sets of

splines, and apply a bead of suitable locking compound to the outer joint splines (VW recommend the use of fluid number D 185 400 A2 - available from VW dealers). **Note:** *On later 2.0 litre (GT specification) models, the hub splines have been modified (the peaks of the splines have been flattened to remove driveshaft backlash) and locking compound should **not** be applied to the outer joint splines.*

11 Manoeuvre the driveshaft into position, and engage the outer joint with the hub. Ensure that the threads are clean, and apply a smear of oil to the contact face of the new driveshaft retaining nut. Fit the washer (where fitted) and nut and use it to draw the joint fully into position.

12 Refit the suspension lower arm balljoint retaining bolts, and tighten them to the specified torque setting, using the marks made on removal to ensure that the balljoint is correctly positioned.

13 Align the driveshaft inner joint with the transmission flange, and refit the retaining bolts and (where necessary) plates. Tighten the retaining bolts to the specified torque.

14 Ensure that the outer joint is drawn fully into position, then refit the roadwheel and lower the vehicle to the ground.

15 On early 2.0 litre models where locking compound has been applied to the outer joint splines, tighten the driveshaft nut to the specified Stage 1 torque setting, and then tighten it through the specified Stage 2 angle **(see Haynes Hint)**.

16 On later 2.0 litre (GT specification) models with modified hubs, first tighten the driveshaft nut to the specified stage 1 torque setting. Fully slacken the nut, tighten it to the stage 2 torque setting, then finally tighten it through the specified stage 3 angle. If an angle-tightening gauge is not available, the angle can be accurately measured by marking the hub and driveshaft nut, tightening the nut so it moves by the equivalent of one point (see earlier Hint).

17 On all other models, tighten the driveshaft nut to the specified torque setting.

18 Once the driveshaft nut is correctly tightened, tighten the wheel bolts to the specified torque and refit the wheel trim/hub cap.

3 Driveshaft rubber gaiters - renewal

1 Remove the driveshaft from the car, as described in Section 2. Continue as described under the relevant sub-heading. On automatic transmission models, driveshafts with a tripod type inner joint can be identified by the shape of the inner CV joint; the driveshaft retaining bolt holes are in tabs extending from the joint, giving it a six-pointed star-shaped exterior, in contrast to the smooth, circular shape of the ball-and-cage joint **(see illustration)**.

Later automatic transmission models - tripod type inner CV joint

Outer CV joint gaiter

2 Secure the driveshaft in a vice equipped with soft jaws, and release the two outer joint gaiter retaining clips. If necessary, the retaining clips can be cut to release them.

3 Slide the rubber gaiter down the shaft to expose the constant velocity joint, and scoop out excess grease.

4 Using a soft-faced mallet, tap the joint off the end of the driveshaft.

5 Remove the circlip from the driveshaft groove, and slide off the thrustwasher and dished washer, noting which way around it is fitted.

6 Slide the rubber gaiter off the driveshaft and discard it.

7 Thoroughly clean the constant velocity joint(s) using paraffin, or a suitable solvent, and dry thoroughly. Carry out a visual inspection as follows.

8 Move the inner splined driving member from side to side to expose each ball in turn at the top of its track. Examine the balls for cracks, flat spots or signs of surface pitting.

9 Inspect the ball tracks on the inner and outer members. If the tracks have widened,

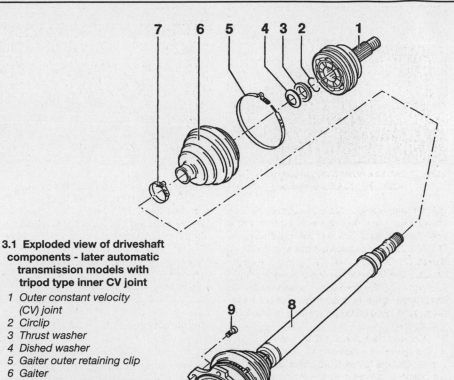

3.1 Exploded view of driveshaft components - later automatic transmission models with tripod type inner CV joint

1 Outer constant velocity (CV) joint
2 Circlip
3 Thrust washer
4 Dished washer
5 Gaiter outer retaining clip
6 Gaiter
7 Gaiter inner retaining clip
8 Driveshaft and inner constant velocity (CV) joint assembly
9 Retaining bolt

the balls will no longer be a tight fit. At the same time, check the ball cage windows for wear or cracking between the windows.

10 If on inspection any of the constant velocity joint components are found to be worn or damaged, it will be necessary to renew the complete joint assembly. If the joint is in satisfactory condition, obtain a new gaiter and retaining clips, a constant velocity joint circlip and the correct type of grease. Grease is often supplied with the joint repair kit - if not, use a good-quality molybdenum disulphide grease.

11 Tape over the splines on the end of the driveshaft, to protect the new gaiter as it is slid into place.

12 Slide the new gaiter onto the end of the driveshaft, then remove the protective tape from the driveshaft splines.

13 Slide on the dished washer, making sure its convex side is innermost, followed by the thrustwasher.

14 Fit a new circlip to the driveshaft, then tap the joint onto the driveshaft until the circlip engages in its groove. Make sure that the joint is securely retained by the circlip.

15 Pack the joint with the specified type of grease. Work the grease well into the bearing tracks whilst twisting the joint, and fill the rubber gaiter with any excess.

16 Ease the gaiter over the joint, and ensure that the gaiter lips are correctly located on both the driveshaft and constant velocity joint. Lift the outer sealing lip of the gaiter to equalise air pressure within the gaiter.

17 Fit the large metal retaining clip to the gaiter. Pull the clip as tight as possible, and locate the hooks on the clip in their slots. Remove any slack in the gaiter retaining clip by carefully compressing the raised section of the clip. In the absence of the special tool, a pair of side cutters may be used, taking care not to cut the clip. Secure the small retaining clip using the same procedure.

18 Check the constant velocity joint moves freely in all directions, then refit the driveshaft to the vehicle, as described in Section 2.

Inner CV joint gaiter

19 At the time of writing, no spare parts were available for the inner CV joint, including the gaiter, and no information was available on dismantling the joint. Refer to your VW dealer for the latest information on parts availability. If the gaiter is now available, take the driveshaft to a VW dealer, who will be able to fit it for a small charge.

All other models

Outer CV joint gaiter

20 Refer to the information given above in paragraphs 2 to 18.

Inner CV joint gaiter

21 A hydraulic press and several special tools are required to remove and refit the inner CV joint. Therefore it is recommended that gaiter renewal is entrusted to a VW dealer.

4 Driveshaft overhaul - general information

1 If any of the checks described in Chapter 1 reveal wear in any driveshaft joint, first remove the roadwheel trim or centre cap (as appropriate) and check that the driveshaft retaining nut is tight.

2 If the nut is tight, refit the centre cap or trim. Repeat this check on the remaining driveshaft nut.

3 Road test the vehicle, and listen for a metallic clicking from the front as the vehicle is driven slowly in a circle on full lock. If a clicking noise is heard, this indicates wear in the outer constant velocity joint. This means that the joint must be renewed; reconditioning is not possible.

4 If vibration, consistent with road speed, is felt through the car when accelerating, there is a possibility of wear in the inner constant velocity joints.

5 To check the joints for wear, the driveshaft must be dismantled. The outer constant velocity joint can be removed and checked, but work on the inner joint should be entrusted to a VW dealer (see Section 3); if any wear or free play is found, the affected joint must be renewed.

8

Chapter 9
Braking system

Contents

Degrees of difficulty

Easy, suitable for novice with little experience	**Fairly easy,** suitable for beginner with some experience	**Fairly difficult,** suitable for competent DIY mechanic	**Difficult,** suitable for experienced DIY mechanic	**Very difficult,** suitable for expert DIY or professional

Specifications

Front brakes
Disc diameter:
  Petrol models:
    1.4 and 1.6 litre models . . . . 239 mm
    1.8 litre models:
      CL and GL models . . . . 239 mm
      GT models . . . . 256 mm
    2.0 litre models . . . . 280 mm
  Diesel models . . . . 239 mm
Disc thickness (new):
  Petrol models:
    1.4 and 1.6 litre models . . . . 12 mm
    1.8 litre models:
      CL and GL models . . . . 12 mm
      GT models . . . . 20 mm
    2.0 litre models . . . . 22 mm
  Diesel models . . . . 12 mm
Disc thickness (minimum):
  Petrol models:
    1.4 and 1.6 litre models . . . . 10 mm
    1.8 litre models:
      CL and GL models . . . . 10 mm
      GT models . . . . 18 mm
    2.0 litre models . . . . 20 mm
  Diesel models . . . . 10 mm
Maximum disc runout . . . . 0.1 mm
Brake pad thickness (all models):
  New . . . . 14 mm
  Minimum . . . . 7 mm

9

Rear drum brakes

Drum diameter:
New	200 mm
Maximum diameter	201 mm

Maximum drum out-of-round .... 0.1 mm

Brake shoe friction material thickness:
New	5.0 mm
Minimum	2.5 mm

Rear disc brakes

Disc diameter .... 226 mm

Disc thickness:
New	10 mm
Minimum	8 mm

Maximum disc runout .... 0.1 mm

Brake pad thickness:
New	12 mm
Minimum	7 mm

Torque wrench settings

	Nm	lbf ft
ABS wheel sensor retaining bolts	10	7
Front brake caliper:		
VW caliper mounting bolts	25	18
Girling caliper:		
Guide pin bolts	35	26
Mounting bracket bolts	125	92
Master cylinder mounting nuts	20	15
Rear brake caliper:		
Guide pin bolts	35	26
Mounting bracket bolts	65	48
Rear brake wheel cylinder bolts	10	7
Roadwheel bolts	110	81
Servo unit mounting nuts	20	15

1 General information

The braking system is of the servo-assisted, dual-circuit hydraulic type. The arrangement of the hydraulic system is such that each circuit operates one front and one rear brake from a tandem master cylinder. Under normal circumstances, both circuits operate in unison. However, if there is hydraulic failure in one circuit, full braking force will still be available at two wheels.

Most large-capacity engine models have disc brakes all round as standard; all other models are fitted with front disc brakes and rear drum brakes. ABS is fitted as standard to some models, and was offered as an option on most other models (refer to Section 22 for further information on ABS operation).

The front disc brakes are actuated by single-piston sliding type calipers, which ensure that equal pressure is applied to each disc pad.

On models with rear drum brakes, the rear brakes incorporate leading and trailing shoes, which are actuated by twin-piston wheel cylinders. A self-adjust mechanism is incorporated, to compensate for brake shoe wear.

On models with rear disc brakes, the brakes are actuated by single-piston sliding calipers which incorporate mechanical handbrake mechanisms.

A pressure-regulating set-up is incorporated in the braking system, this helps to prevent rear wheel lock-up during emergency braking. The system is controlled either by a single load-dependent valve which is linked to the rear axle, or by a pair of pressure-dependent type valves which are screwed into the master cylinder outlet ports, one valve fitted in each rear brake line.

The handbrake provides an independent mechanical means of rear brake application.

Note: *When servicing any part of the system, work carefully and methodically; also observe scrupulous cleanliness when overhauling any part of the hydraulic system. Always renew components (in axle sets, where applicable) if in doubt about their condition, and use only genuine VW replacement parts, or at least those of known good quality. Note the warnings given in "Safety first" and at relevant points in this Chapter concerning the dangers of asbestos dust and hydraulic fluid.*

2 Hydraulic system - bleeding

⚠ *Warning: Hydraulic fluid is poisonous; wash off immediately and thoroughly in the case of skin contact, and seek immediate medical advice if any fluid is swallowed or gets into the eyes. Certain types of hydraulic fluid are flammable, and may ignite when allowed into contact with hot components; when servicing any hydraulic system, it is safest to assume that the fluid IS flammable, and to take precautions against the risk of fire as though it is petrol that is being handled. Hydraulic fluid is also an effective paint stripper, and will attack plastics; if any is spilt, it should be washed off immediately, using copious quantities of fresh water. Finally, it is hygroscopic (it absorbs moisture from the air) - old fluid may be contaminated and unfit for further use. When topping-up or renewing the fluid, always use the recommended type, and ensure that it comes from a freshly-opened sealed container.*

General

1 The correct operation of any hydraulic system is only possible after removing all air from the components and circuit; this is achieved by bleeding the system.

2 During the bleeding procedure, add only clean, unused hydraulic fluid of the recommended type; never re-use fluid that has already been bled from the system. Ensure that sufficient fluid is available before starting work.

3 If there is any possibility of incorrect fluid being already in the system, the brake

components and circuit must be flushed completely with uncontaminated, correct fluid, and new seals should be fitted to the various components.

4 If hydraulic fluid has been lost from the system, or air has entered because of a leak, ensure that the fault is cured before continuing further.

5 Park the vehicle on level ground, switch off the engine and select first or reverse gear, then chock the wheels and release the handbrake.

6 Check that all pipes and hoses are secure, unions tight and bleed screws closed. Clean any dirt from around the bleed screws.

7 Unscrew the master cylinder reservoir cap, and top the master cylinder reservoir up to the "MAX" level line; refit the cap loosely, and remember to maintain the fluid level at least above the "MIN" level line throughout the procedure, or there is a risk of further air entering the system.

8 There are a number of one-man, do-it-yourself brake bleeding kits currently available from motor accessory shops. It is recommended that one of these kits is used whenever possible, as they greatly simplify the bleeding operation, and reduce the risk of expelled air and fluid being drawn back into the system. If such a kit is not available, the basic (two-man) method must be used, which is described in detail below.

9 If a kit is to be used, prepare the vehicle as described previously, and follow the kit manufacturer's instructions, as the procedure may vary slightly according to the type being used; generally, they are as outlined below in the relevant sub-section.

10 Whichever method is used, the same sequence must be followed (paragraphs 11 and 12) to ensure the removal of all air from the system.

Bleeding sequence

11 If the system has been only partially disconnected, and suitable precautions were taken to minimise fluid loss, it should be necessary only to bleed that part of the system (ie the primary or secondary circuit).

12 If the complete system is to be bled, then it should be done working in the following sequence:

  a) *Right-hand rear brake.*
  b) *Left-hand rear brake.*
  c) *Right-hand front brake.*
  d) *Left-hand front brake.*

 Warning: On models with ABS, under no circumstances should the hydraulic unit bleed screws be opened.

Bleeding - basic (two-man) method

13 Collect together a clean glass jar of reasonable size, a suitable length of plastic or rubber tubing which is a tight fit over the bleed screw, and a ring spanner to fit the

2.14 Dust cap (arrowed) over the bleed screw on a rear brake wheel cylinder - models with rear drum brakes

screw. The help of an assistant will also be required.

14 Remove the dust cap from the first screw in the sequence **(see illustration)**. Fit the spanner and tube to the screw, place the other end of the tube in the jar, and pour in sufficient fluid to cover the end of the tube.

15 Ensure that the master cylinder reservoir fluid level is maintained at least above the "MIN" level line throughout the procedure.

16 Have the assistant fully depress the brake pedal several times to build up pressure, then maintain it on the final downstroke.

17 While pedal pressure is maintained, unscrew the bleed screw (approximately one turn) and allow the compressed fluid and air to flow into the jar. The assistant should maintain pedal pressure, following it down to the floor if necessary, and should not release it until instructed to do so. When the flow stops, tighten the bleed screw again, have the assistant release the pedal slowly, and recheck the reservoir fluid level.

18 Repeat the steps given in paragraphs 16 and 17 until the fluid emerging from the bleed screw is free from air bubbles. If the master cylinder has been drained and refilled, and air is being bled from the first screw in the sequence, allow approximately five seconds between cycles for the master cylinder passages to refill.

19 When no more air bubbles appear, tighten the bleed screw securely, remove the tube and spanner, and refit the dust cap. Do not overtighten the bleed screw.

20 Repeat the procedure on the remaining screws in the sequence, until all air is removed from the system and the brake pedal feels firm again.

Bleeding - using a one-way valve kit

21 As their name implies, these kits consist of a length of tubing with a one-way valve fitted, to prevent expelled air and fluid being drawn back into the system; some kits include a translucent container, which can be positioned so that the air bubbles can be more easily seen flowing from the end of the tube.

22 The kit is connected to the bleed screw, which is then opened. The user returns to the

2.22 Bleeding a rear brake caliper using a one-way valve kit

driver's seat, depresses the brake pedal with a smooth, steady stroke, and slowly releases it; this is repeated until the expelled fluid is clear of air bubbles **(see illustration)**.

23 Note that these kits simplify work so much that it is easy to forget the master cylinder reservoir fluid level; ensure that this is maintained at least above the "MIN" level line at all times.

Bleeding - using a pressure-bleeding kit

24 These kits are usually operated by the reservoir of pressurised air contained in the spare tyre. However, note that it will probably be necessary to reduce the pressure to a lower level than normal; refer to the instructions supplied with the kit.

25 By connecting a pressurised, fluid-filled container to the master cylinder reservoir, bleeding can be carried out simply by opening each screw in turn (in the specified sequence), and allowing the fluid to flow out until no more air bubbles can be seen in the expelled fluid.

26 This method has the advantage that the large reservoir of fluid provides an additional safeguard against air being drawn into the system during bleeding.

27 Pressure-bleeding is particularly effective when bleeding "difficult" systems, or when bleeding the complete system at the time of routine fluid renewal.

All methods

28 When bleeding is complete, and firm pedal feel is restored, wash off any spilt fluid, tighten the bleed screws securely, and refit their dust caps.

29 Check the hydraulic fluid level in the master cylinder reservoir, and top-up if necessary (see *"Weekly Checks"*).

30 Discard any hydraulic fluid that has been bled from the system; it will not be fit for re-use.

31 Check the feel of the brake pedal. If it feels at all spongy, air must still be present in the system, and further bleeding is required. Failure to bleed satisfactorily after a reasonable repetition of the bleeding procedure may be due to worn master cylinder seals.

3 Hydraulic pipes and hoses - renewal

Note: *Refer to the note in Section 2 concerning the dangers of hydraulic fluid.*

1 If any pipe or hose is to be renewed, minimise fluid loss by first removing the master cylinder reservoir cap, then tightening it down onto a piece of polythene to obtain an airtight seal. Alternatively, flexible hoses can be sealed, if required, using a proprietary brake hose clamp; metal brake pipe unions can be plugged (if care is taken not to allow dirt into the system) or capped immediately they are disconnected. Place a wad of rag under any union that is to be disconnected, to catch any spilt fluid.

2 If a flexible hose is to be disconnected, unscrew the brake pipe union nut before removing the spring clip which secures the hose to its mounting bracket.

3 To unscrew the union nuts, it is preferable to obtain a brake pipe spanner of the correct size; these are available from most large motor accessory shops. Failing this, a close-fitting open-ended spanner will be required, though if the nuts are tight or corroded, their flats may be rounded-off if the spanner slips. In such a case, a self-locking wrench is often the only way to unscrew a stubborn union, but it follows that the pipe and the damaged nuts must be renewed on reassembly. Always clean a union and surrounding area before disconnecting it. If disconnecting a component with more than one union, make a careful note of the connections before disturbing any of them.

4 If a brake pipe is to be renewed, it can be obtained, cut to length and with the union nuts and end flares in place, from VW dealers. All that is then necessary is to bend it to shape, following the line of the original, before fitting it to the car. Alternatively, most motor accessory shops can make up brake pipes from kits, but this requires very careful measurement of the original, to ensure that the replacement is of the correct length. The safest answer is usually to take the original to the shop as a pattern.

5 On refitting, do not overtighten the union nuts. It is not necessary to exercise brute force to obtain a sound joint.

6 Ensure that the pipes and hoses are correctly routed, with no kinks, and that they are secured in the clips or brackets provided. After fitting, remove the polythene from the reservoir, and bleed the hydraulic system as described in Section 2. Wash off any spilt fluid, and check carefully for fluid leaks.

4 Front brake pads - renewal

⚠️ **Warning: Renew BOTH sets of brake pads/shoes at the same time - NEVER renew the pads/shoes on only one wheel, as uneven braking may result. Note that the dust created by wear of the pads may contain asbestos, which is a health hazard. Never blow it out with compressed air, and DO NOT inhale any of it. An approved filtering mask should be worn when working on the brakes. DO NOT use petrol or petroleum-based solvents to clean brake parts; use brake cleaner or methylated spirit only.**

1 Apply the handbrake, then jack up the front of the vehicle and support it on axle stands. Remove the front roadwheels.

2 Trace the brake pad wear sensor wiring (where fitted) back from the pads, and disconnect it from the wiring connector. Note the routing of the wiring, and free it from any relevant retaining clips. Continue as described under the relevant sub-heading.

VW calipers

3 To improve access, undo the retaining bolts and remove the air deflector shield from the caliper.

4 Slacken and remove the two caliper mounting bolts, then lift the caliper away from the brake pads and hub, and tie it to the suspension strut using a suitable piece of wire **(see illustration)**. Do not allow the caliper to hang unsupported on the flexible brake hose.

5 Withdraw the two brake pads from the swivel hub and recover the anti-rattle springs, noting their correct fitted locations. Note that the springs are different and are not interchangeable.

6 First measure the thickness of each brake pad (including the backing plate). If either pad is worn at any point to the specified minimum thickness or less, all four pads must be renewed. Also, the pads should be renewed if any are fouled with oil or grease; there is no satisfactory way of degreasing friction material, once contaminated. If any of the brake pads are worn unevenly, or are fouled with oil or grease, trace and rectify the cause before reassembly. New brake pad kits are available from VW dealers.

7 If the brake pads are still serviceable, carefully clean them using a clean, fine wire brush or similar, paying particular attention to the sides and back of the metal backing. Clean out the grooves in the friction material (where applicable), and pick out any large embedded particles of dirt or debris. Carefully clean the pad locations in the caliper body/mounting bracket.

8 Prior to fitting the pads, check that the spacers are free to slide easily in the caliper body bushes, and are a reasonably tight fit. Brush the dust and dirt from the caliper and piston, but *do not* inhale it, as it is injurious to health. Inspect the dust seal around the piston for damage, and the piston for evidence of fluid leaks, corrosion or damage. If attention to any of these components is necessary, refer to Section 10.

9 If new brake pads are to be fitted, the caliper piston must be pushed back into the cylinder to make room for them. Either use a G-clamp or similar tool, or use suitable pieces of wood as levers. Provided that the master cylinder reservoir has not been overfilled with hydraulic fluid, there should be no spillage, but keep a careful watch on the fluid level while retracting the piston. If the fluid level rises above the "MAX" level line at any time, the surplus should be syphoned off or ejected through a plastic tube connected to the bleed screw (see Section 2). **Note:** *Do not syphon the fluid by mouth, as it is poisonous; use a syringe or an old poultry baster.*

10 Fit the new anti-rattle springs to the hub, making sure they are correctly positioned and fit the pads, and ensuring that the friction material of each pad is against the brake disc. Note that, where necessary, the pad with the wear sensor wire should be installed as the inner pad **(see illustrations)**.

4.4 On VW calipers, undo the caliper mounting bolts

4.10a Fit the anti-rattle springs to the hub, making sure they are correctly located . . .

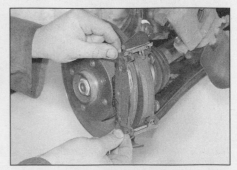

4.10b . . . and install the brake pads with their friction material facing the disc

4.11 With the pads and springs correctly located, slide the caliper back into position

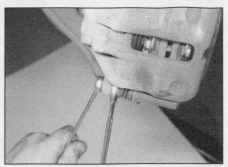

4.18 On Girling calipers, remove the lower guide pin bolt, holding the pin as shown

4.19a Pivot the caliper upwards . . .

4.19b . . . then recover the shim from the caliper piston . . .

4.20 . . . and remove the pads from the caliper mounting bracket

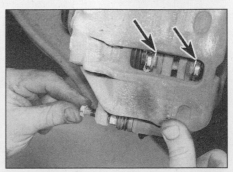

4.23 Ensure the anti-rattle springs (arrowed) are in place, then fit the new guide pin bolt

11 Position the caliper over the pads, and pass the pad warning sensor wiring (where fitted) through the caliper aperture **(see illustration)**.

12 Press the caliper into position sufficiently until it is possible to install caliper mounting bolts. Tighten the mounting bolts to the specified torque setting. **Note:** *Do exert excess pressure on the caliper, as this will deform the pad springs, resulting in noisy operation of the brakes.*

13 Reconnect the brake pad wear sensor wiring connectors, ensuring that the wiring is correctly routed. Where necessary, refit the air deflector shield to the caliper.

14 Depress the brake pedal repeatedly, until the pads are pressed into firm contact with the brake disc, and normal (non-assisted) pedal pressure is restored.

15 Repeat the above procedure on the remaining front brake caliper.

16 Refit the roadwheels, then lower the vehicle to the ground and tighten the roadwheel bolts to the specified torque.

17 New pads will not give full braking efficiency until they have bedded-in. Be prepared for this, and avoid hard braking as far as possible for the first hundred miles or so after pad renewal.

Girling caliper

18 Slacken and remove the lower caliper guide pin bolt, using a slim open-ended spanner to prevent the guide pin itself from rotating **(see illustration)**. Discard the guide pin bolt - a new bolt must be used on refitting.

19 With the lower guide pin bolt removed, pivot the caliper upwards until it is clear of the brake pads and mounting bracket. Remove the shim from the caliper piston **(see illustrations)**.

20 Withdraw the two brake pads from the caliper mounting bracket **(see illustration)**.

21 Examine the pads and caliper as described above in paragraphs 6 to 9, substituting "guide pins" for references to spacers and bushes.

22 Install the pads in the caliper mounting bracket, ensuring that the friction material of each pad is against the brake disc. Note the pad with the wear sensor wiring should be installed as the inner pad.

23 Refit the shim to the caliper piston. Pivot the caliper down into position, and pass the pad warning sensor wiring through the caliper aperture. If the threads of the new guide pin bolt are not already pre-coated with locking compound, apply a suitable thread-locking compound to them. Press the caliper into position whilst ensuring that the pad anti-rattle springs locate correctly with the caliper. Install the guide pin bolt, tightening it to the specified torque setting while retaining the guide pin with an open-ended spanner **(see illustration)**.

24 Reconnect the brake pad wear sensor wiring connectors (where necessary) ensuring that the wiring is correctly routed.

25 Depress the brake pedal repeatedly, until the pads are pressed into firm contact with the brake disc, and normal (non-assisted) pedal pressure is restored.

26 Repeat the above procedure on the remaining front brake caliper.

27 Refit the roadwheels, then lower the vehicle to the ground and tighten the roadwheel bolts to the specified torque.

28 Check the hydraulic fluid level as described in *"Weekly Checks"*.

5 Rear brake pads - renewal

Note: *Refer to the warning at the start of Section 4 before starting work.*

1 Chock the front wheels, then jack up the rear of the vehicle and support it on axle stands. Remove the rear wheels.

2 Slacken the handbrake cable and detach it from the caliper as described in Section 19.

3 Slacken and remove the caliper guide pin bolts, using a slim open-ended spanner to prevent the guide pins from rotating **(see illustration)**. Discard the guide pin bolts - new bolts must be used on refitting.

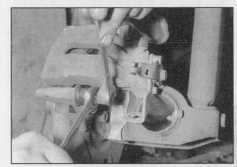

5.3 Hold the guide pin and unscrew the rear caliper guide pin bolts

9

5.4 Lift the caliper upwards and away . . .

5.5a . . . and remove the pads . . .

5.5b . . . and anti-rattle springs from the caliper mounting bracket

4 Lift the caliper away from the brake pads, and tie it to the suspension strut using a suitable piece of wire **(see illustration)**. Do not allow the caliper to hang unsupported on the flexible brake hose.

5 Withdraw the two brake pads from the caliper mounting bracket and recover the anti-rattle springs from the mounting bracket, noting their correct fitted locations **(see illustrations)**.

6 First measure the thickness of each brake pad (including the backing plate). If either pad is worn at any point to the specified minimum thickness or less, **all four** pads must be renewed. Also, the pads should be renewed if any are fouled with oil or grease; there is no satisfactory way of degreasing friction material, once contaminated. If any of the brake pads are worn unevenly, or fouled with oil or grease, trace and rectify the cause before reassembly. New brake pads are available from VW dealers.

7 If the brake pads are still serviceable, carefully clean them using a clean, fine wire brush or similar, paying particular attention to the sides and back of the metal backing. Clean out the grooves in the friction material (where applicable), and pick out any large embedded particles of dirt or debris. Carefully clean the pad locations in the caliper body/mounting bracket.

8 Prior to fitting the pads, check that the guide pins are free to slide easily in the caliper bracket, and check that the rubber guide pin

In the absence of the special tool, the piston can be screwed back into the caliper using a pair of circlip pliers

gaiters are undamaged. Brush the dust and dirt from the caliper and piston, but **do not** inhale it, as it is injurious to health. Inspect the dust seal around the piston for damage, and the piston for evidence of fluid leaks, corrosion or damage. If attention to any of these components is necessary, refer to Section 11.

9 If new brake pads are to be fitted, it will be necessary to retract the piston fully into the caliper bore, by rotating it in a clockwise direction **(see Tool Tip)**. Provided that the master cylinder reservoir has not been overfilled with hydraulic fluid, there should be no spillage, but keep a careful watch on the fluid level while retracting the piston. If the fluid level rises above the "MAX" level line at any time, the surplus should be syphoned off, or ejected through a plastic tube connected to the bleed screw (see Section 2). **Note:** *Do not syphon the fluid by mouth, as it is poisonous; use a syringe or an old poultry baster.*

10 Fit the anti-rattle springs to the caliper mounting bracket, ensuring that they are correctly located. Install the pads in the mounting bracket, ensuring that each pad's friction material is against the brake disc.

11 Slide the caliper back into position over the pads.

12 If the threads of the new guide pin bolts are not already pre-coated with locking compound, apply a suitable thread-locking compound to them. Press the caliper into position, then install the bolts, tightening them to the specified torque setting while retaining the guide pin with an open-ended spanner.

13 Depress the brake pedal repeatedly, until the pads are pressed into firm contact with the brake disc, and normal (non-assisted) pedal pressure is restored.

14 Repeat the above procedure on the remaining rear brake caliper.

15 Reconnect the handbrake cables to the calipers, and adjust the handbrake as described in Section 17.

16 Refit the roadwheels, then lower the vehicle to the ground and tighten the roadwheel bolts to the specified torque setting.

17 Check the hydraulic fluid level as described in *"Weekly Checks"*.

18 New pads will not give full braking

efficiency until they have bedded-in. Be prepared for this, and avoid hard braking as far as possible for the first hundred miles or so after pad renewal.

6 Rear brake shoes - renewal

Note: *Refer to the warning at the start of Section 4 before starting work.*

1 Remove the brake drum (see Section 9).

2 Working carefully, and taking the necessary precautions, remove all traces of brake dust from the brake drum, backplate and shoes.

3 Measure the thickness of the friction material of each brake shoe at several points; if either shoe is worn at any point to the specified minimum thickness or less, **all four** shoes must be renewed as a set. The shoes should also be renewed if any are fouled with oil or grease; there is no way of degreasing friction material, once contaminated.

4 If any of the brake shoes are worn unevenly, or fouled with oil or grease, trace and rectify the cause before reassembly.

5 To renew the brake shoes, continue as follows. If all is well, refit the brake drum as described in Section 9.

6 Note the position of the brake shoes and springs, and mark the webs of the shoes, if necessary, to aid refitting.

7 Using a pair of pliers, remove the shoe retainer spring cups by depressing and turning them through 90°. With the cups removed, lift off the springs and withdraw the retainer pins **(see illustrations)**.

8 Ease the shoes out one at a time from the lower pivot point, to release the tension of the return spring, then disconnect the lower return spring from both shoes **(see illustration)**.

9 Ease the upper end of both shoes out from their wheel cylinder locations, taking care not to damage the wheel cylinder seals, and disconnect the handbrake cable from the trailing shoe. The brake shoe assembly can then be manoeuvred out of position and away from the backplate. Do not depress the brake pedal until the brakes are reassembled; wrap a strong elastic band around the wheel cylinder pistons to retain them **(see illustrations)**.

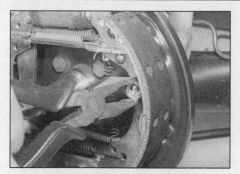

6.7a Using pliers, remove the spring cup . . .

6.7b . . . then lift off the spring . . .

6.7c . . . and withdraw the retainer pin from the rear of the backplate

6.8 Unhook the shoes from the lower pivot point, and remove the lower return spring

6.9a Free the shoes from the wheel cylinder. Note elastic band (arrowed) used to retain pistons . . .

6.9b . . . then detach the handbrake cable and remove the shoe assembly

10 Make a note of the correct fitted positions of all components **(see illustration)**, then unhook the upper return spring, and disengage the wedge key spring.

11 Unhook the tensioning spring, and remove the pushrod from the trailing shoe, together with the wedge key.

12 Examine all components for signs of wear or damage, and renew as necessary. All return springs should be renewed, regardless of their apparent condition. Although linings are available separately (without shoes) from VW dealers, renewal of the shoes complete with linings is to be preferred, unless the necessary skills and equipment are available to fit new linings to the old shoes.

13 Peel back the rubber protective caps, and check the wheel cylinder for fluid leaks or other damage; check that both cylinder pistons are free to move easily. Refer to

Section 12, if necessary, for information on wheel cylinder overhaul.

14 Apply a little brake grease to the contact areas of the pushrod and handbrake lever.

15 Hook the tensioning spring into the trailing shoe. Engage the pushrod with the opposite

end of the spring, and pivot the pushrod into position on the trailing shoe **(see illustrations)**.

16 Fit the wedge key between the trailing shoe and pushrod, making sure it is fitted the correct way around **(see illustration)**.

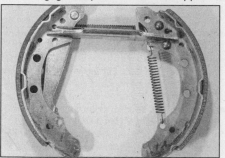

6.10 Prior to dismantling, note the correct fitted location of the shoe components

6.15a Hook the tensioning spring into the trailing shoe . . .

6.15b . . . then engage the pushrod with the opposite end of the spring . . .

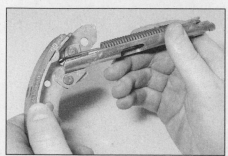

6.15c . . . and pivot the strut into position on the shoe

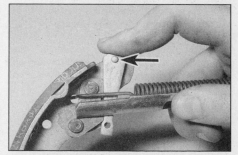

6.16 Slot the wedge key into position. Ensure raised dot (arrowed) is facing away from the shoe

9

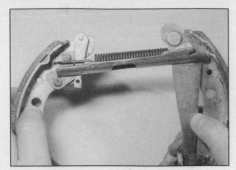

6.17a Locate the leading shoe in the pushrod . . .

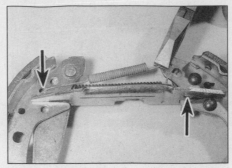

6.17b . . . and hook the upper return spring into the leading shoe and pushrod (arrows)

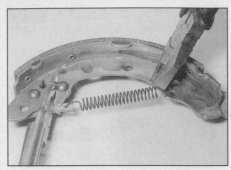

6.18 Fit the spring to the wedge key, and hook it onto the trailing shoe

17 Locate the handbrake lever on the leading shoe in the pushrod, and fit the upper return spring using a pair of pliers **(see illustrations)**.

18 Fit the spring to the wedge key, and hook it onto the trailing shoe **(see illustration)**.

19 Prior to installation, clean the backplate, and apply a thin smear of high-temperature brake grease or anti-seize compound to all those surfaces of the backplate which bear on the shoes, particularly the wheel cylinder pistons and lower pivot point. Do not allow the lubricant to foul the friction material.

20 Remove the elastic band fitted to the wheel cylinder, and offer up the shoe assembly.

21 Connect the handbrake cable to the handbrake lever, and locate the top of the shoes in the wheel cylinder piston slots.

22 Fit the lower return spring to the shoes, then lever the bottom of the shoes onto the bottom anchor.

23 Tap the shoes to centralise them with the backplate, then refit the shoe retainer pins and springs, and secure them in position with the spring cups.

24 Refit the brake drum as described in Section 9.

25 Repeat the above procedure on the remaining rear brake.

26 Once both sets of rear shoes have been renewed, adjust the lining-to-drum clearance by repeatedly depressing the brake pedal until normally (non-assisted) pedal pressure returns.

27 Check and, if necessary, adjust the handbrake as described in Section 17.

28 On completion, check the hydraulic fluid level as described in *"Weekly Checks"*.

29 New shoes will not give full braking efficiency until they have bedded-in. Be prepared for this, and avoid hard braking as far as possible for the first hundred miles or so after shoe renewal.

7 Front brake disc - inspection, removal and refitting

Note: *Before starting work, refer to the note at the beginning of Section 4 concerning the dangers of asbestos dust.*

Inspection

Note: *If either disc requires renewal, BOTH should be renewed at the same time, to ensure even and consistent braking. New brake pads should also be fitted.*

1 Apply the handbrake, then jack up the front of the car and support it on axle stands. Remove the appropriate front roadwheel.

2 Slowly rotate the brake disc so that the full area of both sides can be checked; remove the brake pads if better access is required to the inboard surface. Light scoring is normal in the area swept by the brake pads, but if heavy scoring or cracks are found, the disc must be renewed.

3 It is normal to find a lip of rust and brake dust around the disc's perimeter; this can be scraped off if required. If, however, a lip has formed due to excessive wear of the brake pad swept area, then the disc's thickness must be measured using a micrometer **(see illustration)**. Take measurements at several places around the disc, at the inside and outside of the pad swept area; if the disc has worn at any point to the specified minimum thickness or less, the disc must be renewed.

4 If the disc is thought to be warped, it can be checked for run-out. Either use a dial gauge mounted on any convenient fixed point, while the disc is slowly rotated, or use feeler blades to measure (at several points all around the disc) the clearance between the disc and a fixed point, such as the caliper mounting bracket. If the measurements obtained are at the specified maximum or beyond, the disc is excessively warped, and must be renewed;

however, it is worth checking first that the hub bearing is in good condition (Chapters 1 and/or 10). If the run-out is excessive, the disc must be renewed.

5 Check the disc for cracks, especially around the wheel bolt holes, and any other wear or damage, and renew if necessary.

Removal

6 On models with VW front brake calipers, remove the brake pads as described in Section 4.

7 On models with Girling front brake calipers, unscrew the two bolts securing the brake caliper mounting bracket to the swivel hub, then slide the caliper assembly off the disc. Using a piece of wire or string, tie the caliper to the front suspension coil spring, to avoid placing any strain on the brake hose.

8 Use chalk or paint to mark the relationship of the disc to the hub, then remove the screw securing the brake disc to the hub, and remove the disc **(see illustration)**. If it is tight, tap its rear face with a hide or plastic mallet.

Refitting

9 Refitting is the reverse of the removal procedure, noting the following points:

a) *Ensure that the mating surfaces of the disc and hub are clean and flat.*

b) *Align (if applicable) the marks made on removal, and securely tighten the disc retaining screw.*

c) *If a new disc has been fitted, use a suitable solvent to wipe any preservative coating from the disc, before refitting the caliper.*

7.3 Measuring brake disc thickness with a micrometer

7.8 Undo the retaining screw and remove the front brake disc

d) On models with Girling brake calipers, slide the caliper into position over the disc, making sure the pads pass either side of the disc. Tighten the caliper bracket mounting bolts to the specified torque setting.

e) On models with VW brake calipers, refit the pads as described in Section 4.

f) Refit the roadwheel, then lower the vehicle to the ground and tighten the roadwheel bolts to the specified torque. On completion, repeatedly depress the brake pedal until normal (non-assisted) pedal pressure returns.

8 Rear brake disc - inspection, removal and refitting

Note: Before starting work, refer to the note at the beginning of Section 4 concerning the dangers of asbestos dust.

Inspection

Note: If either disc requires renewal, BOTH should be renewed at the same time, to ensure even and consistent braking. New brake pads should be fitted also.

1 Firmly chock the front wheels, then jack up the rear of the car and support it on axle stands. Remove the appropriate rear roadwheel.

2 Inspect the disc as described in Section 7.

Removal

3 Unscrew the two bolts securing the brake caliper mounting bracket in position, then slide the caliper assembly off the disc. Using a piece of wire or string, tie the caliper to the rear suspension coil spring, to avoid placing any strain on the hydraulic brake hose.

4 Using a hammer and a large flat-bladed screwdriver, carefully tap and prise the cap out of the centre of the brake disc. Renew the cap if it is disfigured during removal.

5 Extract the split pin from the hub nut, and remove the locking cap. Discard the split pin; a new one must be used on refitting.

6 Slacken and remove the rear hub nut, then slide off the toothed washer and remove the outer bearing from the centre of the disc.

7 The disc can now be slide off the stub axle.

Refitting

8 If a new disc is been fitted, use a suitable solvent to wipe any preservative coating from the disc. If necessary, install the bearing races, inner bearing and oil seal as described in Chapter 10, and thoroughly grease the outer bearing.

9 Apply a smear of grease to the disc oil seal, and slide the assembly onto the stub axle.

10 Fit the outer bearing and toothed thrustwasher, ensuring its tooth is correctly engaged in the axle slot.

11 Refit the hub nut, tightening it to the point where it just contacts the washer whilst rotating the brake disc to settle the hub bearings in position. Gradually slacken the hub nut until the position is found where it is just possible to move the toothed washer from side-to-side using a screwdriver. **Note:** Only a small amount of force should be needed to move the washer. When the hub nut is correctly positioned, secure it in position with a new split pin.

12 Fit the cap to the centre of the brake disc, driving it fully into position.

13 Slide the caliper into position over the disc, making sure the pads pass either side of the disc. Tighten the caliper mounting bolts to the specified torque setting.

14 Refit the roadwheel, then lower the vehicle to the ground and tighten the wheel bolts to the specified torque setting.

9 Rear brake drum - removal, inspection and refitting

Note: Before starting work, refer to the note at the beginning of Section 4 concerning the dangers of asbestos dust.

Removal

1 Chock the front wheels, then jack up the rear of the vehicle and support it on axle stands. Remove the appropriate rear wheel.

2 Using a hammer and a large flat-bladed screwdriver, carefully tap and prise the cap out of the centre of the brake drum **(see illustration)**. Discard the cap if it is disfigured during removal.

3 Extract the split pin from the hub nut and remove the locking cap **(see illustration)**. Discard the split pin; a new one must be used on refitting.

4 Slacken and remove the rear hub nut, then slide off the toothed washer and remove the outer bearing from the centre of the drum **(see illustrations)**.

5 It should now be possible to withdraw the brake drum assembly from the stub axle by hand **(see illustration)**. It may be difficult to remove the drum, due to the tightness of the hub bearing on the stub axle, or due to the brake shoes binding on the inner circumference of the drum. If the bearing is tight, tap the periphery of the drum using a hide or plastic mallet, or use a universal puller, secured to the drum with the wheel bolts, to pull it off. If the brake shoes are binding, first check that the handbrake is fully released, then continue as follows.

6 Referring to Section 17, fully slacken the handbrake adjustment, to obtain maximum free play in the cable.

9.2 Lever out the cap from the centre of the brake drum

9.3 Remove the split pin and locking cap . . .

9.4a . . . then unscrew the retaining nut and remove the toothed washer

9.4b Withdraw the outer bearing . . .

9.5 . . . and remove the brake drum

9

9.7a Release the brake shoes by inserting a screwdriver through the drum hole . . .

7 Insert a screwdriver through one of the wheel bolt holes in the brake drum, and lever up the wedge key in order to allow the brake shoes to retract fully **(see illustrations)**. The brake drum can now be withdrawn.

Inspection

Note: *If either drum requires renewal, BOTH should be renewed at the same time, to ensure even and consistent braking. New brake shoes should also be fitted.*

8 Working carefully, remove all traces of brake dust from the drum, but avoid inhaling the dust, as it is injurious to health.

9 Clean the outside of the drum, and check it for obvious signs of wear or damage, such as cracks around the roadwheel bolt holes; renew the drum if necessary.

10 Examine carefully the inside of the drum. Light scoring of the friction surface is normal, but if heavy scoring is found, the drum must be renewed. It is usual to find a lip on the drum's inboard edge which consists of a mixture of rust and brake dust; this should be scraped away, to leave a smooth surface which can be polished with fine (120- to 150-grade) emery paper. If, however, the lip is due to the friction surface being recessed by wear, then the drum must be renewed.

11 If the drum is thought to be excessively worn, or oval, its internal diameter must be measured at several points using an internal micrometer. Take measurements in pairs, the second at right-angles to the first, and compare the two, to check for signs of ovality. Provided that it does not enlarge the drum to beyond the specified maximum diameter, it may be possible to have the drum refinished by skimming or grinding; if this is not possible, the drums on both sides must be renewed. Note that if the drum is to be skimmed, BOTH drums must be refinished, to maintain a consistent internal diameter on both sides.

Refitting

12 If a new brake drum is to be installed, use a suitable solvent to remove any preservative coating that may have been applied to its interior. If necessary, install the bearing races, inner bearing and oil seal as described in Chapter 10, and thoroughly grease the outer bearing.

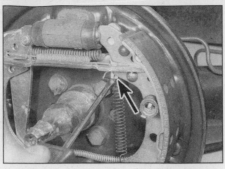

9.7b . . . and levering the wedge key (arrowed) upwards

13 Prior to refitting, fully retract the brakes shoes by lifting up the wedge key.

14 Apply a smear of grease to the drum oil seal, and carefully slide the assembly onto the stub axle.

15 Fit the outer bearing and toothed thrustwasher, ensuring its tooth is correctly engaged in the axle slot.

16 Refit the hub nut, tightening it to the point where it just contacts the washer whilst rotating the brake drum to settle the hub bearings in position. Gradually slacken the hub nut until the position is found where it is just possible to move the toothed washer from side-to-side using a screwdriver. **Note:** *Only a small amount of force should be needed to move the washer.* When the hub nut is correctly positioned, refit the locking cap and secure the nut in position with a new split pin.

17 Fit the cap to the centre of the brake drum, driving it fully into position.

18 Depress the footbrake several times to operate the self-adjusting mechanism.

19 Repeat the above procedure on the remaining rear brake assembly (where necessary), then check and, if necessary, adjust the handbrake cable (see Section 17).

20 On completion, refit the roadwheel(s), then lower the vehicle to the ground and tighten the wheel bolts to the specified torque.

10 Front brake caliper - removal, overhaul and refitting

Note: *Before starting work, refer to the note at the beginning of Section 2 concerning the dangers of hydraulic fluid, and to the warning at the beginning of Section 4 concerning the dangers of asbestos dust.*

Removal

1 Apply the handbrake, then jack up the front of the vehicle and support it on axle stands. Remove the appropriate roadwheel.

2 Minimise fluid loss by first removing the master cylinder reservoir cap, and then tightening it down onto a piece of polythene, to obtain an airtight seal. Alternatively, use a brake hose clamp, a G-clamp or a similar tool to clamp the flexible hose.

3 Clean the area around the union, then loosen the brake hose union nut.

4 Remove the brake pads as described in Section 4.

5 On models with VW brake calipers, unscrew the caliper from the end of the brake hose and remove it from the vehicle.

6 On Girling calipers, slacken and remove the caliper upper guide pin bolt, using a slim open-ended spanner to prevent the guide pin itself from rotating, then unscrew the caliper from the brake hose and remove it from the vehicle. Discard the guide pin bolt - a new bolt must be used on refitting.

Overhaul

7 With the caliper on the bench, wipe away all traces of dust and dirt, but *avoid inhaling the dust, as it is injurious to health.*

8 Withdraw the partially-ejected piston from the caliper body, and remove the dust seal.

> **HAYNES HINT**
> *If the piston cannot be withdrawn by hand, it can be pushed out by applying compressed air to the brake hose union hole. Only low pressure should be required, such as is generated by a foot pump. As the piston is expelled, take great care not to trap your fingers between the piston and caliper.*

9 Using a small screwdriver, extract the piston hydraulic seal, taking great care not to damage the caliper bore **(see illustration)**.

10 Thoroughly clean all components, using only methylated spirit, isopropyl alcohol or clean hydraulic fluid as a cleaning medium. Never use mineral-based solvents such as petrol or paraffin, as they will attack the hydraulic system's rubber components. Dry the components immediately, using compressed air or a clean, lint-free cloth. Use compressed air to blow clear the fluid passages.

11 On VW calipers, withdraw the spacers from the caliper body bushes.

12 On Girling calipers, withdraw the guide pins from the caliper mounting bracket, and remove the rubber gaiters.

13 Check all components, and renew any

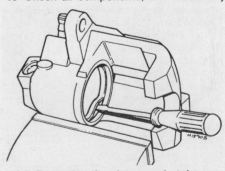

10.9 Extracting the piston seal - take care not to scratch the surface of the bore

that are worn or damaged. Check particularly the cylinder bore and piston; these should be renewed (note that this means the renewal of the complete body assembly) if they are scratched, worn or corroded in any way. Similarly check the condition of the spacers/guide pins and their bushes/bores (as applicable); both spacers/pins should be undamaged and (when cleaned) a reasonably tight sliding fit in their bores. If there is any doubt about the condition of any component, renew it.

14 If the assembly is fit for further use, obtain the appropriate repair kit; the components are available from VW dealers in various combinations.

15 Renew all rubber seals, dust covers and caps disturbed on dismantling as a matter of course; these should never be re-used.

16 On reassembly, ensure that all components are clean and dry.

17 Soak the piston and the new piston (fluid) seal in clean hydraulic fluid. Smear clean fluid on the cylinder bore surface.

18 Fit the new piston (fluid) seal, using only your fingers (no tools) to manipulate it into the cylinder bore groove. Fit the new dust seal to the piston, and refit the piston to the cylinder bore using a twisting motion; ensure that the piston enters squarely into the bore. Press the piston fully into the bore, then press the dust seal into the caliper body.

19 On VW calipers, apply the grease supplied in the repair kit, or a copper-based high-temperature brake grease or anti-seize compound to the spacers and insert them into their bushes.

20 On Girling calipers, apply the grease supplied in the repair kit, or a copper-based high-temperature brake grease or anti-seize compound to the guide pins, and fit the new gaiters. Fit the guide pins to the caliper mounting bracket, ensuring that the gaiters are correctly located in the grooves on both the sleeve and mounting bracket.

Refitting

21 Screw the caliper fully onto the flexible hose union.

22 Refit the brake pads (see Section 4).

23 Securely tighten the brake pipe union nut.

24 Remove the brake hose clamp or polythene, as applicable, and bleed the hydraulic system as described in Section 2. Note that, providing the precautions described were taken to minimise brake fluid loss, it should only be necessary to bleed the relevant front brake.

25 Refit the roadwheel, then lower the vehicle to the ground and tighten the roadwheel bolts to the specified torque.

11 Rear brake caliper - removal, overhaul and refitting

Note: *Before starting work, refer to the note at the beginning of Section 2 concerning the*

dangers of hydraulic fluid, and to the warning at the beginning of Section 5 concerning the dangers of asbestos dust.

Removal

1 Chock the front wheels, then jack up the rear of the vehicle and support on axle stands. Remove the relevant rear wheel.

2 Minimise fluid loss by first removing the master cylinder reservoir cap, and then tightening it down onto a piece of polythene, to obtain an airtight seal. Alternatively, use a brake hose clamp, a G-clamp or a similar tool to clamp the flexible hose.

3 Clean the area around the union, then loosen the brake hose union nut.

4 Remove the brake pads as described in Section 5.

5 Unscrew the caliper from the end of the flexible hose and remove it from the vehicle.

Overhaul

Note: *It is not possible to overhaul the brake caliper handbrake mechanism. If the mechanism is faulty, or fluid is leaking from the handbrake lever seal the caliper assembly must be renewed.*

6 With the caliper on the bench, wipe away all traces of dust and dirt, but avoid inhaling the dust, as it is injurious to health.

7 Using a small screwdriver, carefully prise out the dust seal from the caliper bore, taking care not to damage the piston.

8 Remove the piston from the caliper bore by rotating it in an anti-clockwise direction. This can be achieved using a suitable pair of circlip pliers engaged in the caliper piston slots. Once the piston turns freely but does not come out any further, the piston can be withdrawn by hand.

> **HAYNES HINT** *If the piston cannot be withdrawn by hand, it can be pushed out by applying compressed air to the brake hose union hole. Only low pressure should be required, such as is generated by a foot pump. As the piston is expelled, take care not to trap your fingers between the piston and caliper.*

9 Using a small screwdriver, extract the piston hydraulic seal(s), taking care not to damage the caliper bore.

10 Withdraw the guide pins from the caliper mounting bracket, and remove the guide sleeve gaiters.

11 Inspect all the caliper components as described in Section 10, paragraphs 10 to 16, and renew as necessary, noting that the handbrake mechanism must **not** be dismantled.

12 Soak the piston and the new piston (fluid) seal in clean hydraulic fluid. Smear clean fluid on the cylinder bore surface. Fit the new piston (fluid) seal(s), using only the fingers (no tools) to manipulate into the cylinder bore groove(s).

13 Fit the new dust seal to the piston groove, then refit the piston assembly. Turn the piston in a clockwise direction, using the method employed on dismantling, until it is fully retracted into the caliper bore.

14 Press the dust seal into position in the caliper housing.

15 Apply the grease supplied in the repair kit, or a copper-based brake grease or anti-seize compound, to the guide pins. Fit the new gaiters to the guide pins and fit the pins to the caliper mounting bracket, ensuring that the gaiters are correctly located in the grooves on both the pins and caliper bracket.

16 Prior to refitting, fill the caliper with fresh hydraulic fluid by slackening the bleed screw and pumping the fluid through the caliper until bubble-free fluid is expelled from the union hole.

Refitting

17 Screw the caliper fully onto the flexible hose union.

18 Refit the brake pads as described in paragraphs 10 to 12 of Section 5.

19 Securely tighten the brake pipe union nut.

20 Remove the brake hose clamp or polythene, as applicable, and bleed the hydraulic system as described in Section 2. Note that, providing the precautions described were taken to minimise brake fluid loss, it should only be necessary to bleed the relevant rear brake.

21 Connect the handbrake cable to the caliper, and adjust the handbrake as described in Section 17.

22 Refit the roadwheel, then lower the vehicle to the ground and tighten the roadwheel bolts to the specified torque. On completion, check the hydraulic fluid level as described in Chapter 1.

12 Rear wheel cylinder - removal, overhaul and refitting

Note: *Before starting work, refer to the note at the beginning of Section 2 concerning the dangers of hydraulic fluid, and to the warning at the beginning of Section 4 concerning the dangers of asbestos dust.*

Removal

1 Remove the brake drum (see Section 9).

2 Using pliers, carefully unhook the upper brake shoe return spring, and remove it from both brake shoes. Pull the upper ends of the shoes away from the wheel cylinder to disengage them from the pistons.

3 Minimise fluid loss by first removing the master cylinder reservoir cap, and then tightening it down onto a piece of polythene, to obtain an airtight seal. Alternatively, use a brake hose clamp, a G-clamp or a similar tool to clamp the flexible hose at the nearest convenient point to the wheel cylinder.

4 Wipe away all traces of dirt around the brake pipe union at the rear of the wheel

9

cylinder, and unscrew the union nut. Carefully ease the pipe out of the wheel cylinder, and plug or tape over its end to prevent dirt entry. Wipe off any spilt immediately.

5 Unscrew the two wheel cylinder retaining bolts from the rear of the backplate, and remove the cylinder, taking great care not to allow surplus hydraulic fluid to contaminate the brake shoe linings.

Overhaul

6 Brush the dirt and dust from the wheel cylinder, but take care not to inhale it.

7 Pull the rubber dust seals from the ends of the cylinder body.

8 The pistons will normally be ejected by the pressure of the coil spring, but if they are not, tap the end of the cylinder body on a piece of wood, or apply low air pressure - eg, from a foot pump - to the hydraulic fluid union hole to eject the pistons from their bores.

9 Inspect the surfaces of the pistons and their bores in the cylinder body for scoring, or evidence of metal-to-metal contact. If evident, renew the complete wheel cylinder assembly.

10 If the pistons and bores are in good condition, discard the seals and obtain a repair kit, which will contain all the necessary renewable items.

11 Remove the seals from the pistons noting their correct fitted orientation. Lubricate the new piston seals with clean brake fluid, and fit them onto the pistons with their larger diameters innermost.

12 Dip the pistons in clean brake fluid, then fit the spring to the cylinder.

13 Insert the pistons into the cylinder bores using a twisting motion.

14 Fit the dust seals, and check that the pistons can move freely in their bores.

Refitting

15 Ensure that the backplate and wheel cylinder mating surfaces are clean, then spread the brake shoes and manoeuvre the wheel cylinder into position.

16 Engage the brake pipe, and screw in the union nut two or three turns to ensure that the thread has started.

17 Insert the two wheel cylinder retaining bolts, and tighten them to the specified torque. Now fully tighten the brake pipe union nut.

18 Remove the clamp from the flexible brake hose, or the polythene from the master cylinder reservoir (as applicable).

19 Ensure that the brake shoes are correctly located in the cylinder pistons, then refit the brake shoe upper return spring, using a screwdriver to stretch the spring into position.

20 Refit the brake drum (see Section 9).

21 Bleed the brake hydraulic system as described in Section 2. Providing suitable precautions were taken to minimise loss of fluid, it should only be necessary to bleed the relevant rear brake.

13 Master cylinder - removal, overhaul and refitting

Note: *Before starting work, refer to the warning at the beginning of Section 2 concerning the dangers of hydraulic fluid.*

Removal

1 Disconnect the battery negative terminal. Where necessary, to improve access to the master cylinder, remove the air inlet duct as described in the relevant Part of Chapter 4.

2 Remove the master cylinder reservoir cap, and syphon the hydraulic fluid from the reservoir. **Note:** *Do not syphon the fluid by mouth, as it is poisonous; use a syringe or an old poultry baster.* Alternatively, open any convenient bleed screw in the system, and gently pump the brake pedal to expel the fluid through a plastic tube connected to the screw (see Section 2). Disconnect the wiring plug from the brake fluid level sender unit.

3 Wipe clean the area around the brake pipe unions on the side of the master cylinder, and place absorbent rags beneath the pipe unions to catch any surplus fluid. Make a note of the correct fitted positions of the unions, then unscrew the union nuts and carefully withdraw the pipes. Plug or tape over the pipe ends and master cylinder orifices, to minimise the loss of brake fluid, and to prevent the entry of dirt into the system. Wash off any spilt fluid immediately with cold water.

4 Slacken and remove the two nuts and washers securing the master cylinder to the vacuum servo unit, then withdraw the unit from the engine compartment. Remove the O-ring from the rear of the master cylinder, and discard it.

Overhaul

5 If the master cylinder is faulty, it must be renewed. Repair kits are not available from VW dealer, so the cylinder must be treated as a sealed unit.

6 The only items which can be renewed are the mounting seals for the fluid reservoir; if these show signs of deterioration, pull off the reservoir and remove the old seals. Lubricate the new seals with clean brake fluid, and press them into the master cylinder ports. Ease the fluid reservoir into position, and push it fully home.

Refitting

7 Remove all traces of dirt from the master cylinder and servo unit mating surfaces, and fit a new O-ring to the groove on the master cylinder body.

8 Fit the master cylinder to the servo unit, ensuring that the servo unit pushrod enters the master cylinder bore centrally. Refit the master cylinder mounting nuts and washers, and tighten them to the specified torque.

9 Wipe clean the brake pipe unions, then refit them to the master cylinder ports and tighten them securely.

10 Refill the master cylinder reservoir with new fluid, and bleed the complete hydraulic system as described in Section 2.

14 Brake pedal - removal and refitting

Removal

1 Disconnect the battery negative terminal.

2 Remove the stop-light switch (Section 21).

3 It is then necessary to release the brake pedal from the ball on the vacuum servo pushrod. To do this, reach up behind the pedal and carefully expand the pedal retaining clip lugs until the pedal can be gently pulled off the servo unit pushrod ball.

4 On models with manual transmission, remove the clutch pedal centring spring as described in Chapter 6.

5 Carefully unhook the brake pedal return spring from the pedal bracket.

6 Slide off the pedal pivot shaft right-hand retaining clip, then slide the shaft to the left until the brake pedal is released from its right-hand end. **Note:** *On some models it will be necessary to unclip the plastic wiring bracket from the facia frame to improve access to the retaining clip.*

7 Remove the pedal from the underneath the facia, and recover the return spring.

8 Carefully clean all components, and renew any that are worn or damaged.

Refitting

9 Prior to refitting, apply a smear of multi-purpose grease to the pivot shaft and pedal bearing surfaces.

10 Fit the return spring and manoeuvre the pedal into position.

11 Slide the pivot shaft into position. Make sure the flats on the end of the pivot shaft are positioned vertically, and slide on the shaft retaining clip, making sure it is securely clipped in position. Where necessary, clip the plastic wiring bracket back into position.

12 Hook the return spring onto the bracket, then retain the servo unit pushrod, and clip the pedal back onto its pushrod ball. Make sure the pedal is retained by its spring clip.

13 Where necessary, refit the clutch pedal centring spring as described in Chapter 6.

14 Refit the stop-light switch as described in Section 21 and reconnect the battery.

15 Vacuum servo unit - testing, removal and refitting

Testing

1 To test the operation of the servo unit, depress the footbrake several times to exhaust the vacuum, then start the engine whilst keeping the pedal firmly depressed. As the engine starts, there should be a noticeable "give" in the brake pedal as the vacuum builds up. Allow the engine to run for at least two

minutes, then switch it off. If the brake pedal is now depressed, it should feel normal, but further applications should result in the pedal feeling firmer, with the pedal stroke decreasing with each application.

2 If the servo does not operate as described, first inspect the servo unit check valve as described in Section 16. On diesel models, also check the operation of the vacuum pump as described in Section 25.

3 If the servo unit still fails to operate satisfactorily, the fault lies within the unit itself. Repairs to the unit are not possible - if faulty, the servo unit must be renewed.

Removal

Note: *On left-hand drive models equipped with ABS, it is not possible to remove the vacuum servo unit without first removing the hydraulic unit (see Section 23). Therefore, servo unit removal and refitting should be entrusted to a VW dealer.*

4 Remove the master cylinder (Section 13).

5 On models with manual transmission, remove the clutch master cylinder as described in Chapter 6.

6 On models equipped with ABS, remove the brake pedal position sender unit (Section 23).

7 On all models, remove the heatshield (where fitted) from the front of the servo, then carefully ease the vacuum hose out from the servo unit sealing grommet.

8 From inside the vehicle, remove the stop-light switch as described in Section 21.

9 Undo the four retaining nuts securing the servo unit to the pedal mounting bracket, then return to the engine compartment and manoeuvre the servo unit out of position, noting the gasket which is fitted to the rear of the unit. As the servo is withdrawn, it will be necessary to release its pushrod ball from the brake pedal spring clip (see paragraph 3 of Section 14).

Refitting

10 Check the servo unit vacuum hose sealing grommet for signs of damage or deterioration, and renew if necessary.

11 Fit a new gasket to the rear of the servo unit, and reposition the unit in the engine compartment.

12 From inside the vehicle, ensure that the servo unit pushrod is correctly engaged with the brake pedal, and clip the pedal onto the pushrod ball. Check the pedal is securely retained, then refit the servo unit mounting nuts and tighten them to the specified torque.

13 Carefully ease the vacuum hose back into position in the servo, taking great care not to displace the sealing grommet. Where necessary, refit the heatshield to the servo.

14 On models equipped with ABS, refit the brake pedal position sensor (see Section 23).

15 Refit the master cylinder as described in Section 13 of this Chapter. Where necessary, also refit the clutch master cylinder as described in Chapter 6.

16 Refit the stop-light switch (Section 21).

17 On completion, start the engine and check for air leaks at the vacuum hose-to-servo unit connection; check the operation of the braking system.

16 Vacuum servo unit check valve - removal, testing and refitting

1 The check valve is in the vacuum hose from the inlet manifold to the brake servo. If the valve is to be renewed, the complete hose/valve assembly should be replaced.

Removal

2 Ease the vacuum hose out of the servo unit, taking care not to displace the grommet.

3 Note the routing of the hose, then slacken the retaining clip and disconnect the opposite end of the hose assembly from the manifold/pump and remove it from the car.

Testing

4 Examine the check valve and vacuum hose for signs of damage, and renew if necessary.

5 The valve may be tested by blowing through it in both directions, air should flow through the valve in one direction only; when blown through from the servo unit end of the valve. Renew the valve if this is not the case.

6 Examine the servo unit rubber sealing grommet for signs of damage or deterioration, and renew as necessary.

Refitting

7 Ensure that the sealing grommet is correctly fitted to the servo unit.

8 Ease the hose union into position in the servo, taking great care not to displace or damage the grommet.

9 Ensure that the hose is correctly routed, and connect it to the inlet manifold/pump, tightening its retaining clip securely.

10 On completion, start the engine and check the check valve to servo unit connection for signs of air leaks.

17 Handbrake - adjustment

1 To check the handbrake adjustment, first apply the footbrake firmly several times to establish correct shoe-to-drum/pad-to-disc clearance, then apply and release the handbrake several times.

2 Applying normal moderate pressure, pull the handbrake lever to the fully-applied position, counting the number of clicks emitted from the handbrake ratchet mechanism. If adjustment is correct, there should be approximately 4 to 7 clicks before the handbrake is fully applied. If this is not the case, adjust as follows.

3 Remove the rear section of the centre console as described in Chapter 11 to gain access to the handbrake lever. **Note:** *On some models, the handbrake adjusting nuts*

can be accessed by simply removing the ashtray from the rear of the centre console **(see illustration).**

4 Chock the front wheels, then jack up the rear of the vehicle and support it on axle stands. Continue as described under the relevant sub-heading.

Rear drum brake models

5 With the handbrake set on the 4th notch of the ratchet mechanism, slacken the locknuts and rotate the adjusting nuts equally until it is difficult to turn both rear wheels/drums. Once this is so, release the handbrake lever, and check that the wheels/hubs rotate freely. Check the adjustment by applying the handbrake fully, counting the clicks from the handbrake ratchet and, if necessary, re-adjust.

6 Once adjustment is correct, hold the adjusting nuts and securely tighten the locknuts. Refit the centre console section/ashtray (as applicable).

Rear disc brake models

7 With the handbrake fully released, equally slacken the handbrake locknuts and adjusting nuts until both the rear caliper handbrake levers are back against their stops.

8 From this point, equally tighten both adjusting nuts until both handbrake levers just move off the caliper stops. Ensure that the gap between each caliper handbrake lever and its stop is less than 1.5 mm, and ensure both the right- and left-hand gaps are equal **(see illustration).** Check that both wheels/discs rotate freely, then check the adjustment by applying the handbrake fully, counting the

17.3 Handbrake cable locknuts and adjuster nuts (arrowed)

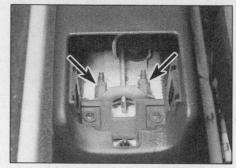

17.8 Adjust the handbrake so that the clearance between the handbrake lever and caliper (arrowed) is as stated

9

clicks emitted from the handbrake ratchet. If necessary, re-adjust.

9 Once adjustment is correct, hold the adjusting nuts and securely tighten the locknuts. Refit the centre console section/ashtray (as applicable).

18 Handbrake lever - removal and refitting

Removal

1 Remove the rear section of the centre console as described in Chapter 11 to gain access to the handbrake lever.

2 Remove both the handbrake cable locknuts and adjusting nuts, and detach the cables from the compensator plate **(see illustration)**.

3 Disconnect the wiring connector from the warning light switch, then undo the retaining nuts and remove the lever from the vehicle.

Refitting

4 Refitting is a reversal of the removal. Prior to refitting the centre console, adjust the handbrake as described in Section 17.

19 Handbrake cables - removal and refitting

Removal

1 Remove the rear section of the centre console as described in Chapter 11 to gain access to the handbrake lever. The handbrake cable consists of two sections, a right- and a left-hand section, which are linked to the lever by a compensator plate. Each section can be removed individually.

2 Slacken the relevant handbrake locknut and adjusting nut to obtain maximum free play in the cable, and disengage the inner cable from the handbrake compensator plate.

3 Chock the front wheels, then jack up the rear of the car and support it on axle stands.

4 From the vehicle underbody, free the front end of the outer cable from the body, and withdraw the cable from its support guide.

5 Working back along the length of the cable, noting its correct routing, and free it from all the relevant retaining clips **(see illustration)**.

6 On models with rear drum brakes, remove the rear brake shoes from the relevant side as described in Section 6. Using a hammer and pin punch, carefully tap the outer cable out from the brake backplate, and remove it from underneath the vehicle **(see illustration)**.

7 On models with rear disc brakes, disengage the inner cable from the caliper handbrake lever, then remove the outer cable retaining clip and detach the cable from the caliper **(see illustrations)**.

Refitting

8 Refitting is a reversal of the removal procedure. Prior to refitting the centre console, adjust the handbrake (Section 17).

20 Rear brake pressure-regulating valves - removal and refitting

Note: *Before starting work, refer to the warning at the beginning of Section 2 concerning the dangers of hydraulic fluid.*

Removal

Note: *Later (February 1995-on) models with ABS are not fitted with any rear brake pressure-regulating valves; the function is automatically controlled by the ABS unit.*

Pressure-dependent valves - 1.4 litre models

1 On 1.4 litre models, the rear brake pressure-regulating valves are of the pressure-dependent type. Depending on model, the valves are either screwed into the master cylinder outlet ports, or are screwed into the brake pipe T-pieces (where the front and rear brake lines join) which are mounted onto the engine compartment bulkhead. Removal is as follows.

2 Minimise fluid loss by first removing the master cylinder reservoir cap, and then tightening it down onto a piece of polythene to obtain an airtight seal.

3 Wipe the area around the regulating valve brake pipe unions, and place rags beneath the pipe unions to catch any surplus fluid.

4 Unscrew the union nuts which connect the brake pipes to the end of the regulating valves, and carefully withdraw the pipes. Plug or tape over the pipe ends.

5 Unscrew the valves, and plug or tape over the master cylinder/T-piece orifices (as applicable) to minimise the loss of brake fluid,

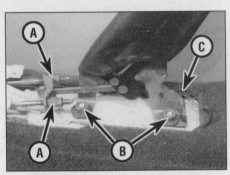

18.2 Handbrake cable locknuts and adjuster nuts (A), lever retaining nuts (B) and warning light switch wiring (C)

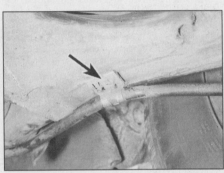

19.5 Release the retaining clips (arrowed) and detach the handbrake cable from the trailing arm

19.6 On drum brakes, remove the shoes and detach the cable from the backplate

19.7a On disc brake models, detach the inner cable from the caliper lever . . .

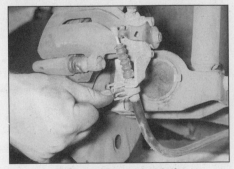

19.7b . . . then remove the retaining clip . . .

19.7c . . . and free the cable from the caliper bracket

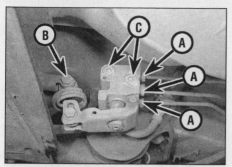

20.6 Load-dependent rear brake pressure-regulating valve brake pipe unions (A), spring pivot bolt (B) and retaining bolts (C)

and to prevent the entry of dirt into the system. Wash off any spilt fluid with cold water.

Load-dependent valve - other models

6 On all models except 1.4 litre, the rear brake pressure-regulating valve is of the load-dependent-type; the valve is mounted next the rear axle, attached to the axle by a spring **(see illustration)**. As the load being carried by the vehicle is altered, the suspension moves in relation to the vehicle body, altering the tension in the spring. The spring then adjusts the pressure-regulating valve lever so that the correct pressure is applied to the rear brakes to suit the load being carried.

7 Minimise fluid loss by first removing the master cylinder reservoir cap, and then tightening it down onto a piece of polythene to obtain an airtight seal.

8 Slacken and remove the nut and bolt securing the valve spring to the axle.

9 Wipe clean the area around the brake pipe unions on the valve, and place rags beneath the pipe unions to catch any surplus fluid. Make identification marks on the brake pipes; these marks can then be used on refitting to ensure each pipe is correctly reconnected.

10 Slacken the union nuts and disconnect the brake pipes from the valve. Plug or tape over the pipe ends and valve orifices, to minimise the loss of brake fluid and to prevent the entry of dirt into the system. Wash off any spilt fluid immediately with cold water.

11 Undo the bolts and remove the pressure-regulating valve and spring from below the car.

Refitting

Pressure-dependent valves - 1.4 litre models

12 Refitting is the reverse of the removal procedure, ensuring that the valves and pipe union nuts are securely tightened. On completion, bleed the complete braking system as described in Section 2.

Load-dependent valve - other models

13 Refitting is the reverse of the removal procedure, noting the following points:

a) If a new valve is being fitted, set the spring adjustment bolt to the same position as the one on the old valve, and tighten it securely.

b) Ensure that the brake pipes are correctly connected to the valve, and that their union nuts are securely tightened.

c) Coat the ends of the spring with grease prior to installation.

d) Bleed the braking system (see Section 2).

e) On completion, take the vehicle to a VW dealer to have the valve operation checked and if necessary adjusted.

21 Stop-light switch - removal and refitting

Removal

1 The stop-light switch is located on the pedal bracket behind the facia.

2 Press in the locking buttons, and unclip the fusebox cover from the underside of the driver's side lower facia panel. Carefully prise the trim panel out from the top of the driver's side lower facia panel, then slacken and remove all the panel retaining screws. Carefully move the panel downwards to release it from the facia, then remove it from the vehicle.

3 Reach up behind the facia and disconnect the wiring connector from the switch

4 Twist the switch through 90° and release it from the mounting bracket.

Refitting

5 Prior to installation, fully extend the stop-light switch plunger.

6 Fully depress and hold the brake pedal, then manoeuvre the switch into position. Secure the switch in position it by twisting it through 90° and release the brake pedal.

7 Reconnect the wiring connector, and check the operation of the stop-lights. The stop-lights should illuminate after the brake pedal has travelled about 5 mm. If the switch is not functioning correctly, it is faulty and must be renewed; no adjustment is possible.

8 On completion, refit the driver's side lower facia panel.

22 Anti-lock braking system (ABS) - general information

Note: *On models equipped with traction control, the ABS unit is a dual function unit, controlling both the anti-lock braking system (ABS) and the electronic differential locking (EDL) system functions.*

ABS is available as an option on all models covered in this manual. The system comprises a hydraulic block (which contains the hydraulic solenoid valves and accumulators), the electrically-driven return pump, and four roadwheel sensors (one fitted to each wheel), the electronic control unit (ECU) and the brake pedal position sensor. The purpose of the system is to prevent the wheel(s) locking during heavy braking. This is achieved by automatic release of the brake on the relevant wheel, followed by re-application of the brake.

The solenoids are controlled by the ECU, which itself receives signals from the four wheel sensors (one fitted on each hub), which monitor the speed of rotation of each wheel. By comparing these signals, the ECU can determine the speed at which the car is travelling. It can then use this speed to determine when a wheel is decelerating at an abnormal rate, compared to the speed of the car, and therefore predicts when a wheel is about to lock. During normal operation, the system functions in the same way as a non-ABS braking system. In addition, the brake pedal position sensor (which is fitted to the vacuum servo unit) also informs the ECU of how hard the brake pedal is being depressed.

If the ECU senses that a wheel is about to lock, it operates the relevant solenoid valve in the modulator block, which then isolates the brake caliper on the wheel which is about to lock from the master cylinder, effectively sealing-in the hydraulic pressure.

If the speed of rotation of the wheel continues to decrease at an abnormal rate, the ECU switches on the electrically-driven return pump, which pumps the hydraulic fluid back into the master cylinder, releasing pressure on the brake caliper so that the brake is released. Once the speed of rotation of the wheel returns to an acceptable rate, the pump stops; the solenoid valve opens, allowing the hydraulic master cylinder pressure to return to the caliper, which then re-applies the brake. This cycle can be carried out at up to 10 times a second.

The action of the solenoid valves and return pump creates pulses in the hydraulic circuit. When the ABS system is functioning, these pulses can be felt through the brake pedal.

The operation of the ABS system is entirely dependent on electrical signals. To prevent the system responding to any inaccurate signals, a built-in safety circuit monitors all signals received by the ECU. If an inaccurate signal or low battery voltage is detected, the ABS system is automatically shut down, and the warning light on the instrument panel is illuminated, to inform the driver that the ABS system is not operational. Normal braking should still be available, however.

If a fault does develop in the ABS system, the car must be taken to a VW dealer for fault diagnosis and repair.

23 Anti-lock braking system (ABS) components - removal and refitting

Hydraulic unit

1 Removal and refitting of the hydraulic unit should be entrusted to a VW dealer. Great care has to be taken not to allow any fluid to escape from the unit as the pipes are disconnected. If the fluid is allowed to escape, air can enter the unit, causing air locks which cause the hydraulic unit to malfunction.

Electronic control unit (ECU)

Removal

2 On vehicles manufactured before January 1993, the control unit is situated underneath the carpet in the right-hand front footwell; on models manufactured between January 1993 and February 1995, it is located underneath the rear seat on the right-hand side of the car. On models manufactured after February 1995, the control unit is mounted onto the base of the hydraulic unit; on these models, the control cannot be removed without first removing the hydraulic unit (see paragraph 1). Prior to removal on earlier models, disconnect the battery negative lead.

3 On models manufactured before January 1993, peel back the carpet to gain access to the ECU; note that it may be necessary to remove the seat (Chapter 11) to gain access. Unclip the ECU, then release the wiring plug clip and carefully pivot the plug out of position. The ECU can then be removed.

4 On models manufactured between January 1993 and February 1995, lift up the right-hand rear seat cushion, and unclip the ECU from its mountings. Release the retaining clip and pivot the wiring connector out of position, then remove the ECU from the car.

Refitting

5 Refitting is a reversal of removal, ensuring that the ECU wiring connector is correctly and securely reconnected.

Front wheel sensor

Removal

6 Chock the rear wheels, then firmly apply the handbrake, jack up the front of the car and support on axle stands. Remove the appropriate front roadwheel.

7 Trace the wiring back from the sensor to the connector, freeing it from all the relevant retaining clips, and disconnect it from the main loom.

8 Slacken and remove the bolt securing the sensor to the swivel hub, and remove the sensor and lead assembly from the car.

Refitting

9 Prior to refitting, apply a thin coat of multi-purpose grease to the sensor tip (VW recommend the use of lubricating paste G 000 650 - available from your dealer).

10 Ensure that the sensor and swivel hub sealing faces are clean, then fit the sensor to the hub. Refit the retaining bolt and tighten it to the specified torque.

11 Ensure that the sensor wiring is correctly routed and retained by all the necessary clips, and reconnect it to its wiring connector.

12 Refit the roadwheel, then lower the car to the ground and tighten the roadwheel bolts to the specified torque.

Rear wheel sensor

Removal

13 Chock the front wheels, then jack up the rear of the car and support it on axle stands. Remove the appropriate roadwheel.

14 Remove the sensor as described in paragraphs 7 and 8.

Refitting

15 Refit the sensor as described above in paragraphs 9 to 12.

Front reluctor rings

16 The front reluctor rings are fixed onto the rear of wheel hubs. Examine the rings for damage such as chipped or missing teeth. If renewal is necessary, the complete hub assembly must be dismantled and the bearings renewed as described in Chapter 10.

Rear reluctor rings

17 The rear reluctor rings are pressed onto the inside of the rear brake drum disc. Examine the rings for signs of damage such as chipped or missing teeth, and renew as necessary. If renewal is necessary, remove the drum/disc as described in Chapter 9 and take it to a VW dealer, who will have access to the necessary tools required to extract the old ring and press on the new one.

Brake pedal position sensor

Removal

18 Release the vacuum from inside the servo unit by depressing the brake pedal several times. Although not absolutely necessary, to improve access to the sensor, remove the master cylinder as described in Section 13.

19 Disconnect the battery negative terminal. Trace the wiring back from pedal position sensor, and disconnect at the connector.

20 Using a small screwdriver, carefully lever off the sensor retaining clip then withdraw the sensor from the front of the vacuum servo unit. Recover the sealing ring and circlip.

Refitting

21 If a new sensor is being fitted, note the colour of the spacer fitted to the original sensor, and fit the relevant colour spacer to the new sensor. This is vital to ensure that the correct operation of the anti-lock braking system.

22 Fit the new circlip to the groove on the front of the vacuum servo unit, positioning its end gap over the servo unit sensor lower locating slot.

23 Fit the new sealing ring to the sensor, and lubricate it with a smear of oil to aid installation.

24 Fit the sensor to the vacuum servo, aligning its locating notch with the servo unit upper groove. Push the sensor until it clicks into position, and check that it is securely retained by the circlip.

25 Reconnect the sensor wiring, and connect the battery negative terminal.

24 Vacuum pump (diesel models) - removal and refitting

Removal

1 Release the retaining clip, and disconnect the vacuum hose from the top of pump.

2 Slacken and remove the retaining bolt, and remove the pump retaining clamp from the cylinder block.

3 Withdraw the vacuum pump from the cylinder block, and recover the O-ring seal. Discard the O-ring - a new one should be used on refitting.

Refitting

4 Fit the new O-ring to the vacuum pump, and apply a smear of oil to the)-ring to aid installation.

5 Manoeuvre the vacuum pump into position, making sure that the slot in the pump drive gear aligns with the dog on the pump drive gear **(see illustration)**.

6 Refit the retaining clamp and securely tighten its retaining bolt.

7 Reconnect the vacuum hose to the pump, and secure it in position with the retaining clip.

25 Vacuum pump (diesel models) - testing and overhaul

1 The operation of the braking system vacuum pump can be checked using a vacuum gauge.

2 Disconnect the vacuum pipe from the pump, and connect the gauge to the pump union using a suitable length of hose.

3 Start the engine and allow it to idle, then measure the vacuum created by the pump. As a guide, after one minute, a minimum of approximately 500 mm Hg should be recorded. If the vacuum registered is significantly less than this, it is likely that the pump is faulty. However, seek the advice of a VW dealer before condemning the pump.

4 Overhaul of the vacuum pump is not possible, since no major components are available separately for it; the only spare part readily available is the pump cover sealing ring. If faulty, the complete pump assembly must be renewed.

24.5 Ensure vacuum pump slot (arrowed) is aligned with the pump drivegear

Chapter 10
Suspension and steering

Contents

Degrees of difficulty

Easy, suitable for novice with little experience	**Fairly easy,** suitable for beginner with some experience	**Fairly difficult,** suitable for competent DIY mechanic	**Difficult,** suitable for experienced DIY mechanic	**Very difficult,** suitable for expert DIY or professional

Specifications

Front suspension
Type . . . . Independent, with MacPherson struts incorporating coil springs and telescopic shock absorbers. Anti-roll bar fitted to most models

Rear suspension
Type . . . . Transverse torsion beam axle with trailing arms. Coil spring struts incorporating telescopic shock absorbers. Anti-roll bar on some models

Steering
Type . . . . Rack-and-pinion. Power assistance standard on certain models, optional on others

Wheel alignment and steering angles
Front wheel:
  Camber angle:
    2.0 litre models:
      GT specification models . . . . -40' ± 20'
      L, CL and GL specification models . . . . -36' ± 20'
    All other models:
      GT specification models . . . . -36' ± 20'
      L, CL and GL specification models . . . . -30' ± 20'
    Maximum difference between sides (all models) . . . . 20'
  Castor angle:
    2.0 litre models:
      GT specification models . . . . 3° 25' ± 30'
      L, CL and GL specification models . . . . 1° 50' ± 30'
    All other models:
      GT specification models . . . . 1° 50' ± 30'
      L, CL and GL specification models . . . . 1° 45' ± 30'
    Maximum difference between sides (all models) . . . . 30'
  Toe setting . . . . 0° ± 10'

10

Wheel alignment and steering angles (continued)

Rear wheel:
Camber angle	-1°30' ± 10'
Maximum difference between sides	20'
Toe setting	20' ± 10'

Roadwheels

Type	Pressed-steel or aluminium alloy (depending on model)

Size:
Roadwheels	5.5J x 13, 6J x 14, 6J x 15 or 6.5J x 15
Spare wheel	3.5J x 14 or 3.5J x 15

Tyres

Pressures - see *"Weekly Checks"*.

Sizes:*

Roadwheels:
5.5J x 13 wheels	175/70 R 13
6J x 14 wheels	185/60 R 14, 195/60 R 14 or 175/65 R 14
6J x 15 wheels	195/50 R 15 or 185/55 R 15
6.5J x 15 wheels	195/50 R 15 or 205/50 R 15

Spare wheel:
3.5J x 14 wheel	105/70 R 14
3.5J x 15 wheel	115/70 R 15

Consult your handbook, a VW dealer or a suitable tyre dealer for the correct size for your vehicle

Torque wrench settings

	Nm	lbf ft
Front suspension		
Anti-roll bar connecting link retaining nut	25	18
Lower arm balljoint:		
2.0 litre (GT specification) models:		
Retaining bolts	35	26
Retaining nut	45	33
All other models:		
Retaining bolts	35	26
Clamp bolt nut	50	37
Lower arm pivot bolt:		
Stage 1	50	37
Stage 2	Angle-tighten a further 90°	
Lower arm rear mounting bolt:		
Stage 1	70	52
Stage 2	Angle-tighten a further 90°	
Subframe mounting bolts:		
Stage 1	70	52
Stage 2	Angle-tighten a further 90°	
Suspension strut spring seat retaining nut:		
2.0 litre (GT specification) models	60	44
All other models	40	30
Suspension strut-to-swivel hub bolt nut	60	44
Suspension strut upper mounting nuts	60	44
Rear suspension		
Rear axle:		
Pivot bolts	80	66
Mounting bracket retaining bolts	70	52
Stub axle/backplate retaining bolts	60	44
Suspension strut:		
Upper mounting bottom nut	15	11
Upper mounting top nut	25	18
Lower mounting bolt	70	52
Spring retaining plate nut	15	11
Steering		
Intermediate shaft clamp bolts	30	22
Intermediate shaft connecting piece nuts	25	18
Power steering pump:		
Swivel bracket and mounting bracket bolts	25	18
Mounting bolts	25	18
Feed pipe union bolt	30	22
Pulley retaining bolts	25	18

Torque wrench settings

	Nm	lbf ft
Steering (continued)		
Steering gear:		
Retaining nuts	30	22
Steering pipe union nuts	30	22
Steering wheel nut	50	36
Track rod balljoint:		
Retaining nut	35	26
Locknut	50	37
Roadwheels		
Roadwheel bolts	110	81

1 General information

The independent front suspension is of the MacPherson strut type, incorporating coil springs and integral telescopic shock absorbers. The struts are located by transverse lower suspension arms, which use rubber inner mounting bushes, and incorporate a balljoint at the outer ends. The front swivel hubs, which carry the wheel bearings, brake calipers and the hub/disc assemblies, are bolted to the MacPherson struts, and connected to the lower arms through the balljoints. A front anti-roll bar is fitted to most models. The anti-roll bar is rubber-mounted, and is connected to both lower suspension arms.

The rear suspension consists of a torsion axle with suspension struts. On larger-engine models, an anti-roll bar is incorporated into the rear axle assembly; this links both trailing arms, and is situated just to the rear of the axle crossmember.

The steering column incorporates a universal joint, and is connected to the steering gear by a second universal joint.

The steering gear is mounted onto the front subframe, and is connected by two track rods, with balljoints at their outer ends, to the steering arms projecting rearwards from the swivel hubs. The track rod ends are threaded, to facilitate adjustment.

Power-assisted steering is fitted as standard on some models, and is available as an option on all others. The hydraulic steering system is powered by a belt-driven pump, which is driven off the crankshaft pulley.

2 Front swivel hub assembly - removal and refitting

Note: *A new driveshaft nut, new suspension strut-to-swivel hub bolt nuts, and a new track rod balljoint nut, will be required on refitting.*

Removal

1 Remove the wheel trim/hub cap (as applicable) and slacken the driveshaft retaining nut with the vehicle resting on its wheels. Also slacken the wheel bolts
2 Chock the rear wheels of the car, firmly apply the handbrake, then jack up the front of the car and support it on axle stands. Remove the front roadwheel.
3 Remove the driveshaft retaining nut and (where fitted) its washer.
4 On models with ABS, remove the wheel sensor as described in Chapter 9.
5 If the hub bearings are to be disturbed, remove the brake disc as described in Chapter 9. If not, on models with VW calipers, remove the brake pads, or on models with Girling calipers, unscrew the two bolts securing the brake caliper assembly to the hub, and slide the caliper assembly off the disc (see Chapter 9). Using a piece of wire or string, tie the caliper to the front suspension coil spring, to avoid placing any strain on the hydraulic brake hose.
6 Slacken the nut securing the steering gear track rod balljoint to the swivel hub, leaving it on by a few threads. Release the balljoint tapered shank using a universal balljoint separator **(see illustration)**. Remove the nut

completely once the taper has been separated.
7 Using a suitable marker pen, draw around the end of the suspension lower arm, marking the correct fitted position of balljoint. Unscrew the balljoint retaining bolts, and remove the retaining plate from the top of the lower arm **(see illustration). Note:** *On most models, the balljoint inner retaining bolt hole is slotted; on these models, the inner retaining bolt can be slackened, leaving the retaining plate and bolt in position in the arm, and the balljoint is then disengaged from the bolt.*
8 Using a suitable marker pen, draw around the outline of each suspension strut-to-swivel hub bolt, marking their positions on the strut. Slacken and remove both nuts and bolts **(see illustration)**.
9 Free the swivel hub from the strut, then carefully pull the hub assembly outwards and withdraw the driveshaft outer constant velocity joint from the hub assembly **(see illustration)**. The outer joint will be very tight -

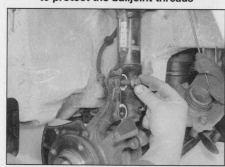

2.6 Separating the track rod balljoint from the swivel hub. Leave on the nut (arrowed) to protect the balljoint threads

2.7 Removing the retaining plate from the top of the lower arm

2.8 Mark their positions on the strut, then remove the swivel hub-to-strut nuts/bolts

2.9 Free the swivel hub from the driveshaft splines, and remove from the car

10

2.12 Fit the washer and driveshaft nut, and use the nut to draw the driveshaft joint fully into position

tap the joint out of the hub using a soft-faced mallet. If this fails to free it from the hub, the joint will have to be pressed out using a suitable tool bolted to the hub.

Refitting

10 Note that all self-locking nuts disturbed on removal must be renewed as a matter of course. These nuts have threads which are pre-coated with locking compound (this is only effective once), and include the driveshaft nut, the track rod balljoint nut, and the suspension strut-to-swivel hub bolt nuts.

11 Ensure that the outer joint and hub splines are clean and dry. On all models except later 2.0 litre (GT specification) models, remove all traces of locking compound from both sets of splines, and apply a bead of suitable locking compound to the outer joint splines (VW recommend the use of fluid number D 185 400 A2 - available from VW dealers). **Note:** *On later 2.0 litre (GT specification) models, the hub splines have been modified (the peaks of the splines have been flattened, to reduce driveshaft backlash) and locking compound should **not** be applied to the outer joint splines.*

12 Manoeuvre the hub assembly into position, and engage it with the driveshaft outer joint. Ensure that the threads are clean and apply a smear of oil to the contact face of the new driveshaft retaining nut. Fit the washer (where fitted) and nut, and use the nut to draw the joint fully into position **(see illustration)**.

13 Engage the swivel hub with the suspension strut whilst aligning the balljoint with the lower arm.

14 Insert the strut-to-swivel hub bolts, and fit the new retaining nuts. Align the bolts with the marks made prior to removal, and tighten the nuts to the specified torque setting.

15 Refit the lower arm balljoint retaining bolts. Align the balljoint with the marks made prior to removal, then tighten the retaining bolts to the specified torque.

16 Engage the track rod balljoint in the swivel hub, then fit a new retaining nut and tighten it to the specified torque.

17 Where necessary, refit the brake disc to the hub, referring to Chapter 9 for further information.

18 On models with VW brake calipers, refit the brake pads. On models with Girling calipers, slide the caliper assembly into position over the disc, then fit the mounting bolts and tighten them to the specified torque (see Chapter 9).

19 Where necessary, refit the ABS wheel sensor as described in Chapter 9.

20 Ensure that the outer joint is drawn fully into position, then refit the roadwheel and lower the vehicle to the ground.

21 Tighten the driveshaft retaining nut correctly as described in Section 2 of Chapter 8, then tighten the roadwheel bolts to the specified torque setting. **Note:** *On completion, it is advisable to have the camber angle checked and, if necessary, adjusted.*

3 Front hub bearings - renewal

Note: *The bearing is a sealed, pre-adjusted and pre-lubricated, double-row roller type, and is intended to last the car's entire service life without maintenance or attention. Never overtighten the driveshaft nut beyond the specified torque wrench setting in an attempt to "adjust" the bearing.*

Note: *A press will be required to dismantle and rebuild the assembly; if such a tool is not available, a large bench vice and spacers (such as large sockets) will serve as an adequate substitute. The bearing's inner races are an interference fit on the hub; if the inner race remains on the hub when it is pressed out of the hub carrier, a knife-edged bearing puller will be required to remove it.*

1 Remove the swivel hub assembly as described in Section 2.

2 Support the swivel hub securely on blocks or in a vice. Using a tubular spacer which bears only on the inner end of the hub flange, press the hub flange out of the bearing. If the bearing's outboard inner race remains on the hub, remove it using a bearing puller (see note above). If necessary, undo the retaining screws and remove the ABS rotor from the rear of the hub. Fit the new rotor and securely tighten the retaining screws.

3 Extract the bearing retaining circlip(s) from the swivel hub assembly **(see illustration)**.

4 Securely support the outer face of the

swivel hub. Using a tubular spacer, press the complete bearing assembly out of the swivel hub.

5 Thoroughly clean the hub and swivel hub, removing all traces of dirt and grease, and polish away any burrs or raised edges which might hinder reassembly. Check both for cracks or any other signs of wear or damage, and renew them if necessary. Renew the circlip, regardless of its apparent condition.

6 On reassembly, apply a light coating of molybdenum disulphide grease (VW recommend Molycote - available from your dealer) to the bearing outer race and bearing surface of the swivel hub.

7 Securely support the swivel hub, and locate the bearing in the hub. Press the bearing fully into position, ensuring that it enters the hub squarely, using a tubular spacer which bears only on the bearing outer race.

8 Once the bearing is correctly seated, secure the bearing in position with the new circlip(s), ensuring that they are correctly located in the groove in the swivel hub.

9 Support the outer face of the hub flange, and locate the swivel hub bearing inner race over the end of the hub flange. Press the bearing onto the hub, using a tubular spacer which bears only on the inner race of the hub bearing, until it seats against the hub shoulder. Check that the hub flange rotates freely, and wipe off any excess oil or grease.

10 Refit the swivel hub assembly as described in Section 2.

4 Front suspension strut - removal, overhaul and refitting

Note: *New suspension strut upper and lower retaining nuts and will be required on refitting.*

Removal

1 Chock the rear wheels, apply the handbrake, then jack up the front of the vehicle and support on axle stands. Remove the appropriate roadwheel.

2 Using a suitable marker pen, draw around the outline of each suspension strut-to-swivel hub bolt, marking their positions on the strut. Slacken and remove both nuts and bolts, and unclip the brake hose from the strut **(see illustration)**.

3.3 Removing the front hub bearing circlip

4.2 Remove the strut-to-swivel hub bolts. Free the brake hose (arrowed)

4.3a Remove the plastic cover . . .

4.3b . . . then unscrew the strut upper mounting nut . . .

4.3c . . . and lift off the mounting plate

3 Unclip the plastic cover (where fitted) from the strut upper mounting, then slacken and remove the upper mounting nut and recover the mounting plate. Note that it may be necessary to retain the strut piston with a suitable Allen key, to prevent it from rotating as the nut is slackened **(see illustrations)**.

4 Free the strut from the swivel hub and manoeuvre it out from underneath the wheel arch. Where necessary, recover the mounting bush from the top of the strut.

Overhaul

 Warning: Before attempting to dismantle the suspension strut, a suitable tool to hold the coil spring in compression must be obtained. Adjustable coil spring compressors are readily available, and are recommended for this operation. Any attempt to dismantle the strut without such a tool is likely to result in damage or personal injury.

5 With the strut removed from the car, clean away all external dirt, then mount it upright in a vice.

6 Fit the spring compressor, and compress the coil spring until all tension is relieved from the upper spring seat. Continue as described under the relevant sub-heading.

2.0 litre (GT specification) models

7 Slacken and remove the spring seat retaining nut, whilst retaining the strut piston with a suitable Allen key, then remove the bearing and upper spring seat.

8 Remove the coil spring, then slide off the damper piston gaiter and rubber damper stop.

9 With the strut assembly now completely dismantled, examine all the components for wear, damage or deformation, and check the bearing for smoothness of operation. Renew any of the components as necessary.

10 Examine the strut for signs of fluid leakage. Check the strut piston for signs of pitting along its entire length, and check the strut body for signs of damage. While holding it in an upright position, test the operation of the strut by moving the piston through a full stroke, and then through short strokes of 50 to 100 mm. In both cases, the resistance felt

should be smooth and continuous. If the resistance is jerky, or uneven, or if there is any visible sign of wear or damage to the strut, renewal is necessary.

11 If any doubt exists about the condition of the coil spring, carefully remove the spring compressors, and check the spring for distortion and signs of cracking. Renew the spring if it is damaged or distorted, or if there is any doubt as to its condition.

12 Inspect all other components for signs of damage or deterioration, and renew any that are suspect.

13 Slide the rubber damper and piston gaiter onto the strut piston.

14 Fit the coil spring onto the strut, making sure its end is correctly located against the spring seat stop.

15 Refit the upper spring seat and bearing, and screw on the retaining nut. Tighten the retaining nut to the specified torque setting whilst retaining the strut piston.

All other models

Note: *A special slotted socket is required to remove and refit the upper spring seat retaining nut; alternatives to the VW tool are available from specialist automotive tool manufacturers (eg. Sykes Pickavant)* **(see Tool Tip)**.

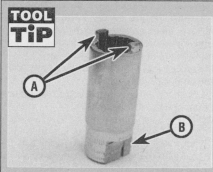

TOOL TiP

In the absence of the special VW tool, a replacement can be fabricated from a long-reach 13 mm socket. Cut the lower end of the socket to leave two teeth (A) which will engage with the slots in the strut nut, and file the upper end of the socket (B) so that it can be held with an open-ended spanner

16 Using the special slotted socket, slacken and remove the upper spring seat retaining nut and lift off the strut mounting, upper spring seat and washer.

17 Lift off the coil spring, and remove the rubber damper and sleeve from the strut.

18 Inspect the strut components as described in paragraphs 9 to 12.

19 To reassemble the strut, follow the accompanying photos, beginning with **illustration 4.19a**. Be sure to stay in order, and carefully read the caption underneath each **(see illustrations)**.

Refitting

20 Ensure that the mounting bush (where fitted) is in position on the top of the strut, then manoeuvre the strut into position and engage it with the swivel hub.

21 Make sure the top of the strut is correctly located, then insert the strut-to-swivel hub bolts and fit the new retaining nuts.

4.19a Slide the rubber damper and protective sleeve onto the strut . . .

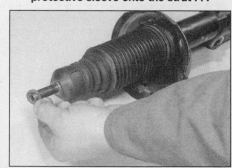

4.19b . . . and refit the washer to the piston (continued overleaf)

10

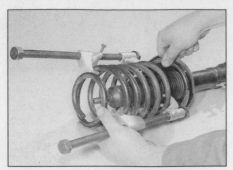

4.19c Fit the coil spring to the strut . . .

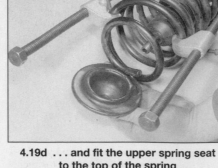

4.19d . . . and fit the upper spring seat to the top of the spring

4.19e Fit the strut mounting assembly . . .

4.19f . . . and screw the slotted nut onto the strut piston

4.19g Tighten the slotted nut to the specified torque setting . . .

4.19h . . . then release the compressors, ensuring the spring ends are located against the stops on the upper and lower seats

4.23 Align the marks made prior to removal, and tighten the strut-to-swivel hub bolts to the specified torque

22 Fit the mounting plate to the top of the strut, and fit the new upper mounting nut. Tighten the nut to the specified torque setting and (where necessary) refit the cover.

23 Align the strut-to-swivel hub bolts with the marks made on removal, and tighten the retaining nuts to the specified torque setting **(see illustration)**. Clip the brake hose back into the strut.

24 Refit the roadwheel, and tighten the wheel bolts to the specified torque. **Note:** *On completion, it is advisable to have the camber angle checked and, if necessary, adjusted.*

5 Front suspension lower arm - removal, overhaul and refitting

Note: *A new lower arm pivot bolt and rear mounting bolt will be required on refitting.*

Removal

1 Chock the rear wheels, firmly apply the handbrake, then jack up the front of the vehicle and support on axle stands. Remove the appropriate front roadwheel.

2 On 2.0 litre (GT specification) models, slacken and remove the nut (or nut and bolt, as applicable) securing the anti-roll bar connecting link to the lower arm, and free the link from the arm.

3 On all other models, remove the connecting link as described in Section 8.

4 On all models, using a suitable marker pen, draw around the end of the suspension lower arm, marking the correct fitted position of balljoint, then slacken and remove the balljoint retaining bolts and lift off the retaining plate from the top of the lower arm.

5 Slacken and remove the lower arm pivot bolt and rear mounting bolt.

6 Lower the arm out of position, and remove it from underneath the vehicle.

Overhaul

7 Thoroughly clean the lower arm and the area around the arm mountings, removing all traces of dirt and underseal if necessary, then check carefully for cracks, distortion or any other signs of wear or damage, paying particular attention to the pivot and rear mounting bushes. If either bush requires renewal, the lower arm should be taken to a VW dealer or suitably-equipped garage. A hydraulic press and suitable spacers are required to press the bushes out of the arm and install the new ones.

Refitting

8 Manoeuvre the lower arm into position, engaging it with the balljoint.

9 Fit the new pivot bolt and rear mounting bolt.

10 Position the retaining plate on the top of the arm, then refit the lower arm balljoint retaining bolts. Align the balljoint with the marks made prior to removal, then tighten the retaining bolts to the specified torque.

11 Tighten the lower arm rear mounting bolt to the specified stage 1 torque setting, then angle-tighten it through the specified stage 2 angle **(see illustration)**. Tighten the pivot bolt lightly only at this stage.

12 On 2.0 litre (GT specification) models, refit the connecting link nut (or nut and bolt) and tighten it to the specified torque setting.

13 On all other models, refit the connecting links as described in Section 8.

5.11 Tighten the lower arm rear mounting bolt to the specified Stage 1 torque

5.14 Tighten the lower arm pivot bolt to the specified torque setting

6.11 Tightening the lower arm balljoint retaining bolts to the specified torque

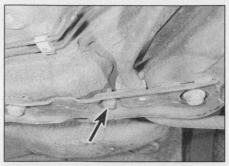

7.3 Anti-roll bar to subframe mounting bolt (arrowed) and clamp

14 Refit the roadwheel, then lower the vehicle and tighten the roadwheel bolts to the specified torque. Rock the vehicle to settle the disturbed components in position, then tighten the lower arm front pivot bolt first to the specified stage 1 torque setting, and then through the specified stage 2 angle (see illustration). Note: *On completion, it is advisable to have the camber angle checked and, if necessary, adjusted*

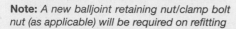

6 Front suspension lower arm balljoint - removal and refitting

Note: *A new balljoint retaining nut/clamp bolt nut (as applicable) will be required on refitting*

Removal

1 Chock the rear wheels, firmly apply the handbrake, then jack up the front of the vehicle and support on axle stands. Remove the appropriate front roadwheel.
2 Slacken and remove the bolts securing the inner driveshaft joint to the transmission flange. Support the driveshaft by suspending it with wire or string, and do not allow it to hang under its own weight.
3 Using a suitable marker pen, draw around the end of the suspension lower arm, marking the correct fitted position of balljoint. Unscrew the balljoint retaining bolts and remove the retaining plate from the top of the lower arm. Note: *On most models, the balljoint inner retaining bolt hole is slotted; on these models the inner retaining bolt can be slackened, leaving the retaining plate and bolt in position in the arm, and the balljoint disengaged from the bolt.*
4 Pull the swivel hub assembly outwards, and disengage the balljoint from the lower arm.
5 On 2.0 litre (GT specification) models, slacken the balljoint retaining nut, and unscrew it until it is positioned flush with the end of the balljoint shank threads. Release the balljoint from the swivel hub, using a universal balljoint separator, then unscrew the nut and remove the balljoint from the vehicle.
6 On all other models, slacken and remove the nut and withdraw the balljoint clamp bolt from the swivel hub. Free the balljoint shank from the hub, and remove it from the vehicle.

7 Check that the balljoint moves freely, without any sign of roughness. Check also that the balljoint gaiter shows no sign of deterioration, and is free from cracks and splits. Renew worn or damaged components as necessary.

Refitting

8 On 2.0 litre (GT specification) models, fit the balljoint to the swivel hub and fit the new retaining nut. Tighten the nut to the specified torque setting, noting that the balljoint shank can be retained with an Allen key if necessary to prevent it from rotating.
9 On all other models, slide the balljoint into the swivel hub and refit the clamp bolt. Fit a new nut to the clamp bolt, and tighten it to the specified torque.
10 Align the balljoint with the lower suspension arm, and slot it into position.
11 Refit the lower arm balljoint retaining bolts. Align the balljoint with the marks made prior to removal, then tighten the retaining bolts to the specified torque (see illustration).
12 Align the driveshaft inner joint with the transmission flange, and tighten its retaining bolts to the specified torque (see Chapter 8).
13 Refit the roadwheel, then lower the vehicle to the ground and tighten the wheel bolts to the specified torque.

7 Front anti-roll bar - removal and refitting

Removal

1 Chock the rear wheels, firmly apply the handbrake, then jack up the front of the vehicle and support on axle stands. Remove both front roadwheels.
2 Remove both connecting links (Section 8).
3 Make alignment marks between the mounting bushes and anti-roll bar, then slacken the two anti-roll bar mounting clamp retaining bolts (see illustration).
4 Remove both clamps from the subframe, and manoeuvre the anti-roll bar out from underneath the vehicle. Remove the mounting bushes from the bar.
5 Carefully examine the anti-roll bar components for signs of wear, damage or deterioration, paying particular attention to

the mounting bushes. Renew worn components as necessary.

Refitting

6 Fit the rubber mounting bushes to the anti-roll bar, aligning them with the marks made prior to removal. Rotate each bush so that its split is positioned at the rear.
7 Offer up the anti-roll bar, and manoeuvre it into position. Refit the mounting clamps, ensuring that their ends are correctly located in the hooks on the subframe, and refit the retaining bolts. Ensure that the bush markings are still aligned with the marks on the bars, then securely tighten the mounting clamp retaining bolts.
8 Refit the connecting links as described in Section 8.
9 Refit the roadwheels, then lower the vehicle to the ground and tighten the wheel bolts to the specified torque.

8 Front anti-roll bar connecting link - removal and refitting

Removal

2.0 litre (GT specification) models

1 Firmly apply the handbrake, then jack up the front of the car and support it on axle stands.
2 Slacken and remove the nut (or nut and bolt, as applicable) securing the anti-roll bar connecting link to the lower arm, and free the link from the arm (see illustration).

8.2 Slacken and remove the nut (or nut and bolt) securing the connecting link to the lower arm . . .

10

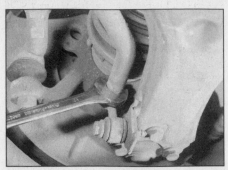

8.3 . . . then unscrew the link from the end of the anti-roll bar

3 Unscrew the connecting link upper balljoint shank from the end of the anti-roll bar, and remove the connecting link from the vehicle (see illustration).

4 On early (pre-April 1992) models, check that each balljoint moves freely, without any sign of roughness. Check also that the balljoint gaiters show no sign of deterioration, and are free from cracks and splits. On later (April 1992-on) models, inspect the balljoint as described, and check the lower bush for signs of damage or deterioration. Renew worn or damaged components as necessary.

All other models

5 Apply the handbrake, then jack up the front of the car and support it on axle stands.

6 Slacken and remove the nut and washer securing the connecting link to the lower arm. Recover the lower mounting rubber, noting which way around it is fitted.

7 Disengage the connecting link from the end of the anti-roll bar, and remove it from the lower arm, complete with the upper mounting rubber.

8 Inspect the mounting rubbers for signs of damage or deterioration, and renew as necessary. The connecting link bush can be pressed out of the link. Coat the new bush with washing-up liquid to ease installation, and press it into position.

Refitting

2.0 litre (GT specification) models

9 Screw the connecting link upper balljoint into the end of the anti-roll bar, and tighten it securely.

10 Refit the lower retaining nut (or nut and bolt) and tighten it to the specified torque setting. Lower the vehicle to the ground.

All other models

11 Apply a smear of washing-up liquid to the connecting link rubber, to aid installation.

12 Fit the upper mounting rubber to the connecting link, making sure its conical side is facing towards the lower arm.

13 Manoeuvre the link into position, and locate it on the end of the swinging arm.

14 Fit the lower mounting rubber with its conical surface facing the lower arm, then refit the washer with its collar facing away from the mounting rubber.

15 Refit the connecting link retaining nut, tighten it to the specified torque setting, then lower the vehicle to the ground.

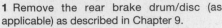

9 Rear hub assembly - removal and refitting

The rear hub is an integral part of the brake drum/disc. Refer to Chapter 9 for removal and refitting details.

10 Rear hub bearings - renewal

1 Remove the rear brake drum/disc (as applicable) as described in Chapter 9.

2 On disc brake models, lever off the cover ring from the rear of the hub.

3 On all models, using a flat-bladed screwdriver, lever the oil seal out of the rear of the hub, noting which way around it is fitted.

4 Remove the inner bearing from the drum/disc.

5 Support the hub, and tap the outer bearing outer race out of position (see illustration).

6 Turn the drum/disc over, and tap the inner bearing outer race out of position.

7 Thoroughly clean the hub, removing all traces of dirt and grease, and polish away any burrs or raised edges which might hinder reassembly. Check the hub surface for cracks or any other signs of wear or damage, and renew it if necessary. The bearings and oil seal must be renewed whenever they are disturbed, as removal will almost certainly damage the outer races. Obtain new bearings, an oil seal and a small quantity of the special grease, from your VW dealer.

8 On reassembly, apply a light film of clean engine oil to each bearing outer race, to aid installation.

9 Securely support the hub, and locate the outer bearing outer race in the hub. Tap the outer race fully into position, ensuring that it enters the hub squarely, using a suitable tubular spacer which bears only on the race outer edge (see illustration).

10 Turn the drum/disc over, and install the inner bearing outer race in the same way.

11 Ensure both outer races are correctly seated in the hub, and wipe them clean.

12 Work grease well into both the taper roller bearings, and apply a smear of grease to the outer races.

13 Fit the taper roller bearing to the inner bearing outer race (see illustration).

14 Press the oil seal into the rear of the hub, ensuring that its sealing lip is facing inwards (see illustration). Position the seal so that it is flush with the hub face, or until its lip abuts the rear of the hub. If necessary, the seal can be tapped into position using a suitable tubular drift with bears only on the hard outer edge of the seal.

15 On disc brake models, press the new cover ring fully onto the rear of the hub.

16 Turn the drum/disc over, fit the taper roller bearing to the outer race, and install the toothed washer.

17 Pack the hub bearings with grease, and install the brake drum/disc as described in Chapter 9.

10.5 Drive the outer races out of position using a hammer and punch

10.9 Drive the outer races securely into position using a socket on the outer edge

10.13 Work grease into the taper roller bearings prior to fitting them to the hub

10.14 Grease the lips of the seal, and press it into the rear of the hub

12.2 Remove the trim panel to improve access to the strut mounting (Hatchback)

12.5 Remove the trim cap from the top of the strut mounting

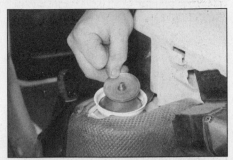

12.6 Unscrew the upper mounting top nut and remove the dished washer . . .

11 Rear stub axle - removal and refitting

Removal

1 Chock the front wheels, then jack up the rear of the car and support it on axle stands. Remove the relevant rear roadwheel.

Rear drum brake models

2 Remove the brake drum as described in Chapter 9.

3 Minimise fluid loss by first removing the master cylinder reservoir cap, and then tightening it down onto a piece of polythene, to obtain an airtight seal. Alternatively, use a brake hose clamp, a G-clamp or a similar tool to clamp the flexible hose at the nearest point to the relevant wheel cylinder.

4 Wipe away all traces of dirt around the brake pipe union at the rear of the wheel cylinder, and unscrew the union nut. Carefully ease the pipe out of the wheel cylinder, and plug or tape over its end to prevent dirt entry. Wipe off any spilt fluid immediately.

5 Slacken and remove the bolts securing the brake backplate assembly in position, and remove it along with the stub axle.

6 Inspect the stub axle surface for damage such as scoring, and renew if necessary. Do not attempt to straighten the stub axle.

Rear disc brake models

7 Remove the brake disc (see Chapter 9).

8 Slacken and remove the bolts securing the disc backplate in position and remove it along with the stub axle.

9 Inspect the stub axle for signs of damage

such as scoring and renew if necessary. Do not attempt to straighten the stub axle.

Refitting

Rear drum brake models

10 Ensure the mating surfaces of the axle, stub axle and backplate are clean and dry. Check the backplate for signs of damage, and remove any burrs with a fine file or emery cloth.

11 Offer up the stub axle and backplate assembly, and fit the washers and retaining bolts. Note that the washers are dished, and should be fitted with their concave surface facing towards the backplate. Tighten the retaining bolts to the specified torque setting.

12 Unplug the brake pipe, wipe it clean, and connect it to the rear of the wheel cylinder. Securely tighten the brake pipe union nut.

13 Remove the hose clamp or polythene, then refit the brake drum (Chapter 9).

14 Bleed the hydraulic system (Chapter 9). Providing precautions were taken to minimise brake fluid loss, it should only be necessary to bleed the relevant rear brake.

Rear disc brake models

15 Refit the stub axle and backplate as described in paragraphs 10 and 11.

16 Refit the brake disc (see Chapter 9).

12 Rear suspension strut - removal, overhaul and refitting

Removal

1 Chock the front wheels, then jack up the

rear of the car and support it on axle stands. Remove the relevant rear roadwheel.

2 To improve access on Hatchback models, tilt the seat back forwards, then unclip and remove the load compartment cover panel. Undo the retaining nuts and remove the trim panel from the side of the luggage compartment **(see illustration)**.

3 To improve access on Saloon models, starting at the bottom of the panel, unclip the left-hand door pillar upper trim panel, and free it from the pillar. Slacken and remove the retaining screw from the top of the rear pillar trim panel. Unclip the rear of the panel from the pillar, then slide the panel towards the front of the car, to disengage its retaining clips. Repeat the procedure on the right-hand side of the car, then carefully unclip the parcel shelf trim panel and remove it from the car.

4 On Estate models, tilt the seat back forwards, then unclip the vent panel from the luggage compartment panel.

5 On all models, remove the trim cap from the top of the strut mounting **(see illustration)**.

6 Slacken and remove the upper mounting top nut and remove the dished washer, noting which way around it is fitted **(see illustration)**.

7 Unscrew the upper mounting bottom nut and lift off the cover plate, upper mounting rubber and shaped washer, noting each component's correct fitted location **(see illustrations)**.

8 From underneath the car, slacken and remove the strut lower mounting nut and bolt, then manoeuvre the strut assembly out of position. Recover the lower mounting rubber from the top of the strut **(see illustrations)**.

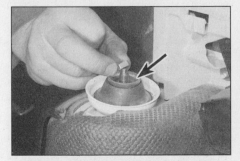

12.7a . . . then unscrew the bottom nut and lift off the cover plate (arrowed) . . .

12.7b . . . followed by the upper mounting rubber . . .

12.7c . . . and shaped washer

10

12.8a Free the lower end of the strut from the trailing arm . . .

12.8b . . . then manoeuvre the strut out from under the wheelarch . . .

12.8c . . . and recover the lower mounting rubber from the top of the strut

12.11 Hold the strut piston with a spanner whilst slackening the spring plate nut

12.14a Ensure that the cap is securely clipped onto the strut . . .

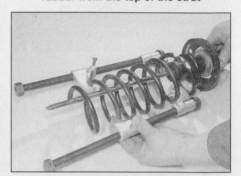

12.14b . . . and fit the coil spring, making sure it is fitted the correct way around

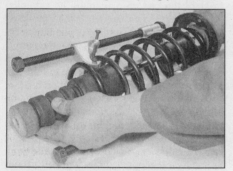

12.14c Slide on the rubber damper and protective sleeve . . .

12.14d . . . and fit the washer to the strut piston

12.14e Fit the rubber spring seat, ensuring it is located with the spring end (arrowed)

12.14f Refit the spring retaining plate

Overhaul

Warning: Before attempting to dismantle the suspension strut, a suitable tool to hold the coil spring in compression must be obtained. Adjustable coil spring compressors are readily available, and are recommended for this operation. Any attempt to dismantle the strut without such a tool is likely to result in damage or personal injury.

Hatchback and Saloon models

9 With the strut removed from the car, clean away all external dirt, then mount it upright in a vice.

10 Fit the spring compressor, and compress the coil spring until all tension is relieved from the upper spring seat.

11 Slacken and remove the spring retaining plate nut whilst retaining the strut piston with an open-ended spanner, then remove the spacer, spring retaining plate, rubber spring seat and washer from the strut **(see illustration)**.

12 Remove the coil spring, and recover rubber damper stop and protective sleeve.

13 Inspect the strut components as described in paragraphs 9 to 12 of Section 4.

14 To reassemble the strut, follow the accompanying photos, beginning with **illustration 12.14a**. Be sure to stay in order, and carefully read the caption underneath each **(see illustrations)**.

Estate models

15 Carry out the operations described in paragraphs 9 and 10.

16 Slacken and remove the spring retaining plate nut whilst retaining the strut piston with an Allen key, then remove the retaining plate and the rubber spring seat.

17 Lift off the spring and remove the rubber damper stop.

18 Inspect the strut components as described in paragraphs 9 to 12 of Section 4.

19 On reassembly, fit the spring and damper stop to the strut, then fit the rubber spring seat, making sure it is correctly located

12.14g Slide on the spacer, and refit the retaining nut. Tighten the nut to the specified torque setting

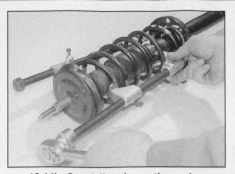

12.14h Carefully release the spring compressors, ensuring the coil spring ends are correctly located

12.23 Ensure that all the upper mounting components are correctly located, and tighten the top nut to the specified torque

against the spring end. Refit the retaining plate, and tighten its retaining nut to the specified torque setting.

Refitting

20 Fit the lower mounting rubber to the top of the strut, and manoeuvre the strut into position. Make sure the strut upper end is correctly located, and refit the lower mounting bolt, tightening its nut by hand only at this stage.

21 From inside the car, refit the washer, upper mounting rubber and cover plate. The rubber should be fitted with its tapered serrated face downwards, and the cover with its convex surface towards the rubber.

22 Fit the upper mounting bottom nut, and tighten it to the specified torque setting.

23 Fit the dished washer with its convex surface downwards, then fit the top mounting nut and tighten it to the specified torque wrench setting **(see illustration)**. Fit any trim panels removed to gain access to the strut mounting.

24 Refit the roadwheel, then lower the car to the ground and tighten the wheel bolts to the specified torque.

25 With the car standing on its wheels, rock the car to settle the strut in position, then tighten the lower mounting bolt to the specified torque setting.

13 Rear anti-roll bar - removal and refitting

The rear anti-roll bar (where fitted) runs along the length of the axle beam. It is an integral part of the axle assembly, and cannot be removed. If the anti roll bar is damaged, which is unlikely, the complete axle assembly must be renewed.

14 Rear axle assembly - removal and refitting

Removal

1 Firmly chock the front wheels, then jack up the rear of the car and support it on axle stands. Remove both rear roadwheels.

2 Referring to Chapter 9, fully slacken the handbrake cable adjuster nut.

3 On models with rear drum brakes, disconnect both cables from the handbrake lever. From underneath the car, work along the length of each cable, and free them from any retaining clips which secure them to the car underbody.

4 On models with rear disc brakes, free the end of the handbrake inner cables from the caliper handbrake levers, then remove the retaining clips and detach the cables from the calipers. Work back along the cables, freeing them from their retaining clips on the axle.

5 On models equipped with ABS, disconnect the ABS wheel sensors at the wiring connectors, and free them from any retaining clips so they are free to be removed with the axle assembly.

6 Referring to Chapter 9, on models with pressure-dependent brake regulating valves, trace the brake pipes back from the caliper/backplate to their unions, which are situated just in front of the rear axle assembly. On models with a load-dependent regulating valve, remove all traces of dirt from the valve, and mark the pipes for identification purposes. On all models, slacken the union nuts and disconnect the pipes. Plug the pipe ends, to minimise fluid loss and prevent the entry of dirt into the hydraulic system. Remove any retaining clips securing the rear section of the pipe to the car underbody.

7 Make a final check that all necessary components have been disconnected and positioned so that they will not hinder the removal procedure, then position a trolley jack beneath the centre of the rear axle assembly. Raise the jack until it is supporting the weight of the axle.

8 Using a suitable marker pen, mark the position of the axle mounting bracket retaining bolts on the bracket.

9 Slacken the remove both the left- and right-hand suspension strut lower mounting nuts and bolts.

10 Slacken and remove the axle mounting bracket retaining bolts, and carefully lower the jack and axle assembly out of position, and remove it from underneath the car. **Note:** *Do not slacken the axle pivot bolts unless*

absolutely necessary; if the bolts are to be slackened, make alignment marks between the mounting bracket and axle prior to loosening. On refitting, ensure that the mounting brackets are correctly positioned in relation to the axle beam, then tighten the pivot bolts to the specified torque.

11 Inspect the axle mountings for signs or damage or deterioration. If renewal is necessary, the task should be entrusted to a VW dealer, who will have the necessary tools required to press out the old bushes and install the new ones.

Refitting

12 Raise the rear axle into position, and insert the mounting bracket retaining bolts.

13 Fit the suspension strut lower mounting nuts and bolts, tightening them by hand only.

14 Position the axle so the mounting bracket bolts are in the centre of their slots. Have an assistant insert a suitable lever between the left-hand axle mounting bracket, and lever the pivot bush inwards until there is only a small clearance between the inner edge of the bush and the mounting bracket. Hold the axle in this position, and tighten the mounting bracket bolts to the specified torque.

15 The remainder of refitting is a reversal of the removal procedure, bearing in mind the following points:

a) *Ensure that the brake pipes, handbrake cables and wiring (as applicable) are correctly routed, and retained by all the necessary retaining clips.*

b) *Securely tighten the brake pipe union nuts.*

c) *Adjust the handbrake cable as described in Chapter 9.*

d) *On completion, lower the car to the ground, and bleed the complete braking system hydraulic circuit as described in Chapter 9.*

e) *Slacken the axle pivot bolts, then rock the car to settle all disturbed components in position. Tighten the strut lower mounting bolts and the axle pivot bolts to their specified torque settings* **(see illustrations)**.

10

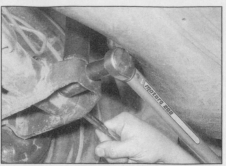

14.15a With the vehicle resting on its wheels, tighten the rear axle pivot bolts . . .

14.15b . . . and the strut lower mounting bolts to their specified torque settings

15.2 On models without an air bag, prise off the horn pad and disconnect its wiring

15.3 Unscrew the retaining nut . . .

15.4 . . . and pull the steering wheel off from the column splines

15 Steering wheel - removal and refitting

Removal

1 Set the front wheels in the straight-ahead position, and release the steering lock by inserting the ignition key.

Models without an airbag

2 Prise the horn pad out from the centre of the wheel, and disconnect the horn wiring connectors **(see illustration)**.
3 Slacken and remove the steering wheel retaining nut **(see illustration)**.
4 Mark the steering wheel and steering column shaft in relation to each other, then lift the steering wheel off the column splines **(see illustration)**. If it is tight, tap it up near the centre, using the palm of your hand, or twist it from side to side, whilst pulling upwards to release it from the shaft splines.

Models with an airbag

5 Remove the airbag unit from the centre of the steering wheel, as described in Chapter 12.
6 Slacken and remove the retaining screws, and remove the steering column upper and lower shrouds.
7 Trace the wiring back from the airbag contact unit in the steering wheel, and disconnect it at the wiring connector.
8 Remove the steering wheel as described above in paragraphs 3 and 4.
9 With the steering wheel removed, rotate the

contact unit ring slightly so its wiring connector is at the bottom (steering wheel in the straight-ahead position); this will lock the contact unit in the central position, and prevent it from being turned.

Refitting

Models without an airbag

10 Refitting is a reversal of removal, aligning the marks made on removal. Tighten the steering wheel retaining nut to the specified torque setting.

Models with an airbag

11 Manoeuvre the wheel into position, making sure the wiring connector is correctly positioned, and engage it with the column splines.
12 Refit the steering wheel retaining nut, and tighten it to the specified torque setting.
13 Reconnect the contact unit wiring

16.4a Unclip the trim panel . . .

connector, making sure the wiring is correctly routed.
14 Refit the steering column shrouds, and securely tighten the retaining screws.
15 Refit the airbag unit as described in Chapter 12.

16 Steering column - removal, inspection and refitting

Note: *New steering column shear-bolts and intermediate shaft retaining plate nuts will be required on refitting.*

Removal

1 Disconnect the battery negative terminal.
2 Remove the steering wheel as described in Section 15.
3 Remove the steering column combination switches as described in Chapter 12, Section 4.
4 Press in the locking buttons, and unclip the fusebox cover from the underside of the driver's side lower facia panel. Carefully prise the trim panel out from the top of the driver's side lower facia panel, then slacken and remove all the panel retaining screws. Carefully move the panel downwards to release it from the facia, then remove it from the car **(see illustrations)**.
5 Disconnect the wiring connector from the ignition switch, then free the wiring harness from its retaining clips on the column.
6 Prise out the retaining clip and remove the trim cover from the base of the steering column **(see illustration)**.

16.4b . . . then undo the retaining screws and remove driver's side lower facia panel

16.6 Prise out the clip and remove the trim cover from the base of the steering column

16.7b . . . then withdraw the retaining plate . . .

16.7a Unscrew the two retaining nuts . . .

16.7c . . . and slide off the connecting piece securing the shaft halves together

7 Slacken and remove the nuts from the intermediate shaft connecting piece, and slide out the retaining plate. Slide the connecting piece upwards, then separate the intermediate shaft halves and recover the connecting piece **(see illustrations)**.

8 The steering column is secured in position with shear-bolts. The shear-bolts can be extracted using a hammer and suitable chisel to tap the bolt heads around until they can be unscrewed by hand **(see illustration)**. Alternatively, drill a hole in the centre of each bolt head, and extract them using a bolt/stud extractor (sometimes called an "easy-out").

9 Pull the column upwards and away from the bulkhead, to release its lower retaining clip, and manoeuvre it out from the car **(see illustration)**.

Inspection

10 The steering column incorporates a telescopic safety feature. In the event of a front-end crash, the shaft collapses and prevents the steering wheel injuring the driver. Before refitting the steering column, examine the column and mountings for signs of damage and deformation, and renew as necessary.

11 Check the steering shaft for signs of free play in the column bushes. If any damage or wear is found on the steering column bushes, the column must be renewed as an assembly. Inspect the intermediate shaft universal joint as described in Section 18.

Refitting

12 Manoeuvre the steering column into

position, and clip the lower retaining clip securely into the bulkhead.

13 Fit the new shear-bolts, and tighten them evenly until both their heads break off **(see illustrations)**.

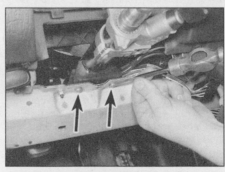

16.8 Tap the shear-bolts (arrowed) around with a hammer and chisel until they can be unscrewed by hand . . .

16.13a Secure the column in position with new shear-bolts . . .

14 Slide the intermediate shaft connecting piece onto the upper half of the shaft, then align the shaft halves and join them with the connecting piece. Insert the retaining plate and fit the new nuts, tightening them to the specified torque setting.

15 Refit the trim cover to the base of the column and secure it in position with the retaining clip.

16 Ensure that the wiring harness is correctly routed then secure it in position with the column retaining clips and reconnect the ignition switch wiring.

17 Refit the lower facia panel, tighten its retaining screws securely, and clip in the trim cover and fusebox cover.

18 Refit the combination switches as described in Chapter 12.

19 Refit the steering wheel (see Section 15).

17 Ignition switch/steering column lock - removal and refitting

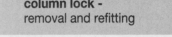

Note: *A new lock assembly shear-bolt will be required on refitting.*

Removal

1 Disconnect the battery negative terminal. Insert the key into the lock, and turn it to release the steering lock.

2 Remove the steering wheel as described in Section 15.

3 Undo the retaining screws, and remove the steering column upper and lower shrouds.

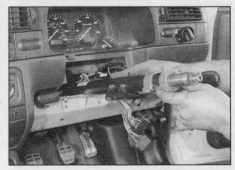

16.9 . . . then lift the steering column out of position and remove it from the vehicle

16.13b . . . and tighten both bolts until their heads break off

10

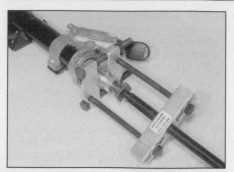

17.5 Draw the splined collar off the steering column using a suitable puller

**(column removed for clarity)
17.8a Undo the retaining screw . . .**

column lock. If all is well, tighten the shear-bolt until its head breaks off.

14 Reconnect the wiring connectors to the combination switches, and securely tighten the switch retaining screws.

15 Refit the steering column shrouds, then fit the steering wheel as described in Section 15. On completion, reconnect the battery and check the operation of the switches.

18 Steering column intermediate shaft - removal and refitting

Note: *New nuts for the intermediate shaft connecting piece retaining plate, and a new clamp bolt nut, will be required on refitting.*

Removal

1 Chock the rear wheels, firmly apply the handbrake, then jack up the front of the car and support on axle stands. Set the front wheels in the straight-ahead position.

2 Release the rubber gaiter from the bulkhead, then cut the cable-tie and free the gaiter from the steering gear. Slide the gaiter downwards to gain access to the intermediate shaft. **Note:** *If necessary, access to the shaft can also be gained from inside the car by prising out the retaining clip and removing the trim cover from the base of the steering column (see Section 16).*

3 Slacken and remove the nuts from the intermediate shaft connecting piece, and slide out the retaining plate. Slide the connecting piece upwards, then separate the intermediate shaft halves and recover the connecting piece.

4 Remove the rubber gaiter from the steering gear.

5 Using a hammer and punch, white paint or similar, mark the exact relationship between the intermediate shaft universal joint and the steering gear drive pinion. Slacken and remove the clamp bolt securing the joint to the pinion, then free the lower half of the intermediate shaft from the steering gear and remove it from the car.

6 Mark the exact relationship between the intermediate shaft upper universal joint and steering column. Slacken and remove the clamp bolt and nut, then disengage the upper

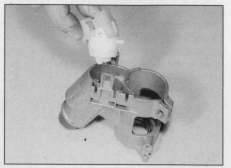

17.8b . . . and remove the ignition switch from the steering column lock assembly

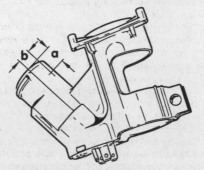

17.9 Drill a 3 mm hole at the point shown to reveal the lock cylinder detent plunger

a 12 mm   b 10 mm

Refitting

10 Fit the ignition switch (where removed) to the lock assembly, making sure it is correctly engaged with the lock cylinder, and securely tighten its retaining screw.

11 Slide the lock assembly onto the column, aligning it with the column lug, and fit the new shear-bolt. Tighten the bolt by hand only at this stage, and reconnect the wiring connector.

12 Fit the spring to the top of the column, and fit the splined collar to the shaft. Fit a washer over the end of the collar, then refit the steering wheel retaining nut, and use the nut to press the collar fully onto the steering column shaft **(see illustrations)**. Once the collar is securely seated, unscrew the nut and remove the washer.

13 Check the operation of the steering

4 Disconnect the wiring connectors from the steering column combination switches. Undo the retaining screws, and remove both switch assemblies.

5 Using a puller, carefully draw the splined collar off from the top of the steering column and recover the spring **(see illustration)**.

6 The lock assembly is secured in position with a shear-bolt. The shear-bolt can be extracted using a hammer and suitable chisel to tap the bolt head around until it can be unscrewed by hand. Alternatively, drill a hole in the centre of the bolt head, and extract it using a bolt/stud extractor (sometimes called an "easy-out").

7 Disconnect the wiring connector, then slide the lock assembly upwards and off the steering column.

8 With the lock assembly removed, slacken the retaining screw and remove the ignition switch from the base of the lock assembly **(see illustrations)**.

9 To renew the lock cylinder, carefully drill a 3 mm diameter hole in the side of the lock casting at the point shown in **illustration 17.9**. Depress the lock detent plunger, and withdraw the cylinder from the casting. Slide the new lock cylinder into position, and check it is securely retained by the detent plunger. **Note:** *Renewal of the lock cylinder is a tricky operation, and it is recommended that it is entrusted to a VW dealer. If the hole is not accurately drilled, the lock assembly casting will be ruined, and the complete lock assembly will have to be renewed.*

17.12a Refit the spring and splined collar to the top of the steering column . . .

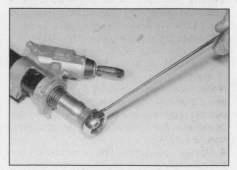

17.12b . . . press them into place by fitting and tightening the steering wheel nut

half of the intermediate shaft from the column splines and remove it from the car.

7 Inspect the intermediate shaft universal joints for signs of roughness in its bearings and ease of movement. If either joint is damaged, it should be renewed. Renew the shaft gaiter if it shows signs of damage or deterioration.

Refitting

8 Check that the front wheels are still in the straight-ahead position and the steering wheel is correctly positioned.

9 Aligning the marks made on removal, engage the upper half of the shaft with the steering column splines. Install the clamp bolt and fit the new retaining nut, tightening it to the specified torque setting.

10 Slide the rubber gaiter into position.

11 Manoeuvre the lower half of the intermediate shaft into position and, aligning the marks made prior to removal, engage it with the steering gear pinion splines. Refit the clamp bolt, and tighten it to the specified torque setting.

12 Slide the intermediate shaft connecting piece onto the upper half of the shaft, then align the shaft halves and join them with the connecting piece. Insert the retaining plate and fit the new nuts, tightening them to the specified torque setting.

13 Seat the rubber gaiter correctly in the bulkhead, then locate it on the steering gear and secure it in position with a new cable-tie. Lower the car to the ground.

---

19 Steering gear assembly - removal, overhaul and refitting

Note: New subframe mounting bolts, track rod balljoint nuts, steering gear retaining nuts, and intermediate shaft connecting piece retaining plate nuts, will be required on refitting

Removal

1 Chock the rear wheels, firmly apply the handbrake, then jack up the front of the car and support on axle stands. Remove both front roadwheels.

2 Slacken and remove the nuts securing the steering gear track rod balljoints to the swivel hubs, and release the balljoint tapered shanks using a universal balljoint separator.

3 Release the rubber gaiter from bulkhead, then cut the cable-tie and free the gaiter from the steering gear. Slide the gaiter downwards to gain access to the intermediate shaft. **Note:** If necessary, access to the shaft can also be gained from inside the car by prising out the retaining clip and removing the trim cover from the base of the steering column (see Section 16).

4 Slacken and remove the nuts, and remove the connecting piece retaining plate from the intermediate shaft. Slide the connecting piece upwards, then disengage the shaft halves and

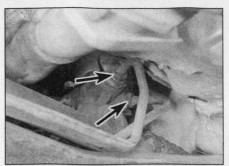

19.11 Power-assisted steering gear union nuts (arrowed)

recover the connecting piece. Remove the rubber gaiter.

5 Place a jack with a block of wood beneath the engine, to take the weight of the engine. Alternatively, attach a couple of lifting eyes to the engine, and fit a hoist or support bar to take the engine weight.

6 On manual transmission models, where necessary, slacken and remove the bolts securing the gearchange linkage pivot to the top of the steering gear (see Chapter 7A).

7 Slacken and remove all the front subframe mounting bolts, whilst making sure that the engine/transmission is adequately supported.

Manual steering gear

8 Slacken and remove the steering gear retaining nuts, and remove the mounting clamps.

9 Lower the subframe slightly, and manoeuvre the steering gear out towards the rear of the subframe. Remove the mounting rubbers from the steering gear, and inspect them for signs of damage or deterioration, renewing them if necessary. **Note:** If the steering rack is to be removed for some time, lift the engine back into position and refit the subframe mounting bolts.

Power-assisted steering gear

10 Using brake hose clamps, clamp both the supply and return hoses near the power steering fluid reservoir. This will minimise fluid loss during subsequent operations.

11 Mark the unions to ensure that they are correctly positioned on reassembly, then unscrew the feed and return pipe union nuts from the steering gear assembly; be prepared for fluid spillage, and position a suitable container beneath the pipes whilst unscrewing the union nuts **(see illustration)**. Disconnect both pipes, and recover their sealing rings. Plug the pipe ends and steering gear orifices, to prevent fluid leakage and to keep dirt out of the hydraulic system.

12 Remove the steering gear as described in paragraphs 8 and 9.

Overhaul

13 Examine the steering gear assembly for signs of wear or damage, and check that the rack moves freely throughout the full length of its travel, with no signs of roughness or excessive free play between the steering gear

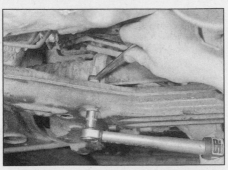

19.15 Tighten the steering gear mounting clamp bolt nuts to the specified torque

pinion and rack. It is not possible to overhaul the steering gear assembly housing components; if it is faulty, the assembly must be renewed. The only components which can be renewed individually are the steering gear gaiters, the track rod balljoints and the track rods. Track rod balljoint and steering gear gaiter renewal procedures are covered later in this Chapter. Track rod renewal should be entrusted to a VW dealer as it is a fiddly task, requiring special tools if it is to be carried out correctly and safely.

Refitting

Manual steering gear

14 Fit the mounting rubbers to the steering gear, and manoeuvre the assembly into position on the subframe.

15 Refit the mounting clamps and fit the new retaining nuts. Tighten the retaining nuts to the specified torque setting **(see illustration)**.

16 Carefully raise the subframe into position, and fit the new mounting bolts. Tighten the subframe mounting bolts first to the specified Stage 1 torque setting, then go around and tighten all the bolts through the specified Stage 2 angle.

17 Slide the intermediate shaft connecting piece onto the upper half of the shaft, then align the shaft halves and join them with the connecting piece. Insert the retaining plate and fit the new nuts, tightening them to the specified torque setting.

18 Seat the rubber gaiter correctly in the bulkhead, then locate it on the steering gear and secure it in position with a new cable-tie.

19 Reconnect the track rod balljoints to the swivel hubs and fit the new retaining nuts, tightening them to the specified torque setting.

20 Refit the front wheels, and lower the car to the ground. On completion check and, if necessary, adjust the front wheel alignment as described in Section 24.

Power-assisted steering gear

21 Refit the steering gear as described in paragraphs 14 and 15.

22 Wipe clean the feed and return pipe unions, then refit them to their respective positions on the steering gear, and tighten the union nuts to their specified torque settings. Ensure that the pipes are correctly routed,

10

and are securely held by all the necessary retaining clips.

23 Carry out the operations described in paragraphs 16 to 20.

20 Steering gear rubber gaiters - renewal

1 Remove the track rod balljoint as described in Section 23.

2 Mark the correct fitted position of the gaiter on the track rod, then release the retaining clip(s) and slide the gaiter off the steering gear housing and track rod end.

3 Thoroughly clean the track rod and the steering gear housing, using fine abrasive paper to polish off any corrosion, burrs or sharp edges, which might damage the new gaiter's sealing lips on installation. Scrape off all the grease from the old gaiter, and apply it to the track rod inner balljoint. (This assumes that grease has not been lost or contaminated as a result of damage to the old gaiter. Use fresh grease if in doubt).

4 Carefully slide the new gaiter onto the track rod end, and locate it on the steering gear housing. Align the outer edge of the gaiter with the mark made on the track rod prior to removal. Make sure the gaiter is not twisted, then lift the outer sealing lip of the gaiter to equalise air pressure within the gaiter.

5 Secure it in position with new retaining clip(s). Where crimped-type clips are used, pull the clip as tight as possible, and locate the hooks on the clip in their slots. Remove any slack in the gaiter retaining clip by carefully compressing the raised section of the clip. In the absence of the special tool, a pair of side cutters may be used, taking care not to actually cut the clip.

6 Refit the track rod balljoint as described in Section 23.

21 Power steering system - bleeding

1 With the engine stopped, fill the fluid reservoir right up to the top with the specified type of fluid.

2 Slowly move the steering from lock-to-lock several times to purge out the trapped air, then top-up the level in the fluid reservoir. Repeat this procedure until the fluid level in the reservoir does not drop any further.

3 Have an assistant start the engine, whilst you keep watch on the fluid level. Be prepared to add more fluid as the engine starts, as the fluid level is likely to drop quickly. The fluid level must be kept above the "MIN" mark at all times.

4 With the engine running at idle speed, turn the steering wheel slowly two or three times approximately 45° to the left and right of centre, then turn the wheel twice from lock to lock. Do not hold the wheel on either lock, as this imposes excessive strain upon the

hydraulic system. Repeat this procedure until bubbles cease to appear in fluid reservoir.

5 If, when turning the steering, an odd noise is heard from the fluid lines, it indicates there is still air in the system. Check this by turning the wheels to the straight-ahead position and switching off the engine. If the fluid level in the reservoir rises, then air is present in the system, and further bleeding is necessary.

6 Once all traces of air have been removed from the power steering hydraulic system, turn the engine off and allow the system to cool. Once cool, check that fluid level is up to the maximum mark on the power steering fluid reservoir, topping-up if necessary.

22 Power steering pump - removal and refitting

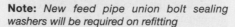

Note: *New feed pipe union bolt sealing washers will be required on refitting*

Removal

1 Slacken the steering pump pulley retaining bolts. Working as described in Chapter 1, release the drivebelt tension and unhook the drivebelt from the pump pulley.

2 Using brake hose clamps, clamp both the supply and return hoses near the power steering fluid reservoir. This will minimise fluid loss during subsequent operations. Continue as described under the relevant sub-heading.

1.4 litre and all 1.6 litre (except AEK engine) models

3 Unscrew the retaining bolts and remove the pulley from the power steering pump, noting which way around it is fitted.

4 Slacken the retaining clip, and disconnect the fluid supply hose from the pump. Where a crimp-type clip is still fitted, cut the clip and discard it; replace it with a standard worm-drive hose clip on refitting. Slacken the union bolt, and disconnect the feed pipe from the pump, along with its sealing washers; discard the washers - new ones should be used on refitting. Be prepared for some fluid spillage as the pipe and hose are disconnected, and plug the hose/pipe end and pump unions, to minimise fluid loss and prevent the entry of dirt into the system.

5 Slacken and remove the three bolts securing the power steering pump to its mounting bracket, and remove the pump from the engine compartment.

1.6 litre (AEK engine) models and all 1.8, 1.9 and 2.0 litre models

6 Carry out the operations described in paragraphs 3 and 4.

7 Slacken and remove the power steering pump pivot bolt and the adjuster bolt, and remove the pump and swivel bracket assembly from the main mounting bracket. If necessary, slacken and remove the pump mounting bolts, and separate the pump and mounting bracket; the mounting bracket can also be unbolted from the engine.

Refitting

1.4 litre and all 1.6 litre (except AEK engine) models

8 Prior to fitting, ensure that the pump is primed by injecting hydraulic fluid in through the supply hose union and rotating the pump shaft.

9 Manoeuvre the pump into position and refit the mounting bolts, tightening them to the specified torque setting.

10 Position a new sealing washer on each side of the feed pipe union, then fit the union bolt and tighten it to the specified torque setting. Refit the supply pipe to the pump, and securely tighten its retaining clip. Remove the brake hose clamps used to minimise fluid loss.

11 Refit the drive pulley, making sure it is the correct way around, and fit its retaining bolts.

12 Refit the drivebelt to the pump pulley, and tension it as described in Chapter 1. Once the belt is tensioned, tighten the pulley retaining bolts to the specified torque setting.

13 On completion, bleed the hydraulic system as described in Section 21.

1.6 litre (AEK engine) models and all 1.8, 1.9 and 2.0 litre models

14 Where necessary, refit the mounting bracket to the engine, and tighten its mounting bolts to the specified torque.

15 Join the pump and swivel bracket, and tighten the mounting bolts to the specified torque setting.

16 Prime the pump as described in paragraph 8.

17 Move the pump assembly into position and insert the pivot bolt and adjuster bolt, tighten them loosely only at this stage.

18 Carry out the operations described in paragraphs 10 to 13.

23 Track rod balljoint - removal and refitting

Note: *A new balljoint retaining nut will be required on refitting.*

Removal

1 Apply the handbrake, then jack up the front of the car and support it on axle stands. Remove the appropriate front roadwheel.

2 If the balljoint is to be re-used, use a straight-edge and a scriber, or similar, to mark its relationship to the track rod.

3 Hold the track rod, and unscrew the balljoint locknut by a quarter of a turn. Do not move the locknut from this position, as it will serve as a handy reference mark on refitting.

4 Slacken and remove the nut securing the track rod balljoint to the swivel hub, and release the balljoint tapered shank using a universal balljoint separator.

5 Counting the **exact** number of turns necessary to do so, unscrew the balljoint from the track rod end.

6 Count the number of exposed threads

23.9 Tightening the track rod balljoint retaining nut to the specified torque

between the end of the balljoint and the locknut, and record this figure.

7 Carefully clean the balljoint and the threads. Renew the balljoint if its movement is sloppy or too stiff, if excessively worn, or if damaged in any way; carefully check the stud taper and threads. If the balljoint gaiter is damaged, the complete balljoint assembly must be renewed; it is not possible to obtain the gaiter separately.

Refitting

8 Screw the balljoint into the track rod by the number of turns noted on removal. This should bring the balljoint locknut to within a quarter of a turn from the locknut, with the alignment marks that were made on removal (if applicable) lined up.

9 Refit the balljoint shank to the swivel hub, then fit a new retaining nut and tighten it to the specified torque **(see illustration)**.

10 Refit the roadwheel, then lower the car to the ground and tighten the roadwheel bolts to the specified torque.

11 Check and, if necessary, adjust the front wheel toe setting as described in Section 24, then tighten the balljoint locknut to the specified torque setting.

24 Wheel alignment and steering angles - general information

Definitions

1 A car's steering and suspension geometry is defined in four basic settings - all angles are expressed in degrees (toe settings are also expressed as a measurement); the steering axis is defined as an imaginary line drawn through the axis of the suspension strut, extended where necessary to contact the ground.

2 **Camber** is the angle between each roadwheel and a vertical line drawn through its centre and tyre contact patch, when viewed from the front or rear of the car. "Positive" camber is when the roadwheels are tilted outwards from the vertical at the top;

"negative" camber is when they are tilted inwards.

3 Camber angle is adjustable, and can be checked using a camber checking gauge.

4 **Castor** is the angle between the steering axis and a vertical line drawn through each roadwheel's centre and tyre contact patch, when viewed from the side of the car. "Positive" castor is when the steering axis is tilted so that it contacts the ground ahead of the vertical; "negative" castor is when it contacts the ground behind the vertical.

5 Castor is not adjustable, and is given for reference only; while it can be checked using a castor checking gauge, if the figure obtained is significantly different from that specified, the car must be taken for careful checking by a professional, as the fault can only be caused by wear or damage to the body or suspension components.

6 **Toe** is the difference, viewed from above, between lines drawn through the roadwheel centres and the car's centre-line. "Toe-in" is when the roadwheels point inwards, towards each other at the front, while "toe-out" is when they splay outwards from each other at the front.

7 The front wheel toe setting is adjusted by screwing the right-hand track rod in or out of its balljoint, to alter the effective length of the track rod assembly.

8 Rear wheel toe setting is not adjustable, and is given for reference only. While it can be checked, if the figure obtained is significantly different from that specified, the car must be taken for careful checking by a professional, as the fault can only be caused by wear or damage to the body or suspension components.

Checking and adjustment

Front wheel toe setting

9 Due to the special measuring equipment necessary to check the wheel alignment, and the skill required to use it properly, the checking and adjustment of these settings is best left to a VW dealer or similar expert. Note that most tyre-fitting centres now possess sophisticated checking equipment.

10 To check the toe setting, a tracking gauge must first be obtained. Two types of gauge are available, and can be obtained from motor accessory shops. The first type measures the distance between the front and rear inside edges of the roadwheels, as previously described, with the car stationary. The second type, known as a "scuff plate", measures the actual position of the contact surface of the tyre, in relation to the road surface, with the car in motion. This is achieved by pushing or driving the front tyre over a plate, which then moves slightly according to the scuff of the tyre, and shows this movement on a scale.

Both types have their advantages and disadvantages, but either can give satisfactory results if used correctly and carefully.

11 Make sure that the steering is in the straight-ahead position when making measurements.

12 If adjustment is necessary, apply the handbrake, then jack up the front of the car and support it securely on axle stands. Adjustment is made on the right-hand track rod (right- and left-hand are as seen from the driver's seat).

13 First clean the track rod threads; if they are corroded, apply penetrating fluid before starting adjustment. Release the rubber gaiter outer clips, peel back the gaiters and apply a smear of grease. This will ensure that both gaiters are free and will not be twisted or strained as their respective track rods are rotated.

14 Retain the track rod with a suitable spanner, and slacken the balljoint locknut fully. Alter the length of the track rod, by screwing them into or out of the balljoints. Rotate the track rod using an open-ended spanner fitted to the track rod flats provided; shortening the track rods (screwing them onto their balljoints) will reduce toe-in/increase toe-out.

15 When the setting is correct, hold the track rod and tighten the balljoint locknut to the specified torque setting. If after adjustment, the steering wheel spokes are no longer horizontal when the wheels are in the straight-ahead position, remove the steering wheel and reposition it (see Section 15).

16 Check that the toe setting has been correctly adjusted by lowering the car to the ground and re-checking the toe setting; re-adjust if necessary. Ensure that the rubber gaiters are seated correctly and are not twisted or strained, and secure them in position with the retaining clips; where necessary, fit a new retaining clip (refer to Section 20).

Rear wheel toe setting

17 The procedure for checking the rear toe setting is the same as described for the front setting in paragraph 10. The setting is not adjustable - see paragraph 8.

Front wheel camber angle

18 Checking and adjusting the front wheel camber angle should be entrusted to a VW dealer or other suitably-equipped specialist. Note that most tyre-fitting centres now possess sophisticated checking equipment. For reference, adjustments are made by slackening the suspension strut-to-swivel hub mounting bolts, and repositioning the swivel hub assembly.

10

Notes

Chapter 11
Bodywork and fittings

Contents

Degrees of difficulty

Easy, suitable for novice with little experience	Fairly easy, suitable for beginner with some experience	Fairly difficult, suitable for competent DIY mechanic	Difficult, suitable for experienced DIY mechanic	Very difficult, suitable for expert DIY or professional

Specifications

Torque wrench settings	Nm	lbf ft
Bonnet lock retaining bolts	12	9
Door hinge retaining bolts	36	27
Door hinge pin grub bolt	23	18
Door check link pivot bolt nut	7	5
Door handle retaining bolt	8	6
Door lock retaining bolts	8	6
Door window glass clamp nuts	10	7
Door window glass regulator retaining bolts	10	7
Front seat mounting bolt nut	8	6

1 General information

The bodyshell is made of pressed-steel sections, and is available in both three- and five-door Hatchback, four-door Saloon and Estate versions. Most components are welded together, but some use is made of structural adhesives; the front wings are bolted on.

The bonnet, door, and some other vulnerable panels are made of zinc-coated metal, and are further protected by being coated with an anti-chip primer before being sprayed.

Extensive use is made of plastic materials, mainly in the interior, but also in exterior components. The front and rear bumpers and front grille are injection-moulded from a synthetic material that is very strong and yet light. Plastic components such as wheelarch liners are fitted to the underside of the vehicle, to improve the body's resistance to corrosion.

2 Maintenance - bodywork and underframe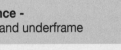

The general condition of a vehicle's bodywork is the one thing that significantly affects its value. Maintenance is easy, but needs to be regular. Neglect, particularly after minor damage, can lead quickly to further deterioration and costly repair bills. It is important also to keep watch on those parts of the vehicle not immediately visible, for instance the underside, inside all the wheelarches, and the lower part of the engine compartment.

The basic maintenance routine for the bodywork is washing - preferably with a lot of water, from a hose. This will remove all the loose solids which may have stuck to the vehicle. It is important to flush these off in such a way as to prevent grit from scratching the finish. The wheelarches and underframe need washing in the same way, to remove any accumulated mud which will retain moisture and tend to encourage rust. Paradoxically enough, the best time to clean the underframe and wheelarches is in wet weather, when the mud is thoroughly wet and soft. In very wet weather, the underframe is usually cleaned of large accumulations automatically, and this is a good time for inspection.

Periodically, except on vehicles with a wax-based underbody protective coating, it is a good idea to have the whole of the underframe of the vehicle steam-cleaned, engine compartment included, so that a thorough inspection can be carried out to see

11

what minor repairs and renovations are necessary. Steam cleaning is available at many garages, and is necessary for the removal of the accumulation of oily grime, which sometimes is allowed to become thick in certain areas. If steam-cleaning facilities are not available, there are some excellent grease solvents available which can be brush-applied; the dirt can then be simply hosed off. Note that these methods should not be used on vehicles with wax-based underbody protective coating, or the coating will be removed. Such vehicles should be inspected annually, preferably just before Winter, when the underbody should be washed down, and any damage to the wax coating repaired. Ideally, a completely fresh coat should be applied. It would also be worth considering the use of wax-based protection for injection into door panels, sills, box sections, etc, as an additional safeguard against rust damage, where such protection is not provided by the vehicle manufacturer.

After washing paintwork, wipe off with a chamois leather to give an unspotted clear finish. A coat of clear protective wax polish will give added protection against chemical pollutants in the air. If the paintwork sheen has dulled or oxidised, use a cleaner/polisher combination to restore the brilliance of the shine. This requires a little effort, but such dulling is usually caused because regular washing has been neglected. Care needs to be taken with metallic paintwork, as special non-abrasive cleaner/polisher is required to avoid damage to the finish. Always check that the door and ventilator opening drain holes and pipes are completely clear, so that water can be drained out. Brightwork should be treated in the same way as paintwork. Windscreens and windows can be kept clear of the smeary film which often appears, by proprietary glass cleaner. Never use any form of wax or other body or chromium polish on glass.

3 Maintenance -
upholstery and carpets

Mats and carpets should be brushed or vacuum-cleaned regularly, to keep them free of grit. If they are badly stained, remove them from the vehicle for scrubbing or sponging, and make quite sure they are dry before refitting. Seats and interior trim panels can be kept clean by wiping with a damp cloth. If they do become stained (which can be more apparent on light-coloured upholstery), use a little liquid detergent and a soft nail brush to scour the grime out of the grain of the material. Do not forget to keep the headlining clean in the same way as the upholstery. When using liquid cleaners inside the vehicle, do not over-wet the surfaces being cleaned. Excessive damp could get into the seams and padded interior, causing stains, offensive odours or even rot. If the inside of the vehicle

gets wet accidentally, it is worthwhile taking some trouble to dry it out properly, particularly where carpets are involved. *Do not leave oil or electric heaters inside the vehicle for this purpose.*

4 Minor body damage - repair

Repairs of minor scratches in bodywork

If the scratch is very superficial, and does not penetrate to the metal of the bodywork, repair is very simple. Lightly rub the area of the scratch with a paintwork renovator or a very fine cutting paste to remove loose paint from the scratch, and to clear the surrounding bodywork of wax polish. Rinse the area with clean water.

Apply touch-up paint to the scratch using a fine paint brush; continue to apply fine layers of paint until the surface of the paint in the scratch is level with the surrounding paintwork. Allow the new paint at least two weeks to harden, then blend it into the surrounding paintwork by rubbing the scratch area with a paintwork renovator or a very fine cutting paste. Finally, apply wax polish.

Where the scratch has penetrated right through to the metal of the bodywork, causing the metal to rust, a different repair technique is required. Remove any loose rust from the bottom of the scratch with a penknife, then apply rust-inhibiting paint to prevent the formation of rust in the future. Using a rubber or nylon applicator, fill the scratch with bodystopper paste. If required, this paste can be mixed with cellulose thinners to provide a very thin paste which is ideal for filling narrow scratches. Before the stopper-paste in the scratch hardens, wrap a piece of smooth cotton rag around the top of a finger. Dip the finger in cellulose thinners, and quickly sweep it across the surface of the stopper-paste in the scratch; this will ensure that the surface of the stopper-paste is slightly hollowed. The scratch can now be painted over as described earlier in this Section.

Repairs of dents in bodywork

When deep denting of the vehicle's bodywork has taken place, the first task is to pull the dent out, until the affected bodywork almost attains its original shape. There is little point in trying to restore the original shape completely, as the metal in the damaged area will have stretched on impact, and cannot be reshaped fully to its original contour. It is better to bring the level of the dent up to a point which is about 3 mm below the level of the surrounding bodywork. In cases where the dent is very shallow anyway, it is not worth trying to pull it out at all. If the underside of the dent is accessible, it can be hammered out gently from behind, using a mallet with a wooden or plastic head. Whilst doing this,

hold a suitable block of wood firmly against the outside of the panel, to absorb the impact from the hammer blows and thus prevent a large area of the bodywork from being "belled-out".

Should the dent be in a section of the bodywork which has a double skin, or some other factor making it inaccessible from behind, a different technique is called for. Drill several small holes through the metal inside the area - particularly in the deeper section. Then screw long self-tapping screws into the holes, just sufficiently for them to gain a good purchase in the metal. Now the dent can be pulled out by pulling on the protruding heads of the screws with a pair of pliers.

The next stage of the repair is the removal of the paint from the damaged area, and from an inch or so of the surrounding "sound" bodywork. This is accomplished most easily by using a wire brush or abrasive pad on a power drill, although it can be done just as effectively by hand, using sheets of abrasive paper. To complete the preparation for filling, score the surface of the bare metal with a screwdriver or the tang of a file, or alternatively, drill small holes in the affected area. This will provide a good "key" for the filler paste.

To complete the repair, see the Section on filling and respraying.

Repairs of rust holes or gashes in bodywork

Remove all paint from the affected area, and from an inch or so of the surrounding "sound" bodywork, using an abrasive pad or a wire brush on a power drill. If these are not available, a few sheets of abrasive paper will do the job most effectively. With the paint removed, you will be able to judge the severity of the corrosion, and therefore decide whether to renew the whole panel (if this is possible) or to repair the affected area. New body panels are not as expensive as most people think, and it is often quicker and more satisfactory to fit a new panel than to attempt to repair large areas of corrosion.

Remove all fittings from the affected area, except those which will act as a guide to the original shape of the damaged bodywork (eg headlamp shells etc). Then, using tin snips or a hacksaw blade, remove all loose metal and any other metal badly affected by corrosion. Hammer the edges of the hole inwards, to create a slight depression for the filler paste.

Wire-brush the affected area to remove the powdery rust from the surface of the remaining metal. Paint the affected area with rust-inhibiting paint; if the back of the rusted area is accessible, treat this also.

Before filling can take place, it will be necessary to block the hole in some way. This can be achieved with aluminium or plastic mesh, or aluminium tape.

Aluminium or plastic mesh, or glass-fibre matting, is probably the best material to use for a large hole. Cut a piece to the approximate size and shape of the hole to be filled, then position it in the hole so that its edges are below the level of the surrounding bodywork. It can be retained in position by several blobs of filler paste around its periphery.

Aluminium tape should be used for small or very narrow holes. Pull a piece off the roll, trim it to the approximate size and shape required, then pull off the backing paper (if used) and stick the tape over the hole; it can be overlapped if the thickness of one piece is insufficient. Burnish down the edges of the tape with the handle of a screwdriver or similar, to ensure that the tape is securely attached to the metal underneath.

Bodywork repairs - filling and respraying

Before using this Section, see the Sections on dent, deep scratch, rust holes and gash repairs.

Many types of bodyfiller are available, but generally speaking, those proprietary kits which contain a tin of filler paste and a tube of resin hardener are best for this type of repair which can be used directly from the tube. A wide, flexible plastic or nylon applicator will be found invaluable for imparting a smooth and well-contoured finish to the surface of the filler.

Mix up a little filler on a clean piece of card or board - measure the hardener carefully (follow the maker's instructions on the pack), otherwise the filler will set too rapidly or too slowly. Using the applicator, apply the filler paste to the prepared area; draw the applicator across the surface of the filler to achieve the correct contour and to level the surface. When a contour that approximates to the correct one is achieved, stop working the paste - if you carry on too long, the paste will become sticky and begin to "pick-up" on the applicator. Continue to add thin layers of filler paste at 20-minute intervals, until the level of the filler is just proud of the surrounding bodywork.

Once the filler has hardened, the excess can be removed using a metal plane or file. From then on, progressively-finer grades of abrasive paper should be used, starting with a 40-grade production paper, and finishing with a 400-grade wet-and-dry paper. Always wrap the abrasive paper around a flat rubber, cork, or wooden block - otherwise the surface of the filler will not be completely flat. During the smoothing of the filler surface, the wet-and-dry paper should be periodically rinsed in water. This will ensure that a very smooth finish is imparted to the filler at the final stage.

At this stage, the "dent" should be surrounded by a ring of bare metal, which in turn should be encircled by the finely "feathered" edge of the good paintwork. Rinse the repair area with clean water, until all the dust produced by the rubbing-down operation has gone.

Spray the whole area with a light coat of primer - this will show up any imperfections in the surface of the filler. Repair these imperfections with fresh filler paste or bodystopper, and again smooth the surface with abrasive paper. If bodystopper is used, it can be mixed with cellulose thinners, to form a thin paste which is ideal for filling small holes. Repeat this spray-and-repair procedure until you are satisfied that the surface of the filler, and the feathered edge of the paintwork, are perfect. Clean the repair area with clean water, and allow to dry fully.

The repair area is now ready for final spraying. Paint spraying must be carried out in a warm, dry, windless and dust-free atmosphere. This condition can be created artificially if you have access to a large indoor working area, but if you are forced to work in the open, you will have to pick your day very carefully. If you are working indoors, dousing the floor in the work area with water will help to settle the dust which would otherwise be in the atmosphere. If the repair area is confined to one body panel, mask off the surrounding panels; this will help to minimise the effects of a slight mis-match in paint colours. Bodywork fittings (eg chrome strips, door handles etc) will also need to be masked off. Use genuine masking tape, and several thickness of newspaper, for the masking operations.

Before starting to spray, agitate the aerosol can thoroughly, then spray a test area (an old tin, or similar) until the technique is mastered. Cover the repair area with a thick coat of primer; the thickness should be built up using several thin layers of paint, rather than one thick one. Using 400 grade wet-and-dry paper, rub down the surface of the primer until it is smooth. While doing this, the work area should be thoroughly doused with water, and the wet-and-dry paper periodically rinsed in water. Allow to dry before spraying on more paint.

Spray on the top coat, again building up the thickness by using several thin layers of paint. Start spraying in the centre of the repair area, and then, using a circular motion, work outwards until the whole repair area and about 2 inches of the surrounding original paintwork is covered. Remove all masking material 10 to 15 minutes after spraying on the final coat of paint.

Allow the new paint at least two weeks to harden, then, using a paintwork renovator or a very fine cutting paste, blend the edges of the paint into the existing paintwork. Finally, apply wax polish.

Plastic components

With the use of more and more plastic body components by the vehicle manufacturers (eg bumpers, spoilers, and in some cases major body panels), rectification of more serious damage to such items has become a matter of either entrusting repair work to a specialist in this field, or renewing complete components. Repair of such damage by the DIY owner is not feasible, owing to the cost of the equipment and materials required for effecting such repairs. The basic technique involves making a groove along the line of the crack in the plastic, using a rotary burr in a power drill. The damaged part is then welded back together, using a hot air gun to heat up and fuse a plastic filler rod into the groove. Any excess plastic is then removed, and the area rubbed down to a smooth finish. It is important that a filler rod of the correct plastic is used, as body components can be made of a variety of different types (eg polycarbonate, ABS, polypropylene).

Damage of a less serious nature (abrasions, minor cracks etc) can be repaired by the DIY owner using a two-part epoxy filler repair material which can be used directly from the tube. Once mixed in equal proportions, this is used in similar fashion to the bodywork filler used on metal panels. The filler is usually cured in twenty to thirty minutes, ready for sanding and painting.

If the owner is renewing a complete component himself, or if he has repaired it with epoxy filler, he will be left with the problem of finding a suitable paint for finishing which is compatible with the type of plastic used. At one time, the use of a universal paint was not possible, owing to the complex range of plastics met with in body component applications. Standard paints, generally speaking, will not bond to plastic or rubber satisfactorily, but professional matched paints, to match any plastic or rubber finish, can be obtained from some dealers. However, it is now possible to obtain a plastic body parts finishing kit which consists of a pre-primer treatment, a primer and coloured top coat. Full instructions are normally supplied with a kit, but basically the method of use is to first apply the pre-primer to the component concerned, and allow it to dry for up to 30 minutes. Then the primer is applied, and left to dry for about an hour before finally applying the special-coloured top coat. The result is a correctly coloured component, where the paint will flex with the plastic or rubber, a property that standard paint does not normally possess.

5 Major body damage - repair

Where serious damage has occurred, or large areas need renewal due to neglect, it means that complete new panels will need welding-in, and this is best left to professionals. If the damage is due to impact, it will also be necessary to check completely the alignment of the bodyshell, and this can only be carried out accurately by a VW dealer using special jigs. If the body is left misaligned, it is primarily dangerous, as the car will not handle properly, and secondly, uneven stresses will be imposed on the steering, suspension and possibly transmission, causing abnormal wear, or complete failure, particularly to such items as the tyres.

11

6.2a Release the upper . . .

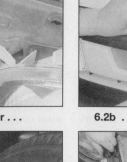

6.2b . . . and lower retaining clips . . .

6.2c . . . then pull the grille forwards

6.3 Remove the fasteners (arrowed) securing the wheelarch liner to the bumper

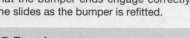

6.4a Slacken and remove the three upper retaining screws (arrowed) . . .

6.4b . . . and the five lower bumper retaining screws (arrowed)

6 Front bumper - removal and refitting

Removal

1 Apply the handbrake, then jack up the front of the vehicle and support it on axle stands (see "*Jacking and vehicle support*").
2 Using a suitable screwdriver, carefully release the radiator grille upper and lower retaining lugs then move the grille forwards and away from the vehicle **(see illustrations)**.
3 Press out their centre pins and remove the fasteners securing the wheelarch liners to the bumper ends. Note that new fasteners will be required on refitting if the centre pins are not recovered **(see illustration)**. Also undo the screws securing the liners to the bumper.
4 Working around the bumper, slacken and remove its eight retaining bolts **(see illustrations)**.

5 Disconnect the wiring connectors from the front direction indicators and (where necessary) foglamps and free the wiring from any relevant retaining clips so that the lamps are free to be removed with the bumper.
6 On models with headlamp washers, remove the washer jets as described in Chapter 12.
7 Carefully release the bumper left- and right-hand ends, and pull the bumper away from the vehicle in a forwards direction.

Refitting

8 Refitting is a reverse of removal, ensuring that the bumper ends engage correctly with the slides as the bumper is refitted.

7 Rear bumper - removal and refitting

Removal

1 To improve access, chock the front wheels,

then jack up the rear of the vehicle and support it on axle stands (see "*Jacking and vehicle support*").
2 Slacken and remove the bolts securing the bottom of the bumper in position.
3 Carefully prise out the trim caps from the top edge of the bumper to gain access to the upper retaining bolts **(see illustration)**.
4 Slacken and remove the upper retaining bolts then pull the bumper away from the vehicle in a rearwards direction. Inspect the bumper shock absorbers, which are mounted onto the rear of the vehicle, for signs of damage or deformation and renew if necessary **(see illustrations)**.

Refitting

5 Refitting is a reverse of the removal procedure, ensuring that the bumper ends engage correctly with the slides as the bumper is refitted.

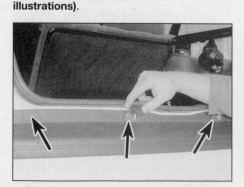

7.3 Unclip the trim caps from the rear bumper to access the screws (arrowed)

7.4a Remove the rear bumper from the vehicle . . .

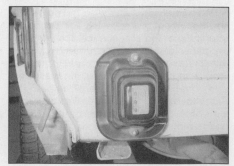

7.4b . . . and inspect the bumper shock absorbers for signs of damage

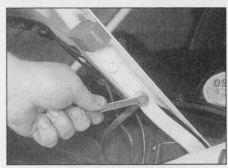

8.2a Unscrew the retaining nut . . .

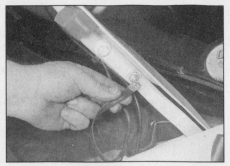

8.2b . . . and free the earth strap from the left-hand side of the bonnet

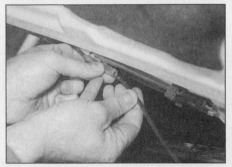

8.3a Disconnect the washer hose from the windscreen jets . . .

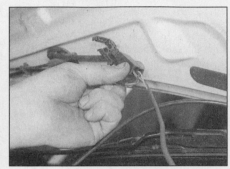

8.3b . . . and on models with heated washer jets also disconnect the wiring connectors

8 Bonnet - removal, refitting and adjustment

Removal

1 Open the bonnet and have an assistant support it. Using a pencil or felt tip pen, mark the outline of each bonnet hinge relative to the bonnet, to use as a guide on refitting.
2 Undo the retaining nut and free the earth strap from the left-hand bonnet retaining bolt **(see illustrations)**.
3 Disconnect the washer hose from the windscreen washer jets and, where necessary, disconnect the wiring from the jet heating elements **(see illustrations)**.
4 Undo the bonnet retaining bolts and, with the help of an assistant, carefully lift the bonnet clear. Store the bonnet out of the way in a safe place.
5 Inspect the bonnet hinges for signs of wear and free play at the pivots, and if necessary renew. Each hinge is secured to the body by two bolts; note that one of the left-hand hinge retaining bolts will have the earth strap attached to it. Mark the position of the hinge on the body then undo the retaining bolts and remove it from the vehicle. On refitting, align the new hinge with the marks and securely tighten the retaining bolts.

Refitting and adjustment

6 With the aid of an assistant, offer up the bonnet and loosely fit the retaining bolts. Align the hinges with the marks made on removal,

then tighten the retaining bolts securely. Reconnect the earth strap and securely tighten its retaining nut.
7 Close the bonnet, and check for alignment with the adjacent panels. If necessary, slacken the hinge bolts and re-align the bonnet to suit. Once the bonnet is correctly aligned, securely tighten the hinge bolts. Once the bonnet is correctly aligned, check that the bonnet fastens and releases satisfactorily.

9 Bonnet release cable - removal and refitting

Removal

1 Mark the position of the bonnet lock on the crossmember with a suitable marker pen then slacken and remove the two bonnet lock

10.2 Slacken and remove the lock retaining bolts (A) and the support strut bolt (B) . . .

retaining bolts. Free the lock from the crossmember then release the outer cable from the lock lever and detach the inner cable from the lock body.
2 Work back along the length of the cable, noting its correct routing, and free it from the retaining clips and ties. Tie a length of string to the end of the cable.
3 From inside the vehicle, slacken and remove the screws securing the bonnet release handle to the vehicle.
4 Release the cable grommet from the bulkhead and withdraw the lever and cable assembly. Once the cable is free, untie the string and leave it in position in the vehicle; the string can then be used to draw the new cable back into position.

Refitting

5 Tie the inner end of the string to the end of the cable, then use the string to draw the bonnet release cable through into the engine compartment. Once the cable is through, untie the string.
6 Manoeuvre the bonnet release lever back into position, and securely tighten its retaining screws. Seat the rubber grommet in the bulkhead.
7 Ensure that the cable is correctly routed, and secured to all the relevant retaining clips.
8 Refit the bonnet lock as described in Section 10.

10 Bonnet lock - removal and refitting

Removal

1 Open up the bonnet then, using a suitable screwdriver, carefully release the radiator grille upper and lower retaining lugs then move the grille forwards and away from the vehicle.
2 Using a suitable marker pen, mark the outline of the bonnet lock on the crossmember then slacken and remove the two lock retaining bolts **(see illustration)**.
3 Undo the retaining bolt and slide the lock support strut out from the bonnet crossmember **(see illustration)**.
4 Free the release outer cable from the lock

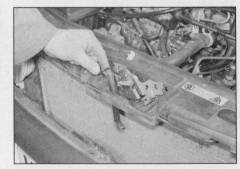

10.3 . . . and remove the support strut from the lock

11

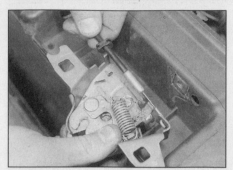

10.4a Detach the release cable from the rear of the lock . . .

10.4b . . . and remove the bonnet lock from the vehicle

lever then detach the inner cable from the lock bracket and remove the lock from the vehicle (see illustrations).

Refitting

5 Before refitting, remove all traces of old locking compound from the bonnet retaining bolts and their threads in the body.

6 Locate the bonnet release inner cable in the lock bracket and reconnect the outer cable to the lever. Seat the lock on the crossmember.

7 Apply a suitable locking compound (VW recommend the use of locking fluid D 185 400 A2 - available from your VW dealer) to the threads of the lock retaining bolts.

8 Align the lock with the marks made prior to removal then refit the bolts and tighten them to the specified torque setting.

9 Refit the support strut and securely tighten its retaining bolts.

10 Clip the radiator grille into position then checking that the lock operates smoothly, without any sign of undue resistance. Check that the bonnet fastens and releases satisfactorily. If adjustment is necessary, slacken the bonnet lock retaining bolts, and adjust the position of the lock to suit. Once the lock is operating correctly, tighten its retaining bolts to the specified torque.

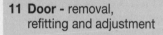

11 Door - removal, refitting and adjustment

Removal

1 Disconnect the battery negative terminal.

2 Open up the door and disengage the wiring gaiter from the door pillar then rotate the connector anti-clockwise and disconnect it from the pillar. On models equipped with central locking also disconnect the vacuum pipe which passes through the connector (see illustrations).

3 Slacken and remove the nut and pivot bolt securing the check link to the pillar (see illustration).

4 There are two possible types of hinges fitted. Where possible, unscrew the two hinge pin grub bolts and, with the aid of an assistant, lift the door upwards and off the hinge pins. Where no grub bolts are fitted to the hinges, first draw around the outline of the

hinge. Have an assistant support the door then slacken and remove the bolts securing the hinges to the door and remove the door from the vehicle (see illustration).

5 Examine the hinges for signs of wear or damage. If renewal is necessary, mark the position of the hinge(s) then undo the retaining bolts and remove them from the vehicle. Fit the new hinge(s) and align with the marks made before removal and lightly tighten the retaining bolts.

Refitting

6 On models where grub bolts are fitted to the hinges, apply a smear of multi-purpose grease to the hinge pins, then, with the aid of an assistant, refit the door to the vehicle. Once the door is correctly positioned, tighten the grub bolts to the specified torque.

11.2a Unscrew the wiring connector . . .

11.3 Unscrew the nut and remove the pivot bolt (arrowed) securing the check link to the pillar

7 On all other models, with the aid of an assistant, offer up the door to the vehicle and refit the hinge bolts. Align the hinges with the marks made before removal and tighten the retaining bolts to the specified torque.

8 On all models, align the check link with its bracket and refit the pivot bolt and nut, tightening it to the specified torque setting.

9 Reconnect the door wiring connector, making sure it is correctly reconnected, and secure it in position. Where necessary, also reconnect the central locking hose making sure the hose connection is pushed firmly together so that the end of the hose aligns with the coloured line.

10 Fold the rubber gaiter back into position, ensuring it is correctly located on the pillar.

11 Check the door alignment and, if necessary, adjust then reconnect the battery negative terminal. If the paintwork around the hinges has been damaged, paint the area with a suitable touch-in brush to prevent corrosion.

Adjustment

12 Close the door and check the door alignment with surrounding body panels. If necessary, slight adjustment of the door position can be made by slackening the hinge retaining bolts and repositioning the hinge/door as necessary. Once the door is correctly positioned, tighten the hinge bolts to the specified torque. If the paint work around the hinges has been damaged, paint the affected area with a suitable touch-in brush to prevent corrosion.

11.2b . . . and disconnect the wiring connector and central locking vacuum pipe (arrowed) from the pillar

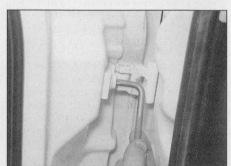

11.4 Where no grub bolts are fitted to the hinges, unscrew the bolts securing the hinge to the door

12.2 Unclip the exterior mirror trim panel and remove it from the door . . .

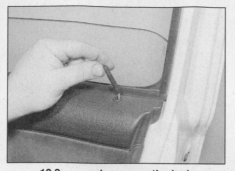

12.3 . . . and unscrew the lock operating knob from its rod

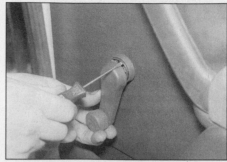

12.4a On manual windows, slide the spacer away from the handle as shown . . .

12.4b . . . then remove the handle and spacer from the door

12.5a Unclip the armrest handle cover from the door . . .

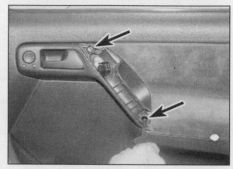

12.5b . . . then slacken and remove the door inner trim panel screws (arrowed)

12 Door inner trim panel - removal and refitting

Removal

Front door

1 Disconnect the battery negative terminal then open the door.

2 Carefully prise out and remove the exterior mirror inner trim panel **(see illustration)**.

3 Unscrew the door lock inner operating knob from its rod **(see illustration)**.

4 On models with manual windows, slide the spacer directly away from the regulator handle, to release the retaining clip. Pull the handle off the spindle, and remove the regulator spacer **(see illustrations)**.

5 Carefully unclip the upper trim cover from

the door armrest handle and remove it from the vehicle, where necessary, disconnecting the wiring connector as it becomes accessible. Slacken and remove the screws securing the armrest to the door **(see illustrations)**.

6 Unclip the trim cover from around the door interior handle, disconnecting the wiring connector (where necessary), as the cover is removed **(see illustration)**.

7 Release the door trim panel studs, carefully levering between the panel and door with a flat-bladed screwdriver. Work around the outside of the panel, and when all the studs are released, ease the panel away from the door, disconnecting the wiring from the speaker as it becomes accessible **(see illustrations)**.

Rear door

8 Disconnect the battery negative terminal then remove the trim panel as described in paragraphs 3 to 7.

Refitting

9 Refitting of the trim panel is the reverse of removal. Before refitting, check whether any of the trim panel retaining studs were broken on removal, and renew them as necessary.

13 Door handle and lock components - removal and refitting

Removal

Interior door handle

1 Remove the door inner trim panel as described in Section 12.

2 Release the handle lower retaining clip with a suitable screwdriver then slide the handle out of the door in a forwards direction and

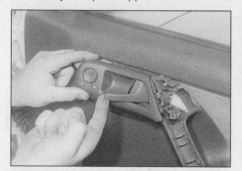

12.6 Unclip the trim cover and remove it from around the door interior handle

12.7a Release the inner trim panel from its retaining clips and remove it from the door . . .

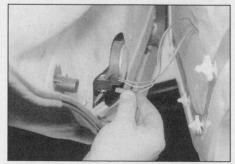

12.7b . . . disconnecting the speaker wiring as it becomes accessible

11

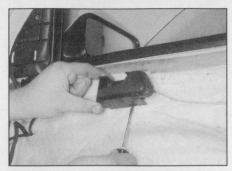

13.2 Release the clip and detach the interior handle from the door and link rod

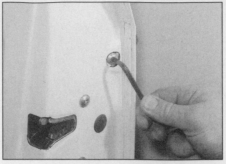

13.4a Slacken and remove the retaining bolt . . .

13.4b . . . then pivot the exterior handle assembly out from the door

13.5a Recover the rubber seals from the handle . . .

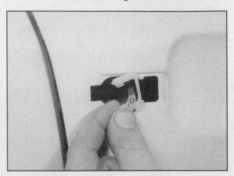

13.5b . . . and remove the handle retaining clip from the door

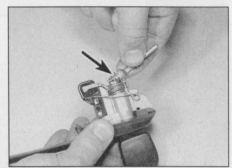

13.7 Unhook the rod from the lock cylinder, and recover its spring (arrowed)

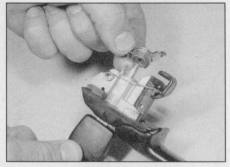

13.8a Remove the coupling and spring assembly . . .

13.8b . . . then withdraw the lock cylinder from the handle . . .

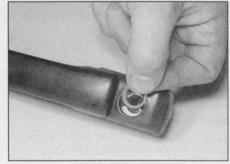

13.8c . . . along with its sealing ring

free it from the end of the link rod **(see illustration)**.

Exterior door handle

Note: *This task can be performed with the door inner trim panel in position.*

3 If work is being carried out on the front door, insert the key into the lock.

4 Slacken and remove the handle retaining bolt from the rear edge of the door then move the handle assembly forwards and pivot it out of position. On the front door, as the handle is being removed, rotate the key through 90° to disengage the handle from the lock operating lever **(see illustrations)**.

5 Recover the handle seals and the lock retaining clip and inspect them for signs of damage or deterioration; renewing them if necessary **(see illustrations)**. **Note:** *Do not drop the clip into the door; if the clip is dropped it will be necessary to remove the inner trim panel to recover it.*

Front door lock cylinder

6 Remove the exterior door handle as described in paragraphs 3 to 5.

7 With the key in the lock, unhook the connecting rod from the rear of the lock cylinder and recover the spring **(see illustration)**.

8 Noting their correct fitted position, release the coupling and spring from the rear of the cylinder then withdraw the lock cylinder from the handle. Recover the sealing ring from the handle and renew it if it is damaged **(see illustrations)**.

Front door lock

9 Ensure that the window is in the fully closed position then remove the interior door handle as described in paragraphs 1 and 2.

10 Carefully lever out the door trim panel retaining clips from the rear edge of the door then peel the polythene insulating panel away from the door to gain access to the lock assembly.

11 Remove the exterior door handle as described in paragraphs 3 to 5.

12 On models with central locking, disconnect the vacuum pipe from the lock assembly and disconnect the wiring from the central locking element **(see illustration)**.

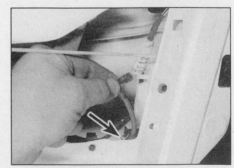

13.12 Disconnect the central locking vacuum pipe and wiring (arrowed)

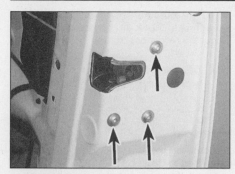

13.13a Slacken and remove the three retaining bolts (arrowed) . . .

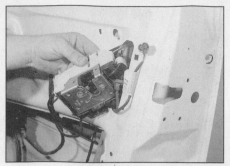

13.13b . . . and manoeuvre the lock assembly out of position

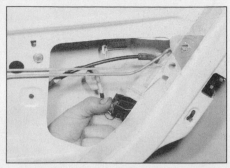

13.14 Disconnecting the rear door lock central locking element wiring connector

13.15a Press out the retaining pin . . .

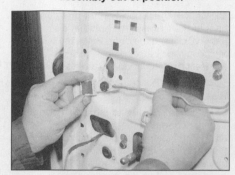

13.15b . . . then free the pivot link from the door and detach it from the link rod

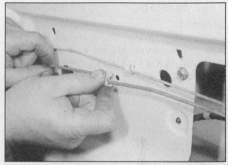

13.16 Remove the guide clips securing both lock link rods to the door

13 On all models, slacken and remove the lock retaining bolts then disengage the lock from the link rod and remove it from the door (see illustrations). Note that on some models it may be necessary to loosen the window regulator retaining bolts and release the guide rail from the door (see Section 14) to gain the clearance required to remove the lock assembly.

Rear door lock

14 Carry out the operations described above in paragraphs 9 to 12 (see illustration).

15 Press out the retaining pin from the centre of the interior lock button pivot link rod and free the pivot from the door. Recover the pin and detach the pivot from the link rod (see illustrations).

16 Unclip the link rod guide clips from the door (see illustration).

17 Slacken and remove the lock retaining bolts and manoeuvre the lock and link rod

assembly out from the door. If necessary, detach the link rods from the lock noting their correct fitted locations; the link rods are different and must not be interchanged (see illustrations).

Refitting

Interior door handle

18 Engage the handle with the link rod and clip it back into position. Make sure the handle operates correctly then refit the trim panel as described in Section 12.

Exterior door handle

19 Fit the lock retaining clip to the door and fit the seals to the rear of the handle. **Note:** *Do not drop the clip into the door; if the clip is dropped it will be necessary to remove the inner trim panel to recover it.*

20 Hook the lock front pivot into place, then clip the rear of the handle into position. On the

front door, rotate the key through 90° as the handle clips it into position, this will engage the handle with the lock operating lever.

21 Check the operation of the handle then refit the retaining bolt and tighten it to the specified torque setting.

Front door lock cylinder

22 Lubricate the outside of the lock cylinder and the locking plates with a suitable lubricant (VW recommend the use of grease G 000 400 - available from your VW dealer).

23 Fit the sealing ring to the handle and insert the cylinder.

24 Refit the coupling and spring to the cylinder, making sure they are correctly located, then check the operation of the lock cylinder (see illustration).

25 Fit the spring to the connecting rod and hook the rod onto the rear of the lock cylinder.

26 Refit the exterior handle as described in paragraphs 19 to 21.

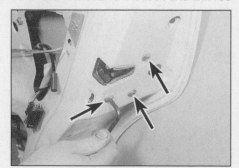

13.17a Undo the retaining bolts (arrowed) . . .

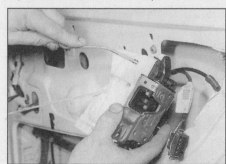

13.17b . . . and remove the lock and link rod assembly from the rear door

13.24 Ensure the coupling spring ends are located over the handle tab (arrowed)

11

13.31a Remove the rubber plug from the rear edge of the door . . .

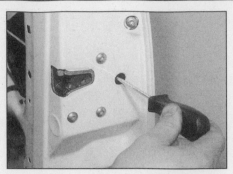

13.31b . . . and adjust the lock as described in text

Front door lock

27 Before refitting, slacken the lock adjusting (Torx) screw; on the left-hand door the screw has a right-handed thread and on the right-hand door it has a left-handed thread.

28 Manoeuvre the lock assembly into position and engage it with the link rod.

29 Refit the lock bolts and tighten them to the specified torque. Where necessary, reconnect the vacuum pipe and wiring connector(s) (as applicable) to the lock assembly.

30 Refit the exterior handle as described in paragraphs 19 to 21.

31 Remove the rubber plug from the door to gain access to the lock adjustment screw. Tighten the screw to 3 Nm (2 lbf ft) (see paragraph 27) then refit the rubber plug **(see illustrations)**.

32 Where necessary, refit the regulator guide rail retaining bolts and adjust as described in Section 14.

33 Check the operation of the lock and handle then press the polythene insulating panel back onto the door. Press the trim panel retaining clips back into position.

34 Refit the interior door handle as described in paragraph 18.

Rear door lock

35 Refit the link rods to the lock making sure they are correctly refitted.

36 Before refitting, slacken the lock adjusting (Torx) screw; on the left-hand door the screw has a right-handed thread and on the right-hand door it has a left-handed thread.

37 Manoeuvre the lock assembly into position and tighten the retaining bolts to the specified torque. Where necessary, reconnect the vacuum pipe and wiring connector(s) (as applicable) to the lock assembly.

38 Attach the link rod to the pivot and clip the pivot into the door. Secure the pivot in position with the retaining pin.

39 Carry out the operations described in paragraphs 30 to 34, ignoring the remark about the regulator bolts.

14 Door window glass and regulator - removal and refitting

Removal

1 Remove the interior door handle as described in Section 13.

2 Carefully lever out the door trim panel retaining clips from the door. Carefully peel the polythene insulating panel away from the door and remove the panel. If the panel is ripped or damaged a new one must be used on refitting; any damaged trim clips must also renewed **(see illustrations)**. Continue as described under the relevant sub-heading.

Front door window glass

3 Position the window glass so the glass clamps on the regulator mechanism are accessible through the door panel cutaways.

4 Carefully ease the window inner sealing strip out from the top edge of the door **(see illustration)**.

5 Slacken the window clamp nuts and release the clamps from the glass then carefully manoeuvre the window glass out through the top of the door **(see illustrations)**.

Rear door window glass

6 Carry out the operations described in paragraphs 3 and 4.

7 Lower the window, then undo the upper

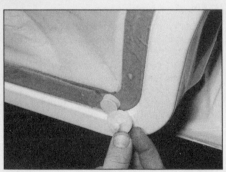

14.2a Slide the door panel clips off the fasteners . . .

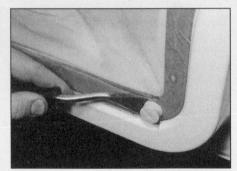

14.2b . . . then carefully prise the fasteners out from the door

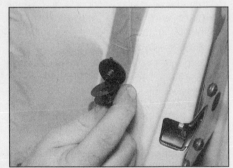

14.2c Remove the panel clip from the upper fastener . . .

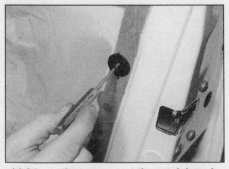

14.2d . . . then press out the retaining pin and unclip the fastener from the door

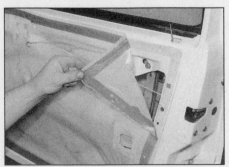

14.2e With all clips and fasteners removed, peel away the polythene panel

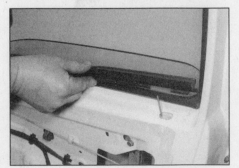

14.4 Unclip the inner sealing strip from the top of the door

14.5a Slacken the window clamp nuts . . .

14.5b . . . then free the glass and remove it through the top of the door

14.7a Undo the upper retaining screw . . .

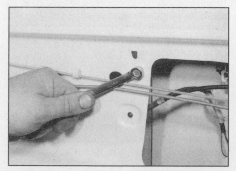

14.7b . . . and the lower retaining bolt . . .

14.7c . . . and remove the window guide rail from the rear door

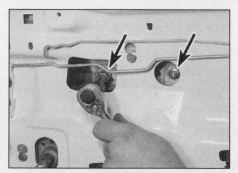

14.8a Slacken the window clamp nuts (arrowed) . . .

and lower retaining screws, and remove the window guide rail from the door **(see illustrations)**.

8 Slacken the window clamp nuts then carefully manoeuvre the glass out through the top of the door **(see illustrations)**.

9 If necessary, the fixed window can then be disengaged from the sealing strip and removed from the door.

Front window regulator

10 Remove the window glass as described earlier.

11 Release the retaining clip and free the regulator cables from the door **(see illustration)**. On models with electric windows disconnect the wiring connector from the regulator motor.

12 Loosen the retaining bolts situated at the top of the regulator guide rails and remove the lower guide rail retaining bolts. Also slacken

the bolt securing the regulator mechanism to the door **(see illustrations)**.

13 Lift the regulator mechanism slightly to disengage it from the door then manoeuvre it downwards and out through the door aperture **(see illustration)**.

Rear window regulator

14 Remove the window glass as described earlier.

15 On models with electric windows, disconnect the wiring connector from the regulator motor.

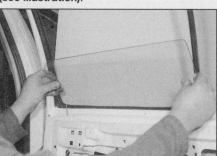

14.8b . . . and manoeuvre the glass out of the top of the rear door

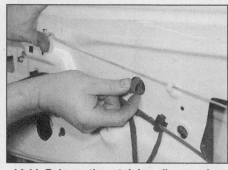

14.11 Release the retaining clip securing the regulator cables to the front door

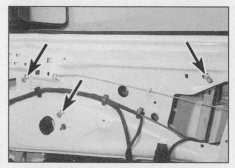

14.12a Slacken the regulator and guide rail upper retaining bolts (arrowed) . . .

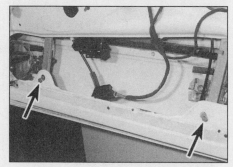

14.12b . . . then remove the guide rail lower bolts (arrowed) . . .

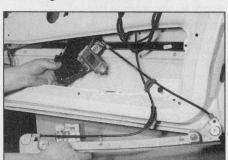

14.13 . . . and manoeuvre the regulator assembly out from the door

11

14.16a Slacken the retaining bolts (arrowed) . . .

16 Slacken the regulator and guide rail retaining bolts then manoeuvre the regulator out through the door aperture **(see illustrations)**.

Refitting

Front door window glass

17 Manoeuvre the window glass into position and engage it with the regulator clamps. Make sure the glass is correctly seated then lightly tighten the regulator clamp nuts.
18 Refit the inner sealing strip to the top of the door.
19 Check that the window glass moves smoothly and easily and closes fully. If necessary, slacken the regulator clamp nuts then reposition the glass as necessary. Once the window operation is correct, tighten the clamp nuts to the specified torque.
20 Once the window is operating correctly, press the polythene insulating panel back into position, making sure it is correctly seated, and refit the trim panel clips. Refit the inner trim panel as described in Section 12.

Rear door window glass

21 Where necessary, ease the fixed window into position making sure it is correctly seated in the sealing strip.
22 Manoeuvre the glass into position, engage it with the regulator clamps and lightly tighten the clamp nuts.
23 Refit the window guide rail to the door, engaging it with the glass, and tighten the retaining screws securely.
24 Carry out the operations described in paragraphs 19 and 20.

Front window regulator

25 Manoeuvre the regulator into position through the door aperture then refit the retaining bolts and tighten all its fixings to the specified torque. Where necessary, reconnect the wiring connector to the regulator motor.
26 Clip the regulator cables into position then refit the glass as described above.

Rear window regulator

27 Manoeuvre the regulator into position through the door aperture then refit the retaining bolts and tighten them to the specified torque. Where necessary, reconnect the wiring connector to the regulator motor.
28 Refit the glass as described above.

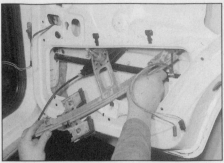

14.16b . . . and remove the regulator assembly from the rear door

15 Tailgate and support struts - removal and refitting

Removal

Tailgate

1 Open up the tailgate then disconnect the battery negative terminal.
2 On Hatchback models slacken and remove the tailgate trim panel retaining screw then release the trim panel clips, carefully levering between the panel and tailgate with a flat-bladed screwdriver. Work around the outside of the panel, and when all the clips are released, remove the panel.
3 On Estate models work around the edge of the tailgate trim panel and remove its retaining clips; to remove the clips, lift their centre pins and then carefully prise them out of position.

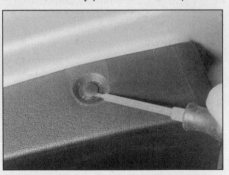

15.3a On Estate models, lift the tailgate trim panel centre pins . . .

15.3c . . . and undo the retaining screw and remove the trim panel

Slacken and remove the trim panel retaining screw then unclip the panel and remove it from the tailgate **(see illustrations)**.
4 Disconnect the wiring connectors situated behind the trim panel and free the washer hose from the tailgate wiper motor **(see illustration)**. Also disconnect the wiring connectors from the heated rear screen terminals and free the wiring grommets from the tailgate.
5 Tie a piece of string to each end of the wiring then, noting the correct routing of the wiring harness, release the harness rubber grommets from the tailgate and withdraw the wiring. When the end of the wiring appears, untie the string and leave it in position in the tailgate; it can then be used on refitting to draw the wiring into position.
6 Using a suitable marker pen, draw around the outline of each hinge marking its correct position on the tailgate.
7 Have an assistant support the tailgate, then using a small flat-bladed screwdriver raise the spring clips and pull the support struts off their balljoint mountings on the tailgate. Slacken and remove the bolts securing the hinges to the tailgate and remove the tailgate from the vehicle **(see illustration)**. Where necessary, recover the gaskets which are fitted between the hinge and tailgate.
8 Inspect the hinges for signs of wear or damage and renew if necessary. The hinges are secured to the vehicle by nuts or bolts (depending on model) which can be accessed once the headlining has been freed from the trim strip and peeled back. On refitting ensure that the hinge gasket is in good condition and secure the hinge in position.

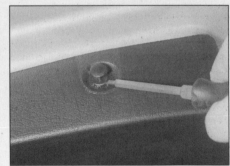

15.3b . . . then prise the retaining clips out of position . . .

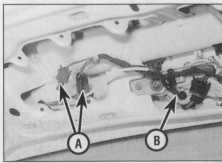

15.4 Disconnect the wiring connectors (A) and detach the washer hose (B) from the wiper motor

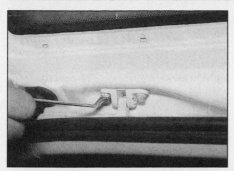

15.7 Unscrew the bolts securing the hinges to the tailgate

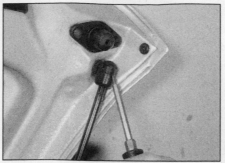

15.10 Carefully lift the spring clip, and free the support strut from the tailgate

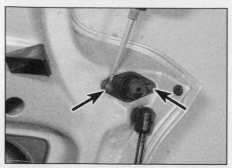

15.13a On Estate models, the tailgate buffers are secured by two pins (arrowed)

Support struts

9 Support the tailgate in the open position, using a stout piece of wood, or with the help of an assistant.

10 Using a small flat-bladed screwdriver raise the spring clip, and pull the support strut off its balljoint mounting on the tailgate **(see illustration)**. Raise the second retaining clip then detach the strut from the balljoint on the body and remove it from the vehicle.

Refitting

Tailgate

11 Refitting is the reverse of removal, aligning the hinges with the marks made before removal.

12 On completion, close the tailgate and check its alignment with the surrounding panels. If necessary slight adjustment can be made by slackening the retaining bolts and repositioning the tailgate on its hinges. On Estate models, if the tailgate buffers are in need of adjustment, continue as follows.

13 Carefully lever out the retaining pins and remove the buffer from the tailgate. Remove the rubber pad from the buffer to gain access to the clamping screw, then slacken the screw and adjust the threaded sleeve to provide a 3 mm clearance as shown. Refit the rubber pad then pull out the buffer slide then push it back in until the lugs engage with the slots in the slide, the distance between the rubber and buffer should be as shown **(see illustrations)**. Refit the buffer to the tailgate and secure it in position with the retaining pins. Close the tailgate to the second lock detent then open it

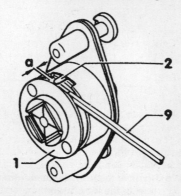

15.13b Tailgate buffer adjustment

1 Threaded sleeve   9 3 mm Allen key
2 Spacer rib   Clearance a = 3 mm

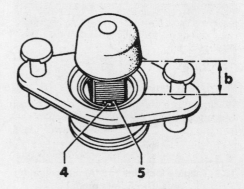

15.13c Tailgate buffer adjustment

4 Lugs   5 Recesses
Clearance b = 10 mm

up again to reset the buffer. Remove the rubber pad and complete the adjustment by tightening the clamp screw lightly (1 to 2 Nm) and refitting the rubber.

Support struts

14 Refitting is a reverse of the removal procedure, ensuring that the strut is securely retained by its retaining clips.

16 Tailgate lock components - removal and refitting

Removal

Tailgate lock

1 Open up the tailgate, then undo the lock

retaining screws. Detach the lock link rod from the button then remove the lock, disconnecting its wiring connector as it is withdrawn **(see illustrations)**.

Tailgate lock button - Hatchback

2 Remove the tailgate trim panel as described in paragraph 2 of Section 15.

3 Disconnect the link rod(s) from the handle assembly and, where necessary, disconnect the wiring from the switch **(see illustration)**.

4 From outside the tailgate, slacken and remove the retaining screws securing the tailgate lock button trim panel in position and remove it from the tailgate **(see illustrations)**.

5 Release the retaining clips and carefully remove the lock button from the tailgate **(see illustration)**.

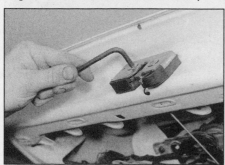

16.1a Undo the retaining screws . . .

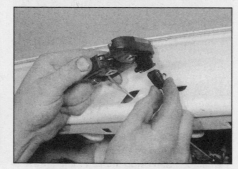

16.1b . . . and remove the lock, disconnecting the wiring and link rod

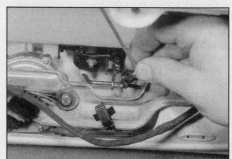

16.3 Release the retaining clips and detach the link rods from the lock button

11

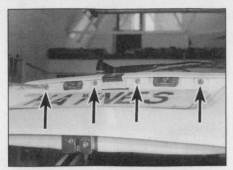

16.4a Undo the retaining screws (arrowed) . . .

16.4b . . . and remove the lock button trim panel from the tailgate . . .

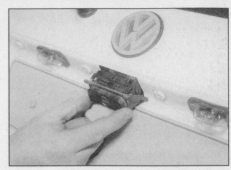

16.5 . . . then release the retaining clips and withdraw the lock button

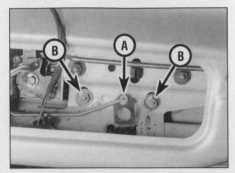

16.7 Tailgate lock link rod (A) and retaining nuts (B) - Estate model

16.10a Remove the retaining clip from the rear of the lock button . . .

16.10b . . . then lift off the link rod cam . . .

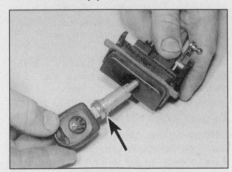

16.10c . . . and withdraw the lock cylinder and sealing ring (arrowed)

Tailgate handle - Estate

6 Remove the tailgate trim panel as described in paragraph 3 of Section 15.

7 Disconnect the link rods from the handle assembly and, where necessary, disconnect the wiring connector from the lock switch **(see illustration)**.

8 Slacken and remove the retaining nuts/bolts (as applicable) and remove the handle from the tailgate. Recover the handle seal (where fitted) and check it for signs of damage, renewing it if necessary.

Tailgate lock cylinder - Hatchback

9 Remove the tailgate lock button as described earlier.

10 Insert the key into the lock then carefully prise off the retaining clip and remove the link rod cam, noting its correct fitted location. Withdraw the lock cylinder from the button and recover its sealing ring. Inspect the

sealing ring for signs of wear or damage and renew if necessary **(see illustrations)**.

Tailgate lock cylinder - Estate

11 Remove the tailgate handle as described earlier.

12 Remove the retaining clip and link rod bracket from the rear of the handle. Insert the key into the lock then turn it to the vertical position and withdraw the lock cylinder from the handle. Recover the lock cylinder seal; the seal should be renewed if it is damaged.

Refitting

13 Refitting is a reversal of the relevant removal procedure. Before refitting the trim panel, check the operation of the lock components and (where necessary) the central locking system.

17 Boot lid and support struts - removal and refitting

Removal

Boot lid

1 Open up the boot lid then disconnect the battery negative terminal.

2 Unclip the plastic covers from the boot lid to gain access to the rear lights. Disconnect the wiring connectors from the lights and tie a piece of string to each end of the wiring. Noting the correct routing of the wiring harness, release the harness rubber grommets from the boot lid and withdraw the wiring. When the end of the wiring appears, untie the string and leave it in position in the

boot lid; it can then be used on refitting to draw the wiring into position.

3 Draw around the outline of each hinge with a suitable marker pen then slacken and remove the hinge retaining bolts and remove the boot lid from the vehicle.

4 Inspect the hinges for signs of wear or damage and renew if necessary; the hinges are secured to the vehicle by bolts.

Support struts

5 Support the boot lid in the open position. Using a small flat-bladed screwdriver raise the spring clip, and pull the support strut off its upper mounting **(see illustration)**. Repeat the procedure on the lower strut mounting and remove the strut from the vehicle.

Refitting

Boot lid

6 Refitting is the reverse of removal, aligning

17.5 Carefully lift the retaining clip and detach the support strut from its upper mounting

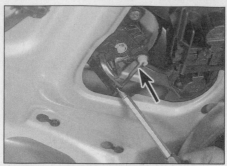

18.2 Unclip the plastic cover from the boot lid to gain access to the lock assembly

18.3 Prise the link rod balljoint off the lock and disconnect the link rod (arrowed) . . .

18.4 . . . then undo the two screws (arrowed) and remove the lock cylinder

the hinges with the marks made before removal.

7 On completion, close the boot lid and check its alignment with the surrounding panels. If necessary slight adjustment can be made by slackening the retaining bolts and repositioning the boot lid on its hinges.

Support struts

8 Refitting is a reverse of removal, ensuring the strut is securely retained by its clips.

18 Boot lid lock components - removal and refitting

Removal

Boot lid lock

1 Open up the boot, then undo the lock retaining screws. Remove the lock, disconnect its wiring connector and detach it from the link rod as it is withdrawn.

Boot lid lock cylinder

2 Unclip the plastic cover from the boot lid to gain access to the rear of the lock cylinder **(see illustration)**.
3 Unclip the link rod from the lock cylinder then free the lock link rod balljoint from its connection **(see illustration)**.
4 Undo the two retaining screws and remove the lock cylinder assembly from the boot lid **(see illustration)**. Recover the lock cylinder sealing ring.
5 Insert the key into the lock then carefully prise off the retaining clip and withdraw the lock cylinder and sealing ring. Inspect the sealing rings for signs of wear or damage and renew if necessary.

Refitting

Boot lid lock

6 Reconnect the wiring connector and securely attach the link rod. Seat the lock in the boot lid and securely tighten the bolts.

Boot lid lock cylinder

7 Fit the sealing ring to the lock cylinder and slide it into position in the housing. Secure the cylinder in position with the retaining clip then check the operation of the lock cylinder assembly.

8 Fit the sealing ring to the lock cylinder assembly. Insert the assembly into the boot lid and refit the retaining screws tightening them securely.
9 Clip the link rod balljoint back onto the lock cylinder and securely reconnect the link rod. Check that the operation of the lock assembly is satisfactory, then refit the plastic cover to the boot lid.

19 Central locking components - removal and refitting

Removal

Central locking pressure pump

1 The central locking operating pump is located in the luggage compartment; on Hatchback and Estate models it is located on the right-hand side, while on Saloon models

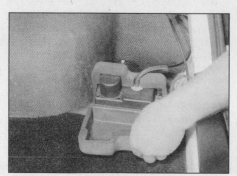

19.3a Remove the insulation around the central locking pump . . .

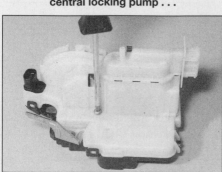

19.5a Remove the retaining screw, then unclip the positioning element . . .

the pump is located on the left-hand side. Before removal disconnect the battery negative lead.
2 Unhook the retaining strap then free the pump from the body.
3 Remove the insulation packing from around the pump then disconnect the wiring connector and vacuum pipe from the pump and remove the pump from the vehicle **(see illustrations)**.

Door lock positioning element

4 Remove the door lock as described in Section 13.
5 Turn the lock latch to the "locked" position then slacken and remove the positioning element retaining screw. Release the retaining clips and remove the positioning element from the lock, noting how the element plunger is engaged with the lock lever **(see illustrations)**.

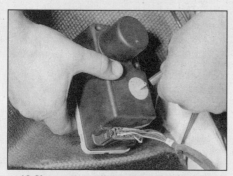

19.3b . . . then disconnect the vacuum pipe and wiring and remove the pump

19.5b . . . noting how the element plunger is engaged with the lock lever (arrowed)

11

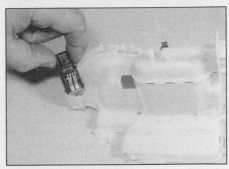

19.7 Removing the front door lock microswitch

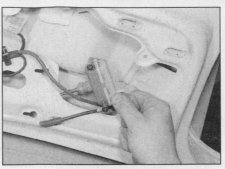

19.10 Removing the tailgate lock positioning element

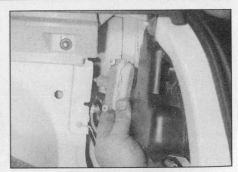

19.14 Removing the fuel filler flap locking element

Front door lock microswitch

6 Remove the door lock positioning element as described in paragraphs 4 and 5.
7 Release the retaining clips and slide out the microswitch **(see illustration)**.

Tailgate lock positioning element - Hatchback and Estate

8 Remove the tailgate trim panel as described in paragraphs 1 to 3 of Section 15.
9 Disconnect the vacuum pipe from the positioning element and free its link rod from the lock/linkage (as applicable).
10 Undo the retaining screws and remove the positioning element and link rod from the tailgate **(see illustration)**.

Boot lid lock positioning element - Saloon

11 Disconnect the vacuum pipe from the positioning element and free its link rod from the lock/linkage (as applicable).
12 Undo the retaining screws and remove the positioning element and link rod from the boot lid.

Fuel filler flap locking element

13 Where necessary, slacken and remove the retaining screws and remove the retaining clips and remove the luggage compartment side trim panel to gain access to the filler flap locking element.
14 Slacken and remove the locking element retaining screws. Remove the element, disconnecting its vacuum hose as it becomes accessible **(see illustration)**.

Refitting

15 Refitting is a reverse of the relevant removal procedure making sure all vacuum pipe connections are securely remade. On completion check the operation of all central locking system components.

20 Electric window components - removal and refitting

Window switches

1 Refer to Chapter 12.

Window winder motors

Removal

2 Remove the regulator assembly as described in Section 14.
3 Remove two of the small Torx-headed motor retaining screws and screw them into the holes shown to secure the baseplate to the regulator assembly **(see illustration)**.
4 Remove the remaining small retaining screws then unscrew the five larger Torx-headed retaining screws. Separate the motor from the regulator and recover the shim; the baseplate will remain on the regulator **(see illustration)**. Ensure that the motor assembly is kept clean.

Refitting

5 If a new motor is being fitted remove the fitting cover.
6 Make sure that the motor drive gear components are sufficiently lubricated (VW recommend grease G 000 450 02 - available from your VW dealer) and free from dust and dirt.
7 Ensure that the regulator and baseplate is free from dirt and fit the shim to the motor shaft. Carefully align the motor and engage it with the regulator.
8 Refit the motor retaining bolts, tightening them loosely only, then unscrew the two bolts used to secure the baseplate in position and refit them to the motor. With all bolts loosely in position, go around and securely tighten the larger bolts in the sequence shown **(see illustration)**. Then securely tighten all the smaller retaining bolts.
9 Refit the regulator assembly as described in Section 14.

21 Exterior mirrors and associated components - removal and refitting

Removal

Manually operated mirror

1 Remove the door inner trim panel as described in Section 12.
2 Remove the insulation from the door frame then undo the retaining screw and free the mirror adjustment mechanism.
3 Slacken and remove the mirror retaining screws and remove the mirror assembly from the door.

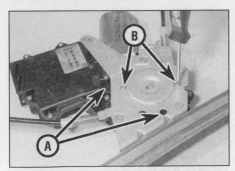

20.3 Unscrew two of the small motor screws (A) and fit them into locations (B) to secure the baseplate to the regulator

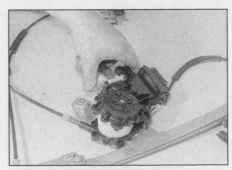

20.4 Slacken and remove the remaining screws and carefully lift the window winder motor off the regulator assembly

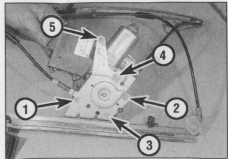

20.8 On refitting tighten the motor large retaining screws in the order shown

21.4 Disconnect the exterior mirror wiring connector . . .

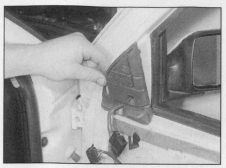

21.5a . . . and remove the insulation panel from the door

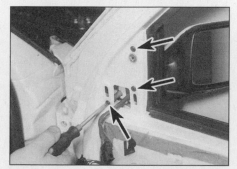

21.5b Remove the three retaining screws (arrowed) . . .

21.5c . . . and lift the mirror and rubber seal assembly away from the door

Electrically operated mirror

4 Remove the door inner trim panel as described in Section 12 and disconnect the mirror wiring connector **(see illustration)**.

5 Remove the mirror insulation from the door frame then undo the retaining screws and remove the mirror assembly from the door. Recover the rubber seal from the mirror; the seal must be renewed if it shows signs of damage or deterioration **(see illustrations)**.

Mirror glass

Note: *The mirror glass is clipped onto the motor. Removal of the glass without the VW special tool (number 800-200) is likely to result in breakage of the glass.*

6 Insert a wide plastic or wooden wedge between the mirror glass and mirror housing and carefully prise the glass from the motor. Take great care when removing the glass; do

not use excessive force as the glass is easily broken.

7 Remove the glass from the mirror, where necessary, disconnect the wiring connectors from the mirror heating element **(see illustration)**.

Mirror switch (electrically operated mirror)

8 Refer to Chapter 12.

Electrically operated mirror motor

9 Remove the mirror glass as described above.

10 Undo the retaining screws and remove the motor, disconnecting its wiring connector as it becomes accessible **(see illustration)**.

Refitting

11 Refitting is the reverse of the relevant removal procedure.

21.7 Unclip the glass from the mirror and (where necessary) disconnect its wiring connectors (arrowed)

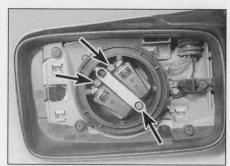

21.10 Exterior mirror motor retaining screws (arrowed)

22 Windscreen, tailgate and fixed rear quarter window glass - general information

These areas of glass are secured by the tight fit of the weatherstrip in the body aperture, and are bonded in position with a special adhesive. Renewal of such fixed glass is a difficult, messy and time-consuming task, which is beyond the scope of the home mechanic. It is difficult, unless one has plenty of practice, to obtain a secure, waterproof fit. Furthermore, the task carries a high risk of breakage; this applies especially to the laminated glass windscreen. In view of this, owners are strongly advised to have this sort of work carried out by one of the many specialist windscreen fitters.

23 Sunroof - general information

Due to the complexity of the sunroof mechanism, considerable expertise is needed to repair, replace or adjust the sunroof components successfully. Removal of the roof first requires the headlining to be removed, which is a complex and tedious operation, and not a task to be undertaken lightly. Therefore, any problems with the sunroof should be referred to a VW dealer.

On models with an electric sunroof, if the sunroof motor fails to operate, first check the relevant fuse. If the fault cannot be traced and rectified, the sunroof can be opened and closed manually using an Allen key to turn the motor spindle (a suitable key is supplied with the vehicle, and should be clipped onto the underside of the sunroof motor). To gain access to the motor, unclip the rear of the access cover then slide the cover to the rear to free it from the headlining. Unclip the Allen key then pivot the spindle cover out of the way and insert the Allen key. Rotate the key to move the sunroof to the required position.

24 Body exterior fittings - removal and refitting

Wheelarch liners and body under-panels

1 The various plastic covers fitted to the underside of the vehicle are secured in position by a mixture of screws, nuts and retaining clips and removal will be fairly obvious on inspection. Work methodically around the panel removing its retaining screws and releasing its retaining clips until the panel is free and can be removed from the underside of the vehicle. Most clips used on the vehicle, except for the fasteners which are used to secure the wheelarch liners in position, are simply prised out of position. The wheelarch liner clips are released by pressing

11

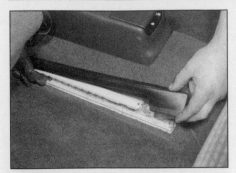

25.1 Removing the seat inner guide rail trim panel

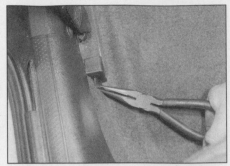

25.2 Pull out the wedge and remove the end plug from the seat outer guide rail

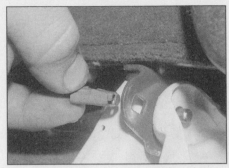

25.3 Remove the spring clip from the front of the seat centre guide rail . . .

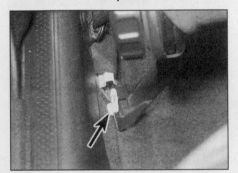

25.4 . . . then slide the seat back and recover the guide piece (arrowed)

25.5 Unscrew the hinge bolts and remove the seat cushion from the vehicle

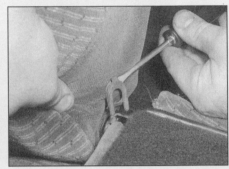

25.7 Prise out the retaining clip from the seat back centre hinge pivot . . .

out their centre pins and then removing the outer section of the clip; new clips will be required on refitting if the centre pins are not recovered.

2 On refitting, renew any retaining clips that may have been broken on removal, and ensure that the panel is securely retained by all the relevant clips and screws.

Body trim strips and badges

3 The various body trim strips and badges are held in position with a special adhesive tape. Removal requires the trim/badge to be heated, to soften the adhesive, and then cut away from the surface. Due to the high risk of damage to the vehicle's paintwork during this operation, it is recommended that this task should be entrusted to a VW dealer.

25 Seats - removal and refitting

Removal

Front seat

1 Slide the seat forwards and unclip the trim cover from the seat inner guide rail **(see illustration)**. On some models the trim cover is secured in position by a clip; the clip is released by pressing out its centre pin then prising out the outer section; if the centre pin is not recovered a new clip will be required on refitting.

2 Release the outer seat rail end plug by pulling out its securing wedge and remove the plug from the end of the rail **(see illustration)**.

3 Slide the seat backwards and remove the spring clip from the front of the seat centre guide rail **(see illustration)**.

4 Slide the seat fully backwards, disengaging it from the outer guide rails and remove it from the vehicle. Recover the plastic guide pieces from each of the seat guides and renew them if they show signs of damage or deterioration **(see illustration)**.

Rear seat assembly

5 Lift up the rear seat cushion(s) then slacken and remove the hinge retaining bolts and remove the seat cushion(s) from the vehicle **(see illustration)**.

6 Fold down the rear seat backs.

7 Carefully prise out the retaining clip out from the top of the centre hinge pivot **(see illustration)**.

8 Using a small flat-bladed screwdriver, release the outer hinge pivot retaining clip

then move the seat cushion upwards to release its pivot pin **(see illustration)**. Disengage the seat back from the centre hinge and remove it from the vehicle. Remove the opposite seat back in the same way.

Refitting

Front seats

9 Before refitting examine the front and rear seat guide pieces for signs of wear or damage and renew if necessary. Refitting is a reverse of the removal procedure, ensuring that the seat adjustment lever engages correctly with the centre guide locking plunger as the seat is refitted **(see illustration)**.

Rear seat assembly

10 Refitting is the reverse of removal making sure the seat backs are clipped securely in position.

25.8 . . . then release the outer hinge pivot clip and remove the seat back

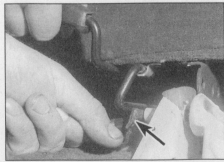

25.9 Ensure the adjustment lever engages with the centre guide plunger (arrowed)

26 Front seat belt tensioning mechanism - general information

Most models covered in this manual are fitted with a front seat belt tensioner system. The system is designed to instantaneously take up any slack in the seat belt in the case of a sudden frontal impact, therefore reducing the possibility of injury to the front seat occupants. Each front seat is fitted with its system, the tensioner being situated behind the sill trim panel.

The seat belt tensioner is triggered by a frontal impact above a pre-determined force. Lesser impacts, including impacts from behind, will not trigger the system.

When the system is triggered, the explosive gas in the tensioner mechanism retracts and locks the seat belt through a cable which acts on the inertia reel. This prevents the seat belt moving and keeps the occupant firmly in position in the seat. Once the tensioner has been triggered, the seat belt will be permanently locked and the assembly must be renewed.

There is a risk of injury if the system is triggered inadvertently when working on the vehicle, and it is therefore strongly recommended that any work involving the seat belt tensioner system is entrusted to a VW dealer. Note the following warnings before contemplating any work on the front seat belts.

 Warning: Do not expose the tensioner mechanism to temperatures in excess of 100° C (212° F).

If the tensioner mechanism is dropped, it must be renewed, even it has suffered no apparent damage.

Do not allow any solvents to come into contact with the tensioner mechanism.

Do not attempt to open the tensioner mechanism as it contains explosive gas.

Tensioners must be discharged before they are disposed of, but this task should be entrusted to a VW dealer.

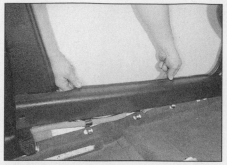

27.1a Remove the centre screw and unclip the fastener from the sill trim panel . . .

27.1c Unscrew the fasteners and release the retaining clip (location arrowed) . . .

27 Seat belt components - removal and refitting

 Warning: On models equipped with seat belt tensioners refer to Section 26 before proceeding; under no circumstances should you attempt to separate the tensioner assembly from the inertia reel.

Removal

Front seat belt - four- and five-door models

1 Unscrew the centre screw from the sill trim panel retaining clip then remove the retaining clip. Press down on the top of the front trim panel, to release its lower edge from the sill, then pull the panel upwards and remove it

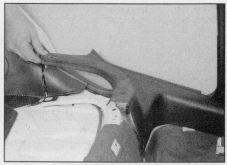

27.1b . . . then unclip the front trim panel and remove it from the vehicle

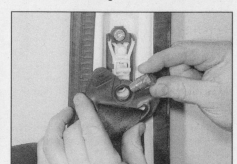

27.1d . . . and remove the rear trim panel from the sill

from the vehicle. Fold the rear seat cushion up then unscrew the fasteners securing the rear section of the sill trim panel in position. Working through the aperture in the seat frame, release the retaining clip by forcing it rearwards, and remove the rear section of the sill trim panel **(see illustrations)**.

2 Starting at the bottom of the panel, unclip the door pillar upper trim panel and free it from the pillar **(see illustration)**.

3 Slacken and remove the seat belt lower mounting bolt and free the seat belt from its lower anchorage **(see illustration)**. The upper trim panel can then be removed.

4 Slacken and remove the upper seat belt mounting bolt and free the belt from the door pillar **(see illustration)**.

5 Slacken and remove the door pillar lower trim panel retaining screw then unclip the panel from the pillar **(see illustrations)**.

6 Undo the retaining screws and remove the

27.2 Unclip the upper trim panel from the door pillar

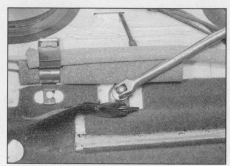

27.3 Unscrew the retaining bolt securing the seat belt to the floor . . .

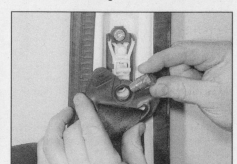

27.4 . . . and the upper retaining bolt securing the seat belt to the pillar

11

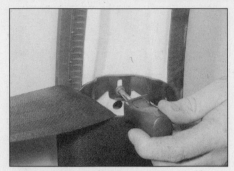

27.5a Unscrew the retaining screw ...

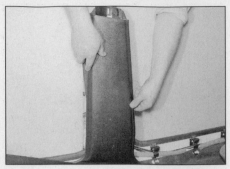

27.5b ... and unclip the lower trim panel from the door pillar

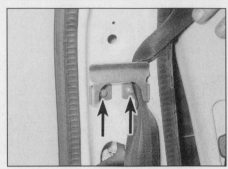

27.6 Undo the screws (arrowed) and remove the seat belt guide from the pillar

27.8a Remove the inertia reel bolt and remove the seat belt from the vehicle

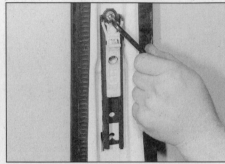

27.8b The height adjuster mechanism is secured to the pillar by one bolt

belt guide from the door pillar **(see illustration)**. The lower trim panel can then be removed.

7 On models with seat belt tensioners, slacken and remove the tensioner assembly retaining nut. This will disable the tensioner making it safe to remove the seat belt assembly.

8 Slacken and remove the inertia reel mounting bolt and remove the seat belt assembly from the vehicle. On models with seat belt tensioners, as the seat belt assembly is removed, release the tensioner assembly from its retaining clip. If necessary, undo the retaining bolt and remove the height adjuster mechanism from the door pillar **(see illustrations)**.

Front seat belt - three-door models

9 Remove the relevant rear seat back as described in Section 25.

10 Remove the sill trim panel and the door pillar upper trim panel as described in paragraphs 1 to 3.

11 Slacken and remove the rear seat back catch pin from the rear of the rear seat side trim panel.

12 Slacken and remove the retaining screws from the front edge of the rear seat side trim panel then prise out the panel retaining clips. Check that all the fasteners have been removed, then unclip the panel and remove it from the vehicle.

13 On models with seat belt tensioners, slacken and remove the tensioner assembly retaining nut. This will disable the tensioner making it safe to remove the seat belt assembly.

14 Slacken and remove the retaining bolt(s) and free the seat belt lower fixing rail from the floor. Disengage the rail from the belt and remove it from the vehicle.

15 Remove the seat belt as described in paragraphs 7 and 8.

Front seat belt stalk - all models

16 Remove the seat (see Section 25).
17 Slacken and remove the bolt securing the stalk to the seat, and remove the stalk.

Rear seat side belt - Hatchback models

18 On three-door models remove the rear seat side trim panel as described in paragraphs 9 to 12.

19 On five-door models remove the sill trim panel and free the door pillar upper trim panel as described in paragraphs 1 and 2.

20 From within the luggage compartment, fold down the rear seat then slacken and remove the retaining nuts securing the relevant side trim panel in position. Unclip the panel from the rear pillar trim panel and remove it from the vehicle; where necessary free the luggage compartment light from the panel as it is removed.

21 Slacken and remove the seat belt lower mounting bolt.

22 On five-door models, slacken and remove the rear seat back catch pin from the body then unscrew the retaining fasteners and remove the trim panel from the side of the seat **(see illustrations)**.

23 Slacken and remove the three retaining nuts from the lower edge of the rear pillar trim panel then undo the retaining screw from the top of the panel. Unclip the rear of the panel from the pillar then slide the panel towards the front of the vehicle, to disengage its upper retaining clips **(see illustrations)**.

27.22a On five-door models, unscrew the seat back catch pin ...

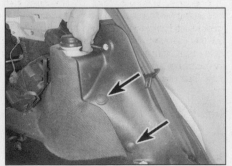

27.22b ... then unscrew the fasteners (arrowed) ...

27.22c ... and remove the rear seat side trim panel

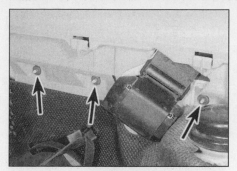

27.23a Undo the lower retaining nuts (arrowed) . . .

27.23b . . . and the upper screw . . .

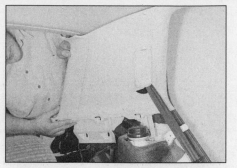

27.23c . . . then unclip the rear pillar trim panel and remove it from the vehicle

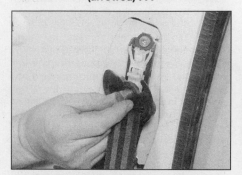

27.24 Unscrew the upper mounting bolt and free the belt from the pillar . . .

27.25 . . . then unscrew the inertia reel retaining bolt and remove the belt assembly from the vehicle

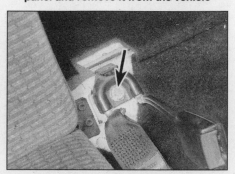

27.35 Rear seat centre belt and buckles are secured to the floor by a single bolt (arrowed)

24 Slacken and remove the seat belt upper mounting bolt and free the belt from the rear pillar **(see illustration)**. Where necessary, recover the spacer from behind the belt anchorage.

25 Undo the inertia reel mounting then free the reel from the pillar and remove the seat belt from the vehicle **(see illustration)**. If necessary, undo the retaining bolt and remove the height adjuster mechanism from the pillar (where fitted).

Rear seat side belt - Saloon models

26 Remove the sill trim panel and free the door pillar upper trim panel as described in paragraphs 1 and 2.

27 Slacken and remove the retaining screw from the top of the rear pillar trim panel. Unclip the rear of the panel from the pillar, then carefully slide the panel towards the front of the vehicle, to disengage its retaining clips.

28 Remove the seat belt as described in paragraphs 21 to 25.

Rear seat side belt - Estate models

29 Remove the rear seat assembly as described in Section 25.

30 Prise out the trim plugs from the luggage compartment cover side support rail to gain access to the retaining screws. Undo the retaining screws and remove the support rail from the vehicle.

31 Slacken and remove the luggage compartment side trim panel retaining nuts and screws and remove its retaining clips. Make a careful check that all fasteners have been removed, then carefully unclip the panel

and remove it from the luggage compartment.

32 Remove the sill trim panel and free the door pillar upper trim panel as described in paragraphs 1 and 2.

33 Slacken and remove the retaining screw from the top of the rear pillar trim panel. Unclip the rear of the panel from the pillar then slide the panel towards the front of the vehicle, to disengage its retaining clips.

34 Remove the seat belt as described in paragraphs 21 to 25.

Rear seat centre belt and buckles

35 Fold the rear seat cushion forwards then slacken and remove the bolt and washers securing the centre belt and/or buckle assembly to the floor, and remove it from the vehicle **(see illustration)**.

Refitting

36 Refitting is a reversal of the removal procedure, ensuring that all the seat belt mounting bolts are securely tightened, and all disturbed trim panels are securely retained by all the relevant retaining clips. When refitting the upper trim panels, ensure that the height adjustment levers engage correctly with the seat belt upper mounting bolt head.

28 Interior trim - removal and refitting

Interior trim panels

Note: *Specific details for most interior panels are contained within Section 27.*

1 The interior trim panels are secured using either screws or various types of trim fasteners, usually studs or clips.

2 Check that there are no other panels overlapping the one to be removed; usually there is a sequence that has to be followed, and this will only become obvious on close inspection.

3 Remove all obvious fasteners, such as screws. If the panel will not come free, it is held by hidden clips or fasteners. These are usually situated around the edge of the panel and can be prised up to release them; note, however that they can break quite easily so replacements should be available. The best way of releasing such clips without the correct type of tool, is to use a large flat-bladed screwdriver. Note in many cases that the adjacent sealing strip must be prised back to release a panel.

4 When removing a panel, **never** use excessive force or the panel may be damaged; always check carefully that all fasteners or other relevant components have been removed or released before attempting to withdraw a panel.

5 Refitting is the reverse of the removal procedure; secure the fasteners by pressing them firmly into place and ensure that all disturbed components are correctly secured to prevent rattles.

Glovebox

6 Slacken and remove the passenger side facia shelf retaining screws. Move the shelf downwards, to release its upper retaining

11

28.6 Undo the screws and remove the passenger side shelf from the facia

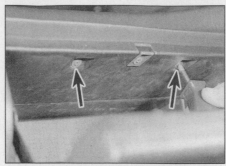

28.7a Slacken and remove the screws from inside the glovebox (arrowed) . . .

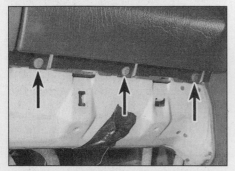

28.7b . . . and those located along the lower edge (arrowed) . . .

28.7c . . . then withdraw the glovebox from the facia

clips and remove it from the facia **(see illustration)**.

7 Open up the glovebox lid then slacken and remove the five retaining screws (two inside the glovebox and three along its lower edge). Slide the glovebox out of position, disconnecting the wiring connector from the glovebox illumination light (where fitted) as it becomes accessible **(see illustrations)**.

8 Refitting is the reverse of removal.

Carpets

9 The passenger compartment floor carpet is in one piece and is secured at its edges by screws or clips, usually the same fasteners used to secure the various adjoining trim panels.

10 Carpet removal and refitting is reasonably straightforward but very time-consuming because all adjoining trim panels must be removed first, as must components such as the seats, the centre console and seat belt lower anchorages.

Headlining

11 The headlining is clipped to the roof and can be withdrawn only once all fittings such as the grab handles, sun visors, sunroof (if fitted), windscreen and rear quarter windows and related trim panels have been removed and the door, tailgate and sunroof aperture sealing strips have been prised clear.

12 Note that headlining removal requires considerable skill and experience if it is to be carried out without damage and is therefore best entrusted to an expert.

29 Centre console - removal and refitting

1 On low specification models, remove the ashtray from the rear of the centre console

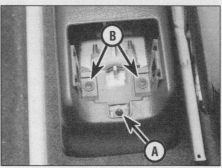

29.1a Unclip the illumination light (A) then undo the retaining screws (B) . . .

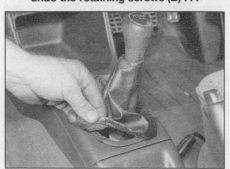

29.3a On manual transmission models, free the gear lever gaiter from the panel . . .

and free the ashtray illumination light (where fitted) from the console. Slacken and remove the two retaining screws located behind the ashtray then lift the rear section of the centre console upwards and off the handbrake lever **(see illustrations)**.

2 On high specification models, slacken and remove the retaining screws and fasteners, located on the side and at the base of the storage compartment, then free the gaiter from the handbrake lever and remove the rear section of the centre console from the vehicle.

3 On manual transmission models, free the gear lever gaiter from the console then carefully unclip the gaiter trim panel and lift it off over the gear lever **(see illustrations)**.

4 On automatic transmission models, undo the retaining screw and remove the handle from the top of the selector lever (Chapter 7B). Carefully unclip the selector lever position display panel from the centre console and slide it off the lever, disconnect the wiring connector from the programme switch (where fitted) as it becomes accessible.

5 On all models, slacken and remove the retaining screws from the left- and right-hand front edges of the console then undo the retaining nuts **(see illustrations)**.

6 Lift up the rear of the console and slide it to the rear to disengage it from the facia. Manoeuvre the console front section out of the vehicle, freeing any relevant wiring from it as it becomes accessible. Recover the spacers from the console mounting studs **(see illustration)**.

7 Refitting is the reverse of removal making sure all fasteners are securely tightened.

29.1b . . . and remove the rear section of the centre console

29.3b . . . then unclip the gaiter trim panel from the centre console

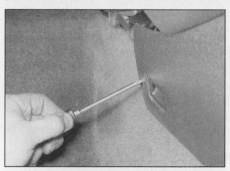

29.5a Slacken and remove the retaining screws from the front edge of the centre console . . .

29.5b . . . then undo the retaining nuts from the rear of the section (arrowed)

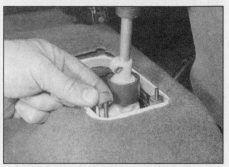

29.6 Remove the front section of the centre console, and recover the spacers from the mounting studs

30 Facia panel assembly - removal and refitting

 HAYNES HiNT *Label each wiring connector as it is disconnected from its component. The labels will prove useful on refitting, when routing the wiring and feeding the wiring through the facia apertures.*

Removal

1 Disconnect the battery negative terminal.
2 Remove the centre console (Section 29).
3 Remove the steering column (Chapter 10).
4 Remove the instrument panel assembly, cigarette lighter and radio/cassette unit as described in Chapter 12. Also remove the front (upper) treble loudspeakers from the facia.
5 On models equipped with a passenger side airbag, remove the airbag unit (Chapter 12).
6 On models not equipped with a passenger side airbag, remove the glovebox as described in Section 28.
7 On Diesel models remove the cold start accelerator cable (where fitted) as described in Chapter 4C.
8 Press in the locking buttons and unclip the fusebox cover from the underside of the driver's side lower facia panel.
9 Carefully prise the trim panel from the top of the driver's side lower facia panel then slacken and remove all the panel retaining screws. Carefully move the trim panel downwards to release it from the facia then remove it from the vehicle.
10 Working along the base of the facia panel slacken and remove the retaining bolts securing the facia to its mounting frame **(see illustrations)**.
11 Remove both windscreen wiper arms as described in Chapter 12.
12 Unscrew the windscreen wiper motor trim cover retaining fastener screws and pull out the fasteners. Peel off the rubber seal the top of the bulkhead then release the two halves of

the trim cover from the windscreen and remove them from the vehicle.
13 Slacken and remove the two facia retaining nuts which are located beneath the centre of the windscreen. If necessary, remove the wiper motor (see Chapter 12) to improve access to the nuts.
14 From inside the vehicle carefully ease the facia assembly away from the bulkhead. As it is withdrawn, release the wiring harness from its retaining clips on the rear of the facia, whilst noting its correct routing (see **Haynes Hint** at the start of this Section). Remove the facia assembly from the vehicle **(see illustration)**. Recover the sealing grommets which are fitted to the facia mounting studs; renew them if they are worn or damaged.

Refitting

15 Refitting is a reversal of the removal procedure, noting the following points:
a) *Fit the sealing grommets to the facia studs and manoeuvre the facia into position. Using the labels stuck on during removal, ensure that the wiring is correctly routed and securely retained by its facia clips.*
b) *Clip the facia back into position, making sure all the wiring connectors are fed through their respective apertures, then refit all the facia fasteners, and tighten them securely.*
c) *On completion, reconnect the battery and check that all the electrical components and switches function correctly.*

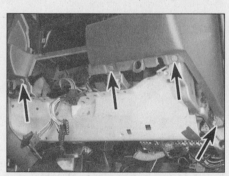

30.10a Slacken and remove the driver's side screws (arrowed) . . .

30.10b . . . the centre retaining screws (arrowed) . . .

30.10c . . . and the passenger side facia retaining screws (arrowed)

30.14 Removing the facia assembly

11

Notes

Chapter 12
Body electrical system

Contents

Degrees of difficulty

Easy, suitable for novice with little experience	Fairly easy, suitable for beginner with some experience	Fairly difficult, suitable for competent DIY mechanic	Difficult, suitable for experienced DIY mechanic	Very difficult, suitable for expert DIY or professional

Specifications

System type	12-volt negative earth
Fuses	See Wiring diagrams at end of Chapter

Torque wrench setting	Nm	lbf ft
Air bag unit	7	5

1 General information and precautions

 Warning: Before carrying out any work on the electrical system, read through the precautions given in "Safety first!" at the beginning of this manual, and in Chapter 5.

The electrical system is of 12-volt negative earth type. Power for the lights and all electrical accessories is supplied by a lead/acid type battery which is charged by the alternator.

This Chapter covers repair and service procedures for the various electrical components not associated with the engine. Information on the battery, alternator and starter motor can be found in Chapter 5.

It should be noted that prior to working on any component in the electrical system, the battery negative terminal should first be disconnected to prevent the possibility of electrical short circuits and/or fires.

2 Electrical fault-finding - general information

Note: Refer to the precautions given in "Safety first!" and in Chapter 5 before starting work. The following tests relate to testing of the main electrical circuits, and should not be used to test delicate electronic circuits (such as anti-lock braking systems), particularly where an electronic control module is used.

General

1 A typical electrical circuit consists of an electrical component, any switches, relays, motors, fuses, fusible links or circuit breakers related to that component, and the wiring and connectors which link the component to both the battery and the chassis. To help to pinpoint a problem in an electrical circuit, wiring diagrams are included at the end of this Chapter.

2 Before attempting to diagnose an electrical fault, first study the appropriate wiring diagram to obtain a complete understanding of the components included in the particular circuit concerned. The possible sources of a fault can be narrowed down by noting if other components related to the circuit are operating properly. If several components or circuits fail at one time, the problem is likely to be related to a shared fuse or earth connection.

3 Electrical problems usually stem from simple causes, such as loose or corroded connections, a faulty earth connection, a blown fuse, a melted fusible link, or a faulty relay (refer to Section 3 for details of testing relays). Visually inspect the condition of all fuses, wires and connections in a problem

12

circuit before testing the components. Use the wiring diagrams to determine which terminal connections will need to be checked in order to pinpoint the trouble spot.

4 The basic tools required for electrical fault-finding include a circuit tester or voltmeter (a 12-volt bulb with a set of test leads can also be used for certain tests); a self-powered test light (sometimes known as a continuity tester); an ohmmeter (to measure resistance); a battery and set of test leads; and a jumper wire, preferably with a circuit breaker or fuse incorporated, which can be used to bypass suspect wires or electrical components. Before attempting to locate a problem with test instruments, use the wiring diagram to determine where to make the connections.

5 To find the source of an intermittent wiring fault (usually due to a poor or dirty connection, or damaged wiring insulation), a "wiggle" test can be performed on the wiring. This involves wiggling the wiring by hand to see if the fault occurs as the wiring is moved. It should be possible to narrow down the source of the fault to a particular section of wiring. This method of testing can be used in conjunction with any of the tests described in the following sub-Sections.

6 Apart from problems due to poor connections, two basic types of fault can occur in an electrical circuit - open-circuit, or short-circuit.

7 Open-circuit faults are caused by a break somewhere in the circuit, which prevents current from flowing. An open-circuit fault will prevent a component from working, but will not cause the relevant circuit fuse to blow.

8 Short-circuit faults are caused by a "short" somewhere in the circuit, which allows the current flowing in the circuit to "escape" along an alternative route, usually to earth. Short-circuit faults are normally caused by a breakdown in wiring insulation, which allows a feed wire to touch either another wire, or an earthed component such as the bodyshell. A short circuit fault will normally cause the relevant circuit fuse to blow.

Finding an open-circuit

9 To check for an open-circuit, connect one lead of a circuit tester or voltmeter to either the negative battery terminal or a known good earth.

10 Connect the other lead to a connector in the circuit being tested, preferably nearest to the battery or fuse.

11 Switch on the circuit, bearing in mind that some circuits are live only when the ignition switch is moved to a particular position.

12 If voltage is present (indicated either by the tester bulb lighting or a voltmeter reading, as applicable), this means that the section of the circuit between the relevant connector and the battery is problem-free.

13 Continue to check the remainder of the circuit in the same fashion.

14 When a point is reached at which no voltage is present, the problem must lie

between that point and the previous test point with voltage. Most problems can be traced to a broken, corroded or loose connection.

Finding a short-circuit

15 To check for a short-circuit, first disconnect the load(s) from the circuit (loads are the components which draw current from a circuit, such as bulbs, motors, heating elements, etc).

16 Remove the relevant fuse from the circuit, and connect a circuit tester or voltmeter to the fuse connections.

17 Switch on the circuit, bearing in mind that some circuits are live only when the ignition switch is moved to a particular position.

18 If voltage is present (indicated either by the tester bulb lighting or a voltmeter reading, as applicable), this means that there is a short circuit.

19 If no voltage is present, but the fuse still blows with the load(s) connected, this indicates an internal fault in the load(s).

Finding an earth fault

20 The battery negative terminal is connected to "earth:"- the metal of the engine/transmission and the car body - and most systems are wired so that they only receive a positive feed, the current returning through the metal of the car body. This means that the component mounting and the body form part of that circuit. Loose or corroded mountings can therefore cause a range of electrical faults, ranging from total failure of a circuit, to a puzzling partial fault. In particular, lights may shine dimly (especially when another circuit sharing the same earth point is in operation), motors (eg. wiper motors or the radiator cooling fan motor) may run slowly, and the operation of one circuit may have an apparently unrelated effect on another. Note that on many vehicles, earth straps are used between certain components, such as the engine/transmission and the body, usually where there is no metal-to-metal contact between components due to flexible rubber mountings, etc.

21 To check whether a component is properly earthed, disconnect the battery and connect one lead of an ohmmeter to a known good earth point. Connect the other lead to

the wire or earth connection being tested. The resistance reading should be zero; if not, check the connection as follows.

22 If an earth connection is thought to be faulty, dismantle the connection and clean back to bare metal both the bodyshell and the wire terminal or the component earth connection mating surface. Be careful to remove all traces of dirt and corrosion, then use a knife to trim away any paint, so that a clean metal-to-metal joint is made. On reassembly, tighten the joint fasteners securely; if a wire terminal is being refitted, use serrated washers between the terminal and the bodyshell to ensure a clean and secure connection. When the connection is remade, prevent the onset of corrosion in the future by applying a coat of petroleum jelly or silicone-based grease or by spraying on (at regular intervals) a proprietary ignition sealer or a water dispersant lubricant.

3 Fuses and relays - general information

Main fuses

1 The fuses are located behind the fusebox cover in the driver's side lower facia panel.

2 To remove the fusebox cover, press in both the cover buttons then unclip the cover from the facia **(see illustration)**.

3 The main fuses are located in a row below the relays. A list of the circuits each fuse protects is stamped on the fusebox cover (a list is also given in the Specifications at the start of this Chapter). On some models (depending on specification), some additional fuses are located in separate holders which can be found either above the relays **(see illustration 3.10)** or in the engine compartment, these are also listed in the Specifications.

4 To remove a fuse, first switch off the circuit concerned (or the ignition), then pull the fuse out of its terminals **(see illustration)**. The wire within the fuse should be visible; if the fuse is blown it will be broken or melted.

5 Always renew a fuse with one of an identical rating; never use a fuse with a different rating from the original or substitute

3.2 Depress the locking buttons (arrowed) and remove the fusebox cover from the underside of the driver's lower facia panel

3.4 Removing a fuse

3.8 Diesel glow plug supply fusible link (early model shown)

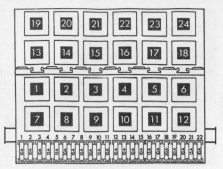

3.10 Fusebox relay and additional fuse locations

1 Air conditioning system relay
2 Tailgate wiper/washer relay
3 Fuel injection/ignition system relay
4 Relief relay for X contact
5 Not used
6 Emergency lighting relay for trailer electrical supply
7 Headlight washer system relay
8 Windscreen wiper/washer relay
9 Seat belt warning system relay/control unit
10 Wiring jumper for foglights
11 Horn relay (models with dual tone horns) or horn wiring jumper
12 Fuel pump relay (petrol models) or preheating system relay (Diesel models)
13 Inlet manifold preheating system relay or starter inhibitor relay
14 ABS relay
15 ABS hydraulic pump relay
16 ABS relay
17 ABS fuse
18 Air conditioning/ electric seat adjustment fuse
19 Not used
20 Starter inhibitor/reversing light relay
21 Lambda sensor heating cut-off relay
22 Not used
23 Not used
24 Not used

anything else. Never renew a fuse more than once without tracing the source of the trouble. The fuse rating is stamped on top of the fuse; note that the fuses are also colour-coded for easy recognition.

6 If a new fuse blows immediately, find the cause before renewing it again; a short to earth as a result of faulty insulation is most likely. Where a fuse protects more than one circuit, try to isolate the defect by switching on each circuit in turn (if possible) until the fuse blows again. Always carry a supply of spare fuses of each relevant rating on the vehicle, a spare of each rating should be clipped into the base of the fusebox.

Fusible links

7 On Diesel models the glow plug electrical supply circuit is protected by a fusible link. On all early models, both petrol and Diesel, the radiator cooling fan run-on supply is also protected by a fusible link (see Specifications for locations).

8 Prior to renewing the link, first ensure that the ignition is turned off. In the case of the glow plug fusible link also ensure that the driver's door is securely shut - the door switch is used to operate the glow plug system. Unclip the cover to gain access to the metal link; if the link has blown it will be broken or melted. Slacken the retaining screws then slide the link out of position (see illustration).

9 Fit the new link (noting the information given in paragraphs 5 and 6) then tighten securely its retaining screws and clip the lid into position.

Relays

10 The relays are located behind the fusebox cover on the driver's side lower facia panel (see illustration).

11 To gain access to the relays, remove, press in the locking buttons and unclip the fusebox cover from the underside of the driver's side lower facia panel. Carefully prise the trim panel from the top of the driver's side lower facia panel then slacken and remove all the panel retaining screws. Carefully move the panel downwards to release it from the facia then remove it from the vehicle. Release the retaining clips and lower the fusebox assembly out from underneath the facia.

12 If a circuit or system controlled by a relay develops a fault and the relay is suspect, operate the system; if the relay is functioning it should be possible to hear it click as it is energised. If this is the case the fault lies with the components or wiring of the system. If the relay is not being energised then either the relay is not receiving a main supply or a switching voltage or the relay itself is faulty. Testing is by the substitution of a known good unit but be careful; while some relays are identical in appearance and in operation, others look similar but perform different functions.

13 To renew a relay, first ensure that the ignition switch is off. The relay can then simply be pulled out from the socket and the new relay pressed in.

14 On refitting ensure that the fusebox is securely retained by the clips then refit the lower facia panel.

4 Switches - removal and refitting

Note: *Disconnect the battery negative lead before removing any switch, and reconnect the lead after refitting the switch.*

Ignition switch/ steering column lock

1 Refer to Chapter 10.

Steering column combination switches

2 Remove the steering wheel (Chapter 10).

3 Undo the retaining screws and remove the steering column upper and lower shrouds (see illustration).

4 Slacken and remove the three retaining screws then disconnect the wiring connectors and remove the switch assemblies from the steering column (see illustrations).

4.3 Undo the screws and remove the steering column upper and lower shrouds

4.4a Undo the screws (arrowed) . . .

4.4b . . . then remove the relevant combination switch assembly

12

4.6 Remove the blanking plate from the side of the lighting switch . . .

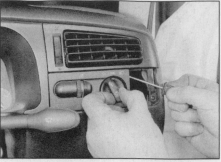

4.7a . . . then depress the retaining lug and withdraw the switch assembly . . .

4.7b . . . disconnecting its wiring connector as it becomes accessible

5 Refitting is a reversal of the removal procedure.

Lighting switch (incorporating instrument panel dimmer and headlight levelling switch)

6 Using a suitable flat-bladed screwdriver, carefully lever out the blanking plate from the side of the lighting switch and remove it from the facia **(see illustration)**. Note: *On models with ABS or an airbag, the blanking plate contains warning lights; it will be necessary to disconnect the wiring connectors from the lights as the plate is removed.*
7 Reaching in through the facia aperture, depress the lighting switch retaining lug and withdraw the switch assembly. Disconnect the wiring connector(s) and remove the switch from the facia **(see illustrations)**.
8 If necessary, release the clips and slide out the instrument panel dimmer/ headlight levelling switch(es) from the lighting switch.
9 Refitting is the reverse of removal.

Heated rear window switch

10 Using a suitable flat-bladed screwdriver, carefully prise out the blanking plug from next to the switch (the blanking plug covers a diagnostic wiring connector).
11 Carefully prise the heated rear window switch out of position, disconnecting its wiring connector as it becomes accessible **(see illustration)**.
12 On refitting securely connect the wiring connector then clip the switch back into the facia. Check the operation of the switch then refit the blanking plug.

Driver's electric rear window switch assembly

13 Remove the heated rear window switch as described above.
14 Carefully prise the rear window switch assembly out of position, disconnecting its wiring connectors as they become accessible.
15 Refitting is the reverse of removal.

Air conditioning system switches (models with standard heating/ventilation controls)

Note: *On models with the Climatronic automatic air conditioning system do not attempt to remove the switches from the control unit; the control unit should be treated as a sealed unit. If any switch fails to work, seek the advice of your VW dealer.*
16 Refer to paragraphs 10 to 12.

Heater blower motor switch (models with standard heating/ventilation controls)

17 The switch is an integral part of the heater control panel assembly and cannot be renewed separately.

Heated front seat switch assembly

18 Using a suitable flat-bladed screwdriver, carefully prise out the small blanking plate from the side of the switch assembly. **Note:** *On models with the Climatronic automatic air conditioning system, the plate will contain a temperature sensor; disconnect the wiring connector from the sensor as the plate is removed.*

19 Carefully prise the switch assembly out of position and disconnect its wiring connector.
20 Refitting is the reverse of removal.

Door electric window switches

21 Carefully unclip the upper trim cover from the door armrest handle and disconnect its wiring connector.
22 Depress the retaining clips and remove the switch from the trim cover.
23 Refitting is the reverse of removal.

Electric mirror switch

24 Unclip the upper trim cover from the door armrest handle and, if necessary, disconnect the wiring from the window switch.
25 Carefully unclip the trim cover from around the interior handle and disconnect the wiring connector from the mirror switch.
26 Release the retaining clips and press the switch out from the trim cover.
27 Refitting is the reverse of removal.

Handbrake warning light switch

28 Remove the rear section of the centre console as described in Chapter 11 to gain access to the handbrake lever.
29 Disconnect the wiring connector from the warning light switch then unclip the switch and remove it from the handbrake lever bracket **(see illustration)**.
30 Refitting is the reverse of removal. Check the operation of the switch before refitting the centre console.

Stop-light switch

31 Refer to Chapter 9.

Courtesy light switches

32 Open up the door and remove the rubber cover from the switch.
33 Carefully prise the switch out of position and withdraw it, disconnecting its wiring connector as it becomes accessible. Tie a piece of string to the wiring to prevent it falling back into the door pillar.
34 Refitting is a reversal of removal.

Luggage compartment light switch

35 The luggage compartment switch is built into the tailgate/boot lock (as applicable).
36 Remove the lock assembly (Chapter 11).

4.11 Removing the heated rear window switch

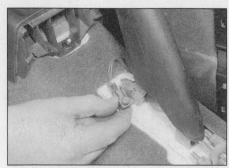

4.29 Unclip the handbrake switch from the lever and disconnect its wiring connector

5.2 Remove the cover (circular cover shown) from the rear of the headlight . . .

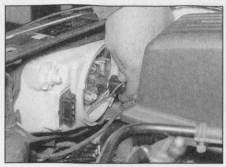

5.3 . . . and disconnect the wiring connector from the bulb

5.4a Unhook the bulb retaining clip . . .

5.4b . . . and withdraw the bulb from the headlight

37 Release the switch retaining clips and remove it from the lock assembly.
38 Refitting is the reverse of removal.

Electric sunroof switch

39 Carefully lever the courtesy light assembly out from the overhead console with a suitable screwdriver. Disconnect the wiring and remove the light assembly.
40 Release the retaining clips and remove the sunroof switch from the light assembly.
41 Refitting is the reverse of removal.

5 Bulbs (exterior lights) - renewal

General

1 Whenever a bulb is renewed, note the following points:
  a) *Disconnect the battery negative lead before starting work.*
  b) *Remember that if the light has just been in use the bulb may be extremely hot.*
  c) *Always check the bulb contacts and holder, ensuring that there is clean metal-to-metal contact between the bulb and its live(s) and earth. Clean off any corrosion or dirt before fitting a new bulb.*
  d) *Wherever bayonet-type bulbs are fitted ensure that the live contact(s) bear firmly against the bulb contact.*
  e) *Always ensure that the new bulb is of the correct rating and that it is completely clean before fitting it; this applies particularly to headlight/foglight bulbs (see below).*

Headlight

2 Working in the engine compartment, remove the access cover from the rear of the headlight unit and recover its seal. On models with a circular cover turn the cover anti-

5.9a Withdraw the sidelight bulbholder from the rear of the headlight . . .

5.11 Removing the front reflector from the bumper (model without foglights shown)

clockwise to release it, and on models with an elongated cover depress the retaining clips to release it **(see illustration)**.
3 Disconnect the wiring connector from the rear of the bulb **(see illustration)**.
4 Unhook and release the ends of the bulb retaining clip and release it from the light unit. Withdraw the bulb **(see illustrations)**.
5 When handling the new bulb, use a tissue or clean cloth to avoid touching the glass with the fingers; moisture and grease from the skin can cause blackening and rapid failure of this type of bulb. If the glass is accidentally touched, wipe it clean using methylated spirit.
6 Install the new bulb, ensuring that its locating tabs are correctly located in the light cut-outs, and secure it in position with the retaining clip.
7 Reconnect the wiring and refit the access cover, making sure it is securely refitted.

Front sidelight

8 Remove the access cover and seal from the rear of the headlight unit (see paragraph 2).
9 Withdraw the sidelight bulbholder from the headlight unit. The bulb is a bayonet fit in the holder and can be removed by pressing it and twisting it anti-clockwise **(see illustrations)**.
10 Refitting is a reversal of removal, making sure the access cover is securely refitted.

Front direction indicator

11 Using a flat-bladed screwdriver, prise the reflector out of the bumper **(see illustration)**.
12 Release the direction indicator light retaining clip and withdraw the light unit from the bumper **(see illustration)**.

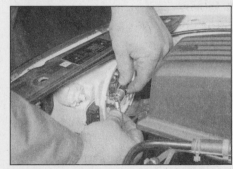

5.9b . . . and remove the bulb by pushing it in and twisting it anti-clockwise

5.12 Depress the clip (arrowed) and withdraw the direction indicator light

12

5.13 Twist the bulbholder anti-clockwise and free it from the light unit

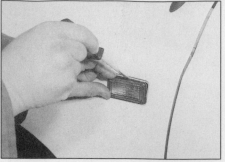

5.15 Ease the side repeater light out of the wing using a screwdriver on its upper edge

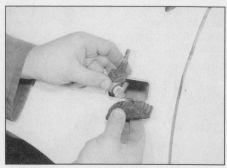

5.16 Twist the bulbholder anti-clockwise to free it from the light unit

13 Twist the bulbholder anti-clockwise and remove it from the rear of the light unit **(see illustration)**. The bulb is a bayonet fit in the holder and can be removed by pressing it and twisting it in an anti-clockwise direction.
14 Refitting is a reverse of the removal procedure making sure the light unit and reflector are securely retained by their clips.

Front direction indicator side repeater

15 Carefully prise the upper edge of the indicator side repeater light out from the wing, taking great care not to damage the painted finish of the wing **(see illustration)**.
16 Withdraw the light unit from the wing then twist the bulbholder anti-clockwise and remove it from the light **(see illustration)**. The bulb is of the capless (push-fit) type and can be removed by pulling it out of the bulbholder.
17 Refitting is a reversal of removal.

Front foglight

18 Insert a flat-bladed screwdriver between the direction indicator light and the reflector and carefully prise the reflector out from the bumper.
19 Slacken and remove the foglight screws and withdraw the light from the bumper.
20 Rotate the foglight cover anti-clockwise and release it from the rear of the light unit.
21 Disconnect the bulb wiring from the cover terminal then release the spring clip and withdraw the foglight bulb.
22 When handling the new bulb, use a tissue or clean cloth to avoid touching the glass with the fingers; moisture and grease from the skin

can cause blackening and rapid failure of this type of bulb. If the glass is accidentally touched, wipe it clean using methylated spirit.
23 Insert the new bulb, making sure it is correctly located, and secure it in position with the spring clip.
24 Connect the bulb wire to the cover terminal then refit the rear cover.
25 Refit the foglight to the bumper, securely tightening its retaining screws. Prior to refitting the reflector cover, check the aim of the foglight beam. If necessary the foglight aim can be adjusted by rotating the adjustment screw situated next to the lower retaining screw. Once the beam aim is correct, clip the reflector back into position.

Rear light cluster

26 From inside the vehicle luggage compartment, unclip the plastic cover (where fitted) to gain access to the rear of the light

cluster **(see illustration)**.
27 Release the retaining catches and free the bulbholder assembly from the rear of the light unit **(see illustration)**.
28 The relevant bulb can then be renewed, all bulbs have a bayonet fitting. Note that the stop/tail light bulb has offset locating pins to prevent it being installed incorrectly.
29 Refitting is the reverse of the removal sequence ensuring that the bulbholder is securely clipped into position.

Number plate light

30 Slacken and remove the retaining screws and withdraw the lens from the tailgate/boot lid. Recover the lens seal and examine it for signs of damage or deterioration, renewing it if necessary **(see illustrations)**.
31 The bulb is of the capless (push-fit) type and can be removed by pulling it out of the bulbholder **(see illustration)**.

5.26 Unclip the plastic cover from the rear light cluster . . .

5.27 . . . then depress the catches and withdraw the bulbholder assembly

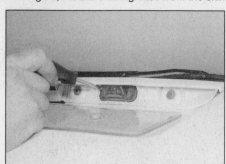

5.30a Undo the retaining screws . . .

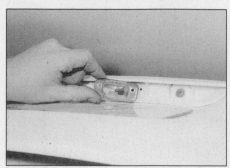

5.30b . . . and remove the lens from the rear number plate light (Hatchback shown)

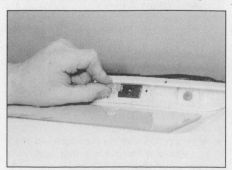

5.31 The number plate light bulb is a push fit in the light unit

32 Press the new bulb into position and refit the seal and lens. Do not overtighten the lens retaining screws as the plastic is easily cracked.

6 Bulbs (interior lights) - renewal

General

1 Refer to Section 5, paragraph 1.

Courtesy light

2 Using a small, flat-bladed screwdriver, carefully prise the light lens out of position and release the bulb from the light unit contacts.
3 Install the new bulb, ensuring it is securely held in position by the contacts, and clip the lens back into position.

Front seat reading light

4 Carefully lever the courtesy light assembly out from the overhead console with a suitable screwdriver. Disconnect the wiring connectors and remove the light assembly.
5 Rotate the reading light bulbholder anti-clockwise and remove it from the rear of the light unit. The bulb is of the capless (push-fit) type and can be removed by simply pulling it out of the bulbholder.
6 Push the new bulb into position and refit the holder to the light unit.
7 Reconnect the wiring connector and clip the light unit back into position.

Rear seat reading light

8 Carefully lever the light assembly out from the pillar with a suitable screwdriver. Disconnect the wiring connectors and remove the light assembly.
9 Rotate the reading light bulbholder anti-clockwise and remove it from the rear of the light unit. The bulb is of the capless (push-fit) type and can be removed by simply pulling it out of the bulbholder.
10 Push the new bulb into position and refit the holder to the light unit.
11 Reconnect the wiring connector and clip the light unit back into position.

Luggage compartment light

12 Refer to the information given above in paragraphs 2 and 3.

Instrument panel illumination/warning lights

13 Remove the instrument panel as described in Section 9.
14 Twist the relevant bulbholder anti-clockwise and withdraw it from the rear of the panel **(see illustration)**.
15 All bulbs are integral with their holders. Be very careful to ensure that the new bulbs are of the correct rating, the same as those removed; this is especially important in the case of the ignition/battery charging warning light.

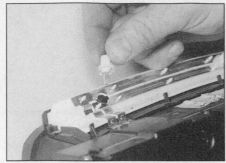

6.14 Removing an instrument panel illumination bulbholder

16 Refit the bulbholder to the rear of the instrument panel then refit the instrument panel as described in Section 9.

Glovebox illumination light bulb

17 Open up the glovebox. Using a small flat-bladed screwdriver carefully prise the top of the light assembly and withdraw it. Release the bulb from its contacts.
18 Install the new bulb, ensuring it is securely held in position by the contacts, and clip the light unit back into position.

Cassette storage box illumination bulb

19 Carefully slide the storage box out from the facia and disconnect its wiring connector.
20 Using a small flat-bladed screwdriver, carefully release the retaining clips and remove the rear cover from the storage box. Remove the bulb from its holder.
21 Refitting is the reverse of removal.

Cigarette lighter/ ashtray illumination bulb

22 On models equipped with standard manual heating/ventilation system controls, carefully prise out the surround from around the control knobs. Slacken and remove the four unit retaining screws and carefully free the control unit from the rear of the switch panel.
23 On models with the automatic "Climatronic" heating system, carefully insert a flat-bladed screwdriver between the bottom of the display panel and the switches and gently ease the panel out of position. Slacken

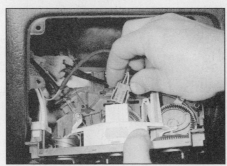

6.28a Disconnect the wiring connector . . .

and remove the four retaining screws and free the electronic control unit from the rear of the switch panel.
24 Remove the ashtray then undo the two facia switch panel retaining screws.
25 Withdraw the switch panel from the facia until access can be gained to the rear of the cigarette lighter. Unclip the bulbholder from the lighter and remove the bulb.
26 Refitting is the reverse of removal.

Heater control panel illumination bulb

27 Withdraw the heater control panel as described in Section 9 of Chapter 3 so that access to the rear of the panel can be gained. Note that there is no need to remove the panel completely, the control cables can be left attached.
28 Disconnect the wiring connector then unclip the bulbholder assembly from the rear of the control panel **(see illustrations)**.
29 Unclip the surround from around the bulb then carefully pull the bulb out of its holder.
30 Refitting is the reverse of removal.

Switch illumination bulbs

31 All of the switches are fitted with illuminating bulbs; some are also fitted with a bulb to show when the circuit concerned is operating. These bulbs are an integral part of the switch assembly and cannot be obtained separately. Bulb replacement will therefore require the renewal of the complete switch assembly.

7 Exterior light units - removal and refitting

Note: *Disconnect the battery negative lead before removing any light unit, and reconnect the lead after refitting the light unit.*

Headlight

1 Using a suitable screwdriver, carefully release the radiator grille upper and lower retaining lugs then move the grille forwards and away from the vehicle.
2 Disconnect the wiring connector from the rear of the headlight unit **(see illustration)**.
3 Slacken and remove the headlight retaining screws and withdraw the headlight from the

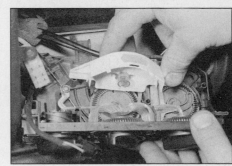

6.28b . . . and unclip the bulbholder from the rear of the heater control panel

12

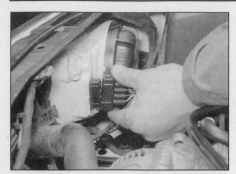

7.2 Disconnecting the headlight wiring connector

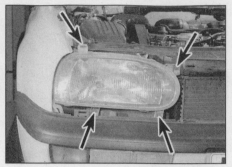

7.3a Slacken and remove the retaining screws (arrowed) . . .

7.3b . . . and remove the headlight from the vehicle

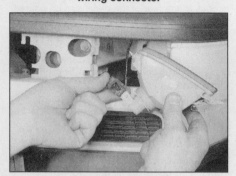

7.7 Removing the front direction indicator light

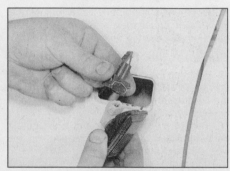

7.9 Removing the front direction indicator side repeater light

Front foglight

11 Insert a flat-bladed screwdriver between the direction indicator light and the reflector and carefully prise the reflector out from the bumper.

12 Slacken and remove the foglight retaining screws then withdraw the light from the bumper and disconnect it from the wiring connector.

13 Refit the foglight to the bumper, securely tightening its retaining screws. Prior to refitting the reflector cover, check the aim of the foglight beam. If necessary the foglight aim can be adjusted by rotating the adjustment screw situated next to the lower retaining screw. Once the beam aim is correct, clip the reflector back into position.

Rear light cluster

14 From inside the vehicle luggage compartment, unclip the plastic cover (where fitted) to gain access to the rear of the light cluster.

15 Disconnect the wiring connectors from the rear of the bulbholder **(see illustration)**.

16 Slacken and remove the rear light unit retaining nuts and withdraw the light unit from the rear of the vehicle. Recover the rubber seal from the rear of the light unit; if the seal shows signs of damage or deterioration, renew it **(see illustrations)**.

17 Refitting is a reverse of the removal procedure. Tighten the retaining nuts securely.

Number plate light

18 Slacken and remove the retaining screws and withdraw the lens from the tailgate/boot

vehicle **(see illustrations)**. On models with a headlight beam adjustment system it will be necessary to disconnect the wiring from the adjustment motor as the headlight is removed.

4 On models equipped with a headlight beam adjustment system, if necessary, rotate the adjustment motor anti-clockwise to free the motor from the rear of the headlight unit and pull the motor squarely away to disconnect its balljoint. On refitting, align the motor balljoint with the light unit socket and clip it into position. Engage the motor assembly with the light and twist it clockwise to secure it in position.

5 Refitting is a direct reversal of the removal procedure. On completion check the headlight beam alignment using the information given in Section 8.

Front direction indicator light

6 Insert a flat-bladed screwdriver between

the direction indicator light and the reflector and prise the reflector out from the bumper.

7 Release the direction indicator light retaining clip then withdraw the light unit from the bumper, disconnecting it from the wiring connector **(see illustration)**.

8 Refitting is a reverse of the removal procedure making sure the light unit and reflector are securely retained by their clips.

Front direction indicator side repeater

9 Carefully prise the upper edge of the indicator side repeater light out from the wing, if necessary using a suitable plastic wedge and taking great care not damage the painted finish of the wing. Disconnect it from the wiring connector **(see illustration)**. Tie a piece of string to the wiring to prevent it falling back into the wing.

10 Refitting is a reversal of removal.

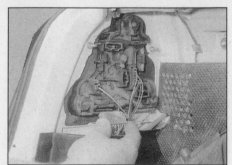

7.15 Disconnect the wiring connectors from the rear of the light unit . . .

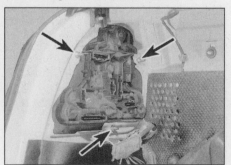

7.16a . . . then undo the retaining nuts (arrowed) . . .

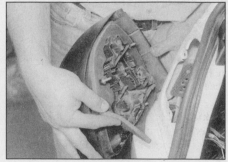

7.16b . . . and withdraw the rear light unit and rubber seal from the vehicle

9.2 On models without heated seats, remove the blanking plate next to the panel

9.4 Undo the two screws (arrowed) and remove the instrument panel shroud

9.5a Undo the two retaining screws (arrowed) . . .

9.5b . . . then withdraw the instrument panel from the facia . . .

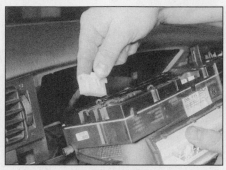

9.5c . . . and disconnect its wiring connector

lid. Recover the lens seal and examine it for signs of damage or deterioration, renewing it if necessary.

19 Withdraw the light unit and disconnect it from the wiring connector.

20 Refitting is the reverse of removal. Do not overtighten the lens retaining screws as the plastic is easily cracked.

8 Headlight beam alignment - general information

Accurate adjustment of the headlight beam is only possible using optical beam setting equipment and this work should therefore be carried out by a VW dealer or suitably equipped workshop.

For reference the headlights can be adjusted using the adjuster assemblies fitted to the top of each light unit. The outer adjuster alters the horizontal position of the beam whilst the inner adjuster alters the vertical aim of the beam.

Some models are equipped , with an electrically operated headlight beam adjustment system which is controlled through the switch in the facia. On these models ensure that the switch is set to the off position before adjusting the headlight aim.

9 Instrument panel - removal and refitting

Removal

1 Disconnect the battery negative terminal.

2 Remove the lighting switch and heated front seat switch as described in Section 4. On models without heated seats, carefully prise out the blanking plate (which is fitted in place of the heated seat switch) from the side of the instrument panel **(see illustration)**.

3 Slacken the retaining screws and remove the steering column shrouds.

4 Undo the two retaining screws and remove the instrument panel shroud from the facia **(see illustration)**.

5 Slacken and remove the two retaining screws from either side of the instrument panel then carefully withdraw the instrument panel from the facia, disconnecting the wiring connector(s) from the rear of the panel **(see illustrations)**.

Refitting

6 Refitting is the reverse of removal making sure that the instrument panel wiring is

11.2a Remove the surround from around the heater controls . . .

securely reconnected. On completion reconnect the battery and check the operation of the panel warning lights to ensure that they are functioning correctly.

10 Instrument panel components - removal and refitting

At the time of writing, no individual components are available for the instrument panel and therefore the panel must be treated as a sealed unit. If there is a fault with one of the instruments, remove the panel as described in Section 9 and take it to your VW dealer for testing. They have access to a special diagnostic tester which will be able to locate the fault and will then be able to advise you on the best course of action.

11 Cigarette lighter - removal and refitting

Removal

1 Disconnect the battery negative terminal.

2 On models equipped with standard manual heating/ventilation system controls, carefully prise out the surround from around the control knobs. Slacken and remove the four retaining screws and free the control unit from the rear of the switch panel **(see illustrations)**.

3 On models with the automatic "Climatronic" heating system, carefully insert a flat-bladed screwdriver between the bottom of the display panel and the switches and

11.2b . . . then undo the four control unit retaining screws (arrowed)

12

11.5 Undo the two screws (arrowed) . . .

11.6a . . . then withdraw the switch panel from the facia

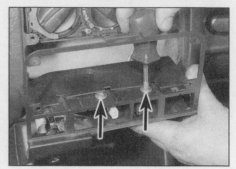

11.6b Undo the diagnostic wiring connector retaining screws (arrowed) . . .

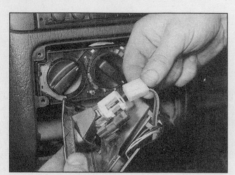

11.6c . . . then disconnect the cigarette lighter wiring and remove the switch panel

11.7 Depress the retaining tangs and push the cigarette lighter out of the switch panel

illustration). Lift the blade off the glass and pull the wiper arm off its spindle. If necessary the arm can be levered off the spindle using a suitable flat-bladed screwdriver.

Note: *If both windscreen wiper arms are to be removed at the same time mark them for identification; the arms are not interchangeable.*

Refitting

4 Ensure that the wiper arm and spindle splines are clean and dry, then refit the arm to the spindle, aligning the wiper blade with the tape fitted on removal. Refit the spindle nut, tightening it securely, and clip the nut cover back in position.

14 Windscreen wiper motor and linkage - removal and refitting

Removal

1 Disconnect the battery negative terminal.
2 Remove the wiper arms as described in the previous Section.
3 Unclip the rubber seal from the top of the engine compartment bulkhead **(see illustration)**.
4 Unscrew the windscreen wiper motor trim cover fastener screws and pull out the fasteners. Release the two halves of the trim cover from the windscreen and remove them from the vehicle **(see illustrations)**.
5 Disconnect the wiring connector from the wiper motor and free the wiring from its retaining clips **(see illustration)**.
6 Slacken and remove the three wiper motor

gently ease the panel out of position. Slacken and remove the four retaining screws and free the electronic control unit from the rear of the switch panel.
4 Prise out the blanking plugs and remove the switch(es) from the facia panel as described in Section 4.
5 Remove the ashtray and cigarette lighter insert then undo the two facia switch panel retaining screws **(see illustration)**.
6 Withdraw the switch panel from the facia and unscrew the retaining screws securing the diagnostic wiring connectors to the panel. Disconnect the wiring connector from the cigarette lighter then release the wiring harness from the panel and remove the switch panel from the facia **(see illustrations)**.
7 Unclip the bulbholder from the lighter then depress the retaining tangs and push out the lighter out of the panel **(see illustration)**.

Refitting

8 Refitting is a reversal of the removal procedure, ensuring that all the wiring connectors are securely reconnected.

12 Horn(s) - removal and refitting

Removal

1 The horn(s) is/are located behind the front bumper. To improve access, apply the handbrake then jack up the front of the vehicle and support it on axle stands (see *"Jacking and vehicle support"*).

2 Undo the retaining bolt and remove the horn, disconnecting its wiring connectors as they become accessible.

Refitting

3 Refitting is the reverse of removal.

13 Wiper arm - removal and refitting

Removal

1 Operate the wiper motor then switch it off so that the wiper arm returns to the at-rest position.
2 Stick a piece of masking tape along the edge of the wiper blade to use as an alignment aid on refitting.
3 Prise off the wiper arm spindle nut cover then slacken and remove the spindle nut **(see**

13.3 Unscrew the retaining nut and remove the wiper arm from its spindle

14.3 Unclip the rubber seal and remove it from the engine compartment bulkhead

14.4a Unscrew the trim cover fastener screws and pull out the fasteners . . .

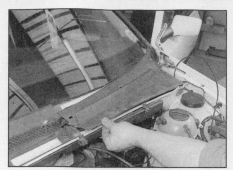

14.4b . . . then remove the passenger's side . . .

14.4c . . . and driver's side of the windscreen wiper motor trim cover

14.5 Disconnect the wiper motor wiring, and free the wiring from its retaining clips

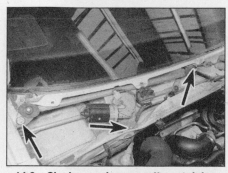

14.6a Slacken and remove the retaining nuts and bolts (arrowed) . . .

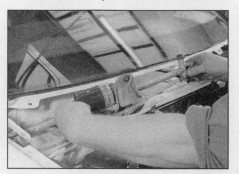

14.6b . . . and manoeuvre the wiper motor assembly out of position

retaining nuts/bolts (as applicable) and manoeuvre the motor and linkage assembly out of position **(see illustrations)**. Recover the washers and spacers from the motor mounting rubbers and inspect the rubbers for signs of damage or deterioration, and renew if necessary.

7 If necessary, mark the relative positions of the motor shaft and linkage arm then unscrew the retaining nut from the motor spindle. Free the wiper linkage from the spindle then remove the three motor retaining bolts and separate the motor and linkage.

Refitting

8 Where necessary, assemble the motor and linkage and securely tighten the motor retaining bolts. Locate the linkage arm on the motor spindle, aligning the marks made prior to removal, and securely tighten its retaining nut.

9 Ensure that the mounting rubbers are in position then manoeuvre the motor assembly back into position in the vehicle. Refit the spacers and washers and tighten the motor mounting nuts/bolts securely.

10 Reconnect the wiring connector and clip it into the retaining clips.

11 Refit the wiper motor trim covers to the vehicle and secure them in position with their retaining clips.

12 Refit the rubber seal to the bulkhead and refit the wiper arms.

15 Tailgate wiper motor - removal and refitting

Removal

1 Remove the wiper arm as described in Section 13.

2 Unscrew the nut from the wiper motor spindle and remove the washer **(see illustration)**.

3 On Hatchback models, slacken and remove the tailgate trim panel retaining screw then release the trim panel clips, carefully levering between the panel and tailgate with a flat-bladed screwdriver. Work around the outside of the panel, and when all the clips are released, remove the panel **(see illustrations)**.

4 On Estate models, work around the edge of the tailgate trim panel and remove its retaining clips; to remove the clips, lift their centre pins and then carefully prise them out of position. Slacken and remove the trim panel retaining screw then unclip the panel and remove it from the tailgate.

5 On all models, disconnect the tailgate washer hose from the rear of the wiper motor then disconnect its wiring connector. Free the

15.2 Unscrew the nut and remove the washer from the wiper motor spindle

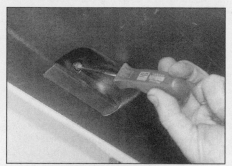

15.3a On Hatchback models, undo the retaining screw . . .

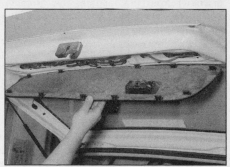

15.3b . . . then unclip the trim panel from the tailgate

12

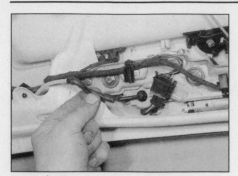

15.5a Disconnect the washer hose . . .

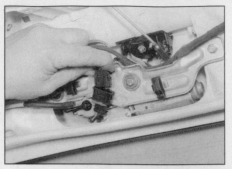

15.5b . . . and wiring connector from the motor, and free the wiring from its clips

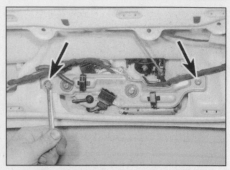

15.6a Undo the two retaining bolts (arrowed) . . .

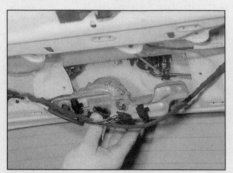

15.6b . . . then remove the motor assembly . . .

15.6c . . . and recover the rubber sealing grommet from the tailgate

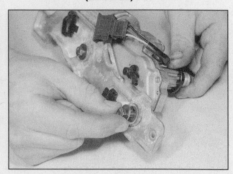

15.7a Unscrew the two bolts, and separate the motor and mounting bracket . . .

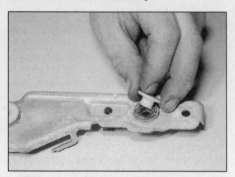

15.7b . . . and recover the spacers from the mounting bushes

wiring from the relevant retaining clips **(see illustrations)**.
6 Slacken and remove the wiper motor retaining bolts and manoeuvre the assembly out from the tailgate. Recover the rubber grommet from the tailgate; the grommet should be renewed if it is damaged **(see illustrations)**.
7 If necessary, slacken and remove the retaining bolts then separate the motor from its mounting bracket and recover the spacers and mounting rubbers **(see illustrations)**. Inspect the rubbers for signs of damage or deterioration and renew if necessary.

Refitting

8 Where necessary, fit the motor to its mounting, making sure the rubbers and spacers are correctly positioned, and tighten the retaining bolts securely.
9 Fit the rubber grommet to the tailgate and

manoeuvre the assembly into position in the tailgate. Refit the motor mounting bolts and tighten them securely.
10 Reconnect the wiper motor wiring connector and the washer hose.
11 Refit the trim panel to the tailgate ensuring that it is securely retained by all of its clips.
12 Slide the washer onto the wiper spindle then fit the retaining nut and tighten it securely.
13 Refit the wiper arm as described in Section 13 and reconnect the battery.

16 Windscreen/tailgate washer system components - removal and refitting

Washer system reservoir

1 Remove the battery (see Chapter 5A).
2 Disconnect the wiring connector and the hose(s) from the washer pump.
3 Slacken and remove the retaining nuts from the top of the reservoir and lift the reservoir upwards and out of position. On models equipped with headlight washers it will be necessary to disconnect the wiring connector and washer hose from the headlight pump as the reservoir is removed. Wash off any spilt fluid with cold water.
4 Refitting is the reverse of removal, ensuring the washer hose(s) are securely connected.

Washer pump

5 Empty the contents of the reservoir or be prepared for spillage as the pump is removed.

6 Remove the battery (see Chapter 5A).
7 Disconnect the wiring connector and washer hose(s) from the pump.
8 Carefully ease the pump out from the reservoir and recover its sealing grommet. Wash off any spilt fluid with cold water.
9 Refitting is the reverse of removal, using a new sealing grommet if the original one shows signs of damage or deterioration. Refill the reservoir and check the pump grommet for leaks.

Windscreen washer jets

10 Open up the bonnet and disconnect the washer hose from the base of the jet. Where necessary, also disconnect the wiring connector from the jet. Carefully ease the jet out from the bonnet, taking great care not to damage the paintwork.
11 On refitting, securely connect the jet to the hose and clip it into position in the bonnet; where necessary also reconnect the wiring connector. Check the operation of the jet. If necessary, adjust the nozzle using a pin, aiming the spray to a point slightly above the centre of the swept area.

Tailgate washer jet

12 Unclip the cover from the wiper arm spindle to gain access to the washer jet and unclip the jet from the centre of the spindle **(see illustration)**.
13 On refitting ensure that the jet is clipped securely in position. Check the operation of the jet. If necessary adjust the nozzle using a pin, aiming the spray to a point slightly above the centre of the swept area.

16.12 Removing the tailgate washer jet

17 Headlight washer system components - removal and refitting

Washer system reservoir

1 Refer to Section 16.

Washer pump

2 Remove the washer reservoir (Section 16).
3 Carefully ease the pump out from the reservoir and recover its sealing grommet. Wash off any spilt fluid with cold water.
4 Refitting is the reverse of removal, using a new sealing grommet if the original one is damaged or perished. Refill the reservoir and check the pump grommet for leaks.

Washer jets

5 On Saloon models, prise out the trim cover

from the front of the washer jet then undo the retaining screws and remove the jet assembly from the bumper.
6 On Hatchback and Estate models, unclip the cover from the top of the jet then undo the retaining screws and remove the jet from the bumper.
7 Refitting is the reverse of removal making sure that the washer jets are correctly aimed at the headlight.

18 Radio/cassette player - removal and refitting

Note: *The following removal and refitting procedure is for the range of radio/cassette units which VW fit as standard equipment. Removal and refitting procedures of non-standard will differ slightly.*

Removal

Early (pre-1994) models

1 The radio/cassette players fitted prior to 1994 have DIN standard fixings. Two special tools, obtainable from most car accessory shops, are required for removal. Alternatively suitable tools can be fabricated from 3 mm diameter wire, such as welding rod.
2 Disconnect the battery negative lead.
3 Insert the tools into the slots on each side of the unit and push them until they snap into place. The radio/cassette player can then be slid out of the facia and the wiring connectors and aerial disconnected **(see illustrations)**.

Later (1994 onwards) models

4 The radio/cassette players fitted from 1994 onwards have special fixings and a special VW radio removal tool (No. 3316) is required for removal **(see illustration)**.
5 Slide tools into the slots on each side of the unit until they snap into place. Slide the radio squarely out of position, disconnecting the wiring connector and aerial as they become accessible. To release the removal tools, push the locating lugs on the side of the unit inwards.

Refitting

6 Reconnect the wiring connector and aerial lead then push the unit into the facia until the retaining lugs snap into place.

19 Loudspeakers - removal and refitting

Front upper (treble) loudspeaker

1 Carefully lever the speaker grille out from the top of the facia, taking great care not to mark either component **(see illustration)**.
2 Prise the speaker out of position and disconnect its wiring plug **(see illustration)**.
3 Refitting is the reverse of removal making sure the speaker is correctly located.

Front lower (bass) loudspeaker

4 Using a flat-bladed screwdriver, carefully prise the speaker grille out from the door panel **(see illustration)**.

18.3a On early (pre-1994) models, insert the removal tools into position . . .

18.3b . . . then withdraw the radio/cassette player and disconnect its wiring connectors and aerial lead (arrowed)

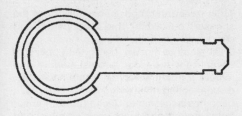

18.4 Radio removal tool (VW No. 3316) required to remove radio/cassette player on later (1994 on) models

19.1 Unclip the speaker grille from the top of the facia . . .

19.2 . . . and carefully prise the front upper loudspeaker out of position

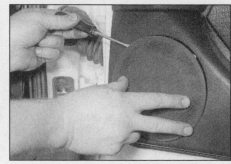

19.4 Unclip the speaker grille

12

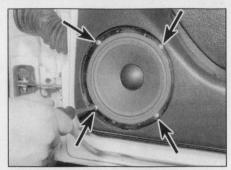

19.5a Undo the four screws (arrowed), withdraw the speaker from the panel . . .

19.5b . . . and disconnect its wiring connector

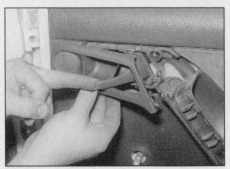

19.8a On 4- and 5-door models, unclip the trim cover around the door handle . . .

19.8b . . . and disconnect the wiring connector . . .

19.8c . . . then release the retaining clips and remove the speaker

5 Slacken and remove the retaining screws then remove the speaker from the door, disconnecting its wiring connector as it becomes accessible **(see illustrations)**.
6 Refitting is the reverse of removal making sure the speaker is correctly located.

Rear upper (treble) loudspeaker

7 On three-door models, carefully prise the speaker out from the trim panel and disconnect it from the wiring connector.
8 On all other models, unclip the upper trim cover from the door armrest handle and remove it from the vehicle, where necessary, disconnecting the wiring connector as it becomes accessible. Unclip the trim cover from around the door inner handle and remove it from the door, disconnecting the wiring connector as it becomes accessible. Unclip the speaker and remove it from the panel **(see illustrations)**.
9 Refitting is the reverse of removal.

Rear lower (bass) loudspeaker

10 Refer to paragraphs 4 to 6.

20 Radio aerial - removal and refitting

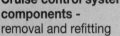

Wing mounted aerial

Removal

1 Open up the bonnet then slacken the retaining nuts and free the earth strap from the left-hand side of the bonnet and wing.
2 Undo the retaining screw(s) then unclip the

left-hand footwell side trim panel from the vehicle to gain access to the aerial lead connection. Separate the two halves of the aerial lead.
3 Undo the retaining screw from the rear of the left-hand wheelarch liner then release the retaining fasteners and remove the liner; the fasteners are released by pressing out their centre pins. If the fastener centre pins are not recovered, new fasteners will be required on refitting.
4 Pull the aerial lead and earth lead through into the wheelarch, noting their correct routing.
5 Unscrew the nut securing the aerial mounting bracket in position then slide the bracket off from the base of the aerial.
6 Slide the aerial downwards and out of position and recover the mounting grommet from the wing. Inspect the mounting grommet and bracket grommet for signs of damage or deterioration and renew as necessary.

Refitting

7 Locate the mounting grommet in the wing and firmly insert the aerial. Slide the mounting bracket into position and securely tighten its mounting nut.
8 Feed the aerial lead and earth lead through their respective apertures in the wing.
9 From inside the vehicle, reconnect the two halves of the aerial lead and refit the footwell side trim panel.
10 Reconnect the earth lead to the bonnet and wing and securely tighten the nuts.
11 Check the aerial operation then refit the wheelarch liner making sure it is securely retained by its fasteners and screw.

Roof mounted aerial

Removal

12 Open up the tailgate (where necessary) and carefully prise out the trim strip securing the rear of the headlining to the roof. Carefully peel the headlining back until access is gained to the aerial retaining nut and aerial lead and wiring connectors.
13 Disconnect the aerial lead and wiring connector then undo the retaining nut and remove the aerial from the roof. Recover the aerial sealing grommet.

Refitting

14 On refitting, locate the sealing grommet and aerial in the roof hole.
15 Refit and tighten the retaining nut.
16 Reconnect the aerial lead and wiring connector then clip the headlining trim strip back into position.

21 Cruise control system components - removal and refitting

1 The cruise control system is a vacuum operated system; the main components being a vacuum pump, an electronic control unit (ECU) and the accelerator pedal position unit. In addition to these there is the operating switch, which is built into the left-hand combination switch, and the vent switch(es) on the clutch and/or brake pedal(s) **(see illustration)**.

Vacuum pump

2 Remove the windscreen washer fluid reservoir as described in Section 16 to gain access to the pump.
3 Disconnect the wiring connector then unscrew the pump retaining bolt.
4 Slide the pump assembly to the rear to disengage its retaining pegs. Disconnect the vacuum hose and remove the pump assembly from the vehicle.
5 Refitting is the reverse of removal making sure that the vacuum hose is securely reconnected.

Electronic control unit (ECU)

6 The cruise control ECU is located behind

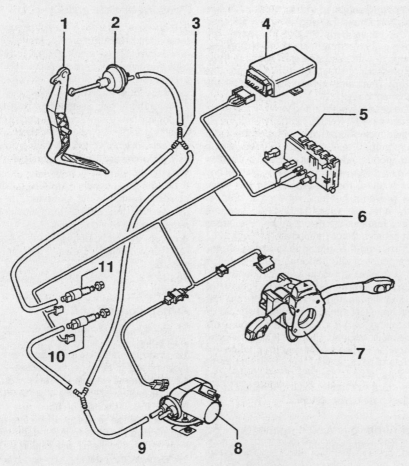

21.1 Cruise control system components

1 *Accelerator pedal*
2 *Accelerator pedal positioning unit*
3 *Vacuum hose connector*
4 *Electronic control unit (ECU)*
5 *Fusebox/relay assembly*
6 *Wiring harness*
7 *System operating switch (integral with steering column switch assembly)*
8 *Vacuum pump*
9 *Vacuum hose*
10 *Brake pedal vent switch*
11 *Clutch pedal vent switch*

the driver's side lower facia panel. Firstly, disconnect the battery negative terminal.

7 Press in the locking buttons and unclip the fusebox cover from the underside of the driver's side lower facia panel.

8 Carefully prise the trim cover from the top of the driver's side lower facia panel then slacken and remove all the panel retaining screws. Carefully move the panel downwards to release it from the facia then remove it from the vehicle.

9 Slacken and remove the retaining nut securing the ECU mounting bracket to the facia and disconnect the ECU wiring connector. **Note:** *On models with an anti-theft alarm system, it will also be necessary to disconnect the wiring connectors from the alarm system ECU as this is mounted on the same plate as the cruise control ECU.*

10 Release the retaining lugs and remove the ECU mounting plate from behind the facia.

11 Undo the retaining screws and separate the ECU and its mounting plate.

12 Refitting is a reverse of the removal procedure making sure the wiring connectors are securely reconnected.

Accelerator pedal positioning unit

13 Remove the driver's side lower facia panel as described in paragraphs 7 and 8.

14 Reach up behind the facia and disconnect the vacuum hose from the unit.

15 Carefully lever the positioning unit rod off its pivot bolt balljoint.

16 Slacken and remove the nut securing the positioning unit to its mounting bracket and manoeuvre the assembly out from underneath the facia.

17 Refitting is the reverse of removal making sure the positioning unit rod is clipped securely onto its balljoint. Prior to refitting the facia panel, adjust the unit as follows.

18 Rotate the adjusting sleeve slightly anti-clockwise and free it from the front of the positioning unit body. Adjust the accelerator cable as described in Chapter 4 then slide the

adjusting sleeve onto the body until there is approximately 1 mm of free play in the positioning unit rod. Hold the sleeve in this position and rotate in slightly clockwise to lock it in position. Once the positioning unit rod free play is correctly adjusted, refit the lower facia panel.

Pedal vent switch

19 Remove the driver's side lower facia panel as described in paragraph 8.

20 Disconnect the wiring connector and pull the vacuum hose off from the switch.

21 Remove the vent valve from the pedal bracket.

22 On refitting, screw the switch fully into the pedal bracket. With the switch in position, pull the pedal back to the at-rest position; this will automatically adjust the position of the vent switch.

23 Reconnect the vacuum hose and wiring connector and refit the lower facia panel.

System operating switch

24 The system operating switch is an integral part of the left-hand combination switch assembly. Refer to Section 4 for removal and refitting details.

22 Anti-theft alarm system - general information

Note: *This information is applicable only to the anti-theft alarm system fitted by VW as standard equipment.*

Some models in the range are fitted with an anti-theft alarm system as standard equipment. The alarm has switches on all the doors (including the tailgate/boot lid), the bonnet and the ignition switch. If the tailgate/boot lid, bonnet or either of the doors are opened or the ignition switch is switched on whilst the alarm is set, the alarm horn will sound and the hazard warning lights will flash. The alarm also has an immobiliser function which makes the ignition (petrol models) or fuel supply system (Diesel models) inoperable whilst the alarm is triggered.

The alarm is set using the key in the driver's or passenger's front door lock. Simply hold the key in the locking position until the warning light near the driver's door lock button starts to flash. The alarm system will then start to monitor its various switches approximately 30 seconds later.

With the alarm set, if the tailgate/boot lid is unlocked, the lock switch sensing will automatically be switched off but the door and bonnet switches will still be active. Once the tailgate/boot lid is shut and locked again, the switch sensing will be switched back on again.

Should the alarm system become faulty the vehicle should be taken to a VW dealer for examination. They will have access to a special diagnostic tester which will quickly trace any fault present in the system.

12

23 Heated front seat components - removal and refitting

Heater mats

1 On models equipped with heated front seats, a heater pad is fitted to both the seat back and the seat cushion. Renewal of either heater mat involves peeling back the upholstery, removing the old mat, sticking the new mat in position and then refitting the upholstery. Note that upholstery removal and refitting requires considerable skill and experience if it is to be carried out successfully and is therefore best entrusted to your VW dealer. In practice, it will be very difficult for the home mechanic to carry out the job without ruining the upholstery.

Heated seat switches

2 Refer to Section 4.

24 Airbag system - general information and precautions

⚠️ **Warning: Before carrying out any operations on the airbag system, disconnect the battery negative terminal. When operations are complete, make sure no one is inside the vehicle when the battery is reconnected.**

Note that the airbag(s) must not be subjected to temperatures in excess of 90°C (194°F). When the airbag is removed, ensure that it is stored the correct way up to prevent possible inflation.

Do not allow any solvents or cleaning agents to contact the airbag assemblies. They must be cleaned using only a damp cloth.

The airbags and control unit are both sensitive to impact. If either is dropped or damaged they should be renewed.

Disconnect the airbag control unit wiring plug prior to using arc-welding equipment on the vehicle.

Both a driver's and passenger's airbag were fitted as standard to some models in the Golf/Vento range; on other models they were available as an optional extra. Models fitted with a driver's side airbag have the word AIRBAG stamped on the airbag unit, which is fitted to the centre of the steering wheel.

Models also equipped with a passenger's side airbag also have the word AIRBAG stamped on the passenger's end of the facia. The airbag system comprises of the airbag unit (complete with gas generator) which is fitted to the steering wheel, an impact sensor, the control unit and a warning light in the instrument panel.

The airbag system is triggered in the event of a heavy frontal impact above a predetermined force; depending on the point of impact. The airbag is inflated within milliseconds and forms a safety cushion between the driver and the steering wheel and (where fitted) the passenger and the facia. This prevents contact between the upper body and the wheel/facia and therefore greatly reduces the risk of injury. The airbag then deflates almost immediately.

Every time the ignition is switched on, the airbag control unit performs a self-test. The self-test takes approximately 3 seconds and during this time the airbag warning light on the facia is illuminated. After the self-test has been completed the warning light should go out. If the warning light fails to come on, remains illuminated after the initial 3 second period or comes on at any time when the vehicle is being driven, there is a fault in the airbag system. The vehicle should then be taken to a VW dealer for examination at the earliest possible opportunity.

25 Airbag system components - removal and refitting

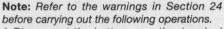

Note: *Refer to the warnings in Section 24 before carrying out the following operations.*
1 Disconnect the battery negative terminal then continue as described under the relevant heading.

Driver's side airbag

Note: *New airbag retaining screws will be required on refitting.*
2 Slacken and remove the two airbag retaining screws from the rear of the steering wheel, rotating the wheel as necessary to gain access to the screws.
3 Return the steering wheel to the straight-ahead position then carefully lift the airbag assembly away from the steering wheel and disconnect the wiring connector from the rear of the unit. Note that the airbag must not be knocked or dropped and should be stored the correct way up with its padded surface uppermost.
4 On refitting reconnect the wiring connector and seat the airbag unit in the steering wheel, making sure the wire does not become trapped. Fit the new retaining screws and tighten them securely. Reconnect the battery.

Passenger side airbag

5 Slacken and remove the passenger side facia shelf retaining screws. Move the shelf downwards, to release its upper retaining clips and remove it from the facia.
6 Unscrew the retaining screws, situated along the lower edge of the facia.
7 Move the airbag assembly downwards to disengage the upper locating pegs from the mounting frame. Remove the airbag unit from the facia, disconnecting the wiring connector as it becomes accessible. Recover the guides from the airbag mounting frame.
8 On refitting, ensure that the guides are correctly seated in the mounting frame then manoeuvre the airbag into position and reconnect the wiring connector.
9 Locate the airbag pegs into the guides then refit the retaining screws, tightening them securely.
10 Refit the facia shelf and reconnect the battery.

Airbag control unit

11 Remove the centre console as described in Chapter 11.
12 Undo the retaining bolts and remove the facia mounting frame centre bracket.
13 Slacken the retaining screws and remove the rear footwell duct joining pieces from the base of the air distribution housing.
14 Remove the retaining screw and fastener and remove the front footwell duct assembly from the base of the air distribution housing.
15 Depress the retaining clip and disconnect the wiring connector from the control unit.
16 Unscrew the nuts securing the control unit mounting bracket to the floor and remove the assembly from the vehicle. Note that it may be necessary to cut the carpet to gain access to the mounting nuts.
17 Where necessary, undo the retaining nuts and separate the bracket and control unit.
18 Refitting is the reverse of removal making sure the wiring connector is securely reconnected.

Airbag wiring contact unit

19 Remove the steering wheel as described in Chapter 10.
20 Taking care not to rotate the contact unit, undo the three retaining screws and remove it from the steering wheel.
21 On refitting, fit the unit to the steering wheel and securely tighten its retaining screws. If a new contact unit is being fitted, cut the cable-tie which is fitted to prevent the unit accidentally rotating.
22 Refit the steering wheel as described in Chapter 10.

Fuse/relay box details

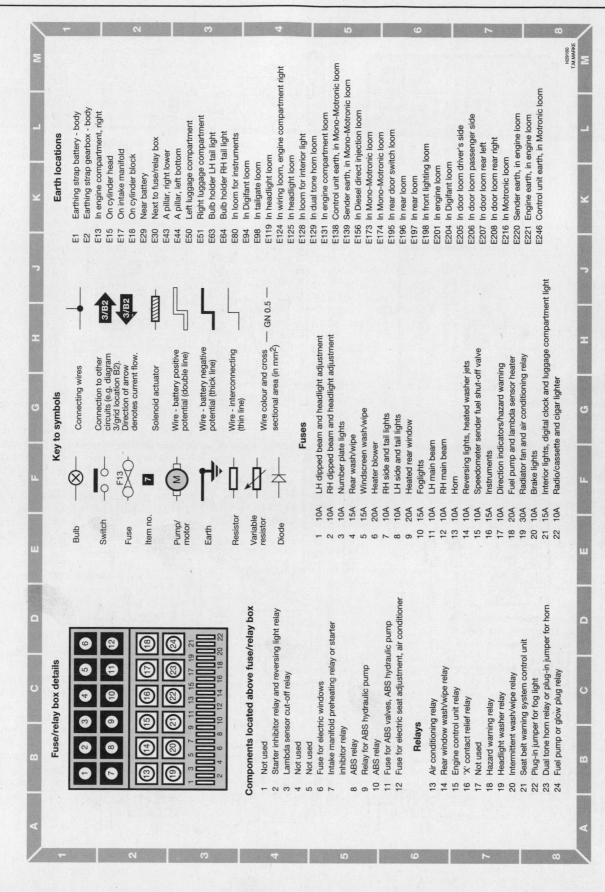

Relay box positions: 1-24

Components located above fuse/relay box

1 Not used
2 Starter inhibitor relay and reversing light relay
3 Lambda sensor cut-off relay
4 Not used
5 Not used
6 Fuse for electric windows
7 Intake manifold preheating relay or starter inhibitor relay
8 ABS relay
9 Relay for ABS hydraulic pump
10 ABS relay
11 Fuse for ABS valves, ABS hydraulic pump
12 Fuse for electric seat adjustment, air conditioner

Relays

13 Air conditioning relay
14 Rear window wash/wipe relay
15 Engine control unit relay
16 'X' contact relief relay
17 Not used
18 Hazard warning relay
19 Headlight washer relay
20 Intermittent wash/wipe relay
21 Seat belt warning system control unit
22 Plug-in jumper for fog light
23 Dual tone horn relay or plug-in jumper for horn
24 Fuel pump or glow plug relay

Key to symbols

Bulb	
Switch	
Fuse	F13
Item no.	7
Pump/motor	M
Earth	
Resistor	
Variable resistor	
Diode	

Connecting wires

Connection to other circuits (e.g. diagram 3/grid location B2). Direction of arrow denotes current flow.

3/B2

Solenoid actuator

Wire – battery positive potential (double line)

Wire – battery negative potential (thick line)

Wire – interconnecting (thin line)

Wire colour and cross sectional area (in mm²) — GN 0.5

Fuses

1 10A LH dipped beam and headlight adjustment
2 10A RH dipped beam and headlight adjustment
3 10A Number plate lights
4 15A Rear wash/wipe
5 15A Windscreen wash/wipe
6 20A Heater blower
7 10A RH side and tail lights
8 10A LH side and tail lights
9 20A Heated rear window
10 15A Foglights
11 10A LH main beam
12 10A RH main beam
13 10A Horn
14 10A Reversing lights, heated washer jets
15 10A Speedometer sender fuel shut-off valve
16 15A Instruments
17 10A Direction indicators/hazard warning
18 20A Fuel pump and lambda sensor heater
19 30A Radiator fan and air conditioning relay
20 10A Brake lights
21 15A Interior lights, digital clock and luggage compartment light
22 10A Radio/cassette and cigar lighter

Earth locations

E1 Earthing strap battery - body
E2 Earthing strap gearbox - body
E13 In engine compartment, right
E15 On cylinder head
E17 On intake manifold
E18 On cylinder block
E29 Near battery
E30 Next to fuse/relay box
E43 A pillar, right lower
E44 A pillar, left bottom
E50 Left luggage compartment
E51 Right luggage compartment
E63 Bulb holder LH tail light
E64 Bulb holder RH tail light
E80 In loom for instruments
E94 In Digifant loom
E98 In tailgate loom
E119 In headlight loom
E124 In wiring loom, engine compartment right
E125 In headlight loom
E128 In loom for interior light
E129 In dual tone horn loom
E131 In engine compartment loom
E138 Control unit earth, in Mono-Motronic loom
E139 Sender earth, in Mono-Motronic loom
E156 In Diesel direct injection loom
E173 In Mono-Motronic loom
E174 In Mono-Motronic loom
E195 In rear door switch loom
E196 In rear loom
E197 In rear loom
E198 In front lighting loom
E201 In engine loom
E204 In Digifant loom
E205 In door loom driver's side
E206 In door loom passenger side
E207 In door loom rear left
E208 In door loom rear right
E216 In Motronic loom
E220 Sender earth, in engine loom
E221 Engine earth, in engine loom
E246 Control unit earth, in Motronic loom

H29160
T.M.MARKE

Diagram 1 : Information for wiring diagrams

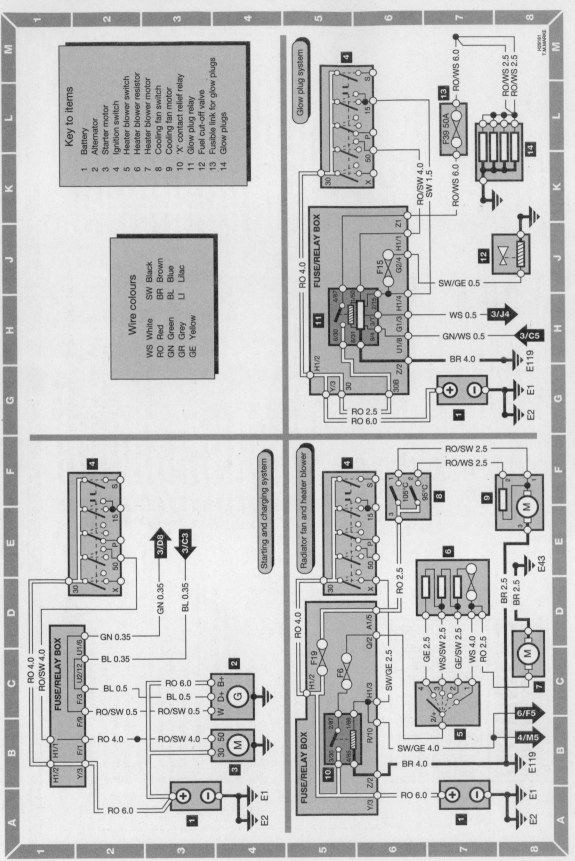

Diagram 2 : Typical starting and charging

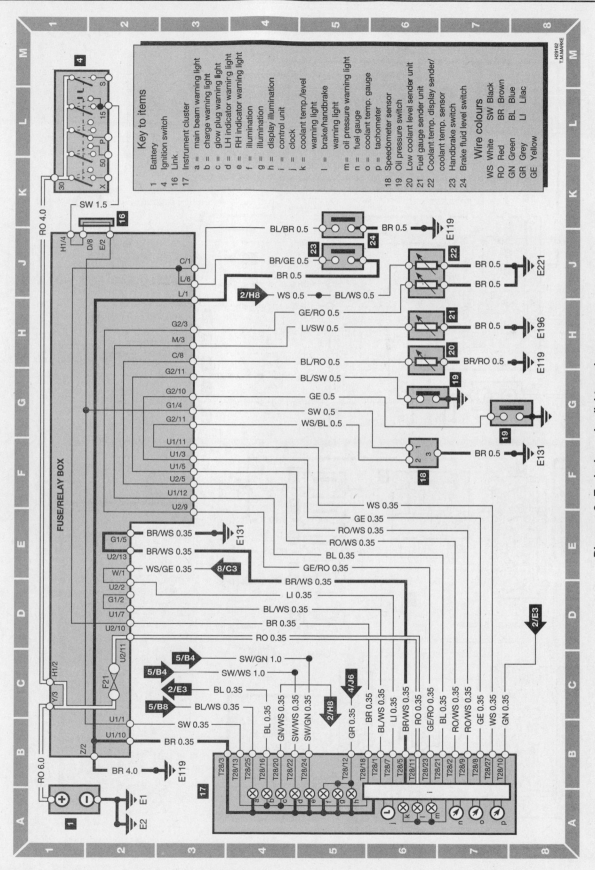

Key to items

1 = Battery
4 = Ignition switch
16 = Link
17 = Instrument cluster
a = main beam warning light
b = charge warning light
c = glow plug warning light
d = LH indicator warning light
e = RH indicator warning light
f = illumination
g = illumination
h = display illumination
i = control unit
j = clock
k = coolant temp./level warning light
l = brake/handbrake warning light
m = oil pressure warning light
n = fuel gauge
o = coolant temp. gauge
p = tachometer
18 = Speedometer sensor
19 = Oil pressure switch
20 = Low coolant level sender unit
21 = Fuel gauge sender unit
22 = Coolant temp. display sender/coolant temp. sensor
23 = Handbrake switch
24 = Brake fluid level switch

Wire colours

WS White   SW Black
RO Red   BR Brown
GN Green   BL Blue
GR Grey   LI Lilac
GE Yellow

Diagram 3 : Typical warning lights and gauges

12

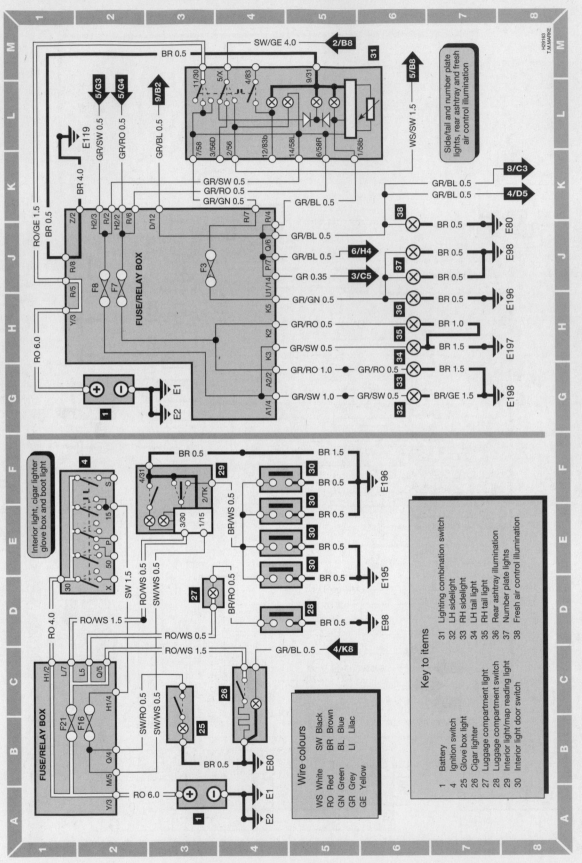

Diagram 4 : Typical interior and exterior lighting

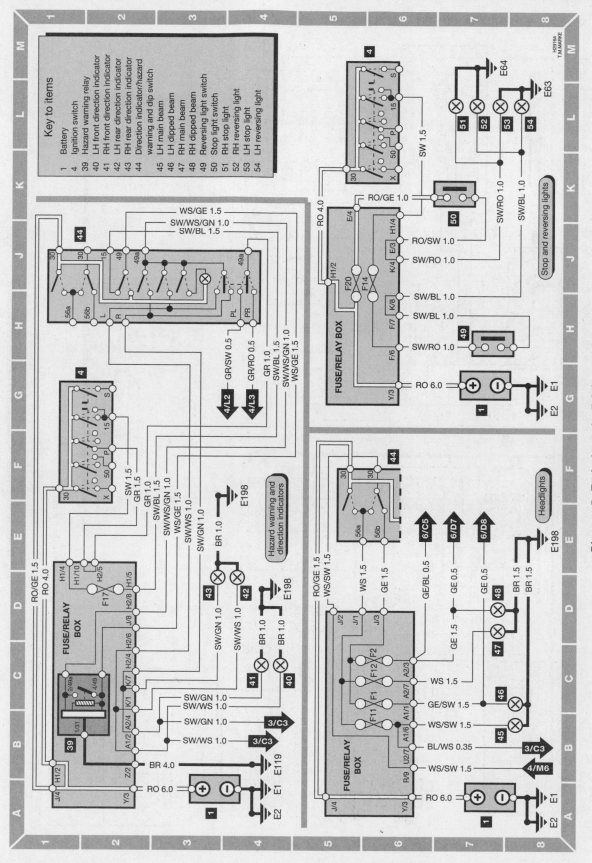

Key to items

1 Battery
4 Ignition switch
39 Hazard warning relay
40 LH front direction indicator
41 RH front direction indicator
42 LH rear direction indicator
43 RH rear direction indicator
44 Direction indicator/hazard warning and dip switch
45 LH main beam
46 LH dipped beam
47 RH main beam
48 RH dipped beam
49 Reversing light switch
50 Stop light switch
51 RH stop light
52 RH reversing light
53 LH stop light
54 LH reversing light

Stop and reversing lights

Hazard warning and direction indicators

Headlights

Diagram 5 : Typical exterior lighting continued

12

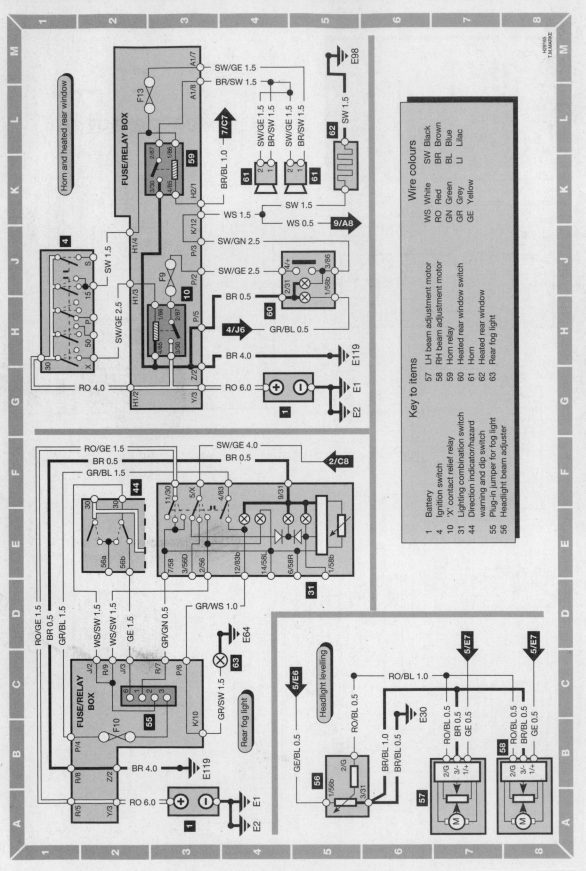

Diagram 6 : Typical exterior lighting and heated rear window

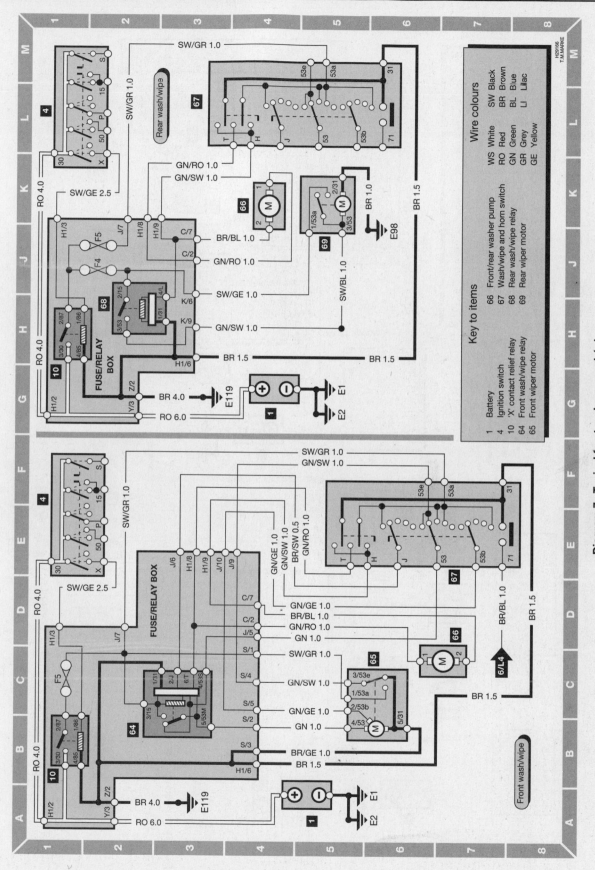

Diagram 7 : Typical front and rear wash/wipe

Wire colours

WS	White	SW	Black
RO	Red	BR	Brown
GN	Green	BL	Blue
GR	Grey	LI	Lilac
GE	Yellow		

Key to items

1	Battery
4	Ignition switch
10	'X' contact relief relay
64	Front wash/wipe relay
65	Front wiper motor
66	Front/rear washer pump
67	Wash/wipe and horn switch
68	Rear wash/wipe relay
69	Rear wiper motor

12

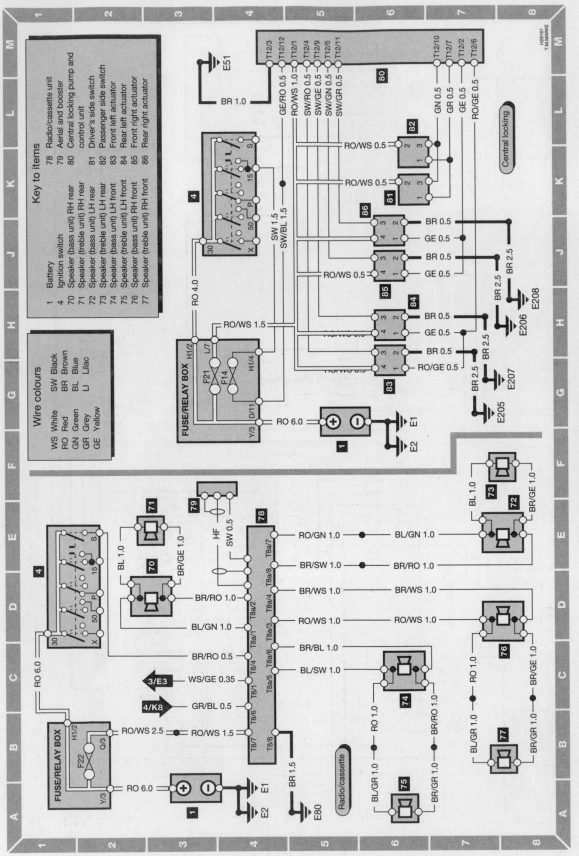

Diagram 8 : Typical radio/cassette and central locking

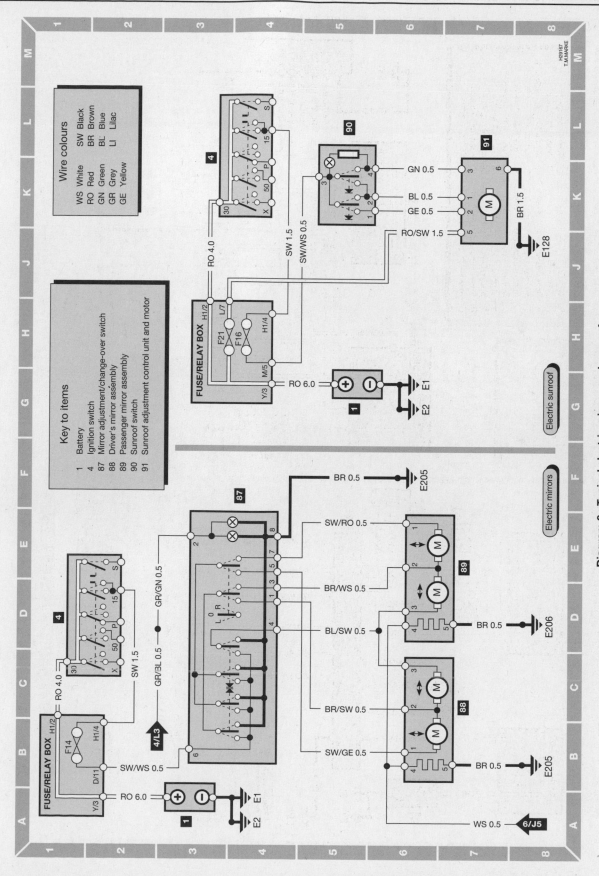

Diagram 9 : Typical electric mirrors and sunroof

Electric sunroof

Electric mirrors

Wire colours

WS White   SW Black
RO Red   BR Brown
GN Green   BL Blue
GR Grey   LI Lilac
GE Yellow

Key to items

1   Battery
4   Ignition switch
87 Mirror adjustment/change-over switch
88 Driver's mirror assembly
89 Passenger mirror assembly
90 Sunroof switch
91 Sunroof adjustment control unit and motor

Notes

Reference REF•1

Dimensions and Weights

Note: *All figures are approximate, and may vary according to model. Refer to manufacturer's data for exact figures.*

Dimensions

Overall length:

    Hatchback models .... 4020 mm

    Saloon models .... 4380 mm

    Estate models .... 4340 mm

Overall width:

    Excluding mirrors .... 1695 mm

    Including mirrors .... 1890 mm

Overall height (unladen):

    Hatchback and Saloon models .... 1425 mm

    Estate models:

        With roof rails .... 1470 mm

        Without roof rails .... 1430 mm

Wheelbase .... 2475 mm

Weights

Kerb weight .... 1000 to 1265 kg*

Maximum gross vehicle weight** .... 1500 to 1725 kg*

Maximum roof rack load:

    Hatchback and Saloon models .... 75 kg

    Estate models .... 85 kg

Maximum towing weight**

    Braked trailer .... 800 to 1200 kg*

    Unbraked trailer .... 500 to 600 kg*

Maximum trailer nose weight .... 50 kg

*Depending on model and specification.

**Refer to VW dealer for exact recommendations.

REF

Conversion Factors

Length (distance)

Inches (in)	x 25.4	= Millimetres (mm)	x 0.0394	=	Inches (in)
Feet (ft)	x 0.305	= Metres (m)	x 3.281	=	Feet (ft)
Miles	x 1.609	= Kilometres (km)	x 0.621	=	Miles

Volume (capacity)

Cubic inches (cu in; in³)	x 16.387	= Cubic centimetres (cc; cm³)	x 0.061	=	Cubic inches (cu in; in³)
Imperial pints (Imp pt)	x 0.568	= Litres (l)	x 1.76	=	Imperial pints (Imp pt)
Imperial quarts (Imp qt)	x 1.137	= Litres (l)	x 0.88	=	Imperial quarts (Imp qt)
Imperial quarts (Imp qt)	x 1.201	= US quarts (US qt)	x 0.833	=	Imperial quarts (Imp qt)
US quarts (US qt)	x 0.946	= Litres (l)	x 1.057	=	US quarts (US qt)
Imperial gallons (Imp gal)	x 4.546	= Litres (l)	x 0.22	=	Imperial gallons (Imp gal)
Imperial gallons (Imp gal)	x 1.201	= US gallons (US gal)	x 0.833	=	Imperial gallons (Imp gal)
US gallons (US gal)	x 3.785	= Litres (l)	x 0.264	=	US gallons (US gal)

Mass (weight)

Ounces (oz)	x 28.35	= Grams (g)	x 0.035	=	Ounces (oz)
Pounds (lb)	x 0.454	= Kilograms (kg)	x 2.205	=	Pounds (lb)

Force

Ounces-force (ozf; oz)	x 0.278	= Newtons (N)	x 3.6	=	Ounces-force (ozf; oz)
Pounds-force (lbf; lb)	x 4.448	= Newtons (N)	x 0.225	=	Pounds-force (lbf; lb)
Newtons (N)	x 0.1	= Kilograms-force (kgf; kg)	x 9.81	=	Newtons (N)

Pressure

Pounds-force per square inch (psi; lbf/in²; lb/in²)	x 0.070	= Kilograms-force per square centimetre (kgf/cm²; kg/cm²)	x 14.223	=	Pounds-force per square inch (psi; lbf/in²; lb/in²)
Pounds-force per square inch (psi; lbf/in²; lb/in²)	x 0.068	= Atmospheres (atm)	x 14.696	=	Pounds-force per square inch (psi; lbf/in²; lb/in²)
Pounds-force per square inch (psi; lbf/in²; lb/in²)	x 0.069	= Bars	x 14.5	=	Pounds-force per square inch (psi; lbf/in²; lb/in²)
Pounds-force per square inch (psi; lbf/in²; lb/in²)	x 6.895	= Kilopascals (kPa)	x 0.145	=	Pounds-force per square inch (psi; lbf/in²; lb/in²)
Kilopascals (kPa)	x 0.01	= Kilograms-force per square centimetre (kgf/cm²; kg/cm²)	x 98.1	=	Kilopascals (kPa)
Millibar (mbar)	x 100	= Pascals (Pa)	x 0.01	=	Millibar (mbar)
Millibar (mbar)	x 0.0145	= Pounds-force per square inch (psi; lbf/in²; lb/in²)	x 68.947	=	Millibar (mbar)
Millibar (mbar)	x 0.75	= Millimetres of mercury (mmHg)	x 1.333	=	Millibar (mbar)
Millibar (mbar)	x 0.401	= Inches of water (inH₂O)	x 2.491	=	Millibar (mbar)
Millimetres of mercury (mmHg)	x 0.535	= Inches of water (inH₂O)	x 1.868	=	Millimetres of mercury (mmHg)
Inches of water (inH₂O)	x 0.036	= Pounds-force per square inch (psi; lbf/in²; lb/in²)	x 27.68	=	Inches of water (inH₂O)

Torque (moment of force)

Pounds-force inches (lbf in; lb in)	x 1.152	= Kilograms-force centimetre (kgf cm; kg cm)	x 0.868	=	Pounds-force inches (lbf in; lb in)
Pounds-force inches (lbf in; lb in)	x 0.113	= Newton metres (Nm)	x 8.85	=	Pounds-force inches (lbf in; lb in)
Pounds-force inches (lbf in; lb in)	x 0.083	= Pounds-force feet (lbf ft; lb ft)	x 12	=	Pounds-force inches (lbf in; lb in)
Pounds-force feet (lbf ft; lb ft)	x 0.138	= Kilograms-force metres (kgf m; kg m)	x 7.233	=	Pounds-force feet (lbf ft; lb ft)
Pounds-force feet (lbf ft; lb ft)	x 1.356	= Newton metres (Nm)	x 0.738	=	Pounds-force feet (lbf ft; lb ft)
Newton metres (Nm)	x 0.102	= Kilograms-force metres (kgf m; kg m)	x 9.804	=	Newton metres (Nm)

Power

Horsepower (hp)	x 745.7	= Watts (W)	x 0.0013	=	Horsepower (hp)

Velocity (speed)

Miles per hour (miles/hr; mph)	x 1.609	= Kilometres per hour (km/hr; kph)	x 0.621	=	Miles per hour (miles/hr; mph)

Fuel consumption*

Miles per gallon (mpg)	x 0.354	= Kilometres per litre (km/l)	x 2.825	=	Miles per gallon (mpg)

Temperature

Degrees Fahrenheit = (°C x 1.8) + 32   Degrees Celsius (Degrees Centigrade; °C) = (°F - 32) x 0.56

It is common practice to convert from miles per gallon (mpg) to litres/100 kilometres (l/100km), where mpg x l/100 km = 282

Spare parts are available from many sources, including maker's appointed garages, accessory shops, and motor factors. To be sure of obtaining the correct parts, it may sometimes be necessary to quote the vehicle identification number. If possible, it can also be useful to take the old parts along for positive identification. Items such as starter motors and alternators may be available under a service exchange scheme - any parts returned should always be clean.

Our advice regarding spare part sources is as follows.

Officially-appointed garages

This is the best source of parts which are peculiar to your car, and are not otherwise generally available (eg badges, interior trim, certain body panels, etc). It is also the only place at which you should buy parts if the vehicle is still under warranty.

Accessory shops

These are very good places to buy materials and components needed for the maintenance of your car (oil, air and fuel filters, spark plugs, light bulbs, drivebelts, oils and greases, brake pads, touch-up paint, etc). Parts like this sold by a reputable shop are of the same standard as those used by the car manufacturer.

Motor factors

Good factors will stock all the more important components which wear out comparatively quickly and can sometimes supply individual components needed for the overhaul of a larger assembly. They may also handle work such as cylinder block reboring, crankshaft regrinding and balancing, etc.

Tyre and exhaust specialists

These outlets may be independent or members of a local or national chain. They frequently offer competitive prices when compared with a main dealer or local garage, but it will pay to obtain several quotes before making a decision. Also ask what 'extras' may be added to the quote - for instance, fitting a new valve and balancing the wheel are both often charged on top of the price of a new tyre.

Other sources

Beware of parts or materials obtained from market stalls, car boot sales or similar outlets. Such items are not invariably sub-standard, but there is little chance of compensation if they do prove unsatisfactory. In the case of safety-critical components such as brake pads there is the risk not only of financial loss but also of an accident causing injury or death.

Vehicle Identification

Modifications are a continuing and unpublicised process in vehicle manufacture, quite apart from major model changes. Spare parts manuals and lists are compiled upon a numerical basis, the individual vehicle identification numbers being essential to correct identification of the component concerned.

When ordering spare parts, always give as much information as possible. Quote the car model, year of manufacture, body and engine numbers as appropriate.

The Vehicle Identification Number (VIN) plate is situated in the engine compartment, riveted to the top of the bonnet lock carrier, on the right-hand side **(see illustration)**.

The chassis number is stamped into the body, along the top edge of the engine compartment bulkhead, and can be viewed with the bonnet open **(see illustration)**.

The engine number is situated on the cylinder block (and on some models can also be found on a sticker attached to the timing belt cover) and can be found in the following locations:

a) *1.4 and 1.6 litre (except AEK engine) petrol models - stamped on the flywheel end of the cylinder block, directly above the flywheel.*

b) *1.6 litre (AEK engine) and 1.8 and 2.0 litre 8-valve petrol models - stamped on the front of the cylinder block, directly below the cylinder head mating surface.*

c) *2.0 litre 16-valve petrol models - stamped on the front face of the cylinder block, directly above the crankcase breather.*

d) *1.9 litre diesel engines - stamped on the front of the cylinder block, between the injection pump and vacuum pump.*

Note: *The first part of the engine number gives the engine code - eg "AAZ".*

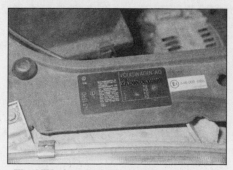

The VIN plate is riveted to the right-hand end of the bonnet lock carrier crossmember

The chassis number is stamped onto the top of the engine compartment bulkhead

Whenever servicing, repair or overhaul work is carried out on the car or its components, it is necessary to observe the following procedures and instructions. This will assist in carrying out the operation efficiently and to a professional standard of workmanship.

Joint mating faces and gaskets

When separating components at their mating faces, never insert screwdrivers or similar implements into the joint between the faces in order to prise them apart. This can cause severe damage which results in oil leaks, coolant leaks, etc upon reassembly. Separation is usually achieved by tapping along the joint with a soft-faced hammer in order to break the seal. However, note that this method may not be suitable where dowels are used for component location.

Where a gasket is used between the mating faces of two components, ensure that it is renewed on reassembly, and fit it dry unless otherwise stated in the repair procedure. Make sure that the mating faces are clean and dry, with all traces of old gasket removed. When cleaning a joint face, use a tool which is not likely to score or damage the face, and remove any burrs or nicks with an oilstone or fine file.

Make sure that tapped holes are cleaned with a pipe cleaner, and keep them free of jointing compound, if this is being used, unless specifically instructed otherwise.

Ensure that all orifices, channels or pipes are clear, and blow through them, preferably using compressed air.

Oil seals

Oil seals can be removed by levering them out with a wide flat-bladed screwdriver or similar tool. Alternatively, a number of self-tapping screws may be screwed into the seal, and these used as a purchase for pliers or similar in order to pull the seal free.

Whenever an oil seal is removed from its working location, either individually or as part of an assembly, it should be renewed.

The very fine sealing lip of the seal is easily damaged, and will not seal if the surface it contacts is not completely clean and free from scratches, nicks or grooves. If the original sealing surface of the component cannot be restored, and the manufacturer has not made provision for slight relocation of the seal relative to the sealing surface, the component should be renewed.

Protect the lips of the seal from any surface which may damage them in the course of fitting. Use tape or a conical sleeve where possible. Lubricate the seal lips with oil before fitting and, on dual-lipped seals, fill the space between the lips with grease.

Unless otherwise stated, oil seals must be fitted with their sealing lips toward the lubricant to be sealed.

Use a tubular drift or block of wood of the appropriate size to install the seal and, if the seal housing is shouldered, drive the seal down to the shoulder. If the seal housing is unshouldered, the seal should be fitted with its face flush with the housing top face (unless otherwise instructed).

Screw threads and fastenings

Seized nuts, bolts and screws are quite a common occurrence where corrosion has set in, and the use of penetrating oil or releasing fluid will often overcome this problem if the offending item is soaked for a while before attempting to release it. The use of an impact driver may also provide a means of releasing such stubborn fastening devices, when used in conjunction with the appropriate screwdriver bit or socket. If none of these methods works, it may be necessary to resort to the careful application of heat, or the use of a hacksaw or nut splitter device.

Studs are usually removed by locking two nuts together on the threaded part, and then using a spanner on the lower nut to unscrew the stud. Studs or bolts which have broken off below the surface of the component in which they are mounted can sometimes be removed using a stud extractor. Always ensure that a blind tapped hole is completely free from oil, grease, water or other fluid before installing the bolt or stud. Failure to do this could cause the housing to crack due to the hydraulic action of the bolt or stud as it is screwed in.

When tightening a castellated nut to accept a split pin, tighten the nut to the specified torque, where applicable, and then tighten further to the next split pin hole. Never slacken the nut to align the split pin hole, unless stated in the repair procedure.

When checking or retightening a nut or bolt to a specified torque setting, slacken the nut or bolt by a quarter of a turn, and then retighten to the specified setting. However, this should not be attempted where angular tightening has been used.

For some screw fastenings, notably cylinder head bolts or nuts, torque wrench settings are no longer specified for the latter stages of tightening, "angle-tightening" being called up instead. Typically, a fairly low torque wrench setting will be applied to the bolts/nuts in the correct sequence, followed by one or more stages of tightening through specified angles.

Locknuts, locktabs and washers

Any fastening which will rotate against a component or housing during tightening should always have a washer between it and the relevant component or housing.

Spring or split washers should always be renewed when they are used to lock a critical component such as a big-end bearing retaining bolt or nut. Locktabs which are folded over to retain a nut or bolt should always be renewed.

Self-locking nuts can be re-used in non-critical areas, providing resistance can be felt when the locking portion passes over the bolt or stud thread. However, it should be noted that self-locking stiffnuts tend to lose their effectiveness after long periods of use, and should be renewed as a matter of course.

Split pins must always be replaced with new ones of the correct size for the hole.

When thread-locking compound is found on the threads of a fastener which is to be re-used, it should be cleaned off with a wire brush and solvent, and fresh compound applied on reassembly.

Special tools

Some repair procedures in this manual entail the use of special tools such as a press, two or three-legged pullers, spring compressors, etc. Wherever possible, suitable readily-available alternatives to the manufacturer's special tools are described, and are shown in use. In some instances, where no alternative is possible, it has been necessary to resort to the use of a manufacturer's tool, and this has been done for reasons of safety as well as the efficient completion of the repair operation. Unless you are highly-skilled and have a thorough understanding of the procedures described, never attempt to bypass the use of any special tool when the procedure described specifies its use. Not only is there a very great risk of personal injury, but expensive damage could be caused to the components involved.

Environmental considerations

When disposing of used engine oil, brake fluid, antifreeze, etc, give due consideration to any detrimental environmental effects. Do not, for instance, pour any of the above liquids down drains into the general sewage system, or onto the ground to soak away. Many local council refuse tips provide a facility for waste oil disposal, as do some garages. If none of these facilities are available, consult your local Environmental Health Department, or the National Rivers Authority, for further advice.

With the universal tightening-up of legislation regarding the emission of environmentally-harmful substances from motor vehicles, most current vehicles have tamperproof devices fitted to the main adjustment points of the fuel system. These devices are primarily designed to prevent unqualified persons from adjusting the fuel/air mixture, with the chance of a consequent increase in toxic emissions. If such devices are encountered during servicing or overhaul, they should, wherever possible, be renewed or refitted in accordance with the vehicle manufacturer's requirements or current legislation.

OIL CARE
FOLLOW THE CODE
OIL BANK LINE
0800 66 33 66

Note: It is antisocial and illegal to dump oil down the drain. To find the location of your local oil recycling bank, call this number free.

The jack supplied with the vehicle tool kit should only be used for changing the roadwheels - see *"Wheel changing"* at the front of this book. When carrying out any other kind of work, raise the vehicle using a hydraulic (or "trolley") jack, and always supplement the jack with axle stands positioned under the vehicle jacking points.

When using a hydraulic jack or axle stands, always position the jack head or axle stand head under one of the relevant jacking points.

To raise the front of the vehicle, position the jack with an interposed block of wood underneath the reinforced hump, which is situated on the front of the floorpan, approximately 150 cm in from the sill edge **(see illustration)**. **Do not** jack the vehicle under the sill, sump, or any of the steering or suspension components. With the vehicle raised, an axle stand should be positioned beneath then vehicle jack location point on the sill. Position a block of wood with a groove cut in it on the jack head to prevent the vehicle weight resting on the sill edge; align the sill edge with the groove in the wood so that the vehicle weight is spread evenly over the surface of the block

To raise the rear of the vehicle, position the jack with an interposed block of wood underneath the reinforced section of the side member, located just in from the sill edge **(see illustration)**. **Do not** attempt to raise the vehicle with the jack positioned underneath the floor pan or axle. With the vehicle raised, an axle stand should be positioned beneath the vehicle jacking location point on the sill. Position a grooved block of wood on the jack as described in the previous paragraph.

Never work under, around, or near a raised vehicle, unless it is adequately supported on stands.

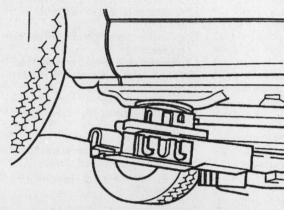

When raising the front of the vehicle, locate the jack underneath the reinforced hump on the front of the floorpan

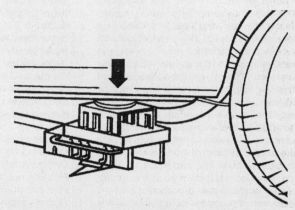

When raising the rear of the vehicle, locate the jack under the reinforced section of the side member located just in from the sill

REF

Introduction

A selection of good tools is a fundamental requirement for anyone contemplating the maintenance and repair of a motor vehicle. For the owner who does not possess any, their purchase will prove a considerable expense, offsetting some of the savings made by doing-it-yourself. However, provided that the tools purchased meet the relevant national safety standards and are of good quality, they will last for many years and prove an extremely worthwhile investment.

To help the average owner to decide which tools are needed to carry out the various tasks detailed in this manual, we have compiled three lists of tools under the following headings: *Maintenance and minor repair, Repair and overhaul*, and *Special*. Newcomers to practical mechanics should start off with the *Maintenance and minor repair* tool kit, and confine themselves to the simpler jobs around the vehicle. Then, as confidence and experience grow, more difficult tasks can be undertaken, with extra tools being purchased as, and when, they are needed. In this way, a *Maintenance and minor repair* tool kit can be built up into a *Repair and overhaul* tool kit over a considerable period of time, without any major cash outlays. The experienced do-it-yourselfer will have a tool kit good enough for most repair and overhaul procedures, and will add tools from the *Special* category when it is felt that the expense is justified by the amount of use to which these tools will be put.

Maintenance and minor repair tool kit

The tools given in this list should be considered as a minimum requirement if routine maintenance, servicing and minor repair operations are to be undertaken. We recommend the purchase of combination spanners (ring one end, open-ended the other); although more expensive than open-ended ones, they do give the advantages of both types of spanner.

☐ *Combination spanners:*
  Metric - 8 to 19 mm inclusive
☐ *Adjustable spanner - 35 mm jaw (approx.)*
☐ *Spark plug spanner (with rubber insert) - petrol models*
☐ *Spark plug gap adjustment tool - petrol models*
☐ *Set of feeler gauges*
☐ *Brake bleed nipple spanner*
☐ *Screwdrivers:*
  Flat blade - 100 mm long x 6 mm dia
  Cross blade - 100 mm long x 6 mm dia
☐ *Combination pliers*
☐ *Hacksaw (junior)*
☐ *Tyre pump*
☐ *Tyre pressure gauge*
☐ *Oil can*
☐ *Oil filter removal tool*
☐ *Fine emery cloth*
☐ *Wire brush (small)*
☐ *Funnel (medium size)*

Repair and overhaul tool kit

These tools are virtually essential for anyone undertaking any major repairs to a motor vehicle, and are additional to those given in the *Maintenance and minor repair* list. Included in this list is a comprehensive set of sockets. Although these are expensive, they will be found invaluable as they are so versatile - particularly if various drives are included in the set. We recommend the half-inch square-drive type, as this can be used with most proprietary torque wrenches.

The tools in this list will sometimes need to be supplemented by tools from the *Special* list:

☐ *Sockets (or box spanners) to cover range in previous list (including Torx sockets)*
☐ *Reversible ratchet drive (for use with sockets)*
☐ *Extension piece, 250 mm (for use with sockets)*
☐ *Universal joint (for use with sockets)*
☐ *Torque wrench (for use with sockets)*
☐ *Self-locking grips*
☐ *Ball pein hammer*
☐ *Soft-faced mallet (plastic/aluminium or rubber)*
☐ *Screwdrivers:*
  Flat blade - long & sturdy, short (chubby), and narrow (electrician's) types
  Cross blade – Long & sturdy, and short (chubby) types
☐ *Pliers:*
  Long-nosed
  Side cutters (electrician's)
  Circlip (internal and external)
☐ *Cold chisel - 25 mm*
☐ *Scriber*
☐ *Scraper*
☐ *Centre-punch*
☐ *Pin punch*
☐ *Hacksaw*
☐ *Brake hose clamp*
☐ *Brake/clutch bleeding kit*
☐ *Selection of twist drills*
☐ *Steel rule/straight-edge*
☐ *Allen keys (inc. splined/Torx type)*
☐ *Selection of files*
☐ *Wire brush*
☐ *Axle stands*
☐ *Jack (strong trolley or hydraulic type)*
☐ *Light with extension lead*

Sockets and reversible ratchet drive

Valve spring compressor

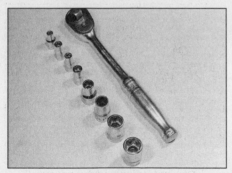

Spline bit set

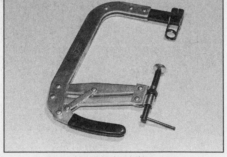

Piston ring compressor

Clutch plate alignment set

Special tools

The tools in this list are those which are not used regularly, are expensive to buy, or which need to be used in accordance with their manufacturers' instructions. Unless relatively difficult mechanical jobs are undertaken frequently, it will not be economic to buy many of these tools. Where this is the case, you could consider clubbing together with friends (or joining a motorists' club) to make a joint purchase, or borrowing the tools against a deposit from a local garage or tool hire specialist. It is worth noting that many of the larger DIY superstores now carry a large range of special tools for hire at modest rates.

The following list contains only those tools and instruments freely available to the public, and not those special tools produced by the vehicle manufacturer specifically for its dealer network. You will find occasional references to these manufacturers' special tools in the text of this manual. Generally, an alternative method of doing the job without the vehicle manufacturers' special tool is given. However, sometimes there is no alternative to using them. Where this is the case and the relevant tool cannot be bought or borrowed, you will have to entrust the work to a dealer.

☐ Valve spring compressor
☐ Valve grinding tool
☐ Piston ring compressor
☐ Piston ring removal/installation tool
☐ Cylinder bore hone
☐ Balljoint separator
☐ Coil spring compressors (where applicable)
☐ Two/three-legged hub and bearing puller
☐ Impact screwdriver
☐ Micrometer and/or vernier calipers
☐ Dial gauge
☐ Stroboscopic timing light
☐ Dwell angle meter/tachometer
☐ Universal electrical multi-meter
☐ Cylinder compression gauge
☐ Hand-operated vacuum pump and gauge
☐ Clutch plate alignment set
☐ Brake shoe steady spring cup removal tool
☐ Bush and bearing removal/installation set
☐ Stud extractors
☐ Tap and die set
☐ Lifting tackle
☐ Trolley jack

Buying tools

Reputable motor accessory shops and superstores often offer excellent quality tools at discount prices, so it pays to shop around.

Remember, you don't have to buy the most expensive items on the shelf, but it is always advisable to steer clear of the very cheap tools. Beware of 'bargains' offered on market stalls or at car boot sales. There are plenty of good tools around at reasonable prices, but always aim to purchase items which meet the relevant national safety standards. If in doubt, ask the proprietor or manager of the shop for advice before making a purchase.

Care and maintenance of tools

Having purchased a reasonable tool kit, it is necessary to keep the tools in a clean and serviceable condition. After use, always wipe off any dirt, grease and metal particles using a clean, dry cloth, before putting the tools away. Never leave them lying around after they have been used. A simple tool rack on the garage or workshop wall for items such as screwdrivers and pliers is a good idea. Store all normal spanners and sockets in a metal box. Any measuring instruments, gauges, meters, etc, must be carefully stored where they cannot be damaged or become rusty.

Take a little care when tools are used. Hammer heads inevitably become marked, and screwdrivers lose the keen edge on their blades from time to time. A little timely attention with emery cloth or a file will soon restore items like this to a good finish.

Working facilities

Not to be forgotten when discussing tools is the workshop itself. If anything more than routine maintenance is to be carried out, a suitable working area becomes essential.

It is appreciated that many an owner-mechanic is forced by circumstances to remove an engine or similar item without the benefit of a garage or workshop. Having done this, any repairs should always be done under the cover of a roof.

Wherever possible, any dismantling should be done on a clean, flat workbench or table at a suitable working height.

Any workbench needs a vice; one with a jaw opening of 100 mm is suitable for most jobs. As mentioned previously, some clean dry storage space is also required for tools, as well as for any lubricants, cleaning fluids, touch-up paints etc, which become necessary.

Another item which may be required, and which has a much more general usage, is an electric drill with a chuck capacity of at least 8 mm. This, together with a good range of twist drills, is virtually essential for fitting accessories.

Last, but not least, always keep a supply of old newspapers and clean, lint-free rags available, and try to keep any working area as clean as possible.

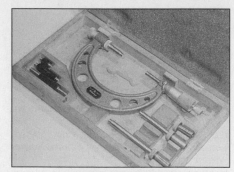
Micrometer set

Dial test indicator ("dial gauge")

Stroboscopic timing light

Compression tester

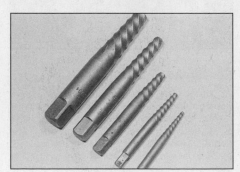
Stud extractor set

This is a guide to getting your vehicle through the MOT test. Obviously it will not be possible to examine the vehicle to the same standard as the professional MOT tester. However, working through the following checks will enable you to identify any problem areas before submitting the vehicle for the test.

Where a testable component is in borderline condition, the tester has discretion in deciding whether to pass or fail it. The basis of such discretion is whether the tester would be happy for a close relative or friend to use the vehicle with the component in that condition. If the vehicle presented is clean and evidently well cared for, the tester may be more inclined to pass a borderline component than if the vehicle is scruffy and apparently neglected.

It has only been possible to summarise the test requirements here, based on the regulations in force at the time of printing. Test standards are becoming increasingly stringent, although there are some exemptions for older vehicles. For full details obtain a copy of the Haynes publication Pass the MOT! (available from stockists of Haynes manuals).

An assistant will be needed to help carry out some of these checks.

The checks have been sub-divided into four categories, as follows:

1 Checks carried out **FROM THE DRIVER'S SEAT**

2 Checks carried out **WITH THE VEHICLE ON THE GROUND**

3 Checks carried out **WITH THE VEHICLE RAISED AND THE WHEELS FREE TO TURN**

4 Checks carried out on **YOUR VEHICLE'S EXHAUST EMISSION SYSTEM**

---

1 Checks carried out **FROM THE DRIVER'S SEAT**

Handbrake

☐ Test the operation of the handbrake. Excessive travel (too many clicks) indicates incorrect brake or cable adjustment.

☐ Check that the handbrake cannot be released by tapping the lever sideways. Check the security of the lever mountings.

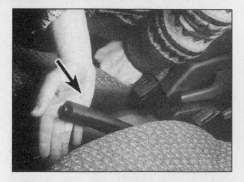

Footbrake

☐ Depress the brake pedal and check that it does not creep down to the floor, indicating a master cylinder fault. Release the pedal, wait a few seconds, then depress it again. If the pedal travels nearly to the floor before firm resistance is felt, brake adjustment or repair is necessary. If the pedal feels spongy, there is air in the hydraulic system which must be removed by bleeding.

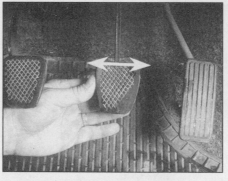

☐ Check that the brake pedal is secure and in good condition. Check also for signs of fluid leaks on the pedal, floor or carpets, which would indicate failed seals in the brake master cylinder.

☐ Check the servo unit (when applicable) by operating the brake pedal several times, then keeping the pedal depressed and starting the engine. As the engine starts, the pedal will move down slightly. If not, the vacuum hose or the servo itself may be faulty.

Steering wheel and column

☐ Examine the steering wheel for fractures or looseness of the hub, spokes or rim.

☐ Move the steering wheel from side to side and then up and down. Check that the steering wheel is not loose on the column, indicating wear or a loose retaining nut. Continue moving the steering wheel as before, but also turn it slightly from left to right.

☐ Check that the steering wheel is not loose on the column, and that there is no abnormal

movement of the steering wheel, indicating wear in the column support bearings or couplings.

Windscreen and mirrors

☐ The windscreen must be free of cracks or other significant damage within the driver's field of view. (Small stone chips are acceptable.) Rear view mirrors must be secure, intact, and capable of being adjusted.

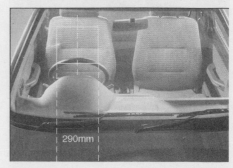

290mm

Seat belts and seats

Note: *The following checks are applicable to all seat belts, front and rear.*

☐ Examine the webbing of all the belts (including rear belts if fitted) for cuts, serious fraying or deterioration. Fasten and unfasten each belt to check the buckles. If applicable, check the retracting mechanism. Check the security of all seat belt mountings accessible from inside the vehicle.

☐ The front seats themselves must be securely attached and the backrests must lock in the upright position.

Doors

☐ Both front doors must be able to be opened and closed from outside and inside, and must latch securely when closed.

2 Checks carried out WITH THE VEHICLE ON THE GROUND

Vehicle identification

☐ Number plates must be in good condition, secure and legible, with letters and numbers correctly spaced – spacing at (A) should be twice that at (B).

☐ The VIN plate (A) and homologation plate (B) must be legible.

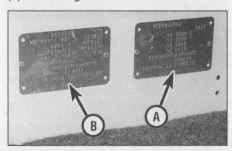

Electrical equipment

☐ Switch on the ignition and check the operation of the horn.

☐ Check the windscreen washers and wipers, examining the wiper blades; renew damaged or perished blades. Also check the operation of the stop-lights.

☐ Check the operation of the sidelights and number plate lights. The lenses and reflectors must be secure, clean and undamaged.

☐ Check the operation and alignment of the headlights. The headlight reflectors must not be tarnished and the lenses must be undamaged.

☐ Switch on the ignition and check the operation of the direction indicators (including the instrument panel tell-tale) and the hazard warning lights. Operation of the sidelights and stop-lights must not affect the indicators - if it does, the cause is usually a bad earth at the rear light cluster.

☐ Check the operation of the rear foglight(s), including the warning light on the instrument panel or in the switch.

Footbrake

☐ Examine the master cylinder, brake pipes and servo unit for leaks, loose mountings, corrosion or other damage.

☐ The fluid reservoir must be secure and the fluid level must be between the upper (**A**) and lower (**B**) markings.

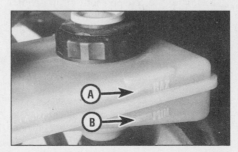

☐ Inspect both front brake flexible hoses for cracks or deterioration of the rubber. Turn the steering from lock to lock, and ensure that the hoses do not contact the wheel, tyre, or any part of the steering or suspension mechanism. With the brake pedal firmly depressed, check the hoses for bulges or leaks under pressure.

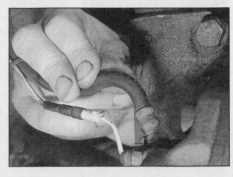

Steering and suspension

☐ Have your assistant turn the steering wheel from side to side slightly, up to the point where the steering gear just begins to transmit this movement to the roadwheels. Check for excessive free play between the steering wheel and the steering gear, indicating wear or insecurity of the steering column joints, the column-to-steering gear coupling, or the steering gear itself.

☐ Have your assistant turn the steering wheel more vigorously in each direction, so that the roadwheels just begin to turn. As this is done, examine all the steering joints, linkages, fittings and attachments. Renew any component that shows signs of wear or damage. On vehicles with power steering, check the security and condition of the steering pump, drivebelt and hoses.

☐ Check that the vehicle is standing level, and at approximately the correct ride height.

Shock absorbers

☐ Depress each corner of the vehicle in turn, then release it. The vehicle should rise and then settle in its normal position. If the vehicle continues to rise and fall, the shock absorber is defective. A shock absorber which has seized will also cause the vehicle to fail.

Exhaust system

☐ Start the engine. With your assistant holding a rag over the tailpipe, check the entire system for leaks. Repair or renew leaking sections.

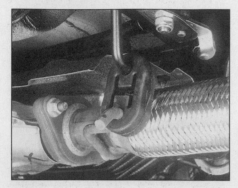

3 Checks carried out WITH THE VEHICLE RAISED AND THE WHEELS FREE TO TURN

Jack up the front and rear of the vehicle, and securely support it on axle stands. Position the stands clear of the suspension assemblies. Ensure that the wheels are clear of the ground and that the steering can be turned from lock to lock.

Steering mechanism

☐ Have your assistant turn the steering from lock to lock. Check that the steering turns smoothly, and that no part of the steering mechanism, including a wheel or tyre, fouls any brake hose or pipe or any part of the body structure.

☐ Examine the steering rack rubber gaiters for damage or insecurity of the retaining clips. If power steering is fitted, check for signs of damage or leakage of the fluid hoses, pipes or connections. Also check for excessive stiffness or binding of the steering, a missing split pin or locking device, or severe corrosion of the body structure within 30 cm of any steering component attachment point.

Front and rear suspension and wheel bearings

☐ Starting at the front right-hand side, grasp the roadwheel at the 3 o'clock and 9 o'clock positions and shake it vigorously. Check for free play or insecurity at the wheel bearings, suspension balljoints, or suspension mountings, pivots and attachments.

☐ Now grasp the wheel at the 12 o'clock and 6 o'clock positions and repeat the previous inspection. Spin the wheel, and check for roughness or tightness of the front wheel bearing.

☐ If excess free play is suspected at a component pivot point, this can be confirmed by using a large screwdriver or similar tool and levering between the mounting and the component attachment. This will confirm whether the wear is in the pivot bush, its retaining bolt, or in the mounting itself (the bolt holes can often become elongated).

☐ Carry out all the above checks at the other front wheel, and then at both rear wheels.

Springs and shock absorbers

☐ Examine the suspension struts (when applicable) for serious fluid leakage, corrosion, or damage to the casing. Also check the security of the mounting points.

☐ If coil springs are fitted, check that the spring ends locate in their seats, and that the spring is not corroded, cracked or broken.

☐ If leaf springs are fitted, check that all leaves are intact, that the axle is securely attached to each spring, and that there is no deterioration of the spring eye mountings, bushes, and shackles.

☐ The same general checks apply to vehicles fitted with other suspension types, such as torsion bars, hydraulic displacer units, etc. Ensure that all mountings and attachments are secure, that there are no signs of excessive wear, corrosion or damage, and (on hydraulic types) that there are no fluid leaks or damaged pipes.

☐ Inspect the shock absorbers for signs of serious fluid leakage. Check for wear of the mounting bushes or attachments, or damage to the body of the unit.

Driveshafts (fwd vehicles only)

☐ Rotate each front wheel in turn and inspect the constant velocity joint gaiters for splits or damage. Also check that each driveshaft is straight and undamaged.

Braking system

☐ If possible without dismantling, check brake pad wear and disc condition. Ensure that the friction lining material has not worn excessively, (A) and that the discs are not fractured, pitted, scored or badly worn (B).

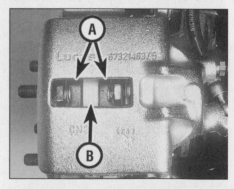

☐ Examine all the rigid brake pipes underneath the vehicle, and the flexible hose(s) at the rear. Look for corrosion, chafing or insecurity of the pipes, and for signs of bulging under pressure, chafing, splits or deterioration of the flexible hoses.

☐ Look for signs of fluid leaks at the brake calipers or on the brake backplates. Repair or renew leaking components.

☐ Slowly spin each wheel, while your assistant depresses and releases the footbrake. Ensure that each brake is operating and does not bind when the pedal is released.

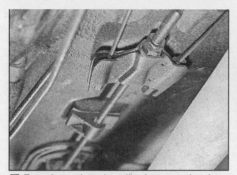

☐ Examine the handbrake mechanism, checking for frayed or broken cables, excessive corrosion, or wear or insecurity of the linkage. Check that the mechanism works on each relevant wheel, and releases fully, without binding.

☐ It is not possible to test brake efficiency without special equipment, but a road test can be carried out later to check that the vehicle pulls up in a straight line.

Fuel and exhaust systems

☐ Inspect the fuel tank (including the filler cap), fuel pipes, hoses and unions. All components must be secure and free from leaks.

☐ Examine the exhaust system over its entire length, checking for any damaged, broken or missing mountings, security of the retaining clamps and rust or corrosion.

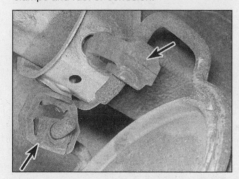

Wheels and tyres

☐ Examine the sidewalls and tread area of each tyre in turn. Check for cuts, tears, lumps, bulges, separation of the tread, and exposure of the ply or cord due to wear or damage. Check that the tyre bead is correctly seated on the wheel rim, that the valve is sound and

properly seated, and that the wheel is not distorted or damaged.

☐ Check that the tyres are of the correct size for the vehicle, that they are of the same size and type on each axle, and that the pressures are correct.

☐ Check the tyre tread depth. The legal minimum at the time of writing is 1.6 mm over at least three-quarters of the tread width. Abnormal tread wear may indicate incorrect front wheel alignment.

Body corrosion

☐ Check the condition of the entire vehicle structure for signs of corrosion in load-bearing areas. (These include chassis box sections, side sills, cross-members, pillars, and all suspension, steering, braking system and seat belt mountings and anchorages.) Any corrosion which has seriously reduced the thickness of a load-bearing area is likely to cause the vehicle to fail. In this case professional repairs are likely to be needed.

☐ Damage or corrosion which causes sharp or otherwise dangerous edges to be exposed will also cause the vehicle to fail.

4 Checks carried out on YOUR VEHICLE'S EXHAUST EMISSION SYSTEM

Petrol models

☐ Have the engine at normal operating temperature, and make sure that it is in good tune (ignition system in good order, air filter element clean, etc).

☐ Before any measurements are carried out, raise the engine speed to around 2500 rpm, and hold it at this speed for 20 seconds. Allow the engine speed to return to idle, and watch

for smoke emissions from the exhaust tailpipe. If the idle speed is obviously much too high, or if dense blue or clearly-visible black smoke comes from the tailpipe for more than 5 seconds, the vehicle will fail. As a rule of thumb, blue smoke signifies oil being burnt (engine wear) while black smoke signifies unburnt fuel (dirty air cleaner element, or other carburettor or fuel system fault).

☐ An exhaust gas analyser capable of measuring carbon monoxide (CO) and hydrocarbons (HC) is now needed. If such an instrument cannot be hired or borrowed, a local garage may agree to perform the check for a small fee.

CO emissions (mixture)

☐ At the time or writing, the maximum CO level at idle is 3.5% for vehicles first used after August 1986 and 4.5% for older vehicles. From January 1996 a much tighter limit (around 0.5%) applies to catalyst-equipped vehicles first used from August 1992. If the CO level cannot be reduced far enough to pass the test (and the fuel and ignition systems are otherwise in good condition) then the carburettor is badly worn, or there is some problem in the fuel injection system or catalytic converter (as applicable).

HC emissions

☐ With the CO emissions within limits, HC emissions must be no more than 1200 ppm (parts per million). If the vehicle fails this test at idle, it can be re-tested at around 2000 rpm; if the HC level is then 1200 ppm or less, this counts as a pass.

☐ Excessive HC emissions can be caused by oil being burnt, but they are more likely to be due to unburnt fuel.

Diesel models

☐ The only emission test applicable to Diesel engines is the measuring of exhaust smoke density. The test involves accelerating the engine several times to its maximum unloaded speed.

Note: *It is of the utmost importance that the engine timing belt is in good condition before the test is carried out.*

☐ Excessive smoke can be caused by a dirty air cleaner element. Otherwise, professional advice may be needed to find the cause.

Engine

- [ ] Engine fails to rotate when attempting to start
- [ ] Engine rotates, but will not start
- [ ] Engine difficult to start when cold
- [ ] Engine difficult to start when hot
- [ ] Starter motor noisy or excessively-rough in engagement
- [ ] Engine starts, but stops immediately
- [ ] Engine idles erratically
- [ ] Engine misfires at idle speed
- [ ] Engine misfires throughout the driving speed range
- [ ] Engine hesitates on acceleration
- [ ] Engine stalls
- [ ] Engine lacks power
- [ ] Engine backfires
- [ ] Oil pressure warning light illuminated with engine running
- [ ] Engine runs-on after switching off
- [ ] Engine noises

Cooling system

- [ ] Overheating
- [ ] Overcooling
- [ ] External coolant leakage
- [ ] Internal coolant leakage
- [ ] Corrosion

Fuel and exhaust systems

- [ ] Excessive fuel consumption
- [ ] Fuel leakage and/or fuel odour
- [ ] Excessive noise or fumes from exhaust system

Clutch

- [ ] Pedal travels to floor - no pressure or very little resistance
- [ ] Clutch fails to disengage (unable to select gears)
- [ ] Clutch slips (engine speed increases, with no increase in vehicle speed)
- [ ] Judder as clutch is engaged
- [ ] Noise when depressing or releasing clutch pedal

Manual transmission

- [ ] Noisy in neutral with engine running
- [ ] Noisy in one particular gear
- [ ] Difficulty engaging gears
- [ ] Jumps out of gear
- [ ] Vibration
- [ ] Lubricant leaks

Automatic transmission

- [ ] Fluid leakage
- [ ] Transmission fluid brown, or has burned smell
- [ ] General gear selection problems
- [ ] Transmission will not downshift (kickdown) with accelerator fully depressed
- [ ] Engine will not start in any gear, or starts in gears other than Park or Neutral
- [ ] Transmission slips, shifts roughly, is noisy, or has no drive in forward or reverse gears

Driveshafts

- [ ] Clicking or knocking noise on turns (at slow speed on full-lock)
- [ ] Vibration when accelerating or decelerating

Braking system

- [ ] Vehicle pulls to one side under braking
- [ ] Noise (grinding or high-pitched squeal) when brakes applied
- [ ] Excessive brake pedal travel
- [ ] Brake pedal feels spongy when depressed
- [ ] Excessive brake pedal effort required to stop vehicle
- [ ] Judder felt through brake pedal or steering wheel when braking
- [ ] Brakes binding
- [ ] Rear wheels locking under normal braking

Suspension and steering systems

- [ ] Vehicle pulls to one side
- [ ] Wheel wobble and vibration
- [ ] Excessive pitching and/or rolling around corners, or during braking
- [ ] Wandering or general instability
- [ ] Excessively-stiff steering
- [ ] Excessive play in steering
- [ ] Lack of power assistance
- [ ] Tyre wear excessive

Electrical system

- [ ] Battery will not hold a charge for more than a few days
- [ ] Ignition/no-charge warning light remains illuminated with engine running
- [ ] Ignition/no-charge warning light fails to come on
- [ ] Lights inoperative
- [ ] Instrument readings inaccurate or erratic
- [ ] Horn inoperative, or unsatisfactory in operation
- [ ] Windscreen/tailgate wipers inoperative, or unsatisfactory in operation
- [ ] Windscreen/tailgate washers inoperative, or unsatisfactory in operation
- [ ] Electric windows inoperative, or unsatisfactory in operation
- [ ] Central locking system inoperative, or unsatisfactory in operation

Introduction

The vehicle owner who does his or her own maintenance according to the recommended service schedules should not have to use this section of the manual very often. Modern component reliability is such that, provided those items subject to wear or deterioration are inspected or renewed at the specified intervals, sudden failure is comparatively rare. Faults do not usually just happen as a result of sudden failure, but develop over a period of time. Major mechanical failures in particular are usually preceded by characteristic symptoms over hundreds or even thousands of miles. Those components which do occasionally fail without warning are often small and easily carried in the vehicle.

With any fault-finding, the first step is to decide where to begin investigations. Sometimes this is obvious, but on other occasions, a little detective work will be necessary. The owner who makes half a dozen haphazard adjustments or replacements may be successful in curing a fault (or its symptoms), but will be none the wiser if the fault recurs, and ultimately may have spent more time and money than was necessary. A calm and logical approach will be found to be more satisfactory in the long run. Always take into account any warning signs or abnormalities that may have been noticed in the period preceding the fault - power loss, high or low gauge readings, unusual smells, etc - and remember that failure of components such as fuses or spark plugs may only be pointers to some underlying fault.

These pages provide an easy-reference guide to the more common problems which may occur during the vehicle's life. These problems and their possible causes are grouped under headings such as Engine, Cooling system, etc. The Chapter and/or Section which deals with the problem is also shown in brackets. Whatever the fault, certain basic principles apply. These are as follows:

Verify the fault. This is simply a matter of being sure you know exactly what the symptoms are before starting work. This is particularly important if you are investigating a fault for someone else, who may not have described it very accurately.

Don't overlook the obvious. For example, if it won't start, is there fuel in the tank? (Don't take anyone else's word on this particular point, and don't trust the fuel gauge either!) If an electrical fault is indicated, look for loose or broken wires before digging out the test gear.

Cure the disease, not the symptom. Substituting a flat battery with a fully-charged one will get you off the hard shoulder, but if the underlying cause is not attended to, the new battery will go the same way. Similarly, changing oil-fouled spark plugs (petrol models) for a new set will get you moving again, but remember that the reason for the fouling (if it wasn't simply an incorrect grade of plug) will have to be established and corrected.

Don't take anything for granted. Particularly, don't forget that a "new" component may itself be defective (especially if it's been rattling around in the boot for months), and don't leave components out of a fault diagnosis sequence just because they are new or recently-fitted. When you do finally diagnose a difficult fault, you'll probably realise that all the evidence was there from the start.

Engine

Engine fails to rotate when attempting to start

☐ Battery terminal connections loose or corroded ("*Weekly Checks*").
☐ Battery discharged or faulty (Chapter 5A).
☐ Broken, loose or disconnected wiring in the starting circuit (Chapter 5A).
☐ Defective starter solenoid or switch (Chapter 5A).
☐ Defective starter motor (Chapter 5A).
☐ Starter pinion or flywheel ring gear teeth loose or broken (Chapters 2A, 2B, 2C and 5A).
☐ Engine earth strap broken or disconnected (Chapter 5A).

Engine rotates, but will not start

☐ Fuel tank empty.
☐ Battery discharged (engine rotates slowly) (Chapter 5A).
☐ Battery terminal connections loose or corroded ("*Weekly Checks*").
☐ Ignition components damp or damaged - petrol models (Chapters 1 and 5B).
☐ Broken, loose or disconnected wiring in the ignition circuit - petrol models (Chapters 1 and 5B).
☐ Worn, faulty or incorrectly-gapped spark plugs - petrol models (Chapter 1).
☐ Preheating system faulty - diesel models (Chapter 5C).
☐ Fuel injection system fault - petrol models (Chapter 4A or 4B).
☐ Stop solenoid faulty - diesel models (Chapter 4C).
☐ Air in fuel system - diesel models (Chapter 4C).
☐ Major mechanical failure (eg camshaft drive) (Chapter 2A, 2B or 2C).

Engine difficult to start when cold

☐ Battery discharged (Chapter 5A).
☐ Battery terminal connections loose or corroded ("*Weekly Checks*").
☐ Worn, faulty or incorrectly-gapped spark plugs - petrol models (Chapter 1).
☐ Preheating system faulty - Diesel models (Chapter 5C).
☐ Fuel injection system fault - petrol models (Chapter 4A or 4B).
☐ Other ignition system fault - petrol models (Chapters 1 and 5B).
☐ Fast idle valve incorrectly adjusted - Diesel models (Chapter 4C).
☐ Low cylinder compressions (Chapter 2A or 2B).

Engine difficult to start when hot

☐ Air filter element dirty or clogged (Chapter 1).
☐ Fuel injection system fault - petrol models (Chapter 4A or 4B).
☐ Low cylinder compressions (Chapter 2A or 2B).

Starter motor noisy or excessively-rough in engagement

☐ Starter pinion or flywheel ring gear teeth loose or broken (Chapters 2A, 2B and 5A).
☐ Starter motor mounting bolts loose or missing (Chapter 5A).
☐ Starter motor internal components worn or damaged (Chapter 5A).

Engine starts, but stops immediately

☐ Loose or faulty electrical connections in the ignition circuit - petrol models (Chapters 1 and 5B).
☐ Vacuum leak at the throttle body or inlet manifold - petrol models (Chapter 4A or 4B).
☐ Blocked injector/fuel injection system fault - petrol models (Chapter 4A or 4B).

Engine idles erratically

☐ Air filter element clogged (Chapter 1).
☐ Vacuum leak at the throttle body, inlet manifold or associated hoses - petrol models (Chapter 4A or 4B).
☐ Worn, faulty or incorrectly-gapped spark plugs - petrol models (Chapter 1).
☐ Uneven or low cylinder compressions (Chapter 2A or 2B).
☐ Camshaft lobes worn (Chapter 2A or 2B).
☐ Timing belt incorrectly tensioned (Chapter 2A or 2B).
☐ Blocked injector/fuel injection system fault - petrol models (Chapter 4A or 4B).
☐ Faulty injector(s) - diesel models (Chapter 4C).

Engine misfires at idle speed

☐ Worn, faulty or incorrectly-gapped spark plugs - petrol models (Chapter 1).
☐ Faulty spark plug HT leads - petrol models (Chapter 1).
☐ Vacuum leak at the throttle body, inlet manifold or associated hoses - petrol models (Chapter 4A or 4B).
☐ Blocked injector/fuel injection system fault - petrol models (Chapter 4A or 4B).
☐ Faulty injector(s) - diesel models (Chapter 4C).
☐ Distributor cap cracked or tracking internally - petrol models (where applicable) (Chapter 1).
☐ Uneven or low cylinder compressions (Chapter 2A or 2B).
☐ Disconnected, leaking, or perished crankcase ventilation hoses (Chapter 4D).

Engine (continued)

Engine misfires throughout the driving speed range

- ☐ Fuel filter choked (Chapter 1).
- ☐ Fuel pump faulty, or delivery pressure low - petrol models (Chapter 4A or 4B).
- ☐ Fuel tank vent blocked, or fuel pipes restricted (Chapter 4A, 4B or 4C).
- ☐ Vacuum leak at the throttle body, inlet manifold or associated hoses - petrol models (Chapter 4A or 4B).
- ☐ Worn, faulty or incorrectly-gapped spark plugs - petrol models (Chapter 1).
- ☐ Faulty spark plug HT leads - petrol models (Chapter 1).
- ☐ Faulty injector(s) - diesel models (Chapter 4C).
- ☐ Distributor cap cracked or tracking internally - petrol models (where applicable) (Chapter 1).
- ☐ Faulty ignition coil - petrol models (Chapter 5B).
- ☐ Uneven or low cylinder compressions (Chapter 2A or 2B).
- ☐ Blocked injector/fuel injection system fault - petrol models (Chapter 4A or 4B).

Engine hesitates on acceleration

- ☐ Worn, faulty or incorrectly-gapped spark plugs - petrol models (Chapter 1).
- ☐ Vacuum leak at the throttle body, inlet manifold or associated hoses - petrol models (Chapter 4A or 4B).
- ☐ Blocked injector/fuel injection system fault - petrol models (Chapter 4A or 4B).
- ☐ Faulty injector(s) - diesel models (Chapter 4C).

Engine stalls

- ☐ Vacuum leak at the throttle body, inlet manifold or associated hoses - petrol models (Chapter 4A or 4B).
- ☐ Fuel filter choked (Chapter 1).
- ☐ Fuel pump faulty, or delivery pressure low - petrol models (Chapter 4A or 4B).
- ☐ Fuel tank vent blocked, or fuel pipes restricted (Chapter 4A, 4B or 4C).
- ☐ Blocked injector/fuel injection system fault - petrol models (Chapter 4A or 4B).
- ☐ Faulty injector(s) - diesel models (Chapter 4C).

Engine lacks power

- ☐ Timing belt incorrectly fitted or tensioned (Chapter 2A or 2B).
- ☐ Fuel filter choked (Chapter 1).
- ☐ Fuel pump faulty, or delivery pressure low - petrol models (Chapter 4A or 4B).
- ☐ Uneven or low cylinder compressions (Chapter 2A or 2B).
- ☐ Worn, faulty or incorrectly-gapped spark plugs - petrol models (Chapter 1).
- ☐ Vacuum leak at the throttle body, inlet manifold or associated hoses - petrol models (Chapter 4A or 4B).
- ☐ Blocked injector/fuel injection system fault - petrol models (Chapter 4A or 4B).
- ☐ Faulty injector(s) - diesel models (Chapter 4C).
- ☐ Injection pump timing incorrect - diesel models (Chapter 4C).
- ☐ Brakes binding (Chapters 1 and 9).
- ☐ Clutch slipping (Chapter 6).

Engine backfires

- ☐ Timing belt incorrectly fitted or tensioned (Chapter 2A or 2B).
- ☐ Vacuum leak at the throttle body, inlet manifold or associated hoses - petrol models (Chapter 4A or 4B).
- ☐ Blocked injector/fuel injection system fault - petrol models (Chapter 4A or 4B).

Oil pressure warning light illuminated with engine running

- ☐ Low oil level, or incorrect oil grade ("Weekly Checks").
- ☐ Faulty oil pressure sensor (Chapter 5A).
- ☐ Worn engine bearings and/or oil pump (Chapter 2C).
- ☐ High engine operating temperature (Chapter 3).
- ☐ Oil pressure relief valve defective (Chapter 2A or 2B).
- ☐ Oil pick-up strainer clogged (Chapter 2A or 2B).

Engine runs-on after switching off

- ☐ Excessive carbon build-up in engine (Chapter 2C).
- ☐ High engine operating temperature (Chapter 3).
- ☐ Fuel injection system fault - petrol models (Chapter 4A or 4B).
- ☐ Faulty stop solenoid - diesel models (Chapter 4C).

Engine noises

Pre-ignition (pinking) or knocking during acceleration or under load

- ☐ Ignition timing incorrect/ignition system fault - petrol models (Chapters 1 and 5B).
- ☐ Incorrect grade of spark plug - petrol models (Chapter 1).
- ☐ Incorrect grade of fuel (Chapter 1).
- ☐ Vacuum leak at the throttle body, inlet manifold or associated hoses - petrol models (Chapter 4A or 4B).
- ☐ Excessive carbon build-up in engine (Chapter 2C).
- ☐ Blocked injector/fuel injection system fault - petrol models (Chapter 4A or 4B).

Whistling or wheezing noises

- ☐ Leaking inlet manifold or throttle body gasket - petrol models (Chapter 4A or 4B).
- ☐ Leaking exhaust manifold gasket or pipe-to-manifold joint (Chapter 4A, 4B or 4C).
- ☐ Leaking vacuum hose (Chapters 4A, 4B, 4C, 5B and 9).
- ☐ Blowing cylinder head gasket (Chapter 2A or 2B).

Tapping or rattling noises

- ☐ Worn valve gear or camshaft (Chapter 2A or 2B).
- ☐ Ancillary component fault (water pump, alternator, etc) (Chapters 3, 5A, etc).

Knocking or thumping noises

- ☐ Worn big-end bearings (regular heavy knocking, perhaps less under load) (Chapter 2C).
- ☐ Worn main bearings (rumbling and knocking, perhaps worsening under load) (Chapter 2C).
- ☐ Piston slap (most noticeable when cold) (Chapter 2C).
- ☐ Ancillary component fault (water pump, alternator, etc) (Chapters 3, 5A, etc).

Cooling system

Overheating

- [ ] Insufficient coolant in system ("*Weekly Checks*").
- [ ] Thermostat faulty (Chapter 3).
- [ ] Radiator core blocked, or grille restricted (Chapter 3).
- [ ] Electric cooling fan or thermoswitch faulty (Chapter 3).
- [ ] Pressure cap faulty (Chapter 3).
- [ ] Ignition timing incorrect/ignition system fault - petrol models (Chapters 1 and 5B).
- [ ] Inaccurate temperature gauge sender unit (Chapter 3).
- [ ] Airlock in cooling system (Chapter 1).

Overcooling

- [ ] Thermostat faulty (Chapter 3).
- [ ] Inaccurate temperature gauge sender unit (Chapter 3).

External coolant leakage

- [ ] Deteriorated or damaged hoses or hose clips (Chapter 1).
- [ ] Radiator core or heater matrix leaking (Chapter 3).
- [ ] Pressure cap faulty (Chapter 3).
- [ ] Water pump seal leaking (Chapter 3).
- [ ] Boiling due to overheating (Chapter 3).
- [ ] Core plug leaking (Chapter 2C).

Internal coolant leakage

- [ ] Leaking cylinder head gasket (Chapter 2A or 2B).
- [ ] Cracked cylinder head or cylinder bore (Chapter 2A or 2B).

Corrosion

- [ ] Infrequent draining and flushing (Chapter 1).
- [ ] Incorrect coolant mixture or inappropriate coolant type (Chapter 1).

Fuel and exhaust systems

Excessive fuel consumption

- [ ] Air filter element dirty or clogged (Chapter 1).
- [ ] Fuel injection system fault - petrol models (Chapter 4A or 4B).
- [ ] Faulty injector(s) - diesel models (Chapter 4C).
- [ ] Ignition timing incorrect/ignition system fault - petrol models (Chapters 1 and 5B).
- [ ] Tyres under-inflated ("*Weekly Checks*").

Fuel leakage and/or fuel odour

- [ ] Damaged or corroded fuel tank, pipes or connections (Chapter 4).

Excessive noise or fumes from exhaust system

- [ ] Leaking exhaust system or manifold joints (Chapters 1 and 4A, 4B or 4C).
- [ ] Leaking, corroded or damaged silencers or pipe (Chapters 1 and 4A, 4B or 4C).
- [ ] Broken mountings causing body or suspension contact (Chapter 1).

Clutch

Pedal travels to floor - no pressure or very little resistance

- [ ] Broken clutch cable - cable-operated clutch (Chapter 6).
- [ ] Incorrect clutch cable adjustment/automatic adjuster faulty - cable-operated clutch (Chapter 6).
- [ ] Hydraulic fluid level low/air in the hydraulic system - hydraulically-operated clutch
- [ ] Broken clutch release bearing or fork (Chapter 6).
- [ ] Broken diaphragm spring in clutch pressure plate (Chapter 6).

Clutch fails to disengage (unable to select gears)

- [ ] Incorrect clutch cable adjustment/automatic adjuster faulty - cable-operated clutch (Chapter 6).
- [ ] Incorrect clutch cable adjustment/automatic adjuster faulty - cable-operated clutch (Chapter 6).
- [ ] Hydraulic fluid level too high - hydraulically-operated clutch
- [ ] Clutch disc sticking on gearbox input shaft splines (Chapter 6).
- [ ] Clutch disc sticking to flywheel or pressure plate (Chapter 6).
- [ ] Faulty pressure plate assembly (Chapter 6).
- [ ] Clutch release mechanism worn or incorrectly assembled (Chapter 6).

Clutch slips (engine speed increases, with no increase in vehicle speed)

- [ ] Incorrect clutch cable adjustment/automatic adjuster faulty - cable-operated clutch (Chapter 6).
- [ ] Hydraulic fluid level too high - hydraulically-operated clutch
- [ ] Clutch disc linings excessively worn (Chapter 6).
- [ ] Clutch disc linings contaminated with oil or grease (Chapter 6).
- [ ] Faulty pressure plate or weak diaphragm spring (Chapter 6).

Judder as clutch is engaged

- [ ] Clutch disc linings contaminated with oil or grease (Chapter 6).
- [ ] Clutch disc linings excessively worn (Chapter 6).
- [ ] Clutch cable sticking or frayed - cable-operated clutch (Chapter 6).
- [ ] Faulty or distorted pressure plate or diaphragm spring (Chapter 6).
- [ ] Worn or loose engine or gearbox mountings (Chapter 2A or 2B).
- [ ] Clutch disc hub or gearbox input shaft splines worn (Chapter 6).

Noise when depressing or releasing clutch pedal

- [ ] Worn clutch release bearing (Chapter 6).
- [ ] Worn or dry clutch pedal bushes (Chapter 6).
- [ ] Faulty pressure plate assembly (Chapter 6).
- [ ] Pressure plate diaphragm spring broken (Chapter 6).
- [ ] Broken clutch disc cushioning springs (Chapter 6).

Manual transmission

Noisy in neutral with engine running

☐ Input shaft bearings worn (noise apparent with clutch pedal released, but not when depressed) (Chapter 7A).*
☐ Clutch release bearing worn (noise apparent with clutch pedal depressed, possibly less when released) (Chapter 6).

Noisy in one particular gear

☐ Worn, damaged or chipped gear teeth (Chapter 7A).*

Difficulty engaging gears

☐ Clutch fault (Chapter 6).
☐ Worn or damaged gearchange linkage/cable (Chapter 7A).
☐ Incorrectly-adjusted gearchange linkage/cable (Chapter 7A).
☐ Worn synchroniser units (Chapter 7A).*

Jumps out of gear

☐ Worn or damaged gearchange linkage/cable (Chapter 7A).
☐ Incorrectly-adjusted gearchange linkage/cable (Chapter 7A).
☐ Worn synchroniser units (Chapter 7A).*
☐ Worn selector forks (Chapter 7A).*

Vibration

☐ Lack of oil (Chapter 1).
☐ Worn bearings (Chapter 7A).*

Lubricant leaks

☐ Leaking differential output oil seal (Chapter 7A).
☐ Leaking housing joint (Chapter 7A).*
☐ Leaking input shaft oil seal (Chapter 7A).*

Although the corrective action necessary to remedy the symptoms described is beyond the scope of the home mechanic, the above information should be helpful in isolating the cause of the condition, so that the owner can communicate clearly with a professional mechanic.

Automatic transmission

Note: *Due to the complexity of the automatic transmission, it is difficult for the home mechanic to properly diagnose and service this unit. For problems other than the following, the vehicle should be taken to a dealer service department or automatic transmission specialist. Do not be too hasty in removing the transmission if a fault is suspected, as most of the testing is carried out with the unit still fitted.*

Fluid leakage

☐ Automatic transmission fluid is usually dark in colour. Fluid leaks should not be confused with engine oil, which can easily be blown onto the transmission by airflow.
☐ To determine the source of a leak, first remove all built-up dirt and grime from the transmission housing and surrounding areas using a degreasing agent, or by steam-cleaning. Drive the vehicle at low speed, so airflow will not blow the leak far from its source. Raise and support the vehicle, and determine where the leak is coming from. The following are common areas of leakage:
  a) *Oil pan (Chapter 1 and 7B).*
  b) *Dipstick tube (Chapter 1 and 7B).*
  c) *Transmission-to-fluid cooler pipes/unions (Chapter 7B).*

Transmission fluid brown, or has burned smell

☐ Transmission fluid level low, or fluid in need of renewal (Chapter 1).

General gear selection problems

☐ Chapter 7B deals with checking and adjusting the selector cable on automatic transmissions. The following are common problems which may be caused by a poorly-adjusted cable:
  a) *Engine starting in gears other than Park or Neutral.*
  b) *Indicator panel indicating a gear other than the one actually being used.*
  c) *Vehicle moves when in Park or Neutral.*
  d) *Poor gear shift quality or erratic gear changes.*
☐ Refer to Chapter 7B for the selector cable adjustment procedure.

Transmission will not downshift (kickdown) with accelerator pedal fully depressed

☐ Low transmission fluid level (Chapter 1).
☐ Incorrect selector cable adjustment (Chapter 7B).

Engine will not start in any gear, or starts in gears other than Park or Neutral

☐ Incorrect starter/inhibitor switch adjustment (Chapter 7B).
☐ Incorrect selector cable adjustment (Chapter 7B).

Transmission slips, shifts roughly, is noisy, or has no drive in forward or reverse gears

☐ There are many probable causes for the above problems, but the home mechanic should be concerned with only one possibility - fluid level. Before taking the vehicle to a dealer or transmission specialist, check the fluid level and condition of the fluid as described in Chapter 1. Correct the fluid level as necessary, or change the fluid and filter if needed. If the problem persists, professional help will be necessary.

Driveshafts

Clicking or knocking noise on turns (at slow speed on full-lock)

☐ Lack of constant velocity joint lubricant, possibly due to damaged gaiter (Chapter 8).
☐ Worn outer constant velocity joint (Chapter 8).

Vibration when accelerating or decelerating

☐ Worn inner constant velocity joint (Chapter 8).
☐ Bent or distorted driveshaft (Chapter 8).

Braking system

Note: *Before assuming that a brake problem exists, make sure that the tyres are in good condition and correctly inflated, that the front wheel alignment is correct, and that the vehicle is not loaded with weight in an unequal manner. Apart from checking the condition of all pipe and hose connections, any faults occurring on the anti-lock braking system should be referred to a VW dealer for diagnosis.*

Vehicle pulls to one side under braking

☐ Worn, defective, damaged or contaminated brake pads/shoes on one side (Chapters 1 and 9).
☐ Seized or partially-seized front brake caliper/wheel cylinder piston (Chapters 1 and 9).
☐ A mixture of brake pad/shoe lining materials fitted between sides (Chapters 1 and 9).
☐ Brake caliper or backplate mounting bolts loose (Chapter 9).
☐ Worn or damaged steering or suspension components (Chapters 1 and 10).

Noise (grinding or high-pitched squeal) when brakes applied

☐ Brake pad or shoe friction lining material worn down to metal backing (Chapters 1 and 9).
☐ Excessive corrosion of brake disc or drum. (May be apparent after the vehicle has been standing for some time (Chapters 1 and 9).
☐ Foreign object (stone chipping, etc) trapped between brake disc and shield (Chapters 1 and 9).

Excessive brake pedal travel

☐ Inoperative rear brake self-adjust mechanism - drum brakes (Chapters 1 and 9).
☐ Faulty master cylinder (Chapter 9).
☐ Air in hydraulic system (Chapters 1 and 9).
☐ Faulty vacuum servo unit (Chapter 9).

Brake pedal feels spongy when depressed

☐ Air in hydraulic system (Chapters 1 and 9).
☐ Deteriorated flexible rubber brake hoses (Chapters 1 and 9).
☐ Master cylinder mounting nuts loose (Chapter 9).
☐ Faulty master cylinder (Chapter 9).

Excessive brake pedal effort required to stop vehicle

☐ Faulty vacuum servo unit (Chapter 9).
☐ Faulty vacuum pump - diesel models (Chapter 9).
☐ Disconnected, damaged or insecure brake servo vacuum hose (Chapter 9).
☐ Primary or secondary hydraulic circuit failure (Chapter 9).
☐ Seized brake caliper or wheel cylinder piston(s) (Chapter 9).
☐ Brake pads or brake shoes incorrectly fitted (Chapters 1 and 9).
☐ Incorrect grade of brake pads or brake shoes fitted (Chapters 1 and 9).
☐ Brake pads or brake shoe linings contaminated (Chapters 1 and 9).

Judder felt through brake pedal or steering wheel when braking

☐ Excessive run-out or distortion of discs/drums (Chapters 1 and 9).
☐ Brake pad or brake shoe linings worn (Chapters 1 and 9).
☐ Brake caliper or brake backplate mounting bolts loose (Chapter 9).
☐ Wear in suspension or steering components or mountings (Chapters 1 and 10).

Brakes binding

☐ Seized brake caliper or wheel cylinder piston(s) (Chapter 9).
☐ Incorrectly-adjusted handbrake mechanism (Chapter 9).
☐ Faulty master cylinder (Chapter 9).

Rear wheels locking under normal braking

☐ Rear brake shoe linings contaminated (Chapters 1 and 9).
☐ Faulty brake pressure regulator (Chapter 9).

Suspension and steering

Note: *Before diagnosing suspension or steering faults, be sure that the trouble is not due to incorrect tyre pressures, mixtures of tyre types, or binding brakes.*

Vehicle pulls to one side

☐ Defective tyre ("*Weekly Checks*").
☐ Excessive wear in suspension or steering components (Chapters 1 and 10).
☐ Incorrect front wheel alignment (Chapter 10).
☐ Accident damage to steering or suspension components (Chapter 1).

Wheel wobble and vibration

☐ Front roadwheels out of balance (vibration felt mainly through the steering wheel) (Chapters 1 and 10).
☐ Rear roadwheels out of balance (vibration felt throughout the vehicle) (Chapters 1 and 10).
☐ Roadwheels damaged or distorted (Chapters 1 and 10).
☐ Faulty or damaged tyre ("*Weekly Checks*").
☐ Worn steering or suspension joints, bushes or components (Chapters 1 and 10).
☐ Wheel bolts loose (Chapters 1 and 10).

Excessive pitching and/or rolling around corners, or during braking

☐ Defective shock absorbers (Chapters 1 and 10).
☐ Broken or weak spring and/or suspension component (Chapters 1 and 10).
☐ Worn or damaged anti-roll bar or mountings (Chapter 10).

Wandering or general instability

☐ Incorrect front wheel alignment (Chapter 10).
☐ Worn steering or suspension joints, bushes or components (Chapters 1 and 10).
☐ Roadwheels out of balance (Chapters 1 and 10).
☐ Faulty or damaged tyre ("*Weekly Checks*").
☐ Wheel bolts loose (Chapters 1 and 10).
☐ Defective shock absorbers (Chapters 1 and 10).

Excessively-stiff steering

☐ Lack of steering gear lubricant (Chapter 10).
☐ Seized track rod end balljoint or suspension balljoint (Chapters 1 and 10).
☐ Broken or incorrectly-adjusted auxiliary drivebelt - power steering (Chapter 1).
☐ Incorrect front wheel alignment (Chapter 10).
☐ Steering rack or column bent or damaged (Chapter 10).

REF

Suspension and steering (continued)

Excessive play in steering

- [ ] Worn steering column intermediate shaft universal joint (Chapter 10).
- [ ] Worn steering track rod end balljoints (Chapters 1 and 10).
- [ ] Worn rack-and-pinion steering gear (Chapter 10).
- [ ] Worn steering or suspension joints, bushes or components (Chapters 1 and 10).

Lack of power assistance

- [ ] Broken or incorrectly-adjusted auxiliary drivebelt (Chapter 1).
- [ ] Incorrect power steering fluid level ("*Weekly Checks*").
- [ ] Restriction in power steering fluid hoses (Chapter 1).
- [ ] Faulty power steering pump (Chapter 10).
- [ ] Faulty rack-and-pinion steering gear (Chapter 10).

Tyre wear excessive

Tyres worn on inside or outside edges

- [ ] Tyres under-inflated (wear on both edges) ("*Weekly Checks*").
- [ ] Incorrect camber or castor angles (wear on one edge only) (Chapter 10).
- [ ] Worn steering or suspension joints, bushes or components (Chapters 1 and 10).
- [ ] Excessively-hard cornering.
- [ ] Accident damage.

Tyre treads exhibit feathered edges

- [ ] Incorrect toe setting (Chapter 10).

Tyres worn in centre of tread

- [ ] Tyres over-inflated ("*Weekly Checks*").

Tyres worn on inside and outside edges

- [ ] Tyres under-inflated ("*Weekly Checks*").

Tyres worn unevenly

- [ ] Tyres/wheels out of balance (Chapter 1).
- [ ] Excessive wheel or tyre run-out (Chapter 1).
- [ ] Worn shock absorbers (Chapters 1 and 10).
- [ ] Faulty tyre ("*Weekly Checks*").

Electrical system

Note: *For problems associated with the starting system, refer to the faults listed under "Engine" earlier in this Section.*

Battery will not hold a charge for more than a few days

- [ ] Battery defective internally (Chapter 5A).
- [ ] Battery terminal connections loose or corroded ("*Weekly Checks*").
- [ ] Auxiliary drivebelt worn or incorrectly adjusted (Chapter 1).
- [ ] Alternator not charging at correct output (Chapter 5A).
- [ ] Alternator or voltage regulator faulty (Chapter 5A).
- [ ] Short-circuit causing continual battery drain (Chapters 5A and 12).

Ignition/no-charge warning light remains illuminated with engine running

- [ ] Auxiliary drivebelt broken, worn, or incorrectly adjusted (Chapter 1).
- [ ] Alternator brushes worn, sticking, or dirty (Chapter 5A).
- [ ] Alternator brush springs weak or broken (Chapter 5A).
- [ ] Internal fault in alternator or voltage regulator (Chapter 5A).
- [ ] Broken, disconnected, or loose wiring in charging circuit (Chapter 5A).

Ignition/no-charge warning light fails to come on

- [ ] Warning light bulb blown (Chapter 12).
- [ ] Broken, disconnected, or loose wiring in warning light circuit (Chapter 12).
- [ ] Alternator faulty (Chapter 5A).

Lights inoperative

- [ ] Bulb blown (Chapter 12).
- [ ] Corrosion of bulb or bulbholder contacts (Chapter 12).
- [ ] Blown fuse (Chapter 12).
- [ ] Faulty relay (Chapter 12).
- [ ] Broken, loose, or disconnected wiring (Chapter 12).
- [ ] Faulty switch (Chapter 12).

Instrument readings inaccurate or erratic

Instrument readings increase with engine speed

- [ ] Faulty voltage regulator (Chapter 12).

Fuel or temperature gauges give no reading

- [ ] Faulty gauge sender unit (Chapters 3 and 4A, 4B or 4C).
- [ ] Wiring open-circuit (Chapter 12).
- [ ] Faulty gauge (Chapter 12).

Fuel or temperature gauges give continuous maximum reading

- [ ] Faulty gauge sender unit (Chapters 3 and 4A, 4B or 4C).
- [ ] Wiring short-circuit (Chapter 12).
- [ ] Faulty gauge (Chapter 12).

Horn inoperative, or unsatisfactory in operation

Horn operates all the time

- [ ] Horn push either earthed or stuck down (Chapter 12).
- [ ] Horn cable-to-horn push earthed (Chapter 12).

Horn fails to operate

- [ ] Blown fuse (Chapter 12).
- [ ] Cable or cable connections loose, broken or disconnected (Chapter 12).
- [ ] Faulty horn (Chapter 12).

Horn emits intermittent or unsatisfactory sound

- [ ] Cable connections loose (Chapter 12).
- [ ] Horn mountings loose (Chapter 12).
- [ ] Faulty horn (Chapter 12).

Electrical system (continued)

Windscreen/tailgate wipers inoperative, or unsatisfactory in operation

Wipers fail to operate, or operate very slowly

☐ Wiper blades stuck to screen, or linkage seized or binding (Chapters 1 and 12).
☐ Blown fuse (Chapter 12).
☐ Cable or cable connections loose, broken or disconnected (Chapter 12).
☐ Faulty relay (Chapter 12).
☐ Faulty wiper motor (Chapter 12).

Wiper blades sweep over too large or too small an area of the glass

☐ Wiper arms incorrectly positioned on spindles (Chapter 1).
☐ Excessive wear of wiper linkage (Chapter 12).
☐ Wiper motor or linkage mountings loose or insecure (Chapter 12).

Wiper blades fail to clean the glass effectively

☐ Wiper blade rubbers worn or perished ("Weekly Checks").
☐ Wiper arm tension springs broken, or arm pivots seized (Chapter 12).
☐ Insufficient windscreen washer additive to adequately remove road film ("Weekly Checks").

Windscreen/tailgate washers inoperative, or unsatisfactory in operation

One or more washer jets inoperative

☐ Blocked washer jet (Chapter 1).
☐ Disconnected, kinked or restricted fluid hose (Chapter 12).
☐ Insufficient fluid in washer reservoir ("Weekly Checks").

Washer pump fails to operate

☐ Broken or disconnected wiring or connections (Chapter 12).
☐ Blown fuse (Chapter 12).
☐ Faulty washer switch (Chapter 12).
☐ Faulty washer pump (Chapter 12).

Washer pump runs for some time before fluid is emitted from jets

☐ Faulty one-way valve in fluid supply hose (Chapter 12).

Electric windows inoperative, or unsatisfactory in operation

Window glass will only move in one direction

☐ Faulty switch (Chapter 12).

Window glass slow to move

☐ Regulator seized or damaged, or in need of lubrication (Chapter 11).
☐ Door internal components or trim fouling regulator (Chapter 11).
☐ Faulty motor (Chapter 11).

Window glass fails to move

☐ Blown fuse (Chapter 12).
☐ Faulty relay (Chapter 12).
☐ Broken or disconnected wiring or connections (Chapter 12).
☐ Faulty motor (Chapter 11).

Central locking system inoperative, or unsatisfactory in operation

Complete system failure

☐ Blown fuse (Chapter 12).
☐ Faulty relay (Chapter 12).
☐ Broken or disconnected wiring or connections (Chapter 12).
☐ Faulty vacuum pump (Chapter 11).

Latch locks but will not unlock, or unlocks but will not lock

☐ Faulty master switch (Chapter 12).
☐ Broken or disconnected latch operating rods or levers (Chapter 11).
☐ Faulty relay (Chapter 12).
☐ Faulty vacuum pump (Chapter 11).

One solenoid/motor fails to operate

☐ Broken or disconnected wiring or connections (Chapter 12).
☐ Faulty operating assembly (Chapter 11).
☐ Broken, binding or disconnected latch operating rods or levers (Chapter 11).
☐ Fault in door latch (Chapter 11).

A

ABS (Anti-lock brake system) A system, usually electronically controlled, that senses incipient wheel lockup during braking and relieves hydraulic pressure at wheels that are about to skid.

Air bag An inflatable bag hidden in the steering wheel (driver's side) or the dash or glovebox (passenger side). In a head-on collision, the bags inflate, preventing the driver and front passenger from being thrown forward into the steering wheel or windscreen.

Air cleaner A metal or plastic housing, containing a filter element, which removes dust and dirt from the air being drawn into the engine.

Air filter element The actual filter in an air cleaner system, usually manufactured from pleated paper and requiring renewal at regular intervals.

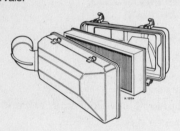

Air filter

Allen key A hexagonal wrench which fits into a recessed hexagonal hole.

Alligator clip A long-nosed spring-loaded metal clip with meshing teeth. Used to make temporary electrical connections.

Alternator A component in the electrical system which converts mechanical energy from a drivebelt into electrical energy to charge the battery and to operate the starting system, ignition system and electrical accessories.

Alternator (exploded view)

Ampere (amp) A unit of measurement for the flow of electric current. One amp is the amount of current produced by one volt acting through a resistance of one ohm.

Anaerobic sealer A substance used to prevent bolts and screws from loosening. Anaerobic means that it does not require oxygen for activation. The Loctite brand is widely used.

Antifreeze A substance (usually ethylene glycol) mixed with water, and added to a vehicle's cooling system, to prevent freezing of the coolant in winter. Antifreeze also contains chemicals to inhibit corrosion and the formation of rust and other deposits that would tend to clog the radiator and coolant passages and reduce cooling efficiency.

Anti-seize compound A coating that reduces the risk of seizing on fasteners that are subjected to high temperatures, such as exhaust manifold bolts and nuts.

Anti-seize compound

Asbestos A natural fibrous mineral with great heat resistance, commonly used in the composition of brake friction materials. Asbestos is a health hazard and the dust created by brake systems should never be inhaled or ingested.

Axle A shaft on which a wheel revolves, or which revolves with a wheel. Also, a solid beam that connects the two wheels at one end of the vehicle. An axle which also transmits power to the wheels is known as a live axle.

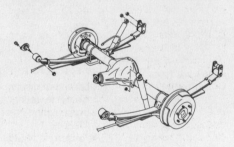

Axle assembly

Axleshaft A single rotating shaft, on either side of the differential, which delivers power from the final drive assembly to the drive wheels. Also called a driveshaft or a halfshaft.

B

Ball bearing An anti-friction bearing consisting of a hardened inner and outer race with hardened steel balls between two races.

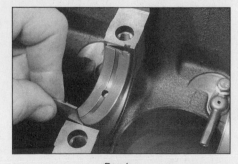

Bearing

Bearing The curved surface on a shaft or in a bore, or the part assembled into either, that permits relative motion between them with minimum wear and friction.

Big-end bearing The bearing in the end of the connecting rod that's attached to the crankshaft.

Bleed nipple A valve on a brake wheel cylinder, caliper or other hydraulic component that is opened to purge the hydraulic system of air. Also called a bleed screw.

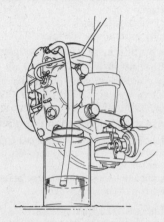

Brake bleeding

Brake bleeding Procedure for removing air from lines of a hydraulic brake system.

Brake disc The component of a disc brake that rotates with the wheels.

Brake drum The component of a drum brake that rotates with the wheels.

Brake linings The friction material which contacts the brake disc or drum to retard the vehicle's speed. The linings are bonded or riveted to the brake pads or shoes.

Brake pads The replaceable friction pads that pinch the brake disc when the brakes are applied. Brake pads consist of a friction material bonded or riveted to a rigid backing plate.

Brake shoe The crescent-shaped carrier to which the brake linings are mounted and which forces the lining against the rotating drum during braking.

Braking systems For more information on braking systems, consult the *Haynes Automotive Brake Manual*.

Breaker bar A long socket wrench handle providing greater leverage.

Bulkhead The insulated partition between the engine and the passenger compartment.

C

Caliper The non-rotating part of a disc-brake assembly that straddles the disc and carries the brake pads. The caliper also contains the hydraulic components that cause the pads to pinch the disc when the brakes are applied. A caliper is also a measuring tool that can be set to measure inside or outside dimensions of an object.

Camshaft A rotating shaft on which a series of cam lobes operate the valve mechanisms. The camshaft may be driven by gears, by sprockets and chain or by sprockets and a belt.

Canister A container in an evaporative emission control system; contains activated charcoal granules to trap vapours from the fuel system.

Canister

Carburettor A device which mixes fuel with air in the proper proportions to provide a desired power output from a spark ignition internal combustion engine.

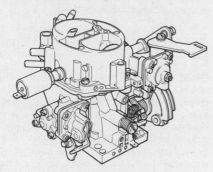

Carburettor

Castellated Resembling the parapets along the top of a castle wall. For example, a castellated balljoint stud nut.

Castellated nut

Castor In wheel alignment, the backward or forward tilt of the steering axis. Castor is positive when the steering axis is inclined rearward at the top.

Catalytic converter A silencer-like device in the exhaust system which converts certain pollutants in the exhaust gases into less harmful substances.

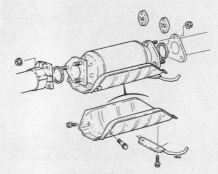

Catalytic converter

Circlip A ring-shaped clip used to prevent endwise movement of cylindrical parts and shafts. An internal circlip is installed in a groove in a housing; an external circlip fits into a groove on the outside of a cylindrical piece such as a shaft.

Clearance The amount of space between two parts. For example, between a piston and a cylinder, between a bearing and a journal, etc.

Coil spring A spiral of elastic steel found in various sizes throughout a vehicle, for example as a springing medium in the suspension and in the valve train.

Compression Reduction in volume, and increase in pressure and temperature, of a gas, caused by squeezing it into a smaller space.

Compression ratio The relationship between cylinder volume when the piston is at top dead centre and cylinder volume when the piston is at bottom dead centre.

Constant velocity (CV) joint A type of universal joint that cancels out vibrations caused by driving power being transmitted through an angle.

Core plug A disc or cup-shaped metal device inserted in a hole in a casting through which core was removed when the casting was formed. Also known as a freeze plug or expansion plug.

Crankcase The lower part of the engine block in which the crankshaft rotates.

Crankshaft The main rotating member, or shaft, running the length of the crankcase, with offset "throws" to which the connecting rods are attached.

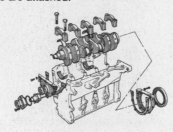

Crankshaft assembly

Crocodile clip See Alligator clip

D

Diagnostic code Code numbers obtained by accessing the diagnostic mode of an engine management computer. This code can be used to determine the area in the system where a malfunction may be located.

Disc brake A brake design incorporating a rotating disc onto which brake pads are squeezed. The resulting friction converts the energy of a moving vehicle into heat.

Double-overhead cam (DOHC) An engine that uses two overhead camshafts, usually one for the intake valves and one for the exhaust valves.

Drivebelt(s) The belt(s) used to drive accessories such as the alternator, water pump, power steering pump, air conditioning compressor, etc. off the crankshaft pulley.

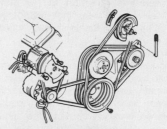

Accessory drivebelts

Driveshaft Any shaft used to transmit motion. Commonly used when referring to the axleshafts on a front wheel drive vehicle.

Driveshaft

Drum brake A type of brake using a drum-shaped metal cylinder attached to the inner surface of the wheel. When the brake pedal is pressed, curved brake shoes with friction linings press against the inside of the drum to slow or stop the vehicle.

Drum brake assembly

E

EGR valve A valve used to introduce exhaust gases into the intake air stream.

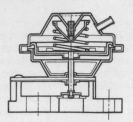

EGR valve

Electronic control unit (ECU) A computer which controls (for instance) ignition and fuel injection systems, or an anti-lock braking system. For more information refer to the *Haynes Automotive Electrical and Electronic Systems Manual.*

Electronic Fuel Injection (EFI) A computer controlled fuel system that distributes fuel through an injector located in each intake port of the engine.

Emergency brake A braking system, independent of the main hydraulic system, that can be used to slow or stop the vehicle if the primary brakes fail, or to hold the vehicle stationary even though the brake pedal isn't depressed. It usually consists of a hand lever that actuates either front or rear brakes mechanically through a series of cables and linkages. Also known as a handbrake or parking brake.

Endfloat The amount of lengthwise movement between two parts. As applied to a crankshaft, the distance that the crankshaft can move forward and back in the cylinder block.

Engine management system (EMS) A computer controlled system which manages the fuel injection and the ignition systems in an integrated fashion.

Exhaust manifold A part with several passages through which exhaust gases leave the engine combustion chambers and enter the exhaust pipe.

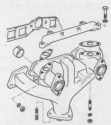

Exhaust manifold

F

Fan clutch A viscous (fluid) drive coupling device which permits variable engine fan speeds in relation to engine speeds.

Feeler blade A thin strip or blade of hardened steel, ground to an exact thickness, used to check or measure clearances between parts.

Feeler blade

Firing order The order in which the engine cylinders fire, or deliver their power strokes, beginning with the number one cylinder.

Flywheel A heavy spinning wheel in which energy is absorbed and stored by means of momentum. On cars, the flywheel is attached to the crankshaft to smooth out firing impulses.

Free play The amount of travel before any action takes place. The "looseness" in a linkage, or an assembly of parts, between the initial application of force and actual movement. For example, the distance the brake pedal moves before the pistons in the master cylinder are actuated.

Fuse An electrical device which protects a circuit against accidental overload. The typical fuse contains a soft piece of metal which is calibrated to melt at a predetermined current flow (expressed as amps) and break the circuit.

Fusible link A circuit protection device consisting of a conductor surrounded by heat-resistant insulation. The conductor is smaller than the wire it protects, so it acts as the weakest link in the circuit. Unlike a blown fuse, a failed fusible link must frequently be cut from the wire for replacement.

G

Gap The distance the spark must travel in jumping from the centre electrode to the side

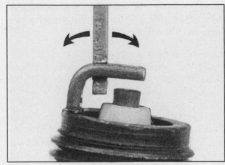

Adjusting spark plug gap

electrode in a spark plug. Also refers to the spacing between the points in a contact breaker assembly in a conventional points-type ignition, or to the distance between the reluctor or rotor and the pickup coil in an electronic ignition.

Gasket Any thin, soft material - usually cork, cardboard, asbestos or soft metal - installed between two metal surfaces to ensure a good seal. For instance, the cylinder head gasket seals the joint between the block and the cylinder head.

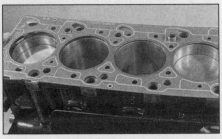

Gasket

Gauge An instrument panel display used to monitor engine conditions. A gauge with a movable pointer on a dial or a fixed scale is an analogue gauge. A gauge with a numerical readout is called a digital gauge.

H

Halfshaft A rotating shaft that transmits power from the final drive unit to a drive wheel, usually when referring to a live rear axle.

Harmonic balancer A device designed to reduce torsion or twisting vibration in the crankshaft. May be incorporated in the crankshaft pulley. Also known as a vibration damper.

Hone An abrasive tool for correcting small irregularities or differences in diameter in an engine cylinder, brake cylinder, etc.

Hydraulic tappet A tappet that utilises hydraulic pressure from the engine's lubrication system to maintain zero clearance (constant contact with both camshaft and valve stem). Automatically adjusts to variation in valve stem length. Hydraulic tappets also reduce valve noise.

I

Ignition timing The moment at which the spark plug fires, usually expressed in the number of crankshaft degrees before the piston reaches the top of its stroke.

Inlet manifold A tube or housing with passages through which flows the air-fuel mixture (carburettor vehicles and vehicles with throttle body injection) or air only (port fuel-injected vehicles) to the port openings in the cylinder head.

J

Jump start Starting the engine of a vehicle with a discharged or weak battery by attaching jump leads from the weak battery to a charged or helper battery.

L

Load Sensing Proportioning Valve (LSPV) A brake hydraulic system control valve that works like a proportioning valve, but also takes into consideration the amount of weight carried by the rear axle.

Locknut A nut used to lock an adjustment nut, or other threaded component, in place. For example, a locknut is employed to keep the adjusting nut on the rocker arm in position.

Lockwasher A form of washer designed to prevent an attaching nut from working loose.

M

MacPherson strut A type of front suspension system devised by Earle MacPherson at Ford of England. In its original form, a simple lateral link with the anti-roll bar creates the lower control arm. A long strut - an integral coil spring and shock absorber - is mounted between the body and the steering knuckle. Many modern so-called MacPherson strut systems use a conventional lower A-arm and don't rely on the anti-roll bar for location.

Multimeter An electrical test instrument with the capability to measure voltage, current and resistance.

N

NOx Oxides of Nitrogen. A common toxic pollutant emitted by petrol and diesel engines at higher temperatures.

O

Ohm The unit of electrical resistance. One volt applied to a resistance of one ohm will produce a current of one amp.

Ohmmeter An instrument for measuring electrical resistance.

O-ring A type of sealing ring made of a special rubber-like material; in use, the O-ring is compressed into a groove to provide the sealing action.

O-ring

Overhead cam (ohc) engine An engine with the camshaft(s) located on top of the cylinder head(s).

Overhead valve (ohv) engine An engine with the valves located in the cylinder head, but with the camshaft located in the engine block.

Oxygen sensor A device installed in the engine exhaust manifold, which senses the oxygen content in the exhaust and converts this information into an electric current. Also called a Lambda sensor.

P

Phillips screw A type of screw head having a cross instead of a slot for a corresponding type of screwdriver.

Plastigage A thin strip of plastic thread, available in different sizes, used for measuring clearances. For example, a strip of Plastigage is laid across a bearing journal. The parts are assembled and dismantled; the width of the crushed strip indicates the clearance between journal and bearing.

Plastigage

Propeller shaft The long hollow tube with universal joints at both ends that carries power from the transmission to the differential on front-engined rear wheel drive vehicles.

Proportioning valve A hydraulic control valve which limits the amount of pressure to the rear brakes during panic stops to prevent wheel lock-up.

R

Rack-and-pinion steering A steering system with a pinion gear on the end of the steering shaft that mates with a rack (think of a geared wheel opened up and laid flat). When the steering wheel is turned, the pinion turns, moving the rack to the left or right. This movement is transmitted through the track rods to the steering arms at the wheels.

Radiator A liquid-to-air heat transfer device designed to reduce the temperature of the coolant in an internal combustion engine cooling system.

Refrigerant Any substance used as a heat transfer agent in an air-conditioning system. R-12 has been the principle refrigerant for many years; recently, however, manufacturers have begun using R-134a, a non-CFC substance that is considered less harmful to

the ozone in the upper atmosphere.

Rocker arm A lever arm that rocks on a shaft or pivots on a stud. In an overhead valve engine, the rocker arm converts the upward movement of the pushrod into a downward movement to open a valve.

Rotor In a distributor, the rotating device inside the cap that connects the centre electrode and the outer terminals as it turns, distributing the high voltage from the coil secondary winding to the proper spark plug. Also, that part of an alternator which rotates inside the stator. Also, the rotating assembly of a turbocharger, including the compressor wheel, shaft and turbine wheel.

Runout The amount of wobble (in-and-out movement) of a gear or wheel as it's rotated. The amount a shaft rotates "out-of-true." The out-of-round condition of a rotating part.

S

Sealant A liquid or paste used to prevent leakage at a joint. Sometimes used in conjunction with a gasket.

Sealed beam lamp An older headlight design which integrates the reflector, lens and filaments into a hermetically-sealed one-piece unit. When a filament burns out or the lens cracks, the entire unit is simply replaced.

Serpentine drivebelt A single, long, wide accessory drivebelt that's used on some newer vehicles to drive all the accessories, instead of a series of smaller, shorter belts. Serpentine drivebelts are usually tensioned by an automatic tensioner.

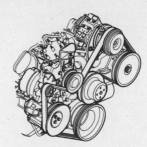

Serpentine drivebelt

Shim Thin spacer, commonly used to adjust the clearance or relative positions between two parts. For example, shims inserted into or under bucket tappets control valve clearances. Clearance is adjusted by changing the thickness of the shim.

Slide hammer A special puller that screws into or hooks onto a component such as a shaft or bearing; a heavy sliding handle on the shaft bottoms against the end of the shaft to knock the component free.

Sprocket A tooth or projection on the periphery of a wheel, shaped to engage with a chain or drivebelt. Commonly used to refer to the sprocket wheel itself.

Starter inhibitor switch On vehicles with an

automatic transmission, a switch that prevents starting if the vehicle is not in Neutral or Park.

Strut See MacPherson strut.

T

Tappet A cylindrical component which transmits motion from the cam to the valve stem, either directly or via a pushrod and rocker arm. Also called a cam follower.

Thermostat A heat-controlled valve that regulates the flow of coolant between the cylinder block and the radiator, so maintaining optimum engine operating temperature. A thermostat is also used in some air cleaners in which the temperature is regulated.

Thrust bearing The bearing in the clutch assembly that is moved in to the release levers by clutch pedal action to disengage the clutch. Also referred to as a release bearing.

Timing belt A toothed belt which drives the camshaft. Serious engine damage may result if it breaks in service.

Timing chain A chain which drives the camshaft.

Toe-in The amount the front wheels are closer together at the front than at the rear. On rear wheel drive vehicles, a slight amount of toe-in is usually specified to keep the front wheels running parallel on the road by offsetting other forces that tend to spread the wheels apart.

Toe-out The amount the front wheels are closer together at the rear than at the front. On front wheel drive vehicles, a slight amount of toe-out is usually specified.

Tools For full information on choosing and using tools, refer to the *Haynes Automotive Tools Manual*.

Tracer A stripe of a second colour applied to a wire insulator to distinguish that wire from another one with the same colour insulator.

Tune-up A process of accurate and careful adjustments and parts replacement to obtain the best possible engine performance.

Turbocharger A centrifugal device, driven by exhaust gases, that pressurises the intake air. Normally used to increase the power output from a given engine displacement, but can also be used primarily to reduce exhaust emissions (as on VW's "Umwelt" Diesel engine).

U

Universal joint or U-joint A double-pivoted connection for transmitting power from a driving to a driven shaft through an angle. A U-joint consists of two Y-shaped yokes and a cross-shaped member called the spider.

V

Valve A device through which the flow of liquid, gas, vacuum, or loose material in bulk may be started, stopped, or regulated by a movable part that opens, shuts, or partially obstructs one or more ports or passageways. A valve is also the movable part of such a device.

Valve clearance The clearance between the valve tip (the end of the valve stem) and the rocker arm or tappet. The valve clearance is measured when the valve is closed.

Vernier caliper A precision measuring instrument that measures inside and outside dimensions. Not quite as accurate as a micrometer, but more convenient.

Viscosity The thickness of a liquid or its resistance to flow.

Volt A unit for expressing electrical "pressure" in a circuit. One volt that will produce a current of one ampere through a resistance of one ohm.

W

Welding Various processes used to join metal items by heating the areas to be joined to a molten state and fusing them together. For more information refer to the *Haynes Automotive Welding Manual*.

Wiring diagram A drawing portraying the components and wires in a vehicle's electrical system, using standardised symbols. For more information refer to the *Haynes Automotive Electrical and Electronic Systems Manual*.

Note: References throughout this index are in the form - "Chapter number" • "page number"

REF

REF

Preserving Our Motoring Heritage

< *The Model J Duesenberg Derham Tourster. Only eight of these magnificent cars were ever built – this is the only example to be found outside the United States of America*

Almost every car you've ever loved, loathed or desired is gathered under one roof at the Haynes Motor Museum. Over 300 immaculately presented cars and motorbikes represent every aspect of our motoring heritage, from elegant reminders of bygone days, such as the superb Model J Duesenberg to curiosities like the bug-eyed BMW Isetta. There are also many old friends and flames. Perhaps you remember the 1959 Ford Popular that you did your courting in? The magnificent 'Red Collection' is a spectacle of classic sports cars including AC, Alfa Romeo, Austin Healey, Ferrari, Lamborghini, Maserati, MG, Riley, Porsche and Triumph.

A Perfect Day Out

Each and every vehicle at the Haynes Motor Museum has played its part in the history and culture of Motoring. Today, they make a wonderful spectacle and a great day out for all the family. Bring the kids, bring Mum and Dad, but above all bring your camera to capture those golden memories for ever. You will also find an impressive array of motoring memorabilia, a comfortable 70 seat video cinema and one of the most extensive transport book shops in Britain. The Pit Stop Cafe serves everything from a cup of tea to wholesome, home-made meals or, if you prefer, you can enjoy the large picnic area nestled in the beautiful rural surroundings of Somerset.

> *John Haynes O.B.E., Founder and Chairman of the museum at the wheel of a Haynes Light 12.*

< *Graham Hill's Lola Cosworth Formula 1 car next to a 1934 Riley Sports.*

The Museum is situated on the A359 Yeovil to Frome road at Sparkford, just off the A303 in Somerset. It is about 40 miles south of Bristol, and 25 minutes drive from the M5 intersection at Taunton.

Open 9.30am - 5.30pm (10.00am - 4.00pm Winter) 7 days a week, *except Christmas Day, Boxing Day and New Years Day*

Special rates available for schools, coach parties and outings Charitable Trust No. 292048